MW00513461

Napoleon

and the Art of Diplomacy

Napoleon le Grand

Napoleon
and the Art of Diplomacy

How War and Hubris

Determined the Rise and Fall of the French Empire

William R. Nester

SB

Savas Beatie

New York and California

Cataloging-in-Publication Data is available from the Library of Congress.

ISBN-13: 978-1-61121-092-7

05 04 03 02 01   5 4 3 2 1
First Savas Beatie edition, first printing

SB

Published by
Savas Beatie LLC
521 Fifth Avenue, Suite 1700
New York, NY 10175

Editorial Offices:

Savas Beatie LLC
P.O. Box 4527
El Dorado Hills, CA 95762
916-941-6896
sales@savasbeatie.com

Savas Beatie titles are available at special discounts for bulk purchases in the United States by corporations, institutions, and other organizations. For more details, please contact Special Sales, P.O. Box 4527, El Dorado Hills, CA 95762, or you may e-mail us at sales@savasbeatie.com, or visit our website at www.savasbeatie.com for additional information.

Proudly published, printed, and warehoused in the United States of America.

Table of Contents

List of Maps

Introduction

"Diplomacy is essential and inseparable from war."

—Napoleon

War is hardly the only subject of diplomacy—only the most dramatic and vital. Depending on who is involved, what they want, and what means they use to get what they want, diplomacy can determine the fate of nations, continents, or, in modern times, every person on the planet. Yet no matter what the stakes are, diplomacy is inseparable from virtually any conflict, whether it is primarily military, economic, ideological, cultural, social, or personal.

Napoleon Bonaparte is best known as a military genius. Was the power that he wielded to assert his foreign policy nothing more than the power to conduct war, or to threaten to do so? Warriors are not generally known for their diplomatic skills; conquerors are accustomed to imposing rather than negotiating terms. Yet, contrary to the popular image, Napoleon often was just as brilliant and successful at diplomacy as he was at war. Indeed, as will be seen, he nearly always thought a dozen or so moves ahead on as many distinct or related diplomatic chessboards. Alas, at times he could also be as disastrous at diplomacy as he was at war. And regardless, depending on circumstances, he could be a model either of decorum or brutality.

For Napoleon, the arts of war and diplomacy meshed. If Karl von Clausewitz famously asserted that "war is the continuation of politics by other means," Napoleon added the truism that diplomacy can be the continuation of war by other means: "Diplomacy is essential and inseparable from war."[1] Ideally, diplomacy makes war unnecessary; if not, it can precede, join, and end a war so that it advances one's interests.

Napoleon therefore usually mapped out his grand diplomatic strategy as carefully as he did his military campaigns. Most of his own correspondence as well as the memoirs of other participants reveal Napoleon to have been a genuine master of diplomacy.[2] When relating to his diplomatic foils, Napoleon at his best paid very careful attention to protocol and was sensitive to the most subtle of nuances even as he systematically presented the rational and emotional arguments for his position—until the other yielded.

Many believed then and have since that Napoleon was an insatiable aggressor who caused all the wars that he fought as head of state. Actually, he entered most wars with reluctance, only when he believed he had exhausted his diplomatic options. He acted thus when he needed a crushing military victory to bolster his diplomatic power, with which he could negotiate a peace that would further bolster French national security. Each war that he fought as the head of France from 1800 to 1815, and the diplomacy surrounding it, had its own distinct set of causes—for which blame can be widely shared among the great powers.

Napoleon's diplomatic skills, like his military skills, varied considerably from one conflict to the next. Not surprisingly, his finesse decreased as he amassed more power. Years of military and diplomatic victories, along with the grandeur of being Emperor Napoleon rather than General Bonaparte, swelled his hubris and blinded him to the vital need for the restraint and symbolic compromises by which he could win his ends without savaging his opponent's pride and provoking an obsession for vengeance.

In Napoleon's mind, there was a clear rationale for that shift in diplomatic approach: the bitter lessons of previous experiences. He concluded that appeasement just did not work. The Austrians especially would not give up. In concluding the first two wars against them, Napoleon offered relatively mild terms, at Campo Formio in 1797 and Luneville in 1801. But Austrian aggression in 1805 forever changed his mind about mild versus harsh peaces. Starting then, Napoleon abandoned a diplomatic strategy of compromise and inducement for one of punishment, containment, and deterrence. No longer would he offer more carrots than sticks. He would instead seek to chastise and weaken rather than reward and entice. He would take much and give little or nothing. His attitude toward diplomacy became, "Take it or leave it." Once a treaty had been negotiated and publicized, the monarch in question had better swiftly ratify it, because any later set of terms would be much harsher.

Napoleon's art of diplomacy also mirrored his art of war at the negotiating level, the tactical level. His axiom, "one engages and then one sees" captures his improvisory approach to tactics. He would probe to provoke a response that revealed the enemy's position, and only then devise a more comprehensive plan.

But when that did not work he unleashed a style of personal diplomacy that can be called "the Napoleon treatment," in which he would wear down his opponent with an unceasing bombardment of mingled threats and allurements, bluster and charm, and arguments rooted in cold reason and warm feelings, before finally marching his most important demands at the enemy's weakest positions. Most of the time the outraged, bewildered, and intimidated foreign envoy would sooner or later capitulate to his demands.

Armand Augustin de Caulaincourt, one of Napoleon's finest diplomats and ministers, left the following lengthy description of what it was like to be on the receiving end:

> The harder the Emperor found it to persuade me, the more art and persistence he put forth to attain that end. His calculated wiles and the language he used would have made anyone believe that I was one of the powers whom he was so much concerned to win over. . . . He acted so towards all whom he wished to persuade, and he always wanted to persuade someone. I enter into these details because they delineate his character. . . . Certain is it that the success which he was accustomed to obtain thus must be his predilection for dealing with sovereigns, and his habit of dealing in any particularly delicate and important matters directly with the ministers and ambassadors of foreign powers. When he so wished there could be a power of persuasion and fascination in his voice, his expression, his very manner, which give him an advantage over his interlocutor as great as the superiority and flexibility of his mind. Never was there a man more fascinating when he chose to be; to withstand him one had to realize, as I did, the political errors which lay concealed beneath his art, often specious but always clever and full of apt comparisons as useful to illustrate his own ideas and to conceal the end he wished to obtain. . . . He never failed to shift the center of argument when he encountered opposition. Woe to him that admitted a single modification, for the adroit interlocutor led him from concession to concession to the end he had in view.[3]

Charisma can at times be so powerful as to sweep away any other position, however grounded in reason or interest. Napoleon's atavistic force of mind and personality mesmerized all who met him, and could sway to his bidding the rawest of recruits in battle or the loftiest of European statesmen in diplomacy. Even his enemies were not immune to his spells. Clement von Metternich insisted that "my admiration for Bonaparte has always been great and sincere." After Tilsit Tsar Alexander considered the emperor his lifelong "friend." Charles Maurice de Talleyrand, a man not known for his sentimentality, admitted his "love for Napoleon." Although a fierce opponent of his policies and power, Rene Chateaubriand explained that the man exuded "the most powerful breath of life that ever animated human clay."[4]

Such diplomatic tactics, which depended as much on the power of Napoleon's personality as on his strategic position, could work—to a point. Diplomacy conducted during a conflict rarely ends with a final, written deal. The treaties that envoys negotiate must later be ratified and then implemented. A sovereign can always dare to spurn a treaty whose tenets exceeded his envoy's instructions, or sign it and drag his feet in fulfilling it. Contrary to Napoleon's own perceptions, deals tended to last longer when he exercised restraint and offered his opponent face-saving provisions rather than crippling impositions of French power.

When Napoleon could not be at the negotiating table, he would instruct his ministers and envoys not only in the broad ends and means of his policies, but often the minute detail of just how to play a particular diplomatic game. Foreign Minister Talleyrand received one such missive in May 1803 as the Peace of Amiens between France and Britain teetered on the brink of collapse. Napoleon coached Talleyrand on an array of subtle mind games with which to manipulate British ambassador Charles, Lord Whitworth:

> Display aloofness, haughtiness, and no little pride!!! If he issues an ultimatum, let him feel the aggression of his words and the arrogance of his condescending manner. If . . . the ultimatum is not withdrawn . . . terrify him of the consequences. . . . If he is unshakeable, have him escort you to your salon and on the point of parting [rhetorically ask] whether Britain had lived up to its treaty obligations by evacuating the Cape of Good Hope and the Isle de Goree. Then soften a bit and invite him to another meeting before he pens an official notice of the break to his court.[5]

There was the Napoleon treatment in a nutshell: the coolly calibrated, constantly shifting blend of intimacy and intimidation intended to impose on the hapless foreign envoy overwhelming feelings of guilt, obligation, and fear regarding both the justness of French demands and the invincibility of French power. Yet in 1803, in this case, those tactics did not work: Napoleon's game of brinksmanship provoked an unwanted war rather than the concessions and peace that he desired. And that, of course, was hardly the only time he overplayed his diplomatic hands.

There is another key to understanding Napoleon's diplomacy. While in other states diplomatic strategy might be made by committee, Napoleon determined his own virtually on his own. He once famously quipped, "I'd rather fight than join a coalition." He rarely asked for advice, and when he did he took the advice offered even more rarely.

That worked fine when his analysis was correct, but could be disastrous when he miscalculated. Although he was renowned for his decisiveness, he often mulled many possible diplomatic ends and means, and at times overlooked others.

Yet another force complicated his diplomacy: making a decision was simple enough for the head of the French empire; getting it carried out was altogether a different, and often vexing, challenge. No matter how much power Napoleon amassed as first consul and then emperor, it was never absolute. Like any leader, he often found an unbridgeable gap between what he wanted to do and what he could do. His ambitions could be thwarted not just by the various international coalitions that arose against him. Within his inner circle, in his government and army, and in Paris and across the empire, he faced individuals and groups with differing powers, ambitions, interests, hopes, and fears. Whether they sought to merely influence him or oppose him outright, the collective weight of their efforts often shifted, whether sharply or minutely, his diplomacy. Time after time, while Napoleon might justify his decisions as "raison d'état," they often reflected as much the quirks and interests (pecuniary and/or ideological) of the individuals and factions contending to shape policy as they did his own vision and strategy.

Nonetheless, Napoleon would insist that all along the key interest for which he maneuvered, bargained, and warred remained constant: French national security. This, in his view, depended on the expansion of French territory, satellite states, and glory. That view was hardly universal among his fellow countrymen, and the number of those who sincerely supported it steadily dwindled with each year of war, as the body count, national debt, prices, and taxes soared.

Over time, ever more bold voices literally begged to differ. How to define and defend French interests was always subject to debate, no matter how much Napoleon tried to stifle it. Talleyrand, the era's leading French diplomat, championed an alternate vision. Peace, prosperity, and security reinforced one another, he believed, and depended on a France satisfied with its "natural frontiers" of the Rhine, Alps, and Pyrenees, buffered by friendly smaller states with relations enriched by mutually advantageous economic, political, cultural, and military ties, and skillfully playing off the other great powers against one another.

Tragically, Napoleon's view prevailed to the bitter end. It did so for many reasons, but mostly because his belief that national security depended on the expansion of French territorial power and satellite states appeared to be true. From the time he took command of the army of Italy in 1796 until his decision to invade Russia in 1812, he won most of his diplomatic conflicts. That string of nearly unbroken successes spoiled him. He dismissed Talleyrand's vision as a completely unwarranted capitulation of all that France had gained at such a terrible cost in blood and treasure.

Napoleon left the bones of a half million of his soldiers strewn across the Russian steppes and watched helplessly as his allies Prussia and Austria turned against him. Even after that he refused to recognize that France's power and thus its interests had radically changed; that it was imperative to compromise to keep something rather than gamble all and lose all. In sum, the reason for his succession of related diplomatic and military catastrophes from 1812 to 1815 was simple: he miscalculated his ends and means relative to those of his enemies.

And that, according to Caulaincourt, was his diplomatic Achilles heel: "Once he had an idea planted in his head the emperor was carried away by his own illusion. He cherished it, caressed it, became obsessed with it."[6] The decision to march into Russia was only the most notorious example of such a self-deluding obsession. He committed many others which eventually destroyed all that he had tried to build. Napoleon ultimately would fail as a conqueror because he failed as a diplomat.

Yet, while hubris ultimately led to his fall, other forces propelled him on his paths. Just because Napoleon had an imperial vision did not mean that he had a long-range plan and timetable. Instead he reacted to changing circumstances by seizing opportunities and blunting challenges. However genuine his brilliance, he could no more foresee the future effects of his decisions in that tumultuous age than anyone else. He could merely assess, act, and then hope for the best.

In that, at least, he was no different from the rest of us. But what makes Napoleon Bonaparte among the great figures of history is that dynamic matrix made up of the astonishing power of his character and the equally astonishing era whose circumstances at once shaped and reflected his choices.

A small library could be stocked with all the books written about Napoleon. As might be expected, most deal with his military campaigns.[7] Astonishingly, no comprehensive exploration of Napoleon's diplomacy exists. *Napoleon and the Art of Diplomacy* provides a vital and neglected dimension to understanding one of history's most complex, influential, and intriguing men.

Introduction Endnotes

1. Bonaparte to Directory, June 21, 1796, Thierry Lentz, ed., *Napoleon Bonaparte, Correspondance Generale: Les Apprentissages, 1784-1797* (hereafter cited as *General Correspondence*)(Paris: Fayard, 2005), 710.

2. Of the hundreds of books, articles, memoirs, and collections of primary sources used for this book, the following were crucial: For primary sources, Thierry Lentz, ed., *Napoleon Bonaparte: Correspondance Generale* (hereafter cited as *General Correspondence*), 3 vols. (Paris: Fayard, 2004, 2005, 2006); Claude Tchou, ed., *Correspondance de Napoleon Ier* (hereafter cited as *Correspondence*), 16 vols. (Paris: Bibliotheque des Introuvables, 2002). Also very helpful was Michel Kerautret's three-volume set of the era's most important treaties and related diplomatic documents: *Les Grands Traites du Consulat, 1799-1804* (Paris: Nouveau Monde Editions/Fondation Napoleon, 2002); *Les Grands Traites de l'Empire, 1804-1810* (Paris: Nouveau Monde Editions/Fondation Napoleon, 2004); *Les Grands Traites de l'Empire, 1810-1815* (Paris: Nouveau Monde Editions/Fondation Napoleon, 2004).

As for secondary sources, none surpasses Thierry Lentz's brilliant and definitive four volumes on Napoleon's years in power: *Le Grand Consulat, 1799-1804* (Paris: Fayard, 1999); *Nouvelle Histoire du Premier Empire: Napoleon et la Conquete de l'Europe, 1804-1810* (Paris: Fayard, 2002); *Nouvelle Histoire du Premier Empire: l'Effondrement du Systeme Napoleonien, 1810-1814* (Paris: Fayard, 2004); *Nouvelle Histoire du Premier Empire: La France et l'Europe de Napoleon, 1804-1814*.

3. Jean Hanoteau, ed., *With Napoleon in Russia: The Memoirs of General de Caulaincourt, Duke of Vicenza* (New York: William Morris, 1935), 26-27.

4. Gregory Dallas, *The Final Act: The Roads to Waterloo* (New York: Henry Holt and Company, 1996), 266.

5. Napoleon to Talleyrand, May 10, 1803, 7629, *General Correspondence*, 4:127.

6. Hanoteau, *With Napoleon in Russia*, 28.

7. Small libraries could be stocked with all the books on the man and his times. Even nearly two centuries after his height of power, the debate among writers over whether Napoleon had a more progressive or destructive impact on France, Europe, and beyond range from the most fawning of hagiography to the most vehement of condemnations, although the vast majority try to offer balanced accounts.

Diplomacy, however, is peripheral to the field of Napoleon studies. Only one English-speaking author and a couple of French authors have attempted to analyze Napoleon's entire diplomatic career. The only book-length attempt in English is a good but dated introduction: Richard B. Mowat, *The Diplomacy of Napoleon* (London: Edward Arnold, 1924). For French authors, see: J. Lovie et A. Palleul Guillard, *L'Episode Napoleonienne: Aspects Exterieurs* (Paris: Seuil, 1972); and Roger Dufraise and Michael Kerautret, *La France Napoleoniene: Aspects Exterieur, 1799-1815* (Paris: Seuil, 1999).

Many more books explore specific diplomatic conflicts or statesmen, of which the most prominent in English are: H.A.L. Fisher, *Napoleonic Statesmanship: Germany* (Oxford: Clarendon Press, 1903); Emile Dard, *Napoleon and Talleyrand* (New York: D. Appleton-Century Company, 1937); Robert B. Holtman, *Napoleonic Propaganda* (Baton Rouge: Louisiana State University Press, 1950); E.E.Y. Hales, *Revolution and the Papacy, 1769-1846* (London: Eyre & Spottiswoode, 1960); E.E.Y. Hales, *Napoleon and the Pope* (London: Eyre & Spottiswoode, 1962); Gabriel H. Lovett, *Napoleon and the Birth of Modern Spain*, 2 vols. (New York: New York University Press, 1965); Michael Glover, *Legacy of Glory: The Bonaparte Kingdom of Spain, 1808-1813* (London: Leo Cooper, 1972); Owen Connelly, *Napoleon's Satellite Kingdoms* (New York: The Free Press, 1965); Harold C. Deutsch, *The Genesis of Napoleonic Imperialism* (Philadelphia: Lippincott, 1975); Edward A. Whitcomb, *Napoleon's Diplomatic Service* (Durham, NC: Duke University Press, 1979); D.G. Wright, *Napoleon and Europe* (London: Longman, 1984); Stuart J. Woolf, *Napoleon's Integration of Europe* (London: Routledge, 1991); Geoffrey Ellis, *The Napoleonic Empire* (Atlantic Highlands, N.J.: Humanities Press International, 1991).

The most prominent studies of specific diplomatic conflicts and statesmen in French are: Albert Vandal, *Napoleon et Alexandre Ier: L'Alliance Russe sous le Premier Empire*, 3 vols. (Paris: Plon, 1891-96); Arthur Levy, *Napoleon et la Paix* (Paris: Plon, 1902); E. Guillon, *Napoleon et la Suisse* (Paris: Plon, 1910); Edouard Driault, *La Politique Orientale de Napoleon, 1806-08* (Paris: F. Alcan, 1904); Edouard Driault, *Napoleon en Italie, 1800-1812* (Paris: F. Alcan, 1905), Edouard Driault, *Napoleon et l'Europe: La Politique Exterieur du premier consul, 1800-1803* (Paris: F. Alcan, 1910); Edouard Driault, *Tilsit: France et Russie sous le Premier Empire* (Paris: F. Alcan, 1917); Andre Fugier, *Napoleon et l'Italie* (Paris: F. Alcan, 1947); Marcel Dunan, *Napoleon et l'Allemagne: le Systeme Continental et les Debuts du Royaume, 1806-1810* (Paris: Plon, 1942); Marcel Dunan, *Le Systeme Continental et des Debuts du Royaume de Baviere* (Paris: Plon, 1943); Marcel Dunan, *L'Allemagne de la Revolution et de l'Empire* (Paris: Plon, 1954); Francois Crouzet, *L'Economie Britannique et le Blocus Continental* (Paris: Economia, 1987); J. Trainie, *Napoleon et l'Angleterre, 1793-1815* (Paris: Pygmalion, 1994); Rodney J. Dean, *Constitutionelle, Napoleon, et le Concordat de 1801* (Paris: University of Paris, Sorbonne, 2004).

Chapter One

The Making of the Man

1769-1796

"Nature, among other talents, has given me a great deal of character."

"Men of genius are meteors destined to burn in order to enlighten the world."

"There are two levers for moving men—fear and interest."

"It was only on the eve of Lodi that I believed myself a superior man, and that the ambition came to me of executing great things which had so far been occupying my thoughts only as a fantastic dream."

—Napoleon Bonaparte

Knowing and Becoming

How does someone become himself?[1] Each of us is a dynamic, changing, unique matrix of constant genes and shifting circumstances. Everyone develops to varying degrees and in varying ways with time, each according to how one's character causes one to react to a succession of choices in and constraints over one's life.

The difference between a choice and a constraint, however, is not always clear. The ability to determine that difference is itself a product of how one's nature collides with and interprets experiences, and later reinterprets them. How many of us look back and think with a sigh: "If only I knew then what I know now?" And how different would each of our lives be had we been armed with that knowledge when we most needed it?

Making the best, worst, or, almost universally, some mix of good and bad choices that define oneself over a lifetime is something everyone does. Yet those who actually deeply understand themselves are rare. Doing so requires the learning and application of both will and skill; most people lack the inclination and time to do so. Instead, most people create a persona or mask that they present not just to the world but to themselves. They fervently believe that persona—composed of a handful of genuine characteristics distorted by wishes and fears—is their true self. But it is merely a caricature that shields them from the much more complex, ambiguous, and evolving self that they really are.

Which brings us to Napoleon Bonaparte. As he rose through the ranks of first military and then political power, the choices he made affected the lives of ever more people. In exile on Saint Helena, his dictated memoirs are filled with justifications, celebrations, and regrets for the choices he made.

So, just who was Napoleon? How did he get to be the way he was? How did he change over time? And how did all that affect his diplomacy?

Napoleon Bonaparte was among those individuals who eventually adopted an ever more obsessively clear vision of who he thought he was and what more he might become. He believed that he was a child of "destiny," that somehow, for unknown and mysterious reasons, he was destined to do great things. That belief animated his reactions to a succession of astonishing opportunities that arose before him throughout most of his life.

Apparently he had inklings of this from an early age. But, as he wrote in his memoirs, it was as a young general, after his victory in the battle of Lodi in 1796, that he shed his lingering uncertainties.[2] The resulting vision would remain unfazed over the next nineteen years, all the way to Waterloo—no matter how many disasters he eventually inflicted on himself, the rest of Europe, and the world.

Yet like most people, Napoleon knew not his true self but only his persona, which became ever more distorted as he amassed more power and glory. Perhaps we can forgive him for that lapse. After all, he was a very busy man until his forced retirement, and lived in an age innocent of psychoanalysis. Indeed, even the scores of historians who have subsequently tackled the subject of Napoleon have often differed widely in their interpretations.[3]

So what, then, was the content of Napoleon's character? Countless contemporaries then and scholars since have struggled to answer that question. Napoleon's may well be history's most debatable character. Nonetheless, most observers share some insights. In addition to his belief that he was destined for greatness, Napoleon had an implacable will, insatiable curiosity, boundless energy, unwavering courage in combat, an ability to think and act outside conventional thought and behavior, and a vision for the revolutionary transformation of France and Europe from feudalism into modernity. All those who met him spoke of his overpowering charisma.

In his personal life he could be tender and loving. His early letters to Josephine are among the most romantic and passionate left to history. He never stopped caring for his family, sharing with them whatever favors he had, whether he was a penniless lieutenant or an emperor with entire kingdoms to bestow. He genuinely adored children, and perhaps was at his happiest when having a carefree romp with them. And he was devoted to his friends, unable to hold back tears as one after another died beside him in battle.

Crucial dimensions of his character, however, did change with time—and not for the better. His dazzling political and military victories, and the brutality involved in fighting what was eventually sixty battles, warped him. As his power swelled, he increasingly tended to overestimate his own powers and underestimate those of others, especially his enemies. He increasingly saw himself as being nearly god-like, invincible, indestructible, omnipotent, and omniscient. And those were his more Olympian faults. On a more pedestrian level, he could be pompous, petty, rude, bullying, and cruel.

Formation of Personality and Character: Initial Family Influences

How much do the time and place of one's upbringing affect the rest of one's life? As with all such questions, the answers vary from one individual, time, and place to another. Obviously the odds of someone realizing his or her full, unique potential improve to the degree that the accompanying circumstances are favorable.

Napoleon Bonaparte was born Napoleone Buonaparte on August 15, 1769, at Ajaccio, Corsica. His "destiny" first manifested itself by ensuring that he was a subject of France, which had taken Corsica from the Republic of Genoa a mere nine months earlier, on May 15, 1768. How different would have been the fate of Napoleone and Europe had Genoa retained the island! He would later change his name's spelling to the familiar French version and his primary language from a Genoan dialect to French.

Each child is an amalgam of the values, ambitions, and attitudes as well as the mingled genes of his or her parents.[4] Napoleon Bonaparte was the second son of an ambitious lawyer, official, and minor noble named Carlo Maria Buonaparte who struggled to advance himself, his wife, and his eight surviving children under the new regime. Indeed, Carlo was so ambitious that he left the woman he loved and married Letizia, the mother of his future children, who was from the far wealthier Ramolino clan. Carlo was away through most of Napoleon's childhood, and became, for all his children, but especially the youngest, largely the image of a distant, benevolent, amiable father. He was also an energetic and impassioned follower of fortune, nobility, and Pascal Paoli, the Corsican nationalist leader, who went into exile after the French takeover. Carlo never quite realized his dreams for ever-higher status, wealth, and power. Bonaparte later complained that his father "was too fond of pleasure."[5]

By necessity and inclination Letizia was the family's core. As Bonaparte later put it, "her tenderness was severe. . . . Here was the head of a woman with the essence of a man."[6] She gave birth to eleven children, of whom Joseph (1768), Napoleon (1769), Lucien (1775), Elisa (1777), Louis (1778), Pauline (1780), Caroline (1782), and Jerome (1784) survived into adulthood.

Education

Although Carlo never lived to see his family achieve a worldly success far beyond even his vivid imagination, he got things started. On December 12, 1778, he set forth from Ajaccio with his two oldest sons to have them educated in France. Accompanying them was their uncle (their mother's half-brother) Joseph Fesch, then fifteen and bound for a seminary at Aix-en-Provence; later he would at times play an important role in Bonaparte's policies toward the Church. Joseph and Napoleon Bonaparte underwent five months of preparatory studies at the Oratorian college of Autun; then they parted. The elder, Joseph, was sent to the same seminary in Aix-en-Provence as Joseph Fesch, while Napoleon was enrolled at the royal military school at Brienne, where he studied from May 1779 to October 1784, before entering the Ecole Militaire in Paris.

Carlo's decision reversed the usual order of vocation for sons, by which the elder generally joined the army and the younger the church. But from an early age Bonaparte's character appeared most appropriate for a military command. His churning mind, restless energy, and dauntless spirit were clear to those who encountered him.

For a boy who was by nature highly intelligent, introspective, proud, melancholy, and passionate, his school years were filled with frustration and loneliness. He spoke hardly a word of French when he first arrived, and would retain a Corsican accent for most of his life. This, combined with a short, scrawny body and quick anger, provoked teasing and bullying by some of his classmates, which only exaggerated his natural characteristics. Indeed, his early failures at love and career at times filled him with such despair that suicide seemed preferable to a wretched existence.

The atmosphere of the two military schools could not have been more different. Brienne was a provincial school for mostly minor nobles. They were subjected to an austere, stoic, and strict regimen. In contrast, the Ecole Militaire was attended by some of France's leading and richest nobles, who could well afford lifestyles of luxury and decadence; Bonaparte could not compete with their elegance or expenses.

He graduated from the Ecole Militaire as a second lieutenant on October 28, 1785. His "genius" was not then apparent—he graduated number 42 in a class of 58 students. Yet that might not be a good measure of his mind. The authorities were so impressed with his intellect that they let him take the graduation exam after one rather than two years. Three days after graduating he began his first assignment with the La Fere artillery regiment at Valence.

Portrait of Napoleon as a Young Man

So what was Napoleon Bonaparte like as a youth and young man? By his own later admission, he was a rambunctious, shrill, high-strung, and demanding brat, nicknamed the "Rabulioni" (the disturber).[7] One of his professors at the Ecole Militaire wrote: "He prefers study to any type of amusement, finding pleasure in the reading of good authors . . . quiet, loving solitude, capricious, arrogant, extremely inclined to egotism, speaking little, spirited in his answers, quick and harsh in his replies. Having much pride and boundless ambition, this young man deserves to be encouraged."[8]

In some ways he never grew up emotionally. The demands and rages of his childhood persisted throughout his adulthood to his deathbed. What made him that way? As a second child, he competed for attention with his older brother Joseph, who lacked his decisiveness, drive, intelligence, and vision. Rather than punish him, his parents, and later the military—which would grant him five extended leaves while he was a young officer—indulged his precociousness. So he was used to having his way.

That sense of privilege was offset by the heavy burden of somehow always being an outsider. At the tender age of nine he was sent away to school in a foreign country where he was mocked and bullied for his foreign origins, puny appearance, fierce pride, and quick temper. At the time, he hated France as much as he loved and romanticized his faraway home of Corsica. So, not surprisingly, he was driven to prove himself and win the approval of others. By his mid-twenties, he had transferred his allegiance to France and language to French, but remained an object of scorn to many for his accent, and to most women because he was undersized, ill-kept, awkward, and brusque. Even after taking power, he was mocked as a parvenu by most European aristocrats, especially after he crowned himself emperor. So Bonaparte spent much of his life trying to assert himself and achieve legitimacy in the eyes of others.

Despite all that emotional baggage, Bonaparte could be compassionate, tender, and loving. Louis Bourrienne, his secretary and school friend, revealed some of the conflicting sides of his complex nature: "He had everything required . . . to be a pleasant man, except the wish to do so. He was far too domineering to entice people." Yet "when removed from the political world, he could be sensitive, good, and capable of showing pity. He liked children very much. . . . He could be genial and even most indulgent so far as human weaknesses were concerned."[9]

It is said that no man is a hero to his butler. Like all rules, that has its exceptions. Bonaparte remained a hero, however flawed and all too human, to his valet of fourteen years (1800 to 1814), Louis Constant, who has left posterity his entertaining, insightful, and largely accurate memoirs. Constant recalled that in private Bonaparte "was nearly always cheerful, friendly, and chatty with his servants."[10] He could be rough in displaying his affection with those close to him; he would pinch an ear or pull a nose. Yet at times he could lapse into an introspective, sullen, or melancholy silence as he mulled ideas, resentments, or the paradoxes of life.

From an early age, Bonaparte displayed an abiding care for his family and did whatever he could to advance its fortunes. His letters to his loved ones are filled with deep concern for their health, happiness, and prosperity, along with constant offers of advice and aid. He rather than Joseph became the family's de facto head when his father died on February 24, 1785. After Bonaparte took over the French government in November 1799, his mingling of family and French fortunes would become ever more central to his diplomacy. Indeed, as will be seen, no one in history practiced nepotism on such a grand and blatant scale.

His first known letter, written when he was fourteen, reveals not only his deep concern for and involvement with his family but also his political savvy and diplomatic skills. In it he was trying to convince his uncle that his brother Joseph was better suited to the priesthood than the army. With keen intelligence, concision, logic, and emotion, he offered a penetrating character study of his brother, mourned for his father who had recently died, and strategized how to advance the family's pecuniary and political interests.[11]

The Romantic

As for romantic love, the young Bonaparte was at once shy and passionate. Desiree Clary was the object of his first prolonged crush, and, like that for many, it was sweet, flirtatious, awkward, innocent, and tormented. She was only fourteen, ten years his junior, when he began courting her. He was a tender suitor, sensitive and nurturing. In his letters, he continually encouraged her to cultivate herself by spending time with elevated minds, serious books, beautiful music, and exhilarating dance. With her, he shared his deepest hopes and fears.

His love for her appears to have climaxed in June 1795 when he fired off to her at least five letters overflowing with longing and passion. The intensity of his love may have exhausted and frightened her; she was too immature, inexperienced, and overwhelmed to return the power and depth of his feelings. He sensed her waning interest. In one letter he chides her for not writing for eleven days, and in another for wanting to put the sea between them by moving with her family to Genoa. He was so desperate to win her love that he even enlisted Joseph, who had married her older sister Julie, and others to assist his courtship. Desiree's inability to return Bonaparte's love agonized him. To Joseph, he wrote this stunning line: "If my relationship with Desiree doesn't work out . . . I will accept a place in the infantry and I will go to the Rhine to find my death."[12]

Eventually he became philosophical about his inevitable loss of her:

Tender [Desiree], you are young. Your sentiments are going to fade, to shift, and after a while you will find yourself changed. Such is the empire of time. Such is the fatal, infallible effect of absence. . . . Don't think that I can accuse you of injustice. A heart bruised by the storms of passion in a virile age is not worthy of you. It is a moment of life that will never return. . . . He who will be solely abandoned to the delicious sentiments of love must not be your lover . . . . The day that you love me no more, promise to tell me. . . . If destiny has linked our destinies as they have our souls, you might become accustomed to the strangeness of my love for you. It is the opposite of that of other men. It begins where others end and ends where others begin. I am nearly twenty-six and command an army with some success and yet it is my love that makes me happy.[13]

Those powerful, passionate feelings were not confined to his love for Desiree. For at least half of his life he was a fervent romantic. As a dreamy, lonely youth, he was inspired by Goethe's novel "Young Werther," along with tales by Rousseau, Ossian, and other romantics. As a young man, he aspired to be a writer, scribbling sonnets, essays, short stories, a play, and even an historical novel, most unpublished in his time. He filled many of his leisure hours as a second lieutenant by seizing his pen and writing a history of Corsica; he never finished it. His writings are far more valuable for what they reveal about him than their expression of style, sentiment, or thought. Bonaparte may well have had Young Werther in mind when he wrote: "Always alone amidst others, I return to dream and immerse myself in a vivid melancholy. In what way do I turn today? Toward death? Since I must die, why shouldn't I kill myself?"[14]

He was tormented by existential doubts about how to live or even whether to continue living in such a tumultuous, treacherous, and transient world. To Desiree, he described himself as a young man with "an imagination of fire, a cool head, a strange heart, and melancholy inclinations, someone who can shine among men like a meteor and then disappear. When one scorns life, there is no point in being virtuous."[15]

Those feelings deepened with time. On the eve of his first Italian campaign, he penned Josephine these heart-rending lines: "My friend, I feel the need to be consoled. It's only in writing you that . . . I can pour out my sorrow. What is the future? What is the past? What are we. . . . We are born, we live, we die amidst marvels. Is it surprising that priests, astrologers, and charlatans have profited from this tendency . . . to parade our ideas and direct them to the will of their passions."[16]

He became ever more cynical about human nature, yet remained vulnerable to its dark side: "Amidst the ferocity and immorality of men, one can win successes without having great merits. . . . When one knows men so well that one no longer esteems them and virtue becomes a problem, the soul will find itself burned."[17]

The Role of Circumstances: History and Fate

In such a world, Bonaparte could feel little more than despair. While posted with his regiment at Valence, he participated in an essay contest held by the Academy of Lyon on the question of what is essential for happiness. His "Discourse on Happiness" yields wonderful insights into his personal and political values at that time.

He spoke in Rousseauian terms of how each individual must develop himself through his passions, interests, and seized opportunities. To do so he must reject those political, social, and religious forces that would repress him and force him to conform to their dictates. Self-doubts and worries render that a difficult journey for even the most aware and determined individual. But "it is essential for my existence and especially my happiness."[18]

Yet few people enjoy the luxury of being able to chart their own respective courses in life. Later, on St. Helena, Bonaparte observed: "If, to be free, it were only enough to desire freedom, then all people would be free. But history shows only that few receive the benefits of freedom because few have the energy, courage, or virtue that it takes."[19]

Obviously there is a dynamic between the circumstances and choices of one's life, with each shaping the other. How truly free are most people to choose their respective paths in life? Any authentic choice can only come when someone completely understands a given situation, and then can and does weigh the possible options. Often a person may not have enough information, or may unconsciously distort the information vital to making a truly free choice.

And then there are the circumstances themselves. Certainly nearly everyone would do everything possible to avoid life's tragedies and limitations if it were possible. One must make the best of what life offers. But what determines those circumstances that are so clearly beyond our control? Ultimately, it is impossible to determine whether purely random chance or supernatural forces govern what Bonaparte often lamented as the "dictatorship of the events" that channel each human life.

After he first achieved fame, Bonaparte acted constantly with an eye toward history and his place in it. He tried to write the history of himself and his times as he lived it. He was obsessed with accomplishing as much as he could in what time he had. He looked continually both to the past and the future. He consciously modeled his policies on those of his heroes, such as Alexander for his dream of carving out an oriental empire, Paoli for modernizing France, Charlemagne for uniting Europe, and all of history's greatest generals for their successful military campaigns.

Yet for a man compelled to launch himself into such whirlwinds of planning and action, whether at war, diplomacy, government, or love, Bonaparte was astonishingly fatalistic. Although he continually struggled to be history's central actor, he felt more like the marionette of forces far beyond his understanding, let alone control. He certainly believed in something he variously called "destiny" or "my star." Throughout his life he was heard to remark that "destiny directs all my operations" or that "I feel myself propelled towards some unknown goal."[20] From a young age he sensed that he was destined for great things, and he did whatever he could to make the most of the opportunities that life presented him. And then, at the height of his successes and powers, he believed that destiny turned its back on him; and thereafter, no matter what he did, he would fail.

He expressed the capriciousness of fate in a letter to Talleyrand in October 1797, after he had finally completed a year and a half military and diplomatic campaign to expel the Austrians from Italy. One might expect him to boast of those deeds which proved to be decisive in that epic struggle. Yet success often left him reflective rather than exultant, especially in his younger years. To Talleyrand, he remarked that "from triumph to a plunge is but a step. I saw in all the greatest circumstances that one does nothing to decide great events."[21] Fatalists tend to dismiss the importance of their choices and acts to both their successes and their failures. Certainly Bonaparte was not someone who readily admitted his mistakes as he made them. Yet he would spend much of his time on St. Helena lamenting his follies.

The Role of Institutions: Church and State

Bonaparte was among those who are profoundly spiritual but not religious. Once when he was asked about his beliefs, he pointed to the sky and replied, "I do not believe in any religion but . . . I speak of God who made all that."[22]

Yet he did not scorn organized religion. Quite the contrary, like most conservatives he believed that religion was crucial to political, economic, and social order. Institutionalized faith was one of many tools by which the few governed the many, by promoting values such as respect for authority, hierarchy, obedience, community, and blind belief—values cherished by any dictator.

So religions should be respected and nurtured—as long as they fulfilled their political duties to support the state and suppress the masses. Unlike most conservatives, Bonaparte did not believe that any one religion was better than the others. He was essentially a deist who believed in some supernatural power that was the first cause of the universe but was largely indifferent to most individual lives. This power did, however, favor a privileged few, such as himself.

So it was in the Henri IV tradition of "Paris is worth a mass" that Bonaparte freely admitted his strategy of appealing to the faith of the people he was trying to conquer: "It was by making myself a Catholic that I won the war in the Vendee, by making myself a Moslem that I established myself in Egypt, by making myself an ultramontane that I turned men's hearts toward me in Italy. If I were to govern a nation of Jews I would rebuild the Temple of Solomon."[23]

Yet Bonaparte did not always practice that sensible policy. One reason for the ferocity of Spain's guerrillas was his policies of confiscating church property, subordinating the church to the state, and even abolishing the Inquisition, which most Spaniards celebrated for purging their country of the unfaithful.

Bonaparte had equally conflicted views over the question of the relation between the state of nature and the nature of the state. As for human nature, like many people when he was younger he embraced Rousseau, but as he aged through the hard school of experience he leaned ever more toward Hobbes: "The natural spirit of man is the wish to dominate. . . . Man in nature knows no other law than self-interest: take care of himself, destroy his enemies, these were his daily tasks."[24]

Yet when it came to ruling, he sought a dynamic mix of Hobbes and Rousseau, a strong state that expressed the general will of the people: "My policy is to govern men as the greatest number wish to be governed. That's the best way, I believe, to recognize the sovereignty of the people." But more than that, he argued that the "goal of government is to lend a strong hand to the weak against the strong, permitting each person to taste sweet tranquility, to find himself on the road to happiness."[25]

Napoleon and the People

By all accounts, Bonaparte had a personal touch with the common soldier or tradesman. He scolded his brother Lucien for talking down to the French in his flowery speeches before the Senate or in other public forums: "Too many words and not enough ideas. You can't speak like that to the ordinary man in the street. He has more common sense and tact than you think."[26] Yet Bonaparte was at times notoriously blunt and even boorish with members of the elite. He did this to intimidate them, personifying Machiavelli's maxim that it is better to be feared than loved.

Exacerbating Bonaparte's conflicted views of life were first the promise and then the terrors of the French Revolution. News of the revolution unfolding in Paris and spreading across the nation initially excited him. Inspired by Rousseau's writings and Paoli's life, he had nurtured liberal and nationalist sentiments, albeit for Corsica rather than France, long before the Estates General convened in May 1789, and he would have loved to be a deputy. He fervently believed in the revolutionary ideals of liberty, equality, fraternity, and careers open to all talents. At first he was able to justify the revolution's excesses: "Blood runs throughout France, but nearly everywhere that has been the impure blood of the enemies of liberty and the nation." With time he realized that violence betrayed rather than fulfilled the revolution's ideals, and he condemned the Jacobins as "crazy and senseless."[27]

It was one thing to be a distant recipient of news of revolutionary events in Paris and elsewhere; quite another to experience the full horrors of mass violence. When he began practicing war it took him took a long time to coarsen himself to its carnage. The death of Felix Joseph Antoine Chauvet, a staff officer, on the eve of Bonaparte's first Italian campaign literally haunted him: "He was very attached to me. He rendered essential services to the nation. His last word was to speak of joining me. . . . I see his shadow. . . . He hisses in the wind; his soul is in the clouds; he will be in charge of my destiny. Insanely, I spill tears on our friendship."[28]

He could be just as sensitive to the fates of others and revealing of his own soul, as in his letter to the widow of Admiral Francois Paul Brueys d' Aigallier, who was killed during the battle of the Nile. Although Brueys died as a result of his own folly, Bonaparte overlooked that and wrote that her husband's death was the sweetest, the most envied by warriors.

> I sense vividly your sorrow. The moment that we are separated from the object of our love is terrible; it isolates us on earth; it punishes us with convulsions and agonies. The powers of our souls are annihilated; we only conserve our relations with the universe by crossing nightmares which alter everything. One can only feel in this situation that if nothing forces us to live, it would be better to die. But then after that first thought, we press our children to our hearts . . . and we live for our children. Yes, Madame, you will cry with them, you will raise them from children, you will cultivate their youths; you will speak with them of their father, of your sorrow, of your loss.[29]

How did Bonaparte manage to pull himself back from his frequent forays to the edge of the abyss? Planning and executing grand plans was the best antidote to the existential poison in his mind. But when that was not possible, he turned for solace to the creations of writers, artists, and composers. Reading the romantics, however, only tended to deepen his brooding. As for painting, he most enjoyed depictions of grand historic moments that inspired him to redouble his own efforts at greatness. Likewise he loved plays and operas that explored the dilemmas of ambitious generals and statesmen. But no art inspired him more than music, which he described as "the soul of love, the sweetness of life, the consolation for grief, and the company of innocence."[30]

In all, when he felt himself dragged down by his past failures, perilous challenges, or life's paradoxes, he tried to find and lose himself in immediate pleasures. To Desiree, he explained: "We cannot, my good friend, demand anything of the future, only of the present; the only good way is not to have any regrets, in not making any sad reflections incompatible with one's nature. Time overthrows all empires, destroys worlds, and changes all our affections. So it is vain to want to anticipate and prejudge the future."[31] As will be seen, two betrayals of his love, one for a man and the other for a woman, would transform him from a romantic into the most worldly and ruthless of cynics.

Napoleon and Corsica: Family, Politics and Allegiance

Although Bonaparte was a commissioned officer in His Majesty's army, his heart lay with his family in Corsica rather than his regiment in France.

Not long after he was commissioned he was somehow able to wangle a leave from his military duties for a year, from September 1786 to September 1787! He spent most of his time in Corsica beset with trying to overcome family problems, such as the vast debts that his deceased father had left and the education of his younger brothers and sisters. With Joseph now studying law in Padua, Bonaparte took over as the family head.

He was no sooner back in Valence than he got another leave, on November 22, 1787. This time he headed first to Paris, where his most notable accomplishment was to lose his virginity to a prostitute in the Palais Royale, before returning to Corsica and re-immersing himself in family matters for the first half of 1788. While he was gone his regiment was transferred to Auxonne. He caught up with it in June 1788. After the revolution broke out he took his third extended leave from his regiment and hurried to Corsica in September 1789. He remained there for twenty months, not returning to his regiment until May 1791. Politics now competed with family for his attention; indeed, from this time forward he would try to advance his family's fortunes through politics.

Bonaparte was only twenty when he plunged into Corsica's political labyrinth; it would be a proving ground in which he could test his ideas, manhood, and ambitions, and develop his political, military, and diplomatic skills. Of all the vital political lessons he learned in Corsica, perhaps the most important was that, although myths rarely reflect realities, they are an essential element of government, war, and diplomacy.

Bonaparte had returned with the hope that somehow, amidst all the revolutionary convulsions, the Corsicans might win at least autonomy, or ideally outright independence, and that somehow he could lead that movement. That anti-colonial struggle received a setback when on November 30, 1789, the National Assembly declared that Corsica would henceforth be an integral part of France and granted Corsicans the same constitutional rights and protections as all other citizens. To guide that transition from colony to province, the government dispatched Antonio Cristoforo Salicetti to his native land.

Bonaparte and Salicetti soon became friends. Among other things they shared the hope that Pascal Paoli could be enticed to return to lead Corsica. Who was this man who so inspired most Corsicans?[32] Paoli was born in 1725, received a classical education centered around Plutarch's lives of virtuous public men, and from his early manhood struggled to liberate Corsica from the Republic of Genoa. In November 1755, he and his followers took power, declared independence, implemented a constitution, cut taxes and corruption, promoted trade and agriculture, founded a university, and curbed the vendetta. In all, he worked to transform Corsica from a feudal, superstitious, clannish, and violent island into a modern state based on Enlightenment ideals of reason and reform. Jean Jacques Rousseau and other luminaries lauded Paoli's efforts. Bonaparte would later try to do all that and more for France and its growing empire.

When, after years of struggle, the Genoese could not crush the rebellion, they gave up and handed the island over to France on May 15, 1768, in exchange for the write-off of their debt to Paris. A massive invasion by French troops eventually managed to rout the rebels and secure Corsica. Paoli escaped aboard a British frigate in June 1769, two months before Napoleon's birth.

Bonaparte grew up hearing tales of Paoli as a political Robin Hood. His father followed Paoli until the French takeover, before reluctantly transferring his loyalty to Corsica's new master; undoubtedly Carlo's loyalties remained conflicted until his last breath. Until his mid-twenties, his second son displayed the same ambivalence, but for now Bonaparte hated France with a passion. He revealed the depths of that rage in a letter to Paoli on June 12, 1789:

> I was born when the country perished; 30,000 Frenchmen, vomited on our shores, drowning the throne of liberty in flows of blood, that was the odious spectacle that first struck my notice. The cries of the dying, the groans of the oppressed, the tears of the desperate surrounded the cradle of my birth. You left your island, and with you disappeared the hopes of happiness; slavery was the price of our submission, crushed beneath the triple chain of soldiers, bureaucrats, and tax collectors.[33]

Inspired by many such appeals from Corsican nationalists, Paoli made a triumphant return on July 17, 1790. He was soon elected president of the Corsican General Council and commander of the National Guard. He called for a federal union with France in which Corsica had political autonomy and its own constitution.

Like many political comebacks, Paoli's could not recapture the success and magic of his first tenure. It was one thing to defy the Republic of Genoa, and quite another revolutionary France. This was the France that had championed many of Paoli's ideals while forging a modern centralized state in which every department would follow the dictates of Paris. So the Paoli who had been a model of dynamism and progress the first time he governed Corsica became a political cipher during his second and last time. He deliberately gave the appearance of leaning in all political directions. That was not just prudent politics as violence and extremism mounted; as a symbol of Corsica itself, he had to be as conciliatory as possible.

Bonaparte understood and supported Paoli's political high-wire act. Yet he gradually cooled to Paoli himself. When Bonaparte began his "History of Corsica" and asked Paoli to send him documents, Paoli's response was curt. Word got back to Bonaparte that Paoli dismissed him as a "ragazzone inspecto," a "big unworldly boy."[34] These words wounded deeply the sensitive, passionate, patriotic youth struggling to become a man. His spirits lifted, however, when he was elected lieutenant colonel of Ajaccio's second volunteer battalion on April 1, 1792.

While Bonaparte had largely resigned himself to the attachment of Corsica and Paoli to France, he could not suppress his own restless idealism, energy, and ambitions. If he could not liberate Corsica, he reasoned, he could at least help nurture the revolution in France. As a result, when he left Corsica he did not return to his regiment but headed instead to Paris, where he arrived on May 28, 1792. The National Assembly had declared war on Austria the previous month, on April 20, and the radical Jacobins were amassing ever more power while squeezing out more moderate rivals. Bonaparte did what he could to curry favor with the Jacobins, of whom one presciently observed, "I do not see him stopping short of either the throne or the scaffold."[35] Still, his latest loyalty cooled when he witnessed the mob butcher the Swiss Guards at the Tuileries Palace on August 10. It was time to return to his regiment.

Bonaparte's commander not only welcomed him back but promoted him to lieutenant. The promotion reflected not so much Bonaparte's merits but the regiment's needs. The steady stream of officers into exile opened more opportunities for those who stayed behind—especially artillery officers, with their special skills. Napoleon was one of only six of his fifty-six classmates who remained in France.[36]

Before long Bonaparte longed for his native land and began a fifth leave in Corsica in October 1792. This would be his most eventful sojourn of all. On February 18, 1793, he embarked as the second-in-command of his first military expedition, this one to conquer Sardinia. It was an ignominious failure. Under orders from Colonna Cesari, he landed his troops on the tiny island of San

Stefano and prepared to invade neighboring Magdalena Island, but the troops mutinied and forced Cesari to let them re-embark and sail back to Corsica.[37]

That failure and rumors that Paoli was increasingly leaning toward the royalists and the English prompted the Convention to condemn him, on April 2, 1793, as an ambitious conspirator who would sell out Corsica and the revolution to England. The order for Paoli to come to Paris to account for his actions arrived in Ajaccio on April 12.

Although Bonaparte's faith in Paoli had been fissuring since 1790, the condemnation provoked him into penning to the Convention a passionate defense of Paoli against all charges. The letter reveals his budding diplomatic skills. He began by singing the Convention's praises, and only then countered all the attacks against Paoli. He flattered the bloated, hyper-sensitive, and quick-triggered egos of the Convention by lauding them as "the true organs of the people's sovereignty. All your decrees are dictated or immediately ratified by the Nation. Each of your laws is a benefit and gives you a new title in the recognition of posterity which you owe to the Republic and to the world, to which you gave liberty." He then pointed to the Convention's only mistake: accusing "an old man in his seventies, afflicted with infirmities, devoted to fulfilling his mission" as a "scandalous, vile, and ambitious villain." After his point-by-point rebuttal, he concluded: "We owe him everything."[38]

Despite that courageous defense of his tarnished hero, within weeks Bonaparte had not just broken with Paoli but was fleeing with his family from the wrath of Paoli's followers. It happened because Paoli had responded to the Convention's condemnation and summons to Paris by spurning that demand and mobilizing 5,000 troops. The Convention declared him an outlaw.

Bonaparte now faced a cruel choice. Even in the unlikely event that Paoli and his forces could somehow stave off the French and declare independence, Bonaparte reckoned he had no future in that regime. As was typical, Corsican politics had become thoroughly entangled in clan rivalries. Joseph and Lucien had joined Bonaparte in struggling at once to advance the fortunes of their family and Corsica. The Bonapartes had forged a tight alliance with Salicetti and his clan, dedicated to nurturing Corsican autonomy within the French republic.

Their worst political enemies were the allied Pozzo di Borgo and Buttafuoco clans; their leader was Charles Andre Pozzo di Borgo, who had served as a lawyer, Paoli's secretary, deputy to the National Assembly, and president of the Corsican state council.

Salicetti received orders from Paris to arrest Paoli. To defy those orders would undoubtedly take him and the Bonaparte brothers to the scaffold; to obey them would provoke a civil war in Corsica. As he was mulling that dilemma, Lucien publicly denounced Paoli as a counter-revolutionary and an English agent. Paoli's government condemned the Bonapartes to "civil death," which meant that the state would confiscate their property and status. They actually arrested Bonaparte on May 5, but somehow he was able to escape. He fled from Ajaccio to Bastia, arriving on May 10. Paoli and his provisional government declared independence for Corsica on May 17. After a mob wrecked the Bonapartes' home in Ajaccio on May 23, the family fled to Calvi, where Bonaparte joined them on June 2. They sailed from Corsica on June 11 and landed at Golfe Juan near Antibes on June 13. Bonaparte helped his family settle in a house they had previously purchased in Marseilles. Then he rejoined his regiment, which was now stationed at Nice.

This was a decisive turning point in Bonaparte's life. He had forever abandoned his hero Paoli and the dream of an independent republic of Corsica. From now on he would dedicate himself to France and the revolution—a revolution that he would eventually hijack and reinvent in his own image.

Yet that was an unimaginable future when he and his family set foot in France as refugees, with only their meager belongings, a burning rage at the Paolists, sorrow at leaving their shattered home and nation, and immense gratitude for having escaped with their lives. Each of them would have to do whatever he or she could to rebuild the family fortunes in a new land.

The Nature of France

The Bonapartes did not pull themselves up by their bootstraps all by themselves. They were among a wave of Corsican refugees who fled to France. Among them was their friend and ever-more-influential political ally Salicetti. He would soon get Bonaparte promoted to captain, and eventually won him command of the artillery at Toulon.

It was soon evident that the Bonapartes had escaped one peril only to plunge into another. As they mulled their options, France was being torn apart between nationalists who favored centralized power, federalists who favored regional autonomy, and royalists who mostly advocated a constitutional monarchy. With the nationalists firmly rooted in power in Paris, the federalists and royalists cooperated. In the summer of 1793, those allies took over

Avignon, Marseilles, and eventually Toulon, and declared their autonomy from Paris.

Thus were the Bonapartes trapped in another civil war. When Bonaparte received orders on July 3 to rejoin his regiment, he could not have imagined that he would play a leading role in that war. But within half a year the unknown artillery captain would be promoted to general and celebrated as a national hero.

Bonaparte's views on politics and life were rapidly changing. If his "Discourse on Happiness" had expressed his young Rousseauian views, his "The Supper at Beaucaire," published on July 29, 1793, reflected his development into a fervent French revolutionary and nationalist.

In the "Discourse" he wrote of a debate he had over dinner with four merchants who were "federalists" and supported the recent declaration of autonomy by Marseilles from Paris. Bonaparte now as fervently favored a powerful state as he had once favored first Corsican independence and then autonomy within a federalist France. He condemned the federalists as royalist dupes who were trying to weaken France before its enemies. He also condemned Paoli for tricking the people and betraying Corsica.

Nonetheless, he called for national reconciliation, lamenting that "we tear each other to pieces, we hate each other, and we kill each other without knowing what our opponents are like." He called for "all parties to put aside their differences and unite against their common foreign enemies. . . . Better to risk oneself with the possibility of victory than to become a victim without hope." He observed wisely that "the most dangerous counselor is self-esteem." Alas, he would fail to heed his own advice in the years ahead.

He ended with this appeal:

> Listen to me, my friends from Marseilles, shake off the yoke of the few criminals who are leading you into the counter-revolution. Reestablish your constitutional authorities. Accept the Constitution. Restore to the deputies their liberty. Let them go to Paris to plead for you. You have been led astray. It is nothing new for the people to be led by a small number of conspirators. . . . In all ages the gullibility and ignorance of the mob have been the cause of most civil wars.

Having convinced the federalists, he lauded them for seeing reason. They resumed their discussion at breakfast the following morning, "when the Marseillais had several more doubts to put forward, and I plenty of interesting truths to bring home to them."[39]

Initial Military Successes

Bonaparte's regiment was part of General Jean Francois Carteaux's force, which was assigned the mission of retaking the rebel towns and pacifying the region. Avignon capitulated on July 26 and Marseilles on August 25. That left the Toulon federalists, who had not only allied with royalists but invited in a British armada under Admiral Samuel Hood on August 27. Toulon was the home port of France's Mediterranean fleet. In addition to its deep, protected waters and complex of warehouses and shipyards, Toulon was ringed by forts on the surrounding hills. The British field commander, General Charles O'Hara, had manned those positions with his own mixed force of British, Piedmontese, Neapolitan, Spanish, federalist, and royalist troops, which so far had repulsed every French assault.

When the position to command the artillery at Toulon opened, Salicetti secured it for Bonaparte, even though he was a mere captain. Bonaparte received his orders on September 6, 1793, and would be promoted to major on October 18.

It was at Toulon that Bonaparte first revealed his genius for war and diplomacy. It was also there that he formed a group of devoted comrades who would follow him, often until their deaths: Duroc, Junot, Desaix, Marmont, Leclerc, and Suchet.

Within days after taking command, Bonaparte had carefully examined the enemy's defenses, identified the weakest and most strategic point, and devised a plan that would systematically evict the English. All that was easy enough for him. The real challenge was in convincing General Carteaux to adopt the plan. Jealous that after weeks of siege he and his aides had not reached the same sensible conclusions, Carteaux dismissed the plan as unworkable.

It was then that Bonaparte had to resort to diplomacy. He submitted his plan to the local revolutionary committee, which forwarded it to Paris. The Committee of Public Safety enthusiastically approved the plan and replaced Carteaux with General Doppet. Although the new commander proved to be every bit as inept as his predecessor, Doppet did later have nice things to say about Bonaparte: that he "joins many talents with a rare courage and indefeatible energy."[40] The Committee replaced Doppet with General Jacques Dugommier.

After arriving on November 16, Dugommier approved Bonaparte's plan and gave him full powers to implement it. Bonaparte set to work massing guns, munitions, and troops at key points. O'Hara understood the significance of Bonaparte's work and ordered a sortie on November 30. Bonaparte directed the repulse of that attack.

Finally, after months of preparation and diplomacy, the decisive battle came on December 17. Bonaparte gave the order for his massed guns to open a bombardment. He then led the assault which captured the fort and killed or captured over 400 British and their allies, and took O'Hara prisoner, at a cost of 50 French dead and 150 wounded. Bonaparte was among the casualties, having suffered a bayonet wound in his calf. Just as darkness fell he ordered the captured guns turned on the British fleet massed in the harbor below. That night Admiral Hood prudently withdrew his troops from the surrounding hills into his ships, along with as many munitions and provisions as possible; torched the arsenal, warehouses, and those French ships that he could not man; and sailed away.

Bonaparte was celebrated as the hero of Toulon and was promoted to brigadier general on December 22. He had learned valuable lessons in war and diplomacy. But he also saw first-hand how ruthless the revolution could be: the commissars ordered the execution of 800 federalist and royalist prisoners.

During this time Augustin Robespierre, Pierre's younger brother, squeezed out Salicetti to become the region's chief commissar and Bonaparte's mentor. Robespierre gave Bonaparte command of the Army of Italy's artillery on February 7, and shortly thereafter assigned him the task of inspecting France's coastal defenses along the Mediterranean from the Rhone River to the Italian frontier. Bonaparte spent the next six weeks systematically examining that region's forts and ports, and then wrote reports on just how to strengthen them.[41]

Robespierre recalled Bonaparte to the Army of Italy's headquarters at Nice in April 1794 and put him in charge of devising a plan for an invasion of Italy. In his plan, Bonaparte revealed some of the principles of war that would guide him for the next two decades:

> One should not at all disperse but instead concentrate one's attacks. A campaign should be like a siege which masses fire at a single point; once the breach is made, the enemy's equilibrium is broken and can do nothing more as the position is taken.

But he was just as canny in understanding the grand strategic picture. He advised a coordinated offensive of four French armies against its enemies along the German and Italian fronts. To do so, he proposed withdrawing troops from the Spanish frontier.[42]

Augustin Robespierre took Bonaparte's plan to Paris and personally presented it to the Committee of Public Safety. Although the committee and War Minister Lazare Carnot were impressed with the plan, they finally rejected it due to lack of resources to devote to that distant, secondary front and protests by the Army of the Alps that the plan gave it only a supporting role in the campaign.

However, General Pierre Dumerbion, the Army of Italy's commander, did approve Bonaparte's plan, which he received on April 2, for a limited offensive in the Maritime Alps. Under Bonaparte's supervision, the French took the fort at Oneglia on April 8, defeated the Piedmontese at Saorgio on April 28, and captured the strategic Col de Tend on May 11. This small-scale offensive was the perfect training ground and first step up the ever grander scales of warfare that Bonaparte would master in the years to come.

Falling Outs: Personal, Political, Governmental

It was during this time that Bonaparte and Salicetti had a falling out. Salicetti was jealous of being superseded by Robespierre in authority, over both the region and the young general. Then, apparently, Bonaparte bested Salicetti in love as they both vied for the affections of Desiree Clary. Although just what transpired is unclear, Salicetti not only lost out to Bonaparte but was transferred to serve as commissar of the Army of the Alps. He would soon avenge his humiliations.

It was also during this time that Bonaparte received his first diplomatic mission. In July, the Committee of Public Safety sent him to Genoa to assess the nature of its relationship with revolutionary France and the degree of Austrian influence in its policies. He left for Genoa on July 11 and spent a couple of weeks there trying to learn all that he could and convince that government to remain neutral. He returned to Nice on July 29.

Two days before he returned to headquarters, the latest convulsion broke out in Paris. Jean Paul Barras, Jean Tallien, and Joseph Fouche led a coup which recaptured the government from the Jacobins, put its leaders on trial, and purged their followers from positions of power across France. Suddenly the "hero of Toulon" was under suspicion for his Jacobin ties and became one of seventy-four officers arrested for their links to the Jacobin leaders of the Terror.

Bonaparte was placed under arrest on August 9 and imprisoned at Fort Carre at Antibes. Salicetti was the chief instigator behind the charges that his diplomatic mission to Genoa had actually been a cover for the Jacobins to betray the revolution. Bonaparte was philosophical about his incarceration: "Men can be unjust toward me . . . but it's sufficient to be innocent; my conscience is the tribunal where I evoke my conduct. This conscience is calm when I am interrogated."[43] He delivered a powerful defense of himself which appealed both to reason and emotion:

> You have suspended my work, arrested and declared me a suspect. . . . In a revolutionary state, there are two classes, suspects and patriots. . . . To declare a patriot a suspect is a judgment that wrenches him from all that is most precious. . . . In which class will you put me? From the beginning of the revolution, haven't I always devoted myself to its principles? . . . I abandoned my property and gave up everything for the revolution. Then, I served at Toulon with some distinction. . . . Thus no one can ever dispute my title of being a patriot.[44]

His appeal worked: he was released on August 20.

The British had captured Corsica on August 9, ironically the same day that the island's most famous son was incarcerated. To rehabilitate himself, Bonaparte asked to plan and command an expedition to retake Corsica. He also refined and resubmitted his plan for the invasion of Italy. Once again he had to get the Committee's approval. This time he would do so in person.

In Paris all his impassioned reason was to no avail. Although he had been acquitted, he remained suspect. For now the new government decided to sideline rather than cashier him. Starting with being named head of the Topographical Bureau on August 19, 1794, he was given a series of minor posts in Paris, where he would remain in bureaucratic limbo until he once again had a chance to display his brilliance. In May 1795 he was given command of the artillery of the Army of the West, which struggled to crush the Vendean and Chouan uprisings, but he never entered that field.

A five-man Directory led by Barras replaced the Committee of Public Safety as France's government in September 1795. The new regime's hold on power was shaky. Despite the purge, plenty of Jacobins remained free to plot revenge. On October 5, 1795, the Jacobins rallied over twenty thousand followers to converge on Paris and retake the government.

Key Triumphs

In response, the Directory urgently called on Bonaparte to organize the city's defense. Bonaparte massed guns and troops at critical points, bloodily repulsed the mob, and saved the Directory. Once again Napoleon Bonaparte was celebrated as a French hero. Barras rewarded him with command of the Army of Italy.

But that was not all. Barras also passed on to the young general his former mistress, Rose de Beauharnais, whom Bonaparte called and history recalls as Josephine. She was pretty, vivacious, and, having passed her childhood in Martinique, exuded a natural, beguiling sensuality. She was also six years older than Bonaparte, had two young children, and had lost her husband to a guillotine's blade. It would be Josephine whose unfaithfulness would eventually inflict the knock-out blow to Bonaparte's romanticism.

Bonaparte was instantly smitten. For him, Josephine's charms trumped any notion that she was among the discards of someone as dissolute as Barras, whose sexual hungers were unrestricted by gender or age. To Josephine he wrote some of history's most fervent love letters—until proof of her infidelity destroyed his passion for her. In his first known missive to her, he writes:

> I awaken filled with you. Your intoxicating vision and memories of last night will not leave my feelings. Sweet and incomparable Josephine, what a strange effect you've had on my heart! . . . My soul is bursting with sorrow. . . . I take from your lips and your heart a flame that burns me. . . . I am waiting to receive a thousand kisses, but don't give me them because they'll scorch my blood.[45]

Josephine at first was as much repulsed as intrigued by him. She saw him as an idle amusement that Barras had tossed in her lap. But she bored easily, especially when comparing Bonaparte to others with whom she had shared her charms. The two could not have been more ill-matched. She had enjoyed a succession of skilled lovers over a dozen or more years; he had had a few sporadic, fleeting encounters with street prostitutes, hardly the best training for a would-be lover. Most likely his skill at love-making fell far short of his passions. In his nights with her, his desires were fulfilled, while hers were not. They were both ever more frustrated, her from boredom, him from her coquettish distance.

And then there was his personality. He was certainly no polished aristocrat who could fill a crowded salon or locked boudoir with wit, gaiety, and finesse. Indeed, he was naturally taciturn and ill-at-ease, especially in elite social settings, and could at times become outright boorish. Yet he impressed her with the passion of his love for her, and more so by the widespread belief that he was bound for glory and its accompanying riches and power.

So, despite her doubts, Josephine agreed to Bonaparte's pleas that they marry. She could console herself with knowing that he would soon be far away on the Italian front, where he might well meet his death. Regardless, she could reimmerse herself in the whirl of lovers, parties, and shopping in Paris. A simple civil ceremony attended by only four friends legally united them on March 6, 1796.

Two days later Bonaparte raced off to Nice to take command of the campaign which would dramatically shift Europe's power balance, propel France toward eventual domination of the continent, and gain him eternal fame as one of history's greatest commanders.

Chapter One Endnotes

1. The literature on personality and politics is vast. Among the works that informed this book are: Jerrod M. Post, *Leaders and Their Followers in a Dangerous World: The Psychology of Political Behavior* (Ithaca, N.Y.: Cornell University Press, 2004); Martha L. Cottam, et al., *Introduction to Political Psychology* (Mahwah, N.J.: Lawrence Erlbaum Associates, 2004); Russell Dalton, ed., *The Oxford Handbook of Political Behavior* (New York: Oxford University Press, 2007); David Haughton, *Political Psychology: Situations, Individuals, and Cases* (London: Routledge, 2008); Greg Ogden and Daniel Meyer, *Leadership Essentials: Shaping Vision, Multiplying Influence, Defining Character* (Downers Grove, Ill.: Intervarsity Press, 2007); Catherine Fitzgerald, *Developing Leaders: Research and Applications in Psychological Types and Leadership* (New York: Davies-Black, 1997); Oliver Woshinksky, *Explaining Politics: Cultural Institutions and Political Behavior* (London: Routledge, 2007).

2. Emmanuel Auguste Dieudonne Las Cases, *Memorial de Sainte Helene* (Paris: Editions de Seuil, 1968), 193.

3. Napoleon may well be history's most debatable character. For excellent literature reviews of that debate, see: Pieter Geyl, *Napoleon: For and Against* (New Haven, Conn.: Yale University Press, 1949); Charles J. Esdaile, "The Napoleonic Period: Some Thoughts on Recent Historiography," *European History Quarterly* 23 (1993), 415-32; Leigh Ann Whaley, *The Impact of Napoleon, 1800-1815* (Lanham, Md.: Scarecrow Press, 1997). Hundreds of books have been written on Napoleon. Among the more prominent recent biographies that I have used for this study are: Jean Tulard, *Napoleon ou le Mythe du Sauveur* (Paris: Fayard, 1987); Alan Schom, *Napoleon Bonaparte* (New York: HarperCollins, 1997); Robert Asprey, *The Rise of Napoleon Bonaparte* (New York: Basic Books, 2000); Steven Englund, *Napoleon, A Political Life* (Cambridge, Mass.: Harvard University Press, 2004). By far, the most up-to-date analysis of Napoleon as a ruler is the three-volume modern classic by Thierry Lentz: *Le Grand Consulat, 1799-1804* (Paris: Fayard, 1999); Nouvelle Histoire du Premier Empire: *Napoleon et la Conquete de l'Europe* (Paris: Fayard, 2002); Nouvelle Histoire du Premier Empire: *l'Effondrement du Systeme Napoleonien, 1810-1814* (Paris: Fayard, 2004).

4. For the best book which explores such questions, see: Dorothy Carrington, *Napoleon et ses Parents: Au Seuil de l'Histoire* (Paris: Editions Alain Piazzola & La Marge, 2000). A more detailed if not psychologically penetrating study is Arthur Chuquet, *La Jeunesse de Napoleon*, 3 vols. (Paris: Armand Colin, 1897).

5. Englund, *Napoleon*, 13.

6. Carrington, *Napoleon et ses Parents*, 102.

7. Carrington, *Napoleon et ses Parents*, 80.

8. Asprey, *Rise of Napoleon*, 13.

9. Louis Antoine Fauvelet de Bourrienne, *Memoires de M. de Bourrienne sur Napoleon*, 5 vols. (Paris: Garnier, 1899-1900), 1:424-25.

10. Louis Constant, *Memoires Intimes de Napoleon Ier par Constant, son valet de chambre*, 2 vols. (Paris: Mercure de France, 1967), 1:223.

11. Napoleon to Joseph Fesch, June 25, 1784, Thierry Lentz, ed., *General Correspondence* (Paris: Fayard, 2004), 1.

12. Napoleon to Joseph, June 24, 1795, *General Correspondence*, 232.

13. Bonaparte to Desiree, June 14, 1795, *General Correspondence*, 303.

14. Tulard, *Napoleon*, 42.

15. Bonaparte to Desiree Clary, June 14, 1795, *General Correspondence*, 303.

16. Napoleon to Josephine, April 5, 1796, *General Correspondence*, 461.

17. Bonaparte to Desiree Clary, June 14, 1785, *General Correspondence*, 303.

18. Tulard, *Napoleon*, 62.

19. Las Cases, *Memorial de Sainte Helene*, 115.

20. Philippe Paul de Segur, *Histoires et Memoires*, 8 vols. (Paris: Firmin Didot, 1873), 4:74.

21. Bonaparte to Talleyrand, October 7, 1797, *General Correspondence*, 2149.

22. Owen Chadwick, *The Popes and European Revolution* (New York: Oxford University Press, 1981), 485.

23. Pierre Louis Roederer, *Oeuvres du Comte Pierre Louis Roederer*, 8 vols. (Paris: Firman Didot Freres, 1853-59), 3:334.

24. Roederer, *Oeuvres*, 2:102-03.

25. Roederer, *Oeuvres*, 3:334.

26. Gregor Dallas, *The Final Act: The Roads to Waterloo* (New York: Henry Holt, 1997), 266.

27. Bonaparte to Joseph Fesch, August 29, 1788, *General Correspondence*, 21; Bonaparte to Joseph, August 9, 1789, *ibid.*, 34; Bonaparte to Joseph, June 22, 1792, *ibid.*, 65.

28. Napoleon to Josephine, April 5, 1796, *General Correspondence*, 461.

29. Bonaparte to Madame Brueys, August 19, 1798, *General Correspondence*, 2869.

30. Napoleon to Desiree Clary, September 10, 1794, *General Correspondence*, 244.

31. Napoleon to Desiree Clary, August 10, 1795, *General Correspondence*, 321.

32. Peter A. Thrasher, *Pasquale Paoli: An Enlightened Hero, 1725-1807* (London: Constable, 1970); Antoine Maria Graziani, *Pascal Paoli Pere de la Patrie Corse* (Paris: Talladier, 2002).

33. Bonaparte to Pascal Paoli, June 12, 1789, *General Correspondence*, 29.

34. Eugene Deprez, "Les Origines Republicaines de Bonaparte," *Revue Historique*, 97, (1908), 319.

35. Asprey, *Rise of Napoleon*, 44.

36. Asprey, *Rise of Napoleon*, 60.

37. Bonaparte to Paoli, March 2, 1793, *General Correspondence*, 77.

38. Bonaparte to National Convention, April 18, 1793, *General Correspondence*, 79.

39. Somerset de Chair, ed., *Napoleon on Napoleon: An Autobiography of the Emperor* (London: Cassell, 1992), 59-70.

40. Tulard, *Napoleon*, 65. See also, Bonaparte to Bouchotte, War Minister, November 14, 1793, *General Correspondence*, no. 111; Bonaparte to Carteaux, mid-October, 1793, *ibid.*, 94; Bonaparte to Chauvet, ordnance commissioner, mid-October 1793, *ibid.*, 95; Bonaparte to Representatives of the People, October 16, 22, 1793, *ibid.*, 96, 102; Bonaparte to Committee of Public Safety, October 25, *ibid.*, 105; Bonaparte to Gassendi, chief of brigade, October 18, December 22, 1793, *ibid.*, 101, 126; Bonaparte to Bouchotte, war minister, November 14, 1793, *ibid.*, 111; Bonaparte to Duppin, adudant to war minister, November 30, 1793, *ibid.*, 113.

41. Bonaparte to Bouchotte, war minister, January 4, 20-25, 1794, *General Correspondence*, 139, 142; Bonaparte to Committee of Public Safety, February 12, 1794, *ibid*; 147; Bonaparte to People's Representatives, February 12, 28, 1794, *ibid.*, 148, 154;

Bonaparte to Mazurier, war ministry adudant, February 23 (2 letters), 1794, *ibid.*, 150, 151; Bonaparte to Maignet, people's representative, February 23, 28, 1794, *ibid.*, 152, 155; Bonaparte to General Pille, June 16, 1794, *ibid.*, 183.

42. Bonaparte's plan, June 20, 1794, *Correspondence*, 30; for a sampling of insights into his planning, see: Bonaparte to Multedo, Corsican deputy, *General Correspondence*, 248; Bonaparte to Berlier, under-director of artillery, October 17, 1794, *ibid.*, 257; Bonaparte to Andreossey, November 23, 1794, *ibid.*, 268, Bonaparte to Montfort, chief of brigade, November 22, 1794, *ibid.*, 267.

43. Bonaparte to Junot, August 12 or 19, 1794, *General Correspondence*, 235.

44. Napoleon to the Representatives of the People, August 12, 1794, *General Correspondence*, 236.

45. Bonaparte to Josephine, December 1795, *General Correspondence*, 387. For the most passionate and revealing of his letters, see Bonaparte to Josephine, December 1795, March [n.d.], 14, 30, April 3, 5, 7, 24, 29, June 8, 11, 14, 15, July 19, 22, October 17, 1796, *General Correspondence*, 387, 411, 414, 439, 454, 461, 467, 526, 547, 662, 677, 688, 693, 785, 811, 1,005.

The Rise of Bonaparte

1796-1799

"Italy is yours."

"Egypt calls me."

"What have you done to the country I left so powerful?"

—Napoleon Bonaparte

From Nice to Rivoli

Bonaparte's celebrated seizure of Toulon and defense of Paris revealed that he had the potential to do great things. Yet in both cases he had been subordinated to those with lesser ability and daring. With the grant of a field command in 1796, he finally enjoyed the means to display the full array of his military and diplomatic powers. He would make the very most of it.

The first step after arriving at his headquarters at Nice on March 26, 1796, was to actually take command of his army. That was no easy task. Nearly all his generals were not only older but, more importantly, far more experienced in war. Their initial reaction was to sneer at his youth, inexperience, and appearance. But he soon won them over through the sheer atavistic power of his mind, will, energy, and vision. General Charles Augereau, then a grizzled, cynical, twenty-two year veteran, admitted to General Andrea Massena, himself a similarly disposed twenty-one year veteran, that the "little bastard of a general frightened me."[1]

Then Bonaparte had to inspire his soldiers. That too was a challenge. The Italian front was the neglected stepchild of French policy. The 40,000 troops were little more than scarecrows; they lacked nearly everything they needed to make war: munitions, muskets, food, uniforms, tents, wagons, draft animals, medicine, and so forth.

The government's disinterest was understandable. The priorities were the nearby fronts in the Low Countries and along the Rhine, where the fortunes of war had seesawed between France and its enemies ever since the September 1792 invasion by the Austrians and Prussians. By offering invaders the shortest route to the capital, those northeastern fronts clearly presented the worst dangers to France. So naturally Paris funneled most of its resources to the armies defending them. In stark contrast, the distant Italian front had not just stalemated, it had stagnated. Neither side could muster the will or resources to march against the other.

Yet that front did have strategic potential. If the French army could march over the Maritime Alps into the Po valley and somehow defeat the Piedmontese and Austrian armies encamped there, Vienna would have to divert crucial numbers of troops, transport, and supplies from its northern to its southern front. That was obvious. Nonetheless, those who devised the French government's grand strategy could not envision the Italian front ever playing more than a secondary role in the war; at best it could be an useful diversion, but could certainly never be decisive. Bonaparte's campaign would stunningly disprove that assumption.

Bonaparte began to win over his troops with stirring proclamations, drills, and parades to instill discipline and pride. He also redoubled the efforts of his quartermaster corps to scour the countryside for provisions, and he browbeat Paris into sending him as many arms and munitions as possible. Yet even on the campaign's eve the army was still short of nearly everything vital. But Bonaparte knew how to convert his men's grumbling and lethargy into unbridled enthusiasm. In one of his most memorable proclamations, he announced that the solution to all their problems lay in conquest: "Soldiers! . . . The government owes us much but can give us nothing. . . . Rich provinces, wealthy towns, all will be yours for the taking. There you will find honor and glory and riches."[2]

His efforts worked. He wrote to War Minister Lazare Carnot that "I was very well received by the army, which showed me a confidence that obligates me to an eager gratitude." Although he faced "many grand obstacles, the biggest are surmounted." He admitted that the "new organization has made many malcontents." He was sensitive to the fate of his predecessor, General Barthelemy Scherer, who "seemed to be exhausted from the war which ruined his health." Bonaparte asked if Scherer could not be made an ambassador somewhere. In fact, Scherer would replace Carnot as war minister on July 22.[3]

To boost his campaign's chance of success, his diplomacy had to extend beyond inspiring his own generals and soldiers. The Directory had armed him with plenipotentiary powers, and he was not shy about using them. From the beginning he would not confine his diplomacy to dealing with his immediate enemies or allies, but acted within the grander strategic horizon that embraced Europe, the Mediterranean, and beyond.

On his immediate front, Bonaparte faced a coalition of three kingdoms, Austria, Sardinia-Piedmont, and Naples. Its forces were organized in two armies: General Michelangelo Alessandro Colli-Marchi's 15,000 Piedmontese; and General Jean Pierre Beaulieu's 28,000 troops, which were mostly Austrians but included a Neapolitan division. Bonaparte hoped to weaken that coalition before the campaign began. He reckoned that there was no point in launching a diplomatic initiative with either Austria or Naples, which had the least to lose and most to gain from trying to contain France beyond the maritime Alps. Piedmont, however, as a French neighbor, was the state in the coalition most vulnerable to a successful French offensive.

So Bonaparte tried to detach Piedmont from the coalition by sending General Colli a plea for peace that both flattered his vanity and placed the blame for war on him: "I will seize every chance . . . to give you marks of my esteem that I carry for the brave soldiers of your army. I have too high an opinion of you to think that you would go to extremes that any man of honor should disavow by unleashing tides of blood. You will be responsible in the eyes of all Europe and your army in particular."[4] Although Colli spurned that appeal, he would hear similar words from Bonaparte in just a few weeks. Indeed, Bonaparte would make such messages—ones that both conferred honor and heaped guilt—a standard ploy in his diplomatic repertoire.

The Republic of Genoa was the region's diplomatic wild card. To this point the Genoans had maintained a fragile neutrality. At the very least, Bonaparte had to ensure that Genoa did not join Austria, Piedmont, and Naples. Ideally, he could induce the Genoans into an alliance that would allow him to outflank his enemies and supply his forces much easier across northwestern Italy. But even the more modest goal demanded the most delicate and sensitive of diplomacy. Genoa was split among factions; although most wanted to stay out

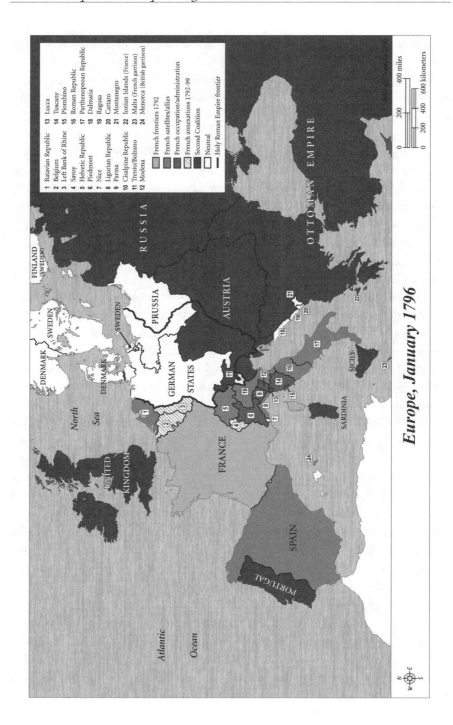

Europe, January 1796

Key:

1 Batavian Republic
2 Belgium
3 Left Bank of Rhine
4 Savoy
5 Helvetic Republic
6 Piedmont
7 Nice
8 Ligurian Republic
9 Parma
10 Cisalpine Republic
11 Trento/Bolzano
12 Modena
13 Lucca
14 Tuscany
15 Piombino
16 Roman Republic
17 Parthenopean Republic
18 Dalmatia
19 Ragusa
20 Cattaro
21 Montenegro
22 Ionian Islands (France)
23 Malta (French garrison)
24 Menorca (British garrison)

French frontiers 1792
French satellites/allies
French occupation/administration
French annexations 1792–99
Second Coalition
Neutral
Holy Roman Empire frontier

of the war, there were those who leaned toward the Austrians or the French. A further complication was rising anti-French sentiments, including the harassment of residents and merchants.

In such a political powder keg Bonaparte's most important task was to avoid any provocation. He sent general reassurances of French good will to the Genoan government. But it also was essential to learn as much as possible about the positions and strengths of the various political factions. For that he depended mostly on reports that arrived several times a week from France's ambassador to Genoa, Guillaume Charles Faipoult de Maisoncelles. Eventually, he would act decisively toward Genoa, but only after thoroughly studying the situation, nurturing pro-French political factions, and winning a series of battlefield victories that gave him the prestige and power to advance French interests there.[5]

The campaign opened on April 2, 1796, when Bonaparte ordered his army to march against the enemy. It would end over a year and a half later, on October 18, 1797, when he concluded the Treaty of Campo Formio with Austria. In between Bonaparte fought a frenzied series of military and diplomatic battles whose outcomes were often in doubt. The final result in Italy would be a titanic shift in the distribution of power, from Hapsburg Austria and Bourbon Naples to France. Bonaparte would enrich France strategically, by creating satellite republics across northern Italy, as well as financially and culturally, by sending caravans laden with coins and art back to Paris.

The first phase of Bonaparte's Italian campaign revealed the military and diplomatic strategies that he would repeat in numerous versions in the years ahead. Essentially he sought to split, encircle, and destroy the enemy both on the battlefield and at the negotiating table. In this first instance, his enemies unwittingly played into his hands: although their 43,000 troops slightly outnumbered his own 38,000 troops, they were scattered across the region. Bonaparte divided his army in two, with General Andre Massena marching with half the soldiers while he led the rest over the Maritime Alps. He quick-marched his converging forces to overwhelm each enemy force in turn before it could be reinforced by the others. The French defeated the Austrians and Piedmontese in a series of battles from April 11 to April 26, at which point Bonaparte united his troops between the remnants of the two enemy armies. Beaulieu withdrew his forces eastward, while Colli wearily agreed to Bonaparte's call for an armistice.

Bonaparte made it clear that he would grant a cease-fire only with the understanding that it would be the first step to a peace treaty: "The military and moral position of the two armies makes impossible all suspension of arms pure and simple. Yet since I am convinced that the Directory will accord reasonable peace conditions to your King, I can . . . halt my march [only as] . . . a means of reaching the goal which conforms to the genuine interests of your realm, and thus spare an useless flow of blood contrary to reason and the laws of war." To that end, "you have the choice of putting in my power two of the three fortresses" of Coni, Ceva, and Tortone in the Maritime Alps, along with the strategic fortress city of Alexandria on the Po River. "We can then wait, without hostilities, for the diplomats to begin work. This proposition is very moderate. The mutual interests which must exist between Piedmont and the French Republic bring me the desire to see distanced from your country all kinds of evils which could unfold."[6]

Bonaparte's diplomacy worked. Colli passed his message on to King Victor Amadeus III, who was eager to comply. A temporary cease-fire took place on April 24; it took another four days to hammer out the details of an armistice. In what would become typical of his diplomacy, Bonaparte raised his demands and threats the longer it took to cut a deal. At Cherasco on April 28, he talked the king's envoys into accepting an armistice whereby Piedmont would surrender all three strategic fortresses in the Maritime Alps to France and allow the French army and its supply convoys free passage across the entire kingdom. Those terms laid the foundation for a treaty signed in Paris on May 15.[7]

In a few weeks of hard marches, battles, and bargaining Bonaparte had single-handedly revolutionized the nature of war and diplomacy. In all he had "won six victories, captured 21 flags, 55 pieces of artillery, several fortresses, and 15,000 prisoners, had inflicted 10,000 casualties, and had conquered the richest part of Piedmont."[8]

Yet he was still adjusting to war's full spectrum of horrors. He apologized to the Directory that, despite his efforts to prevent them from doing so, his troops had committed atrocities that "make one blush to be a member of the human race."[9] While he would eventually become relatively inured to witnessing the aftermath of robbery, rape, and murder, he issued a steady stream of orders forbidding his troops from doing so and had those caught tried and punished, often with execution. He was motivated to do so more by practical than moral qualms: it was in French interests to win the hearts and minds of the peoples it was trying to conquer.

Bonaparte's victory was so swift and the subsequent diplomatic possibilities so fluid that he had to slow down. At this stage of his career, he was careful not to carry his diplomacy too far. One reason was that his army's position could not have been more vulnerable. Although the king had signed an armistice, he could break it and resume war against the French army's rear. Bonaparte explained the delicacy of the situation to Paul Barras, the head of the Directory: "The war in Italy at this time is half military and half diplomacy. To put one enemy to bed with an armistice while having the time to crush the other, or to obtain passage and provisions, is the grand art of war in Italy."[10]

And then there was an even more distant front to worry about: at times his diplomacy with his own government was the most trying of all. He felt constrained by the distance and time it took to communicate with Paris and the vague and at times conflicting instructions the Directory issued to him. He was sensitive not to offend any of the directors or other influential politicians in Paris. He was well aware of the fate of generals who failed to meet the government's expectations: if they were lucky, they were merely cashiered; but many were shot, "to encourage the others."

So he sent back regular reports to the Directory, informed the members in detail of his actions, and asked for instructions. On April 26, he wrote to them of his "eagerness to know if my diplomatic efforts conformed to your intentions." He explained to Barras that "if you can explain to me what you want, I can cease worrying about whether I am fulfilling your intentions and of being accused of mixing my desires with diplomacy."[11]

Although his letters to the Directory are filled with respect and tact, he took off his diplomatic gloves on one crucial issue. He threatened to resign when the Directory wrote that he would have to share his command with General Francois Kellermann. "I can only be useful here if you invest me with your complete confidence."[12] The Directory backed off.

Bonaparte soon learned how to outmaneuver his own government as skillfully as he did enemy armies. He did so by creating situations in which the Directory had no choice but to follow his lead. The directors would find that the only way they could keep up with his whirlwind of military and diplomatic victories was to expand his plenipotentiary powers. But for now their most helpful act was to quickly elaborate the terms of his armistice into a peace treaty with the kingdom of Piedmont-Sardinia on May 15. That let him face the Austrians with relative confidence that his rear was secure.

Nor was Bonaparte shy about asking for more powers or giving advice. He implored Carnot that "If you desire peace with Sardinia, prescribe for me the authority to deal with Genoa, Parma, and Rome." He explained to the Directory that "I cannot doubt that you approve my conduct since . . . a suspension of arms gives me time to battle the" Austrians. Victor Amadeus "is a king who put himself absolutely in my hands, gave me three of his strongest places and the richest half of his state. We can dictate peace as the masters of the king of Sardinia." To be lasting, that peace had to be just and moderate. He warned the Directory that "if you don't want peace with the king of Sardinia, if your project is to dethrone him," it would take several decades to overcome the subsequent political instability.[13] He would soon lose such qualms about overthrowing governments and imposing revolutions.

Bonaparte saw a chance for France to aggrandize itself beyond the kingdom of Piedmont and Sardinia. "As for Genoa," he informed the Directory, "I believe that you must demand 15 million in indemnities for the [French] frigates and vessels impounded in its ports." Yet here too he was sensitive to not go too far. Peace and security depended on winning friends rather than subjects for France, at least for the present.[14]

Bonaparte gave his troops a brief pause for breath before issuing orders for his campaign's second phase. He quick-marched most of his army down the Po River's south bank, then crossed over at Piacenza in an attempt to get behind the Austrian army. However, Beaulieu got word of the maneuver and fled eastward toward the "quadrilateral" fortresses of Mantua, Legnano, Peschiera, and Verona.

The battle of Lodi on May 10, 1796, in which Bonaparte clipped the tail of the retreating Austrian army, was a decisive turning point—not in the campaign, but in his psyche. Strategically, had Bonaparte lost that battle, Beaulieu might well have halted his retreat, and subsequent battles would have been fought in the region. But more importantly, Bonaparte's vision that he was destined for greatness would certainly have been delayed and perhaps lost altogether.

The Austrians had 7,500 infantry, 2,500 cavalry, and 14 cannons on the east side of the Adda river, with one battery pointing straight down the bridge leading to Lodi on the west bank. After swiftly assessing the situation, Bonaparte brought up his guns to pin down the enemy; split his cavalry in two, with each wing searching for a ford up or down stream to cross, so as to encircle the Austrians; and then, upon judging the moment right, ordered his troops to charge across that bridge. Under the barrage of Austrian fire the French faltered, then fell back. Bonaparte grabbed a flag, rallied his troops, and led them forward. The Austrians, having lost ever more troops to French cannon fire, with their flanks threatened by the French cavalry, and now facing a determined assault across the bridge, fled the field. They left behind 153 killed, 182 wounded, and 1,701 prisoners.[15]

Bonaparte raced his army after Beaulieu, but the Austrians retreated safely into the fortress of Mantua. Bonaparte set his men to work zigzagging entrenchments and redoubts forward for a prolonged siege. But a crisis in his rear forced him to leave the siege's supervision to his subordinates.

The very atrocities Bonaparte had condemned and feared had provoked mass uprisings at Como on May 22, Varese and Pavia on May 23, and Lodi and Binasco on May 24. The worst was at Pavia, where the rebels had massacred the 400-man French garrison after it surrendered. Bonaparte galloped back, reversed the march of contingents heading to the front, slaughtered 700 insurgents at Binasco on May 25, and then unleashed his troops for the sack of Pavia. That ended the revolt—but undoubtedly swelled the collective hatreds.[16]

By mid-June Bonaparte had concluded his campaign's second phase. He had routed the Austrians, opened the siege of Mantua, crushed an uprising in his rear, and subdued most other potential or actual enemies via diplomacy. Beaulieu was bottled up in Mantua, and there were no other Austrian armies on the horizon.

So Bonaparte could concentrate on diplomacy. In the short term, he hoped to detach the Kingdom of Naples or the Two Sicilies from the coalition while ensuring that the other Italian states remained neutral. He sent word to Ferdinand IV at Naples to yield to his demands or face invasion. The king was eager to get out of the war, at least for the present. He authorized his envoy, Fabrizio di Belmonte, to negotiate an armistice. Belmonte and Bonaparte began haggling at Peschiera on June 1 and signed a deal on June 5. By withdrawing into neutrality, Ferdinand forced both Austrian troops and British warships to leave his territory. That secured Bonaparte's southern flank, so that he could concentrate on defeating the Austrians to the eastward.[17]

Yet another successful target of Bonaparte's diplomacy was the would-be Louis XVIII, the Count of Provence, who had been living in exile with an entourage at Verona since May 1794. His was hardly a passive retirement. From his palazzo he oversaw the efforts of royalist agents to slip back into France and provoke dissent, disorder, and, ideally, revolt. On April 21, the Venetian Republic agreed to Bonaparte's request to expel him.[18]

It took Louis a while before he and his followers could find a new home. One might imagine that Europe's royal rulers would be happy to welcome one of their own who had been "unjustly" deprived of his throne as a government-in-exile that could one day be restored to a France purged of revolutionaries and imperialists. But that was not the case. They were all painfully aware of how inept and hated the Bourbons were in France, and thus saw Louis, his younger brother Charles, the Count of Artois, and the entire extended family as more an embarrassment and a burden than a potential asset. Eventually Karl, the Duke of Brunswick, who had led the 1792 invasion of France which ended at Valmy, took pity on the two men and invited them to his chateau at Blankenburg in July of that same year, 1796.

Bonaparte did not spare Rome his powerful mix of war and diplomacy. On June 19 he dispatched forces into the Papal Legations, or protectorates, of Bologna, Modena, and Ferrara, and into the strategic Adriatic seaport of Ancona, in the northeastern corner of the Papal States. He justified that invasion as the liberation of exploited people from autocracy into a new regime founded on French revolutionary ideals.

Meanwhile he pursued a parallel diplomatic offensive. He had the Cardinal legate at Bologna, Francois Vincenti, arrested. Then he released him to return to Rome carrying Bonaparte's terms for peace and a promise to halt his army if they were met. He explained his diplomacy: "To make Rome tremble and believe that their magic hold on the people will have no effect against us, I authorized the senate of Milan to ignore all of Rome's decrees."[19] Since there were then no formal diplomatic relations between Paris and Rome, he used Spanish envoy Jose Nicolas de Azara as a further go-between. Pope Pius VI and his miniscule army could do nothing but submit. On June 20 envoys signed an armistice at Bologna which tentatively pledged Pius to free his political prisoners and donate 15.5 million livres, 5.5 million livres of provisions, and 100 paintings to France. In return Bonaparte would withdraw French forces from Ancona. A formal treaty would be negotiated with the terms of the armistice as its foundation.[20]

Bonaparte next used a rapid-fire series of threats, marches, and talks to get the Duchy of Tuscany to submit. Theoretically, France and Tuscany had been at peace since the treaty of Basel on February 9, 1795. But Bonaparte charged Ferdinand III, the duke and younger brother of Austrian king and Holy Roman Emperor Francis II, with ignoring that treaty by allowing French envoys and merchants to be "constantly insulted at Livorno . . . each day is marked by outrages contrary to French interests and the rights of man."[21] In violation of Tuscany's neutrality, a British frigate captured two French merchant ships under the guns of Livorno's port. Finally, the duke openly supported French émigrés who were conspiring against the revolutionary government in Paris. To the Directory, Bonaparte explained his strategy for dealing with Ferdinand and other minor states: "These little princes need to be led; they esteem more a note from our army than from our diplomats; only fear makes them honest and respectful to what we say."[22]

So Bonaparte ordered troops to occupy Livorno on June 27. That got the duke's attention. Ferdinand sent his minister, the Marquis de Manfredini, to Bologna, where he protested the invasion of Tuscany. He argued that the duke had actually cooperated fully with France, most notably by preventing the Neapolitans from marching through his territory to northern Italy. Bonaparte countered that he was protesting the duke's blind eye toward the harassment of French merchants in his realm. Regardless, French troops would remain—with or without the duke's approval. Ferdinand grudgingly gave his permission.[23]

To Genoa, Bonaparte sent periodic warnings when he learned of swelling anti-French sentiments, whether in the government or in the streets. In mid-June, he wrote to the Genoan Senate demanding that it "purge the territory of the assassins who fill it. If you don't take those measures I will. I will burn the cities and towns in which a single Frenchman is murdered. I will burn the homes which shelter the murderer. I will punish the magistrate who violates the first of the principles of neutrality."[24]

Whether from powerlessness or pride, the Genoese did not yield. A month later, Bonaparte wrote to Faipoult, France's envoy at Genoa, of his outrage at the "insolent and absurd behavior of the Genoan people."[25] He told him to insist that the insults to French residents and interests end. If they did not, he was to leave the republic with the warning that the French would impose a military solution where diplomacy had failed. Faipoult promptly issued the ultimatum, the Genoan government made a serious effort to crack down on crimes against the French, and the crisis passed.

Bonaparte did not invent the policy whereby the vanquished paid for their defeat with huge indemnities to the victors; the practice is as old as humanity. But he was certainly among its most ruthless practitioners. By the end of 1796 alone he had extracted from Italy 45,706,493 francs in cash, 12,132,909 francs in gold, silver, and jewels, and hundreds of paintings and other artworks which were priceless in value.[26] Assisting him in the selection and transfer of those riches was the Commission of Arts and Science, newly created by the Directory. Although two scientists, the chemist Claude Louis Bertollet and the mathematician Gaspard Monge, led the commission, judging by the former Italian paintings hanging in the Louvre and other French museums, they had a keen eye for art.

As if looting Italy's artistic heritage were not brazen enough, Bonaparte sought to scour Italy of its finest minds as well. To the Italian astronomer Barnaba Oriani, he wrote a letter that revealed his Enlightenment values:

The sciences, which honor the human spirit, and the arts which embellish life and transmit great acts into posterity, must be especially honored in a free government. All men of genius, all those who have obtained a distinguished rank in the republic of letters, are French, regardless of the country of their birth. . . . Thought has become free in Italy. There is no more inquisition, intolerance, or tyranny. I invite all the savants to join together and share with me their views on what they want to do and what they need to do to give to the sciences and arts a new life. . . . All those who would like to go to France will be welcomed with distinction by the government. The French people attach more value to the acquisition of a wise mathematician, a famous painter, indeed to any distinguished man, no matter what his calling, than to the conquest of the richest and most prosperous city.[27]

Bonaparte's diverse diplomatic efforts were disrupted in July 1796 by the first of four Austrian campaigns launched that year to defeat him and relieve Beaulieu at Mantua. Although he was outnumbered every time, he defeated each of those offensives by racing his troops to mass against an enemy prong, rout it, and then dash on to attack the next. Whenever the Austrians retreated, he and his weary army would have a few weeks respite before mustering to stave off the next onslaught. The most decisive of those battles were the seven days of fighting around Rivoli beginning July 29 and the three days at Arcole beginning November 15.

Bonaparte penned his first appeal to Francis II for peace on October 2: "Your Majesty, all of Europe wants peace. This disastrous war has lasted far too long. I have the honor of warning Your Majesty that if you do not send envoys to Paris to open peace negotiations the Directory has ordered me to capture Trieste and destroy all your Adriatic ports." He went on to note, "Until now I have restrained myself from executing this plan with the hope of not adding to the number of this war's innocent victims. I wish that Your Majesty were sensitive to the evils that menace his subjects, and give ease and tranquility to the world."[28] He did not receive a reply.

All along Bonaparte had to scan the horizons south and west to ensure that the other Italian states were not rising against him. In early October his spies brought word that Venice, Naples, and Rome might be conspiring to join

Austria against France. He sent a new round of warnings to the leaders of those states. Of the three countries, only Naples reacted by agreeing to conclude a peace treaty, which was signed at Paris on October 10, based on the terms of the armistice. Venice reiterated its pledge of neutrality.

Only Rome did not give a definitive answer. Bonaparte warned Rome to uphold the armistice and convert it into a lasting treaty. His letter to Cardinal Alessandro Mattei was a model of his approach to diplomacy. He first cited a litany of the other side's offenses, claiming that they violated not just the interests of France but all of humanity. He then appealed to the other side's sense of morality. Finally, he warned of the most dire consequences if his demands were not met. His contrast of his own devotion to peace with the pope's seeming tolerance for war was at once eloquent and ironic: "Anticipating those ruins and deaths, I owe it to my nation and humanity to try one last time to return the pope to more moderate sentiments that conform to his true interests, his sacred character, and to reason." He reminded the cardinal of his ability to destroy Rome's worldly power. He ended with the warning that "war, so cruel for humanity, has terrible results for the vanquished." Four days later he followed up that letter by instructing Francois Cacault, the French envoy at Rome, to call on Pius VI to open negotiations for a peace treaty.[29] But the pope stonewalled any serious talks for the present.

Bonaparte's most successful diplomacy was to act as the godfather of and midwife to Italian liberalism and nationalism. In principle if not in practice, he still believed in the French revolution's ideals of liberty, equality, and fraternity. He encouraged Italian liberals to unite and convert their states into republics with French-style constitutions under French protection.[30]

He initiated that movement in Milan, whose eight-hundred member "Society of Friends of Liberty and Equality" had welcomed the French as liberators from Austrian rule. In September the group renamed itself the Academy of Literature and Public Instruction; adopted red, white, and green cockades; and issued a proclamation proposing a convention that would create a republic. That inspired similar groups to form in Italy's other relatively prosperous, literate, and learned northern cities. Bonaparte authorized the Milanese to create a 3,500-man legion commanded by French and Italian officers.

Bonaparte helped form additional forces elsewhere. In the Papal Legations of Bologna, Modena, and Ferrara he convinced prominent liberals to send delegations to Paris with petitions for French annexation. His most decisive act that year was to help organize at Modena a Congress of liberals from the Papal

Legations and Reggio. On October 16, the Congress called for the formation of a Cispadane Confederation and an Italian Legion of 25,000 troops allied with France. A Convention of 110 deputies reaffirmed those goals and adopted the green, white, and red tricolor flag at Reggio on December 27, 1796. On March 27, 1797, the Convention unveiled a French-style constitution that would govern the republic. Bonaparte's dream had been dramatically realized.

Yet Bonaparte's latest diplomatic coup set off alarm bells in Paris. All along the Directory had viewed the young general's diplomacy with very mixed feelings. Its members cheered each caravan packed with gold, silver, and art that plodded into Paris, but worried that Bonaparte's sponsorship of Italian unity and liberalism was creating a monster that might one day turn against its creator. Speaking for the Directory, Barras raised that fear in a letter to Bonaparte, arguing that Italian unification was "impossible. If we tried to achieve it, we would cause an uproar in Europe. Anyway what would be the point in creating a giant whose great size would be a cause of embarrassment for us one day? Let us leave Venice, Tuscany, Naples, Rome, and Piedmont independent from each other."[31]

In a series of letters, Bonaparte demolished those and other arguments.[32] He sharply criticized the Directory for trying to micromanage events that they did not understand in a region hundreds of miles from Paris. Italian unification only posed a danger if it was done too hastily, thus fostering institutional weaknesses in and widespread resentment of the new regime. He then outlined a diplomatic strategy he was confident would prevent that. It called for France to offer immediate protection to the northern Italian states liberated from Austrian or Papal rule, alliances with the Kingdom of Sardinia and Republic of Genoa, and generous peace treaties with the Republic of Venice, Kingdom of the Two Sicilies, and Duchy of Parma. The immediate effect of those policies would be to shift decisively their respective orientations from Austrian, Papal, or British influence to French influence. Over the long term it would allow for Italian unification under France's benevolent guidance and revolutionary ideals. He concluded one letter with the explanation: "I have done my duty; the army has done its duty. My soul is torn apart but my conscience is at rest."[33]

In any event, the Directory apparently could spare little time to ponder the implications of Bonaparte's diplomacy in Italy, let alone his soul ravaged by seven months of fighting, negotiating, building, and destroying. Notwithstanding that, the accomplishments of his blitzkrieg were astonishing: he had won most of northern Italy into alliance with or occupation by France before the two French armies on the northeastern front had even begun their campaigns.

Nonetheless, the Directory persisted in viewing Italy as a secondary front that merely diverted Austrian power from the crucial battles along the Rhine. But the French generals there just could not muster Bonaparte's energy, skills, and vision. Each of those armies—Jean Victor Moreau's 79,000-man Army of the Rhine and Moselle and Jean Baptiste Jourdan's 78,000-man Army of the Sambre and Meuse—was twice the size of Bonaparte's and far better equipped and supplied. But when those armies finally crossed the Rhine in June, they initially suffered humiliating defeats at the hands of Archduke Charles' 101,000 troops. They were saved only when 25,000 reinforcements under General Dagobert Wurmser, slated to reinforce Charles, were diverted to Italy. When Moreau and Jourdan advanced, Charles drew them deeper into Bavaria before turning and routing first Jourdan and then Moreau, forcing them back across the Rhine in a succession of battles. By late October, Charles could safely put most of his army into winter quarters even while sending contingents to Italy.

Despite those military failures in the north, the Directory was able to score some diplomatic successes of its own in 1796. On August 19, French and Spanish envoys signed the Treaty of Ildefonso by which Charles IV publicly allied with France and secretly pledged to pressure the Portuguese to close their ports to the British or else risk invasion. That was an extraordinary diplomatic flip-flop for Spain, which had joined the coalition against the French in 1792. But the Spanish had been wearied by four years of inconclusive and ever more expensive war, and in July of 1795 had signed a peace treaty whereby they ceded their half of the island of Saint Domingue to France. But now they jumped off the diplomatic fence to side with the French revolutionaries. The incentive was to recoup their previous losses by plundering a vulnerable Portugal. Or at least, that was the rationale. The French sealed the deal with an extremely generous "gift" to Manuel de Godoy, the king's chief minister and the queen's former lover. In accepting an alliance with France, Charles IV not only betrayed the royalist cause but defied history: nearly every previous alliance between France and Spain had gone badly. Nonetheless, Charles officially declared war against Britain on October 4, 1796.

The predictable happened. With no direct means of attacking Britain, the Spanish could only seethe in helpless rage as report after report reached Madrid of the superior British navy scouring the seas of Spanish war and merchant ships. And as for Portugal, when Madrid issued an ultimatum, Lisbon conceded by promising to close its ports to the British. This prevented a Spanish invasion, even though the Portuguese never kept their promise, instead continuing to trade with the British.

The Directory also bolstered the previous year's peace treaty with Prussia by which Berlin had withdrawn from the coalition. In a treaty signed on August 5, Paris recognized Berlin's protectorates over northern Germany, including Nassau, with its ties to the Dutch House of Orange. In return Prussia recognized French conquests west of the Rhine. The Prussians, however, politely rebuffed a French request to join them against Austria.

The most potentially beneficial diplomacy of all lay in the Directory's attempts to reach a peace accord with Britain. Prime Minister William Pitt was willing to consider peace—at the right price. British expeditions that year that had taken Dutch Guyana in April and French St. Lucia in May gave him some valuable bargaining chips. Talks began at Lille, but died when the French refused to abandon the Low Countries.

France's strategic position brightened significantly after November 6 when a stroke killed Catherine, Russia's tsarina. Her estranged son Paul, whom Catherine had not only exiled to a remote chateau but disinherited from the throne, managed to seize and destroy the offending document and have himself crowned tsar. He gleefully reversed most of his mother's policies, including withdrawing Russia from the coalition against France and sending an envoy to Berlin to talk with the Prussians about sponsoring a general peace congress.

However, like virtually all of France's amphibious expeditions during that era, an armada dispatched to invade Ireland met with a series of disasters. Wretched seamanship, storms, fogs, and a lone British frigate resulted in the loss of three ships of the line, four frigates, and four transports and the scattering of the others. The remaining captains had no choice but to sail home. Had nature been kinder and the seamen more skilled, the armada could have landed an army of 15,000 veterans and the Irish revolutionary Wolf Tone—on an Ireland defended by only 12,000 redcoats, split among widely scattered garrisons, amidst a largely hostile population longing for liberty. Most likely the French would have captured Ireland, and thus held a nearly priceless bargaining chip for French diplomats to deal with London.

Such was the strategic and diplomatic context within which Bonaparte battled, haggled, and triumphed in Italy. In a few months he had accomplished military and diplomatic marvels. He had done so by wielding at once the most extreme brutality and most diplomatic finesse. Many of those deeds weighed on his conscience as well as provoked fears that some in Paris might condemn him. He sought understanding and sympathy from the Directory:

Today Italy is French. With a mediocre army I had to face everyone: constrain the Austrian army, besiege fortresses, guard our rear, and impose myself on Genoa, Venice, Tuscany, Rome, and Naples; it was essential to be powerful everywhere with an unified military, diplomatic and financial front. Here it is necessary to burn and execute, to wield terror and give shocking examples. . . . Yet . . . diplomacy is essential and inseparable from war to advance French interests.[34]

From Rivoli to Leoben

The battle for Italy was finally decided in three desperate days of fighting at Rivoli from January 24 to 26, 1797. Bonaparte had no sooner shattered that Austrian army when he got word that on February 1 Pius VI had ordered General Colli (who had been given the command of the 15,000-man Papal army after being fired by King Victor Amadeus) to march against the French. The pope's timing could not have been worse. Unaware of that approaching relief force, Beaulieu surrendered Mantua to General Claude Victor on February 2. Had Rome entered the war earlier—at almost any time over the preceding seven months—the Papal army might have tipped the balance. Instead Pius failed to coordinate his offensive with Vienna. Bonaparte galloped down to join General Victor, defeated the Papal forces at Imola, Castel Bolognese, and Faenza, and then recaptured Ancona.

The pope asked for terms. What Bonaparte demanded was predictably stiff; after all, Pius had broken the armistice he had ratified with Bonaparte the previous summer. Under the Treaty of Tolentino, signed between Bonaparte and Cardinal Mattei on February 19, the pope ceded Avignon, Comtat Venassin, Ferrara, Bologna, and Romagna to France; reduced his army to a skeleton force; shut his ports to all enemies of France; accepted a French garrison in Ancona; herded 1,600 horses to the French army; handed over another 15 million livres plus a hundred paintings chosen by the Commission of Arts and Science; sent an envoy to Paris with compensation and apologies to the family of French minister Hugo de Bassville, who had been murdered by a Roman mob four years earlier; and freed his political prisoners. To ensure that the pope did not break his latest promise, Bonaparte sent to Rome his older brother Joseph as his ambassador, guarded by a force under General Auguste Marmont.[35]

Bonaparte had been on the strategic defensive for ten months. Now there was neither a huge enemy garrison nor a papal army in his rear, and the remnants of the Austrian army, now commanded by Archduke Charles, were retreating before him. Bonaparte led his army across northeast Italy toward Vienna, sent a contingent to occupy Venice, and sent another under General Barthelemy Joubert up the Adige valley into the Tyrol.

The Directory did not experience unalloyed elation at the news of Bonaparte's latest triumphs in Italy. The members resented the general's habit of ignoring their carefully prepared diplomatic instructions. His effort to redraw the map of Italy was complicating the diplomacy of French envoy Henri Jacques Guillaume Clarke in Vienna. Austrian foreign Minister Johann, Baron Thugut had rejected Clarke's demands that Austria surrender Belgium and all its lands on both sides of the Rhine, including the strategic city of Mainz (Mayence), to France. Thugut impatiently pointed out that Archduke Charles had defeated the attempts of Moreau and Jourdan to seize and hold territory east of the Rhine. He then noted that Bonaparte rather than Paris seemed to be determining French diplomacy; perhaps Clarke might want to consult with the general. Clarke hurried to join Bonaparte.

In early March, Bonaparte launched an offensive east of the Tagliamento River in an attempt to encircle the Austrians. Charles and his army barely escaped the trap. Bonaparte would have liked to march after the Austrians, but he knew that could be the road to disaster. He had only 35,000 troops while the Austrian army, despite nearly a year of defeats in Italy, continued to swell with reinforcements. Meanwhile his rear was potentially threatened when Joubert retreated back down the Adige valley before a superior Austrian army in his front and through a rebellion in his rear. On the Rhine front the Austrians had once again blunted French offensives led by Moreau and Lazare Hoche, who had replaced Jourdan.

So instead Bonaparte unleashed a diplomatic rather than a military campaign. On March 31 he penned Charles a model of diplomatic communication, one which appealed to the archduke's sincere humanitarianism even as it gently reminded him that he was facing an invincible general. "Haven't we killed enough people and committed enough evils for humanity to mourn?" Bonaparte asked. He warned that, should Charles spurn peace, Austria would be ravaged. He ended his appeal with the sentiment that "if the approach which I have had the honor to make to you can save the life of just one man, I shall take greater pride in the peacemaker's crown than in all the somber glory which military success brings."[36]

Despite his worsening strategic position, when Bonaparte did not receive a reply he resumed his advance. He reasoned that maintaining the illusion of military superiority represented his best chance of winning a diplomatic victory. The bluff worked. Alarmed at reports of the fast-approaching French steamroller, Thugut sent General Maximilien Merveldt and Marzio Nostrilli, Duke Gallo, to negotiate a ceasefire with Bonaparte. On April 7 they reached his headquarters at Iudenburg in Styria, just eighty miles—a four-day steady march—from Vienna.

Bonaparte accepted a six-day truce, which would give the Austrians enough time to prepare for formal negotiations at Leoben, about midway between the two armies. He then marched his troops on to Leoben. The Austrian envoys would negotiate surrounded by the French army.

It took four days of tough bargaining before a deal was struck. The Treaty of Leoben, signed on April 18, 1797, would be a preliminary agreement upon which to negotiate a permanent peace within three months. Like most treaties of the era, it had both public and secret provisions. Paris openly promised to withdraw from and not foment revolution within the Austrian empire, in return for which Vienna recognized France's territorial expansion over the Austrian Netherlands (Belgium) along with the west bank of the Rhine, Savoy, and Nice. Secretly Paris acquiesced in Austria's takeover of the Republic of Venice, while France would receive the Papal Legations and the quadrilateral fortresses. In addition Austria would accept, if not officially recognize the Cisalpine Republic (with Lombardy at its core and Milan as its capital) and the Cispadane Republic (with Emilia Romagna at its core and Modena as its capital).

The Directors were shocked when they read the treaty brought back to them by Clarke. Although what Bonaparte had gained for France in the treaty exceeded the Directory's original instructions to Clarke, the Directors had expected to gain even more. They initially rejected the treaty by a vote of three to two, with Barras among those casting a negative vote. However, within a week the arguments for the treaty overcame those against it; in a second vote they ratified the treaty, with only Reubell dissenting.

Bonaparte helped turn that tide with a diplomatic offensive directed toward his own government. He fired off a series of letters which systematically made the case for the treaty and the grave consequences for spurning it.[37] Leoben would be just the first step. A mild peace would make France appear benevolent while giving it a desperately needed breathing space. It would be able to consolidate control over what it had taken and rebuild its depleted finances, troops, provisions, and munitions for the inevitable next round of fighting. Had

Bonaparte demanded more, the Austrians would have broken off the talks and renewed the war. His army, neglected by Paris, was stretched to the snapping point. Should the Austrians attack with the overwhelming numbers they were massing against him, he feared he would have to retreat back to central northern Italy, or even further. That would encourage the Austrians to launch offensives along the Rhine. In the worst case, France risked losing all that it had gained through immense sacrifices of treasure and blood. And, speaking of the Rhine front, France could have won far more had its northern armies been led as decisively as the Army of Italy.

Here Bonaparte revealed his very profound understanding of the mingled arts of war, psychology, politics, economics, and diplomacy. Alas, those gifts were lost on the Directory—which sought to renegotiate the treaty: it sent Clarke back to Vienna with new instructions. Although mercifully the Austrians did not renew the war, it would be another half year before another treaty was signed.

Not just the treaty's terms were controversial; Bonaparte had negotiated and signed it without permission. Essentially he had assumed Clarke's role and powers. He rather sheepishly explained to the Directory that Clarke "had arrived twenty-four hours after the signing because of accidents en route." He asked the Directory to grant Clarke new powers to open talks with the Austrians for a definitive peace.[38]

And that was not all. Apparently even then there were rumors and fears by some of the directors that Bonaparte's dazzling victories in war and peace had given him the confidence and popularity to take power. He tried to reassure them that "I have justified the confidence that you placed in me. I never considered myself in all my operations. . . . The slander will only make me more resistant to any treacherous intentions. My civil career will be like my military career, one and simple."[39]

Meanwhile, the latest crisis erupted in his rear. The Doge of Venice, learning that France had agreed to Austria's takeover of the Republic, had encouraged a revolt against the French occupiers. A mob murdered over 400 French troops, mostly convalescents, in Verona on April 17, while another slaughtered the crew of a French ship moored in Venice itself.[40]

Bonaparte declared war against the Republic of Venice on May 2 and sent General Charles Augereau to systematically march his division through that realm, wipe out any resistance, impose martial law, and garner all the treasure of the state and church in each city. The Doge did not give in until Augereau prepared to bombard Venice itself. The price for peace was high. With the

Treaty of Milan, signed on May 16, the Venetians agreed to surrender the Ionian islands of Corfu, Cephalonia, Zante, Cergio, and Santa Maura; three million livres in cash and a million livres worth of naval supplies; three men-of-war and three frigates; and 20 paintings and 500 manuscripts. French troops would occupy the republic until the Venetians fulfilled their promises.[41]

Having imagined a prolonged siege of Venice, Bonaparte had summoned Admiral Francois Paul Brueys d'Aigailliers and his squadron from Toulon. Although the Doge surrendered before the squadron's arrival, Bonaparte packed it with 2,000 troops led by General Antoine Gentili and ordered it to set sail for the Ionian Islands. Bonaparte issued Brueys his mission: "It is indispensable for the operations of the army of Italy that I be absolute master of the Adriatic, in all circumstances and in all operations that I would like to undertake."[42]

Anticipating the Directory's objections, Bonaparte explained the economic and strategic logic behind his diplomacy. With considerable exaggeration, he argued that the Ionian islands "are more important to us than all of Italy put together . . . [as] a source of wealth and prosperity for our commerce. . . . The time is not far off when, in order to truly ruin England, we shall have to take over Egypt. The vast Ottoman Empire, which decays more each day, obliges us to think of a good time to seize the means of preserving our trade with the Levant."[43]

Once again the Directory had mixed feelings about Bonaparte's diplomacy. The Directors welcomed the loot, but feared that France would be overextended in the Ionian Islands. They eventually sent their reluctant and bewildered approval.

Bonaparte was dreaming big. Undoubtedly inspired by Alexander the Great, one of his heroes, he envisioned carving a French empire out of the eastern Mediterranean. He intended to neutralize and eventually supplant British naval superiority in the region by steadily extending French control over ever more strategic islands. That would at once cut off Britain's ships from shelter and provisions, and provide French warships with secure bases from which to pick off British merchant ships and, if necessary, withdraw to shelter before superior British naval forces.

By seizing the Ionian Islands, Bonaparte could largely seal off the Adriatic and begin to convert it into a French sea. The next step would be to seize all its borders while reaching eastward into the Greek mainland and Aegean Sea. To that end, as Brueys and Gentili occupied the Ionian Islands, he sent an agent to Greece to plot with local rulers a revolt against the Ottoman Empire, and an envoy to Ali Pasha, Albania's ruler at Janina, with the offer of an alliance with France.[44]

When Bonaparte envisioned the Mediterranean, he did not just face east. How far west should France's sphere of influence over the Mediterranean extend? A glance at a map reveals Malta's strategic importance. It lies roughly halfway between Sicily and Tunisia, and midway between the Mediterranean Sea's eastern and western halves. Bonaparte wrote to the Directory for permission to prepare an expedition to take Malta, and included spy reports that if France did not act promptly the Russians might launch their own expedition there. Malta could eventually be a stepping stone from Toulon and other French ports to Egypt and the Levant. The Directory would eventually approve his grandiose plans.[45]

Those plans were disrupted when once again a threat emerged in Italy south of the Po River. Anti-French foment worsened in Rome and Ferdinand IV threatened to invade the Papal States. Joseph Bonaparte had been named ambassador to the Holy See on May 15, 1797. Bonaparte urged his brother to be tough toward both the Romans and the Neapolitans. He was especially concerned that Pius VI had named an Austrian general, Giovanni Provera, to command the papal army. Bonaparte had Joseph make it clear to Rome that France would not tolerate that appointment. As for Ferdinand, "the moment he crossed the frontier, the Roman people would come under French protection." He reassured his brother that should a crisis break out he would rush to back him up. Yet another fear was that the sickly pope would soon die. That would open Rome to all kinds of covert intrigues and overt foreign pressures.[46]

Bonaparte then immersed himself in the latest stage of his reorganization of Italy. He continued to nurture the development of the Cispadane Republic, which had been founded at Modena in January, by allowing Bologna, Ferrara, and Romagna to join it rather than Venice, which had been his original intention; the Venetian revolt let him cancel that promise. Meanwhile, yet another uprising against French troops, this time in the Republic of Genoa, played into his hands. After suppressing the insurgents, he reorganized and renamed the Republic of Genoa the Ligurian Republic on June 6, 1797. He oversaw the amalgamation of an enlarged Cispadane Republic with the Cisalpine Republic on July 9, 1797.[47]

To the new provisional government which he helped to install at Genoa, he issued congratulations, instructions, and a thinly disguised warning. He was especially concerned that the Ligurian Republic would be headed by a weak government torn by factions, emotions, and greed. "Your principal duty is to silence all passions" and rule with "wisdom and moderation." Economic prosperity and political stability are inseparable. The republic "can only exist with commerce; commerce can only exist with confidence. Weak governments do not give confidence."[48]

As always, he saw the grander diplomatic and strategic picture. He hoped eventually to unite the Cisalpine and Ligurian republics. That future grand Italian republic would give France varying degrees of influence over the entire peninsula, the surrounding seas, the Ionian Islands, and Malta. Meanwhile, it would be good diplomacy to enlist Spain, whose king Charles IV was not just allied with France but was the brother of Ferdinand IV, into pressuring the courts of Rome, Naples, Florence, and Parma to cooperate with the revolutionary political changes engulfing Italy. He saw the chance that a revolution might sweep the inept Charles Emmanuel IV, who had taken the throne of Sardinia and Piedmont after his father Victor Amadeus died in 1796, from power in Turin, which would give an opening to France. Thus was the Italian peninsula being radically transformed from either Habsburg or Bourbon control into a French sphere of influence.[49]

Bonaparte explained to the Directory some of his goals for his new creations. Typically his diplomacy mingled both humanitarian ideals and hard French interests: "My first act is to recall all those who fled during the war. I have pressed the government to make peace with all those citizens and destroy all vestiges of hate which could exist. I will cool the hot heads and warm the cold heads. I hope that the inestimable worth of freedom that I will give this people will stir in them a new energy to help the French Republic in future wars."[50]

Peace Talks, Coup Plots, and a Partnership

From the time that Bonaparte took command of the Army of Italy, his influence with Paris grew with his military and diplomatic victories. All along, he understood his own struggles within a strategic context that stretched across Europe and beyond, and he did not hesitate to share that understanding with the Directory. His advice increasingly acquired the air of commands and became a prolonged dress rehearsal for the time when he would rule France. The Directors may have resented his instructions, but nonetheless more often than not followed them because they made sense.

Yet Bonaparte passed on more than fait accomplis and advice to Paris. In the summer of 1797, he saved the Directory a second time from being overthrown, this time from a conspiracy masterminded by British and Bourbon agents.

Whitehall was in a quandary. The cabinet got word of the Leoben Treaty within weeks of its signature. Reports received of Bonaparte's ambitions and intrigues in Italy and the Mediterranean were sporadic and sketchy, but disturbing for their dire potential consequences for Britain. News of the former inclined the cabinet toward peace; news of the latter stiffened the will to fight on.

After Bonaparte knocked Austria out of the war, Britain no longer had an ally capable of attacking France, and thus would have to fight alone. That made little sense to ever more Britons, including the prime minister and most of his cabinet. After four years of war there was little to cheer other than the capture of several strategic and lucrative foreign colonies including St. Lucia from France, Cape Town and Ceylon from Holland, and Trinidad from Spain, as well as scores of French and other foreign war and merchant ships. In contrast, there was much to lament, including a soaring national debt and inflation and a plummeting stock market. Naval mutinies erupted at one home port after another in April and May as the sailors demanded better pay, food, and leave, and a larger cut of the prize money. The crisis abated after Parliament swiftly passed a bill promising the sailors a portion of their request, while the admiralty rounded up and hanged twenty-eight ringleaders.

After order was restored in the fleet, William Pitt sent James Harris, the Earl of Malmesbury, to Lille, where he negotiated first with Charles Delacroix from June through July 1797, and then with Charles Maurice de Talleyrand-Perigord through September. Malmesbury rejected first Delacroix's position that peace was possible only if Britain recognized France's conquests and returned the colonies it had taken, then Talleyrand's offer to trade Holland's Cape Town and Ceylon for St. Lucia and recognition of French expansion on the continent. Malmesbury was willing to return France's colonies only if France evacuated the Low Countries. And there the negotiations died.

Although thwarted at Lille, Talleyrand brilliantly reversed Portugal's alliance with Britain that summer. He spread rumors that he was going to do what he had already done—ally with Spain to fight Portugal. When Portugal's ambassador asked him to verify or deny those rumors, he did neither, but warned that it was a likelihood that could be forestalled if Lisbon not only severed its alliance but all trade with Britain. The Portuguese agreed to do so in a treaty signed with France on August 10, 1797.

Despite Talleyrand's success atop France's conquests and favorable peace treaties on the continent, the Directory was hard-pressed that year. France too was exhausted from war. Ever more people demanded peace at any price, even if it meant yielding to all of Britain's demands. Royalist candidates won 182 seats in the Council of Five Hundred's spring election. They then elected one of their own, General Jean Charles Pichegru, to be president of the chamber. The Directory split between Paul Barras, Jean Francois Reubell, and Jean Marie La Revelliere-Lepeaux who allied with the Jacobin minority, while Lazare Carnot and Francois Barthelemy leaned toward the royalists.

Although Bonaparte was far away in Milan, he became a decisive player in the French capital's political intrigues. On May 21, his secret police arrested the royalist spymaster Emmanuel de Launay, Count d'Antraigues, with incriminating papers in Trieste, and brought him to Milan. Napoleon supervised the interrogation during the night of May 31 to June 1. As dawn broke he offered Antraigues a deal: he would be allowed to "escape" if he told all that he knew and agreed to act as a double agent for France; otherwise, of course, he would be hanged as a spy. Antraigues swiftly agreed and began talking. The most damning information that he spilled was that Pichegru was a royalist agent and was plotting a coup. Bonaparte sent that word by a fast courier back to Barras in Paris. Although Antraigues was allowed to flee Milan on August 29, his role as a double agent never got off the ground, since Louis XVIII and other royalists thereafter shunned him as undoubtedly compromised.[51]

Once again Barras was beholden to Bonaparte for keeping him in power. Barras recalled the reliable General Lazare Hoche from Holland to command all troops in and around Paris. Fearing that Hoche himself might take advantage of the situation for his own coup, Bonaparte sent General Augereau to the capital to counter him. Barras, Hoche, and Augereau then carefully planned the arrest of Pichegru and all others that Antraigues had fingered in the conspiracy. Early on the morning of September 4 the police nabbed 53 suspects, including Pichegru, Carnot, Barthelemy, and eighteen others from within the Council of Five Hundred. Those suspects were eventually found guilty of treason and exiled to the "dry guillotine" of Guyana; Carnot was allowed to escape. The purge did not end there. Under interrogation or in return for reduced sentences, many of those implicated named other names. Eventually over 160 émigrés were rounded up and executed as spies, while over 1,800 priests were jailed for refusing to take the oath of allegiance to the government; 263 were sentenced to Guyana. Any potential threat the nakedly ambitious Hoche posed to the Directory disappeared when he died of tuberculosis in late September. To replace all the vacancies in the legislature, that year's election was annulled and a new election called. Finally, Malmesbury was sent packing. Apparently he had used his diplomatic cover to become a key link in the plot.[52]

While that effectively ended the official peace talks, Talleyrand and Barras immediately opened a back channel. Through intermediaries in Hamburg and London, those two ever-venal and opportunistic characters passed on word that they were willing to accept the British terms for peace—for a price: 15 million pounds sterling! Pitt counter-offered 450,000 pounds sterling, and refused to raise the price despite protests from Talleyrand and Barras that their "service" was worth much more than that. The talks, such as they were, ended on January 21, 1798.[53]

It was during the late summer of 1797 that one of the most creative and destructive relationships in diplomatic history began, after Talleyrand replaced Delacroix as foreign minister on July 16. Talleyrand and Bonaparte each initiated a relationship with the other by sending a celebratory letter that crossed in the mail as the former announced his new post and the latter sent his congratulations. Each was eager to get to know the other. Bonaparte, of course, was by now a national hero. Talleyrand's reputation was far more controversial, with his diplomatic brilliance lauded and his decadence and venality widely condemned. In the coming years, they would open their vast intellects to each other, sharing visions and insights. Bonaparte's first letter included an especially haunting line, given subsequent events: "Who will end the revolution? It's a problem that time keeps secret and will be resolved by reason and necessity."[54]

To Campo Formio and Rastadt

Throughout the summer of 1797, Bonaparte faced a time constraint. Under the preliminary treaty of Leoben, a permanent peace treaty had to be negotiated, signed, and ratified within three months; a follow-up agreement on May 24 officially designated an August 18 deadline. A number of forces largely beyond Bonaparte's control forced him to miss that date.

The biggest obstacle was in Vienna, which was split between those who called for warring until victory and those who sought peace at some to-be-determined price. Johann, baron Thugut, was the formidable, outspoken leader of the "let's give war another chance" camp. Having been bested by Bonaparte in one prolonged, expensive, humiliating campaign, Francis and most of his advisors were little inclined to a second round, at least for the present. However, they varied over how much they were willing to pay for peace. The most influential of this group were Thugut's chief rival for the king's ear, Johann Philippe, Count Cobenzl; his cousin, Ludwig Cobenzl; and the king's younger brother, Archduke Charles.

Although Thugut championed a minority view, he found a rather petty but effective way to block the path to peace. He ensured that one of the two envoys tapped to represent Austria at the "peace" talks was his protégé Johann Merveldt, Marquis de Courelles, to counter the other envoy, Marzio Mastrilli, Marquis de Gallo, who hoped to end the war. Thugut also ensured that those envoys lacked the power to conclude a definitive treaty. In doing so, he apparently hoped to run out the clock beyond the August 18 deadline, and use that as an excuse to renew the war.

That infuriated Bonaparte, who found himself trapped in the Kafkaesque dilemma of trying to negotiate with diplomats who claimed to want peace but lacked the power to make it. Actually, it was soon evident that Gallo and Courelles respectively fronted the peace and war factions. Bonaparte condemned Gallo for hesitating to confront Thugut, and Courelles for parroting Thugut's more outlandish positions. To Talleyrand, he complained that "it's not possible to conduct such vital negotiations with men so timid and even worse logicians, and who have no support at the court. Gallo . . . would never dare confront Thugut . . . while Merveldt never blushes" when he utters his boss's nonsense. "Thugut is a rascal who should be hanged; but Thugut is the true ruler in Vienna. I predict nothing but bad for the negotiations."[55]

Weeks were lost as both Bonaparte and Gallo sent a series of appeals to Vienna requesting that the appropriate negotiating power be granted. Thugut must have smiled wickedly as he filed away those petitions without bringing them to the king's attention. In late July Bonaparte tried to outflank Thugut by sending General Auguste Marmont as his envoy to Vienna. But Marmont's blunt demeanor and demands complicated rather than forced the resolution of the standoff within the Austrian government.[56]

Thugut found yet another way to abort any movement toward peace. He insisted that because Francis headed both the kingdom of Austria and the Holy Roman Empire, any talks had to be multilateral rather than bilateral. But that contradicted the Leoben treaty, under which a bilateral treaty between France and Austria would first be negotiated and only then followed by talks at Rastadt with envoys of the Holy Roman Empire for a general peace treaty. Thugut pushed for skipping the first stage, which was tentatively agreed to take place at Udine, and jumping straight into talks at Rastadt. There he hoped to spike any talk of peace by the sheer ponderousness of forging a consensus among the emperor and scores of princes. Most of those envoys would refuse to recognize France's conquest of the Holy Roman Empire west of the Rhine. Bonaparte, in his turn, hoped to sidestep Thugut's "trap" by presenting an unified French government condemnation and refusal to go to Rastadt until a binding treaty was forged with Vienna.[57]

There was another reason why the Austrians dragged their diplomatic feet. Whitehall, Vienna's paymaster, cheerleader, and very distant ally, had dispatched envoys to talk with the French at Lille. The Austrians naturally wanted to know which way the diplomatic winds were blowing before they spread their own sails.

Meanwhile, Bonaparte's bargaining power diminished somewhat when he was forced by the Leoben treaty to withdraw his army from Austrian to Venetian territory in northeastern Italy. Nonetheless, those delays actually played into Bonaparte's hands, at least in regard to his vision for Italy. As he put it in a letter to the Directory, "If the emperor [Francis II] is an imbecile and delays concluding a definitive peace, all of Italy will escape his hands and the yoke of the other princes who submit to him."[58] The general typically used the down time to ready his army should the August 18 deadline pass with Austria poised to renew the struggle.

Bonaparte tried to cut the Gordian diplomatic knot on July 23 with his latest direct appeal to Francis II. His letter was a minor diplomatic masterpiece in which he systematically recounted the horrors of war, his own string of victories that had brought him ever closer to Vienna, his moderation and benevolence during the talks which had culminated in the Leoben treaty, and the subsequent bad faith of Thugut and his man Courelles at Udine. "We are in the fourth month after signing the preliminaries and your chancellery has still not sent plenipotentiary powers to its envoys. . . . Will the scourge of war be renewed? Will Your Majesty give the word for Germany to be ravaged?" Bonaparte pretended to refuse to believe that Francis himself wanted to renew such horrors on his own people, since "your virtues are too well known; but I deplore those kings who let themselves be mastered by malicious others around them. . . . I do not doubt that Your Majesty has been tricked." He begged the king to consider the situation between France and Austria, which between them determined Europe's power balance and thus the happiness of all Europeans.[59]

That letter failed to break the political impasse in Vienna. The August 18 deadline passed. On August 27, Bonaparte pointedly moved his headquarters from Milan to the chateau of Manin at the village of Passariano, about twenty miles from the Austrian headquarters in Udine in northeastern Italy. The message in that move was clear: Bonaparte was ready for war or peace.

Thugut's maneuvers continued to infuriate Bonaparte. To Talleyrand, the general explained the dilemma and his strategy: "The emperor and the nation want peace; M. Thugut does not want peace but dares not openly push for war. One must cut with a sword all the sophisms by which he twists each event to the end of war. One must present the consequences of his machinations to him as if it were the head of Medusa and only then will he be reduced to reason."[60] But the Austrian minister was not solely to blame—"Thugut's bad faith is equaled by the stupidity of his envoys."[61]

The diplomatic breakthrough came in mid-September after personnel shakeups in both the Austrian and French camps. In Vienna, the peace faction finally bested the war faction in their tug-of-war over Francis. The Emperor sent Ludwig Cobenzl with full powers to represent Austria to Bonaparte; Courelles and Gallo would assist Cobenzl.[62]

Bonaparte's own diplomatic powers were boosted in late September when the Directory made him the sole plenipotentiary and recalled Clarke, who as a Carnot protégée had been implicated, unfairly it seems, in the royalist coup plot. Clarke's removal provoked mixed feelings in Bonaparte. While he welcomed the powers he received, he had developed a close working relationship with Clarke and valued his talents. He had used Clarke as a kind of diplomatic chief of staff or foreign minister who worked out the details of the grand diplomatic strategy that he fed him, much as Louis Alexander Berthier served as his military chief of staff. Bonaparte defended Clarke against charges that he was Carnot's spy.[63]

So what would Bonaparte do with his new powers? Alas, they still fell short of what he needed to fulfill his grand vision, which he sketched out for Talleyrand. The foreign minister was familiar with some of his ideas, such as systematically taking over the eastern Mediterranean, including the Adriatic basin, Ionian Islands, Malta, and Egypt. To that Bonaparte added new ideas, the most startling of which was to foment a revolution and overthrow the king of Sardinia, "who never ratified the treaty of alliance with France and has actually been our secret enemy. During my absence, he has conducted chicaneries with the Cisalpine Republic." He also wanted to expand the Cisalpine Republic to include Mantua and Brescia, and reorganize the Venetian republic into a French protectorate. He justified all this with the argument that "a wise and true policy must suit a great nation which has a great destiny to fulfill and powerful enemies in its way." For those who might protest that his vision was too ambitious, Bonaparte had a reply: "You don't have to be a great captain to understand all that: a sole glance at a map with a compass would be convincing evidence for all that I am saying."[64]

Bonaparte and Cobenzl squared off on September 27 for the first of a series of prolonged discussions. Although Bonaparte was irritated by Cobenzl's condescending manner, he was able to craft a face-saving treaty with him that appeared to advance the interests of both France and Austria. The first step was to ascertain that Cobenzl had both the power and will to negotiate a peace treaty. Then he got Cobenzl to agree that a general treaty with the Holy Roman Empire at Rastadt should only follow and be built upon the foundations of a treaty between France and Austria. With those broad issues out of the way, the men immersed themselves into laboriously working out the nitty-gritty details. That done, they symbolically capped their compromises by choosing Campo Formio, a tiny village which had played no role in the negotiations but was situated halfway between the French and Austrian armies, as the name for the treaty. The treaty was actually signed at the chateau of Manin, Bonaparte's headquarters, just before midnight on October 17.[65]

Under the treaty, Paris acquiesced in Austria's takeover of the Venetian Republic west to the Adige River, Istria, Dalmatia, the Archbishopric of Salzburg, and Bavaria's Inn valley. Vienna publicly accepted France's hold over Belgium, the fortresses of Mantua, Peschiera, and Ferrara, the port of Ancona, the Ionian Islands, and its protectorates over the Cisalpine and Ligurian republics. Austria also secretly recognized France's conquests west of the Rhine. The treaty bound the Austrian king as Holy Roman Emperor to call to Rastadt a congress of member states which would negotiate and sign its own peace treaty with France. For that congress, Bonaparte managed to squeeze an astonishing concession from Cobenzl. Vienna granted Paris the power to name one of the Holy Roman Empire electors. Finally, it was the emperor's duty somehow to compensate those German princes who had lost realms to France with lands elsewhere within the empire.[66]

Bonaparte had Louis Alexandre Berthier, his chief of staff, and Gaspard Monge, the commissioner for sciences and arts, carry that treaty to Paris and present it to the Directory for ratification. To the Directory he wrote: "I beg you to accept with equal distinction, a distinguished general and savant. Both illustrate the nation and celebrate the name French. It is impossible for me to send you a peace treaty via two men more distinguished in such different ways."[67]

How could the directors criticize, let alone reject, a treaty that was filled with so many goodies for France and was so artfully packaged? Berthier and Monge arrived on the night of October 25 and presented the treaty to the Directory at six o'clock the following morning. Not surprisingly, the Directors ratified the treaty without debate.

Nonetheless, a few directors later raised some misgivings. Once again Bonaparte was forced to explain what he assumed was the obvious logic behind his seeming "concessions" to Vienna. The treaty had subtlety but decisively bolstered France's strategic position. By accepting Austria's takeover of Bavaria's Inn valley, he had made Bavarian Elector Maximilien Joseph a natural French ally. By accepting Austrian control over Istria and Dalmatia, he had stretched Vienna's commitments deeper southeast into the Balkans, and thus exacerbated long-standing conflicts with the Ottoman and Russian empires over their overlapping spheres of influence and ambitions in that region. By winning the power to name a Holy Roman Empire elector, he gave France eyes and ears, along with a vote, in that realm's inner circle for the first time. To Talleyrand, Bonaparte wrote that he "had no doubt that critics would depreciate the treaty that I just signed. However, all those who understand Europe and its affairs will be convinced that it was impossible to reach a better treaty without fighting and conquering two or three provinces of Austria."[68]

Francis II ratified the treaty and sent out invitations for imperial delegates to meet in a congress at Rastadt. Eager to begin negotiations, Bonaparte reached Rastadt on November 25. To his disappointment, he received there a letter from the Directory recalling him to Paris. After working with the Viennese and German delegations to set up the congress's agenda, he turned over his duties to the French delegation on December 2.[69]

Three days later he was in Paris. No parade awaited him, nor did he want one. He did hope that his wife would be there for him, but Josephine had spurned his earnest letters so that she could stay in Milan and there indulge her frivolities and flirtations without disruption.

He had been away twenty months, having devoted much of that time to war and nearly all of it to diplomacy. He was only twenty-eight years old, but had crammed several lifetimes of adventures and horrors into his last half dozen years. He was world-weary to the depths of his soul.

He shut himself up in a small house on the rue Chanterine where he spent weeks mulling all that he had done and not done, and what more he hoped to do. While he received visits from his family and friends, along with leading generals, politicians, and ministers, he avoided attending the dozens of soirees to which he received invitations.

He emerged from his den to pay two important visits that December. The first was to a man he had never before met but with whom he had been corresponding since August. On December 6, Napoleon and Talleyrand bent their heads for the first of countless discussions between them in the years ahead as they sought to forge a common vision and strategy for France. The second was even more meaningful for Napoleon. The National Institute of Sciences and Arts had offered him a membership. In his acceptance speech before several hundred of France's leading intellectuals in the Luxembourg Palace on December 26, he expressed a wisdom far beyond his years—but one, tragically, that would steadily drain from him in the nearly two decades ahead. "True conquests," he sincerely explained, "the only ones which leave no regret, are those made over ignorance. The most honorable occupation for nations, as well as the most useful, is to contribute to the extension of human knowledge. The true power of the French Republic should consist henceforth in allowing no single new idea to escape its embrace."[70]

Between War and Peace

In those fleeting weeks of well-deserved leisure in Paris, Napoleon Bonaparte certainly could look back over the previous twenty months and feel an enormous sense of accomplishment. Through the mingled arts of war and diplomacy, he had repeatedly trounced the Austrians both on the battlefield and at the diplomatic table; began the process of transferring ever more of Italy from Habsburg or Bourbon domination to French satellite status; and gained Vienna's grudging acceptance of French territorial expansion west of the Rhine, in western Switzerland, in northwest Italy, and the Ionian Islands.

Those were stunning achievements. But forces beyond his control threatened to unravel all of it. A series of intrigues, crimes, and aggressions and Whitehall's promises of huge subsidies enticing Vienna into another coalition edged France and Austria back toward and eventually over the brink of war.

Austria's previous defeat allowed France to expand its influence in many realms. From his embassy in Rome, Joseph Bonaparte conspired to strip the pope of all worldly power and transform the Papal States into a Roman Republic. That provoked riots on December 28, 1797, during which French General Leonard Duphot was murdered, Papal troops took over the French embassy, and Joseph barely escaped to Florence. But like his brother, Joseph knew how to turn a tragedy to France's advantage. He ordered General Berthier at Ancona to use Duphot's murder as an excuse to conquer the Papal States. Berthier mustered all available troops, routed the Papal army, and, on February 18, marched into Rome and seized the pope. Two days later Pius was transferred to a monastery near Sienna.

Although Berthier did not declare a Roman Republic, he did impose a series of liberal decrees which abolished feudalism and declared legal equality for all, including Jews. That was provocative enough. Then General Andre Massena replaced Berthier as commander and allowed himself and his troops to indulge their greed by looting. An uprising broke out on February 25. Although after days of fierce fighting Massena eventually managed to crush the rebellion in Rome, revolts broke out in Orvieto in March; Umbria in April, when a mob massacred 130 French soldiers in Citta di Castello; and Abruzzi in May. The French restored order in all those regions, but at an enormous cost in destroyed lives and property.

Yet another target of French ambitions was the Swiss Confederation, which had maintained a strict but ever more strained neutrality since the revolutionary wars had broken out in 1792. In 1797, Bonaparte had pressured the Confederation to cede the Grison cantons of Bormio, Chiavenna, and Valtelina to the Cisalpine Republic in return for taking over the Frickthal region in southern Germany; the Swiss balked at his demand that they surrender the Simplon Pass and Valais region. Then in December 1797 the Directory embraced the cause of Swiss radicals Frederic Cesar La Harpe, Peter Ochs, and Jean Francois Reubell, who asked for the French army to back what they claimed was widespread support for a Swiss republic.

The Directory assigned General Guillaume Brune the mission of aiding the uprising promised by the radical leaders. But no joyous mass rebellion greeted Brune and his French army when they marched into the western Swiss cantons of the Vaud and Valais in the new year of 1798. Nonplused, Brune linked up with the relative handful of rebels, helped them write a French-style constitution, and declared the birth of the Helvetian Republic on March 22. With the aim of creating a secular, unified society, the new government then adopted French-style policies by abolishing all internal trade barriers, guilds, and corporations, confiscating Church property, and ending feudalism.

Pent-up Austrian rage at these latest French aggressions and humiliations atop all those which had preceded them exploded on April 15, when a Viennese mob ripped down and burned the tricolor raised before France's embassy. Ambassador Jean Baptiste Bernadotte demanded compensation for the insult and sent a report to Paris. Talleyrand was worried that too adamant a stand on a relatively trivial issue could jeopardize the concrete issues that the French were pushing at the Rastadt Congress, which had opened on January 19. He asked Vienna to make some face-saving gesture while redoubling its efforts to resolve the weighty agenda at Rastadt.

With the Rastadt Congress and European peace teetering on the brink of collapse, Bonaparte sent Ludwig Cobenzl a letter pleading with him "that France desires to avoid the horrors of war whose evils will be incalculable for our poor continent. . . . This peace must, it seems to me, endure, since I can see nothing in the interests of our two countries to cause its demise. I know, monsieur, your pacific intentions. . . . I would like you to understand the calm that the French government has displayed" despite repeated provocations. He then ended by warning that should Austria start another war, France would have no choice but to impose a revolution on Vienna as it had on other realms.[71] Fearing the worst, Bonaparte readied himself once again to lead a war against Austria.[72]

Fortunately, the shaky peace held and the crisis passed. Indeed, the Congress eventually made some progress. Most delegates reluctantly agreed on March 11 to accept France's takeover of the German territories, and on April 4 to compensate the Catholic Church for property secularized by the French in those territories.

Then, as the Congress went into a recess on April 28, a vicious crime was committed. Although all the details of the conspiracy will never be known, it involved British agents with pockets full of gold, a network of mostly Swiss patriots enraged at French imperialism, and Colonel Barbaczy who commanded Austria's Szechkler Hussar regiment garrisoned in nearby Gernsbach. Barbaczy led his regiment to Rastadt, forbade all but the French delegation to leave, and delayed their departure until well after nightfall. The French diplomats, families, and servants set off in three carriages toward Paris. In the countryside just a kilometer from Rastadt, four hussars stopped the caravan, yanked out the three diplomats, drew their sabers, and cut them down, murdering two and mutilating the third. They then galloped away into the dark.[73]

Yet even then the renewal of war would be delayed a bit longer.

In Alexander's Footsteps

During those months Bonaparte was planning his greatest adventure yet. Who first conceived the notion of conquering Egypt is impossible to determine. Certainly Talleyrand was the first to publicly call for doing so, in a lecture entitled "Essay on the Advantages of Retaking Colonies under the Present Circumstances," which he delivered before the Institute of France in July 1797.

Reading that report crystallized a vague notion of taking Egypt that Bonaparte had long harbored. Word that the Directory had dismissed the idea prompted a letter from Bonaparte on his August 15 birthday begging to differ.[74] He explained that his entire military and diplomatic strategy was aimed at transforming the eastern Mediterranean from Malta to Constantinople and Toulon to Alexandria into a French sea. Egypt would sooner or later be a crucial element of that grand strategy.

When the Directory remained noncommittal, Bonaparte bluntly pitched the idea to Talleyrand: "Why don't we take over Malta? . . . We should also take over Egypt. That country has never belonged to an European country. . . . I would like you to . . . seek information on the reaction of the Porte if we invade Egypt." As for any fears about provoking a religious war, he argued: "With armies like ours all religions are equal—Muslims, Copts, Arabs, Pagans; all will be complaisant; we will respect each in turn."[75] His letter is curious in that he does not acknowledge and seems to have forgotten that it was Talleyrand who had first publicly called for an invasion of Egypt.

But romanticism was as important as geopolitics in animating Bonaparte's vision. Conquering Egypt would be the first stage in emulating Alexander the Great's attempts to conquer Asia. He later admitted that "I could see myself en route for Asia, riding on an elephant, wearing a turban and bearing a new Koran in my hand, which I would have composed to my liking. I would have united in my enterprise the experience of two worlds, digging about in the ground of all history, attacking English power in India while renewing in that conquest my relationship with old Europe."[76] After his return to Paris in December, he devoted himself to working with Talleyrand to talk the Directory into approving and mobilizing an expedition to Egypt.

Meanwhile, Bonaparte kept a keen eye on France's grand strategic and diplomatic situation. Indeed, he took more than an interest in all of it by behaving as if he already headed France. He did not hesitate to fire off letters filled with advice not just to the Directory, the foreign minister, and the war minister, but to diplomats and generals in the field! And even more astonishingly, those directors, ministers, ambassadors, and commanders more often than not followed his advice![77]

The Directors provided Bonaparte with something concrete to do on January 12, 1798, when they gave him command of an expedition to invade not Egypt but England. On February 8 he embarked on an inspection of the army and naval forces along the Channel. On February 23 he presented to the Directory a report which buried the idea: "To invade England without mastering the sea is about as bold and difficult a mission [as] possible. . . . The expedition to England only appears possible next year. . . . The true moment for preparing ourselves for this expedition has been lost, perhaps forever."[78]

The following day, the Directory let Bonaparte make his pitch for the expedition he really wanted to command. His presentation typically was rooted in tight logic seasoned with emotional appeals. He argued that Egypt would first help anchor French hegemony over the eastern Mediterranean Sea, and then serve as a jumping-off point to conquer British colonies in India and elsewhere in the Indian Ocean. All along Britain's superior seapower could be evaded if the French expedition and supply convoys made short, swift cruises from port to port in southern Europe or between Mediterranean islands. To questions about just where the money would come from to launch and sustain those expeditions, he replied that France's colonization of Egypt would reap revenues that would underwrite his ambitious vision. The final objection offered was that by invading Egypt France would alienate the Turks, who had incorporated that province into their empire in 1517. Here Bonaparte's reply was less assured. He argued that a war was not inevitable, given how overextended the Turks were in the Balkans and elsewhere. At this point Talleyrand interrupted to announce his willingness to go to Constantinople and talk Selim III, the sultan, into ceding Egypt without a war.[79]

The Directory asked Bonaparte to submit a detailed plan of just what troops, ships, and supplies he would need. He did so on March 5.[80] That very same day the Directors appointed him the commander, assigned him Admiral Paul Brueys d'Aigailliers to command the armada, and allocated the necessary funds and forces. It is quite likely that in addition to Bonaparte's rationale for the expedition, the attraction of ridding Paris of that brilliant, ambitious general played an important role in the Directory's decision.

Bonaparte set to work on the monumental challenge with his usual whirlwind of eighteen-hour days that exhausted his subordinates but seemed only to bolster his own energy and enthusiasm. Two months later he packed 167 of France's leading intellectuals along with 36,826 troops, 1,330 horses, and 171 field and siege guns aboard 365 transports which would be escorted by thirteen ships of the line, six frigates, and 50 lesser warships manned by 13,000 sailors.

At first luck sided with the French. Most of the armada set sail from Toulon, and elements from Marseilles, Ajaccio, Genoa, and Civitavecchia from May 19 through the 21st.[81] The voyage of Bonaparte's expedition to Egypt was one of France's rare naval ventures of that epoch that evaded both the British fleet and Neptune's wrath, at least initially. Inevitably spies had learned of the preparations for that massive undertaking, but could not pry out its objective. Prime Minister William Pitt and his cabinet pondered the most likely targets, with Malta, Ireland, and the West Indies heading the list, and how to reposition his majesty's ships to protect them.

On April 29 Pitt ordered eight ships of the line from the Channel squadron to head to Gibraltar, where most of the Mediterranean fleet was refitting, with hopes of plugging that strait so that the French could not escape into the Atlantic. On May 2 Rear Admiral Horatio Nelson received orders to break off his blockade of Cadiz and sail for Toulon. Then, a day before the French armada lifted anchor, a storm fortuitously blew away lurking British frigates; by the time those warships tacked back against the winds to their posts, the main fleet was far to the south en route to a rendezvous with the other divisions at Malta.

The armada dropped anchor just beyond cannon shot of the batteries and forts guarding the deep, narrow bay of Valetta, Malta's capital, on June 8. The Maltese refused Bonaparte's request to crowd his entire armada into the bay for shelter and to take on water; they would allow no more than four ships at a time to enter. Bonaparte protested that this was contrary to the laws of neutral nations, and thus would be added to long-standing French complaints that Ferdinand Joseph Hermann Antoine de Hompesch, the Grand Master of the Knights of St. John, refused to recognize France's revolutionary government and discriminated against French merchants, constituting an act of war.[82]

It did not take long for Bonaparte to conquer Malta. He landed his troops and siege guns on an undefended sandy cove, marched them around to sever the neck protecting the peninsula of Valetta, and demanded that the Maltese surrender. After a brief, face-saving cannonade, the Maltese complied on June 11. The treaty netted France Malta and eleven million francs in return for a pledge to find the Knights of St. John another realm to rule and allowing 300 French knights to return to their ancestral homeland. Thinking of the complex diplomacy which lay ahead, Bonaparte freed 2,000 Muslim galley slaves and had them returned to North Africa. Recognizing that conquering Malta, a protectorate of Tsar Paul I, would undoubtedly spark a diplomatic row, he advised the Directory to offer St. Petersburg the rather lame excuse that by taking Malta off the tsar's hands he was annually sparing Russia a 400,000 ruble subsidy. Bonaparte garrisoned Malta with 3,053 troops and General Charles Vaubois as governor. With all that done, the expedition lifted anchor on June 18. The whole business of conquering and occupying Malta had taken a mere nine days.[83]

En route to Egypt Bonaparte issued a proclamation to his soldiers on June 22. It celebrated their glorious adventure but also explained the alien nature of the civilization they were about to invade and emphasized how vital it was to be sensitive and diplomatic at all times:

> You are about to undertake a conquest which will have incalculable consequences for civilization and world trade. . . . The peoples with whom we are going to live are Muslims; the first article of their faith is this: 'There is no God but God, and Mohammad is his prophet.' Do not contradict them. Respect their muftis and their imams, as you have respected rabbis and priests. Be tolerant towards the ceremonies prescribed by the Koran, as you were tolerant to the convents, the synagogues, the religion of Moses and of Jesus Christ. The Roman legions protected all religions. Here you will encounter ways that are different from Europe. You must get accustomed to them. The peoples whose land we are entering treat their women differently from us; but in all countries, one thing is universal: rape is a monstrosity. . . . Looting . . . dishonors us, destroys our resources and makes us the enemies of the people we need to keep as our friends.[84]

The armada's longboats began landing troops at Marabout, west of Alexandria, on July 1. Hoping to occupy first Alexandria and then the rest of Egypt without a fight, Bonaparte sent ahead letters to various rulers justifying his invasion and explaining his good intentions. He wrote Abou-Bekr, the Pasha of Cairo and the Ottoman envoy, that France would liberate Egypt from Mameluke rule, and so "you must see my arrival with pleasure . . . so come then to meet me and join against the beys" (governors). He warned Idris-Bey, Egypt's naval commander, not to resist. Alexandria surrendered without a fight. While the fleet anchored in Aboukir Bay, Bonaparte paraded his army through the city. He assured local officials that he had come to free Egypt under French protection; promised to respect the local religion, women, and riches; and had a proclamation to that effect printed and distributed in Alexandria and sent on to other cities.[85]

He then marched his army up the Nile. Along the way many a straggler died from the oven-like heat or Egyptian cutthroats mounted on swift Arabian horses which shadowed the French like wolves. But no enemy army blocked Bonaparte's path until he was within a score of miles of Cairo. There, on July 21, with the pyramids on the horizon, he faced a horde of Mameluke warriors led by Ibrahim-Bey and Mourad-Bey. The Mamelukes valiantly and repeatedly charged the French army but were decimated by volleys of musket fire and barrages of canister.

The battle of the Pyramids shattered but did not destroy Mameluke power. Ibrahim-Bey fled with his followers to the Sinai, while Mourad-Bey withdrew with his men to upper Egypt. Both would remain painful thorns in the side of the French for as long as they clung to the Egyptian earth. The Mamelukes would evade numerous expeditions sent to search out and destroy them, reject nearly as many entreaties to negotiate, and launch scores of raids that gnawed away at French power. From early in the occupation, Bonaparte realized that his best chance for peace was to buy rather than conquer it from the rebels. He sent periodic pleas to the guerrilla leaders to join him and enjoy "fortune and happiness."[86] But the Mameluke leaders knew that time was on their side and ignored the offers.

Bonaparte encamped his army just beyond cannon shot of Cairo and sent a letter to its "sheiks and nobles": "Yesterday, the Mamelukes had been for the most part killed or captured, and I am pursuing the rest. Let my boats pass on the river. Send me a deputation to give me word of your submission. Have bread, meat, straw, and barley prepared for my army. And be without worry, because no one desires more to contribute to your happiness than me."[87]

Abou-Bekr, the pasha of Cairo and Ottoman envoy, fled with some followers to join Ibrahim-Bey. Bonaparte futilely tried to entice them back. The rest of the leaders, knowing that resistance would only lead to their destruction, agreed to surrender.[88]

Installing himself and his army in Cairo, Bonaparte was determined to make that city a model of enlightened rule. He purged the Mamelukes from their posts and confiscated and sold off their estates for over three million francs. He then tried to reorganize the government on the principles of a modern civil service, with "careers open to all talents" and dedicated to problem-solving, equality, and justice for all. He had the streets cleaned of heaps of rotting garbage, wells dug for fresh water, and hospitals built for the sick and lame. He appointed a military governor to each province and city, and had them follow the same progressive policies. He established an Administrative Commission to take charge of taxation, sell property confiscated from the Mamelukes, and establish a sound currency. He cut loose his scientists to explore, under heavy guard, Egypt's ancient and natural heritage, and on August 22, 1798, set up the Institute of Egypt for the Arts and Science in which they could herald and debate their findings. Also on his "to do" list was having a canal dug at Suez to link the Mediterranean and Red Seas.[89]

Bonaparte was attempting nothing less than the imposition of a political, economic, social, and cultural revolution on Egypt. For that revolution to succeed, he knew he had to first capture the hearts and minds of both Egypt's elite and its masses. He explained to General Kleber, the governor of Alexandria, his intention to "accustom the people little by little to our ways of acting and thinking, and . . . give them the latitude to run their interior affairs, especially not at all getting mixed up in their conception of justice which is founded on the divine laws incorporated entirely in the Koran." He called on Kleber to "have the highest regard for the muftis and principal sheiks of the country."[90]

Bonaparte was living out his vision in exhilarating days and sultry nights. His secretary Louis de Bourrienne would later write that "only those who saw him in the vigor of his youth can form an idea of his extraordinary intelligence and activity. Nothing escaped his observation. . . . In a few weeks he was as well acquainted with the country as if he had lived in it for ten years." Looking back from St. Helena, Bonaparte reflected: "In Egypt I found myself free of the drags of inconvenient civilization. I dreamt all things and I envisioned the means of fulfilling them. . . . The time I passed in Egypt was the most beautiful in my life, for it was the most ideal. But fate decided different."[91]

The idyll was indeed fleeting. Word arrived that on August 1 Lord Horatio Nelson's squadron had surprised and virtually destroyed the French fleet anchored at Aboukir Bay. It was a stunning victory: Nelson's warships sank two French warships and forced nine others to strike their colors while only two escaped, and killed 1,700 sailors and wounded 1,500 others. With that victory the entire balance of power in the eastern Mediterranean shifted decisively from France to Britain. Bonaparte and his expedition were now marooned in Egypt as prisoners of their own conquest.

How could that have happened? Bonaparte had ordered Admiral Brueys either to crowd the French fleet within Alexandria's harbor or, if that were not possible, to sail to Corfu; but, regardless of his anchorage, to erect shore batteries and be constantly vigilant for the enemy.[92] But Brueys did none of that during the four weeks between when the expedition landed and Nelson arrived. Brueys neither tried to cross the shallow sandbar into the shelter of Alexandria Bay nor set sail for Corfu; he neither dug in an appreciable number of cannons at the bay's west end nor posted any frigates a score or so miles to sea. Most of his crews were lounging ashore at the time of the attack.

Bonaparte could have been forgiven for condemning and despising Brueys for the murderous disaster his incompetence had inflicted on France and the Egyptian expedition. Instead that paradoxical man wrote the most tender letter of condolence to the admiral's widow. From the depths of a naturally loving heart, even as it became ever more calloused by years of waging war and the most brutal forms of power, he spoke of love, life, death, children, posterity, and the search for meaning in an unpredictable and often violent world.[93]

He was also surprisingly philosophical about the disaster in his report to the Directory. After explaining that Brueys had spurned his repeated warnings and instructions about the fleet's disposition, he raised the issue of chance. After stating that the "setback cannot be attributed to the inconsistency of Fortune," he then argued the opposite, that "the fates wanted, in this circumstance like so many others, to test us. . . . [Yet Fortune] has not yet abandoned us; far from that, it has served us throughout this operation beyond our own efforts. When I arrived before Alexandria and I learned that superior English forces had passed that way several days before, despite the terrible tempest which raged and at the risk of shipwreck, I threw my forces on land. I recall that amidst the preparations for the landing . . . I cried to myself, 'Fortune, have you abandoned me?' . . . So it was only when Fortune saw that all its favors were useless that it abandoned our fleet to its destiny."[94]

The debacle at Aboukir Bay was the worst of a series of setbacks that France suffered that year, although it would be months before Bonaparte would learn of them. Pitt was able to entice not just Austria's Francis II but also

Russia's Paul I into a coalition. With his official title as the protector of the Knights of St. John, Paul was incensed when he got word of Bonaparte's conquest of Malta and exile of its rulers. The tsar not only promised to send armies west to join the fight against France but allowed the would-be Louis XVIII and his entourage to take refuge at a palace at Mittau near Riga.

The worst event, the one that would directly affect Bonaparte in Egypt, was the sultan's reaction. On September 2, Selim III had France's ambassador and the rest of the delegation at Constantinople arrested and tossed into the prison of Seven Towers, where they would rot for the next three years. On September 9, he formally declared war on France and joined the coalition. He named the pasha of Acre, Ahmed al-Jazzar—he of the well-deserved nickname Djezzar, or "the Butcher"—to command all Ottoman forces in Palestine.

For the first time in history the Russians and Turks fought on the same rather than opposite sides. On October 1 a Russo-Turkish armada sailed west from Constantinople; by November 20 it had taken the Ionian Islands of Cerigo, Zante, and Cephalonia, and was preparing to invade Corfu. Bonaparte's efforts to establish French hegemony over the eastern Mediterranean were crumbling behind him, and he was helpless to do anything about it.

As if all those related challenges were not daunting enough, Bonaparte faced an insurgency throughout the Nile valley. In what will sound eerily familiar, he issued this warning to Kleber: "The worst thing that we feared is at hand . . . terror."[95] Although the maxim that "one person's terrorist is another person's freedom fighter" had not yet been coined, it was just as true then as now. Likewise the tactics, if not the technologies, for an insurgency were essentially the same: the insurgents tried to provoke indiscriminate and vicious retaliation so that it would alienate ever more natives to take up arms. They also enjoyed international support. As elsewhere, the English bought the allegiance of locals with promises, weapons, and gold, and had them infiltrate the cities occupied by the French and instigate rebellions. In all, Bonaparte faced virtually the same bewildering dilemmas as more recent attempts by various western powers to conquer and transform parts of the Middle East.

How do you fight a thriving insurgency? Then as now, systematic, simultaneous reform and repression offer the best chance. Bonaparte had successfully applied that strategy to the revolutions he imposed on parts of Italy, and now tried to do the same in Egypt.

As Bonaparte supervised his sweeping reforms, he was utterly ruthless in fighting terror with terror: "Every day I order five or six heads cut off in Cairo's streets. Until recently we had to be careful to avoid our reputation for terror which preceded us. Today, in contrast, it is necessary to take measures which are suitable for getting these people to obey; and to obey, for them, is to fear."[96] In addition to ordering executions of proven or suspected terrorists, he had village leaders held as hostages, villages which rebelled burned, suspects tortured into revealing other conspirators, and native military and police formed to suppress their own people. But he did not just impose a harsh, Biblical, "eye for an eye" justice. Amnesty was granted either to award or induce good behavior.

Yet no matter what he did, nothing worked for long, if at all. For instance, the French held in custody the wives and children of prominent Mamelukes, including Mourad-Bey; but that only hardened the resolve of the guerrillas to avenge their humiliations. The enemy baffled Bonaparte: "The Arabs . . . are all mounted and live in the middle of the desert. They pillage equally the Turks, Egyptians, and Europeans. Their ferocity equals the miserable life they lead, exposed all their days amidst the burning sands, the relentless sun, without water to quench their thirst. They are without pity or honesty. They are a spectacle of the most savage men that are imaginable." Nonetheless, he bore his foes a grudging admiration: "The Mamelukes are extremely brave and make an excellent light cavalry, richly dressed, armed with great care, and mounted on horses of the best quality."[97]

A rebellion broke out in Cairo itself on October 21. Although the uprising caught the French by surprise, they brutally crushed it within twenty-four hours. The French lost 16 killed in the fighting and a convoy of 21 sick who were slaughtered, while as many as 2,500 Egyptians may have died. Bonaparte admitted he "had to fire cannon and mortar shells on the Grand Mosque. . . . The city has had a good lesson which it will remember a long time, I believe."[98]

Religious differences, of course, compounded the occupiers' challenges. Bonaparte walked a delicate line between trying to assuage both the majority Muslim and minority Christian Copt populations. He could certainly not afford to show a special favor toward the Copts. Yet the Copts were increasingly targeted by enraged Muslims who, unable to easily kill well armed and alert French soldiers, instead turned their knives on the infidels in their midst. So when the Copt community asked for Bonaparte's protection, he granted it.[99]

All along, diplomacy within and beyond Egypt was a key component of Bonaparte's policies. As usual his diplomacy extended in all relevant directions, the most vital of which was toward Constantinople. For a long time he clung to the naive hope that Selim III would shrug off the French conquest of his province of Egypt. He called on Pierre Ruffin, the French envoy at Constantinople, to explain that the French republic desired no trouble with the

Ottoman Empire, but was simply launching a punitive expedition against the Mamelukes for their years of abuse against French merchants; Alas Ruffin and his staff could conduct little meaningful diplomacy while imprisoned in the Seven Towers. He also harbored dwindling hopes that Talleyrand had made good on their understanding that he would journey to Constantinople and smooth things over with the Sultan. To Nassif, the Grand Vizier, he wrote that Talleyrand should by now have arrived at Constantinople, armed with powers to bridge all differences between France and the Ottoman Empire. If by chance he was not there, Bonaparte called on Nassif to send to Cairo an envoy empowered with full negotiating powers. Bonaparte would not receive a direct reply, and would later learn that Talleyrand had never left Paris.[100]

Bonaparte also tried to win the hearts and minds of neighboring Muslim rulers, including the Ottoman beys in Tunis, Tripoli, and Algiers in North Africa; Acre, Damascus, and Mecca in the Middle East; and even the pasha of Albania. He also enlisted any French envoys stationed there and elsewhere in the region into his diplomatic campaign. From most of those rulers he received nothing but a contemptuous silence. However, he would eventually learn that the "Butcher," Ahmed al-Jazzar, the pasha of Acre, had lived up to his disturbing nickname by torturing to death one of Bonaparte's envoys. Only Ghalib ibn Mussaid, the sheik of Mecca, offered respectful and regular replies.[101]

Bonaparte's diplomacy with Djezzar was the most infuriating. For three months Bonaparte tried to forge a good relationship by sending him letters and envoys which conveyed praise and promises in the most flowery language. In return, he received word that the pasha's response was to harass French envoys and merchants. With the axiom that Arabs only respect and obey strength, Bonaparte tried a firmer tack in a November 19 letter: "I don't want to war with you if you are not my enemy; but it is time that you explain yourself. If you continue to give refuge on Egypt's frontiers to Ibrahim-Bey, I will regard that as a mark of hostility and I will go to Acre. If you want to live in peace with me, you will distance Ibrahim-Bey . . . from the Egyptian frontier, and you will free commerce between Damietta and Syria."[102]

But it did not matter what Bonaparte tried. After all, what could he offer someone from the Muslim world other than humiliation and rage provoked by an invasion and occupation by infidels? Nonetheless, he tried to prove his benevolence by pointing to his freeing of the Muslim galley slaves of Malta; liberating of Egypt from Mameluke rule; respecting the major tenets of the Muslim religion; helping organize a grand fete to celebrate Mohammed's birthday; flirting with the notion of converting himself and his army to Islam; extending protection to caravans of pilgrims bound for Mecca; and bringing order, efficiency, and justice to Egypt. Indeed, his interest in Islam and his respect for the Mamelukes as warriors were genuine.

The lack of response to most of his initiatives was not completely deliberate. The British naval blockade was nearly impenetrable. Squadrons sealed off Alexandria and the mouths of the Nile's west and east branches. His Majesty's warships picked off most vessels trying to run the gauntlet from or to Egypt. The British also regularly bombarded and occasionally raided French positions around Aboukir and Alexandria.

That made it nearly impossible for Bonaparte to communicate regularly with French garrisons on Malta or Corfu, let alone the government in faraway Paris. For months the French marooned in Egypt might get no word at all from their homes. The Ionian Islands were the nearest of France's stepping stones across the Mediterranean. Bonaparte sent numerous letters to General Louis Chabot, who governed the Ionian Islands from Corfu, seeking news of the outside world and such vital supplies as wine and wood. He got very little of either.[103]

In Bonaparte's diplomacy with the Directory, he all along emphasized his military and political victories while downplaying defeats and asking for more men, munitions, and provisions. No matter how bad things got, he incessantly promoted his venture: "Never did a colony offer more advantages. I have no doubt that Egypt will be the means of overcoming England and bringing the peace that we desire. By mastering Egypt France will master India. The English cabinet understands this perfectly. I have no doubt that [our occupation of Egypt] will at the very least guarantee a general peace."[104] He also never lost sight of the grand strategic picture, and did not hesitate to share his policy views with the Directory. Indeed, he tended to present his proposals as orders rather than suggestions: "You will not abandon your army in Egypt; you will pass it supplies, news, and you will take all measures . . . to send a powerful fleet in these waters. You will send an ambassador via Vienna to Constantinople; that is essential. Talleyrand must keep his promise and take himself there; and, if the Porte wants war, you will have an army at Corfu."[105]

France and Bonaparte at Bay

In early 1799 all of France's conquests, satellite republics, and protectorates were imperiled. Revolts broke out against the French "liberators" in southern Italy, Switzerland, the middle Rhine valley, Luxembourg, and Belgium, as well as once again in the Vendee of France itself. The Directory tried to simultaneously crush those revolts and launch four offensives against Austria, with generals Jean Jourdan and Jean Bernadotte leading armies into Germany, Andre Massena into Switzerland, and Barthelemy Scherer into northern Italy. But the Austrians, bolstered by a Russian army in Italy and British gold, staved off all four offensives and then counterattacked. A British expedition, meanwhile, helped Ferdinand IV retake his capital of Naples after French-backed revolutionaries had driven him into exile in Sicily the previous December. The Russo-Turkish expedition took Corfu, the last French holdout in the Ionian Islands. Then it split up, with the Turks sailing toward Egypt and the Russians heading up the Adriatic to cooperate with the Russian army commanded by General Alexander Suvorov. He, with the Austrians, was driving the French from northern Italy. Additional good news for the coalition eventually came from the far side of the world, where General Arthur Wellesley, the future Duke of Wellington, was systematically wiping out France's colonies and protectorates in India. The only allied expedition to fail was the Anglo-Russian effort which landed on Holland's Walcheren Island but was bottled up there. That setback, combined with real or imagined slights from all his allies, prompted the mercurial Paul to withdraw abruptly from the coalition in November.

Bonaparte, meanwhile, had consolidated his power in Egypt and was preparing to fulfill yet another vision. In December he began carefully massing supplies and fortifying a series of positions across the Sinai for an invasion of Palestine. On February 10, 1799, he led 13,000 troops eastward from Cairo to conquer the Holy Land, which he hoped would force Selim III to make peace with him. That quest revived the romanticism that had originally driven Bonaparte to the Middle East. He thrilled at entering the door of Asia at Gaza on February 25. He found his promised land "a very beautiful country," although he was disappointed that it was as cold and rainy as Paris.[106] The weather would soon dramatically change to a quite different extreme.

As always, Bonaparte conducted his military campaign within a grander strategic and diplomatic context. Not only did he try to conciliate the sultans of

Mecca and Oman to his invasion of the Holy Land, he actually tried to contact Tipoo Sahib, a Muslim leader who was leading a revolt against the British in India: "I am filled with desire to liberate you from the iron yoke of England."[107]

His Palestine campaign started out well enough. Upon reaching the province he defeated the Ottoman army in a half dozen engagements, although none were decisive. However, provisions were scarce, often nonexistent; his troops were frequently reduced to eating dogs, donkeys, and camels. Water was even scarcer, and often fouled. Rather than feed his prisoners, he freed them on parole—which they promptly broke. When he recaptured 2,000 of those parolees at Jaffa, he ordered them executed on the beach. Despite his victories, he steadily lost men from battle, exhaustion, and disease. He faced a swelling guerrilla movement which hid amidst a sullen population.[108]

To win over hearts and minds, Bonaparte's diplomatic rhetoric was increasingly that of an avenging warrior of Islam rather than a champion of the Enlightenment. His letter to the sheiks, religious leaders, and people of Palestine opened with the words: "God is lenient and merciful." He then explained that he had come to rid the region of Palestine's governor, "Djezzar" or "the Butcher," and his Mameluke supporters. "He provoked me to war, I will carry it to him." For those who did not resist, he promised to respect their property, well-being, and, above all, religion. "It is from God that all wealth comes; it is him who grants victory. . . . It is good that you know that all human efforts are useless against me, because all I undertake must succeed. Those who declare themselves my friends will flourish. Those who declare themselves my enemies will perish. . . . I am terrible to my enemies and I am good to my friends and I am especially lenient and merciful to the poor." The image he tried to convey was one of an avenging, invincible general bearing all the finest attributes of God and Islam.[109]

He penned many of the same vivid phrases to Pjezzar himself. He recounted his victories and attributed them to God. He explained his mercy toward those who yielded. He then called for peace between them: "You have no real reason to be my enemy." He would march against Acre in a few days to meet the governor—either as an enemy or a friend.[110]

But despite those diplomatic efforts, it was before Acre that his campaign ground to a bloody halt. Pjezzar replied to Bonaparte's letter by having the courier's head chopped off. As if Pjezzar was not a formidable enough enemy, he was backed by William Sydney Smith, a Royal Navy captain on a mixed military-diplomatic assignment, who had arrived with two warships crammed with supplies and munitions just days before Bonaparte and his dwindling army.

Then on March 18 Smith led his warships out and captured a French convoy that was bringing Bonaparte desperately needed siege guns, munitions, provisions, and reinforcements.

At that point Bonaparte would have been better off giving up his siege and withdrawing to Egypt. But another supply flotilla was expected in a week or so, and he gambled that it might evade Smith's warships. So he ordered his battery commanders to mass their field guns and blast away at a key part of the city's wall. Meanwhile, he sought to split the Arabs by promising the Druze emir, Bechir Chihab, independence for his people in return for an alliance. He also called Mourad Radeh, the Mullah of Damascus, to rally the other mullahs and sheiks to join him in liberating the region from Pjezzar, "for his aggressions against God." Not surprisingly, neither took the offer. By March 28 the French guns had opened a small breach in the wall. Bonaparte ordered an assault, but the Turks repelled it with heavy French losses. The French flotilla safely reached Jaffa on April 15, but it would take another two weeks to transport all those heavy guns and munitions to Acre. Meanwhile an Ottoman relief army was reported advancing from Damascus. Bonaparte dispatched General Jean-Baptiste Kleber with several thousand troops to block it. Kleber routed the Ottomans at Mt. Tabor on April 16. The siege guns finally reached the French lines and were put into place. The bombardment tore ever more gaps in the walls. A mine was laboriously inched toward a key tower, and the end was filled with gunpowder kegs and detonated; but the damage was minimal. The Turks repelled five assaults from May first to the tenth.[111]

Bonaparte finally gave up. He ordered his army to begin the long march back to Egypt on May 20. To the Directory he glossed over what was actually a defeat: "Having reduced Acre to a pile of rubble, I will return across the desert and prepare to receive an European or Turkish army," which spies had brought word would invade Egypt in a month or so. "Furthermore, the season is too advanced; the goal that I had proposed has found itself fulfilled. Egypt calls me."[112]

Although he safely reached Cairo on June 14, his situation was grim. He was clinging to power with only 13,000 out of the 35,000 soldiers he had disembarked the previous year. A joint British, Russian, and Turkish fleet had trapped him in Egypt and was massing reinforcements for an eventual invasion. While preparing for that inevitable attack, he also had to shore up his political and military power across all the territory that his troops occupied.

Word of Bonaparte's defeats and atrocities had reached the Nile valley. To counter that, Bonaparte promoted the notion to Egypt's leaders and people that his expedition to the Holy Land had been a glorious victory rather than a dismal failure. He described his behavior all along as irreproachable: "Have I not followed the true spirit of the Koran! . . . The Divan and the people of Egypt must therefore see in this conduct a special proof of the feelings that I nourish in my heart for their happiness and prosperity, and, if the Nile is the first among the Orient's rivers, the people of Egypt, under my government, must be the first of its peoples." To the emir of Mecca, Bonaparte essentially declared himself a Muslim: "In the name of a most lenient and merciful God! There is no god but God and Mohammad is his prophet!"[113]

But Bonaparte soon had a public relations rival. William Sydney Smith and his warships had shadowed the French retreat across the Sinai, then dropped anchor off Alexandria. Under a flag of truce, he cheerfully sent ashore the latest newspapers filled with stories of French disasters on the continent. It was also rumored that he had been among the truce party, disguised as a common sailor. Smith's exploits of first trouncing Bonaparte in Palestine and then locking and mocking him in Egypt provoked the general's ire. To General Marmont, his commander at Alexandria, he dismissed Smith "as a young fool who wants to make his fortune. . . . The best way to punish him is to ignore him. It is necessary to treat him like a captain of arsons."[114]

The expected invasion finally occurred on July 11, when General Mustafa Pasha landed at the head of 15,000 men at Aboukir Bay. But there, inexplicably, he encamped rather than advanced against Alexandria. As Bonaparte mustered as many soldiers as possible, he wrote the Divan of Cairo that the invaders were enemies of Islam, and thus all Egyptians had to unite against them; "I desire that you make that known to all the divans of Egypt." He quick-marched 10,000 troops down the Nile valley. On July 25 he launched his army on what became a slaughter of the Turks.[115]

Bonaparte followed up that victory with an appeal for peace to Youssef-Pasha, the Ottoman Empire's Grand Vizier. Bonaparte related the news of the Turkish debacle and capture of their general, Mustafa Pasha, who was celebrated for his victories against the Russians in previous wars. Bonaparte once again justified his invasions first of Egypt and then Palestine as attempts to punish the Mamelukes for their misrule and their attacks on French interests. He explained his efforts to protect Muslims everywhere. And he called not just for peace but an alliance between France and the Ottoman Empire against the Russians and British.[116]

Despite his victory, Bonaparte recognized that his vision of reconquering Alexander's empire had become a chimera. There was nothing more he could do in Egypt. It was time somehow to slip past the enemy blockade and sail back to France and save his country from its massed enemies. After all, the Directory had originally asked him to return after he had accomplished his mission in Egypt. Indeed, although he would not learn of it until after his arrival in France, the directors had actually renewed their instructions that he return in a letter sent on May 26. So technically, in heading for France he was merely following orders.

Secret diplomacy allowed him to do so. The same man who had prevented him from conquering Palestine helped him escape from Egypt. As William Sydney Smith explained, "I engaged General Bonaparte, in leaving him a free passage to return to take command of the Army of Italy, which no longer exists."[117]

On the night of August 23, Bonaparte turned over command of his army to General Kleber and set sail in two swift ships with his circle of generals and scientists. They landed at Frejus on October 9. When he arrived at Paris on October 16, he was celebrated as the conqueror of Egypt and savior of France. His reply struck most as pertinent, a few as impertinent: "What have you done with the country I left so powerful?"[118]

Chapter Two Endnotes: The Rise of Bonaparte

1. Alan Schom, *Napoleon Bonaparte* (New York: HarperCollins, 1997), 38-41.

2. Proclamation, March 27, 1796, Claude Tchou, ed., *Napoleon I, Correspondance de Napoleon 1er* (hereafter cited as *Correspondence*), 16 vols. (Paris: Bibliotheque Introuvable, 2002), 91.

3. Bonaparte to Carnot, March 28, 1796, Thierry Lentz, ed., *Napoleon Bonaparte: Correspondance Generale*, (hereafter cited as *General Correspondence*), 3 vols. (Paris: Fayard, 2004, 2005, 2006), 424.

4. Bonaparte to Colli, April 8, 1796, *General Correspondence*, 470.

5. Bonaparte to Faipoult, March 27, April 1, 1796, *General Correspondence*, 422, 449.

6. Bonaparte to Colli, April 23, 1796, *General Correspondence*, 520.

7. Bonaparte to Directory, April 28, 1796, *General Correspondence*, 1:541.

8. T. C. W. Blanning, *The French Revolutionary Wars, 1787-1802* (New York: Arnold Books, 1996), 151.

9. Bonaparte to Directory, April 24, 1796, *General Correspondence*, 522.

10. Bonaparte to Barras, end of April 1796, *General Correspondence*, 553.

11. Bonaparte to Barras, May 14, 1796, *General Correspondence*, 596; Bonaparte to Carnot, May 14, 1796, *ibid.*, 597.

12. Bonaparte to Directory, April 26, 1796, *General Correspondence*, 530; Bonaparte to Barras, April [n.d.], 1796, *General Correspondence*, 553.

13. Bonaparte to Carnot, April 29, 1796, *ibid.*, 545; Bonaparte to Directory, April 29, 1798, *General Correspondence*, 546.

14. Bonaparte to Directory, April 29, 1796, *General Correspondence*, 546; Bonaparte to Barras, end of April 1796, *ibid.*, 555.

15. Blanning, *French Revolutionary Wars*, 146.

16. Bonaparte to Berthier, May 25, 1796, *General Correspondence*, 629; Bonaparte to Directory, June 1, 1796, *ibid.*, 639.

17. Bonaparte to Directory, June 1, 7, 1796, *General Correspondence*, 643, 656; Bonaparte to Belmonte-Pignatelli, June 7, 1796, *ibid.*, 655.

18. Bonaparte to Directory, June 5, 1796, *General Correspondence*, 651.

19. Bonaparte to Directory, June 21, 1796, *General Correspondence*, 711; Bonaparte to Directory, June 26, July 2, 1796, *ibid.*, 725, 744.

20. Bonaparte to Ferdinand III, June 29, 1796, *General Correspondence*, 732.

21. Bonaparte to Directory, May 6, 1796, *General Correspondence*, 575.

22. Bonaparte to Directory, July 2, 1796, *General Correspondence*, 743.

23. Bonaparte to Genoa Senate, June 15, 1796, *General Correspondence*, 697.

24. Bonaparte to Faipoult, July 20, 1796, *General Correspondence*, 793.

25. Robert Asprey, *The Rise of Napoleon* (New York: Basic Books, 2000), 147-48; Blanning, *French Revolutionary Wars*, 160.

26. Bonaparte to Oriani, May 24, 1796, *General Correspondence*, 627.

27. Bonaparte to Francis II, October 2, 1796, *General Correspondence*, 962.

28. Bonaparte to Mattei, October 24, 1796, *General Correspondence*, 1007.

29. Bonaparte to Cacault, October 28, 1796, *General Correspondence*, 647.

30. For some key letters to Italian leaders nurturing Italian development, see Bonaparte to Garrau, October 9, 1796, *General Correspondence*, 983; Bonaparte to Facci, January 1, 1796, *ibid.*, 767.

31. Jacques Godeschot, *La Grande Nation: L'Expansion Revolutionaire de la France dans le Monde de 1789 a 1799* (Paris: Auber, 2004), 1:298.

32. For key letters explaining his ends and means, see Bonaparte to Directory, October 2, 11, 17, 1796, *General Correspondence*, 960, 988, 1002.

33. Bonaparte to Directory, November 15, 1796, *General Correspondence*, 1059.

34. Bonaparte to Directory, June 21, 1796, *General Correspondence*, 710.

35. Bonaparte to Mattei, January 22, 1797, *General Correspondence*, 1315; Bonaparte to Directory, February 15, 19, 1797, *ibid.*, 1:1579, 1591.

36. Bonaparte to Charles, March 31, 1797, *General Correspondence*, 1484.

37. Bonaparte to Directory, April 16, 19, 22, 30, 1797, *General Correspondence*, 1514, 1516, 1517, 1519.

38. Bonaparte to Directory, April 19, 1797, *General Correspondence*, 1516.

39. Bonaparte to Directory, April 19, 1797, *General Correspondence*, 1516.

40. Bonaparte to Lallement, April 9, 30, 1797, *General Correspondence*, 1499, 1523; Bonaparte to Envoys of the Venetian senate, April 30, 1797, *ibid.*, 1522.

41. Bonaparte to Venetian Doge, May 27, 1797, *General Correspondence*, 1589. Bonaparte to Directory, May 27, 1797, *ibid.*, 1587.

42. Bonaparte to Brueys, September 17, 1797, *General Correspondence*, 2035; Bonaparte to Brueys, August 4, 1797, *General Correspondence*, 1864.

43. Bonaparte to Directory, August 16, 1797, *General Correspondence*, 1908. See also, Bonaparte to Directory, June 1, 3, 1797, *ibid.*, 1608, 1615; Bonaparte to Talleyrand, August 16 (two letters), 1797, *ibid.*, 1910, 1911.

44. Bonaparte to Ibrahim, August 16, 1797, *General Correspondence*, 1909.

45. Bonaparte to Directory, August 16, September 23, 1797, *General Correspondence*, 1908, 2077; Bonaparte to Talleyrand, September 13, 1797, *ibid.*, 2019.

46. Bonaparte to Joseph, September 2 (four letters), September 29, November 14 (two letters), 1797, *General Correspondence*, 1955, 1956, 1957, 1958, 2105, 2245, 2246.

47. Bonaparte to Directory, May 14, 19, 30, June 6, 1797, *General Correspondence*, 1549, 1561, 1600, 1630; Bonaparte to Lombardy administration, May 27, 1797, *ibid.*, 1590; Bonaparte to Brignolle, Doge of Genoa, June 7, 1797, *ibid.*, 1642; Bonaparte to Antonio Garruchio, July 6, 1797, *ibid.*, 1765; Bonaparte to Berthier, July 23, 1797, *ibid.*, 1808.

48. Bonaparte to Genoan government, June 16, 1797, *General Correspondence*, 1691; see also Bonaparte to Genoan government, *ibid.*, 2214.

49. Bonaparte to Directory, May 26, July 11, 1797, *General Correspondence*, 1580, 1774.

50. Bonaparte to Directory, May 8, 1797, *General Correspondence*, 1538.

51. Bonaparte to Berthier, May 30, June 4, 7, 26, September 11, 1797, *General Correspondence*, 1589, 1620, 1538, 1731, 2000; Bonaparte to Directory, June 3, 1797, *ibid.*, 1618. See also, Jacques Godeschot, *Le Comte d'Antraigues: Un Espion dans l'Europe des émigrés* (Paris: Fayard, 1986).

52. Elizabeth Sparrow, *Secret Service: British Agents in France, 1792-1815* (London: Boydell, 1999), 123-24, 131, 138.

53. Sparrow, *Secret Service*, 139-44.

54. Bonaparte to Talleyrand, July 26, 1797, *General Correspondence*, 1822.

55. Bonaparte to Talleyrand, September 6, 1797, *General Correspondence*, 1973.

56. Bonaparte to Directory, June 20, 22, July 2 (two letters), 23, 1797, *General Correspondence*, 1699, 1714, 1745, 1746, 1811; Bonaparte to Austrian envoys, June 21,

July 28, (two letters), July 29 (three letters), 1797, *ibid.*, 1704, 1818, 1819, 1832, 1833, 1834; Bonaparte to Gallo, June 21, 1797, *ibid.*, 1706.

57. Bonaparte to Talleyrand, September 19, 1797, *General Correspondence*, 2047.

58. Bonaparte to Directory, July 11, 1797, *General Correspondence*, 1774.

59. Bonaparte to Francis, July 23, 1797, *General Correspondence*, 1812.

60. Bonaparte to Talleyrand, September 3, 1797, *General Correspondence*, 1965. For his diplomatic strategy, see also Bonaparte to Talleyrand, September 13, 1797, *ibid.*, 2021.

61. Bonaparte to Talleyrand, September 19, 1797, *General Correspondence*, 2047.

62. Bonaparte to Directory, September 19, 1797, *General Correspondence*, 2045.

63. Bonaparte to Clarke, July 17, 18, 23, 26, 1797, *General Correspondence*, 1790, 1797, 1810, 1815; Bonaparte to Talleyrand, September 26, 1797, *ibid.*, 2099.

64. Bonaparte to Talleyrand, September 26, 1797, *General Correspondence*, 2098.

65. Bonaparte to Talleyrand, September 28, October 7, 1797, *General Correspondence*, 2101, 2149; Bonaparte to Austrian envoys, September 28 (two letters), *ibid.*, 2102, 2103; Bonaparte to Cobenzl, October 8, 1797, *ibid.*, 2150.

66. Bonaparte to Directory, October 10, 1797, *General Correspondence*, 2153.

67. Bonaparte to Directory, October 18, 1797, *General Correspondence*, 2169.

68. Bonaparte to Talleyrand, October 18, 1797, *General Correspondence*, 2170.

69. Bonaparte instructions for French envoys to Rastadt, December 9, 1797, *General Correspondence*, 2276.

70. Bonaparte to National Institute, December 26, 1797, *General Correspondence*, 2280.

71. Bonaparte to Cobenzl, April 25, 1798, *General Correspondence*, 2431; Bonaparte to Talleyrand, April 26, 1798, *ibid.*, 2432.

72. Bonaparte to Merlin de Douai, president of Directory, May 1, 1798, *General Correspondence*, 2437.

73. Sparrow, *Secret Service*, 168-73.

74. Bonaparte to Directory, August 16, 1797, *General Correspondence*, 1908; Talleyrand to Bonaparte, August 23, 1797; Lacour-Gayet, *Talleyrand,* 4 vols. (Paris: Payot, 1928-34), 1:304.

75. Bonaparte to Talleyrand, September 13, 1797, *General Correspondence*, 2019.

76. Dard, *Napoleon and Talleyrand*, 22. See also, Jacques Benoist-Mecin, *Bonaparte en Egypt ou la Reve Inassouvi* (Paris: Perrin, 1978); Thierry Lentz, *Savary, le Seide de Napoleon* (Paris: Fayard, 2001), 42.

77. Bonaparte to Directory, January 16, April 13, 1798, *General Correspondence*, 2301, 2390; Bonaparte to Talleyrand, January 14, 16, 1798, *ibid.*, 2300, 2302; Bonaparte to Brune, January 11, 1798, *ibid.*, 2296; Bonaparte to Berthier, Commander of Army of Italy, January 11, 24 (two letters), March 8, 1798, *ibid.*, 2298, 2306, 2307, 2326; Bonaparte to General Gentili, Governor of Ionian Islands, January 17, 1798, *ibid.*, 2303, 2304, 2305; Bonaparte to Faipoult, minister of the Republic of Genoa, January 11,

1798, *ibid.*, 2297; Bonaparte to Directory of Cisalpine Republic, February 6, 1798, *ibid.*, 2310; Bonaparte to Treilhard, French envoy to Rastadt, March 18, 1798, *ibid.*, 2338.

78. Bonaparte to Scherer, January 9, February 7, 1798, *General Correspondence*, 2295, 2313; Bonaparte to Directory, February 12, 1798, *ibid.*, 2314.

79. Yves Laissus, *L'Egypte: Une Aventure Savante, Avec Bonaparte, Kleber, Menou, 1798-1801* (Paris: Fayard, 1998), 134.

80. Bonaparte to Directory, March 5, 1798, *General Correspondence*, 2322.

81. Bonaparte to Directory, April 13, May 19, 24, 27, 1798, *General Correspondence*, 2390, 2496, 2498, 2505; Bonaparte to Berthier, March 15, 1798, *ibid.*, 2330; Bonaparte to Treasury Commissioners, March 11, 1798, *ibid.*, 2328; Bonaparte to Brueys, March 30, April 17, 1798, *ibid.*, 2348, 2398; Bonaparte to Commission on Mediterranean Coasts, March 30, 1798, *ibid.*, 2349; Bonaparte to Sucy, Commissary General, March 30, April 17, 1798, *ibid.*, 2352, 2399; Bonaparte to Monge, April 19, 1798, *ibid.*, 2415; La Jonquiere, *L'Expedition L'Egypte*, 1:246-81, 324-53.

82. Bonaparte to Berthier, June 9, 1798, *General Correspondence*, 2514.

83. Bonaparte to Directory, June 13, 17, 1798, *General Correspondence*, 2523, 2547; Bonaparte to Garat, French minister at Naples, June 13, 1798, *ibid.*, 2524; Bonaparte to Najac, Commissary General, June 12, 1798, *ibid.*, 2515; Bonaparte to Bishop Gabini, June 12, 1798, *ibid.*, 2517; Bonaparte to Berthier, June 14, 1798, *ibid.*, 2525.

84. Napoleon Proclamation to Army of Italy, June 22, 1798, *General Correspondence*, 2710.

85. Bonaparte to Abou-Bekr, June 30, 1798, *General Correspondence*, 2560; Bonaparte to Idris-bey, July 1, 1798, *ibid.*, 2561.

86. Bonaparte to Ibrahim-Bey, August 12 1798, *General Correspondence*, 2814.

87. Bonaparte to Sheiks and Nobles of Cairo, July 22, 1798, *General Correspondence*, 2616.

88. Bonaparte to Abou-Bekr, July 22, 23, 1798, *General Correspondence*, 2617, 2622.

89. Bonaparte to Directory, July 6, 1798, *General Correspondence*, 2593; Bonaparte to Administrative Commission, July 28 (three letters), August 1, 1798, *ibid.*, 2669, 2670, 2671, 2715.

90. Bonaparte to Kleber, July 7, 1798, *General Correspondence*, 2601; see also Bonaparte to Menou, July 7, 1798, *ibid.*, 2602.

91. Louis Antoine de Bourrienne, *Memoires de M. de Bourrienne sur Napoleon, le Directoire, le Consulat, l'Empire, et la Restauration*, 10 vols. (Paris: Lavocate, 1829), 1:143; Emmanuel Auguste Dieudonne Las Cases, *Memorial de Sainte Helene* (Paris: Editions de Seuil, 1968), 367.

92. Bonaparte to Brueys, April 22, July 27, 30 (two letters), 1798, *General Correspondence*, 2425, 2654, 2676, 2677; Bonaparte to Directory, July 6, August 19, 1798, *ibid.*, 2593, 2878; Bonaparte to Kleber, July 7, 1798, *ibid.*, 2601.

93. Bonaparte to Madame Brueys, August 19, 1798, *General Correspondence*, 2869.

94. Bonaparte to Directory, August 19, 1798, *General Correspondence*, 2879.

95. Bonaparte to Kleber, July 30, 1798, *General Correspondence*, 2680.

96. Bonaparte to Menou, July 31, 1798, *General Correspondence*, 2699.

97. Bonaparte to Directory, October 17, 1798, *General Correspondence*, 3476; Bonaparte to Directory, August 19, 1798, *ibid.*, 2870.

98. Bonaparte to Marmont, October 23, 1798, *General Correspondence*, 3532; Bonaparte to Directory, October 27, 1798, *ibid.*, 3554.

99. Bonaparte to Girges-el-Gouhary, December 7, 1798, *General Correspondence*, 3872.

100. Bonaparte to Nassif-Pasha, Grand Vizier, August 22, 1798, *General Correspondence*, 2906; Bonaparte to Youssef-Pasha, Grand Vizier, November 9, December 11, 1798, *ibid.*, 3647, 3920; Bonaparte to Ruffin, July 1, 6, November 9, 1798, *ibid.*, 2562, 2592, 3639; Bonaparte to Talleyrand, August 22, 1798, *ibid.*, 2904.

101. Bonaparte to Ghalib-ibn-Mussaid, August 25, September 6, 1798, *General Correspondence*, 2931, 3099; Bonaparte to Ali of Janina, June 17, 1798, *ibid.*, 2539; Bonaparte to Abadallah, Pasha of Damascus, August 31, 1798, *ibid.*, 3035; Bonaparte to French envoys at Tunis, Tripoli, and Algiers, June 15, 1798, *ibid.*, 2532; Bonaparte to Alphonse de Guy, August 18, 1798, *ibid.*, 2860; Bonaparte to Beauvoisins, August 22, 1798, *ibid.*, 2895; Bonaparte to French envoys at Jaffa, August 27, 1798, *ibid.*, 2960; Bonaparte to Mure, French consul at Cyprus, August 28, 1798, *ibid.*, 2986.

102. Bonaparte to Ahmed Djezzar, August 22, September 12, 1798, *General Correspondence*, 2894.

103. Bonaparte to Chabot, June 15, August 5, 1798, *General Correspondence*, 2531, 2748.

104. Bonaparte to Directory, September 8, 1798, *General Correspondence*, 3112.

105. Bonaparte to Directory, October 7, 1798, *General Correspondence*, 3404.

106. Bonaparte to Marmont, February 26, 1799, *General Correspondence*, 4261.

107. Bonaparte to Tipoo-Sahib, January 25, 1799, *General Correspondence*, 4167; Bonaparte to Said Ibn Sultan, Iman of the Ibadites, January 25, 1799, *ibid.*, 4164; Bonaparte to the Sultan of Mecca, January 25, 1799, *ibid.*, 4166.

108. Bonaparte to Directory, March 13, 1799, *General Correspondence*, 4294.

109. Bonaparte to Sheiks, Ulemas, and People of Gaza, Ramleh, and Jaffa, March 9, 1799, *General Correspondence*, 4276; see also, Bonaparte to Sheik, Ulema, and Commander of Jerusalem, March 9, 1799, *ibid.*, 4277; Bonaparte to Guerar, sheik of Naplouise, March 9, 1799, *ibid.*, 4278.

110. Bonaparte to Ahmed Djezzar, March 9, 1799, *General Correspondence*, 4280.

111. Bonaparte to Directory, May 10, 1799, *General Correspondence*, 4346; Bonaparte to Grezieu, April 5, 1799, *ibid.*, 4316; Bonaparte to Emir Bechir Chihab, March 20, 1799, *ibid.*, 4301; Bonaparte to Mullah Mourad-Radeh, March 27, 1799, *ibid.*, 4312.

112. Bonaparte to Directory, May 10, 1799, *General Correspondence*, 4346.

113. Bonaparte to Divan of Cairo, June 27, 1799, *General Correspondence*, 2:4476; Bonaparte to Sherif of Mecca, June 30, 1799, *ibid.*, 4489.

114. Bonaparte to Marmont, June 26, 1799, *General Correspondence*, 4470.

115. Bonaparte to Divan of Cairo, July 21, 1799, *General Correspondence*, 2:4633; Bonaparte to Directory, July 28, 1799, *ibid.*, 4659.

116. Bonaparte to Youssef-Pasha, August 17, 1799, *General Correspondence*, 4743.

117. Sparrow, *Secret Service*, 192-93, 203.

118. Louis Madelin, *Histoire du Consulat et de l'Empire*, 16 vols. (Paris: Hachette, 1937-54), 1:34-46.

Chapter Three

The Rise of Napoleon

1799-1805

*"Who will end the revolution? It's a problem that time keeps secret and
will be resolved by reason and necessity." (to Talleyrand)*

*"What do you hope to gain from going to war? The world is large enough that our two
nations can live in it, and reason is sufficiently powerful for one to find a means
of reconciliation if both sides have the will to seek it." (to George III)*

*"I did not usurp the Crown. I picked it out of a ditch
and the people placed it on my head."*

—Napoleon Bonaparte

Coup and Consulate

The timing of Bonaparte's return and grab for power could not have been
better.[1] The war was dragging on inconclusively, and with it came a rising body
count, ever more crippling debt, prices, taxes, scarcity, and despair. The five
directors were not merely incapable of bringing an end to all that, their
corruption and ineptness grossly worsened matters. The Directory's backers
had dwindled to few more than its immediate beneficiaries.

But to whom could those disgusted with the Directory turn? Ironically, both the royalists and the Jacobins were slowly crawling their way back from the political wilderness to be seen as viable alternatives by different but growing audiences. The royalists, however, were still largely an underground movement. In contrast, the Jacobins had become the largest party in the Council of Five Hundred, the National Assembly's lower house, following the spring 1799 election.

The Jacobins had no sooner taken their seats when they began to flex their political muscles. On June 5 they rallied a majority to vote for a resolution condemning the Directory for its string of military defeats abroad, inability to quell the Vendee insurgency, and ever more autocratic measures. After the Directory pointedly ignored the resolution, the Council of Five Hundred declared itself in permanent session from June 15. Then, to bolster its popularity, the Jacobins on August 5 issued a resolution calling for the distribution of property from the rich to the poor.

That gesture certainly pleased the poor and inspired mobs in the squalid quarters of Paris and other cities. It also sent a chill up the spines of not just those with property, but everyone who recalled that such rhetoric had been the prelude to the bloodbath the Jacobins had inflicted on France the last time they were in power. Could anything prevent another Terror?

Those who looked toward the army for protection were not reassured by what they saw; its loyalties were bitterly divided. Legally it was committed to upholding the constitution and thus the Directory, yet the rumors circulating of the unbridled greed of the directors and their confederates enraged most officers and soldiers along with almost everyone else. From the barracks and camps a murmur arose and grew ever louder that perhaps only a military dictator could flush France's Augean stables of corruption and secure the nation from all its enemies, foreign and domestic.

And who could best accomplish that mission? Each regional army tended to favor its own best general, if it had one, as a possible contender. At that point General Jean Victor Moreau, who commanded the Army of the North, stirred the most enthusiasm among the rank and file. After Moreau, General Jean Baptiste Bernadotte was among the Jacobins' leading voices, and only poorly hid his lust for power; but his checkered military record and imperious manner limited his popular appeal.

And then Napoleon Bonaparte returned from Egypt. For those French who longed for a savior who would bring prosperity, unity, and peace to the nation, ever more imagined him in that role. He certainly appeared to be the ideal candidate. He was as brilliant at administration and diplomacy as he was at war. No other general or politician came close to matching his achievements or sheer ability to inspire. A circle of prominent generals, politicians, and thinkers were actively urging him to take over. Countless others would rally enthusiastically to his rule, and most of the rest would shrug off the latest shift in power. Few would dare openly oppose him. Indeed, among Bonaparte's supporters was Moreau himself, whom Emmanuel Sieyes, one of the directors, had earlier approached to lead a coup; Moreau had declined. After Bonaparte reappeared in Paris on October 16, Moreau noted to Sieyes, "There is your man; he will be better at making a coup than me."[2] With such widespread sentiments, if the plot were done right the takeover could be swift and bloodless.

Lucien, the most gifted of the Bonaparte brothers after Napoleon himself, was a key conspirator and, as the newly elected president of the Council of Five Hundred, could not have been better placed. There he had wielded his influence to get Sieyes and Roger Duclos elected as directors; both men agreed to share power with Bonaparte in a triumvirate. Also prominent in the plot were Charles Maurice de Talleyrand-Perigord, who had resigned as foreign minister on July 18 amidst a corruption scandal but was eager to retrieve his portfolio; Police Minister Joseph Fouche; Admiral Estache Bruix; and prominent politicians Jean Jacques Regis de Cambaceres, Pierre Louis Roederer, and Pierre Francois Real. As for the other directors, Louis Gohier and General Jean Moulin would adamantly oppose a coup. Paul Barras was the wild card, but was likely to go along. He had genuinely supported Bonaparte in the past by giving him the command of armies and a wife. Plus, his loyalty was clearly for sale, as rumors spread that he had recently pocketed a 12 million franc bribe to work for a Bourbon restoration; his head might well roll if he were charged with treason.

Now all that remained was for the plotters to contrive a crisis in which the National Assembly could be stampeded into suspending the Directory and granting Bonaparte emergency powers. The catalyst to justify their coup would be the fictitious need to counter another, imaginary coup. On November 9 Sieyes and Duclos warned the Council of Ancients of a brewing Jacobin conspiracy. A majority of the alarmed legislators agreed to transfer both houses of the National Assembly from Paris to the relative safety of the Palace of St. Cloud on the city's outskirts, and to give Bonaparte the command of all troops in and around Paris. To ensure that the National Assembly safely reached its new quarters, Bonaparte would himself escort them there at the head of a

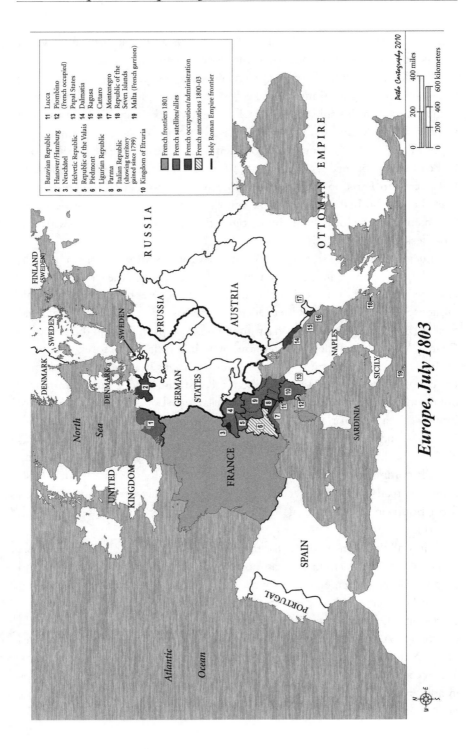

Europe, July 1803

Delta Cartography 2010

1 Batavian Republic
2 Hanover/Hamburg
3 Neuchâtel
4 Helvetic Republic
5 Republic of the Valais
6 Piedmont
7 Ligurian Republic
8 Parma
9 Italian Republic (showing territory gained since 1799)
10 Kingdom of Etruria
11 Lucca
12 Piombino (French occupied)
13 Papal States
14 Dalmatia
15 Ragusa
16 Cattaro
17 Montenegro
18 Republic of the Seven Islands
19 Malta (French garrison)

French frontiers 1801
French satellites/allies
French occupation/administration
French annexations 1800–03
Holy Roman Empire frontier

grenadier battalion. What a classic case of a fox getting appointed to guard the chicken coop! Meanwhile, Talleyrand and Bruix convinced Barras to retire with a two million livre pension. Bonaparte informed Gohier and Moulin that the Directory was no more and asked them to resign; when they refused, he had them arrested.

So far, so good for the conspirators. But trying a two-day coup was a mistake. While it had not been difficult to bribe Barras and arrest Gohier and Moulin among the directors, it would be far tougher to manipulate 750 legislators in two separate but adjacent bodies into yielding power. The best chance to do so would have been when the legislators were still stunned from the "threat" of that "Jacobin conspiracy." The delay of their move until the following day gave them time to compose themselves and think.

They raised sharp questions and voices the next morning, November 10, when Bonaparte appeared before the Council of Ancients, which was meeting in the Gallery of Apollo. He started his pitch for them to abolish the Directory and replace it with a three-man consulate led by himself; but he was nervous, and it showed. When angry voices began to shout him down, he lost his cool and coherence. Having failed with the Council of Ancients, he strode angrily over to the Council of Five Hundred in the separate building, the Orangery, to try to convince them. That was the political equivalent of jumping from the frying pan into the fire, since the Council of Five Hundred, with its Jacobin majority, was the more radical of the two houses. They not only jeered but mobbed him. A half dozen grenadiers managed to surround Bonaparte and push their way through the enraged crowd to safety outside.

Bonaparte was about to give up when his brother rescued him from the brink of political extinction. Before the grenadier battalion massed on parade outside, Lucien declared that the radicals had attacked their general and had to be rousted to save France; the grenadiers charged into the assembly halls. Most legislators fled; the forty or fifty who remained voted to grant emergency powers to Bonaparte, Sieyes, and Duclos. That done, they voted their institutions into an indefinite recess.

The triumvirate immediately put their shadow government into power, with Talleyrand as foreign minister, Louis Alexandre Berthier as war minister, Lucien as interior minister, Martin Gaudin as finance minister, and Fouche as police minister. Sieyes headed a fifty-man commission, with half drawn from each legislative house, charged with writing a new constitution.

The constitution that was unveiled on December 15 was billed as the latest French version of a republic. But beneath its democratic trappings, it essentially conferred dictatorial powers on First Consul Bonaparte, with the other two consuls playing no more than advisory roles and the National Assembly largely reduced to rubber-stamp status. The First Consul was granted a ten-year, renewable term during which he was empowered to issue unchallengeable decrees; initiate or approve all laws; appoint all senators, state councilors, ministers, prefects, sub-prefects, and mayors; exercise all executive authority; and command the army and navy.

Elections would be held every three years. However, universal manhood suffrage (for all those at least twenty-five years old) existed only at the local commune, or arrondissement, level. From there a plurality sent a representative, or "notable", to a departmental electoral college; its members then chose one of their own to send to the national college. From that pool Bonaparte picked a Senate of at first 60, eventually 100, members, aged at least 40 years, who would enjoy lifetime tenure. They in turn would annually choose two new members and replace older members. The Senate picked a Legislative Corps of 300 members aged 30 or more years and a Tribunate of 100 members aged 25 or more years. The Senate also voted for the consuls and appeals court judges, and had the power to issue decrees. The State Council originally had 29 members, eventually expanded to 40, all handpicked by Bonaparte. Lawmaking was split among those institutions: the Consuls or State Council introduced laws; the Tribunate debated them; the Legislative Corps voted on them; and the Senate determined whether they were constitutional. While the departments, communes, and arrondissements were preserved, henceforth each would be governed by, respectively, a prefect, mayor, or subprefect—all named by Bonaparte. Glaringly absent from the constitution was a bill of rights.

The rump assemblies of Ancients and Five Hundred overwhelmingly endorsed the new constitution. It then was presented to France's electorate. Had the votes been fairly counted, the constitution would have been overwhelmingly rejected, by over two to one, with 3.5 million opposed and only 1.5 million in favor. But once again Lucien came to the rescue. As Interior Minister he simply announced on February 17, 1800, that 3,011,007 had approved and only 1,562 rejected the proposal.[3]

Bonaparte now had his official government. He had devised it largely for show, to present a pantomime of republican institutions and practices. In reality, he now had virtually uninhibited powers to govern France. And his first step was to amass yet more power. He pressured Sieyes and Duclos to resign and replaced them with the much more politically docile Jean Jacques Regis de Cambaceres and Charles Francois Lebrun. He transferred his office from the

Luxembourg to the Tuileries Palace on February 19, 1800, and would make ample use of the St. Cloud Palace when he wanted to get out of the heart of Paris to its fringe.

Over the next couple of years Bonaparte would get the National Assembly to pass constitutional amendments which empowered him to appoint the other two consuls and his own successor, and to override the votes of the Legislative Assembly and Tribunate. Meanwhile, he steadily emasculated the power of the assemblies. From 1802 he would name all of the Senate's new members, and added 40 more members to dilute the power of the originals. He allowed the most autonomous of the assemblies, the Tribunate, to atrophy by filling no vacant seats, and abolished it outright in 1807. As for the Legislative Corps, he simply dismissed it when it disappointed him and recalled it ever more rarely; it met only seventeen days in 1811 and never in 1812.

Of the assemblies, Bonaparte would diminish the State Council's powers the least. Unlike the other three bodies, which met at Bonaparte's pleasure, the State Council was in permanent session. He packed it with talented men who often became experts in fields he had no time to study, and for many years he encouraged wide-ranging, in-depth, and frank discussions whenever he needed advice.

Two other bodies existed to advise him, the Privy Council and the so-called "Black Cabinet." During the consulate the Privy Council at first included only the two other consuls, but he expanded its members until during the empire it included archchancellor Cambaceres, two ministers, two senators, two state councilors, and two grand officers of the Legion of Honor. He used the Privy Council for (usually) genuine debate on relatively mundane matters. For crucial questions of war, diplomacy, terrorism, and subversion, he turned to his Black Cabinet, which usually included his ministers of foreign affairs, war, police, and interior, and the Paris police prefect.

In all, Napoleon Bonaparte ruled through technocrats rather than lawmakers. He sought a streamlined, muscular, problem-solving administration of experts guided by his energetic, meticulous leadership. He frequently exhorted his ministers to cut more wasteful spending, practices, and personnel. He urged one minister to "form your bureau especially of men who are just, moral, and tough."[4] He surrounded himself mostly with talented, energetic individuals who shared his zeal to develop France. His ideal official had a keen intelligence, quiet confidence, and unshakeable loyalty, and remained unperturbed by any challenges, crises, or Bonaparte himself. Those who were timid, uncertain, or wishy-washy were soon ushered to the street.

On most issues, at most times, he listened closely if curtly to his advisors. Indeed, he would often pick their brains for hours before he made a decision. But it was always his decision. There was no collective decision making in the cabinet or Council of State. Meetings were mostly held at the Tuileries or St. Cloud, although at times he would summon officials to Malmaison, Fontainebleau, the Petite Trianon at Versailles, or another residence if a problem arose unexpectedly. And his willingness to ponder opinions that conflicted with his own instincts dwindled as his power and ego swelled. Once he made up his mind, he tended to shun information or advice that undercut his decision. Ultimately, for better or worse, he was the source of virtually all of France's decrees, policies, and laws during his latter years in power.

Having ensured that virtually everyone in the government would cooperate with rather than challenge him, Bonaparte then turned to the most obvious source of potential dissent elsewhere. The revolution had inaugurated freedom of the press, and in the decade after 1789 hundreds of pamphlets, journals, and books were published. That freedom essentially ended on January 17, 1800, when the First Consul ordered all but thirteen of sixty political journals shut down. Those allowed to publish had to buy a license and take a loyalty oath. He made it clear to the editors of the survivors that their persistence depended on their ability to adhere to the most rigorous self-censorship. Nonetheless, censors pored over every line of every publication from the surviving presses—and they still managed to find plenty to censor, even though the publishers rigorously combed their own works for anything remotely offensive. By 1811 only four presses were left for all of Paris; none were allowed to print political news unless it had already appeared in *Le Moniteur*, the government's quasi-official newspaper.[5]

Manipulating the press to project images and messages that enhanced his administrative, military, and diplomatic initiatives and power was only part of Napoleon Bonaparte's public relation campaigns. He mastered what previous rulers had pioneered: the art of the "big lie," propagated through the mass media, monuments, parades, awards, and titles. For instance, it was not enough for Bonaparte to win battles; he had to envelop those victories in legend. He explained why propaganda was so vital to his rule: "Everybody reasons in France. Flighty and frivolous, yes; but nobody forgets anything here. This country needs to be governed with a firm hand. A strong will is needed, but one that must draw its force from public opinion—and to that end all minds must be enlisted, all factions held in unison, so as to give them all a stake in the success of the government which protects them."[6]

He also did not hesitate to imprison those who appeared to pose a threat to his rule. By 1814 there were about 2,500 political inmates in state prisons and perhaps 4,000 others in internal exile. That may seem like a lot, until it is compared to 30 million people living in France itself and the 300,000 to 500,000 who had been imprisoned and perhaps 50,000 executed by the Convention. Historian Steven Englund argues that "though the Napoleonic police were perhaps everywhere, the justice given out by the Empire was far less unjust than in the later Revolution. To call the regime a police state is to exaggerate."[7]

Yet, despite all the power at Bonaparte's disposal, it was never total, even later after he became emperor. Like any modern leader, he demanded two things when he was making a decision: the most accurate possible information, and the utmost vigor in implementing his subsequent decision. And therein lay the rub. Just because he asked for information did not mean that what he got was true; nor when he issued a decree could he be certain that it would be realized. While he made great strides in professionalizing the bureaucracy, he could not eliminate all its pettiness, incompetence, corruption, and intrigues. Even worse, Bonaparte unwittingly drew two men into his inner circle who would do all they could to check and eventually destroy his rule.

Charles Maurice de Talleyrand-Perigord sincerely believed that he always put France's interests foremost in his efforts.[8] He would later defend his betrayal by insisting that, although he "loved Napoleon," he loved his nation all the more. Thus he worked for Bonaparte only as long as the emperor's policies advanced what he believed were France's genuine interests.

Most of those who knew him would mock that notion and assert that he loved one thing above all, including France. As Madame Anne Louise Germaine de Stael bluntly put it: "You have never had any opinions, Monsieur, you have only interests, and the vilest of all. They have been the sole motive of your conduct under every regime. Money and more money, that's all you have ever looked for."[9] Indeed, Talleyrand would eventually have his hand deep in the pockets of the British, Russians, Spanish, Austrians, Bourbons, and most likely many other states and numerous businesses.

Talleyrand begged to differ with that very common view of him. In his mind his notorious reputation for using his public power to aggrandize his private fortune was simply a happy coincidence of national and private interests. And despite his corruption he always remained firmly his own man. Indeed, it was Talleyrand's overabundance of charm, intelligence, and ruthlessness, along with a lot of luck, that allowed him not only to survive but generally thrive throughout the ancien regime, revolution, empire, and restoration.

His public career had begun inappropriately—in the Catholic Church. As an incorrigible free-thinker and free-spirit, few people were less suited to the priesthood, but a club foot kept him from the military career he would have loved to pursue. He took his vows in 1779, most likely with his fingers crossed. He rose rapidly through the ranks, being named Agent-General of the Clergy in 1779, bishop of Autun in 1788, and representative to the Estates General in 1789. Then he not only joined but led the revolution's dechristianization of France; for his efforts he was elected president of the National Assembly in 1790. He resigned as bishop in 1791. As terror began to saturate the revolution he escaped France in September 1792. He stayed away until 1796, when he was convinced the Directory would welcome his talents with a ministry rather than the scaffold. Within days of meeting Barras, he was appointed foreign minister.

Joseph Fouche was Bonaparte's other bete noire.[10] Like Talleyrand, he was a master of intrigue and a political chameleon who grabbed hold of the core of national power and, through guile and luck, somehow survived the various regimes of the revolution, consulate, empire, and restoration. He conspired against everyone who sought or held power, especially those he supposedly served. Although he was purged several times, he always managed to crawl and claw his way back. He was utterly ruthless and supervised some of the revolution's worst massacres. Yet he was known to be a faithful husband and doting father.

Before the revolution he had been a teacher with the Oratory of Jesus brotherhood. When the Legislative Assembly closed all Catholic schools, he entered politics. He was elected to the Convention as a moderate "constitutional royalist." When the Terror seized the body politic he became one of its most voracious practitioners. At Lyon he commanded the murder of 1,905 people and the destruction of 1,600 homes. He coldly explained his crimes as vital examples of revolutionary justice: "Terror is now the order of the day here. . . . We are causing much impure blood to flow, but it is our duty to do so, it is for humanity's sake."[11] The Directory recognized his talents by naming him police minister. He joined Bonaparte's conspiracy and was reappointed police chief.

It was Fouche who alienated Bonaparte from the most politically gifted of his brothers, Lucien. The interior minister went to Napoleon with damning evidence that Fouche was abusing his power. The police minister countered with his own damning evidence of Lucien's pocketing of public funds for private purposes, most ostentatiously by bedecking a string of mistresses with gowns and jewels, and allowing the publication of a book which compared Bonaparte to Cromwell. Although angry at both, Bonaparte was hardest on his brother. Lucien resigned in disgust. The First Consul tried to assuage him by appointing him ambassador to Spain on November 7, 1800. With Lucien out of the way, Fouche then intrigued to force War Minister Lazare Carnot's early retirement.

Both Talleyrand and Fouche found Josephine an easy mark, and thus a source of pillow talk from and influence over Bonaparte. How did they get to her? Mostly with money—Josephine was an incorrigible shopaholic. The two men's influence over her grew with the amount of her monetary debt to each of them. At times Talleyrand was physically by her side: at receptions for the diplomatic corps, he would escort Josephine and formally present her to each envoy.[12]

Although Bonaparte was aware of many of the machinations of Talleyrand and Fouche, he never got the crucial evidence of their eventual conspiracy to overthrow him. Regardless, why would he keep them in power through so much of his tenure? He did so for the same reason a politician pays off an organized crime gang: he gains a sort of protection, and fears the consequences if he does not. He was especially nervous of Fouche, who had extensive files hidden away on each of the Bonaparte clan's corrupt financial and sexual relations, knew literally and figuratively where all the bodies were buried, and commanded a network of thugs and assassins.

As First Consul, Bonaparte tried to rid himself of one of the two, but was politically stung so badly that he would tolerate them both in his inner circle until years after he became emperor. On September 14, 1802, he fired Fouche, abolished the Police Ministry, and gave its duties to the Interior Ministry. Rather than jail Fouche, Bonaparte hoped to coopt him with a 1.2 million franc retirement package and seats in the State Council and Senate. But Fouche was not content to be an idle spectator in the consulate's chambers. He passed word to his police agents to neglect their duties and let the criminals and conspirators know it. Crime soared, rumors of royalist plots swirled, and dissent simmered in ever more provinces.

Bonaparte bowed to that power. He reluctantly reinstated both the Police Ministry and Fouche as its head on July 10, 1804. Thereafter he tried to check Fouche's power by naming the incorruptible, loyal, and skilled Louis Nicolas Dubois as the police prefect for Paris; but that had little effect.

Yet despite the nearly incessant machinations of Talleyrand and Fouche, the regime's achilles heel was Bonaparte himself. The entire system revolved around his brilliant mind and implacable will. While he sincerely sought peace most of the time, he also ruthlessly waged war, and at times did not hesitate to lead from the front.

People, especially those who were ambitious and well-placed, naturally speculated about what should happen if Bonaparte were killed either by soldiers or assassins, or decisively defeated in battle. After Bonaparte left for his 1800 Italian campaign, Moreau, La Fayette, and Bernadotte formed the first known group which prepared to fill that void. Talleyrand, Fouche, and Murat would make similar preparations during his 1808 Spanish campaign. Talleyrand would actually pull the political rug from beneath him in 1814, and Fouche would do the same in 1815.

So that was the regime by which Napoleon Bonaparte ruled France and his empire for nearly fifteen years. While it took months to get his government up and running, and years to fine-tune it, Napoleon Bonaparte was immersed in diplomacy from the very beginning of his rule.

The Search for Peace

The First Consul reasoned that the search for peace should begin within France itself. Two major rebel groups, the Vendeans in the lower Loire Valley and the Chouans in Brittany, fought for the restoration of the monarchy. Rather than lead an army against them, Bonaparte sought instead to get them to give up their arms by addressing their grievances. On November 13 he revoked the law of hostages by which the state imprisoned the families and friends of armed rebels. On November 24 he announced that he would suspend operations and called for peace talks. The Vendean rebels came in from the cold. A truce was signed on December 2 between General Gabriel, Count Hedouville, and a Vendean delegation at the chateau of Angers. The Vendean leaders then journeyed to Paris, where Bonaparte met them on December 26.

The Vendeans hoped to talk Bonaparte into working with them for a Bourbon restoration, inspired by the notion that he would play a role for France similar to that of General George Monk who, after taking power in England when Oliver Cromwell died, restored the monarchy to power. The First Consul swiftly disillusioned them of that dream.

Instead Bonaparte embraced them with an amnesty, a promise to protect the Catholic Church, and an appeal to their patriotism: "The Bourbons no longer have a chance. You have done everything you could have for them. You are good men. Ally yourselves with the side of glory; yes, come under my banner, my government will be that of youth and spirit."[13] They then returned to the Vendee, where they succeeded in convincing a handful of other rebel leaders to accept the peace. Meanwhile Bonaparte reinforced those efforts by issuing, on December 28, 1800, a proclamation calling for reconciliation and offering amnesty.[14]

But the leading Vendean rebel, George Cadoudal, with his forces freshly supplied by British money, arms, munitions, and provisions, broke the truce with renewed attacks. The First Consul ordered Hedouville to crush the rebels as ruthlessly "as if you were in the middle of Germany."[15] When incompetence, moral qualms, or some combination kept Hedouville from doing so, Bonaparte replaced him on January 14, 1800, with General Guillaume Brune. He empowered Brune to "welcome anyone who submits but . . . do not spare the villages which resist" and summarily execute anyone caught with arms. To another general he boasted that "we have carried terror among the Chouans. . . . Hereafter do not lend your ear to any plea for talks. . . . To negotiate for any length of time is a sign of weakness."[16]

Brune launched a full-scale offensive that swiftly broke the backbone of both rebel groups. George Cadoudal and other Vendean and Chouan leaders asked for terms. Negotiations opened and continued until February 14, when an armistice was signed. Bonaparte had his field commanders "make it known to the chiefs . . . that my intention is to do them no harm but instead to win them confidence in the government by being generous to them." To that end he once again brought the rebel leaders to Paris and tried to win them over with meetings on March 5 and 29.[17]

Whether or not the rebels were sincere, they all tried to appear contrite—except Cadoudal, who did not disguise his defiance and scorn as he scribbled his signature on an oath of allegiance. Bonaparte understood that and privately condemned Cadoudal as "the veritable chief of the English party which is the most dangerous of all our enemies." Yet he had no choice but to free him along with the rest. Cadoudal promptly fled to Britain, where he was soon plotting to murder the man who had granted him clemency.[18]

As his peace offensive with the rebels unfolded, Bonaparte launched a similar effort with the governments which continued to war against France. On Christmas Day 1799 he offered the gift of peace to George III, Paul I, Francois

II, and even the would-be Louis XVIII. His letters were typically eloquent and powerful appeals at once to reason, feeling, vanity, and morality. To Francis II he wrote: "Alien to all sentiment of vain glory, the first of my vows is to stop the flow of blood. . . . The known character of Your Majesty leaves me without any doubt that . . . I can glimpse the possibility of reconciling the interests of our two nations." George III received these, among other words: "Must the war which has ravaged all parts of the world last forever? Is there no way to resolve our differences?. . . Peace is the first of our needs and the first of our glories. These sentiments cannot be alien to Your Majesty . . . [and] can only see in this overture my sincere desire to contribute to a general peace."[19]

None of the sitting monarchs stooped to reply. British Foreign Secretary William Wyndam, Baron Grenville, wrote on the king's behalf that peace would be possible only if the Bourbons were restored to power. Austrian Foreign Minister Johann von Thugut indirectly endorsed that British position when he rejected any notion of a peace separate from Vienna's allies. Furthermore, with Austria's armies having regained northern Italy and the Rhineland after Bonaparte had departed on his Egyptian odyssey, Vienna was dead set to retain those conquests. For now there was no message from the Russian court. But rather than give up, Bonaparte ordered Talleyrand to keep trying.[20]

Bonaparte did receive a formal request from former king Louis, penned on February 20, 1800, that he be restored to power. To disillusion Louis from that dream, he did not reply for seven months, and then, on September 7, issued a tough rebuke: "You must not hope for your return to France; to do so you would have to walk over a hundred thousand corpses. Sacrifice your interest to the peace and happiness of France. History will uphold you." He then offered an inducement: "I am not insensitive to the sufferings of your family. I would contribute with pleasure to the sweetness and tranquility of your retirement" if Louis would renounce all claims to the throne.[21]

The 1800 Campaign

With his enemies so adamant for war, Bonaparte felt he had no choice but to accommodate them. He devoted the early months of 1800 to preparations for a campaign intended to retake all of Austria's conquests since 1798 and force Francis II to beg for peace. Two outstanding individuals, Lazare Carnot as war minister and Louis Alexandre Berthier as chief of staff, assisted his planning.

The strategy involved the coordinated launching of two land offensives against Austria and four naval expeditions to distract and tie down British forces. On land, Moreau would lead his army across the Rhine and Bonaparte himself an army over the Alps toward the Austrians in northwestern Italy. At sea, Admiral Eustache Bruix would carry troops and supplies for General Kleber in Egypt; Admiral Jean Lacrosse would sail first to Madeira and then on to the West Indies to capture as many British merchant ships as possible; a fleet of French and Spanish warships would sail from Brest, first to relieve General Vaubois at Malta and then to capture Port Mahon, Minorca; and Christoforo Salicetti would invade Sardinia.[22]

With the planning done, Bonaparte left Paris on May 6 for Geneva, where the 40,000-man Army of the Reserve awaited him; his carriage halted before his headquarters three days later. Both to skirt the constitutional ban on the First Consul leading armies and to fool the Austrians, Berthier was in official command; but Bonaparte fully intended to lead that army against the Austrians. On May 1 he and his army began the long march toward Italy. The crossing of the Alps was dramatic but unopposed. On the other side the French advance was briefly checked by the Austrians at Aosta and Fort Bard before it reached the plains of the Po River Valley.[23]

Bonaparte had hoped to pulverize General Michael Melas' 50,000 Austrians against Massena's 30,000 troops besieged in Genoa, like a hammer against an anvil. But Massena was hemmed in by Austrian forces on land and British forces at sea. Bonaparte was well aware of how tenuous Massena's position was and authorized him to fall back on Savona if the Austrians tried to trap him in Genoa. As for provisions, it would be safer and easier to send bags of coins rather than shiploads of grain. In early March the First Consul sent Massena 1,500,000 francs to distribute directly to the troops so that they could buy what they needed from the locals. Given Massena's well-deserved reputation for corruption, venality, and brutality, Bonaparte may have wondered just how much the general would siphon off into his own very deep pockets.[24]

Massena's capitulation on June 4 completely upset the First Consul's strategy. Melas was now free to turn on Bonaparte and await him at Alessandria. Then Bonaparte made a nearly disastrous mistake. Believing that Melas would be too timid to attack, he spread his army's divisions across a broad front. Melas hurled his army against Bonaparte's center at Marengo on June 14, and by mid-afternoon appeared on the verge of a crushing victory. At that decisive moment Bonaparte's other divisions, which he had sent couriers galloping to recall, reached the field and turned the tide of battle.

In fact the French routed the Austrians so thoroughly that Melas was willing to do anything to prevent what he feared would be his army's annihilation, so on June 15 he signed terms dictated by Bonaparte. Under the Convention of Alessandria, he would cede Lombardy, Genoa, and Ancona to France, and withdraw all Austrian troops east of the Mincio and north of the Po Rivers.[25] Bonaparte was typically generous in victory; he offered Melas a beautifully designed Mameluke saber that he had taken during his Egyptian campaign.

Bonaparte followed up that armistice with his latest conciliatory letter to Francis II. He humbly asked that they forge a lasting peace based on the Campo Formio treaty, pointed out that he had allowed Melas a face-saving capitulation when he could have destroyed his army, and blamed Britain for instigating the war. He appealed just as powerfully to Francis' heart: "War has taken place. Thousands of French and Austrians live no more. Thousands of desolated families mourn the loss of their fathers, husbands, and sons! The evil that caused all this . . . so afflicts my heart . . . that I am directly writing Your Majesty to come up with the means of ending the horrors on the continent. . . . Let us bring peace and tranquility to the present generation. If future generations are crazy enough to fight each other, well, they will soon learn after several years of war to become wise and live in peace." He put the onus for war or peace squarely on the Austrian monarch's shoulders: "If Your Majesty wants peace, it is done." However, if Francis chose to continue to wage war he would be solely responsible "in the eyes of the world."[26]

Bonaparte's 1800 campaign may have appeared dazzling and was certainly portrayed as such, but actually it was a pale imitation of his brilliant 1796 campaign. His strategic and tactical blunders leading up to Marengo almost lost him that decisive battle. Then, rather than follow up that victory by a relentless pursuit that might have annihilated the Austrians, he settled for an armistice which allowed Melas to withdraw his army intact beyond the Mincio River.

A key problem was that Bonaparte was distracted. He kept looking over his shoulder at events in faraway Paris. This was not due to idle paranoia. A rumor that he had been killed and the army routed inspired a number of factions to jostle for power. The ink was no sooner dry on the armistice than he left General Brune in command and raced back to Paris to reassert power. On the way he tarried briefly in Milan, where he presented the Cisalpine Republic with a constitution—and a bill for two million francs to pay for its latest liberation from Austria.[27]

Bonaparte's Lombardy campaign hardly ended the war. Victory and peace now depended on how well Moreau, with his 80,000 troops, did in Germany. The First Consul had unleashed Moreau on April 22 with these words: "The season is beautiful, your troops are numerous and well-led. You have our complete confidence. Unfurl your banners and take many prisoners. Do not stop advancing until you have retaken all that we have lost."[28]

Moreau lived up to that command. After crossing the Rhine on April 25, he sidestepped General Paul Kray's 70,000 troops in Bavaria and then trounced him in a series of small battles before marching triumphantly into Munich. Having driven the Austrians from nearly all of Bavaria, Moreau then paused to offer Kray terms. After two weeks of haggling, the commanders on July 15 signed the Truce of Pasdorf, which ceded most of Bavaria to French occupation while the Austrians retained the fortresses of Ulm, Philipsburg, and Ingolstadt.

At that point Francis had little choice but to accept the First Consul's offer of peace negotiations. However, he did so only with the deepest reluctance. He genuinely believed that French aggression was the war's sole reason and that Austria was bound by interests and honor to resist. He explained his outlook in a July 5 letter: "Without equilibrium in Europe, it is necessary for several states to unite against one. What can one expect when [France] adds more to its already unheard of immense conquests and seizes even more influence on most other states? To propose peace in such circumstances provides nothing useful for humanity or even a sincere desire for peace."[29]

In nurturing such a belief Francis deluded himself, including to justify what in reality had been the violation of the Treaty of Campo Formio by Austria, not France. Francis' regrets were especially troubling because on June 23 his government had signed a treaty with Britain whereby London was to give Vienna monthly installments of what could have become a 666,666 pound sterling subsidy to underwrite its war against France. Those payments ceased after London learned of the truce.

Count St. Julien, Austria's peace envoy, faced an impossible mission. His instructions allowed him to negotiate a peace based on the Campo Formio Treaty, but forbade him from doing so without Whitehall's approval. He accomplished half of that. Bonaparte and Talleyrand took turns wearing him down in a series of intense negotiating sessions. Using classic bad cop/good cop tactics, Bonaparte was as brusque as Talleyrand was silken in battering St. Julien with the same accusations, inducements, and demands.

The hapless envoy finally yielded on July 28 by signing a treaty which essentially reinstituted Campo Formio. The Austrians thereby actually got off rather lightly, considering that they had resumed and then lost the war. Francis was ready to ratify that treaty when at the last moment he gave in to Chancellor Thugut's arguments that for Austria to violate its promise to Britain of no separate peace would forever dishonor the nation. That rationale was boosted by Prime Minister Pitt's desperate, last-minute offer of another two million pounds sterling for Austria to spurn peace and keep fighting. So Francis set aside the treaty, even though he knew that if France again triumphed during the war's next round the consequences for Austria would be far harsher.[30]

Pitt faced his own moral quandaries. The latest expedition to Brittany to aid French rebels was defeated by poor planning, inadequate supplies, timid leadership, and storms. Indeed, the troops crammed aboard the transports never even set foot on French soil. Learning that the expedition was merely hovering offshore, with its commander hesitant to land on unknown beaches, Pitt ordered it to sail on to the Mediterranean and join General Ralph Abercromby's expedition bound to invade Egypt. Pitt was painfully aware that the failure to launch a successful land campaign against France made it appear that his government was merely the dispenser of blood money, but for now there was nothing he could do about that.

Bonaparte gave Pitt a way out of that morass in July when he sent an envoy to London with an offer for an armistice followed by peace talks. Pitt mulled the offer. Not just pride kept him from accepting it. There were genuine concerns that Bonaparte would use the armistice to reinforce his beleaguered garrisons in Malta and Egypt. So he sent word that he was willing to open talks while the war continued.

That was a bold reply, seeing that once again Britain appeared to be on the verge of fighting alone. The coalition that Pitt had so laboriously tried to stitch together was unraveling. From Whitehall's view, the allies who were so eager to palm British subsidies tended to cut and run when things got tough. After suffering its latest round of defeats, Austria was once again being lured to the peace table. And Russia seemed ever more eager to do something even more damaging to British interests.

Bonaparte's envoys and spies in St. Petersburg had passed him accurate assessments of Tsar Paul's character and his worsening rift with his allies. The First Consul did what he could not just to widen that rift but to entice the mercurial and hyper-sensitive tsar into switching sides. On July 4, 1800, he had Talleyrand write Paul a letter reporting that the First Consul praised his leadership and the fighting rigor of his troops, and offered to repatriate 7,000 Russian prisoners of war. Along with that letter his envoy was to present Paul the ceremonial sword of the Knights of St. John that he had captured at Malta. A half year later, on December 21, Bonaparte wrote directly to Paul and asked him to consider an alliance devoted to peace.[31]

Bonaparte knew his man. Even more than most royals, Paul had an excessive weakness for flattery and generosity. He sent Count Kolichev and General Joram Sprengporten to negotiate with Talleyrand and General Henri Clarke in September. The alliance Paul was willing to join against Britain, however, would be economic rather than military. The League of Armed Neutrality would economically unite the Baltic states against Britain.

Bonaparte was certainly intrigued, and would eventually adopt that idea with his Continental System. But for now he needed Russian help to launch a decisive blow against Britain and end the war once and for all. In return he promised Paul Malta and whatever lands he could rip from the Ottoman Empire.[32]

That was hardly a generous offer. Bonaparte had just received word that the French garrison on Malta had surrendered on September 5. While that was certainly a blow to France's strategic and thus diplomatic position, Bonaparte further widened the rift between Russia and Britain by encouraging Paul to press his claim to what he believed was rightfully his. He knew well that Britain had bought Paul's allegiance with 1.9 million pounds sterling and a promise that, as grand master of the Knights of St. John, he could keep Malta if he helped take it. A joint Anglo-Russian expedition had besieged Malta in 1799, but the island appeared impregnable. Wearying of the expedition's cost and seeming futility, Paul ordered the Russian armada to withdraw. The British carried on until they finally captured Malta. As expected, Whitehall would soon rebuff Paul's demand that Malta be transferred to his rule.

The enraged tsar ordered the withdrawal of Alexander Suvorov's army from Austria and 25,000 troops billeted in the Channel Islands of Jersey and Guernsey, although Russian troops still garrisoned the Ionian Islands. He also approved the French reoccupation of southern Italy with garrisons at Naples, Tarento, Otranto, and Brindisi, and pledged to send aid to the beleaguered French in Egypt. Like Bonaparte, Paul could dream big. He envisioned Russia someday displacing Britain in south Asia. As a first step in that journey, he sent 22,000 Cossacks into Central Asia to solidify Russian influence there. He tried to pique Bonaparte's interest in a joint expedition against British India. By mid-autumn Paul had completely withdrawn Russia from the coalition. He would soon commit an even more harmful set of acts against Britain.[33]

As the Russians were exiting the war, the Austrians seemed ever more likely to rejoin it. The Pasdorf truce was to expire on September 20. Although Francis had not ratified the treaty that St. Julian had signed, his intentions remained unclear to Bonaparte. The word was that he was still torn over what to do. His younger brother and Austria's best general, Archduke Charles, favored peace and prevailed on Francis to allow him to sit with Chancellor Thugut whenever he was summoned for a royal council.

Bonaparte took advantage of those divisions in the Austrian camp by offering to extend the truce so that Vienna had more time to convince London that peace was in everyone's interests. Charles eagerly embraced the idea and talked Francis into accepting it. Thugut angrily threatened to resign. Francis kept him in office for the present, but diluted his power by bringing the more conciliatory Philip Cobenzl and Franz Colloredo into his inner circle, and sent Cobenzl's younger brother Ludwig to Luneville in Alsace to meet with Joseph Bonaparte. Talks opened on October 24. Joseph essentially reoffered the same treaty that had been signed in Paris. Cobenzl demanded concessions in Italy and Germany that Bonaparte was unwilling to make. With no apparent way around the impasse, Cobenzl left for Vienna on November 4. Bonaparte sent a courier to Vienna with a message extending the truce to November 22. But with Vienna's rejection of the peace treaty, he ordered Moreau, Macdonald, and Brune to prepare their armies in Germany, Switzerland, and Italy, respectively, to renew the war.[34]

Meanwhile Bonaparte also sought peace with virtually all those who had fled France during the revolution. On October 20, 1800, he offered an amnesty to those who would sign a loyalty oath to the French constitution. That enticed over 100,000 émigrés eventually to return to France. Most of them would live up to their pledge; a few, however, would conspire for Bonaparte's demise and the return of the Bourbons to power.

The truce's deadline expired. On November 27 Archduke John, another of Francis' younger brothers, led 100,000 Austrian troops against Moreau. He defeated Moreau at Ampfing on December 1; but then, overconfident, he divided his forces and, on December 3, was crushed by Moreau at Hohenlinden. Austria lost 10,000 troops and 50 guns compared to 2,500 for the French. Francis replaced John with Charles, but the latter could do little more than try to keep a few steps ahead of Moreau's relentless pursuit. The French trounced the Austrians in a series of skirmishes that by Christmas Day brought them only thirty miles from Vienna. Charles signed at Steyr a forty-day armistice which yielded to France the fortresses of Ulm, Philipsburg, and Ingolstadt.

The French were equally victorious on the Italian front. Brune's 66,000 troops eventually routed General Heinrich Bellegarde's 40,000 at the battle of the Mincio River, which raged on December 25 and 26. The armistice on that front was signed on January 15, 1801. In central Italy General Joachim Murat forced Ferdinand IV, the King of Naples, to sign on February 6, 1801, an armistice that would last for thirty days, during which peace talks would take place.

Bonaparte nearly did not live to see all the stunning victories of his generals and the subsequent diplomatic revolutions. The first royalist attempt to murder him came on Christmas Eve 1800 when he was in a cavalcade of coaches clattering through the narrow, crowded streets from the Tuileries to the opera. An "infernal machine"—a horse-drawn cart packed with gunpowder and a burning fuse—partly blocked his coach's path. The driver, sensing danger, whipped the horses into a canter around the wagon. The bomb exploded seconds later, killing four bystanders—including the young girl whom the assassin had paid to hold the horse while he scurried to safety—and wounding sixty others.

Fouche's investigation found that royalists were behind the plot. That discovery complicated Bonaparte's diplomacy. Naively he still hoped to convince the royalists to renounce their own ambitions to return to power and instead endorse his rule. But he had to make an example of someone. There was plenty of evidence that the Jacobins were plotting their own murderous comeback. He ordered a purge in which over 700 received prison terms and 129 were exiled.[35]

All that was for public consumption. A deeper and secret investigation confirmed Fouche's initial findings. In mid-April Bonaparte had Talleyrand issue a letter to Whitehall condemning the British government for employing "monsters who dishonor human nature" and calling for it to "act in these circumstances according to the sentiments of conscience, the laws of religion, and political principles" by "arresting and delivering to justice the perpetrators of that crime."[36] Whitehall did not respond. The British could only watch in helpless despair as Bonaparte survived and Austria was once again being knocked out of the war.

But it was Whitehall's inept policy that provoked the shutting of the Baltic to British war and merchant ships and thus gave Bonaparte another opening.

The trouble had started the previous summer when the British began retaliating against neutral Denmark for renting its flag to merchant ships registered in France or its allies to evade the British blockade. The British boarded and seized ever more ships and crews flying the Danish flag, and in July even captured a convoy and its escort, a Danish frigate. Copenhagen turned to Russia for help. Paul called on Prussia, Denmark, and Sweden to join Russia in closing its ports to British trade, and to make the boycott more effective even encouraged them to take Hanover, Hamburg, and Lubeck, respectively. Russia, Sweden, and Denmark signed on December 16, 1800, a treaty forming the League of Armed Neutrality; Prussia joined two days later. The Prussians then marched into Hanover and the Danes into Hamburg. The British replied by declaring war on the League of Armed Neutrality. Paul's final blow to the now-dead coalition came on January 22, 1801, when he sent word to Louis XVIII that he and his entourage were no longer welcome and thus would have to find someone else, ideally Britain, to harbor them. The exiles actually found their latest refuge in Warsaw under Prussian protection.

Amidst all these stunning diplomatic developments, Bonaparte sent Joseph back to Luneville to meet again with Cobenzl. This time he would be far less magnanimous in victory. The Austrians had broken the Campo Formio treaty, and they would pay for that perfidious violation. As always, the key diplomatic question was, how much?[37]

Under the Treaty of Luneville, signed between Joseph Bonaparte and Ludwig Cobenzl on February 9, 1801, Austria's Francis II not only openly recognized France's conquests west of the Rhine but also its "sister" Batavian, Helvetian, Ligurian, and Cisalpine Republics. He also acceded to his younger brother Ferdinand III being deprived of the duchy of Tuscany. Austria in turn would be allowed to retain Venetia, Friuli, Istria, Dalmatia, and Cataro. The Adige River would be the frontier between Italy and Austria. As for all those rulers who had lost their realms west of the Rhine and elsewhere, Francis was obligated to somehow find them new thrones from within the Holy Roman Empire or the Austrian kingdom; he would eventually compensate his brother with the ecclesiastical city-states of Passau, Berchtesgaden, and Salzburg.

Peace and French hegemony would extend over central and southern Italy as well, at the expense of the Papal States and the Kingdom of Naples. Joachim Murat commanded the army which marched against Naples. On February 6 French and Neapolitan envoys signed the armistice of Foligno. By its terms not only did the fighting stop but Ferdinand IV agreed to close all his ports to British ships in return for French recognition of his continued rule. As negotiations began for a peace treaty, Bonaparte instructed Murat to keep pressure on the Neapolitans and "not prolong the armistice. Peace must be concluded, and you must march General Soult immediately to occupy" those ports "which are essential to supplying our army in Egypt." Knowing Murat's weakness for flattery and bribes, he warned him not to "receive a single distinction or present whatever, neither from the king of Naples nor [prime minister] Acton. That is the only government which, because of its horrible conduct, deserves the opprobrium of all Europe. It is said that Cardinal Ruffo wants to offer you a horse; you must refuse; that man plays a despicable game."[38]

Despite his contempt for the Neapolitan king and court, Bonaparte remained polite in his letters to Ferdinand IV. As he explained to Murat, his primary goal with Ferdinand was to convert him into an ally. Under the Treaty of Florence signed on March 28, Ferdinand IV would withdraw his troops from Rome, cede to France his claims to Tuscany, Elba, Lucca, and Piombino, close all ports to British shipping, join the League of Armed Neutrality, and underwrite the presence of 10,000 French troops split among Pescara, Brindisi, and Taranto. Those troops supposedly would be in those ports temporarily before being shipped to reinforce Egypt. But if that was not possible, Ferdinand would be obligated to provide them hospitality until a general peace was negotiated.

Bonaparte kept trying to entice Tsar Paul into an alliance. As a stepping stone to that end he concluded with Ambassador Sprengporten on March 9 a convention by which 7,000 Russian prisoners would be repatriated. He followed that up two days later with a direct appeal to Paul.[39] However, the word that he finally received from St. Petersburg could not have been worse: Paul had been strangled in a coup on March 24, 1801. This brought his son, Alexander, to the throne. Paul's sadism, paranoia, and tyranny had certainly given the conspirators ample cause for rage and terror, if not outright murder. But Alexander had not just been a passive victim of his bullying, for his father had been in the process of replacing him with a German prince as the successor to the Russian crown.

With the advice of his ministers, the new tsar reversed virtually all his father's foreign policies. He recalled that Cossack army riding toward India, shrugged off the title of being Grand Master of the Knights of St. John, denounced the claim to Malta, sent word to the other members of the League of Armed Neutrality that he was withdrawing Russia, and recalled the French royal family to Mittau. That resolved the most troubling conflicts with Britain. On June 5 St. Petersburg and London restored diplomatic relations.

Nonetheless Bonaparte did what he could to impede all that. He sent General Gerard Christophe Duroc to St. Petersburg to deliver to Alexander a letter from Bonaparte offering his condolences and an alliance. Although Alexander declined, he did, on October 8 and 10, sign treaties by which St. Petersburg recognized France's republic, "natural frontiers," protectorates, and "sister republics." It also granted independence to the Ionian Republic, which a Russian armada had seized from France, although for now Russian troops would linger there. And in return for all that, Russia got nothing more than peace. The First Consul redoubled his efforts to entice the tsar into an alliance.[40]

That left Britain as France's sole enemy. If directly attacking Britain was all but impossible, how could France's most elusive and persistent enemy be indirectly damaged? Bonaparte increasingly eyed Portugal as a possible bargaining chip. He considered that kingdom, with its centuries-old commercial and strategic ties to London, to be a British quasi-colony. Indeed, Lisbon had acted as an enemy by harassing French merchants and residents and contributing to the blockade of Alexandria. Malta's capitulation on September 5, 1800, made it imperative that France and Spain grab Portugal as compensation. Bonaparte sent word to Charles IV to invade and conquer Portugal before October 15. That, of course, was easier said than done, especially for the notoriously timid, lethargic, and venal Spanish court.[41]

The First Consul needed a special envoy who could bolster the alliance with Spain so as to take Portugal. He did not look far for his choice. After Lucien lost his interior ministry portfolio, Bonaparte tried at once to both rehabilitate him and advance French interests by appointing him ambassador to Madrid on November 7, and arming him with plenipotentiary powers.[42]

Lucien arrived in Madrid on December 6, 1800, and quickly got to work. He soon forged close ties with Charles IV and his chief minister Manuel de Godoy. Under a treaty signed between Godoy and Lucien on January 6, 1801, France and Spain agreed to conquer and partition Portugal if it did not agree to break its alliance with Britain and join them. Bonaparte ratified that treaty on January 29 and sent General Gouvion St. Cyr to act as the French commander in the alliance.[43]

Lisbon subsequently refused the ultimatum. Charles IV dutifully declared war on Portugal on February 27, 1801, but a Franco-Spanish army did not invade until May 19. After the allies captured the frontier fortress of Elvas,

Lisbon asked for terms. Lucien and Godoy revealed them to Portugal's envoy Pinto de Souza at Badajoz. Souza had little choice but to submit.

Under the Treaty of Badajoz, signed on June 6, 1801, Portugal had to break its alliance with and close its ports to Britain, ally with and pay a 15 million livres indemnity to France and Spain, and hand over the city of Olivenza to Spain and a portion of Guyana to France. Those terms were certainly onerous enough, but they were not all that Bonaparte had instructed Lucien to win. He ordered Lucien to renegotiate the treaty, and explained just why he had rejected the first draft: "Portugal interests us only so far as it provides us a lever for making a general peace." France would take three provinces, or a quarter of Portugal, as bargaining chips. The French knew that the British would not resist, because if they did the French would take Lisbon. Under the second version of the treaty, signed on September 29, the indemnity rose to 25 million livres, and France took all of Guyana. That same month Lucien also signed a secret treaty with Godoy whereby Spain would allow a French army passage across its soil to attack Portugal if Lisbon violated the Treaty of Badajoz.[44]

France, meanwhile, lost its North African toehold. General Abercromby's expedition invaded Egypt in March 1801, battered the French in three battles, besieged Alexandria, and marched up the Nile. Cairo capitulated on June 27 and Alexandria on September 2. The British repatriated the 8,000 remaining French soldiers and civilians, and took their place as Egypt's rulers.

That loss weakened Bonaparte's diplomatic strategy. The previous October he had sent General Louis Otto to London to propose a prisoner exchange and dangle Spain's Trinidad and Holland's Ceylon as possible trades for peace. When the British hinted their interest, he reinforced Otto with Marquis Casimir Montrond in January 1801. But Pitt remained stubbornly wed to his demand that France withdraw to its 1789 borders. That human obstacle disappeared on February 3 when Pitt and his government resigned after George III rejected a bill that would have allowed Irish Catholics full political rights if they swore an allegiance to the crown.[45]

The king asked Henry Addington to form a new government on February 5. Ironically, the madness of King George, after a dozen years' dormancy, returned in full fury on February 18. Once again the Prince of Wales, the future George IV, took over as regent.

Although the Addington government was ready to conclude peace with France, it would take another half year of tough negotiations before a treaty was hammered out. The official word that Whitehall was interested came on March 19 in a meeting between Robert Jenkinson, Baron Hawkesbury (later Lord

Liverpool), and Otto. Although each side eagerly embarked on the negotiations at London, neither side was willing to make the first concession that might break the stalemate. That came only after an ultimatum by Bonaparte on September 29 that a deal must be cut by October 2 or France would withdraw from the talks.[46]

Under the preliminary treaty signed in London on October 1, 1801, France and Britain agreed to end all fighting on land or sea in Europe immediately, in the Americas and Africa within three months, and in Asia within a half year. All colonies taken by Britain would be restored except Spain's Trinidad and Holland's Ceylon. The British would evacuate Malta and return it to the Knights of St. John. Egypt would be evacuated and restored to the Ottoman Empire. The French would evacuate the Kingdom of Naples and the Papal States. All prisoners would be returned.

It then took another five months to convert that bilateral treaty into a multilateral treaty which would be accepted by France's allies Spain and the Batavian Republic. For that, the negotiating teams and location changed, with Joseph Bonaparte and Edward Cornwallis replacing Otto and Hawkesbury, while the action shifted from London to Amiens in northern France. They were joined by a Dutch envoy, Jean Roger Schimmelpenninck, and a Spanish envoy, Don Joseph Nicolas d'Azara. Although Schimmelpenninck could be relied upon to go along with the French position, not so Azara, who raised a range of issues to ensure that Spanish interests were protected. Bonaparte protested repeatedly at his ally's objections, but to no avail. Yet the Treaty of Amiens, signed on March 25, 1802, did not differ in substance from the preliminary treaty, but simply included details for its implementation.

Virtually everyone on both sides of the Channel rejoiced at news of the Amiens treaty. France and Britain had been at war for nine years, and most people were exhausted emotionally and economically. Yet that peace, which seemed so promising, would prove to be fleeting.

The Concordat

The promise to evacuate Rome helped Bonaparte resolve yet another war, this one over religion. The French Revolution had waged total war against the Catholic Church: nationalized or destroyed its property; jailed, exiled, or outright murdered its priests; invaded the Papal States; and even imprisoned the pope. For practical rather than sentimental reasons, Bonaparte was determined to end that persecution which helped keep alive the royalist cause. But he sought a Catholic Church which championed rather than defied the state and remained firmly under the state's thumb.[47]

As so often happens in diplomacy, the removal from power of one leader committed to a deal-killing position can open the way for a breakthrough with a more flexible successor. Pius VI had died on August 29, 1799, after suffering eighteen months as a French prisoner. High on Bonaparte's agenda after taking power two and a half months later on November 10 was reconciliation with Rome. But even if Bonaparte was willing to compromise, a new pope might simply defend his predecessor's position that a concordat was possible only if the French government restored the Church to the power, property, and prestige it had enjoyed before 1789. Of course, the best way to finesse that probability was to determine just who would next sit on the papal throne.

Just how could Bonaparte pull off that coup? After all, the First Consul was hardly the only ruler who would do virtually anything to engineer the election of a pope favorable to his realm's interests.

Of all the Catholic monarchs, Francis II was the most keenly determined to be the pope-maker. And he had the means to do so. Under the Campo Formio Treaty, Vienna was allowed to annex the Venetian Republic. Francis cleverly got the cardinals to hold their conclave at the Benedictine monastery on the Venetian Island of San Giorgio. Of the thirty-five cardinals who gathered, only five were not Italians, and none of them were French. Finally, his donation of 24,000 ducats to underwrite the conclave left few doubts as to the political orientation of whomever was selected. Francis made it clear that Ravenna's Archbishop Alessandro Mattei was Vienna's favorite candidate. Mattei despised everything about the French Revolution. He also could never forgive Bonaparte for forcing him to sign the Treaty of Tolentino, by which Rome had ceded the Papal Legations, which France then merged into the Cispadane Republic.[48]

Yet, despite all those Austrian machinations, most cardinals remained independent and wanted to stay that way. When the conclave convened on November 30, 1799, the Austrians were in the process of reestablishing their control over northern Italy, which they had retaken from France while Bonaparte was on his Egyptian adventure. During the first vote, a majority sent a clear signal to Vienna when Bishop Bellisomi of Cesena got eighteen votes, only nine supported Mattei, and the rest backed other candidates. The conclave remained stalemated for months, as no one was able to muster the two-thirds vote necessary to win.

Bonaparte meanwhile made three conciliatory gestures. On November 29 he annulled the deportation of priests who refused to pledge loyalty to the constitution; on December 28 he authorized the opening of churches on Sundays; and he ordered that Pope Pius VI, whose body was still at Valence, be given an elaborate state funeral. He then sent word that he was willing to do much more if Rome were willing to compromise with him on their differences.

Word of those steps electrified the cardinals in Venice. But they needed a pope to respond. They finally broke the deadlock on March 13, 1800, when they elected Cardinal Barnabe Chiaramonte, the Bishop of Imola, as Pope Pius VII. Although officially Chiaramonte was Spain's candidate, the French had talked their ally into championing that choice. Of all the candidates, none had the potential to be more amenable to French interests. It was Chiaramonte who on Christmas Day 1797 had preached a sermon with two political assertions, one long established and the other revolutionary. First, he presented the familiar Church argument that all governments are divinely sanctioned and thus must be obeyed by the people under their rule. Then, astonishingly, he asserted that Catholicism and republicanism could be compatible. After getting a copy of the sermon, French officials mass-produced and distributed it.

Having lost the battle for the new pope, the Austrians tried to talk Pius into accepting Venetian Cardinal Flangini, one of their supporters, as his secretary of state, and to come to Vienna for his first state visit. Pius politely declined both invitations. Instead he hurried to Rome to take the papal throne.

Within a month Bonaparte was leading an army over the Alps and onto the Lombardy plains. As always, while he appeared to be single-mindedly focused on waging war, he was juggling a half dozen or so other diplomatic issues. Among those was a possible detente with Rome. He paused briefly in Milan to proclaim "my firm intention that the Christian, Catholic, and Roman religion shall be preserved in its entirety, that it shall be publicly performed. . . . No society can exist without morality; there is no good morality without religion. It is religion alone that gives to the State a firm and durable support. . . . As soon as I am able to confer with the new Pope, I hope to have the happiness of removing every obstacle which will hinder complete reconciliation between France and the head of the Church."[49]

He paused again at Milan on June 25, eleven days after crushing the Austrians at Marengo and forcing Melas to sign an armistice whereby he retired the remnants of his shattered forces east of the Mincio. Following a Te Deum mass at the cathedral, he met with Cardinal Martiniana for a long talk in which he shared his sincere desire for reconciliation between Paris and Rome, offered suggestions for the sort of concessions each side could give to make compromise possible, and asked that a papal envoy be sent to Paris. The cardinal made a detailed report on his encounter to the pope.

Pius VII was interested, and instructed the cardinal to open talks about what to talk about. With that done, he sent Cardinal Joseph Spina to Paris. Shortly after Spina's arrival on November 5 he began talks with Talleyrand. Bonaparte somewhat naively believed that the talks could be wrapped up and a treaty drafted within a few weeks. To his growing irritation, they would sputter along for seven months.

The key issue was, who would determine the personnel and policies of the Catholic Church in France? The French Constitution's "Organic Articles" strengthened the state's control over all religions. The law forbade any papal bull from being valid in France without the state's permission; reduced the number of bishops to sixty and empowered the state to appoint them; let bishops select the clergy in the parishes; legalized divorce; granted freedom of religion, with none superior to the others; made priests, ministers, and rabbis salaried state officials; and reaffirmed the legality of the nationalization of Church property.

The cardinal condemned all those policies, and insisted that the Catholic Church should once again be France's supreme religion. The foreign minister was just as adamant that Rome should simply accept those revolutionary changes. As if bridging that gulf was not daunting enough, Spina detested Talleyrand. The cardinal viewed with horror the excommunicated former priest, revolutionary zealot, and fervent libertine sitting across the table as the epitome of evil. While the foreign minister was well aware of the cardinal's attitude and may have idly regarded him as the envoy of a religion he believed was rooted in hypocrisy, superstition, and corruption, he was better at concealing his feelings.

Strategy rather than sentiment explains Talleyrand's unyielding position, not just with Rome but on most diplomatic issues. Like Bonaparte, Talleyrand had a "take it or leave it" attitude toward diplomacy. Unlike the general, who sought a swift, decisive victory, Talleyrand was a patient negotiator who tried to wear down his counterparts with an insouciant attitude that it was all the same to him, since he had so many other pressing issues on his agenda. He would also drop hints that the matter might be expedited by a generous "gift." Although that infuriated most envoys, they usually gave in sooner or later.

This time the gift Talleyrand sought did not glitter. His excommunication hampered both his professional and private life. Not only did it offend devoted envoys from Catholic realms, it prevented him from marrying his lover Catherine Grand in the joyous church wedding for which she increasingly longed. She sought to end five years of living in sin with an excommunicate and its accompanying ostracism by her religion and many in high society. But Spina adamantly rejected any notion of lifting the excommunication. Pius would later uphold Spina's ruling, even after Bonaparte directly appealed to him to grant grace to his foreign minister. So Talleyrand grew more contemptuous, and more indifferent to the negotiations.[50]

Bonaparte had Francois Cacault supersede Talleyrand as the chief negotiator. Cacault was a good choice: he did not have Talleyrand's moral baggage, and had worked on the Treaty of Tolentino. But the talks still went nowhere but in circles for the next two months. Bonaparte finally lost the last of his patience. Summoning Spina and Cacault to his home at Malmaison on May 12, he issued one of the ultimatums which had worked well in other stalled talks. By June 5 they could either present an acceptable list of compromises or the talks would end. Spina would have been happy to pack his bags, but Cacault convinced him first to consult the pope.

Pius promptly dispatched Cardinal Ercole Consalvi, his secretary of state, to Paris. Bonaparte received Consalvi shortly after he arrived on June 29. Once again he shook up his diplomatic team by putting his brother Joseph in charge of negotiations. Yet the papal team was still not eager to compromise. It took yet another of Bonaparte's ultimatums before they finally cut a deal.

A last-minute snag threatened to destroy that achievement. On June 13, just as the cardinal was about to sign the document, he discovered that the text was different from the preliminary one he had approved. He threatened to leave with his delegation. Bonaparte dictated another version and then tried to get Consalvi to accept it. The cardinal refused. They heatedly worked out the details.

Under the Concordat, signed on July 15, 1801, Bonaparte got most of what he sought while yielding little in return. Rome recognized France's constitution, which guaranteed religious freedom and financially underwrote the salaries and houses of worship for the major faiths. The Catholic Church would simply be a, rather than the, religion of France. The state would appoint its priests, bishops, and archbishops, and would accept as candidates only those who swore allegiance to the constitution. None of that vast hierarchy could assemble together or even leave their dioceses without official leave. The pope would then perfunctorily approve each list of new appointees or dismissals sent from Paris. Civil marriage and divorce remained French rights. All confiscated Church property would stay legally in the hands of the state or others who now held it, and it could be sold to others. No papal bull, decree, or encyclical would be valid in France without the state's approval. In return Bonaparte acknowledged that most French were Catholic and their right to worship as they pleased.

Pius issued a bull ratifying the treaty on August 15, 1801, both the Day of the Assumption and Bonaparte's birthday. Upon receiving word of the pope's action, the First Consul promptly signed the treaty on September 10. The relevant chambers of the National Assembly put the Concordat on their busy respective agendas and scrutinized it carefully when it finally came before them. That time-consuming process tried the patience of both the notoriously impatient First Consul and even the famously serene pope. The Tribunate finally accepted the Concordat by a 228 to 7 vote on April 1, 1802, and the Legislative Corps by a 220 to 21 vote two days later. The First Consul proclaimed the Concordat on Easter, April 18, 1802. Prestigious ambassadors were exchanged, with Cardinal Jean Caprara heading to Paris and Joseph Fesch, the Cardinal of Lyon and Bonaparte's uncle, to Rome.

Bonaparte then initiated and supervised talks in Paris for a similar Concordat between Milan and Rome. At crucial points he did not hesitate to give the pope himself a nudge: "I see with pain that Your Holiness believes it is not necessary to establish a concordat with the Republic of Italy."[51] All along he reassured Pius that the Italian state and Catholic Church shared a common interest in forging a Concordat. Nonetheless it took over a year before Cardinal Caprara and envoy Ferdinando Marescaldi struck a deal. This time, Rome got much more. The Italian Republic would repeal some of its more nettlesome laws that hampered the Church's operations and threatened its property.

In France the Catholic Church was officially restored but was a pale shadow of its pre-revolution self in power and prestige. In 1789 there had been over 130,000 priests in 135 dioceses governed by 150 bishops; now there were only 36,000 priests and 60 bishops in 60 dioceses. The Church had once owned about one-quarter of France; almost all of that had been nationalized.[52]

Bonaparte's Concordat realized most of his goals. He had reestablished Catholicism in a France whose state at once guaranteed freedom for all faiths and carefully regulated all religions. Unlike the American Revolution, the French Revolution did not separate church and state, it established the government's role as the warden of all religions. He had gotten Rome either to officially accept or to stop actively opposing all the religious changes in France since 1789. He simultaneously inflicted a powerful blow to the royalist cause and boosted his own power. Yet the new relationship with Rome was fragile, and eventually would break down completely in the most dramatic way.

Reforms Across France and the Empire

Victories in diplomacy, as in war, depend on the relative powers of the states and their envoys involved in the struggle. Bonaparte was always well aware that his own prowess at the negotiating table or battlefield was ultimately rooted in France's total power. Thus was the nurturing of French administrative, legal, financial, economic, educational, entrepreneurial, cultural, and, yes, military power both an end and a means of his policies. Developing France rather than fighting wars was his true vocation, what he most enjoyed doing, and what he was most proud of having done.[53]

Critics accuse Napoleon Bonaparte of destroying the Revolution after he took power on November 10, 1799. Actually the Terror, starting with the massacres of September 1792 and culminating with the actions of Pierre Robespierre and his henchmen from April 1793 to July 1794, literally mass-arrested and murdered the Revolution. Whether Bonaparte then buried or revived the Revolution will forever be debated. Certainly he and his supporters would passionately argue that he not only saved the Revolution but personified its highest ideals.

If so, what then were those ideals? His slogan of "careers open to all talents" surpassed and eventually effaced the revolution's core values of "liberty, equality, and fraternity." Modernity and democracy are hardly inseparable. Bonaparte did indeed systematically carry out France's political, economic, social, and psychological modernization. Yet he did so while transforming France into an ever more efficient police state. That was perhaps most pointedly symbolized when in 1811 he ordered the inscription "Liberty, Equality and Fraternity" chiseled out of the Hotel de Ville's façade in Paris.

Bonaparte initiated most of his modernization policies as First Consul rather than emperor. The Peace of Amiens was among those rare interludes between wars that let him devote himself and his administrators fully to the mission of reforming and strengthening France. They did so in eighteen-hour days that exhausted everyone except seemingly Bonaparte himself.

That a nation's military and diplomatic power can only be as strong as its economic power is an often-neglected truism in international politics. How many governments have mortgaged the economy by piling up the nation's debt to fund an ever larger military, only ultimately to weaken both?

Bonaparte understood that. He was determined that France would match and eventually surpass Britain as an economic powerhouse. To accomplish that he needed to revamp France's financial system, nurture an array of industries that could go head-to-head with their British rivals, and foster the ability of creative people to invest their minds and money in new, dynamic businesses. On February 13, 1800, he founded the Bank of France as a joint venture between the state and private investors to strictly oversee government spending, regulate the money supply, raise revenues, issue low-interest loans to key industries and firms, create a viable currency, and sell bonds. The next major step came in 1803 when the Bank of France issued the "franc germinal," whose value of five grams of gold created a solid currency for the French economy. If money is a modern economic system's blood, the infrastructure and industries are its skeleton and muscle, respectively. All along Bonaparte ensured that public and private funds were invested in infrastructure such as roads, ports, canals, bridges, sewers, water pipes, warehouses, and public buildings, while providing low-interest loans to industrialists, entrepreneurs, inventors, and scientists. In addition to cheap money, he further nurtured industries with government procurement and high tariffs against foreign rivals.

But that was not enough. Bonaparte understood the essential link among learning, investing, and serving. In 1802 he developed a lycee system across France of forty-five secondary schools with high standards and scholarships for 2,400 talented students, with each school manned by eight professors and equipped with a library stocked with classic and contemporary books on the humanities and sciences. His vision was to eventually expand that system so that lycees would educate all children so uniformly that each age class would learn the same thing in the same way at the same time. In 1808 he created the Ecole Normale as a boarding school to train 300 teachers annually; the student-teachers paid back their scholarships with ten years' service to the state. In 1809 he introduced the baccalaureate, a national examination system which awarded degrees only to those who passed the rigorous test. Lycee teachers qualified only after passing the aggregation, or national examination, designed for them. As for higher education, he improved standards, salaries, and facilities for the two existing national universities, the Ecole Normale Superieure and the Ecole Polytechnique, and in 1806 founded Imperial University as a federation which provided common standards and exchanges among the other universities across France. To enhance research he reorganized and expanded the facilities at the National Library and National Archives. Finally, he boosted military education in 1802 by founding the Academy of St. Cyr to provide advanced studies for Ecole Militaire graduates.

He similarly revamped the administrative and judicial systems. He purged inefficient bureaucracies and inept and/or corrupt bureaucrats, beefed up existing or established new, essential offices, and tried to ensure that only those best qualified took office. To that latter end he hand-picked the nation's judges, prefects, sub-prefects, and mayors based on the strength of their dossiers. Perhaps his most enduring achievement was to modernize France's civil, criminal, and commercial codes into a system of justice known ever since as the Code Napoleon. To that end in 1800 he set up and presided over several legal reform committees that for years regularly met and debated just what laws to keep, revise, or discard. The Civil Code took effect on New Year's Day of 1804; it was renamed the Code Napoleon in 1807. The Commercial Code and Criminal Code were unveiled in 1807 and 1808, respectively. Bonaparte in turn supplemented those law codes with over 15,000 decrees that he and his government issued during his fifteen years in power.

As a soldier Bonaparte understood the power of incentives to inspire people to sacrifice and strive to achieve beyond what they otherwise would. So on May 19, 1802, he founded the Legion of Honor to reward those soldiers and civilians who brought glory to France. Over the next dozen years he would bestow 38,000 Legions of Honor. To those who worried that such distinctions violated the revolutionary ideal of equality, Bonaparte replied: "Well, men are led by toys. I don't think that the French love liberty and equality. The French are not at all changed by ten years of revolution. . . . They must have distinctions."[54]

Bonaparte extended his reforms to the satellite "sister republics" and those regions annexed to France's budding empire. He took a special interest in the Cisalpine Republic. After all, he had created that state, crafted its constitution, and hand-picked many of its key leaders. In December 1801 a delegation from Milan arrived in Paris with a petition that the Cisalpine Republic be renamed the Republic of Italy and that Napoleon Bonaparte be its first president. The First Consul was thrilled at the blossoming of an idea that he had planted with the Cisalpine Republic's State Council, or Consulta. After a show of feigned reluctance, he approved the petition and asked all the delegates to convene at Lyon, half-way between Paris and Milan. Thus empowered, the Consulta issued a decree on January 26, 1802, giving birth to the Republic of Italy, with Bonaparte its first president.[55]

Bonaparte was nearly as zealous in developing Italy as he was France. Over the next decade he issued a stream of nearly daily directives, first to vice-president Francesco Melzi d'Eril, then later to vice-king Eugene de Beauharnais, his stepson; each of them faithfully worked out and implemented the details. With his conflicting goals of reform and exploitation, Bonaparte was well aware of the diplomatic juggling act that his regime trod in Italy and all other conquered regions. Nearly everyone begrudged the French administrative and military presence, especially the recruiters and taxmen. He had to be extra careful not to alienate liberals, who were a sliver of the population but the republic's backbone. He also recognized that his creation, arming, and expansion of what had become the Italian Republic with himself as president was "a political irritation" to other European powers. But he persisted in those policies because they appeared to serve French interests.[56]

There were limits to his vision for Italy. He could have joined other conquered regions to the Italian Republic, but he wanted a subordinate, not a potentially rival, state. Instead, he annexed to France Elba on August 26, 1802, and Piedmont on September 11, 1802. Both acts were the culmination of complex, overlapping diplomatic paths.

Bonaparte had first taken territory, fortresses, and the right of passage for French troops from the King of Piedmont and Sardinia in May 1796. When the French invaded in late 1798 in response to the Austro-Russian offensive in Italy, Charles Emmanuel signed a treaty on December 9 whereby he abdicated his rule over Piedmont and then retired with his family and court to Caligari, the capital of Sardinia, the other half of his realm. In February 1799 Piedmontese liberals declared a republic and demanded annexation to France. Thus was the way open for annexation—until Austria's takeover later that year aborted the process. Once Bonaparte retook Piedmont in 1800 the issue of annexation was reopened. A deal was cut whereby Charles Emmanuel would accept France's annexation of Piedmont if he were compensated with lands elsewhere in Italy. However, Charles Emmanuel, already burdened by the loss of half of his kingdom, was further devastated by his wife's death in July 1802, and he abdicated to his brother Victor Emmanuel. The new king would have to wait another dozen years before he received any justice for his family's losses at the hands of French armies and Italian liberals.[57]

The diplomacy that determined Piedmont's fate was relatively straightforward compared to that regarding a nearby region of Italy. After

Bonaparte had first conquered Parma and Piacenza in 1796, he took a payoff from Duke Ferdinand I of six million livres and 25 of his finest paintings to retain his throne for the rest of his life. When Ferdinand died in 1802 Bonaparte decided to annex those lands to France. He was, however, careful to compensate Ferdinand's heir, Louis, who was married to Marie Louise, the third daughter of France's ally, Charles IV, the King of Spain. That was why he converted the Duchy of Tuscany into the Kingdom of Etruria and placed Louis on that throne. That was part of a grand swap with Spain in which Bonaparte received in return Parma, Elba, Louisiana, ten ships of the line, and joint and separate military campaigns against the British and Portuguese. That complex deal was legalized with two treaties, Ildefonso on October 1, 1800, and Aranjuez on March 21, 1801.

Negotiating those treaties was a tough diplomatic challenge. Although Bonaparte first charged Talleyrand with the mission on July 22, 1800, he typically micro-managed the details. In mid-August he sent Berthier to hand-deliver to Charles his formal proposal for the campaigns and grand swap, and then negotiate a treaty. It took Berthier nearly two months to cut the Ildefonso treaty with Manuel de Godoy, the forever-conniving and greedy prime minister. After an exhausted Berthier returned in November, Bonaparte replaced him with his brother Lucien. It took three additional months of persistent diplomacy before Lucien was able to sign with Godoy the Aranjuez treaty.

Thus did Bonaparte play kingmaker for the first time; he would acquire an insatiable appetite for the practice. But when Europe's newest royal couple visited Paris from mid-May 1801 to June 30, he was not pleased with the puppet king he had tapped to reign over his puppet realm. Louis was stingy, arrogant, and a bit of a nitwit. Nonetheless, the First Consul had no choice but to make the most of his creation. He tried to share his leadership secrets and policy expectations with Louis during several prolonged private sessions. He also showered expensive presents on the couple, and ensured that they received all the formal protocol due to their rank throughout a whirl of Parisian balls, concerts, and plays capped by a grand fete in their honor hosted by Talleyrand at the chateau of Neuilly on June 8.[58]

Louis was crowned the King of Etruria in Florence on July 28, 1801. His reign would be short and pathetic. Bonaparte's first king was no sooner installed than he began displaying ever-worsening signs of not just disease but madness.[59] That greatly disturbed the First Consul, who foresaw a "grand evil for Tuscany and for a prince who we are honor-bound to protect, because in a city like Florence the prince has many enemies." He then mulled various options over what to do if the king became incapacitated or died. He concluded that what was best for the present was to remain a supportive but light presence as the Tuscan government dealt with the problem. He informed Charles IV of the disturbing news of his son-in-law. He wrote Louis himself encouraging letters. He had Talleyrand warn their key man in Florence, Henri Clarke, that "he is an ambassador to Florence, not the governor of Florence." But there was little more that he could do. When Louis died on May 27, 1803, his infant son Charles Louis was named king, with Marie Louise as regent.[60]

Not all the peoples affected by Bonaparte's reshuffled leaders, imposed constitutions, or annexations to France were quite so complacent. The Dutch, for instance, were ever more resentful of having to uphold a treaty signed on May 16, 1795, which bound the Batavian Republic to be a French protectorate. To that end, the Dutch had to underwrite annually with 100,000 florins the cost of a 25,000-man French army scattered in garrisons across their land. That burden was compounded by the British blockade of Holland's ports, which battered that seafaring nation into a chronic depression.

Unable to rise against the French, the Dutch instead simply cut back their payments and upped their pleas to reduce their troops. They also dared to reject a French-style constitution, by a vote of 55,000 to 17,000. As in France's plebiscites, a creative counting of ballots in the United Provinces resulted in an official announcement that the Dutch had overwhelmingly approved the proposed constitution; that was accomplished by the inclusion of the 400,000 people who had not bothered to vote at all in the "yes" column. The constitution was promulgated on October 6, 1801. Theoretically, the Batavian Republic was independent; in reality, it was a protectorate of France, whose officials vetted all the key office-holders and watched like hawks every move made by those in power, or who wanted power.

Bonaparte responded to the Dutch defiance by pressuring their ambassador, Roger Jean Schimmelpenninck, and through blunt letters to their government, to live up to their legal duties. But he also gave the nod to French commander Charles Augereau to rattle his saber: "In the position we find ourselves we have several grand goals to assert with the Batavian government, and the conduct of the French government will determine what comes from these negotiations."[61]

The Dutch Directory complained of Augereau's belligerent and uncouth conduct and asked Bonaparte to replace him. The First Consul politely refused that request, asking them not to "dishonor someone who has commanded your troops with glory and success, and contributed to your independence." Like countless diplomatic and political messages throughout history, Bonaparte's letter had a surreal, "through the looking glass" air to it. None of it was true; but all of it was what Bonaparte wanted everyone, especially the directors, to believe. In actuality, Augereau was there to subject rather than protect them, and had hardly won any laurels in that pedestrian duty. For now the Dutch leaders had no choice but to go along with the fiction. Bonaparte's goal with the Batavian Republic was clear. To Talleyrand he wrote: "I just want no movement in Holland, no change in government."[62] He got what he wanted.

He was just as successful with the Helvetian Republic, but it took more effort. Switzerland was torn apart by linguistic, regional, and political factions. The French and Austrians were especially active in trying to woo support from the respective French-and German-speaking regions. As in the Batavian Republic, the French had in August 1798 imposed a constitution which created a centralized state and a treaty by which the two countries became allies. In September 1802 the Federalist Party in power in Bern sent a delegation to Paris to explain that, while they appreciated all the "help" from Paris, most cantons wanted to restore both their traditional political distance from each other and from France.

Given Switzerland's strategic location between Germany and Italy, Bonaparte was determined to deepen rather than lessen that land's dependence on and integration with France. His gut reaction was to condemn the Federalists as ingrates: "Certainly it would be a strange ineptitude on my part of cutting loose a country that we have defended against Russian and Austrian armies." Ideals would yield to security: "What I need above all is a frontier that covers Franche-Comte and France. That is my first desire. . . . French interests dictate my policies to me."[63]

So the First Consul wrote out an ultimatum and had General Michel Ney deliver it to Bern: "Citizen deputies of the eighteen cantons of the Helvetian Republic, the situation of your country is critical. Moderation, prudence, and the sacrifice of your passions are essential to saving it. I offer, before the eyes of Europe, my timely mediation." He went on to laud their special and unique attributes, explain why they had fallen into chaos, and to their problems offered a solution based on a new, specially designed constitution—and French troops to maintain order while it took effect.[64]

After several months of negotiations, Bonaparte signed two treaties on February 19, 1803, an Act of Mediation, which abolished the 1798 system, and a Federal Act, which created a decentralized system among the cantons, with a capital at Bern; each canton would receive its own French-style constitution tailored to its specific traditions, needs, and desires. In return, the Swiss would supply France with 16,000 troops in peacetime and another 8,000 in war, and France committed itself to the Helvetian Republic's protection.[65]

Bonaparte even tried to manipulate events in lands beyond immediate French control. The Treaty of Campo Formio had given France a seat among the Holy Roman Empire's electors. In 1802 the Austrians effectively retook that seat by blocking France's candidate for the archbishopric of Cologne and settling the Habsburg Archduke Anton there. Francis II then sent Prince Karl Schwarzenberg and Count Philip Stadion to Russia and Prussia, respectively, to seek those countries' support against France on the elector and other German issues.

Bonaparte sternly rebuked Francis for his intrigues: "I entreat your majesty to end promptly your business in Germany so that tranquility can be restored to all those nations."[66] He then journeyed to Rastibonne (Regensburg) for the meeting of the German Diet in August 1802. The Diet was still working on how to reorganize the empire in accordance with the Treaties of Campo Formio and Luneville. Bonaparte set out a vision for Germany's future and left a delegation to work out the details with their counterparts. The resulting treaty was called the "Imperial Recess." After prolonged and often rancorous debate, it was approved by the Diet on February 25, 1803. The Diet eliminated 112 states and merged those lands with the survivors. In all over three million people learned that they were subjects of new rulers. Two assemblies would preside over the empire, the electorate of ten states (four catholic and six protestant) that would choose the emperor, and a college of 130 states (53 catholic and 77 protestant) that would debate and decide on all other issues. Bonaparte was able to get the largest states, Austria, Prussia, Bavaria, Saxony, and Hanover, to accept the plan because he had enlarged them with many of the abolished states.[67]

Bonaparte's guidance of Germany's reorganization was hardly altruistic. French influence expanded across western Germany and in seaports such as Hamburg, Bremen, and Lubeck. But he was not content with that. He ordered the march of French troops into the minor ports of Ritzelbuttel and Cuxhaven, which were generally acknowledged to be in Prussia's sphere of influence. It was a deliberate test of Prussian resolve.

Had Frederick William III protested and made signs of military and diplomatic mobilization, Bonaparte most likely would have cut some face-saving deal for them both. But the king and his ministers had no stomach for a fight, diplomatic or otherwise. They turned the other cheek and looked the other way. Despite the expansion of French influence, it was still Austria that was Prussia's greatest rival for influence over Germany. Frederick William sent Johann Wilhelm Lombard to Paris to try to prevent any further French inroads into northern Germany, and to encourage instead French expansion into southern Germany to provoke Austria.

That was exactly what Bonaparte had hoped would happen. He loosened Talleyrand on Lombard, with instructions to forge a treaty whereby Prussia recognized not only all of France's existing annexations and satellites, but its expanded sphere of influence over ever more of Germany, northern as well as western and southern. Over the next ten months Talleyrand would make steady progress toward those goals—until a notorious murder abruptly ended the talks.

Amidst these stunning political developments, the Senate rewarded Bonaparte for all the peace, prosperity, and pride that he had brought to France. On May 6, 1802, when the First Consul presented the Treaty of Amiens to the senators, they noted their deep gratitude by voting to extend his tenure in office for another decade. Bonaparte replied that fulfilling all the dazzling goals that he envisioned for France would demand a lifetime of powers. At this point the Senate balked; it voted to hold a plebiscite to see what the people thought of the notion.

With Bonaparte's officials counting the votes, the plebiscite's results were not in doubt. The announcement came on August 2, 1802, that the French nation had voted overwhelmingly, by 3,568,885 to 8,374, to extend the consulate to Napoleon Bonaparte for life.[68] The Senate accordingly granted him that power two weeks later, on his August 15 birthday when he turned thirty-three years old. There was only one other gift that could surpass what he had just received—and he would soon ask for that.

The American Dream

Those dazzling achievements in developing power for France and himself only left Bonaparte aching for more. But where and how? Wherever Bonaparte scanned the geopolitical horizon, British power blocked his view, either partly or wholly. So what could be done about that?

At least one thing was certain. Sooner or later war would re-erupt between France and Britain. On the continent British diplomats with treasure chests filled with gold would once again forge a coalition against France. On the high seas the British fleet would most likely stymie any French attacks on England's colonies, Ireland, or the home island itself, while plucking one by one France's vulnerable, far-flung colonies, scouring its merchant ships from the seas, and landing supplies, money, and troops to aid rebels in France itself.

A hard look across the Channel revealed the secret of that power. Over the course of centuries the British had mastered a dynamic, virtuous cycle of ever-greater commercial, financial, entrepreneurial, industrial, imperial, and naval power. Britain's population was less than a third that of France, but it was more prosperous and enterprising, and was integrated with an expanding global commercial and territorial empire. A nation's power thus depended on a population for much more than just troops and taxes. People also demand goods and services; the more prosperous and numerous a population, the more it buys. Buying power, however, can work for or against national power. If people buy foreign goods, they enrich foreigners. If people buy goods produced at home, they enrich those producers directly, and themselves indirectly by creating more and better-paying jobs which circulate more money through the economy, and produce more revenues for the government. Britain limited its imports mostly to the raw materials which fed the voracious factories that produced high-quality, low-cost products which were sold at home and exported to markets around the world. Contrary to what liberals such as Adam Smith said, trade clearly was a type of warfare, in which one side's gain was at once its rivals' loss.

In drawing those conclusions, Bonaparte was simply reformulating the rationale for a mercantilist strategy which France had been consciously practicing, albeit far less adeptly than Britain, for a couple of centuries. He understood that, but was determined to succeed where France's previous rulers had failed. The reforms that Bonaparte would institute in France and the expansion of French influence in the Low Countries, Germany, Switzerland, and Italy were essential first steps in trying to emulate Britain's success. But French industrialists needed access to more markets across the continent and around the world.

To that end, unfortunately, Bonaparte looked first to a vast region which not only had virtually no market at all but had been a chronic drain on French power the last time Paris owned it. Starting with its first settlement at Biloxi in 1699, Versailles had tried to develop its claim to the entire Mississippi River watershed, which it called Louisiana. But it had made little progress in the six decades leading up to its defeat in the Seven Years' War. Under the Treaty of

Paris which ended that war in 1763, France ceded Canada and all of Louisiana east of the Mississippi, except New Orleans, to Britain; and all of Louisiana west of that river, along with New Orleans, to Spain. Since then Spain had found that Louisiana was at once an economic liability and a strategic asset in blocking the relentless westward march of the restless Americans.

Bonaparte knew that Louisiana's poor, sparse population would cost France far more to administer and defend than any taxes it might reap. It would take decades to transform that colony with numbers of people, wealth, and dynamism. But it was military rather than economic strategy that immediately attracted him to Louisiana. He believed that New Orleans would be a vital base for invading Britain's sugar island colonies in the Caribbean and aiding France's reconquest of Saint Domingue (Haiti), which had been in rebellion since 1792.

So it was Bonaparte's American dream which inspired his grand swap of Tuscany for Louisiana, Elba, and ten ships of the line. Charles IV at once brightened at the thought of the financial gain that deal could bring to Spain, while regretting the strategic loss. Under the secret Treaty of Ildefonso, signed on October 1, 1800, Spain agreed to the trade in return for France's promise not to transfer Louisiana to any third country. Bonaparte insisted on a secret treaty so that France could establish itself firmly in power there before the British and Americans learned of that presence and began to muster expeditions to oust the French. It would only be after he had forged peace treaties with Austria, Britain, and the United States that Bonaparte could confidently unveil his grand deal with Spain with the public Treaty of Aranjuez, signed on March 21, 1801.

The United States was potentially a far greater threat to Louisiana than Britain. Throughout the late 1790s France and the United States had been fighting an undeclared naval war, as French warships continued to seize American merchant ships bound for the ports of France's enemies, especially Britain. Should the Americans learn that France held legal title to Louisiana, they might well invade and conquer that vast region. Somehow a peace treaty had to be signed with the United States.

And peace would only be the first step. Bonaparte had long recognized the strategic and economic value of close ties with the United States. Paris and Washington shared the interest of somehow containing and ideally eroding British power. Indeed, on Bonaparte's first day as First Consul he wrote Foreign Minister Charles Reinhard that "it is indispensable that we find ourselves as promptly as possible on the best foot with the United States."[69]

The opportunity for better relations came in early 1800 when President John Adams sent to Paris three envoys—Williams Vans Murray, Oliver

Ellsworth, and William Richardson Davis—to demand an apology, compensation, and a promise to stop seizing American merchant ships.[70] Bonaparte had Joseph negotiate with the envoys parallel to the secret talks with Spain over Louisiana. On September 30, 1800, after half a year of hard bargaining and just two days before the Treaty of Ildefonso, Joseph and two colleagues signed the Treaty of Mortefontaine with the Americans. It was a rare instance of Bonaparte seeming to concede more than he took. France promised to end all privateering against American ships, and allowed American merchants to sue for damages in French courts. In fact, he could not have taken Louisiana without first establishing peace with the United States.

During the celebratory party which Joseph threw at his chateau where they had signed the treaty, Murray had a chance to meet Bonaparte. He found the First Consul "grave, rather thoughtful, occasionally severe—not inflated nor egotistical—very exact in all his motions which show at once an impatient heart & a methodical head . . . of a most skilful fencing master. . . . He speaks with a frankness so much above fear that you think he has no reserve."[71]

Another parallel step in Bonaparte's strategy for the New World was to end the Haitian independence movement threatening the French colony of St. Domingue, which was the world's richest sugar producer, accounting for three-quarters of all production.[72] During the 1790s that island had steadily dissolved into chaos, in parallel to the ever more convulsive and violent revolution in France. The struggle was not just between republicans and royalists, but among whites, mulattoes, and blacks as well. A slave rebellion erupted in 1791 and continued for years. That struggle did not diminish after the arrival of word that the National Assembly had abolished slavery on February 4, 1794. Led by Pierre Domingue Toussaint L'Ouverture, the blacks demanded land and national independence as well as personal liberty.

Bonaparte had viewed the news of anarchy, massacres, and devastation from St. Domingue with ever more dismay. He mulled various plans for running an armada through the gauntlet of prowling British squadrons and retaking the colony, but finally concluded that the odds of succeeding were not worth the risk. Instead he decided to coopt rather than conquer the rebels.

He took his first step on December 25, 1799; this was just six weeks after he took power. He issued a proclamation which confirmed his commitment to slavery's abolition and civil rights for all, but insisted that St. Domingue remained a French colony and that he was determined to reestablish the rule of law to halt the violence and anarchy. He had three envoys—General Michel, Colonel Vincent, and the mulatto leader Raymond—journey to Port au Prince to issue that proclamation and deliver a letter granting L'Ouverture the title of Captain General. But the title was symbolic; the three envoys were intended to wield genuine power behind the scenes.[73]

Bonaparte's letter to L'Ouverture was another of his minor diplomatic masterpieces. In it he lauded all L'Ouverture's talents and achievements, embraced him as a savior of the islands, promised him glory and riches, then warned him of the consequences should he fail in his duty to France. L'Ouverture, however, insisted on retaining all power in his hands. The First Consul had no choice for the present but to continue to treat him with the utmost respect. Yet, just to remind him of who was really the boss, he instructed Marine Minister Pierre Forfait to ensure that his envoys handed any letter to the rebel chief with "a certain hauteur."[74]

Having failed to enlist the rebel leader and the masses of former slaves behind him, Bonaparte increasingly viewed abolition as a mistake; it had at once alienated the powerful class of slave owners, fueled the war that had engulfed the island ever since, and encouraged most Haitians to seek independence. If slavery were reinstated it might be easier to reassert control over the colony. But for the present he left a decision in abeyance; there were too many other pressing diplomatic issues to resolve.[75]

But within two years, two sets of forces, one positive and the other negative for France, stirred Bonaparte to action. Under the Treaty of Amiens, signed on March 27, 1801, Britain agreed to restore France's Caribbean islands that it had captured. Then Bonaparte learned that L'Ouverture had invaded the eastern side of the island, which Spain had ceded to France in 1795; L'Ouverture declared a republic on July 8, 1801. And atop that, Bonaparte received an insulting letter from the rebel leader himself.

The First Consul devised and issued to Marine Minister Denis Decres on October 31, 1802, a detailed, three-part strategy for retaking St. Domingue, along with Guadeloupe.[76] During the first phase, "the blacks must be flattered and well treated, but overall we must remove their popularity and power." During the second phase, L'Ouverture and his followers would be arrested and deported, with whites sent to prisons in Guyana, mulattoes to Corsica, and blacks to Brest, while the white prostitutes would be released into Europe. And during the final phase, all civilians would be disarmed. For the present, all blacks on the French side of the island would enjoy liberty as long as they resumed their former jobs; but slavery would be restored on the Spanish-speaking side of the island. The Americans would be allowed to continue trading for the time being, but after the third period they would be barred, with only French merchants allowed access.

To carry out that mission, Bonaparte mobilized at Brest a 19,000-man army led by his brother-in-law, General Victor Leclerc, and another of 3,000 men led by General Antoine Richepanse. The first expedition set sail for St. Domingue on December 14, and the second on January 7, 1802, to retake Guadeloupe. By spring 1802 both forces had landed. On April 27 Bonaparte succumbed to pressure from the colonial lobby and issued a decree restoring slavery; the decree became law on May 20. Although his wife Josephine, a Martinique native, was clearly an influential voice for that policy, actually nearly all of his State Council, for practical and/or venal reasons, had reached the same conclusion.

The initial news from both islands was good. Richepanse restored control over Guadeloupe and Leclerc's forces captured L'Ouverture on June 7. But tropical diseases steadily devoured the French forces, including Leclerc, who died in November 1802. The Haitian rebels, now led by the mulatto Jean Jacques Dessalines and enflamed by word that they would be returned to slavery, retook ever more of St. Domingue in an orgy of mass destruction, looting, rape, and murder. After war with Britain resumed in early 1803, British expeditions soon captured St. Lucia, Tobago, Goree, and Guyana, then St. Domingue itself on November 30, 1803. Dessalines triumphantly declared Haiti's independence on January 1, 1804. A couple of decades later on St. Helena, Bonaparte would call his Caribbean strategy "a huge stupidity on my part."[77]

With his American dream dying, Bonaparte decided to cut his losses. Louisiana was now a strategic as well as an economic curse, just another expensive French investment that the British would capture sooner or later. It would be far better to sell it to the Americans than lose it to the British.

The Americans would eagerly accept that offer.[78] The notion that Spain had sold Louisiana to France enraged knowledgeable Americans. The fact that Spain had controlled New Orleans, and thus the flow of American trade down the Mississippi River and out to international waters beyond, had been exasperating enough. But at least Spain posed no military threat to the United States; France was another problem altogether. If a veteran French army were garrisoned in New Orleans or, even worse, St. Louis, it could threaten all of America's nascent states west of the Appalachian Mountains.

President Thomas Jefferson instructed Robert Livingston, his minister in Paris, to see if Bonaparte was willing to sell the city of New Orleans. Livingston did so in a letter to Talleyrand on February 20, 1802. In his reply, Talleyrand asked how much the Americans might be interested in paying.

Now it was Livingston's turn to be coy. There was no need to begin laborious negotiations and pay a huge price for something that the United States might just take for free. As French losses in the Caribbean mounted, that potential French threat to the United States from Louisiana eroded to the vanishing point. Meanwhile, pressure in the United States among belligerent congressmen and newspaper editors was mounting on Jefferson to declare war on France and seize Louisiana. In a public statement designed to be relayed to Paris, Secretary of States James Madison said: "How sad it would be if French intransigence forced us to conquer the country west of the Mississippi."[79]

Fearing Livingston was unreliable, Jefferson sent Pierre Samuel du Pont, a naturalized American who was born in France, to Paris with word that if Bonaparte did not sell New Orleans at a reasonable price to the United States, then the Americans might just ally with Britain and take that city and all of the vast Louisiana territory by force. He followed that up by sending to Paris James Monroe with instructions to offer to buy the city of New Orleans for not more than $9 million.

Bonaparte was eager to cut a deal. At a State Council meeting on April 11 he announced his willingness to sell all of Louisiana for 100 million francs, about $20 million. His Treasury Minister, Francois Marbois, explained that the Americans could not afford to pay that much. Bonaparte abruptly cut his demand in half. Talleyrand would later call that "the fastest decline in property values in the history of the world."[80]

That same day Talleyrand asked Livingston how much he would be willing to pay for all of Louisiana. Livingston offered $4 million. Talleyrand countered with 100 million francs. Neither side budged for another two weeks; then Monroe and Marbois took over as each side's chief negotiators. They finally agreed on a price of $15 million, or 80 million francs. As they sealed the deal with a treaty on April 30, 1803, Talleyrand remarked with grace and prescience: "You have made a noble bargain for yourselves, and I suppose you will make the most of it."[81]

The Road to War

Disinformation can be a vital strategy in war or diplomacy. Spreading distorted or false tales can make one seem stronger or weaker than is actually the case, sow dissent in the enemy's ranks, or mask one's true intentions while diverting the enemy's attention in the wrong direction. Bonaparte was a master of all that.[82]

While he never abandoned his dream of asserting French power over the entire Mediterranean basin, his belief that he could achieve that anytime soon would die in Egypt. Yet he wanted the other great powers to believe that dream was still his priority. The more of a distraction he stirred there, the better his chance of advancing other goals elsewhere. Or so he believed.

To that end, in 1801 he spread rumors that he was secretly preparing another expedition to invade Egypt. He let slip the news that he had sent Colonel Horace Sebastiani there to assess how to reassert French rule. The government newspaper, *Le Moniteur*, then published Sebastiani's subsequent report. Talleyrand boasted to the English ambassador that Egypt would soon not only once again be part of the French Empire, but that eventually all of North Africa to the straits would come under French protection. To reinforce that impression, Bonaparte sent envoys to seek trade and peace accords with all the beys across the region; they signed treaties with Algiers on December 28, 1801, and Tunis on December 23, 1802. When Algiers reneged on the treaty with demands for 200,000 piastres in bribes, Bonaparte demanded reparations and an apology, and explained how he had destroyed the Mamelukes of Egypt for similar acts of piracy: "I will land at the head of 80,000 troops and I will destroy your regime." The pasha yielded. In the autumn of 1802 Bonaparte dispatched the intrepid Sebastiani on a diplomatic odyssey down the Balkan side of the Adriatic, through the Ionian Islands, and finally to Istanbul.[83]

All along, Bonaparte's propaganda mill resurrected the image of the Mediterranean as the stepping stone to India. India actually was among Bonaparte's targets should war break out again with Britain, but he had no intention of following the stepping-stone strategy, which would take years to implement. Instead he wanted that attack to occur quickly, ideally even before the British in India got word that war had resumed. So he secretly sent an expedition under Captain-General Decaen to the French enclave at Pondicherry in what is now southeast India to ready itself for an immediate attack.

Bonaparte twice sent envoys to St. Petersburg with the proposal that France and Russia split the Ottoman Empire between them. Alexander spurned the offer; he was then conducting secret talks with Francis for dividing the Ottoman Empire between Russia and Austria. Reports from Bonaparte's spies informed him of those talks. He must have smiled as he read the reports. That was exactly what he had hoped would happen and had encouraged with the "concessions" of his various treaties with Austria which lured it deeper into the Balkans, and the envoys he sent to St. Petersburg.

Bonaparte's saber-rattling over a second descent on Egypt and rumors that he was mulling the conquest and division of the Ottoman Empire hardly helped, but did not destroy, a relationship that he was trying to nurture with Istanbul. The Turks, isolated on Europe's geographic, cultural, and religious fringe, could not be too picky about "friends," let alone allies. A peace treaty between France and the Ottoman Empire was signed on June 26, 1801. Bonaparte dispatched General Guillaume Brune to serve as France's ambassador at Istanbul. Brune informed his hosts that Alexander and Francis were plotting the Ottoman Empire's demise.[84]

Yet for now Brune could get no diplomatic traction over Russian envoy Andrei Italinsky for influence with the Porte. Selim III was still enraged over Bonaparte's campaigns in Egypt and Palestine, during which the Russians had fought beside the Turks against the French. And Italinsky eagerly fed him Bonaparte's own propaganda about preparations to retake Egypt. It was not hard to convince the sultan that France remained a clear and present danger. Selim rebuffed Brune's attempts to get him to recognize the French Republic and block Russian warships from sailing through the straits. In yet another sting to French interests, he allowed the tsar to establish an embassy with Ali Pasha, Albania's ruler, whom Bonaparte had been trying to entice into an alliance.[85]

For Bonaparte, the ideal result of the Austrian and Russian intrigues in the Balkans would be to entangle them in war with the Turks. To foster that end he sent General Pierre Roederer on a mission, first through the Austrian Empire to assess its readiness for war, and then through the Balkans to promise gold and perhaps troops to local rulers if they rose against the Austrians and Russians.

Yet that mission was more likely to provoke Austria into a war with France. That possibility became greater when Bonaparte authorized Francesco Melzi d'Eril, the Italian Republic's vice-president, to parade his Austrian Legion, composed of Austrian deserters, along the Adige River frontier between the two realms.

That was hardly the only instance of contradictions in Bonaparte's diplomacy. In many ways Bonaparte unwittingly fouled his diplomacy with his own propaganda. The worst instance was over Malta, which he genuinely wanted Britain to evacuate. From the viewpoint of British interests, if Bonaparte was determined to carve out a Mediterranean empire during the next war, then it made perfect sense to hold onto rather than relinquish Malta as required under the Treaty of Amiens. So that is what Whitehall did when the deadline for Malta's reversion passed in September 1802.

Bonaparte raised the issue at the most opportune time to embarrass the British and promote France's case. During a banquet for the diplomatic community he noisily confronted Charles Fox and Henry Holland about that violation, and pointed out that France had complied with the Treaty of Amiens by withdrawing troops from ports in the Kingdom of Naples. Under the circumstances their only reply was a promise to convey the First Consul's protest to their government. After two weeks without a response, Bonaparte had Talleyrand fire off to Whitehall a tough letter demanding the immediate evacuation of Malta, resumption of bilateral trade, and cutoff of aid to the royalists.[86]

Prime Minister Henry Addington promptly sent Charles Whitworth to Paris. From November 1802 to May 1803 Whitworth and Talleyrand engaged in a series of talks which resolved nothing, but did reveal two starkly different diplomatic styles: Whitworth's red-faced bluster versus Talleyrand's insinuating grace. It was a classic diplomatic standoff. Neither side wanted war, but was even more determined to uphold a misguided sense of national honor that refused to make the concessions that could prevent a war.

To pressure Britain, Bonaparte played to the diplomatic gallery. On March 11, 1803, he launched a miniature diplomatic offensive with letters to Frederick William III of Prussia, Alexander I of Russia, and Charles IV of Spain. Although each letter addressed specific bilateral issues, they all explained the Amiens Treaty's tenets; insisted that France was fulfilling its terms, including the evacuation of the Kingdom of Naples and the Papal States; and condemned the British for violating the treaty, most notably by retaining Malta. Finally, Napoleon asked each sovereign to help pressure Whitehall into living up to its promises. He was especially keen to get Alexander to act as a mediator in the peace talks. But he did not get any takers.[87]

Ironically, the two sides of that chasm could have been bridged with relatively symbolic gestures. Whitworth stood firm on Britain's retention of Malta for a decade, as well as independence for Holland and Switzerland. If the

French complied, Britain would recognize the Italian and Ligurian Republics, the Kingdom of Etruria, and the annexation of Elba.

Talleyrand advised Bonaparte to take the offer. If the British were dead set to hold Malta, there was nothing France could do about that. Why not accept that reality? As for the "independence" of Holland and Switzerland, that could be feigned simply by reducing the French garrisons; the French-style republics appeared relatively well rooted. But Bonaparte could not abide Britain's control of Malta; he still harbored dreams of expelling the British beyond the Gibraltar Straits and converting the Mediterranean into a French sea.[88]

Bonaparte conveyed his rejection of any compromise with a public insult to a man he despised for so obviously despising him. During a diplomatic reception on March 13, 1803, he tongue-lashed the character of both Whitworth and his country. If Bonaparte thought his assault would rally the diplomatic community behind him, he could not have been more mistaken. Whatever the ambassadors thought of Bonaparte's position, his behavior appalled them.[89]

Over the next few days Bonaparte tried to make up for his tirade by contriving a strained pleasantness with Whitworth, but the damage was done. Whitworth restated his position and dismissed Bonaparte's suggestion that they invite Russia to mediate their talks. Bonaparte typically responded with loud and prolonged saber-rattling by ordering his administration and military to openly prepare for war.[90]

Whitworth explained the standoff to his government and asked what he should do next. Whitehall instructed him to issue an ultimatum that Bonaparte accept Britain's position or else, then hurry back to London after the dictator's inevitable refusal. Whitworth dutifully issued the ultimatum on May 1, but had to wait until May 4 for a reply.

Bonaparte re-explained why the British position was unacceptable, but suggested that they finesse the Malta issue by placing the island under the joint protection of Austria, Prussia, and Russia. As always in his diplomacy, he tried to paint his opponent as the villain: "If this proposal is not accepted, it will be clear to all that England never had any intention of executing the Treaty of Amiens."[91]

Whitworth rejected the notion. Bonaparte declared the talks over. Hoping that Bonaparte might strike a last-minute deal, Whitworth lingered in Paris until May 11, then had his coachman head toward Dunkirk at a leisurely pace.

The following day Bonaparte sent a courier galloping after him with his last offer: France would accept Britain's occupation of Malta for a decade, in return for France's occupation of Otranto for the same time. Whitworth might have accepted that trade had Bonaparte made it a couple of months earlier. But from the viewpoint of British honor it was too late for any more compromises, however reasonable others might find them. Whitworth boarded a vessel bound for Dover. Britain officially declared war on May 16, 1803. Somewhat stunned at finding himself in a war that he did not want at that time, Bonaparte issued his own declaration to the National Assembly on May 25.[92]

It should have been a war that Whitehall also would not have wanted at that time, for now Britain stood alone. Diplomats hurriedly dispatched to Vienna, Berlin, St. Petersburg, and Lisbon with pleas for them to join another coalition against France were gently rebuffed. None of those governments saw a vital national interest threatened that justified war.

Meanwhile, Bonaparte swiftly mustered the forces of France and his satellites. He ordered the reoccupation of the Neapolitan ports of Brindisi, Otranto, and Taranto, and massed an army around Boulogne on the English Channel. Yet none of those forces could strike the enemy as long as Britain commanded the sea. At best the armies of France and its allies might intimidate states on the continent from siding with Britain; at worst they might provoke those states into war. For the present there was only one way the First Consul could hurt Britain. He issued hundreds of licenses to privateers, who would reap a rich harvest of British merchant ships. Yet although the damage they inflicted was ever more painful to Britain's economy, it could never be fatal. And all along British privateers and warships would gut the even more vulnerable merchant ships of France and its allies, as well as those of neutral countries with suspicious cargos and destinations. It would be a prolonged, indecisive, pinprick type of war that drained the strength from both sides.

That was unacceptable for a man always impatient to land a crushing blow against his enemies. Not long after his war declaration he decided to try to mount expeditions against Britain. He reasoned that he had little to lose and potentially much to gain, especially if he got his allies to share the costs. Under the Franco-Batavian Convention signed on June 25, 1803, the Dutch reluctantly agreed to supply two French expeditions, one with five ships of the line, five frigates, and transports for 25,000 troops, and the other with a score of warships and transports for 36,000 troops, 2,500 horses, and vast amounts of supplies. But Bonaparte had not yet decided where to send them.[93]

As those expeditions were being mobilized, Bonaparte found another target. His spy network picked up a diplomatic double game being played by Ferdinand IV and Marie Caroline of the Kingdom of the Two Sicilies. They had promised to remain neutral, yet were secretly negotiating with British and Russian envoys to join the latest coalition. That was quite a gamble to take, given the strength of French forces stationed in their own kingdom as well as elsewhere across Italy, and the weaknesses of their own army, finances, and administration.

Emotion rather than reason and the triumph of an iron-willed wife over her spineless husband best explains the policy. The queen had hated the French ever since they had imprisoned and eventually beheaded her younger sister, Marie Antoinette; thereafter she eagerly grabbed at any chance for vengeance. The royal couple's prime minister was John Acton, an English expatriate who retained his English patriotism; he never missed a chance to use his power to advance British interests, even at the expense of the royal house he served.

Bonaparte knew that the queen was the power behind the king. Several times he posted them separate letters on the same day, with his message to Marie Caroline far blunter than his to Ferdinand. His July 28, 1803, letter to the queen was a thinly veiled ultimatum: "I see a man heading your government who is foreign to your country and whose policies serve English interests. . . . I have thus decided . . . to consider Naples as a country governed by an English minister."[94] He insisted that she expel Acton and let more French troops march across her territory to reinforce those already there. Although she angrily bowed to the demands, she secretly kept plotting with the English and Russians.

A similar intrigue was being played out in Madrid. Charles IV certainly had good cause for complaint. In selling Louisiana to the Americans, Bonaparte had broken the 1800 Treaty of Ildefonso and the 1801 Treaty of Aranjuez with Spain, which had forbidden that very act. And now Bonaparte was trying to squeeze a commitment from Charles to ally openly against the British and Portuguese, based on the 1796 Treaty of Ildefonso which formed an alliance between France and Spain. The king did not want to provoke anyone, especially Bonaparte. Instead it was Manuel de Godoy, his chief minister, who pushed him over the edge. As usual, Godoy's loyalties were available to the highest bidder; this time it was the British who won the bid by filling his pockets with enough gold. He got the king to mobilize his army and 100,000 militiamen, seize French ships anchored in Spanish harbors, and suspend subsidy payments to Paris required under their alliance treaties and subsequent agreements.

Bonaparte put Talleyrand to work convincing Madrid to reverse course. The foreign minister warned Godoy that a French army of 80,000 men would invade Spain by September if Charles IV did not agree to pay 24 million francs that he already owed that year and an additional 72 million francs the following year, release all French ships and crews that had been seized, break all diplomatic and trade relations with Britain, confiscate all British ships then in Spanish harbors, and attack Gibraltar and Portugal. With Godoy acting as his backbone, Charles demurred.[95]

That prompted Bonaparte to fire off a letter to Charles on September 18, 1803, in which he detailed all the French complaints against Spain and demanded that the king fulfill his treaty duties. In a tactic typical of his diplomacy, he at once tried to save the sovereign's face by pointing to a scapegoat within his government who was causing all the problems, while chiding him for allowing someone to seize his power: "In effect, if your Majesty permits me to say it to him, all of Europe is afflicted with indignity at the assumptions that the Prince of Peace [Godoy] has usurped. . . . It is him who is the true king of Spain."[96] Charles finally caved in to Bonaparte's pressure, and negotiations began. On October 19, 1803, the Treaty of Paris committed Spain to pay France six million francs a month and restore all that had been confiscated, in return for neutrality.

Although war had been declared and armies and navies mobilized, no fighting had yet occurred. Tsar Alexander sent envoys to London and Paris with a sweeping peace proposal. All six European great powers would recognize France's annexations since 1792. Russia would occupy Malta for a decade and then return its rule to the Knights of St. John. Britain would be appeased with the island of Lampedusa from the Kingdom of Sardinia, which would be compensated with land on the Italian mainland. Britain and France would have to return all the merchant ships each had seized. France would have to withdraw all its troops from Italy, Switzerland, and Holland. A congress of Europe's great powers would convene to resolve all outstanding differences. Tragically, neither London nor Paris was willing to accept that sensible compromise.[97]

Word in the summer of 1803 that the Irish might be on the verge of revolt gave the First Consul a potential target for one of the two expeditions he was organizing. To Irish exile leaders he promised to land 25,000 troops—if 20,000 rebels joined them against the British. Much as the Irish would have liked to make such a promise, they could not in good faith do so. That expedition was postponed indefinitely.

The year ended without any fighting on any front other than skirmishes on the high seas. Armies massed but had no place to march. The most interesting maneuvers were those of diplomats and spies in various capitals. A grand compromise that restored the fragile peace was still possible, if unlikely.

George III buried that possibility during his 1804 New Year's address to Parliament, in which he essentially committed Britain to a crusade to restore the Bourbons to power in France. Although Addington and most of his cabinet were aghast at the notion, they did not repudiate the king's words; instead they worked toward his stated end by the only means at their disposal. In a covert action Whitehall code-named "the factory," British agents worked with royalist agents to organize a coup against Bonaparte's rule.[98] The plot included the defector General Jean Charles Pichegru, Chouan leader Georges Cadoudal, and Charles, the Count of Artois and younger brother of the future Louis XVIII. A British warship would land Cadoudal, Pichegru, and a dozen others in Brittany, where they would be met by local rebels. The conspirators would then head to Paris, where they would try to enlist ambitious generals such as Moreau and Bernadotte in a coup that would kill Bonaparte, take power, and bring the Bourbons back to rule within a constitutional monarchy.

Word of that plot soon reached Paris; the French exile community in London and elsewhere was riddled with spies. Mehee de la Touche proved to be among police minister Joseph Fouche's best agents. He was accepted into the cabal and sent to Munich, where British spymaster Francis Drake gave him papers and hurried him to Paris. Upon reaching the capital he immediately reported to Fouche before disappearing into the underground. Fouche fed Touche a series of carefully doctored documents designed to confuse the British about Bonaparte's power and intentions. The reports pleased Drake, who passed on to Touche more details of the plot.

Cadoudal, Pichegru, and their men reached Paris in January 1804. On January 28 Cadoudal and Pichegru met with Moreau on the Boulevard de Madeleine. Although Moreau refused to join their plot, he did swear to keep it secret. That same day, acting on Touche's information, the police arrested a conspirator who soon confessed names and safehouses. The next arrest came on February 8 when the police nabbed one of Cadoudal's underlings. That interrogation revealed yet more crucial names and safehouses. Over the next few weeks a small army of police spread out across the city and eventually rounded up Pichegru, Cadoudal, Moreau, and 356 others. The subsequent interrogations reaped scores of confessions and accusations. That led Bonaparte to order his officials to cast the net for émigré plotters beyond France to Munich, Freiburg, Hamburg, Zurich, and other cities. His most immediate success was to get Maximilien Joseph of Bavaria to expel Drake.

The trial lasted from May 28 to June 10. With a small mountain of evidence and 150 witnesses, its results were not in doubt. Of the forty-five formally charged with being part of the conspiracy, twenty-five were convicted and the rest acquitted. Cadoudal was among twenty who were executed for treason on June 28. Pichegru would have joined them had he made it to trial; he was strangled in his cell on May 25, most likely by suicide. Moreau was among five who received lesser sentences. Bonaparte would eventually pardon and release Moreau into a life-long banishment from France. Moreau would repay Bonaparte's mercy by eventually becoming an advisor to the coalition. He would be killed at Leipzig in October 1813.

The crackdown on royalists did not end with the trials in Paris. Among the exiles fingered in the conspiracy was Louis Antoine Henri de Bourbon Conde, Duke Enghien, who was living just across the frontier in Ettenheim, Baden.[99] Enghien had served with Louis, Duke Conde, and his army of exiles, which had been disbanded as part of the Amiens treaty. It only made sense to snatch the most accessible and highest-ranking Bourbon, whose chateau had been revealed to be a link in the royalist chain of spies and assassins. The more that were brought to justice, the more the ring would be disrupted, discouraged, and intimidated, and thus the more secure would be France and Bonaparte's life.

The Council of State made that decision on March 10. Bonaparte at first hesitated. It was Talleyrand, backed by Lebrun, Real, Murat, and Regnier (only Cambaceres demurred) who talked him into approving the operation. Talleyrand secretly warned Charles Frederick, Duke Baden, that a contingent of French troops would arrest Enghien, along with General Charles Dumouriez, who was said to be lurking there with him. (The "rendition" of terrorist suspects with the host government's secret nod and later public denial is hardly a recent practice.)[100]

Bonaparte had his aide, General Armand de Caulaincourt, and General Michel Orderer carry out the raid with several hundred dragoons and gendarmes. They crossed the Rhine in pontoon boats on the night of March 15, nabbed Enghien, eleven other suspects, and a trove of documents, and hustled them back over the border. While the other suspects were interrogated in Strasbourg, the prime catch was brought directly to Vincennes Castle just outside Paris on the night of March 20.

So far, so good—but there was a problem. The charges against Enghien may not have won a conviction in a fair trial. There was no doubt that he was on the British payroll and a part of the web striving for a Bourbon restoration. Yet he vociferously denied any knowledge of the recent conspiracy in Paris. The evidence was ambiguous, and any finding of his guilt would hardly be beyond a reasonable doubt. So the decision was made to try Enghien by a secret court martial of seven generals rather than via a public criminal trial. He was found guilty and executed on the early morning of March 21.

As Talleyrand was later said to have remarked, "It was worse than a crime, it was a blunder." The news of Enghien's summary execution shocked all the courts of Europe. Although Bonaparte would defend that decision, it haunted him politically and perhaps emotionally for the rest of his days. After all, Bonaparte had let off Moreau, who had actually met in Paris with Cadoudal and Pichegru, and yet he accepted the commission's judgment that Enghien was somehow guilty of a capital offense. Years later on St. Helena, he declared that "I had Enghien arrested and judged because it was necessary for the security, interests, and honor of the French people. . . . In the same circumstances, I would act the same." But at the time, his stepdaughter Hortense de Beauharnais heard him mutter, "It was a useless crime."[101]

The news of the execution certainly tainted Bonaparte's diplomacy. Although only Britain, Russia, and Sweden issued official condemnations, France's relations with most states suffered to varying degrees. Yet each state, when forced to choose, tended to put its concrete interests before its principles.

For instance, Prussia's King Frederick William simply wanted to avoid getting caught up in the swelling wave toward war which seemed to be surging across the continent. So the king used the execution as an excuse to end talks over a possible alliance with France. Yet he was careful not to alienate Bonaparte. When the would-be Louis XVIII on June 6 issued a proclamation calling on all the crowned heads of Europe to overthrow Bonaparte and restore the Bourbons, Frederick William expelled him and his followers from Warsaw. Once again that peripatetic court needed a new home; it eagerly accepted an offer from Swedish King Gustav IV to occupy a chateau at Kalmar.

Russia's tsar Alexander did officially express his indignation. The First Consul retorted with a protest at the tsar's embrace of émigrés at his court, the advice of some in his council, and even his employment of a few as diplomats and spies. But the atmosphere between Paris and St. Petersburg had been worsening for months anyway. As if the array of geopolitical issues were not grounds enough for acrimony, the relationship was further fouled by personal animosity between Talleyrand and Russian ambassador Arkadi Markov. The First Consul finally yielded to Talleyrand's complaints by expelling Markov. For the present Alexander did not appoint a successor.

The tsar made a personnel change of his own that would affect relations with Paris. He retired with honors his aged chancellor, Alexander Vorontsov, who sought to avoid an unnecessary war with France. He replaced him with his childhood friend, the Polish patriot Adam Czartoryski. Czartoryski was among the most influential among those urging Alexander to become a "moral force" in European diplomacy by resisting French ambitions and championing Polish liberties under Russian suzerainty. It was Czartoryski who had urged the tsar to issue, on April 17, a condemnation of France and order that his court go into a period of mourning. Furthermore, if Paris did not issue some sort of apology, Russia's chargé d'affairs, Pavel Oubril, was promptly to return to St. Petersburg. Although Talleyrand's assurance that Enghien was a British agent did not convince Oubril, he chose to remain in Paris for the present.[102]

So often Bonaparte disrupted his own diplomacy by letting his passions overwhelm his reason. The tsar's condemnation filled him with indignation. He could have sent Alexander a personal letter in which he explained his decision with conciliatory words. Instead he had Talleyrand write a stinging rebuttal and had it published in *Le Moniteur*, the government's semi-official newspaper. The most damning content accused Alexander of hypocrisy, given his participation in the overthrow and murder of his own father. That may have been true, but it did not serve French interests to blare it so publicly.[103]

Those were fighting words to Alexander. He fired off an appeal to Francis of Austria for an alliance between them against France, and promised to bring 100,000 Russian troops into the field. Francis too was appalled by Enghien's execution, but, like Frederick William of Prussia, was not prepared to war over it. Austria was still recovering from its most recent defeat at the hands of Bonaparte; for the present, few Austrians were eager to give him another chance to repeat his performance. Francis offered a defensive alliance.

That was not good enough for Alexander. He turned to Prussia for an offensive alliance. Like Francis, Frederick William gently declined that offer, but would accept a defensive alliance, although the conditions he presented were designed to force the tsar to reject them. If Russia committed 50,000 troops and got Saxony, Denmark, and all the other German states into the coalition, then Prussia would join. As expected, the tsar dismissed that notion.

Learning of the tsar's efforts, Bonaparte had Talleyrand issue a tough message to Russian envoy Oubril. The letter listed all Russian violations of the treaty and other understandings between them, and demanded that Alexander adhere to its commitments. Bonaparte gave the tsar a face-saving way out by identifying former Russian ambassador Markov as "the true author of the disunion and the cold relations which exist between our two states. During his time in Paris, he constantly stirred up all sorts of intrigues which could exist against the public tranquility . . . from the French émigrés and other agents in

England's pocket." The letter concluded: "The French emperor wants peace on the continent; he has done all that he could to reestablish peace with Russia; he has spared nothing to maintain it, but, with the aid of God and his arms, he fears no one."[104]

Neither his inability to get allies nor Bonaparte's warning cowed Alexander. If Russia had to fight alone, so be it. He issued a demand that France withdraw from Hanover and the Neapolitan ports and compensate the King of Sardinia for annexing Piedmont and Savoy. After getting Bonaparte's angry dismissal of those demands, the tsar severed diplomatic relations on September 15.

The ultimatum stirred Bonaparte to initiate his next stage for Germany's reorganization. On August 25 he dispatched Talleyrand on a diplomatic journey through the German states to rally them as allies. The foreign minister's itinerary included Aachen, Cologne, Bonn, Coblenz, Mainz, and Trier. He would gather all the foreign ministers and as many sovereigns as possible to meet at Mainz in September. Although most of the German foreign ministers appeared, Bonaparte was disappointed to find that no sovereigns showed up at the congress. Nonplused, he proposed that the states combine in what would be known as the Rhine Confederation under French protection. The proposal stunned most of the leaders. Essentially, he was asking them to exchange their shelter under either Prussian or Austrian hegemony for French hegemony. Yet for a few that made perfect sense. Why not ally as a junior partner with the most powerful state on the continent? But most foreign ministers sidestepped any action by citing the need to consult with their respective sovereigns. So Bonaparte appealed directly to the princes.[105]

Bavaria's chancellor, Maximilian Monteglas, embraced the idea and urged his counterparts to do the same. Bonaparte then, typically, went too far. In addition to the Rhine Confederation, he offered an offensive alliance with Bavaria against Austria, with himself in command of the combined armies. Monteglas insisted on a defensive alliance and autonomy for the Bavarian army. They shelved the idea for the present, but eventually Napoleon's version would prevail.[106]

Word of Bonaparte's German diplomatic offensive tipped the balance from the peace to the war faction in Vienna. Francis acceded to the consensus among his advisors that he should seek a defensive alliance with Russia. Alexander agreed, and they consummated that idea with a treaty on November 4, 1804.

The work of those diplomats was accelerated after news arrived of Bonaparte's latest provocation. On October 24 a French detachment marched into Hamburg and arrested Britain's envoy, Sir George Rumbold, confiscated all his documents, and hustled the haul back across the Elbe. That violation of diplomatic immunity outraged not just the British but virtually everyone.

The abduction was especially a slap in the face to the Prussians, who still considered Hamburg part of their sphere of influence. The British and Russian ambassadors at Berlin urged Frederick William to protest the violation. During a meeting of his state council on October 30, the king agreed to send a tough letter to Bonaparte demanding the envoy's immediate release; to back that demand the Prussian army would be mobilized. Bonaparte defused the crisis by releasing Rumbold—without, however, his papers, which were an intelligence bonanza for France. He also sent a conciliatory letter to Frederick William in which he justified the rendition as a reaction to English provocations. He called for continued good relations between France and Prussia. To the disappointment of the British, Russians, and Austrians, Frederick William ordered his troops to stand down. Foreign Minister Karl von Hardenburg justified the decision with the quip that Prussia would not go to war over "a box of papers."[107]

By now France and Britain had officially been at war for over eighteen months. Yet, other than desultory actions at sea, not a battle had been fought. That began to change after Henry Addington resigned and King George III asked William Pitt on May 18 to once again be his prime minister. Pitt was eager to strike France; but the question, as always, was how. He finally decided to launch an attack on Spain, which he was sure was to convert its defensive alliance with France into an offensive one in the near future. He issued an ultimatum that Madrid repudiate its alliance and subsidiary treaties with France. When Charles IV refused, Pitt decided to initiate war against Spain without a formal declaration. He ordered a squadron to attack Spain's annual treasure fleet as it approached Cadiz in October. During the battle the British sank the flagship, but captured three other ships packed with silver. Once coined, all that silver would help subsidize Britain's war effort.

Despite that enormous loss, Charles IV did not immediately declare war on Britain. He knew that if he did so the British would swiftly sweep the seas of Spanish ships and capture one by one its most vulnerable colonies. So the king protested the unprovoked attack and demanded that Britain compensate Spain for its losses. The British replied with a blockade of Spanish naval bases at Cadiz, Port Mahon, and Ferrol. Even then, despite the urging of the French, Charles IV did not declare war until December 12. It would be another month of negotiations before Talleyrand was able to work out the details of an offensive alliance between France and Spain with Ambassador Don Frederico Gravina, which they signed into a treaty on January 4, 1805.

Emperor and King

The crowned heads of Europe had yet another reason to hate Napoleon Bonaparte: from May 18, 1804, he pretended to be one of them. On that day the Senate proclaimed him Emperor Napoleon I. That was the first formal step. It would take another half year, until November 6, before the French people's "will" was determined. According to the plebiscite's announced "vote" of 3,572,329 to 2,569, 99.993 percent of the French wanted him to be their emperor. Although the exact figures will never be known, it is quite likely that most had voted for him. At that point and for the next couple of years, his popularity apparently peaked. So he was being quite truthful when he claimed that "I did not usurp the Crown. I picked it out of a ditch and the people placed it on my head."[108]

That would not be the only crown that he was promised in 1804. On May 7, eleven days before the Senate vote, a delegation from the Republic of Italy led by Foreign Minister Ferdinando Marescalchi petitioned him to let them transform their republic into a kingdom over which he would serve as their monarch. The petition was, of course, no surprise to the emperor; he had secretly planted the seed and nurtured it over the preceding months.

Napoleon promptly agreed to their first request. The Republic of Italy was transformed into the Kingdom of Italy on May 28, 1804. As for becoming their king, to avoid the appearance of having too voracious an appetite for power, Napoleon spent three months directing a diplomatic charade in which he played coy to the idea. He first asked his brother Joseph and then his stepson Eugene de Beauharnais to accept that crown. They faithfully followed the script and refused an honor that only Napoleon himself was worthy of fulfilling. The emperor feigned reluctance to become Italy's king, but promised to do so at some point the following year. For the present he was too busy preparing for his coronation as the Emperor of France.[109]

The ceremony he wanted for the coronation on December 2, 1804, demanded deft diplomacy. Napoleon increasingly saw himself as, and justified his policies as those of, a Charlemagne for modern times. Like his hero, he was not only trying to reorganize and unify Europe, but wanted to legitimize his ambitions with a papal blessing. For that he hoped to do his esteemed predecessor one better: Charlemagne had journeyed all the way to Rome to be crowned by the pope; if all went according to plan, Pius VII would journey all the way to Paris to bless Napoleon as he crowned himself.

And that was what happened, although it took some hard bargaining to pull it off. In July 1803 Napoleon sent his uncle, Cardinal Joseph Fesch, to Rome, where he spent the next four months trying to talk secretary of state Cardinal Consalvi into the idea. Rome had gotten little and given much in the Concordat. Fesch promised that after the coronation Napoleon would be amenable to making generous concessions to the Church, but ones he could not commit to until he had amassed all the legitimacy granted by a papal blessing as he received the imperial crown. That would soften the hardened hearts of the French toward Rome, and they would welcome the return of the Church to its former prominent status in their nation. And France would be only the first step. Papal power would soon after be restored to the Kingdom of Italy and other Catholic satellites. How could Consalvi say no to such promises? Napoleon tried to break the impasse by writing to Pius with the promise "to submit all that you propose to the most scrupulous examination."[110]

Relations with Rome remained a sticky issue for diehard revolutionaries within the government, such as Talleyrand and Fouche, and prominent people throughout Parisian society. So Bonaparte had to tread a diplomatic tightrope between granting the pope all the protocol due him, while asserting all the splendor and power of his throne and the nation he led. So all the minute details of dress, words, gestures, and positions of all official meetings and ceremonies had to be choreographed beforehand.

One other diplomatic matter—this one initiated by Josephine—was raised shortly after Pius and his entourage of five cardinals, two Roman princes, four bishops, and 97 prelates and lesser officials packed into a cavalcade of ornate carriages clattered into the courtyard of Fontainebleau Palace on November 25. The empress convinced the pope to back her in an issue that had become ever more important to her over the years, as her husband's powers grew and her apparent ability to bear him a child dwindled to the vanishing point. She rightfully feared that one day she would have to yield her crown and husband to a more fertile empress and wife. Their marriage had only been a short civil ceremony. Josephine convinced Pius not to bless the coronation unless she and Napoleon were married within the Church. The pontiff eagerly agreed. That news irritated the emperor, who had indeed been agonizing over whether he should find a fecund royal womb that could produce an imperial heir.[111]

Outflanked by his wife and facing the pope's unassailable position, Napoleon had no choice but to yield, at least partially. The night before the coronation Cardinal Fesch married them in a private ceremony. Only Talleyrand and Berthier were present, but they pointedly did not sign the register as legal witnesses. That, Napoleon hoped, would give him a legal loophole to wiggle through, if need be.

The ceremony at Notre Dame Cathedral, crammed with a thousand high officials, officers, and other supporters of the new imperial regime, was a dream come true for Napoleon and Josephine. At the decisive moment, Napoleon raised the crown from a pillow on the altar, turned his back on the pope and, facing the audience, placed it on his own head. He then did the same for Josephine. Following acclamations from the Legislative Corps, Tribunate, and Senate, Napoleon swore to uphold and defend the constitution.

After all the diplomacy that it had taken to bring Pius there, he was merely the closest spectator. Napoleon wanted him near enough to confer an air of legitimacy, but not near enough to seem superior. For Napoleon to don his own crown certainly asserted his independence. And the idea that the pope was there to consecrate, not crown, the emperor had already been worked out.

Having gotten what he wanted, Napoleon had no need to concede anything important. Pius lingered in Rome for another four months, pleading with Napoleon to make Catholicism the state religion, outlaw divorce, increase state subsidies to the Church, return Church property, let the Church educate the young, and restore the Papal Legations and papal enclaves of Avignon and Venassin. The emperor did no more than toss him a few diplomatic bones: a jewel-studded tiara, a small endowment to repair the crumbling Lateran Palace, laws that restricted work on Sundays, and the abandonment of the revolutionary calendar and return to a standard year with Sundays an official day of rest, starting on January 1, 1805. A disappointed, weary, and humiliated Pius finally left Paris on April 4, 1805; he was well aware that Parisian wits derided him as the "imperial chaplain."[112]

The pope's failed mission made him the butt of jokes among a cruel few. In contrast, the excessive pomp and pretension of Napoleon's coronation may have dazzled most French, but they provoked scorn and fear across the rest of Europe. For Europe's crowned heads, France's revolution, which had murdered a royal couple along with thousands of other nobles and championed universal ideals of republicanism, had been terrifying enough. Compounding that was the ability of some minor noble from a remote island to fight and finagle his way to an imperial crown. If that could happen in France, what prevented it from happening elsewhere?

Indeed, a vital part of Napoleon's diplomacy over the next decade would consist of imposing himself or his brothers and even a brother-in-law on thrones across the continent. The first would be for Napoleon to accept the Iron Crown of Lombardy, presented by the Kingdom of Italy on May 26, 1805. This time Pius refused to preside over the coronation. The decision on January 26, 1805, by the kingdom's vice-president, Melzi d'Eril, to suspend key tenets of the 1803 Concordat with Rome and re-inaugurate secular laws provoked a crisis. Pius, however, did allow Cardinal Caprara to be with Napoleon when he was crowned in Milan's cathedral.

In his acceptance speech, Napoleon tried at once to allay fears that he was amassing too much power and hint that his ambitions were hardly fulfilled. He promised to uphold the "separation of the crowns of France and Italy"; and he said, "I will see with pleasure the arrival of the moment when I can place it on a younger head than mine, animated with my spirit, continuing my work, and always ready to sacrifice himself and his interests for the security and happiness of the people."[113]

For the present, only Britain and Sweden dared not recognize the new emperor and king. The other governments trembled at his power, and eventually acquiesced to his rule. Francis of Austria was among those who sent him a letter of congratulations upon his coronation. For Napoleon that was an especially welcome surprise. With his coronation as the Emperor of France, he had claimed the crown of Charlemagne—which the Habsburgs had considered their own for several centuries. Also, in taking the Iron Crown of Lombardy, he had violated the Treaty of Luneville.

It had taken two letters from Napoleon to Francis to secure his approval. While he also extolled the virtues of peace and condemned the horrors of war, the heart of his letters was an attempt to get Francis to recognize Napoleon's pending coronation as the King of Italy. He claimed that the Italian crown had been thrust upon him, and that only duty forced him "to carry such a heavy burden." He tried to put the event of a French emperor becoming an Italian king in an historical context with other kings, including Francis, who wore two crowns. He promised not to unite his two kingdoms into one. With his dedication to peace, Francis need fear nothing. Finally, he asked for help in expelling the British from Malta and the Russians from the Ionian (Seven Island) Republic. While Francis spurned the alliance offer, he not only recognized Napoleon's latest coronation, but was so inspired by the example that he would promote himself from the King to the Emperor of Austria in August 1805.[114]

The new King of Italy had no sooner taken the throne than he embarked on his latest whirlwind of action to transform that realm from feudalism to modernism. He adjusted the constitution, laws, and administration to reinforce his new powers as king. He reinforced the subjection of the church to the state with new laws, including one allowing civil divorce; consolidated and reorganized the parishes so that they were fewer in number and more equal in population; shut down most monasteries and convents; and banned most religious orders. To rule Italy when he was away, he named his stepson Eugene to be his viceroy; to reinforce the viceroy's status, he began looking for a royal princess to be his bride.[115] Finally, and most controversially of all, on June 4, 1805, he accepted a petition by the Ligurian Republic to be annexed—not to Italy, but to France itself.

To a letter from Pius condemning those actions, Napoleon issued this revealing reply: "My intention has been to better everything....The Court of Rome is very slow and follows a policy which, although good for past centuries, is not adapted to the century in which we live. I beg your Holiness to immerse himself in the spirit which animates the Italian people." Although the emperor regretted the destruction and nationalization of Church property, he could not afford financially or politically to restore the past.[116]

The 1805 Campaign

As the year 1805 dawned, only one major irritant clouded Napoleon's heady joy at holding ultimate power. Much against his preference, France and Britain were still at war. It all seemed so senseless; neither side had the power decisively to defeat the other. Since Britain had declared war nearly two years earlier in May 1803, the only military actions had been isolated naval engagements. The diplomatic battles, however, were as heavy as the military battles were sporadic. The French and British daily dueled in tugs-of-war for loyalties in courts and chancelleries across Europe. As yet neither side had gained a notable edge; that would change this year.

Napoleon longed to end the war and concentrate on governing. He had opened the new year by writing to his fellow monarch George III a sincere and rather plaintive appeal for peace: "My brother, called to the throne of France by

Providence and the demands of the Senate, people, and army, my first sentiment is a vow of peace. France and England are wasting their prosperity. They can struggle for centuries. . . . And so much blood spilled uselessly. . . . I attach no dishonor to taking the first step for peace. . . . What do you hope to gain from going to war?. . . The world is big enough for our two nations to share, and reason is powerful enough for one to find a means to reconcile if each of us has the will."[117] But the king remained figuratively and literally deaf to the emperor's reason; Napoleon never received a reply.

In the international struggle for hearts and minds, the British occupied a far stronger diplomatic position than Napoleon. In early 1805 Whitehall redoubled its efforts to entice other great powers, with promises of gold and other concessions, into the latest grand coalition against France. St. Petersburg was the first to enlist. Envoys signed on April 11, 1805, a treaty by which Russia would field 100,000 troops in return for a British promise of 1,250,000 pounds sterling and eventual withdrawal from Malta. Impressive as that deal may have seemed, it was essentially meaningless unless some way were found to actually deploy those troops against the French in battle. While the British and Russians mulled various joint naval expeditions, they could cram only so many troops into the available transports, and then safely land them only at sites far from concentrations of France's swift-marching troops. Instead, the most practical way to employ all those Russians would be to send them through the territory of an ally such as Austria, Prussia, or, ideally, both.

The news that Napoleon had annexed the Ligurian Republic and divided it into three new French departments pushed Austria into the coalition. Francis promised to contribute 235,000 troops to the coalition if the Russians increased their contingent to 180,000. Alexander agreed.

If the coalition could then enlist Prussia, it would field armies so vast that they would overwhelm anything that even Napoleon's military genius could muster against it. At best the French would have to fight a delaying action on the Rhine and then fall back as superior allied armies crossed at various points up and down stream. So Napoleon wrote to Frederick William several letters during 1805, offering him Hanover in return for his neutrality, and in August sent his aide Gerard Duroc to elaborate his plea for peace. To the emperor's relief, the king for now dismissed offers to add the Prussian army to the coalition.[118]

Several minor powers did join the coalition. Sweden, in a treaty signed on August 31, promised to contribute 12,000 troops, and its Baltic islands of Rugen and Stralsund as staging areas. The even more minor realms of the

Kingdom of Sardinia and Electorate of Hanover also pledged to do what they could. Ferdinand IV and Marie Caroline of the Kingdom of the Two Sicilies typically played a double game. They secretly agreed to let the allies land and march through its territory, in a treaty signed on September 10, and then pledged their neutrality in a treaty with France on September 22.

Ferdinand and Marie Caroline were well aware of the potentially disastrous consequences of their perfidy, should Napoleon defeat the alliance. The emperor's spies kept him well informed of most intrigues in the Naples court. Just after the new year of 1805 he had greeted each monarch with a letter; he filled that for the queen with blunt accusations: "I have in my hands several letters of Your Majesty which leave no doubt of your true secret intentions. Why does Your Majesty appear to harbor such a hatred for France . . . ? Your Majesty, who seems to have a spirit so notable among women . . . can she treat affairs of state as if they were affairs of the heart?" Napoleon went on to remind her: "She has already lost her kingdom one time; twice she has been the cause of a war which brought ruin from top to bottom of her paternal home; does she therefore want to be the cause of a third?" He urged her to break with Britain. If she refused to do so, he warned that "the first war that she causes, she and her posterity will have ceased to reign; her children will be rendered beggars across the countries of Europe."[119]

As war with Austria and Russia seemed ever more likely, Napoleon stepped up his diplomacy toward the Turkish Sultan and Persian Shah. He told the Ottoman ambassador that the Porte "would lose itself through weakness" unless it stood up to the Russians and Austrians, who were determined to take European Turkey. He wrote Selim III a formal request that he curtail Russian influence in his capital, close the straits against Russian warships, and form an alliance with France. After lauding him with flowery language, he then ended his letter by chiding him: "You, descendent of the grand Ottomans, emperor of one of the great empires of the world, have you ceased to reign?"[120] The Sultan chose to stay neutral, but tilted toward the coalition by agreeing in September to allow the Russian fleet to sail freely through the straits.

Perhaps the most unusual and unique among Napoleon's letters to his fellow heads of state was that sent to the Persian Shah. Inexplicably, he wrote it in familiar rather than formal French. His opening line to the king is curious enough: "I have everywhere agents who inform me on all that is important to know." Assuming that he has gotten the king's attention, he next relates what he believes he knows about Persian affairs, and then boasts of French power. All that is a very circular way of preparing to ask for a commercial and strategic alliance: "All peoples have need of one another. The men of the Orient have courage and ingenuity; but ignorance of certain arts and negligence of certain disciplines. . . . If we work in concert we will render our peoples more powerful, rich, and happy." He elaborated his views six weeks later: "I must believe that the genies who preside over the destiny of states demand that I second the efforts that you make to assure the power of your empire, because, at the same time, our spirits have been striking us with the same thoughts. . . . Persia is the most noble country in Asia. France is the premier empire of the West." An alliance between them could not be more natural or mutually beneficial.[121] Napoleon would receive a favorable reply—but it would take two years to reach him.

Napoleon was not one to sit tight and await his enemies. He had massed most of the French army in camps centered at Boulogne on the English Channel to intimidate, and ideally invade, Britain. Yet that was a fruitless effort: as long as His Majesty's fleet commanded the Channel, Napoleon would be prevented from crossing. That did not deter the emperor. He had devised and revised a series of elaborate schemes to send out French naval squadrons in various directions to draw off the British fleet long enough for those 167,000 troops, 9,149 horses, scores of cannon, and thousands of tons of munitions and provisions to be loaded into 2,343 vessels, including 1,016 flatboats, and rowed across the Channel.[122]

Spain was an important part of Napoleon's plan. Throughout 1805 he expended enormous diplomatic efforts on Charles IV. First, he sought and eventually got Charles to agree to joint operations of the French and Spanish fleets against the British navy, and to send the Spanish army against Portugal if it did not sever its economic and military ties with Britain. He then spent as much time trying to ensure that Charles did not renege on the deal. His own letters to Charles were pep talks that appealed to the king's sense of honor and sovereign duties as well as Spanish interests.[123]

Meanwhile, Napoleon tried to convince John, Portugal's regent, to live up to his promises made in the 1801 Treaty of Badajoz by breaking all military and trade ties with Britain and at least becoming neutral, but ideally by allying with France and Spain. That was easier demanded than done. Portugal and Britain had enjoyed a flourishing bilateral trade for centuries, and frequent alliances when faced with a mutual enemy. Since Napoleon took power he had issued periodic protests, both to Ambassador Souza and Prince Regent John, over the unofficial alliance with Britain and discrimination against, and at times outright harassment of, French merchants. The Portuguese replies were invariably polite but maddeningly noncommittal. To no avail, Bonaparte had warned in August 1803 that if French grievances were not overcome, he "would be obliged to consider the Portuguese administration governed not by the prince but by English influence", and thus he would be obliged to "make a severe example" of the realm. But the Portuguese dismissed that as an empty threat, given France's distance, the ineptness of its ally Spain, and the steadfastness of Portugal's ally Britain.[124]

To spearhead his diplomacy, Napoleon sent his aide Andoche Junot first to Spain and then on to Portugal. His instructions were typically very precise, outlining minute details about the days he should spend in each capital, the times he should meet with each minister, the points he should make, and how he should make them.[125] Junot's mission partly succeeded. He bolstered the alliance with Spain and accelerated planning for joint naval operations. Portugal, however, remained defiant.

Ultimately, Napoleon's diplomatic exertions with Spain and Portugal mattered little. Any alliance with Spain and neutrality with Portugal was intended to assist Napoleon's plan to invade England; and that plan was absolutely daft.

First of all, Britain's Channel Fleet would stay on station and fight all comers. Even in the unlikely event of the French fleet briefly driving it off, the longboats that the soldiers were supposed to row nearly twenty-five miles across the English Channel, with its treacherous tides, currents, and winds, were leaky, unwieldy, and low-slung; countless would sink, and countless heavily laden soldiers would drown long before they reached the other side. And even in the unlikely event of a sizable French army getting ashore, they would leave the empire denuded of most of its troops, and would eventually be cut off when the superior English fleet retook command of the Channel. The coalition armies, which spies reported were gathering to march first into Germany and then westward, would find very few French forces to oppose them.

Napoleon eventually bowed to those inescapable realities. On August 13 he wrote to Talleyrand that "I want to attack Austria and be in Vienna before November, and then square off with the Russians, if they present themselves." His foreign minister's job was to obscure that intention through talks. Yet "I prefer above all that Austria puts itself in a truly peaceful situation." So Talleyrand was to offer Francis peace—if he allied with France, evacuated the Tyrol, and sent home all his newly mobilized troops.[126]

While the emperor still hoped for peace with Austria, he began to prepare for war on August 24 when he issued radically changed plans to Louis Berthier, his chief of staff.[127] His new strategy was to force-march his "Grand Army" from the Channel toward Vienna and defeat the Austrians before the Russians could come to their rescue. To do so he first had to secure a free passage across the intervening realms. He set his diplomats to work. In return for promises of land and other booty, Bavaria's King Maximilien Joseph formally allied with France on August 24, Baden's Duke Charles Frederick on September 5, and Wurttemberg's Duke Frederick on October 5.

But a free passage to the Austrian frontier did not ensure peace of mind. Berlin was the greatest threat to Napoleon's strategy: all would be lost if the Prussians fell on his rear while he was marching against the Austrians and Russians down the Danube Valley. He sent his aide Christophe Duroc to Berlin to ask Frederick William for an alliance. The king demurred, but did agree to stay on the sidelines for the present.

Although none of the coalition partners would actually field the number of troops it promised, the total was nonetheless formidable. The plan was for Austrian General Karl Mack to overrun Bavaria with 72,000 troops and await a Russian army of 35,000 troops commanded by General Mikhail Kutuzov. To distract Napoleon, a Russo-Swedish army of 32,000 troops would march from Straslund to Hanover. Austrian Archduke John would invade the Kingdom of Italy with 22,000 troops. An armada packed with 25,000 Russians and 8,000 British would rendezvous at Corfu and then sail to Naples, from which they would march north to help liberate Italy.

The portion of that grand strategy which would unfold in Germany unwittingly played right into Napoleon's hands. By marching their armies piecemeal toward France, the allies subjected those armies to being defeated one by one by Napoleon. They appear to have recalled nothing about how swiftly the emperor could move and mass troops against his enemy's critical points.

Instead the allies, especially the Austrians, became bloated with a false sense of euphoria as Mack's conquest of Bavaria, beginning September 8, was quick and largely unopposed. On September 14 he captured Munich; Maximilien Joseph fled with his court and many of his troops to Wurzburg. Mack then marched his army to Ulm, where he awaited Austrian reinforcements and Kutuzov's Russians.

As Napoleon prepared the epic march that would take his army from the English Channel to the heart of Bavaria in a few weeks, he anxiously awaited word from Admiral Pierre Villeneuve, who commanded the fleet that had been intended to clear the Channel for a crucial few days. Either from ineptness, cowardice, or some mix of the two, Villeneuve had failed to fulfill each of the emperor's orders which caught up to him. After a battle with an English squadron in which he lost two ships, Villeneuve holed up his fleet at Ferrol and refused to budge. Upon learning his location, Napoleon sent him a command on July 26 to sail to Cadiz, combine with the Spanish fleet, and head north to the Channel. On August 11 Villeneuve weighed anchor for Cadiz—where he remained. On September 16 the emperor sent an order to Villeneuve demanding that he turn over his command to Admiral Rosily, who would then sail to Genoa rather than the Channel. Somehow Villeneuve got word informally of those orders. Determined to retain his command, he directed the thirty-three captains of the combined Franco-Spanish fleet to set sail. The resultant voyage would end at Trafalgar on October 21.

Leaving a 30,000-man observation corps on the coast, Napoleon issued orders on September 20 for seven infantry corps, the Imperial Guard, and a cavalry corps to set off on a huge arc across the middle Rhine and toward the Danube north and east of Mack. Joachim Murat's cavalry corps screened that advance and prevented the Austrians from knowing exactly where the French army was and where it was going. In Italy, meanwhile, Marshal Andre Massena and Eugene de Beauharnais would slow Archduke John's army along the Adige while awaiting the arrival of General Gouvion St. Cyr's 25,000 troops marching north from their garrisons in southern Italy.[128]

The emperor left St. Cloud for Germany on September 24. As his coach rapidly conveyed him toward his army, Napoleon was confident of victory. Having repeatedly defeated the Austrians in battle, he had no doubt that he would do so again. The question was, what sort of peace to impose on the vanquished? Guided by the idea that peace would be more enduring if it were gentle rather than harsh, he had been deliberately lenient in the treaties of Campo Formio in 1798 and Luneville in 1801. But the Austrians had returned his generosity with renewed aggression. This time he would insist on terms that sharply pared Vienna's power to make war, as Austria's losses would directly aggrandize France. That would deter not just the Austrians but other monarchs who did not want to suffer the same fate. He outlined his ideas to Talleyrand and asked him to incorporate them in his negotiations and the final treaty.

Napoleon's terms appalled Talleyrand, who clung to the notion that mild peaces endured the longest and best served French interests. Typically he remained tight-lipped as he listened. Among the attributes which made him a great diplomat was knowing when and how to respond to people with whom he disagreed. Certainly the worst time was when the other person was passionately expressing his position. Talleyrand would let that enthusiasm subside, drop a few hints that sowed doubts, and only later offer a systematic rebuttal.

And that was how he handled Napoleon's vision. In a memorandum he penned at Strasbourg on October 17, the foreign minister begged the emperor to reconsider. Yes indeed, Austria's latest belligerence should be punished. But those lands of Venetia, the Tyrol, Vorarlberg, the Adriatic littoral, and the rest of southwest Germany that Napoleon was determined to strip from Austria should go not to France but to satellites or client buffer states. Meanwhile, Napoleon should offer a painless compromise by promising to keep his two crowns separate during his lifetime, and then bequeathing them to different lineages. Finally, Talleyrand agreed with Napoleon that Austria should be encouraged to make up for its territorial losses in the west with gains in the east down the Danube Valley into Moldavia, Wallachia, Bessarabia, and Bulgaria, which would put Vienna in perpetual conflict with St. Petersburg and Constantinople.[129]

For the present, both visions of peace depended on the war's outcome. The initial phase of Napoleon's campaign unfolded almost perfectly according to his plan. By October 6 his corps had cut off Mack and caught him in a giant, killing vise. Over the next two weeks the French routed each Austrian attempt to break out. On October 18 Mack surrendered 27,000 troops and 60 cannons. That was the largest haul in the campaign's first phase, which altogether netted 60,000 prisoners of war. Napoleon then paused a few days to allow his footsore troops to rest, bring up reinforcements and supplies, learn how the Italian front was faring, and, most importantly, let his spies pass back intelligence of just where the other Austrian and Russian armies were located.[130]

Napoleon's victory at Ulm inspired him to embrace an even more grandiose vision for peace. When Talleyrand caught up to him at Munich on October 26, the emperor brusquely rejected his memorandum and related his vision to transform southern and central Germany from an Austrian into a French sphere of influence. He would at once aggrandize Bavaria, Baden, Wurttemberg, Hanover, and Saxony with territory and bind them as French satellites. Finally, in addition to all the lands and peoples he would strip from Vienna's rule, he would ally with Russia to deter Austrian aggression. Talleyrand again, for the present, bit his tongue at a scheme that he believed would entangle France in perpetual wars that could lead eventually to the downfall of them all.

Napoleon's vision depended on his ability to keep racking up decisive victories against his enemies. Of course, the odds of that happening depended on many things. Among those, perhaps the most vital was for Frederick William to keep his promise that Prussia would remain neutral.

The Prussian king remained the rope in an ongoing diplomatic tug-of-war between France and its enemies that had persisted for years. He preferred peace, but the allies and ever more of his ministers urged him to war against France. The British, as usual, were the most persuasive, as they gilded their reasons with gold—the king would get 250,000 pounds sterling upon signing a treaty of alliance, and 100,000 a month for the war's duration. Tsar Alexander, however, nearly nullified that deal when he issued a virtual ultimatum to Frederick William to allow the Russian army to cross Prussian territory. Frederick William responded by forbidding any violation of his realm, backed that stand by ordering his army to mobilize, and invited Alexander to a summit. Realizing his folly, the tsar apologized and accepted the invitation.

Napoleon committed the act which Alexander had been prudent enough to sidestep. He ordered Marshal Bernadotte to march his corps via a short-cut through the Prussian dependencies of Ansbach and Bayreuth. When Frederick William protested the invasion, Napoleon sent to him, on October 3, a short letter which acknowledged the violation and asked for the king's understanding. He soon began getting reports that Frederick William was enraged by the violation, and even more so at the perfunctory nature of Napoleon's letter. The emperor responded in two ways. First, he recalled Duroc on October 24, and had him deliver tough talk to the king as he departed. Then, three days later, he sent the king a long, mostly conciliatory letter in which he denied knowing anything about the intrusion before it happened, hoped that they could put the incident behind them, and presented the arguments for peace and alliance between them.[131]

Nonetheless, the Prussian king used that violation as an excuse to join the coalition. In a mystical, torch-lit meeting before the tomb of Frederick the Great at Potsdam on November 3, Frederick William, his strong-willed wife Louise, and Alexander pledged themselves to work toward Napoleon's eventual destruction. To that end, the king promised that in about a month, after his army had completed its preparations, he would issue Napoleon an unacceptable ultimatum, and upon receiving the inevitable rejection would declare war.

Napoleon, meanwhile, was heartened by good news from Italy. Massena and Eugene had crossed the Adige, defeated Archduke Charles at Caldiero on October 30, and then followed him into Carinthia. On November 3 Napoleon wrote to Francis that he was "ready to forget the injustice of this third war of aggression, and to try again a third treaty." But he would only accept peace if Francis immediately broke with his allies and forced the Russians to withdraw from Austrian territory. With his armies defeated on two fronts, Francis sent Napoleon a plea for an armistice. Napoleon welcomed the plea as a sign of desperation in Vienna; but in his reply he turned him down.[132]

Indeed, Napoleon was urging his corps to race down the Danube Valley after the retreating Austrian and Russian armies. Marshal Ney clipped the tail of Archduke John at Scharnitz on November 5. Marshal Adolphe Mortier blunted an attack by Kutuzov at Loiben on November 11, and General Gazan staved off another Russian attack at Durrenstein the same day. John and Kutuzov retreated toward Olmutz, where Alexander joined them. As the French neared Vienna, Francis and his court abandoned the city and fled to Olmutz as well. Murat's cavalry cantered into the undefended capital on November 13. Within a week much of the rest of the French army filed through Vienna to replenish their provisions and munitions from the captured Austrian stores, and then marched into Moravia.

Four problems darkened Napoleon's elation at the successful conclusion of his campaign's second phase. He received word of Villeneuve's devastating defeat by Admiral Horatio Nelson at the Battle of Trafalgar; in all, the French and Spanish had lost twenty-two ships. Trafalgar crushed Napoleon's dream of following up his eventual defeat of the Austrians and Russians with an invasion of Britain the following year. And then there was the reality that defeating the allies would be no easy matter. The two enemy armies hovering in the region—the 90,000 Austrians and Russians at Olmutz, and the 50,000 troops of Charles in Carinthia—outnumbered his own 75,000-man army, although for now they were widely separated while his army was concentrated. Finally, the news arrived of the perfidy of Ferdinand IV and Marie Caroline. On November 20 an allied army of 6,000 British, 11,000 Russians, and 1,600 Greek and Albanian militiamen had disembarked at Naples and was preparing to march north. Massena and Eugene would have to catch up to Charles and decisively defeat him before turning south to face that latest threat. But the most ominous problem was the mobilization of Prussia's 200,000-man army. Somehow Napoleon would have to destroy the Austrians and Russians at Olmutz before the Prussians entered the field.

Napoleon desperately needed time for a military victory. To gain that, he first needed a diplomatic victory. Frederick William unwittingly gave him that opportunity. The king felt that he could honorably withdraw from his promise of neutrality in return for Hanover only if Napoleon rejected his call for a general peace congress. So he sent one of his closest advisors, Christian von Haugwitz, with that ultimatum to the emperor. On November 28 Napoleon received Haugwitz, listened to the ominous message, and replied by both agreeing to a congress and repeating his previous requests for an alliance between France and Prussia. It would take time for Haugwitz to carry that message back to Frederick William, for the king and his ministers to forge a consensus on a reply, and then to convey that reply to Napoleon.[133]

As Frederick William was timidly tip-toeing toward war, Francis was ever more eager for peace on almost any terms. After all, he had lost an army and his capital, and feared that he would soon lose even more. He sent another envoy to Napoleon requesting an armistice, or even peace based on the previous Treaty of Luneville. Napoleon's answer was polite, but firmly the same as his previous letters—except now he would not enter any negotiations unless Francis promised to transfer Venetia to the Kingdom of Italy. And that would only be the first of his demands.[134]

Among Napoleon's strengths as a diplomat, as well as a general, was his ability to shift his strategy with circumstances.[135] He realized that Francis' reluctance to continue the war was as great as Alexander's enthusiasm to do so. He launched a diplomatic initiative that he hoped would have two effects. One was to widen the gulf between the two sovereigns; the other was for them to interpret his diplomacy as a sign of weakness that might eventually entice them to attack him. To those ends he dispatched to Olmutz General Jean Savary. There Savary first conferred privately with Francis and offered him essentially a return to the Treaty of Luneville—if he immediately agreed to ally with France. Savary then met with Russian Prince Pierre Dolgorouski and asked him to pass on Napoleon's request for a summit with Alexander.

Alexander and Francis interpreted Napoleon's initiative as he had intended. To Napoleon they sent Dolgorouski, who with deliberate arrogance demanded an armistice during which a treaty would be negotiated by which France abandoned Italy, the Rhineland, and Belgium. Although they knew he would reject those terms, they hoped that he would begin bargaining. They too were playing for time, so that the armies of Prussia and Charles would converge on Napoleon from different directions.

Napoleon pretended that he was eager for a deal, although not the one they demanded. He let Dolgorouski pass unblindfolded through his camp so that he could observe the French soldiers preparing for winter rather than battle, and gain the impression that he was seeing the entire diminished French army, rather than a few corps with the others camped a day or two's march away. To encourage an allied attack as soon as possible, the emperor warned the envoy that he was expecting reinforcements within a week or so. Finally, rather than react in kind, he displayed measured calm to Dolgorouski's bluster and demands that the emperor withdraw his army back to France.

The diplomacy and subterfuge worked perfectly. Without waiting for the Prussians or Charles, Alexander and Francis issued orders on November 29 for their troops to march swiftly against the French. Napoleon sent couriers galloping to his marshals to join the main army deployed along the Goldbach stream near the village of Austerlitz. To lure the enemy onward he even abandoned the Pratzen Heights east of that stream. Alexander and Francis eagerly took the bait. On the morning of December 2 the Russian and Austrian corps marched down into the valley and attacked the French line. The French repelled them with heavy losses. Napoleon ordered an attack on a gap in the enemy line. The French broke through, re-took the Pratzen Heights, and routed the allies. In all, the French inflicted over 30,000 casualties on the Russians and Austrians while suffering only 10,000 of their own.

The following morning, while Alexander retreated with his mauled army eastward, Francis sent Prince Lichtenstein with a request to Napoleon for an immediate armistice. Napoleon called for a summit between them; Francis agreed. They met for two hours at a windmill near Ziaroschitz on December 4. Francis agreed to all of Napoleon's terms for an armistice, but it took another two days for their diplomats to work out the details. The sovereigns signed the armistice on December 6. Meanwhile, Napoleon sent Savary galloping after the Russian army to ask Alexander for a similar truce. The tsar was noncommittal, but did invite Savary to St. Petersburg for further talks. It was clear that the Russians were heading for winter quarters in their own land. Napoleon then retired to the Schonbrunn Palace outside Vienna. There he would conduct negotiations, first with his allies, and then with his enemies.[136]

The emperor worked new clauses into his separate treaties with Bavaria, Baden, and Wurttemberg whereby each would supply more troops should war resume, but sweetened that by generously granting them lands taken from Austria and immediately recognizing Bavaria and Wurttemberg as kingdoms and the following summer Baden as a grand duchy. He then proposed to King Maximilien Joseph a marriage between the king's daughter Auguste Amelie and his stepson Eugene. The king promised to consult his daughter's feelings on the proposal.[137]

Napoleon was naturally tough on Prussia for its threats and mobilization, even if no fighting had occurred. Under the Treaty of Schonbrunn, signed on

December 15, Prussia would not only recognize all the changes that Napoleon had brought to Europe, but would cede Cleves and Neuchatel to France and Ansbach to Bavaria, and pay Bavaria for its cession of the province of Berg for Joachim Murat and Napoleon's sister Caroline to rule. In addition, Prussia would join France in an offensive alliance. Finally, Frederick William had to immediately wield diplomacy or force to rid northern Germany of all the Russian, Swedish, and British troops. If the Prussians did all that, then Napoleon would recognize their takeover of Hanover.[138]

Frederick William and his ministers were horrified at the humiliating treaty that Haugwitz unveiled to them. The king sent him back to Napoleon with instructions to renegotiate the treaty so that Prussia could immediately take Lubeck, Hamburg, and Bremen, along with Hanover, with no strings attached. Talleyrand made it clear that Frederick William was making a very grave mistake in not ratifying the treaty as it was, but then invited Haugwitz to discuss any amendments he proposed.

In his diplomacy, Napoleon deliberately left Austria's monarch for last. He wanted Francis to brood over all the humiliation and devastation that his decision for war had brought upon his realm. He also wanted Francis to witness how generous Napoleon could be with his allies and how harsh he could be with his enemies.[139]

The terms that the emperor had his foreign minister negotiate were neither as tough as the former nor as lenient as the latter had envisioned beforehand. Under the Treaty of Pressburg, which Talleyrand and Ludwig Cobenzl signed on December 26, Austria would cede Venetia and the Dalmatian coast down to Cattaro to the Kingdom of Italy; those cessions would largely complete the transformation of the Adriatic into a French sea. Vienna would also grant the Tyrol, Vorarlberg, and a scattering of small holdings to Bavaria, the division of its lands in southwest Germany between Baden and Wurttemberg, and the recognition of the promotions of the rulers of those lands in noble status. Austria would pay France an indemnity of 40 million francs, 2,000 cannons, and enough horses to double the size of France's cavalry. French troops would occupy Austria until that payment was completely made. In return, Napoleon tossed a few bones to Vienna, including allowing Salzburg and Berchtesgaden to return to Austrian control.[140]

Napoleon had largely achieved his grand diplomatic design. Austria was weakened and humbled, with its geopolitical center of gravity shifted from Germany toward the Balkans; yet it was still strong enough to counter Russia. France's power over Germany was strengthened both through its allies and possessions. Prussia was in the process of learning a harsh lesson about betraying a deal with France. The Russians and British withdrew their troops from southern Italy and parted company. Napoleon envisioned that French control of the Adriatic would be the first step in the eventual transformation of the entire Mediterranean basin into a French sphere of influence.

Napoleon's treaties with Prussia and Austria in December 1805 represented a turning point in his approach to diplomacy. Until then he had sought to convert enemies into neutrals or actual allies by treating them gently with the terms of the final treaty. But years of bitter experience finally taught him that letting an enemy off lightly only made it easier for the ingrate to rearm and return to war. Henceforth his treaties with his enemies would be examples of vengeance rather than restraint.

Was Napoleon's new diplomacy an improvement? At a glance, it may have appeared to work better, at least for a while. It would take Vienna four years and Berlin five years after having been devastated militarily, economically, and psychologically for them to dare rise again against Napoleon. Yet appearances can indeed be deceiving. After all, French diplomats had induced Prussia to peace with light terms in 1795, and there Berlin had stayed until even the timid Frederick William could no longer resist the temptation of the strategic opportunity that unfolded in late autumn 1805. The effects of Napoleon's new diplomatic strategy varied just as widely with other countries. A harsh peace could cow one people into a sullen apathy, like the Venetians, and provoke another into years of guerrilla warfare, like the Spanish.

All decisions for war or peace depend on circumstances that are unique. People—whether they are diplomats, dictators, generals, mobs, or characterized by some other dominant characteristic—do what they perceive is best. Regardless of whether his diplomacy overall served or undermined his interests, Napoleon always felt that he had no choice but to conduct it as he did.

Chapter Three Endnotes: The Rise of Napoleon

1. Albert Oliver, *Le Dix-Huit Brumaire* (Paris: Gallimard, 1959); Jean Paul Bertaud, *1799: Bonaparte Prend Le Pouvoir* (Bruxelles: Comptexe, 1987); Thierry Lentz, *Les Coups de Napoléon* (Paris: Jean Picollec, 1997); Jean Tulard, *Le 8 Brumaire* (Paris: Perrin, 1999).

2. Thierry Lentz, *Le Grand Consulat, 1799-1804* (Paris: Fayard, 1999), 51.

3. Antonello Pietromarchi, *Lucien Bonaparte, Prince Romain* (Paris: Perrin, 1980), 30-31, 75-76; Claude Langlois, "Le plebiscite de l'an VIII ou le coup d'Etat du 18 puviose an VIII," *Annales historique de la Revolution Francaise, 1792*, 45-63, 231-46, 390-415.

4. Bonaparte to Abria, July 18, 1800, Thierry Lentz, ed., *Napoleon Bonaparte: Correspondance Generale* (hereafter cited as *General Correspondence*) (Paris: Fayard, 2006), 5535. See also Bonaparte to Carnot, September 1, 1800, *ibid*, 3:5625; Bonaparte to Forfait, October 26, 1800, *ibid.*, 5721.

5. June K. Burton, *Napoleon and Clio: Historical Writing, Teaching, and Thinking During the First Empire* (Durham, NC: Carolina Academic Press, 1979); Michael Polowetzky, *A Bond Never Broken: The Relations Between Napoleon and the Authors of France* (Rutherford, NJ: Fairleigh Dickinson University Press, 1993).

6. Jean Hanoteau, ed., *No Peace with Napoleon: Concluding the Memoirs of General de Caulaincourt, duke of Vincenza, from the original memoirs* (New York: W. Morrow and Company, 1936), 192.

7. Steven Englund, *Napoleon: A Political Life* (Cambridge, Mass.: Harvard University Press, 2004), 316. See also Michael Sibalis, "The Napoleonic Police State," in Philip G. Dwyer, ed., *Napoleon and Europe* (London: Longman, 2001).

8. For the best biography to date, see Emmanuel de Waresquiel, *Talleyrand* (Paris: Fayard, 2003).

9. Gregor Dallas, *The Final Act: The Roads to Waterloo* (New York: Henry Holt, 1997), 117.

10. E.A. Arnold, *Fouche* (Washington DC: University Press of America, 1979); Jean Tulard, *Joseph Fouche* (Paris: Fayard, 1998).

11. Alan Schom, *Napoleon Bonaparte* (New York: HarperCollins, 1997), 253.

12. Louis Constant, *Memoires Intimes de Napoleon Ier*, 2 vols. (Paris: Mercure de France, 1967), 1:97; Tulard, *Fouche*, 194.

13. Jacques Godechot, *The Counter-Revolution: Doctrine and Action, 1789-1804* (New York: Howard Fertig, 1971), 364-65.

14. Bonaparte to the People of the western Departments, December 28, 1799, *General Correspondence*, 4823.

15. Bonaparte to Hedouville, December 28, 1799, *General Correspondence*, 4824; Bonaparte to Berthier, December 29, 1799, *General Correspondence*, 4824.

16. Bonaparte to Brune, January 14, 1800, *General Correspondence*, 4872; Bonaparte to La Baroliere, January 22, 1800, *ibid.*, 4898.

17. Bonaparte to Gardanne, February 20, 1800, *General Correspondence*, 5016.

18. Bonaparte to Brune, February 8, 1800, *General Correspondence*, 4944; Bonaparte to Bernadotte, May 1, 1800, *ibid.*, 5219.

19. Bonaparte to Francis II, December 25, 1799, *General Correspondence*, 3:4815; Bonaparte to George III, December 25, 1799, *General Correspondence*, 3:4817.

20. Bonaparte to foreign minister, January 16, 1800, Talleyrand to Thugut, February 27, 1800, April 7, 1800, in *Correspondance de Napoleon 1er* (hereafter cited as *Correspondence*), 16 vols. (Paris: Bibliotheque des Introuvables, 2002), 4:4445, 4446, 4530, 4623, 4708.

21. Bonaparte to Louis, September 7, 1800, *General Correspondence*, 5639.

22. Bonaparte to Berthier, January 25, March 3, April 26, May 2, 4, 1800, *General Correspondence*, 4903, 5040, 5202, 5223, 5229; Bonaparte to Carnot, April 24, 1800, *ibid.*, 5195; Bonaparte to Talleyrand, March 12, May 15, 1800, *ibid.*, 5096, 5317.

23. Bonaparte to Carnot, June 4, 1800, *General Correspondence*, 5398.

24. Bonaparte to Massena, March 12, 1800, *General Correspondence*, 5094.

25. Bonaparte to Melas, June 20, 1800, *General Correspondence*, 5458.

26. Bonaparte to Francis, June 16, 1800, *General Correspondence*, 5440.

27. Bonaparte to Fouche, May 24, June 4 (2 letters), 1800, *General Correspondence*, 5365, 5400, 5401; Bonaparte to Cambaceres and Lebrun, June 15, 1800, *ibid.*, 5435.

28. Bonaparte to Moreau, April, 22, 1800, *General Correspondence*, 5190. See also Bonaparte to Moreau, March 1, 12, April 1 (of questionable authenticity), 1800, *ibid.*, 5033, 5095, 5156.

29. Francis to Bonaparte, July 5, 1800, Prince Napoleon et Jean Hanoteau, eds., *Lettres Personelles des Souverains a l'Emperor Napoleon Ier* (Paris: Plon, 1939), 8-10.

30. Bonaparte to Talleyrand, July 11, 1800, *General Correspondence*, 5506; Bonaparte to Francis, July 29, 1800, *ibid.*, 5578; Bonaparte to Carnot, August 2, September 15, 1800, *ibid.*, 5592, 5643.

31. Bonaparte to Talleyrand, July 19, 1800, *General Correspondence*, 5545; Bonaparte to Paul, December 21, 1800, *ibid.*, 5833; see also Bonaparte to Talleyrand, June 4, July 4, 19, August 4, 1800, January 20, 1801, *ibid.*, 5411, 5491, 5545, 5595, 5949.

32. Bonaparte to Talleyrand, January 27, 1801, *General Correspondence*, 5975; Bonaparte to Joseph, January 21, 1801, *ibid.*, 5950; Bonaparte to Paul, February 27, March 12, 1801, *ibid.*, 6076, 6119.

33. Norman E. Saul, *Russia and the Mediterranean, 1797-1807* (Chicago: University of Chicago Press, 1970), 149-51.

34. Bonaparte to Joseph, October 20, 1800, *General Correspondence*, 5700; Bonaparte to Carnot, September 24, 1800, *ibid.*, 5651.

35. Owen Connelly, *The French Revolution and Napoleonic Era* (New York: Harcourt Inc., 2000), 207. For good overviews of the plot and investigation, see: Jean Tulard, *Napoleon* (Paris: Fayard, 1998), 145-64; Isser Woloch, *Napoleon and his Collaborators: The Making of a Dictatorship* (New York: W.W. Norton, 2001), 66-80.

36. Bonaparte to Talleyrand, April 12, 1801, *Correspondence*, 6207.

37. Bonaparte to Joseph, January 21, February 13, 1801, *General Correspondence*, 5950, 6017; Bonaparte to Talleyrand, February 2, 1801, *ibid.*, 5982.

38. Bonaparte to Murat, March 24, 1801, *General Correspondence*, 6154.

39. Bonaparte to Paul, March 12, 1801, *General Correspondence*, 6119.

40. Bonaparte to Alexander, April 26, 1801, February 16, 1802, *General Correspondence*, 6238, 6770.

41. Bonaparte to Talleyrand, September 30, 1800, *General Correspondence*, 5682.

42. Bonaparte to Charles IV, November 7 (3 letters), 1800, *General Correspondence*, 5749, 5750, 5751.

43. Bonaparte to Berthier, February 4, 1801, *General Correspondence*, 5990; Bonaparte to Talleyrand, February 4 (2 letters), 13 (2 letters), March 2, 1801, *ibid.*, 5996, 5998, 6019, 6020, 6094; Constant, *Memoires*, 1:352.

44. Bonaparte to Lucien, June 17, 22, 1801, *General Correspondence*, 6335, 6339.

45. Bonaparte to Talleyrand, March 10, September 30, 1800, *General Correspondence*, 5083, 5681; Bonaparte to Talleyrand, May 9, 28, September 17, 1801, *General Correspondence*, 6262, 6305, 6494; Bonaparte to Caillard, July 23, 1801, *ibid.*, 6372.

46. Bonaparte to Joseph, January 7, February 2, March 8, 12, 1802, *General Correspondence*, 6713, 6749, 6800, 6805; Bonaparte to Talleyrand, February 19, 1802, *ibid.*, 6780; Bonaparte to Hauterive, December 26, 1801, *ibid.*, 6693.

47. E. E. Y. Hales, *Napoleon and the Pope: The Story of Napoleon and Pius VII* (London: Eyre & Spottiswoode, 1962), 7-8.

48. Andre Latreille, *L'Eglise Catholique et la Revolution Francaise*, 2 vols. (Paris: Editions des Cerfs, 1970), 2:7-11.

49. William Doyle, *The Oxford History of the French Revolution* (New York: Oxford University Press 1989), 386.

50. Bonaparte to Talleyrand, December 14, 1800, February 2, 1810, *General Correspondence*, 5833, 5981.

51. Bonaparte to Pius VII, August 28, 1802, *General Correspondence*, 7113.

52. Steven Englund, *Napoleon: A Political Life* (Cambridge, Mass.: Harvard University Press, 2004), 184.

53. Pieter Geyl, *Napoleon For and Against* (New Haven, Conn.: Yale University Press, 1963); J. Kaplow, ed., *New Perspectives on the French Revolution* (New York: Wiley, 1965); Robert B. Holtman, *The Napoleonic Revolution* (Philadelphia: Lippincott, 1967); D.M.G. Sutherland, *France, 1789-1815: Revolution and Counterrevolution* (London: Fontana, 1985); Jean Tulard, *Napoleon ou le Mythe du Sauver* (Paris: Fayard, 1987); Colin Lucas, ed., *The Political Culture of the French Revolution* (New York: Oxford University Press, 1991); Martyn Lyons, *Napoleon Bonaparte and the Legacy of the French Revolution* (New York: Palgrave, 1994); Isser Woloch, *The New Regime: Transformations of the French Civic Code, 1789-1820s* (New York: W.W. Norton, 1994).

54. D.M.G. Sutherland, *France, 1789-1815: Revolution and Counterrevolution* (New York: Oxford University Press, 1986), 367; Robert Asprey, *The Rise of Napoleon* (New York: Basic Books, 2000), 430.

55. Bonaparte to Cambaceres and Lebrun, January 24, 25, 26, 1802, *General Correspondence*, 6738, 6739, 6745; Bonaparte to Talleyrand, October 14, 1801, *ibid.*, 6579; Bonaparte to Cisalpine Republic Government, October 31, 1801, *ibid.*, 6626.

56. Bonaparte to Melzi, May 22, October 16, 1802, *General Correspondence*, 6904, 7216.

57. Bonaparte to Piedmont Executive, October 29, 1800, *General Correspondence*, 5735; Bonaparte to Talleyrand, November 2, 1802, *ibid.*, 7261.

58. Bonaparte to Talleyrand, April 25, July 22, 28, August 2, 1800, January 27, 1801, *General Correspondence*, 5192, 5554, 5574, 5602, 5975; Bonaparte to Ferdinand I, Duke of Parma, June 20, 1800, *ibid.*, 5455; Bonaparte to Charles IV, August 15 (2 letters), 1800, *ibid.*, 5604, 5606; Bonaparte to Lucien, December 22, February 28, *ibid.*, 5862, 6083.

59. Constant, *Memoires*, 131-37, 534-35.

60. Bonaparte to Louis I, Etrurian king, July 27, October 10, 1801, May 23, 1802, *General Correspondence*, 6382, 6553, 6911; Bonaparte to Murat, April 24, July 27, 1801, *ibid.*, 6234, 6383; Bonaparte to Talleyrand, May 22, 1802, *ibid.*, 6905; Bonaparte to Charles IV, May 23, 1802, *ibid.*, 6908.

61. Bonaparte to Talleyrand, January 13 (3 letters), 1800, *General Correspondence*, 4867, 4868, 4869; Bonaparte to Augereau, February 5, March 5, 1800, *ibid.*, 4934, 5045; Bonaparte to Amsterdam government, March 8, 1800, *ibid.*, 5075.

62. Bonaparte to Batavian directory, April 9, July 25, 1801, *General Correspondence*, 6198, 6379; Bonaparte to Talleyrand, April 9, 1801, *ibid.*, 6200; Bonaparte to Talleyrand, October 6, 1802, *ibid.*, 7199.

63. Bonaparte to Talleyrand, September 23, 1802, *General Correspondence*, 7174.

64. Bonaparte to 18 Helvetian Republic cantons, December 10, 1802, *General Correspondence*, 7545.

65. Act of Mediation for Switzerland, February 19, 1803, *Correspondence*, 6590; Napoleon to Talleyrand, May 21, July 30, August 4, 1804, *ibid.*, 7762, 7884, 7895.

66. Bonaparte to Francis, October 19, 1802, *Correspondence*, 6382.

67. John C. Gagliardo, *Reich and Nation: The Holy Roman Empire as Idea and Reality* (Bloomington: University of Indiana Press, 1980), 225-26, 290-305.

68. Englund, *Napoleon*, 218.

69. Bonaparte to Reinhard, November 10, 1799, *General Correspondence*, 4765.

70. William Garrott Brown, *The Life of Oliver Ellsworth* (New York: Macmillan, 1905), 305-08; Ruhl J. Barlette, *The Record of American Diplomacy* (New York: Knopf, 1964); 100-02; Peter P. Hill, *William Vans Murray* (New York: Macmillan, 1975), 195-96.

71. Andrew J. Montague, ed., *The American Secretaries of State and Their Diplomacy* (New York: Knopf, 1927), 2:254.

72. For the best account to date, see Pierre Branda and Thierry Lentz, *Napoleon, L'Esclavage, et les Colonies* (Paris: Fayard, 2006).

73. To the Citizens of St. Domingue, December 25, 1799, *General Correspondence*, 4455; Bonaparte to Lacrosse, January 4, 1800, *ibid.*, 4843.

74. Bonaparte to Toussaint-L'Ouverture, March 4, November 18, 1801, *General Correspondence*, 6102, 6647; Bonaparte to Forfait, marine minister, May 10, October 5, 25, November 5, December 22, 1800, February 18, 1801, *ibid.*, 5265, 5686, 5717, 5745, 5860, 6049.

75. Bonaparte to Decres, October 31, 1801, *General Correspondence*, 6627. See also Bonaparte to Barbe Marbois, finance minister, October 23, 1801, *ibid.*, 6600; Bonaparte to Decres, October 23, 1801, *ibid.*, 6603; Bonaparte to Berthier, October 27, 1801, *ibid.*, 6608; Bonaparte to Leclerc, November 19, 1801, *ibid.*, 6648.

76. Bonaparte to Cambaceres, April 27, 1802, *General Correspondence*, 6863.

77. G. Gourgand, *Journal de Sainte Helene*, 2 vols. (Paris: Flammarion, 1947), 1:278.

78. Charles A. Cerami, *Jefferson's Great Gamble: The Remarkable Story of Jefferson, Napoleon, and the Men Behind the Louisiana Purchase* (Naperville, Il.: Sourcebooks, 2003), 58.

79. Cerami, *Great Gamble*, 222.

80. Cerami, *Great Gamble*, 166.

81. Cerami, *Great Gamble*, 180.

82. Robert B. Holtman, *Napoleonic Propaganda* (Baton Rouge: Louisiana State University Press, 1950).

83. Bonaparte to Talleyrand, August 29, 1802, *General Correspondence*, 7125; Bonaparte to Sebastiani, September 5, 1802, *ibid.*, 7142; Bonaparte to Hamouda Pasha, bey of Tunis, May 5, 1800, December 5, 1801, May 7, 1802, *ibid.*, 5243, 6670, 6887; Bonaparte to Mustapha Pasha, bey of Algiers, November 25, 1801, July 8, 27, 1802, *ibid.*, 6655, 7028, 7052; Bonaparte to Talleyrand, July 18, 1803, *Correspondence*, 7029.

84. Bonaparte to Decres, April 15, 1802, *General Correspondence*, 6848.

85. Bonaparte to Talleyrand, May 10, 1800, *General Correspondence*, 5271; Bonaparte to Selim III, October 11, 1801, *ibid.*, 6561.

86. Bonaparte to Talleyrand, November 4, 1802, *Correspondence*, 6414.

87. Bonaparte to Frederick William, March 11, 1803, *Correspondence*, 6626; Bonaparte to Alexander, March 11, 1803, *ibid.*, 6625; Bonaparte to Charles IV, March 11, 1803, *ibid.*, 6627.

88. Bonaparte to Talleyrand, August 23 (2 letters), 1803, *Correspondence*, 7032, 7033; Observations, *ibid.*, 7034, Note, *ibid.*, 7035.

89. Hortense de Beauharnais, *Memoires*, 1:146.

90. Bonaparte to Berthier, March 25, March 30, 1803, *Correspondence*, 6654 and 6658.

91. Bonaparte to Whitworth, May 4, 1803, *Correspondence*, 6725.

92. Bonaparte to Whitworth, May 12, 1803, *Correspondence*, 6740; Bonaparte to Talleyrand, May 13, 1803, *ibid.*, 6740; Bonaparte to Senate, March 20, *ibid.*, 6755; Bonaparte to Senate, Tribunate, and Legislative Corps, May 25, 1803, *ibid*, 6766.

93. Schom, *Napoleon Bonaparte*, 319-21.

94. Napoleon to Marie Caroline, July 28, 1803, *Correspondence*, 6951.

95. Talleyrand to Godoy, July 26, 1803, August 14, 1803, August 16, 1803, *Correspondence*, 6942, 7007, 7008.

96. Bonaparte to Charles IV, September 18, 1803, *Correspondence*, 7113.

97. Bonaparte to Decres, August 8, 1803, *Correspondence*, 6994; Bonaparte to Berthier, January 13, 1804, *ibid.*, 7475.

98. For excellent overviews of the plot, arrests, and trial, see: Sparrow, *Secret Service*, 276-304; Thierry Lentz, *Savary: Le Seide de Napoleon* (Paris: Fayard, 2001), 98-136.

99. For an excellent overview of the Enghien affair, see: Lentz, *Grand Consulat*, 539-57; see also: Waresquiel, *Talleyrand*, 322-30; Lentz, *Savary*, 108-112; Jean Tulard, *Joseph Fouche* (Paris: Fayard, 1998), 168-72; Emile Dard, *Talleyrand and Napoleon* (New York: Appleton-Century Company, 1937), 65-70.

100. Bonaparte to Regnier, March 27, April 4 (2 letters), 27, 1804, *Correspondence*, 7647, 7661, 7662, 7717; Bonaparte to Chaptal, April 4, 1804, *ibid.*, 7663; Bonaparte to Talleyrand, March 18, 22, 1804, *ibid.*, 7630, 7642; Bonaparte to Real, March 19, 1804, *ibid.*, 7631; Bonaparte to Fouche, July 28, August 6, 13, 30, September 5, 1804, *ibid.*, 7880, 7905, 7923, 7974, 7988.

101. Waresquiel, *Talleyrand*, 324; Lentz, *Savary*, 125, 123.

102. W.H. Zawadzki, *Man of Honor: Adam Czartoryski as a Statesman of Russia and Poland, 1795-1831* (New York: Oxford University Press, 1993), 104.

103. Lentz, *Consulat*, 556.

104. Napoleon to Talleyrand, August 24, 1804, *Correspondence*, 7959.

105. Napoleon to Talleyrand, August 25, 1804, *Correspondence*, 7961; Napoleon to Bavarian Elector, October 1, 1804, *ibid.*, 8066; Napoleon to Hesse-Cassel Elector, October 2, 1804, *ibid.*, 8067; Napoleon to Hesse-Darmstadt Landgrave, October 2, 1804, *ibid.*, 8068; Napoleon to Frankfort Burgermeister, October 2, 1804, *ibid.*, 8069.

106. Napoleon to Bavarian Elector, August 25, October 2, 1805, *Correspondence*, 9134, 9314.

107. Napoleon to Frederick William III, August 30, 1804, *Correspondence*, 7973; Brendan Simms, *The Impact of Napoleon: Prussian High Politics, Foreign Policy, and the Crisis of the Executive, 1797-1806* (Cambridge: Cambridge University Press, 1997), 159-68.

108. Jean Tulard, *Napoleon, ou le Mythe du Sauveur* (Paris: Fayard, 1977), 172; Dallas, *Final Act*, 269.

109. Napoleon to Melzi, June 23, 1804, *Correspondence*, 7814.

110. Napoleon to Pius VII, August 3, 1804, *Correspondence*, 7899; Napoleon to Fesch, November 5, 1803, *ibid.*, 8161.

111. Constant, *Memoires*, 1:566.

112. Napoleon to Pius VII, March 21, 1805, *Correspondence*, 8457.

113. Napoleon's Response to Delegation, March 17, 1805, *Correspondence*, 8444.

114. Napoleon to Francis II, January 1, March 17, 1805, *Correspondence*, 8250, 8445; Francis to Napoleon, August 28, 1804, J. Hanoteau, ed., *Lettres Personelles,* 17.

115. Napoleon to Genoan Delegation, June 4, 1805, *Correspondence*, 8836.

116. Napoleon to Pius VII, August 19, 1805, *Correspondence*, 9091.

117. Napoleon to George III, January 2, 1805, *Correspondence*, 8252.

118. Napoleon to Frederick William III, August 23, 1805, *Correspondence*, 9116; Napoleon to Duroc, August 24, September 11, 1805, *ibid.*, 9126, 9199; Napoleon to Talleyrand, August 22, 24, September 5, 19, 1805, *ibid.*, 9104, 9127, 9180, 9240.

119. Napoleon to Marie Caroline, January 2, 1805, *Correspondence*, 8255; Napoleon to Ferdinand IV, January 2, 1805, *ibid.*, 8254.

120. Napoleon to Selim III, January 30, 1805, *Correspondence*, 8298.

121. Napoleon to King of Persia, February 16, March 30, 1805, *Correspondence*, 8329, 8502.

122. For insights into his diplomatic and strategic outlook, administrative skills, and ability to shift his plans with circumstances, see Napoleon to Decres, March 10, April 11, 12, 13, 23, 30, May 4, 29, 31, June 9, August 13, 14, September 13, 1805, *Correspondence*, 8410, 8568, 8575, 9071, 9076, 8582, 8618, 8659, 8685, 8809, 8817, 8871, 9209; Napoleon to Villeneuve, December 12, 1804, March 2, April 14, May 8, August 13, September 14, 1805, *ibid.*, 8206, 8381, 8583, 8700, 9073, 9210.

123. Napoleon to Charles IV, June 14, 1804, January 2, February 23, 1805, *Correspondence*, 7809, 8253, 8351.

124. Bonaparte to Prince Regent of Portugal, August 4, 1803, *Correspondence*, 6979, Bonaparte to Prince Regent of Portugal, January 14, 1803, *ibid.*, 6540; Bonaparte to Talleyrand, January 12, August 4, 1803, *ibid.*, 6537, 6978.

125. Napoleon to Junot, February 23, 1805, *Correspondence*, 8350; Napoleon to Prince Regent of Portugal, February 19, 1805, *ibid.*, 8337.

126. Napoleon to Talleyrand, August 13, 1805, *Correspondence*, 9070.

127. Napoleon to Berthier, August 24, 26, September 21, 1805, *Correspondence*, 9128, 9137, 9248.

128. Order to the Army, September 20, 1805, *Correspondence*, 9245; Napoleon to Songis, September 20, 1805, *ibid.*, 9246.

129. Talleyrand Memorandum, October 17, 1805, Pierre Bertrand, ed., *Lettres Inedites de Talleyrand a Napoleon, 1800-1809* (Paris: Perin, 1989), 156-74.

130. 7th Bulletin of the Grand Army, October 19, 1805, *Correspondence*, 9398; 9th Bulletin of the Grand Army, October 21, 1805, *ibid.*, 9408.

131. Napoleon to Bernadotte, October 2, 1805, *Correspondence*, 9312; Napoleon to Otto, October 3, 4, 1805, *ibid.*, 9319, 9334; Napoleon to Frederick William, October 5, 27, 1805, *ibid.*, 9342, 9434; Napoleon to Duroc, October 24, 1805, *ibid.*, 9420.

132. Napoleon to Francis II, November 3, 8, 1805, *Correspondence*, 9451, 9464.

133. Napoleon to Talleyrand, November 22, 1805, *Correspondence*, 9516.

134. Napoleon to Francis II, November 17, 1805, *Correspondence*, 9503; Napoleon to Talleyrand, November 25, 1805, *ibid.*, 9523.

135. For accounts of Napoleon's diplomatic and military strategy which culminated with Austerlitz, see Napoleon to Alexander I, November 25, 1805, *Correspondence*, 9524; Napoleon to Talleyrand, November 30, 1805, *ibid.*, 9532; 30th, 33rd Bulletins of the Grand Army, December 3, 6, 7, 1805, *ibid.*, 9541, 9550.

136. Napoleon to Talleyrand, December 4, 1805, *Correspondence*, 9542; 31st, 34th Bulletin of Grand Army, December 5, 10, 1805, *ibid.*, 9546, 9556,

137. Napoleon to Talleyrand, December 13, 1805, *Correspondence*, 9560; Napoleon to Wurttemberg Elector, December 13, 1805, *ibid.*, 9567; Napoleon to Bavarian Elector, December 21, 27, 1805, *ibid.*, 9599, 9620; Napoleon to Baden Elector, December 27, 1805, *ibid.*, 9623.

138. Napoleon to Talleyrand, December 14, 15, 16, 1805, *Correspondence*, 9573, 9578, 9582; Napoleon to Frederick William, December 15, 1805, *ibid.*, 9577.

139. Napoleon to Talleyrand, December 20, 1805, *Correspondence*, 9594.

140. Napoleon to Francis II, December 25, 1805, *Correspondence*, 9612; Napoleon to Talleyrand, December 25, 27, 1805, *ibid.*, 9613, 9617; Napoleon to Archduke Charles, December 25, 1805, *ibid.*, 9615.

Chapter Four

Napoleon Invincible

1806-1809

"My intention is to place the kingdom of Naples in my family. This will be along with Italy, Switzerland, Holland, and the three German kingdoms . . . or in truth the French empire."

"My family does not back me up. They are all insanely ambitious, ruinously extravagant, and devoid of talent."

"The English declare that they will no longer respect neutrals at sea; I will no longer recognize them on land."

—Napoleon Bonaparte

Family Values and the Fate of Europe

Napoleon devoted the first nine months of 1806 to doing what he seemed to enjoy the most in life: nation-building. He was determined to create states that were not just models of efficiency but loyalty. To Joseph he explained his "intention . . . to place the kingdom of Naples in my family. This will be along with Italy, Switzerland, Holland, and the three German kingdoms . . . or in truth, the French empire."[1]

Family members, both as players and pawns, were essential to Napoleon Bonaparte's diplomacy throughout most of his political life. His brothers, stepson, and brother-in-law would serve as diplomats, soldiers, politicians, and eventually rulers of states. His sisters would play a more subtle although at times just as vital a game; all along they would wield their formidable feminine charms, backed by the promise of a hand in Napoleon's generosity, to entice powerful men to share secrets and alter their allegiances. Eventually Caroline and Elisa would assert the power of state, but behind rather than atop thrones crowded by their husbands; Pauline was the least clever of the clan, but at least knew not to meddle in complex issues beyond her understanding.

Like most autocrats, Napoleon saw marriage primarily as a means to promote national and family interests by cementing alliances and spawning the requisite heir and spare; both lust and love were best satisfied with someone other than one's spouse. To that end he made and broke marriages, including his own. The most notorious was when he bullied his wayward youngest brother Jerome to trade his beloved, pregnant, American wife for a Wurttemberg princess. Nearly as heartless was forcing Louis to give up the woman he adored for a bitter marriage to Josephine's daughter Hortense.

Yet he did not always get his way. He initially opposed the marriage of Caroline, perhaps the most Machiavellian of the Bonapartes after himself, to his valiant but rather dense cavalry commander Joachim Murat. He later despaired when they plotted against him. And then there was Lucien, the most politically astute and courageous of Napoleon's brothers, who was eventually driven into exile. What was his crime? On the eve of Napoleon's transformation from First Consul into Emperor, Lucien put love before international diplomacy by refusing to divorce his commoner wife for the promise of being united one day with a princess. Instead he fled with his family to Rome. When Napoleon found out he stripped Lucien of his Senate seat and his place in the line of succession. It seems that most of the family secretly sided with Lucien. Letizia, their formidable mother, did so openly. She was so disgusted by Napoleon's behavior that she pointedly joined Lucien and his family in Rome and refused to return for the coronation.

While, as the saying goes, blood may be thicker than water, it guarantees neither competence nor loyalty. Napoleon conquered and awarded realms to his brothers and sisters; then, to his irritation, he found himself as mired in diplomacy with those new rulers as if he were dealing any other regime. In all it was about as easy for the emperor to coordinate policies among those of his siblings that he had plopped on thrones as it was to herd as many cats.

Napoleon would actually deprive Louis of his Dutch crown after he ignored repeated demands to desist from putting his subjects' interests before those of France.

While his siblings mocked or bristled at his commands, Napoleon fumed at their ingratitude. Where would they be without all his sacrifices, his prowess on scores of battlefields and at countless negotiating tables, his endless eighteen-hour work days devoted to advancing his vision for France, Europe, and their family? He lamented that "my family does not back me up. They are all insanely ambitious, ruinously extravagant, and devoid of talent."[2]

And even when they actually bothered to follow his directions, they often got lost along the way. Not only did none of them enjoy his natural gift to command and create, they often made a mess of things when they tried to emulate him. Lucien was perhaps the only one who might have neared Napoleon's dynamism as a ruler, but was lost forever to such plans after the squabble over his choice of a wife.

Ironically, the most loyal and dependable of Napoleon's family was not related by blood. His stepson Eugene Beauharnais far exceeded the others as a general and statesman.[3] That was understandable, for two reasons. The lad had lost his aloof father to the guillotine. Undoubtedly he had mixed feelings when Napoleon began courting his mother, but the awkward and passionate suitor proved to be far more loving and interested in Eugene and his sister Hortense than their real father had ever been. Moreover, Napoleon would carefully groom Eugene for and install him in a succession of ever more important military, diplomatic, and government posts until he finally became the viceroy of Italy. So Eugene's gratitude was kindled when at age fifteen he found himself apprenticed as a staff officer to one of history's greatest generals and statesmen; the feeling swelled into life-long devotion. He would be at Napoleon's side through both campaigns in Italy, as well as the Egyptian odyssey squeezed in between. As important were the lessons in statecraft he learned from observing his stepfather in the field or at Paris as he dealt decisively with the endless array of political and diplomatic challenges.

After nine years together, Napoleon was confident that his understudy was ready to rule. On February 1, 1805, he named Eugene the archchancellor of Italy and promoted him to brigadier general. Then on June 7, 1805, the newly crowned king of Italy raised his son's status to viceroy. In his own version of *The Prince*, Napoleon issued Eugene with a very wise set of instructions for ruling Italy on his behalf:

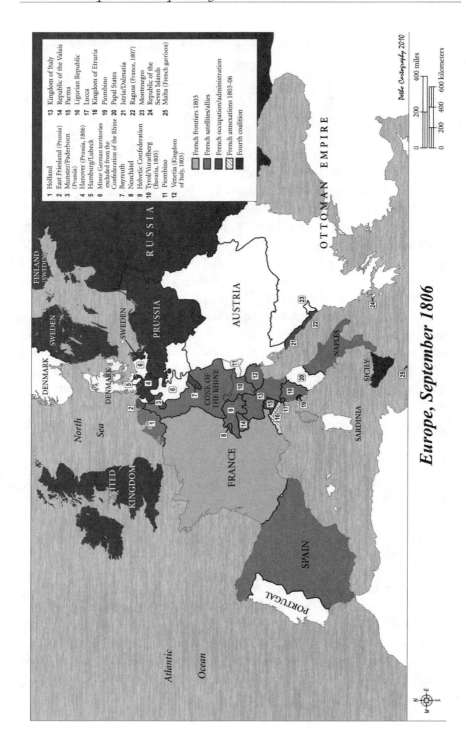

Europe, September 1806

1 Holland
2 East Friesland (Prussia)
3 Munster/Paderborn (Prussia)
4 Hanover (Prussia, 1806)
5 Hamburg/Lubeck
6 Minor German territories excluded from the Confederation of the Rhine
7 Bayreuth
8 Neuchâtel
9 Helvetic Confederation
10 Tyrol/Vorarlberg (Bavaria, 1805)
11 Piombino
12 Venetia (Kingdom of Italy, 1805)
13 Kingdom of Italy
14 Republic of the Valais
15 Parma
16 Ligurian Republic
17 Lucca
18 Kingdom of Etruria
19 Piombino
20 Papal States
21 Istria/Dalmatia
22 Ragusa (France, 1807)
23 Montenegro
24 Republic of the Seven Islands
25 Malta (French garrison)

French frontiers 1803
French satellites/allies
French occupation/administration
French annexations 1803–06
Fourth coalition

Pete Cartography 2010

0   200   400 miles
0 200 400 600 kilometers

Be very prudent and circumspect. Never give anyone your complete confidence. . . . The less you talk, the better. . . . Learn to listen and remember that silence is often as impressive as knowledge. But do not hesitate to ask questions. You are only twenty-three, and however much people will try to flatter you, they know all too well your limitations. Do not try to imitate me. You must be more reserved. . . . Take the greatest care not to expose yourself to any insult. However, should that happen . . . no matter whom the offender is, have him arrested on the spot. . . . Cultivate the younger Italians. The older ones are all useless. Italians are naturally more deceitful than the French. Nonetheless show respect for them, and all the more so as you become more disillusioned. There really is little difference among countries. You will gradually realize this. Your duty is to make my Italian subjects happy. . . . Consider yourself a failure if you cannot get the Italians to love you. They know there is no love without respect. Learn to speak good Italian. Go around and show yourself. Find valuable people as assets. Admire what they admire. Get to know them and their families. Never form a clique. . . . See that your orders are obeyed . . . never allow them to be disobeyed.[4]

And so on.

From Eugene's arrival at Milan in March 1805, he would consciously follow that advice and prove his mettle as chief of the Consulta, or State Council, with much of his stepfather's dynamism. Thanks largely to Eugene's efforts there, for nearly another decade the Kingdom of Italy would be among the best run of Napoleon's satellites. Indeed, Eugene was so diligent that at times Napoleon, the ultimate workaholic and slave-driver, actually implored him to take it easier: "My son, You are working too hard; your life is too monotonous. . . . You have a young wife. . . . I think you should arrange to pass the evening with her. . . . Why not go to the theater once a week. . . . I have more work to do than you, yet I can honestly say that I set aside more time for pleasure and fun than you."[5]

Of all the marital bonds the emperor forged, perhaps only that between Eugene and Auguste Amelie, the Bavarian elector's beautiful and accomplished daughter, was truly happy. Yet few of Napoleon's matchmaking efforts demanded more persistent and prolonged diplomacy. He expressed his interest as early as July 14, 1804, when he asked Ambassador Louis Guillaume Otto to get all the information he could on the girl as a possible wife. Hints of his intentions to her father began not long after. At first, Maximilien Joseph was dead-set against the match. Although he would not dare say so openly, he disdained losing his daughter to the stepson of some Corsican parvenu as much as he feared being straitjacketed within that upstart's ever more powerful empire. So he deftly sidestepped ever more obvious hints by both Napoleon and Talleyrand throughout 1805 that Eugene and Auguste would make a wonderful pair. He used the excuse that his daughter was already promised to Charles Louis Frederick, the heir to the duchy of Baden.[6]

As it did for other rulers across the continent, Austerlitz changed Maximilien's emotional and political calculus. When Napoleon again raised the issue with a formal request penned on December 21, and had Gerard Duroc, his chief aide-de-camp, hand-deliver it, the man he had newly promoted to king was eager to discuss the terms. The stickiest issue was what to do about Auguste's hapless fiancé. Napoleon promised to compensate Charles by marrying him within his own clan. The king then talked his daughter into breaking her engagement.[7]

With that done, the emperor sent a courier galloping to Milan with the wedding announcement. His December 31 letter was curt but promising: "I have arranged your marriage with Princess Auguste; it has been announced.. . . She is very pretty." The summons came with a letter penned on January 3, 1806: "Twelve hours after receiving this letter you will with all diligence embark for Munich."[8]

Eugene faithfully followed his orders. He swiftly organized his packing, transportation, and a military escort, and then set forth on that long road across the winter-bound Alps. Eugene and Auguste were undoubtedly nervous when they met for the first time on January 10, 1806; but, as a close observer put it, "they loved each other as if they had known each other for years because never were two persons better made for loving each other."[9] On the morning of January 13, Napoleon officially adopted Eugene. Then, a little later that day, with Napoleon and Josephine beaming happily, the couple were wed in a civil ceremony; the church wedding came the next day.[10]

Napoleon had not forgotten poor Charles of Baden, who was heart-broken and resentful at having his fiancé snatched away. The emperor sent his condolences and fixed him up with Josephine's niece, Stephanie de Beauharnais, whom Napoleon adopted on March 3, 1806. That match was not made in heaven. Like Hortense, Stephanie was noted for her beauty and gaiety, whereas Charles was a cold, stern, corpulent young man. Stephanie wept throughout the wedding ceremony on April 7, 1806. Napoleon later sent her a letter beseeching her to "love your husband. . . . Be friendly with the [father]; this is your first duty; he is your father now. Moreover, he is a prince whom I have always esteemed. Treat your subjects well; sovereigns are only made for the welfare of their people."[11]

From Napoleon's point of view, linking with marriage the throne of France with Baden and Bavaria made perfect strategic sense as territorial stepping stones to the Austrian frontier and heart of Germany. And his Italian subjects would thrill at having such a lovely couple reign so graciously over them on his behalf. For a wedding gift to Eugene and Auguste, Napoleon sent General Auguste Marmont with a small army to occupy Istria and Dalmatia which, along with Venetia, he took from Austria under the Pressburg treaty and annexed to the kingdom of Italy.

That was hardly the only change he had in mind for the peninsula. The emperor was determined that Ferdinand IV and Marie Caroline of Naples would suffer severely for betraying their neutrality agreement with him by inviting that 25,000-man Anglo-Russian expedition into their realm. What led them to dare violate their promise to Napoleon? Although the queen served as the king's political backbone, she in turn had been influenced by three powerful men, all English. Sir William Hamilton had been England's ambassador there from 1768 until his recent death in April 1803; Hugh Eliot replaced him. Then there was Lord Admiral Horatio Nelson, whose attempts to defend the kingdom may have been guided as much by his love for the ambassador's wife, Lady Emma Hamilton, as British strategic interests; Nelson perished at Trafalgar in October 1805—and Nelson was irreplaceable. Finally, the redoubtable Sir John Acton remained very much their prime minister.

Napoleon was well aware that Marie Caroline wore the political pants in that Bourbon family. "I am going to punish that bitch," he promised Talleyrand. And so he did. On December 27, 1805, the emperor publicly declared that the "dynasty of Naples has ceased to reign. Its existence is incompatible with the repose of Europe and the honor of my crown." He gave Marshal Gouvion St. Cyr orders to carry out the mission. The *Moniteur*, Napoleon's official newspaper, elaborated the justification for conquering the Kingdom of Naples, denouncing the queen as "vicious and immoral," a woman who "has brought humiliation to her husband" for conspiring with foreign powers. Such an enraged tone and fervor suggests that the emperor may have had some issues with the queen beyond geopolitics. Although many rulers would betray his trust over his years in power, none provoked quite the rage in him that Marie Caroline did.[12]

The Anglo-Russian force was not strong enough to resist St. Cyr's rapidly approaching army. The British packed their troops aboard most of the fleet and sailed away from Naples on January 14, 1806, for Gibraltar; two days later the Russians embarked their troops and lifted anchor for Corfu.

While the trembling king sailed for Palermo aboard a British warship on January 21, his tougher half lingered and sought to defend her throne by appealing to Napoleon's sense of mercy. On February 7 Marie Caroline wrote him a letter in which she confessed her mistake and begged his forgiveness. He replied with silent contempt. She waited with worsening anxiety until February 11, when Acton finally convinced her to flee aboard a British warship before it was too late. Three days later St. Cyr's army marched into Naples.

The man who would soon be the new king of that realm arrived on February 15. Napoleon had tapped his elder brother for that role on New Year's Eve, 1805. It was perhaps the best choice under the circumstances. Joseph had already proven his political worth as a skilled diplomat, legislator, and advisor. As a genuine liberal and romantic, he was eager to bring progressive changes to the kingdom. Yet he was hardly the perfect match for the mission. He tended toward indecision, indolence, and, in times of danger, timidity.[13]

Nonetheless, the two generally worked well together. Of all his brothers, Joseph was the closest to Napoleon. In scores of heart-felt letters from their boyhood onward, Napoleon revealed his deepest feelings and thoughts, exchanged views on a range of subjects, plotted to advance the family's fortunes, and even asked Joseph's aid in his courtship of Desiree Clary, the younger sister of Julie, whom Joseph had married in August 1794. And from an early age, Napoleon had dominated Joseph, giving him advice on career, love, politics, writing style, family, and, later, the craft of government and diplomacy.

Napoleon helped Joseph land a series of ever more powerful posts, including commissary general of Bonaparte's army on the first Italian campaign, ambassador first to Parma and then Rome, and a member of the Council of Five Hundred. After the November 1799 coup, the First Consul named him a state councilor and senator, and gave him such important diplomatic missions as negotiating the 1801 Concordat with Rome, the 1802 peace treaty of Amiens with Britain, and the 1803 sale of Louisiana to the United States. In 1804 the new emperor named him a prince and grand elector, and in 1805 left him to run the empire while he embarked on his campaign that would be capped by Austerlitz. After such a distinguished apprenticeship, Joseph was a natural choice to rule the kingdom of Naples. On March 30, 1806, after the French army had secured southern Italy, Napoleon officially decreed that his brother was now Joseph I, King of Naples.

As with other French possessions across Europe, the mission in Naples was to modernize the realm and integrate it into the empire. Joseph certainly had his work cut out for him. Southern Italy was a feudal backwater, with a population of mostly poverty-stricken, superstitious peasants; a bureaucracy renowned for being corrupt, inept, and brutal; and an armed, uniformed mob which passed for an army. Although the new king was no workaholic, he did know how to study a problem, make a decision, and then delegate the policy to those who could best carry it out. Napoleon hand-picked a talented group to serve as Joseph's state council.

Gradually the reforms began to take effect. Government was revolutionized with a French-style constitution and the Code Napoleon. Well-trained police and inspectors began to root out petty crime and corruption. The economy was stimulated with investments that bettered transportation and communications by land and sea. Revenues from taxes and tariffs rose and were reinvested in the economy and administration. The army was professionalized. Two years later Napoleon would be so pleased that he would tap Joseph to try to perform similar wonders as the king of another very backward realm. However, Joseph would not be quite as successful atop his second throne.

Joseph was not the only brother who received a crown in 1806. Louis would also be so blessed—or cursed—by Napoleon's ambitions. Napoleon tapped Louis to rule the former United Provinces of the Netherlands, which had been transformed into the Batavian Republic during the French Revolution, and would soon be the Kingdom of Holland. In 1805 the emperor had abolished the republic's directory, replaced it with an executive "Great Committee" led by a "grand pensioner," and entrusted that post to Rutger Jan Schimmelpenninck, who had served as Dutch ambassador to Paris. That leader would soon be pensioned off, as soon as he and the committee had fulfilled the latest decree from Paris. On March 14, 1806, Napoleon had Talleyrand write a letter to the Dutch leaders directing that they either invite Louis to be their king or agree to have their land annexed to France.[14]

It took another two months of bitter debate before the Great Committee chose the lesser of two evils, on May 3. French and Dutch envoys then began to negotiate the details of life under King Louis. On May 24 a treaty was signed whereby Schimmelpenninck would resign and a delegation would journey to Paris to beseech the emperor to grant them both independence and his brother as their monarch. The catch was that the Kingdom of Holland would be independent in name only, and the monarch not at all. The delegation arrived on June 5 and presented its petition to the emperor.

That same day Napoleon announced his latest royal creation to the Senate. After citing the familiar sophism that the Dutch had freely chosen to dissolve their republic into a monarchy, he explained the real reasons. The most vital was to bolster the Bonaparte clan's lineage, since he had adopted Louis' son as his heir. Holland, of course, had strategic military and economic importance as well. Finally, he explained that Louis, "being without a single personal ambition," was making a sacrifice for France. There were certainly worse sacrifices that the emperor would call upon his subjects to make![15]

Napoleon's parting words to his brother were: "Never cease being French." Louis was formally enthroned as the king of Holland at The Hague on June 23. One line in particular of his inaugural speech was designed at once to sooth his subjects and irritate his brother: "From the moment I set foot on Dutch soil I became Dutch."[16] He would soon prove wrong the emperor's hope that he was merely uttering an insincere platitude. Over the next four years the relations between the two brothers would fray to the snapping point as Louis found an array of passive-aggressive ways to defy virtually every one of Napoleon's demands.

The source of that political estrangement was thoroughly personal. Louis now had the means of getting back at his big brother for years of real, exaggerated, and imagined affronts. Louis was bright, modest, honest, secretive, hard-working, peace-loving, and apparently kind-hearted to nearly everyone but his wife. He suffered from bouts of depression and ill health. Although he was fit to be neither a soldier nor a statesman, Napoleon had tried to mold him into both. Like Eugene, Louis had been attached to Napoleon's staff during his first three campaigns. The two young aides were complete opposites, with Eugene as energetic, courageous, and charismatic as Louis was lethargic, moody, and sickly. Napoleon bullied Louis to be as outstanding as Eugene, which of course only worsened his brother's hatred for them both.

That barely concealed rage culminated when Napoleon forced him to end his courtship of Emilie de Beauharnais and marry her cousin Hortense, Josephine's daughter. Like her mother, Hortense was pretty, vivacious, and passionate. She was no more attracted to Louis than he was to her. Louis was twenty-four and Hortense a mere eighteen years old when they were wed on the bitterly cold day of January 4, 1802. The ceremony was hardly a girl's dream come true. Louis made no secret that he despised Hortense, and she naturally returned the contempt. They also had to share the stage with another tempestuous couple, Murat and Caroline, who picked that day and place to renew their vows. Throughout the ceremony, Louis' face was an angry mask, while Hortense wept uncontrollably. The relationship deteriorated from there.[17] Beyond court ceremonies they stayed far apart, him to brood mostly alone or with a few confidants, and her to share her natural vivacity and intelligence with others, including, eventually, lovers.

Napoleon pestered Louis continually about fulfilling the unceasing flow of decrees that he sent him. Louis had been in power only a month when Napoleon complained that "every day you write me things that make me miserable."[18] He would eventually depose Louis for his failure to follow his commands.

The problems that Napoleon had with Louis went beyond state affairs. He received ever more reports from various sources, especially an upset Josephine, that Louis mistreated Hortense. Amidst his 1807 campaign, Napoleon sent his brother a long letter in which he systematically denigrated him as a king and a husband: "Your quarrels with the queen have penetrated the public. You have in your household the same authoritarian and effeminate character that you show in your government, and have in those affairs a rigidity that you show in your family. You treat a young woman as if you were heading a regiment. . . . You have the best and most virtuous woman, and you make her unhappy. Let her dance as much as she wants. . . . Make happy the mother of your children."[19]

Ah yes, the children. That last line may have been the most cutting of all. Hortense would give birth to three sons; only the second was undoubtedly her husband's. It is quite possible that Napoleon fathered her first son, Napoleon Louis Charles, who was born on October 10, 1802. Louis Constant, Napoleon's valet, hinted strongly and repeatedly that this was so, and insisted that "I knew better than anyone the emperor's loves."[20] Certainly Napoleon always expressed a love for Hortense beyond that of a doting stepfather. Was it possible that Josephine, herself unable to bear any more children, was happy to have her daughter act as a surrogate, especially since the lad who was at once her grandson and secret stepson would inherit the French empire?

Napoleon legally adopted that son as his own and designated him as his successor to the French throne, with Louis and Hortense acting as regent should he be less than eighteen years old. Napoleon was a doting father to his heir. He would be less affectionate with the next two boys, Napoleon Louis, who was born on October 11, 1804, and Charles Louis Napoleon, the future Napoleon III, on April 20, 1808; the third son's paternity would also be questioned. Napoleon was heart-broken when his heir died of croup on May 5,

1807. Although the second son took his older brother's place in the succession, the emperor chose not to adopt him. Instead, the death precipitated his goal of eventually divorcing Josephine and finding a fertile royal womb to marry. That second son would be disinherited from the French crown in 1811 when a son was born to Napoleon and Marie Louise.[21]

Elisa was the third beneficiary that year of Napoleon's family ambitions. After his coronation he had granted all his siblings royal titles; it would take a bit longer to find them lands and peoples to rule. On March 18, 1805, he granted his least favorite sister Elisa and her husband Felix Bacciochi the minor city-state of Piombino. On March 30, 1806, he joined an expanded duchy of Lucca to Piombino to create a grand duchy.[22]

Although Elisa was not pretty, coquettish, and conniving like Caroline and Pauline, she proved to be an able ruler. She had no sooner asserted power over her expanded realm when she became embroiled in a conflict with Rome. The catalyst was her implementation of her brother's orders to subordinate the church to the state and nationalize its property, as had been done in France and the Kingdom of Italy. The Archbishop of Lucca and the Pope condemned her actions. Napoleon told her to hang tough and, along with his other policies that offended Catholicism, defended her in his letters to the pope and the archbishop. Elisa herself wrote a powerful defense of her actions to Pius VII. She also embarked on a policy of economic and social reforms for her people, which prompted a letter of glowing praise from her brother. Napoleon would eventually reward Elisa's loyalty and competence by giving her all of Tuscany.[23]

Among the Bonaparte sisters, Pauline was the most beautiful, least talented, and closest to Napoleon. Her first husband, Victor Leclerc, actually bore a physical resemblance to and had a lively personality similar to that of her brother.[24] She accompanied Leclerc when he led the expedition to retake St. Domingue. Her mourning did not last long after yellow fever killed him on October 22, 1802. She returned to France and soon wed Camillo Borghese, a rich, powerful Roman noble. Marriage hardly curbed her gaiety and frivolity. Indeed, her excesses were so great that in April 1804 Napoleon wrote her a stern letter demanding that she behave with dignity, and asked Cardinal Fesch, their uncle and his ambassador to Rome, to keep her in line.[25] Although her behavior changed little, Napoleon granted her the duchy of Gustalla on March 30, 1806. With a realm of her own, Pauline could now party to her heart's content, and there was nothing Napoleon's subsequent diplomacy could do to stop her.

One last sibling, Caroline, along with her husband Joachim Murat, would receive a realm in 1806, the Duchy of Berg and Cleves. Napoleon's other siblings as rulers were merely, at worst, inept and corrupt; whereas Caroline and Murat would eventually be outright treacherous after they took the throne of Naples in 1808.

And before that, Murat's impetuousness would bring France to the brink of war with Prussia.

Revolutionizing Germany

Of all the clouds on the diplomatic horizon as 1806 unfolded, none was more ominous to Napoleon than the one hovering over Prussia. There the emperor faced another one of those royal couples composed of a dithering husband and a vengeful wife who hated all things French and Napoleon most of all. Prussia's state council was split between those who would appease and those who would oppose any more French demands on Prussia and expansion over Germany. The hard-line faction had convinced Frederick William to repudiate the Treaty of Schonbrunn that Count Christian Haugwitz had set before him in December. The British and Russian ambassadors were urging the king to join their coalition against France.

The war that eventually broke out between France and Prussia in October 1806 was not inevitable, but became ever more likely as the year advanced. The two states were locked in a classic security dilemma. Neither the emperor nor the king wanted war; but each took measures which the other perceived as aggressive, and thus needed to be countered with even tougher measures. The result was a vicious cycle of worsening fears, resentments, and affronts that would dead-end in war.

With his ever more uncompromising approach to conducting diplomacy, Napoleon believed he had no choice but to make an example of Prussia. After all, the king had broken his promise of neutrality and mobilized his army against France, even if Austerlitz had ended the war before the Prussians could draw blood. To not punish that transgression would encourage other rulers to do the same with impunity if they saw an advantage in it. So when Haugwitz appeared in Paris with a list of treaty revisions, Napoleon brushed them aside. The treaty was non-negotiable. Prussia had only one choice: ratification or war. He backed that threat by mobilizing allies and massing troops near Prussia.[26]

Once again Haugwitz wilted before the emperor's diplomatic barrage. Under the Treaty of Paris, signed by Duroc and Haugwitz on February 15, 1806, Prussia would ally with France; cede to France Wesel, Ansbach, Neuchatel, Cleves, and Valengin; break relations with Britain; and recognize all the territorial and political changes for France, Italy, and Naples. In return Prussia could take Hanover, an action guaranteed to provoke a diplomatic rupture with Britain, since it was the royal family's ancestral home.

When Frederick William balked at ratifying such a treaty, Napoleon sent him a very pointed reminder of his duties and the consequences if he evaded them: "I cannot convey the pain that I received after learning of the treaty's reception in Berlin. Your Majesty more than anyone knows that a treaty is the result of a competition between two wills." The emperor's will obviously had prevailed, and thus the king must yield to that reality. He then hinted that the alternative would be a war that he hoped would never happen.[27]

The emperor's diplomacy got exactly what he wanted: peace with Prussia and war between Prussia and Britain. Upon learning that Frederick William had marched into Hanover, Whitehall announced a blockade of Prussia's ports on May 21 and a war declaration on June 21. The Prussian king and his council had no choice but to reluctantly issue their own declaration.

So far, so very good, from Napoleon's perspective. Then he did a very stupid thing. He sent an emissary to London with a proposal to swap Hanover for Sicily, transfer Malta to a neutral power, and recognize Britain's possession of the Cape of Good Hope in return for Whitehall's recognition of Napoleon's conquests and king-making on the continent. He was especially concerned to take Sicily, because with that island along with Malta in English hands, they "would have drawn an insurmountable barrier across the Mediterranean which would prevent our communications with the Adriatic and Constantinople." Naturally the British not only spurned that proposal, but revealed Napoleon's Hanover offer to the Prussians. That would eventually push Frederick William into a decision for war.[28]

But that provocation occurred in August. Napoleon had committed another earlier that year when he united the duchies of Berg and Cleves into a Grand Duchy and awarded it to Murat and Caroline on March 15, 1806. With its capital at Dusseldorf and location in central Germany, the gift made strategic if not diplomatic or administrative sense. Murat was a gallant, if at times foolhardy, cavalry commander. As a diplomat he was merely foolhardy, all bluster and swagger and no common sense. He offended rather than enticed his diplomatic foils. As an administrator he was inept in executing the detailed instructions, explanations, and lessons in statecraft that Napoleon sent him. The emperor would forever chide him for his incompetence, but to no avail.

Murat had no sooner settled into his new realm than he began to enlarge it by ordering his troops into Werden, Essen, and Elten, each a patch of land centered on an abbey. He justified those seizures by claiming that they were legally a part of the Cleves which Prussia had ceded to France. Berlin rejected the claim and marched troops to the frontier. Napoleon had Talleyrand offer to clean up the mess. Although the foreign minister was obviously not a disinterested party, he convinced the Prussians that Murat's claim to those lands was rooted in more than the fact that he simply wanted them. When the conflicting legal claims were sorted out, it seemed that Cleves did indeed enjoy title.[29]

Alas, Murat could not leave well enough alone. He now insisted that the Prussians had offended his honor, an offense which could only be erased with compensation. Once again the Prussians protested. Napoleon had Talleyrand try to appease them by encouraging them to take Pomerania from Sweden. That, of course, would have embroiled Prussia in a war with Sweden; the king demurred, and tried to calm his enraged ministers.

Napoleon, in turn, tried to appease Murat by annexing the Principality of Dulenberg to his duchy in July 1806. When Murat continued to bluster, Napoleon chastised him for "insulting Prussia," which "is very contrary to my intentions. I am in good friendship with that power. . . . Don't make a single offense or give a single pretext. . . . I cannot express the anxiety I feel in reading your letters. You are hopelessly rash."[30]

Napoleon's instigations did not stop with Berlin. Among his list of demands for Vienna was that the Austrians join the French in driving the Russians from Cattaro, Montenegro's seaport, which Vienna had ceded in the Treaty of Pressburg. That, of course, would have launched Vienna into a war with St. Petersburg. In a convention signed between France and Austria on April 16, Francis committed himself merely to try to talk the Russians out. However, he did agree to Napoleon's other demands, including allowing the French to build a military road, with supply depots, linking Italy with Istria and Dalmatia; shutting all remaining Austrian Adriatic ports to British and Russian ships; and opening the Austrian ports of Trieste and Fiume to French and Italian commerce.[31]

Francis believed that he had no choice but to grant these latest concessions. There was certainly a hard practical reason not to resist. The Austrian army was in no condition to fight, having been routed, scattered, and depleted. Across his realm, French troops occupied key strategic points, and were emptying the treasury, arsenals, warehouses, and stables. Yet there was perhaps a moral as well as a practical reason to go along. In less than a decade, Austria had suffered three humiliating defeats at Napoleon's hands. Francis recognized that ultimately he had been responsible for each loss, by letting his more belligerent advisors talk him into war. The emperor had let him off fairly easily in the first two peace treaties, and only imposed painful terms with the third. For now Vienna had no choice but to turn the other cheek, go along, and patiently await an opportunity to take back all that had been lost, and more.

To that end, Francis took one more humiliating step. In May 1806 he announced his plans to eventually abdicate his throne as Holy Roman Emperor, and that henceforth he would simply be the Emperor of Austria. Who would the Holy Roman Empire then turn to for its leader? Most assumed that Napoleon was impatiently awaiting an opportunity to consider such an opening as an offer.

Those who did not fathom Napoleon's strategy were stunned when he renounced any intention of doing so. After catching their breath, they then assumed that he was just playing hard to get, as he had with the kingdom of Italy. But actually his goal was not to rule over but to abolish the Holy Roman Empire and absorb most of its lands into the French empire.[32]

The first diplomatic step to that end had occurred the previous November when Charles, the Duke of Dalberg and the Holy Roman Empire's chancellor, requested that the Rhineland states secede from the Holy Roman Empire and form an independent Rhine Confederation under French protection. Napoleon was happy to harvest this latest diplomatic initiative he had planted. The Rhine Confederation was founded on July 12, 1806, by a treaty signed by the foreign ministers of France, the new kingdoms of Bavaria and Wurttemberg, the new grand duchies of Baden, Berg, and Hesse-Darmstadt, the new duchy of Nassau, and ten city-states in the Rhine valley. Under a constitution adopted by the members on August 1, Frankfort would be the capital, with a prince primate and a diet of two "colleges," one made up of the six kings and the other of the ten princes. In gratitude for French protection, the Confederation would pay an annual fee to Paris and supply 88,400 troops in war. Napoleon tapped the pliant yet capable Dalberg as the Confederation's prince primate.

The Holy Roman Empire imploded shortly after those sixteen states defected. Dalberg resigned his post as chancellor on July 31. The Imperial Diet dissolved itself on August 1, 1806. Francis II officially abdicated as Holy Roman Emperor on August 6; henceforth he would be Francis I, Emperor of

Austria. Napoleon then rolled up his sleeves and consolidated the over one hundred remaining states into thirty-seven, which included, of course, all sixteen Rhine Confederation members. He had Talleyrand issue a declaration that the Rhine Confederation was "inviolable." Finally, he wrote to Dalberg a letter expressing his own political vision, as well as extending protection to the Rhine Confederation.[33]

Berlin condemned the Holy Roman Empire's destruction and Rhine Confederation's creation. Talleyrand replied by encouraging the Prussians to create their own north German confederation—while separately warning Saxony, Hesse-Cassel, Hamburg, Bremen, and Lubeck never to join. When Napoleon got word that Prussia and Saxony were negotiating an alliance, he made it clear that war would result if they did so.[34]

Overall, Napoleon's diplomacy had succeeded brilliantly. He had shifted Germany's power balance decisively in France's favor, first by crippling Austria and then by trimming Prussia. He had shattered and then shoveled onto history's dustbin the Holy Roman Empire, despite its thousand-year legacy. He had fathered the Rhine Confederation, which gave France a strategic buffer against eastern enemies, 84,000 troops, an annual income, and a huge, affluent market for French products. What more could he want?

War or Peace

Even as Napoleon was revolutionizing Germany, he sought to forge peace with Russia. Technically, Russia and France were still at war. However, there was only one small spot over which the belligerents could still spill blood: Montenegro's strategic seaport of Cattaro. This was among the long list of lands to which Vienna had transferred title to Paris under the Treaty of Pressburg.

Grand dreams of Napoleon and Alexander alike revolved around that remote stretch of rugged coast. The emperor sought to transform the Adriatic into a French sea.[35] The tsar hoped, by dominating the Adriatic's eastern seaboard, to anchor Russia's expansion across the Balkans and strengthen its protectorate over the Ionian Republic at the Adriatic's southeastern end. The Russians had previously occupied Cattaro.

Napoleon had elicited a promise from Francis to try to convince Alexander to leave. On May 12 Alexander had replied with a firm no, and ordered Admiral Dimitri Siniavin to reinforce Cattaro.[36] So Napoleon's indirect diplomacy through Vienna had failed. The only path now was to drive out the Russians, and from that position of strength begin talks.

To that end he ordered General Gabriel Molitor to occupy Ragusa (Dubrovnik). Molitor and his troops marched into Ragusa on May 26, and Siniavin promptly blockaded it. French reinforcements arrived under General Jacques Lauriston, who took over command from Molitor. A Russian and Montenegrin army led by General Viazemsky disembarked at Ragusa-Vecchia on June 3 and marched on to besiege Ragusa on June 17. Lauriston counterattacked on July 3, routed the Russians, and took Vecchia-Ragusa.

Alexander had Pierre d'Oubril, his envoy in Paris, offer a deal to Napoleon. The tsar would recognize France's kingdom of Naples, to include southern Italy and Sicily, if the emperor would grant Ferdinand IV title to a kingdom consisting of Dalmatia, Ragusa, and Albania, under Russian protection. Meanwhile Alexander had to bolster his vulnerable military, and thus diplomatic, position at Cattaro. If he failed to do so, the French would eventually be able to muster enough sea and land power to take by force what Russia did not yield with grace. The only way to forestall that would be to strike a deal with the British for a massive joint expedition in the Adriatic. But for that Whitehall would undoubtedly demand an expansion of influence for Britain there and elsewhere in the eastern Mediterranean. For now, neither Austria nor Prussia was capable of resisting France. Indeed, Napoleon had diplomatically driven Prussia into war against Britain. Alexander had to change that.

During May and June the tsar sent a series of letters to King Frederick William of Prussia reminding him of the vow they had made before Frederick the Great's tomb and beseeching him to resume peace with Britain and war against France. In his diplomatic offensive Alexander had an ally in the vacillating king's uncompromising wife Louise. Frederick William finally succumbed and agreed to a defensive alliance between Prussia and Russia on June 30.[37]

The word of the Russo-Prussian alliance and the tsar's Adriatic deal hit Napoleon hard. He certainly did not want war at that time. But to agree to Alexander's offer would mean abandoning his Adriatic dreams. He got Talleyrand to pressure d'Oubril into signing a treaty on July 20 by which Ferdinand would be compensated with the Balearic Islands at Spain's expense; the Russians would withdraw from Cattaro and eventually from the Ionian Republic; and the French would withdraw from Ragusa, reduce their troops east of the Rhine, and resume trade with Russia.

In the likely event that Alexander rejected that treaty, Napoleon hoped for diplomatic breakthroughs on two other fronts. The best way to counter the Russians in the Balkans was once again to stir up the Turks against them. In June 1806 Napoleon appealed to Selim III for an alliance, in typically stirring language: "One of the most grand and precious goals which I want to achieve with my military, is to support the most useful as well as ancient of our allies. . . . My enemies are also yours. Never fear me; united with me, there will never be any doubt of our power against our enemies." He proposed a grand scheme that involved a united front of France, Turkey, and Persia against Russia. To that alliance, France would send 25,000 troops under General Marmont to aid the Turks against the Russians in Wallachia, and six ships of the line to sail with the Turkish fleet against the Russian fleet in the Black Sea. The sultan was actually considering that deal—until he got word of French double-dealing: at the same time that Napoleon was trying to foster an alliance with Istanbul, he was trying to talk Ali Pasha of Janina into warring against the Turks. Eventually Selim III, inspired by Napoleon's letter recounting his conquest of Prussia, would declare war on Russia in December 1806 and Britain in January 1807; but he would do so without a formal alliance with France.[38]

Far more important than an alliance with Turkey was peace with Britain, with which France had officially been at war since May 1803. William Pitt, France's most indomitable foe, had died on January 23, 1806, of what many believed was a heart broken by his failure to defeat his nemesis. George III asked William Wyndam, Baron Grenville, to form a government. That took several weeks of haggling among various parliamentary factions. Eventually Grenville was able to form a coalition, most notably with Charles Fox as foreign secretary.

Fox had opposed war with France ever since the revolution began. He was determined to forge a lasting peace with France. To do so he needed some way to break the stalemate. He soon stumbled upon a startling possibility. With access to secret papers and briefings by experts, he learned to his horror about Britain's dozen years of covert operations with royalists and other rebels against first the French Revolution and then Napoleon. At that moment the latest plot was unfolding to assassinate the emperor. For both practical and moral reasons, Fox believed it was better to stifle than nurture that plot. If the plot failed, it would simply be another propaganda coup for Napoleon. If the emperor was murdered, his place most likely would be taken by just another dictator, and the war would sputter on to no nation's benefit. So he tipped off Talleyrand on February 20.[39]

Talleyrand conveyed both his gratitude and a desire for peace to Fox via the release of British General Francis, Earl Yarmouth, the highest-ranking prisoner of war held by France. Fox was happy to resume peace talks, but unfortunately chose to send Yarmouth back to Paris to conduct them. When Yarmouth proved unfit for that job, Fox reinforced him with James Maitland, Earl Lauderdale.[40]

The pressure on Fox to negotiate a lasting peace tightened during the summer. First, Whitehall felt compelled to declare war on Prussia, on June 21, for its takeover of Hanover. Then came word of the peace treaty signed between Talleyrand and d'Oubril on July 20. Once again it seemed that Britain was fated not only to fight on alone, but possibly even with the continent's great powers united against it.

The French-British talks stalled on a number of points, of which the most implacably held were Talleyrand's demands that Britain withdraw from Malta, recognize Joseph as King of the Two Sicilies, compensate Ferdinand IV with the Balearic Islands, and accept Prussia's takeover of Hanover. After weeks of stalemate on those issues, Talleyrand suddenly offered a grand compromise: southern Italy would go to Joseph, Sicily to Ferdinand, and Malta to Britain. Fox insisted that Hanover be restored to independence. When Talleyrand shrugged off that land as well, Fox suddenly found himself agreeing to a deal.

It was Napoleon who killed that chance for peace. First he insisted on his original position; then, after the British delegation left for home on August 11, a peace based on the Treaty of Amiens. That was unacceptable to Whitehall. The pressure for peace lifted somewhat when word arrived in London on September 3 that Alexander had spurned d'Oubril's treaty and recalled him to St. Petersburg. The last chance for peace died with Fox on September 13. Charles Grey, Lord Howick, took his place, but without Fox's will to somehow find a formula to end the war. Indeed, dramatic recent events were transforming the political calculus for war or peace, with the former increasingly seen as preferable.

Word of some notable triumphs on land and sea that summer calmed some of the British public's swelling resentment against the war. A British expedition under General John Stuart and Admiral Sydney Smith had routed a French army under General Jean Reynier at Maida in Calabria, Italy, on June 30. That was the first time in decades that British troops had trounced French troops in an open field fight. Then came word that Commodore Home Popham and General David Baird had captured the Cape of Good Hope in January 1806.

Closer to home, France and Prussia were stepping ever closer to war's brink. Russia was mustering its own armies to march west as Prussian's ally. All Whitehall needed was a pledge from Berlin to disgorge Hanover; with that, it would be happy to throw its financial and military weight behind Prussia. The final push of Frederick William toward war came with the British revelation that Napoleon had offered to restore Hanover.

The 1806 Campaign

Unusually cautious King Frederick William was furious when he learned on August 6 of Napoleon's betrayal. Three days later he called for a general mobilization. Within a month much of the army was ready. He was further emboldened with the transformation of the alliance with Alexander from defensive to offensive on August 26. On September 12 he ordered troops to march into Saxony to pressure his reluctant ally, Elector Frederick Augustus III, to muster his own men for war.

That same day Napoleon sent a conciliatory letter to Frederick William urging him to keep the peace: "I consider that a war between us would be like a civil war given how entwined our interests are. . . . I rest unshakeable in my dedication to our alliance." However, Napoleon continued, if the war party in Berlin persists in mobilizing and menacing my army and allies in Germany, "I will be obliged to receive the war which is declared against me." He asked Ambassador Antoine Laforest to elaborate that message to Haugwitz: "If they want war they can stay armed; if they want peace they must demobilize." He cautioned Laforest "to communicate this with prudence, moderation, and wisdom, because the emperor [Napoleon] truly desires not to fire a shot against Prussia. He would regard that event as an evil, since it would just worsen our interests which are already complicated enough."[41]

That message provoked only derision from the swelling war party in Berlin. Its members pressured the reluctant king to dismiss the emperor's sentiments and take the final step. On September 25 Frederick William issued Napoleon an ultimatum demanding that by October 8 he promise to abandon all lands east of the Rhine, withdraw all his troops to west of that river, and recognize the North German Confederation which the Prussians were then organizing—or else.[42]

That ultimatum put Napoleon in a bind. He did not want war, but even less did he want to give up his German lands. He fired off to Berlin a letter to his ambassador with instructions to do anything possible short of an actual concession to placate the Prussian king. Meanwhile, he positioned six corps a day or so march from the southern frontiers of Prussia and Saxony, called up 33,000 Rhine Confederation contingents, and had the Imperial Guard raced from Paris to that front in horse-drawn wagons. In all he assembled 129,000 troops to the 114,000 Prussians and Saxons near the frontier. On September 25 the emperor left Paris for his army.[43]

War was still not inevitable, and Napoleon still hoped to prevent it. On October 5 he sent Frederick William a request for a clear declaration of peace by October 8. The king answered with silence.[44]

Two days later Napoleon ordered his army to attack. What followed was his quickest and most devastating victory. The French routed the enemy's advance guard at Saalfeld on October 10, and within days overran Saxony. On October 12, as his corps continued their relentless and rapid march toward Berlin, Napoleon fired off his latest letter to Frederick William asking for peace. On October 14 he crushed the Prussians at the twin battles of Jena and Auerstadt, and relentlessly pursued the remnants. On October 15 he submitted a bill for 159,424,000 francs to Prussia to underwrite the cost of his campaign. He began to integrate Saxony into the Rhine Confederation.[45]

Napoleon was hardly surprised to receive on October 18 a letter from Frederick William requesting an armistice. What offended him was the messenger rather than the message. Conveying that letter was Marquis Girolamo de Lucchessini, the former ambassador to France. Napoleon despised Lucchessini on two counts: his haughty attitude toward the emperor, and his exaggerated reports to Berlin (whose contents were intercepted by French spies), which had convinced the king that he could win a war against France. Thus, ironically, one of the war's worst instigators was now the conduit by which the Prussian king begged for an end to it.[46]

Napoleon's reply to Frederick William stated the obvious: "Any suspension of arms which would give time for the Russian armies to arrive . . . would be too contrary to my interests for me to allow it." He then tried to soften the king to embrace peace by expressing his sorrow "that two nations which for so many reasons were meant to be friends have been drawn into a conflict so meaningless."[47]

The king agreed to hear the emperor's terms. Napoleon sent Duroc to open talks with Lucchessini at Magdeburg on October 21. The terms that Duroc presented were harsh but appropriate: Prussia would surrender all its lands west of the Elbe, except the Duchy of Magdeburg and the Mark of Brandenburg, which would be split among the Rhine Confederation; pay a huge indemnity of 160 million francs; renounce all pretensions to influence over Germany; and ally with France against Russia and Britain. Accept these terms now, Duroc warned, or face even tougher terms later. He then held up the fate of Austria as an example not to follow.

The war faction won out over the peace faction in the tug-of-war for Frederick William's royal consent. Recognizing that French animosities toward Lucchessini were not helping his cause, the king dispatched Count Friedrich Zastrow to catch up with the negotiators, who themselves were trying to keep up with the quick-marching French army. The talks convened briefly at Wittenberg, then continued at the king's palace of Charlottenburg at Berlin.

Frederick William kept rejecting the emperor's terms despite the reality that Napoleon was systematically destroying his army and kingdom. Within a month of the invasion the French had overrun most of the country, killed or captured 135,000 Prussian troops, and taken such key fortresses and arsenals as Stettin, Custrin, Magdeburg, Glogau, Hameln, Lubeck, and Posen.[48]

Napoleon paid homage to Frederick the Great at his tomb at his Palace Sans Souci at Potsdam on October 26. However, rather undiplomatically, the emperor also carried away some souvenirs that were sure to enrage the Prussians: Frederick's sword, belt, and Black Eagle decoration, which he sent to Paris for "safe-keeping."[49]

The following day Napoleon rode triumphantly at the head of his Imperial Guard into Berlin. His determination to devastate Prussia as thoroughly as he had Austria was bolstered when he gained access to the diplomatic archives at Berlin. His aides brought him irrefutable proof of the king's double game throughout that year, pretending to pursue peace with Paris while preparing for war.[50]

Frederick William, his court, and 35,000 troops barely escaped to East Prussia, first to Konigsberg and then to Memel, the eastern-most city of his realm. There, on November 7, he finally made his first concession. He sent the emperor a letter in which he requested an armistice and reported that he had asked Alexander to halt the advance of his armies to aid Prussia. It took Duroc and Zastrow a week to work out the details of an armistice. Under the Truce of Charlottenburg, signed on November 16, the relentless French advance halted abruptly.[51]

But meanwhile, to keep the pressure on Frederick William, Napoleon issued a decree on November 3 that organized his conquered territory into four districts, Berlin, Custrin, Stettin, and Magdeburg; named a military governor to each; and began milking them for provisions and taxes. He pointedly pardoned the Saxon elector Frederick Augustus III as the first step in converting him and the 6,300 captured soldiers he freed into allies. The next step came at Posen on December 11, 1806, when Frederick Augustus signed a treaty whereby he broke his alliance with Prussia, allied with France, and joined the Rhine Confederation. In return, Napoleon promoted Frederick Augustus from elector to king. He would soon give that new king a new realm to reign over.[52]

The Continental System

To Napoleon there was one ultimate cause for the wars plaguing Europe. It was British gold that made mercenaries of Europe's monarchs. Who could resist those English envoys with their promises of that huge initial lump sum followed by monthly payments for the duration, especially when they were also generously slipping bags of coins into the pockets of those ministers who were either genuinely or insincerely opposed to war?

The emperor understood all too well that Britain's prosperity and security ultimately rested on its vast fleet of war and merchant ships. If Napoleon could not get to the British, he could at least prevent the British from getting to a vital source of their wealth, European markets. That in turn would diminish their power to fund wars against France.

To that end, on November 21, 1806, he issued the Berlin Decree, which called for the closure of all ports of France, its allies, and its conquests to trade with Britain; the seizure of all Britons, their ships, and other property in those lands; the capture of all British shipping on the high seas; and the blockade of the British Isles themselves. He reinforced those measures two days later by decreeing that any ship that traded with Britain was also liable to seizure. Then, on December 17, he included in those sanctions any ship whose captain allowed it to be searched by or paid any fine or fee to the British. To bolster the enforcement of those decrees, he sent troops into the ports of Hamburg, Bremen, Mecklenburg, and Lubeck, and demanded that neutral Denmark conform to the same measures.[53]

In doing all that, Napoleon did not initiate economic warfare against Britain; that dated from the early 1790s, when the French and British cut off trade with each other and bullied others to do the same. After taking power, Napoleon had made a trade embargo against Britain a key tenet of treaties with

Naples in 1800, Spain in 1801 and 1803, Portugal in 1801, Russia in 1801, the Ottoman Empire in 1802, and Italy in 1803 and 1806. His Berlin Decree and its amendments combined all those bilateral deals into one grand, universal system—at least theoretically.

Napoleon knew that his Continental System, as it came to be called, would initially devastate the ports of Europe as well as those of Britain. He hoped that the economic depression would stir privateers to sail forth against British shipping and bring back their booty for sale in the deprived marketplaces. That would alleviate some of the squeeze caused by the collapse of trade. The rest, he hoped, would be made up by entrepreneurs manufacturing at home what they could no longer buy from Britain. Over the long term, the trade cutoff would stimulate a tidal shift of wealth and power from Britain to the continent, especially France.

However, Napoleon's dream was largely a chimera.[54] The embargo hurt mainland Europe much more than Britain. Whitehall retaliated with new Orders in Council on January 7, 1807, which reinforced the navy's power to scour the seas of neutral shipping. British merchants and manufacturers gradually diversified their markets away from Europe, and thus restored their profits after an initial plunge. But much of the excess production of British factories was consumed at home, as the population rose from 15.7 million in 1801 to 18 million in 1811. As for Europe, smugglers and privateers sporadically brought in shiploads of banned goods to European ports and sold them for sky-high prices. Ever more factories did open across Europe, although consumers often complained of the high costs and low quality of their goods. But overall, the Continental System rendered Europe's ports all but ghost towns as ships rotted in harbors, once-bustling businesses shut their doors, and the ranks of the jobless, homeless, and criminal swelled. All that, combined with Napoleon's insatiable demand for taxes and troops, fostered ever more hatred for the emperor and French imperialism.

But Napoleon would not admit defeat. Indeed, his stubbornness at enforcing and expanding the system worsened as its economic, political, and social costs became ever more evident. His obsession with bringing Britain to its knees through economic warfare warped and stunted his diplomatic strategy. The Continental System's "logic" was crucial in driving his decisions to invade Portugal in 1807, Spain in 1808, and Russia in 1812, all of which ultimately ended in disaster.

The 1807 Campaign

The French pursuit of the retreating Russian and Prussian forces continued into the ever more bitter winter. Murat led the advance into Warsaw on November 28, 1806. Soon Murat's corps and others which arrived marched north of the Vistula and camped in an arc covering the city. Napoleon himself rode into Warsaw on December 18. After a week he joined his army in pursuit of the enemy. The French advance guards and allied rear guards fought sharp skirmishes. But Napoleon soon called off his offensive. The main Russian and Prussian armies were far away, supplies were scarce, and the cold and snow bogged down his army. He withdrew his corps to positions closer to Warsaw's supply depots, and himself returned to the city by New Year's Eve.[55]

As always, while the battles were sporadic, the diplomacy was incessant. Napoleon dangled an offer to discuss peace. The Prussian and Russian camps were split over whether to keep fighting or get the best terms possible. Frederick William and his ministers mourned the loss of virtually all of Prussia's army and kingdom. Alexander's armies were scattered among three far-flung fronts: against the French in Poland, the Turks in the lower Danube, and the Persians in the Caucasus. Yet while the king was ready to accept defeat, the tsar stood firm. Alexander brushed off his advisors who dismissed Prussia as a lost cause that would only drag Russia down into another defeat. He and Queen Louise bolstered Frederick William's sagging backbone.

Napoleon found himself having to bolster the backbone of one of his own allies. Among the damning letters French officials found while rummaging in the Prussian archives was one from Manuel de Godoy, Spain's prime minister, to Frederick William, proposing to attack France while Napoleon was in Germany. The emperor had Talleyrand issue a severe rebuke to Madrid. The revelation of Godoy's betrayal of Spain's alliance with France deeply embarrassed Spanish King Charles IV. Charles and Godoy sent letters to Napoleon begging for forgiveness. Although the emperor was furious at Spain's bad faith, he could do nothing at that point but welcome the penitents back into the fold. The Spanish would, however, pay a price for their aborted defection. Napoleon forced Charles to recognize Joseph, rather than his own cousin Ferdinand IV, as the King of Naples; pay promptly all of Spain's debts to Paris; send 15,000 of his best troops to Hamburg and northern Germany to bolster the French rear; cut off all trade with Britain; and pressure Portugal to join the Continental System—or else face invasion. Those concessions could not have made Napoleon happier. But within a couple of years he would demand far more from that hapless king.[56]

For now, with the allies having spurned any negotiations, the key diplomatic question was what to do about Poland. Napoleon at first found the Poles "showing so much circumspection and demanding so many guarantees before declaring themselves." That was certainly understandable. Most of those who dreamed that Napoleon would restore their ancient kingdom may have worried about the depth of his commitment, when France was so far away—whereas Russia, Prussia, and Austria, which had devoured Poland in three huge gulps in 1772, 1793, and 1796, were so close. And then, many others were genuinely tied economically, culturally, and politically to St. Petersburg.

In a letter to Murat discussing his options, Napoleon made it clear that "My grandeur is not founded on helping thousands of Poles. It's for them to profit with enthusiasm from the present circumstances. It's not for me to take the first step. If they show a firm resolution of making themselves independent, if they commit themselves to supporting the king that they will be given, then I will see what I should do. . . . For now it is necessary to hold the patriots at arm's length." Then he held out a veiled promise to Murat: "I don't lack for thrones to give to my family."[57]

But for now, would it really be appropriate for one of his relatives to rule a reconstituted Poland? On second thought, Napoleon dismissed the notion. Traditionally the Saxon elector had also served as the Polish king in that elected rather than inherited monarchy. Asking the newly minted King Frederick Augustus to hold another throne would at once advance two goals: it would reinforce Napoleon's budding relationship with him; it would also create a huge swath of territory across two adjacent states, Saxony and Poland, which would drive a huge wedge between Prussia, Austria, and Russia.

But just what should that new Poland be called? Despite swelling pressure by Polish patriots, he stopped short of recreating an independent kingdom of Poland. Had he done so he would have forever alienated Prussia, Russia, and Austria. Instead in the future the very threat that he would convert the duchy of Warsaw into the kingdom of Poland might help keep those three great powers in line.[58]

Napoleon announced his decision on January 14, 1807. Frederick Augustus would reign over the Duchy of Warsaw, with most of its territory taken from Prussia. Real power would lie in a seven-man commission which Napoleon hand-picked. He granted to the duchy a French-style constitution and law code. Finally, he created a corps of troops known as the Polish Legion.[59]

His ties to Poland soon became more than strategic. Talleyrand and a coterie of Polish nobles encouraged his affair with the Countess Marie Walewska, a twenty-one year old, charming, blond beauty and passionate Polish patriot, who was married to a seventy year old man. The Emperor and countess first met when she presented a petition for Polish independence to him on January 1, 1807. He was smitten, and had Duroc try to discover her identity. It finally took the resources of Polish police chief Bielinski to learn the mystery woman's identity. She refused his demand for a private meeting, but did agree to attend a ball on January 17. They danced; she remained coy; the emperor's lust began to deepen into something greater. Constant recalled that Napoleon's belief that she was some sort of sacrificial lamb made him "more passionate than he had ever been for a woman." She succumbed to his request to meet. Despite, or perhaps because of, his "unaccustomed agitation," he respected her virtue the next day, but overwhelmed her during their rendezvous on January 19. Thereafter he spent as much time as he could with her until he left Warsaw for the front on January 30. Napoleon genuinely loved Marie. In the coming years their visits were sporadic and fleeting, and thus all the more poignant. Within months he would learn the stunning news that he had seeded a child with his Polish lover. That would eventually have vital diplomatic repercussions.[60]

Given his growing love for Marie and the horrendous weather, it was likely with considerable reluctance that Napoleon roused his scattered corps and ordered them forward in search of another Austerlitz. He would eventually find it at a town called Friedland, but only after his army had suffered a nearly seven-month hemorrhage of lives from frost, hunger, disease, and the occasional battle after first entering Poland. And at certain points along the way Napoleon would wonder whether those costs were worth what he was pursuing.

The battle of Eylau on February 7, 1807, gave the allies cause for hope. Napoleon held the field at the end of that blood-soaked day, but at a loss of 25,000 troops to the 15,000 borne mostly by the Russians. After that both sides went into winter camp. Napoleon's own strategy for that battle was sound, but was miscarried by his marshals. He had planned a grand double envelopment, but the corps of Bernadotte and Ney did not show up on time, while Lefebvre's fell not on the enemy's flank but its front, and was decimated by massed Russian cannons. Only a massive cavalry attack led by Murat prevented a decisive allied victory. The Russians and Prussians finally withdrew from the field of devastation.[61]

Eylau only reinforced Napoleon's eagerness for peace; but of course, any peace had to be on his terms. As always, in diplomacy as in war, he sought to split his enemies and deal separately with each. General Henri Bertrand acted as his envoy during much of the new year. On January 29, 1807, Bertrand took to Prussia's envoy Zastrow a letter written by Talleyrand calling for the renewal of talks and hinting at a less severe peace. The hardliners around Frederick William forced him to reject the offer. In his reply of February 16, the king merely called for a prisoner exchange. Napoleon meanwhile sent Bertrand to Alexander with a secret, oral offer to split Europe and most of Prussia between them, with the French taking Germany and much of western Prussia, and the Russians much of eastern Prussia and as much of eastern Europe as they wished. That would have eliminated the Duchy of Warsaw that Napoleon had just created and reduced Prussia to an impotent rump state. Alexander angrily rejected that scheme.[62]

Resisting the emperor's attempts to split them, the tsar and king jointly called for a general peace congress to settle all of Europe's affairs. In that they got Whitehall's backing. Napoleon agreed to participate as long as the Turks were included, and called for the congress to be held at Memel. But the allies spurned any inclusion of the Ottomans in the congress, and the notion died.[63]

Eylau and the brutal winter had plunged Napoleon into a deep funk. He felt trapped in the vast, snow-bound Polish countryside, so barren of bustling cities, good roads, and ample supplies. He was often moody, lethargic, and short-fused. His spirits began to lift on April 1 when he transferred his headquarters from the crowded, dark residence at Osterode to the airy, refined castle at Finkenstein. As the snow melted, the trees budded, and the days grew longer, his natural driving energy and ambitions reemerged.

He threw himself into readying his army for the spring 1807 campaign. This one had to be decisive. On the Polish front the Russian army swelled steadily with reinforcements and supplies while the Prussians retained a small but tough fighting force. Spies sent word that Sweden and Britain might be planning to launch expeditions against his rear in northern Germany. There was always the fear that Austria might rejoin the coalition.

Yet his own army was growing too. His allies were doing their share: one-third of his soldiers were German or Polish. By April 18 four other German states had joined the Rhine Confederation. They too would provide small contingents of troops, mostly to defend the emperor's hundreds of miles of supply lines.

Then there were the more distant allies. Napoleon's oriental dream never quite died, no matter how impractical or impossible its fulfillment proved to be. In early April he received a report from his embassy in Constantinople of the fortunes of Turkey's war with the Russians. Napoleon sent Selim III a letter extolling his efforts, exaggerating the successes of his own campaign, and urging the sultan to retake Moldavia and Wallachia and ally with Persia. He warned that the Greeks were actually conniving with the Russians to undermine Turkish rule over their provinces. He urged him to close the straits against the Russian fleet. He then explained that his recent takeover of Dalmatia was solely to help him contain Russian power and posed no threat to the Ottomans in the Balkans. Shortly thereafter he got word that Selim had been murdered in a coup; it remained unclear whether the new sultan would carry on the war.[64]

That same week the emperor and his army were both amused and heartened by the unexpected arrival of an envoy from an even more exotic land, Persia. Shah Fatah Ali sent an urgent request for aid against the Russians in Georgia and the British in India. Napoleon united France and Persia as allies with the Treaty of Finkenstein on May 4. Soon he would dispatch General Claude Gardane to head a seventy-man military and diplomatic mission. They would not only advise the shah but map routes both south to India and north to Central Asia.[65]

Although Napoleon was sincere in trying to nurture a grand alliance with Turkey and Persia for both strategic and sentimental reasons, all those efforts and hopes could never be more than a diplomatic sideshow. The decisive front lay before him.

Amidst his 1807 campaign yet another issue arose that demanded delicate diplomacy. Josephine had heard the disturbing rumors about his deepening relationship with Marie Walewska. So he wrote her his assurance that she need never fear anyone stealing his feelings for her: "I love my little Josephine, good, sulky, and capricious, who knows how to make a quarrel with grace . . . because she is always amiable, except when she is jealous—then she becomes a devil."[66] What he did not say, of course, was that he could love more than one woman at the same time in different ways.

In mid-April the emperor received the latest invitation for a general congress, this one to be held at Copenhagen and confined to Russia, Prussia, Britain, and France. Talleyrand urged him to accept that offer along with its accompanying armistice in place. Napoleon sharply chided his foreign minister with the argument that he first had to strengthen his bargaining position by taking Danzig.[67] In his April 29 reply to the allies, he declined their invitation, with the excuse that honor permitted him to attend only if joined by his allies: "The participation in the work of peace by Spain, Turkey, and other warring states and French allies in the present conflict is as necessary as it is just. I raise no barrier to allowing England and Russia to make common cause, although France has always regarded this as contrary to its policy's primary principles. Why do you refuse me the same thing with" my allies?[68] Frederick William saw the reason in that, but Alexander and British envoy Hutchinson convinced him to turn a blind eye to it.

So the fighting resumed in late May; but this time, mercifully, was over in less than three weeks. After a half year's siege the French captured Danzig on May 26. The allies won a limited victory at Heilsberg on June 10. Then, four days later on June 14, Napoleon concentrated his army and hurled it at the Russians at Friedland. In the rout the Russians lost 20,000 men and 80 guns. The French then captured Konigsberg with over 200 Russian ships packed with supplies.[69]

Alexander was still determined to fight on. But now a majority of his advisors joined with Frederick William and most of his advisors to urge him to seek the best terms. The tsar accepted an armistice on June 21 as preparations were made for a peace conference at Tilsit.[70]

With the imperial guards of the two rulers lining their respective shores of the Niemen River, Napoleon and Alexander embraced on a large raft anchored midstream on June 25. Each was accompanied by a retinue of his closest aides and generals, all dressed immaculately, their uniforms bedecked with glittering medals and their hats with fluttering plumes. The monarchs spoke animatedly for two hours. The emperor's diplomatic powers were at their height. Soon he had beguiled a tsar bitter at his latest defeat and fearful of his realm's fate to trust, admire, and follow him. It was all, as Alexander later put it, "like a dream." He was especially struck by Napoleon's ability always to be "in the midst of the greatest excitement" with "a calm, cool head; all his rages are for others and most often they are only calculated."[71]

Having conquered the tsar's heart and mind, the emperor's next step was to harness him into lockstep against a common enemy, Britain. He soon had Alexander exclaiming that "I hate the English no less than you do and I shall second you in everything you undertake against them." Napoleon could not have scripted those words better himself. To that he replied, then "everything can be settled and peace is made."[72]

The terms Napoleon offered were relatively light. Under the Treaty of Tilsit, signed on July 7, Alexander agreed to yield Cattaro and the Ionian Islands to France; withdraw from Wallachia and Moldavia; recognize Napoleon's radical reorganization of Europe from the North to the Tyrrhenian Seas, including the annexations to France, the thrones of Joseph in Naples, Louis in Holland, Murat in Berg, and eventually Jerome in Westphalia, the Rhine Confederation, the Duchy of Warsaw, and French occupation of the duchies of Mecklenburg-Schwerin, Saxe-Coburg, and Oldenburg; and finally, to expel Louis XVIII and his court from Mittau. As usual, the emperor tossed the vanquished a token concession; in this case, Alexander could take the Polish province of Bialystok.[73]

Those provisions were all publicly displayed. Secretly the emperor and tsar pledged to help each other resolve their respective wars with Britain and Turkey. They would first try diplomacy by offering to act as mediators in the other's war. If by November 1 that peace offensive had failed, the tsar was to break diplomatic relations with London and join the Continental System, and the emperor would do the same with Istanbul. They also built into their treaty the recognition of each other's future planned conquests, Sicily for France and Finland for Russia.

Napoleon made a series of gestures to honor and influence the tsar. He had his Imperial Guard throw a dinner for Alexander's Imperial Guard; the banquet and toasts ended with the French and Russians exchanging uniforms! Another day, after reviewing a parade of Alexander and his Guard, Napoleon pinned his own Legion of Honor on the soldier the tsar considered his bravest.

In contrast to his gentle treatment of Alexander, Napoleon intended to punish Frederick William harshly for starting a war against France and refusing to accept defeat until he had no other choice. That intention was nearly derailed by Queen Louise's appearance on July 6. As she knelt before him and beseeched him to be merciful to Prussia, he was nearly as enchanted by her as the tsar had been by him. She continued her charm offensive at an elaborate banquet later that night. Napoleon confessed to Josephine that "I had to resist not giving in to her and making even more concessions to her husband. But while I was gallant I held on to my policy." He reassured his wife that, although she "was really charming and full of coquetry toward me . . . don't be at all jealous."[74]

Constant paints a vivid picture of the sexual and political tensions between Napoleon and Louise: "The queen was beautiful and gracious, maybe a bit haughty and severe; but that did not prevent her from being adored by everyone around her. The emperor looked for ways to please her, and she did not neglect any of those innocent coquetries of her sex to soften her husband's conqueror. I saw the queen several times . . . sitting between the two emperors, who plied her with longing attentions and gallantries. . . . One day Napoleon offered her a superb rose, which she finally accepted after hesitating a while."[75] But her price for taking it was high: the return of the fortress city of Magdeburg. There Napoleon politely drew the line.

All the queen's beauty, charm, and cunning could only briefly cloud the utter contempt Napoleon harbored for her husband and their kingdom. Typically he neither hid his feelings nor minced his words. To Alexander he sneered at Frederick William as "a contemptible king" of "a contemptible nation" with "a contemptible army, a country which has deceived everyone and does not deserve to exist."[76] He refused to allow the king to join the negotiating sessions between him and the tsar. When he had the king ushered before him, Napoleon unleashed all his pent-up rage on him for his bad faith and stubbornness. Stunned by that barrage, Frederick William could only "in vain" appeal "to his heart and his magnanimity, and I trooped out all the fine phrases and promises that my feeble eloquence could prompt."[77]

The treaty of Tilsit, signed on July 9, elaborated by the treaty of Konigsberg on July 12, imposed devastating losses on Prussia. Frederick William was forced to cede all lands west of the Elbe to a new kingdom of Westphalia to be led by Jerome, while Prussia's eastern frontier shrank to its 1771 border, and the Duchy of Warsaw regained all that it had lost to Berlin since then. In all, Prussia's population would plummet from 9,752,731 to 4,938,000, and its territory from 5,570 square miles to 2,877. French troops would occupy Prussia until Berlin paid off to Paris an indemnity whose amount remained to be assessed.[78]

There was no question in the minds of Frederick William or anyone else at that time, or of anyone since, that Prussia had suffered an enormous blow at Tilsit. Yet the Treaty of Tilsit between France and Russia was a diplomatic victory for both sides. Napoleon and Alexander would each come away from Tilsit believing that he had outwitted the other.

Certainly Napoleon had reason to be ecstatic. Much as he had with Austria, the emperor had reoriented Russia away from conflicts with France over its conquests or protectorates to conflicts over lands with other great powers elsewhere, such as the Baltic, Balkans, and Caucasus. Most importantly, he had committed the tsar to break with Britain and join the Continental System.[79]

Yet Alexander also had reason to be pleased. He had lost nothing of substance while extracting himself from a debilitating war. He would bide his time, rebuild his troops and treasury, and, when the time was right, help forge what he could only hope would be the last coalition against France. In his friend Frederick William's ear, he whispered for him to "have patience. We shall take back what we have lost. He will break his neck. In spite of my demonstrations of friendship and my external actions, at heart I am your friend and I hope to prove it to you by acts."[80]

Talleyrand

Only one prominent Frenchman then in the inner circle of power did not gloat over Napoleon's diplomatic triumphs at Tilsit. During those negotiations the emperor had pointedly limited the role of his foreign minister, Charles Maurice de Talleyrand-Perigord, to simply writing up the terms he dictated. The reason was that the emperor and his foreign minister held diametrically opposed views of the ends and means of French foreign policy. Napoleon insisted that France's wealth, power, and security were best advanced by conquering an empire so vast that none would dare challenge it. Talleyrand countered that such an ambition would simply invite other states to ally with each other and war continuously against France, to no one's benefit and France's inevitable defeat. Instead, France should confine itself to its easily defensible and non-threatening natural frontiers. Paris could then master the balancer role in European politics by playing the other great powers off against each other in war and trading with them all to everyone's betterment in peace. The emperor and foreign minister even disagreed over which country would make the best ally for France. Napoleon would split all of Europe asunder between himself and Alexander. Talleyrand sought to unite Paris and Vienna in an axis of cooperation, since French interests overlapped more with those of Austria than the other great powers', and thus demanded more attention in managing them to their mutual benefit.

Tilsit deeply embittered Talleyrand. He later recalled that "I was indignant with everything I saw and heard, but I was obliged to conceal my indignation at Tilsit." Had Napoleon followed Talleyrand's vision rather than his own, the man who "held the destiny of Europe in his hands" could have achieved "true glory," but tragically that was something that he "simply did not understand."[81]

Talleyrand was partly right. There is no question that Napoleon bloated himself on his triumphs and blinded himself to the ultimate nature and limits of power. Eventually he would choke to death on his own hubris. History would have been far different had Napoleon chosen not to take over Spain in 1808 and, especially, to invade Russia in 1812. Had the emperor been content with the gains of Pressburg and Tilsit, he might have kept those conquests and his throne for a lifetime and established a virtuous cycle of peace, prosperity, and security for France. Eventually Paris and London would have wearied of the chronic military and diplomatic stalemate between them and found some way to finesse their differences. But Talleyrand's own vision too is open to criticism. There is no guarantee that his notion of a France confined to its "natural frontiers" would have made the nation any more secure. Indeed, it most likely would have more readily invited the aggression of others, as happened in 1870, 1914, and 1940.

Talleyrand was so disgusted with Napoleon's strategy that he offered to resign amidst the negotiations at Tilsit. Napoleon would certainly have weakened his position had he accepted his foreign minister's request at that time and word leaked over its cause. He ordered Talleyrand to stay put and do his job. It was only on August 9, after they had returned to Paris, that Napoleon replaced Talleyrand with Jean Baptiste de Nompere de Champagny, who would serve more as a clerk than an advisor. Napoleon then "promoted" Talleyrand to the sinecure of "vice-grand elector," with an annual income of 330,000 francs.

Talleyrand was not the only recipient of a new title and stipend. After his return from Tilsit the emperor sought to further consolidate his power in France. He decreed the abolition of the Tribunate, the most assertive of the three national assemblies, on August 19, 1807. But a more subtle way to bolster his power was to award both his supporters and potential influential dissidents with empty ranks and hefty incomes. His empire would eventually include seven princes, twenty-one dukes, 452 counts, 1,500 barons, and 1,474 knights—all dependent for their wealth and prestige on their emperor.[82]

The emperor soon missed Talleyrand's diplomatic expertise. To his aide Armand Augustin de Caulaincourt, Napoleon later admitted that "business was transacted efficiently as long as Talleyrand was in charge. It was his fault that I became prejudiced against him. Why did he insist on leaving office? He knew France and Europe better than anyone else and could still have stayed in office had he wanted."[83]

Napoleon was well aware that Talleyrand had persisted in criticizing his emperor's foreign policies even while he abetted them as a member of his government. The emperor's spies kept him informed of Talleyrand's latest witty, eloquent, and biting critiques via pen or tongue of the man whom he supposedly served. But for years Napoleon tolerated his presence in his administration's inner circle. He did so because he at once respected and feared Talleyrand: the man was clearly as devious as he was brilliant. It was better to try to coopt him with titles and wealth than to push him into opposition.

What Napoleon's spies did not uncover was that Talleyrand was not merely critical, he was traitorous. He would eventually be on the payroll of as many as half a dozen foreign governments and groups, all devoted to destroying Napoleon and his empire. Like most traitors, Talleyrand would justify his betrayal by citing his allegiance to a higher cause: "I served Bonaparte as emperor with devotion . . . so long as I felt he himself was solely devoted to the interests of France."[84]

Westphalia

Napoleon's reorganization and consolidation of Germany continued after he returned from his latest campaign. On November 16, 1807, he announced that he was going to transform the duchy of Westphalia into a constitutional monarchy by adding to it parts of Saxony, Brunswick, Hesse-Cassel, and Hanover, and presenting to that new realm a French-style constitution and his brother Jerome as king. Jerome settled on that throne at Cassel on December 7. On New Year's Day, 1808, the emperor granted the Code Napoleon to Westphalia.[85]

The emperor had grand hopes for Westphalia. To France the kingdom would contribute troops, taxes, and a strategic location in the heart of northern Germany. To the Rhine Confederation it would serve as the leader and model state. All that the kingdom of Westphalia now needed was leadership.

Jerome was only twenty-two years old when he was suddenly expected to personify all the dignity, wisdom, and decisiveness expected of a model constitutional monarch of a model state. Unfortunately, he still had a lot of growing up to do. The youngest son of the Bonaparte family never knew his father, and until his late teens barely knew his older brothers, who were off pursuing their respective destinies. He was left to be pampered by his mother and three sisters, and to hear tales of his brothers' exploits, especially those of the general and statesman who was fifteen years his senior. Jerome naturally hero-worshipped Napoleon, and Napoleon in turn regarded Jerome more as the adoring, bright, and fun-loving son he longed to have than a younger brother. So the lad's pampering persisted during the two years he lived with Napoleon and Josephine at Malmaison, their home outside Paris. Napoleon had ambitions for Jerome similar to those for his other brothers, but first the boy had to shed his childhood and be hardened to manhood by a succession of worldly challenges.

When Jerome was nineteen the First Consul secured him a berth as an ensign on a warship bound for the Caribbean. After that shake-down cruise he was promoted to lieutenant and given command of a brig. In 1803 he was indulging in the sensualities of Martinique when he suddenly received orders to sail back to France. Instead he abandoned his command to a junior officer and caught a ship bound for the United States. By flaunting his family name and exuberant personality, he was eagerly welcomed into America's elite circles, and soon ran up debts of over $30,000 to the French consulate and fawning friends.

In Baltimore Jerome was beguiled by the beauty, charm, and wealth of Elizabeth Patterson, the daughter of one of the city's leading merchants. They were married on Christmas Eve, 1803, by Archbishop John Carroll. The French consul promptly certified their marriage. They sent their happy news back to the Bonaparte clan in Paris.

Napoleon, predictably, was incensed. It was bad enough that his brother had deserted his post, but to marry a common American! He launched a merciless diplomatic campaign to force his prodigal brother to renounce his folly and devote himself to serving the interests of the Bonaparte clan. To Baltimore he dispatched two frigates to convey his command that Jerome embark for the long sail back to France. Napoleon insisted that his legal code nullified Jerome's marriage: according to the Code Napoleon, no one younger than twenty-five could marry without the consent of his parents or legal guardians. Jerome replied that French law was null and void in America; and besides, their own mother had sent her blessing when she heard of his marriage. Napoleon then tried to get Pius VII to annul the marriage; the pope eventually did so on May 24, 1806.[86]

Napoleon had only two more cards in his hand, but they proved to be trumps. On March 11, 1805, he issued an imperial decree declaring that the marriage between Jerome and Elizabeth was annulled. He also declared that if Jerome did not divorce Elizabeth and return to Paris, he would not only lose all his considerable allowance and inheritance, but would promptly be imprisoned if he ever again set foot on French soil.

That worked. On May 6, 1805, Jerome pledged to divorce his wife, strip her of the name Bonaparte, and deprive their forthcoming child, a son who would be born in London on July 7, of any claims against the Bonaparte family or France. In return, Napoleon promoted him to captain and gave him 150,000 francs; a year later the emperor raised his rank to admiral and his annual allowance to one million francs! Perhaps never before in history did a man benefit so handsomely from abandoning his wife. The divorce was the easy part of Napoleon's diplomacy; Elizabeth would be compensated with a lifelong annual alimony of 60,000 francs. It took another eighteen months for Napoleon to convince the Catholic Church to grant an annulment. But after October 6, 1806, Jerome was free for Napoleon to impose his own choice of a wife upon him.

Yet Jerome had to undergo one last trial to prove his worthiness: prowess on the field of battle. Napoleon made him a general and gave him command of three German divisions for his 1807 campaign. Jerome proved to be an inspiring and brave leader.

Napoleon thereupon judged his brother to be ready for a royal marriage and kingdom. He found a suitable political match in Princess Frederika Catherine Sophia Dorthea, the King of Wurttemberg's second daughter. At the Tuileries they celebrated a civil marriage on August 22, 1807, and a religious marriage the next day. It would be an adequate enough marriage for him, if not her. He would enjoy all the perks of being married into royalty, yet remained an insatiable womanizer, despite the fact that his wife was beautiful and adored him. They honeymooned in Cassel, Westphalia's capital.

The emperor had provided his brother with more than a wife and a realm. Naturally, he had designed a constitution especially for Westphalia. What's more, as with all those siblings and others to whom he had entrusted thrones, he issued a stream of minutely detailed instructions to his brother for properly governing his kingdom.[87]

Despite all that, Jerome's rule over Westphalia was stormy from the start. The reason was simple: he remained a child in the guise of a man—impetuous, spoiled, and stubborn. When the parliament refused to implement some of his ideas, he suspended it and issued decrees. If he succeeded with anything, it was his army, which became renowned for its polish on the parade ground and élan in battle. Like his brother monarchs, his worst challenge as king was dealing with Napoleon; he continually found himself trapped between the emperor's commands and his kingdom's needs. When he could get away with it, he put Westphalia first. The levies of taxes and troops were onerous enough, but the Continental System was a terrible burden. Like Joseph and Louis, Jerome turned both a blind eye and an open palm to the pervasive smuggling. And like them, Napoleon blistered Jerome with letters criticizing his failures.[88]

Sewing Up the Continent

Maintaining an empire was endless work. No sooner would Napoleon seem to resolve one problem within a colony, protectorate, or ally than another would arise. Word arrived from spies that ever more prominent Prussians, led by Baron Heinrich Fredrich Karl von Stein, insisted that honor and interest demanded that they overthrow French rule. That discontent was understandable. The territory lost by the treaties of Tilsit and Konigsberg was devastating enough. Then the French intendant at Berlin, General Pierre Daru, submitted an indemnity bill for 150 million francs.[89]

Frederick William pleaded with Daru that the amount was not only unjust but far beyond Berlin's means to pay. Daru twice agreed to cut back the bill, but each time was overruled by Napoleon. Instead, Napoleon had Daru present to his counterpart a copy of one of Stein's letters that had been intercepted by a French spy as proof of Prussian deceit and justification for the sternest measures against Berlin. The emperor demanded that the king banish Stein from Prussia. When Frederick William wearily complied, Napoleon rewarded him by reducing the indemnity by 10 million francs.[90]

Nonetheless, the three Conventions of Ebling signed on October 13, November 10, and December 6, 1807, were harsh enough. A French army would occupy Prussia until Berlin paid the entire bill of 140 million francs. Although most troops would be withdrawn at that point, the French would garrison the fortress cities of Magdeburg, Custrin, Stettin, and Glogau, and designate and use military roads, garrisons, and depots across the kingdom. The Prussian army would be reduced to 42,000 men. As a French ally, Prussia would have to supply a 16,000-man corps should war again break out with Austria.[91]

Frederick William had no choice but to bow to all these humiliating and debilitating demands. But the king agreed with his advisors that they had to embark on wide-ranging administrative, military, and economic reforms that would empower Prussia one day to rebel against, defeat, and exact a harsh vengeance upon France. And indeed, all that would come to pass.

Even after Napoleon repeatedly defeated Britain's allies and gradually united much of the continent behind him, Whitehall still spurned his calls for peace. George Canning, the foreign secretary, explained why: Peace "would sanction . . . some dozen of green and tottering usurpations and leave Bonaparte to begin anew. And that is why he is anxious for it. . . . Our interest is that until there can be a final settlement that shall last, everything should remain as unsettled as possible: that no usurper should feel sure of acknowledgement; no people confident of their new masters; no kingdom sure of its existence; nor spoliator secure of his spoil; and even the plundered not acquiescent in their losses."[92]

On the continent only Sweden and Portugal refused to join Napoleon's economic blockade of Britain. Among the deals struck at Tilsit, Alexander was to take care of Sweden while Napoleon dealt with Portugal. However, before either monarch could launch his campaign, the British struck a harsh blow at the Continental System. In July 1807 Canning sent an ultimatum to Copenhagen, demanding that the Danes surrender their fleet and ally themselves with Britain. Upon hearing their refusal, he gave the nod to Admiral James Gambier, whose expedition set sail on July 26, disembarked 18,000 troops on Zealand on August 16, opened a bombardment of Copenhagen on September 2, and received the Danish surrender on September 7. Under the treaty the Danes had to give up their entire fleet of sixteen ships of the line, ten frigates, eight brigs, and thirty other vessels to Britain, and torch eight ships of the line under construction.[93]

The Danes belatedly agreed to a formal treaty of alliance with France on October 31, long after it could do them any good. Napoleon followed that up by pretending to act as Sweden's protector. This included issuing a demand to garrison with French troops Swedish Pomerania in northern Germany and the island of Rugen in the Baltic. Knowing that the emperor simply took what he was not given, the Swedes complied.

Around that time Napoleon got word that Alexander might already be wobbling in his commitment to the Continental System. Apparently the tsar's council was split over the question, with the weight of British gold causing ever more of his advisors to lean toward a break with France.

That was the pull. The push was the emperor's own ambassador to St. Petersburg, General Jean Savary. Savary's gifts as a fierce warrior poisoned his diplomacy. His arrogance and brusqueness would alienate ever more in the tsar's inner circle and court, as well as the diplomatic corps. In so doing he violated the clear instructions that Napoleon had issued him "to fine-tune the alliance" and displace British with French influence in St. Petersburg. Knowing all too well Savary's temperament, Napoleon warned him to "carefully avoid anything that could shock. For example, never speak of war, be critical of anyone or anything, or engage in ridicule. . . . Write every letter as if the tsar were reading it." Talleyrand's instructions to Savary were more succinct: "Try to learn much and demand little."[94]

When Savary arrived in St. Petersburg on July 23, 1807, he was the first French ambassador to Russia since Gabriel Hedouville packed his bags in 1804. Although Alexander liked Savary, nearly everyone else at the court soon despised him. But that was not the fault of Savary's belligerent manner alone. As in Berlin, Naples, Madrid, and Palermo, a formidable woman was the power behind the throne in St. Petersburg.

It seems that Alexander was a bit of a mama's boy. Not only that, but the Dowager Tsarina, Maria Feodorovna, surrounded herself with French émigrés and imbibed their hatred of all that had convulsed France since 1789. One of her favorites, Nicolay Rumiantsev, was the foreign minister and a fervent Slavophile. To worsen matters, Alexander's defeats in 1805 and 1807 hardly endeared him to his court or countrymen. Finally, the tsar was literally haunted by the murder of his father, against whom he had conspired and whose dying screams he had heard. All that political and psychological baggage made Alexander unreliable.

Of that array of diplomatic challenges, Napoleon could control only one. In November 1807 he sent Armand de Caulaincourt to replace Savary. Caulaincourt arrived on December 10, 1807. For a while the new ambassador ameliorated the relationship. Meanwhile, through letters to Alexander, Napoleon tried to keep alive the fading spirit of Tilsit by offering his political analysis, encouragement, suggestions, and hopes. A typical letter began: "In these few lines I express to Your Majesty my entire soul."[95]

In Paris, Alexander's ambassador was no less irritating. Count Peter Tolstoi had bitterly opposed Tilsit and did everything he could to undermine that treaty. He even conspired with French émigrés, British agents, and all others who hated Napoleon in Paris. Napoleon convinced the tsar to replace Tolstoi with someone committed to Tilsit. Alexander complied by sending him Prince Alexander Kurakin.[96]

Having settled diplomatic disputes with Sweden, Denmark, and Russia, Napoleon then turned westward. Earlier that summer, on July 19, amidst the heady elation of Tilsit, he had Talleyrand issue an ultimatum to Lisbon either to join the Continental System by September 1, 1807, or suffer conquest by French and Russian armies.[97]

Although disturbed by Napoleon's threat, Prince John, who was serving as regent for his mad mother, Queen Maria I, and his ministers were puzzled by the notion that a Russian army posed any threat to their realm. Actually, a formidable Russian force would indeed come, but by sea rather than land, and as guests rather than conquerors: Russia's Mediterranean fleet, commanded by Admiral Siniavin, having been barred by war with the Turks from returning to its Black Sea anchorage, was en route to the Baltic; it would winter in Lisbon.

The September 1 deadline passed with no word received in Paris from the Portuguese court. In a September 8 letter to Prince John, the emperor urged him to yield. Still silence reigned. On October 12 Napoleon sent orders to General Andoche Junot at Bayonne to lead his 28,000 French to Burgos. On October 22 the emperor formally declared war on Portugal. Apparently, until they received that declaration the Portuguese had thought Napoleon was bluffing. Prince John sent word that Portugal would comply with his demands.[98]

That message arrived too late. Napoleon was putting the finishing touches on just how Portugal would be divvied up. The fate of Portugal and parts of Italy were sealed by the Treaty of Fontainebleau, signed on October 27, 1807. Spain agreed that France could annex the kingdom of Etruria in Italy. In return for this Portugal would be split into three parts: the northern third would go to the dethroned King of Etruria as the new King of Lusitania; the southern third would go to, of all people, the ever-conniving and greedy Manuel de Godoy, who would henceforth be known as the Prince of Algarve; and the middle third would be occupied by the French and used as a bargaining chip for the return of all the French and Spanish colonies the British had taken since 1793, along with Gibraltar which they had taken in 1713. The treaty projected three military expeditions against Portugal. The Spanish would add 11,000 troops, nominally commanded by Crown Prince Ferdinand, to the 28,000 French at Burgos, and Junot would lead that army toward Lisbon. Two other forces, both Spanish, would also move against Portugal, 10,000 troops toward Oporto in the north and 6,000 along the Algarve coast in the south; but neither would reach its objective.[99]

Napoleon sent Junot his orders on October 31, covering just how to get to, take over, and govern Portugal. Junot led his army from Burgos on the long, grueling march to Lisbon. Along the way a diplomatic tussle broke out when

Charles complained that his son Ferdinand should head that army across Spain. In his reply Napoleon made it clear that only Junot would be in charge.[100]

Meanwhile, Prince John sent an urgent appeal to London for help. Whitehall replied by dispatching Napoleon's old bugbear, Admiral William Sydney Smith, and his fleet to anchor off Lisbon. The Portuguese court squeezed aboard for a long voyage, and an even longer sojourn in Brazil. They weighed anchor and disappeared over the horizon just a day before Junot's army marched into the capital on November 30. Admiral Siniavin's Russian fleet arrived a little later. Although the Portuguese royal family had escaped, they had not been able to take everything with them. Junot quickly secured Lisbon and began extracting a 100 million franc indemnity.[101]

Without then having sufficient naval and land forces available to drive the French from Portugal, Canning tried a diplomatic ploy. He hoped to break apart the fragile alliance between Napoleon and Alexander by dangling a false peace proposal before the nose of each. In January 1808 he asked Maksim Alopeus, the tsar's ambassador, who was about to embark for home, to carry a message to Paris before returning to St. Petersburg. The deal was straightforward enough: peace founded on the principle of uti possedetis, or "each could keep what had been taken" since the war began. Canning assumed that Napoleon would spurn and Alexander would seize the offer, and thus Britain could gain propaganda points and perhaps further estrange the emperor and tsar.

But Canning had grossly misunderstood Britain's nemesis. Napoleon not only eagerly accepted the offer, but sweetened it by promising to free Hanover, Portugal, and Swedish Pomerania. An embarrassed Canning never replied. An ever more impatient emperor finally realized that Canning's offer had been a trick. That spurred him to redouble his military and diplomatic efforts to mobilize all of Europe against Britain. He ordered the Continental System tightened, Rome occupied, Portugal reinforced, and Irish rebels aided with shipments of arms and munitions to wield against their British occupiers. In the latest instance of his own penchant for diplomatic perfidy, he secretly offered President Thomas Jefferson Spanish Florida if he would ally the United States with France against Britain. Jefferson demurred.

The emperor was well aware that the tsar's enthusiasm for the French alliance and the Continental System was being spoiled by some of his hawkish advisors. He tried to divert Alexander by entangling him in schemes, one outlandish, the other quite practical.

Napoleon penned a proposal early in 1808 for a Franco-Russian expedition to capture Constantinople, split up the Ottoman Empire, and then "if an army of 50,000 men, Russian, French, and perhaps even partly Austrian were to set off from Constantinople into Asia it would need get no further than the Euphrates to make England tremble and fall at the feet of the continent." But if the British did not yield, the allies would march down the Euphrates valley through Baghdad to the Persian Gulf and then set sail for India. His mission to the Persian Empire had already partly reconnoitered a different route which would carry that Franco-Russian army across Central Asia to Herat, Kabul, and down the Khyber Pass to Peshawar and then on to India. Either itinerary may provoke a chill down the spine of the contemporary reader.

It undoubtedly provoked a diversion in the tsar's court, but one rooted in derision rather than inspiration. Yet the hare-brained scheme inspired Alexander. Rather than wonder whether Napoleon had flipped his lid, he remarked happily to Caulaincourt that "This is the language of Tilsit." In his reply Alexander lauded "a genius so superior that he could conceive of so vast a plan," but then tried to bring the emperor down to earth by saying that for now his immediate objective was to take Finland from Sweden, something Napoleon had previously encouraged.[102]

For St. Petersburg to conquer Finland would serve the geopolitical interests of both Russia and France. Napoleon had an added motivation for Russia to humble and diminish Sweden: Gustav IV, the Swedish king, hated Napoleon with a nearly unhinged zeal. That monarch truly believed that Napoleon was the anti-Christ predicted by the New Testament Book of Revelation, and he preached that message either directly or through his undoubtedly embarrassed envoys to as many fellow rulers as possible, especially those in Germany.

Gustav gave Alexander his hoped-for excuse for war. In January 1808 he formally broke with the Continental System and allied with Britain. In February he agreed to accept an 11,000-man British force under General John Moore to man Sweden's more vulnerable ports, and a 1.2 million pound sterling subsidy. Those British troops and treasure provoked rather than deterred Alexander. The tsar issued an ultimatum to the king to break his alliance and revert to the Continental System; Gustav rejected the ultimatum; Alexander sent his army into Finland. Napoleon ordered General Bernadotte to complete France's takeover of Swedish Pomerania.

Gustav blamed all his troubles on the British, actually ordered General Moore's arrest, and demanded that Whitehall give him two million pounds sterling to compensate for his territorial losses. Although Moore responded by withdrawing his expedition to England, Whitehall would later agree, on March 1, 1809, to underwrite the alliance with 1.2 million pounds sterling. But Gustav would never get a chance to spend a penny of it: he was overthrown and murdered in a coup on March 12. The Riksdag, or national assembly, replaced Gustav with his senile uncle, who would reign as Charles XIII.

And that would be the end of that royal line. Then the Riksdag would have to choose someone else to be their king. They would settle on someone from a curious choice of realms—France. Although Napoleon's diplomacy would be decisive in shaping that choice, it would have unforeseen and disastrous consequences for himself and his empire.

The Fate of Spain

Junot's takeover of Portugal, or at least its capital, Lisbon, had been swift and relatively bloodless. It would also be brief. During the summer of 1808 Whitehall mobilized an expedition to retake Portugal, and gave that command to General Arthur Wellesley, who had made a reputation for himself by successfully warring in India, and who would be named the Duke of Wellington for his even greater achievements on the Iberian Peninsula. Meanwhile, to worsen matters for the French hold on Portugal, its supply and communications across Spain would soon be severed.

The Bourbons who ruled Spain were among Europe's more dysfunctional royal families. The king's queen, Maria Luisa, and his first minister, Manuel de Godoy, had enjoyed a notorious affair when they were younger, and remained close if no longer amorous. The king's son, Ferdinand, the Prince of Asturias, despised his father for his tolerance of being cuckolded and his intolerance of those like himself who advocated an administrative, military, and economic overhaul of Spain. Ferdinand was conspiring to deprive his father of the throne. Had Shakespeare been around to write a play on those intrigues and how they turned out, he may have been torn over whether to depict them as tragedy or farce.

Napoleon naturally was pleased to learn of the ever more poisonous relations within Madrid's House of Bourbon. He played his classic divide-and-conquer diplomatic strategy by making conflicting promises to the king, prince, and minister who, respectively, could become the king of all of Iberia, the king of all Iberia if he married a French princess, and the prince of southern Portugal. Each would then see Napoleon as an ally, and they would all come to him to settle their differences. Then the emperor would be able to decide the fate of Spain.[103]

Napoleon's strategy effectively thickened the plot. Ferdinand was emboldened to press harder for some sort of coup against his father. He wrote Napoleon a letter on October 11, 1807, requesting to marry a French princess from the emperor's own family, and asking for support to depose Godoy. Napoleon was happy to help him against Godoy, but had no intention of marrying off one of his own family to someone he considered a fool.[104]

Charles learned of his son's machinations and had him arrested on October 27, 1807. The prodigal threw himself at his father's feet and begged forgiveness; the king released him. And then, exactly as the emperor had hoped, Charles appealed to Napoleon to resolve their conflicts.

Napoleon was eager to oblige. On February 20, 1808, he declared that Spain was dissolving into anarchy, and he ordered Marshal Joachim Murat to lead an army to Madrid to restore order. Murat began massing troops from French garrisons in Barcelona, Pamplona, San Sebastian, and Figueras. Reinforcements swelled his army to 118,000 men. He would enter Madrid on March 23.[105]

The king's envoy, Eugenio Izquierdo, arrived in Paris bearing a proposal that Napoleon amend their treaty of Fontainebleau signed on October 27, 1807. It requested the transfer of northern Portugal to the king of Etruria and the granting of southern Portugal to Spain rather than Godoy. The emperor rejected that request. Instead, he had Talleyrand and Duroc meet with Izquierdo on February 24 and pass him an astonishing letter for Charles IV: an offer to give him Portugal in return for turning Spain over to France!

Meanwhile, the Bourbon family in Spain continued to play into Napoleon's hands by disintegrating. When the king, queen, and minister learned that their son's repentance had been a sham and that he was conspiring once again to dethrone them, they panicked and tried to escape to their empire in America. Troops loyal to Ferdinand arrested them at Aranjuez. What followed from March 17 to 19 became known as the Revolution of Aranjuez. Charles IV abdicated in favor of his son, who was named Ferdinand VII. Godoy resigned as chief minister. Riots and uprisings favoring the old or new king erupted in ever more cities, including Madrid, which Ferdinand entered on March 24. Murat's troops crushed the insurgents in the cities they occupied.[106]

News of the abdication and violence in Spain swiftly reached Paris. At first Napoleon was perplexed. He sent Murat a long analysis of the political situation and the policy options.[107] How could order be restored to Spain? Charles and his government "are so thoroughly discredited that they will not last three months." Godoy was especially "detested because he was accused of delivering Spain to France." Ferdinand lacked "a single quality needed to be a head of state, but that does not prevent him from opposing us if we make him a hero." Nonetheless, the Spanish army fielded 100,000 troops. The English would undoubtedly take advantage of Spain's chaos to undercut the French there, and eventually strike at Junot in Portugal. For the present, Napoleon urged Murat to show caution and not take sides: "I want no violence used against the royal family." Above all, they had to avoid the worst-case scenario: "The nobles and the clergy are the masters of Spain. If they fear for their privileges and their very existence, they will raise the masses against us in an eternal war." Yet somehow, in the tumultuous weeks and months to come, Napoleon lost sight of his own sage advice.

What then should be done? "Only a revolution can change the state of that Country. . . . In my empire's interests I could do much better for Spain. But what are the best means to take it?"[108] The answer soon came to him.

He dispatched Savary to Spain with letters to Charles and Ferdinand inviting them, along with the queen and prime minister, to Bayonne, where he promised to resolve all their problems. He spurred each to hurry to Bayonne by pretending that he favored him to be the rightful king of Spain. Yet he also hinted at a different outcome than either hoped for: "I will float various ideas which need to be settled."[109]

After arriving there on April 14, the emperor chose the chateau of Marracq in which to play out the diplomacy which would win for Joseph the crown of Spain—and for his empire a "cancerous ulcer" that would eat away its wealth and power over the next five years.[110]

Ferdinand and his younger brother Charles arrived on April 20. Napoleon had them to dinner and saw the would-be king frequently over the next ten days as they awaited the king, queen, and minister. No passions had cooled when that party finally arrived on April 30. The king, and especially the queen, vented their rage at their son for his betrayal.[111]

Napoleon had to be especially careful to separate his diplomatic performance from his private feelings. He utterly loathed them all, especially the queen, who extolled her former lover and demanded that her son be executed for treason. As worrisome were how all his machinations in Bayonne would play in Madrid and the rest of Spain. He sent Murat careful instructions on how to orchestrate delivery of the news that the Bonapartes were to replace the Bourbons on the throne.[112]

The emperor's "solution" was essentially to pension off the royal family to luxurious retirements in France while he took the crown to dispose of as he pleased. In a series of agreements which culminated with separate Treaties of Bayonne signed with Charles on May 5 and Ferdinand on May 10, each renounced his respective claims to the Spanish throne. In return Charles would get an annual pension of 7.5 million francs, Louise Marie two million francs, Ferdinand one million francs, and 400,000 francs each to the two youngest sons and Charles' brother. The chateaux of Compiegne and Chambord would be provided to Charles, Louise Marie, the youngest boy and Charles' brother, and Godoy; Valencay, Talleyrand's chateau, to Ferdinand and the second son Charles. Meanwhile, Charles sent separate proclamations back to the Supreme Council, the Junta, and his former subjects, asking them to welcome their new king and his army. Napoleon issued his own proclamation justifying his mediation and solution to the political crisis in Spain.[113]

The ink was no sooner dry on that deal than Napoleon informed Joseph that he would fill the empty throne and be the new king of Spain: "It is for you that I have destined this crown." Joseph did not want the job, being quite content to rule the kingdom of Naples; but he obeyed his emperor's command. Nor was Joseph Napoleon's first choice; Louis had earlier politely but firmly turned down the notion.[114] Joseph set sail from Naples on May 23 and arrived at Bayonne on June 8 in preparation for the announcement.

Spain, meanwhile, erupted in revolt against French rule. Murat's troops slaughtered a mob of rioters in Madrid on May 2. Elsewhere rebels assassinated the French military governors of Cadiz, Cartagena, and Badajoz. Upon learning of the abdication at Bayonne, Spanish generals mustered their troops and began to march against the French.

To make a success of the transfer of power, Napoleon ordered Marshal Jean Baptiste Bessieres to march with an army to Murat's relief; Bessieres routed a Spanish army under the joint command of generals Gregorio de la Cuesta and Joachim Blake at Medina del Rio Seco on July 14. Napoleon called on May 25 for the Spanish Cortes, or parliament, to assemble at Bayonne; 91 of 150 delegates would eventually reach that alien city. Only after seemingly securing Spain militarily and politically did Napoleon announce on June 6 that he was awarding the throne of Spain to Joseph.[115]

Napoleon and Joseph approved a treaty on July 5 between their respective realms whereby the emperor granted the king the kingdom of Spain in return for the kingdom of Naples. On July 7 the Cortes voted its approval of its new king and a French-style constitution for Spain, and issued declarations for the Spanish people to pledge their loyalty to the new government. An army escorted that new government to Burgos, where on July 7 Joseph was officially crowned the King of Spain. The government then journeyed on to reach Madrid on July 19.

Joseph's initial reign in his capital was fleeting. General Francisco Castanos defeated General Pierre Dupont in several battles, bottled Dupont up at Bailen, and forced him to surrender his 22,000 troops on July 22. That panicked Joseph, who ordered a retreat of his government and army from Madrid to north of the Ebro River on July 31. He sent Napoleon the first of numerous letters over the next five years asking to be allowed to resign; Napoleon pointedly ignored them all.

The Spanish began to reestablish rule over most of their country. The army reoccupied Madrid on August 13. Thirty-five nobles formed a provisional government under the leadership of Count Floridablanca. They in turn created a Supreme Junta at Cadiz on September 25, 1809. The Supreme Junta would consist of two deputies from each provisional junta and one from the Canary Islands. Its first act was to acclaim Ferdinand VII as Spain's rightful king. That was about all they agreed upon; the junta soon split into five antagonistic factions.

Napoleon's ambitions for Spain would be a godsend for the British, although it would take a while before that became apparent. Upon learning of these events, Foreign Secretary George Canning dispatched Charles Stuart to Cadiz to dispense the first installments of over 2.5 million pounds sterling and 160,000 muskets that would reach Spain that year alone. Wellesley's expedition set sail from Cork on July 12 and disembarked at Mondego Bay, fifty miles up the coast from Lisbon, on August 1. He marched his 14,000 troops south on August 9, defeated the French at Rollica on August 15 and Vimiero on August 21, then followed hard on Junot's heels toward Lisbon.[116]

Junot asked for terms. Fortunately for him, General Harry Burand, the British theater commander, showed up at that moment to negotiate. Junot proved to be a much better diplomat than general. He talked Burand into sailing him and his army back to France. In compensation, he had no objection to the British desire to confiscate all the Russian warships under Admiral Siniavin; the sailors too would be carried back to their homes, courtesy of the British fleet. The Convention of Cinta formalizing those terms was signed on August 30.

Although pleased that all those Russian warships had augmented his king's fleet, Canning was incensed when he learned that Burand had let an entire French army escape spending the war in rotting prison hulks. Burand, Wellesley, and another general were recalled to London for an official inquiry. Although Wellesley would be acquitted, the British campaign in the Peninsula would be deprived of his leadership for the interim. His replacement, General John Moore, might have been just as great a general had he lived for the war's duration. He disembarked with 20,000 men at Lisbon on October 6 and began marching up the Tagus River. General David Baird landed at Coruna on October 13 and headed toward Valladolid, where he met Moore in November.

Junot's capitulation provoked a different reaction in Napoleon. Although he was naturally disappointed at losing Portugal, he recognized that Junot's army had been isolated and overwhelmed by numbers. He reassured his ever-faithful friend and officer that he had fulfilled his honor and duty in all respects. Napoleon was rarely so understanding of people's failures, except his own.[117]

Murat and Caroline

Napoleon's choice to replace Joseph as the king of Naples was at first a hit with most Neapolitans. Joachim Murat seemed to have stepped out of an Italian opera. Gaudy in dress, extravagant in gesture, passionate in his loves and hates, generous to the needy, and utterly fearless in battle, Murat personified how Neapolitans envisioned themselves.

He was born in 1767 as the eleventh and last child of a poor, struggling, bourgeois family in Dordogne. His parents sent him away to seminary, but he dropped out to join the cavalry. With the departure of ever more royalist officers after 1789, he rose rapidly through the ranks. Murat had endeared himself to Napoleon by aiding him at a crucial moment in his astonishing rise to power. It was Murat whom Napoleon sent galloping with his cavalry to retrieve cannons and return to Paris just in time to rout a mob threatening the Directory on October 5, 1795. The grateful directors then assigned Napoleon to command the army of Italy. Murat accompanied Napoleon as his cavalry commander and thereafter served valiantly on dozens of battlefields, nowhere more so than at Eylau where he led the charge that converted a Russian victory into a retreat.

Impressive as his early career was, Murat, alas, exemplified the notion that many people rise until they reach their level of incompetence. He was brilliant at inspiring his men and leading charges. But he was not only hopeless as a strategist or tactician, he failed as a cavalryman regarding the number one rule: take care of your horse. He literally rode his mounts into the ground; starved, lame, dying horses littered Murat's passages across Europe, and left ever more of his men afoot. But he would prove to be an even worse king and diplomat.

So why would Napoleon entrust a throne to such a man? Mostly he did so because of the woman Murat married in a civil ceremony on January 20, 1800. His sister Caroline had fallen in love with the dashing cavalryman and had rejected Napoleon's protests that she should wed some equal to her in intelligence and to his own ambitions for the Bonaparte clan. Although Bonaparte refused to attend their wedding, he eventually reconciled himself to the mismatch.[118]

Caroline excelled at the arts of politics and diplomacy in which her husband was so wanting. She was definitely her own woman. Not only was she the brains behind the thrones of first the Grand Duchy of Berg and then the Kingdom of Naples, but as a woman of voracious passions she bedded numerous luminaries and lovers of that era, including, most notably, Talleyrand and Metternich. From those liaisons she garnered wealth, power, and prestige as well as immediate pleasures. Among other qualities, she was a master of discretion; Murat only learned of her affairs in their eleventh year of marriage. And, like all the Bonapartes, she was a survivor. When all was lost she would cut and run, even if it meant abandoning her own brother, Napoleon.

Certainly the men in her life admired her talents in and out of bed. Talleyrand once described Caroline as "the head of Cromwell on the shoulder of a pretty woman."[119] Women were less appreciative, especially Laura Junot, who quipped that Caroline was "the only one who had not learned to become a princess; she could not leave off the satirical giggle and sneering of the schoolgirl, while her manners were undignified, and her walk the most ungraceful possible."[120] However, the fact that Caroline not only had a fling with Madame Junot's husband but, even worse, stole her lover Metternich from her might have skewed Laura's judgment.

The emperor reasoned that things would work out as long as Murat followed Napoleon's own grand commands and Caroline's tactical advice. But things did not work out as he had hoped. Although Napoleon mostly epitomized cold, even ruthless calculation, he could also at times be too trusting. He certainly never recognized the depths of deceit and intrigue fostered against him by Talleyrand and Fouche. Murat and Caroline would end up betraying him nearly as badly.

Caroline had finagled the Neapolitan crown for herself and her husband by skillfully laying the groundwork over the previous years. In 1805 she had raised a storm with Napoleon when he gave the Dutch throne to Louis rather than her. In 1806 she made it clear to her brother that she was hardly mollified by his gift to her of the Duchy of Berg. She pressured him into expanding Berg's territory and subjects. He complied, even though it nearly provoked a premature war with Prussia. When the throne of Naples was vacant, Caroline lobbied hard to take it. It took her two weeks of haggling with her brother at Bayonne until, on July 15, their respective foreign ministers signed a treaty which would transfer Murat's throne from Berg to Naples on August 1, 1808.

Murat headed straight for his new realm while Caroline returned to Berg to settle affairs and pack everything for the long journey south. The streets of Naples were thronged with adoring people when Murat arrived as King Joachim Napoleon I on September 6. They expected great things of that renowned warrior and veritable peacock of a man. Within a month he obliged them with the first and only victory of his seven years as their ruler. In the dead of night on October 3 he sent an elite force of two thousand crack troops to land on Capri Island twenty miles from Naples. The garrison's British commander, General Hudson Lowe, finally surrendered on October 16. Years later Lowe would cruelly enjoy his vengeance when Whitehall entrusted to him the governorship of another island, St. Helena, where he became Napoleon's jailor and tormenter.

Such are the quirks of history. In retrospect, Napoleon might have been better off entrusting Spain rather than Naples to Murat and Caroline. While the queen would have kept a steely hand on the tiller of government in Madrid, the king could have ridden forth against at least one of the allied armies steadily grinding down French control over the Peninsula. Although the impetuous Murat would have undoubtedly fared even worse against Wellington than first-rate generals such as Massena and Soult, he certainly would have been ruthless in running down any Spanish army in his way.

Yet Napoleon's choice to crown Joseph rather than Murat as the king of Spain made perfect sense at the time. First of all, the throne in Madrid was far more prestigious than that in Naples. After all, Spain still had its vast New World empire from which each year ships filled with silver sailed to the mother country. Handing that crown to his older brother rather than his younger brother-in-law was diplomatically appropriate. Secondly, Joseph had initiated important reforms in the kingdom of Naples that had generated popularity and undercut opposition to French rule. Napoleon hoped Joseph would be just as successful in Spain. Finally, the assumption that the French would soon establish order in Spain, as they had elsewhere, meant that the emperor did not anticipate the ensuing prolonged guerrilla and conventional war that might have made a battle-hardened soldier rather than a mild-mannered lawyer more fitting for the job. All that, however, does not explain why, over the coming years, Napoleon retained Joseph despite his obvious unsuitability for that vital post and repeated requests to resign.

Murat himself was bitterly disappointed when the throne went to Joseph. He would angrily declare that he was "robbed" of his rightful throne.[121] That may have been the most important reason why he would later betray Napoleon. In retrospect, Napoleon could have saved himself enormous grief had he dropped the virtually impossible mission—that of quelling a Spanish insurgency and repelling repeated offensives by British and Spanish armies—into the lap of Murat rather than Joseph. By keeping Murat and Caroline busy clinging to power in Spain, they would have had far less time and opportunity to intrigue and ultimately betray Napoleon than they would in their relatively tranquil kingdom of Naples. But that reality would only strike Napoleon long after it was far too late to change.

Erfurt

The war hawks in Vienna viewed with rising glee the transfer of ever more French divisions from central Germany to faraway Spain. It was increasingly evident that a decisive knockout victory was unlikely there: the land was too vast; Cadiz, the provisional capital, was too distant; the Spanish armies were too scattered; Spanish guerrillas were too bloodthirsty; and British munitions, gold, and ever more troops were too numerous. The French marshals could not conquer Spain on their own with what they had. The emperor would have to commit far more troops to guard the ever longer and more vulnerable supply and communications lines against the guerrillas and mass against the enemy armies. But to do so, the emperor would have to strip his forces elsewhere to the bone. And so much the better, Vienna knew, if Napoleon journeyed to the Peninsula to take personal command.

And when that happened, Austria could swiftly muster its armies and not only regain all that it had lost in three previous wars against Napoleon but smite a blow so severe that it might topple that upstart from his throne. Of course, the chances of all that happening would swell significantly if Vienna could entice Berlin or St. Petersburg back into the field to pursue their own vengeance.

As usual, the emperor's spies kept him well informed of such belligerent mutterings within the Austrian court. That news would be disturbing at any time, but Napoleon was indeed planning to go to Spain in search of a decisive victory. That campaign would be complicated if he was continually looking back over his shoulder at what the Austrians were doing in Germany. Before he could leave for Spain he had to secure his rear.

The first step was to issue the sternest possible warning. In meetings with ambassador Clement von Metternich on August 15 and 25, the emperor angrily explained that Austria would be crushed if its leaders were foolish enough once again to embrace aggression. In its inevitable defeat Austria would suffer the same fate as Prussia: it would be carved down to a rump state and army, with most of its lands and peoples transferred to France and its grateful allies.

He then summoned the sovereigns of Russia and nearly all the German states to a congress at Erfurt; by not inviting the Prussian king and Austrian emperor, he pointedly snubbed them. Napoleon explained his strategy to Talleyrand: "We are going to Erfurt so that I can be free to do in Spain what I want. I want to be sure that Austria will be quiet and content. . . . Prepare me a convention that will please Tsar Alexander and divert him against England. That will leave me at ease."[122]

The sovereigns met from September 27 to October 14, 1808, for a series of talks broken by banquets, hunts, balls, concerts, parades, and plays. The emperor's diplomatic agenda was typically ambitious. To strengthen his empire he sought to bolster ways to keep the British out and the Austrians and Prussians down, and to welcome in the new kings of Spain and Naples. That was the public diplomacy. He also had the word whispered that he was in the market for a new wife.[123]

Napoleon expected that the Congress of Erfurt would be a replay of Tilsit but on a grander and more glittering scale—Russia would be his diplomacy's keystone in an arch of fawning French allies and protectorates. However, although he did gather his intended audience, Alexander was not acting according to the script. The tsar had changed in the sixteen months since the shock and awe which had driven him to Tilsit. Then he had been dazzled and humbled by the charismatic military genius who had defeated him; now he was serenely confident. Russia itself, after all, was surely beyond Napoleon's grasp. The emperor needed the tsar much more than the reverse.

There was another reason why Alexander was non-committal at Erfurt. The emperor had included Talleyrand in his procession to the congress. Although Napoleon had shorn his former foreign minister of formal power, he still kept him around for his sage advice on tactical if not strategic diplomatic questions. Talleyrand used the opportunity to secretly work against the emperor, whom he believed was violating France's true interests. He managed to meet privately with the tsar and made this powerful plea: "Sire, what did you come to do here? It's for you to save Europe. . . . The French people are civilized, their sovereign is not. It's therefore the Russian tsar who must ally with the French people." He went so far as to encourage Russia to ally with Austria against France. He also crafted a response for Alexander to make when Napoleon popped the question about marrying his sister Catherine. To those who would later condemn him for his double game, Talleyrand would reply: "At Erfurt I saved Europe."[124]

So Alexander was evasive and even mildly dismissive of Napoleon's demands. He refused the emperor's request for an alliance against Austria. That sent Napoleon into a fury, to the point where he stomped his own hat. The tsar would not be bullied. As if talking to a petulant child, he replied: "You are violent. I am stubborn. So anger will get you nowhere with me. Let us talk. Let us reason or I shall leave."[125]

With his rage spent and recognizing his own folly, Napoleon tried to make up to Alexander with gentle charm. Alexander replied in kind. One day the emperor pinned a Legion of Honor on the tsar and received the Saint Andrew's cross in return. Napoleon had an audience with all of Alexander's staff officers one morning; the tsar reciprocated with all of the emperor's the next. When the tsar admired the emperor's iron campaign bed, Napoleon had one made and presented it to him the following day. During one ball Johann Wolfgang von Goethe was presented to the sovereigns; the philosopher had kind and wise words for them both. The tsar was smitten with a French woman of apparently loose virtues and even looser tongue, but the emperor dissuaded him from pursuing her to avoid ridicule. The tsar wondered if the emperor had either a special rancor for or interest in her; Napoleon insisted that he was acting solely to protect Alexander. He assuaged the tsar's disappointment by encouraging a liaison between him and his sister Pauline. The result was that the emperor was beguiled by the tsar even as he deluded himself into believing that Alexander was still enthralled with him. To Josephine he wrote: "If he were a woman I believe I would make him my mistress."[126]

That remark on the surface was odd enough. What made it doubly so was that Napoleon had revealed to Alexander his intention to divorce Josephine and marry a fecund princess. He had heard wonderful things about the beauty, intelligence, and vivacity of the tsar's sister, Catherine. Would Alexander consider reinforcing their alliance with a marriage that made them brothers-in-law? Alexander hid his disgust at the proposal and said he would see what plans Catherine and their formidable mother might already have for her marriage. Although disappointed that the tsar did not immediately seize the opportunity, the emperor bit his tongue and turned the talk in other directions.

It was Talleyrand who beforehand had fed the tsar that face-saving line to fend off Napoleon's request to wed his sister. He had guided their secret discussion to another possible marriage, that of his nephew Edmond de Perigord to the Duchesse of Courland's daughter, Dorothee, who was one of Europe's richest heiresses. That match would gain Talleyrand yet another back channel to the exiled Louis XVIII and his entourage; the duchesse had hosted them at her chateau at Mittau and remained in close contact even though Napoleon had forced Alexander to expel them from his realm. The tsar was happy to oblige. The duchesse and her daughter proved to be enthusiastic. Talleyrand then arranged the ceremony in a way that would forge the latest strand in his web of conspirators against Napoleon. The priest who presided over the wedding at Frankfort in April 1809 was none other than the Rhine Confederation's Prince Primate, Karl von Dalberg, who was also an old friend. Talleyrand enticed Dalberg into the network and put him in direct contact with the tsar. In all, Talleyrand's secret diplomacy at Erfurt thwarted Napoleon on virtually all fronts.[127]

The Convention of Erfurt, which was signed on October 12, 1808, mostly elaborated existing commitments. Russia agreed to war with France against Britain until Whitehall accepted all of the continent's territorial and dynastic changes. Should Austria once again war against France, the tsar would declare a common cause with Paris against Vienna; here Napoleon had failed to get Alexander explicitly to commit to a military alliance. France in turn would recognize Russia's acquisition of Finland, Wallachia, and Moldavia, withdraw troops from the Duchy of Warsaw, and reduce Prussia's indemnity by 20 million francs.[128]

That same day they signed an eloquent joint plea to George III for peace:

The present European circumstances unite us at Erfurt. Our first thought is to serve the wishes and needs of all peoples, and to find a prompt peace with Your Majesty. . . . The long and bloody war which has torn the continent apart has ended. . . . Many changes have taken place in Europe. Many states have been overthrown. . . . And more changes can take place, all contrary to English interests. Peace is therefore in the interests of the British people. We are united in pleading with Your Majesty to listen to the voice of humanity, of looking forward with the interest of realizing, the reconciliation of all interests, to guarantee the existing powers, and assure the happiness of Europe and this generation at whose head providence has placed us.[129]

They would never receive a direct response.

Two days later in October 1808, the emperor and tsar made a very public show of feigned affection as they bid each other farewell. Their carriages rolled off in opposite directions. They would never meet again.

Spain and Conspiracy

When Napoleon left Erfurt he was in an even greater hurry than usual. Having shored up his rear as best he could, he was dashing off toward what he hoped would be a decisive campaign in Spain. After a brief sojourn at Paris to tie up loose political ends, he hurried onward and reached the army's headquarters at Vitoria on November 5.

Napoleon's military offensive was successful, if not decisive. He led his army across the Ebro on November 6, routed the Spanish at Burgos on November 10, Tudela on November 23, and Somosierra on November 30, and marched triumphantly into Madrid on December 4. At the capital he reinstalled a sheepish Joseph on the throne. He also launched a diplomatic offensive that he believed would at once soften Spanish hearts and minds to French rule while swelling his government's treasury: he decreed the abolition of feudalism and the Inquisition, and ordered one-third of the realm's monasteries confiscated and sold. But in doing so he grossly misjudged the people he was trying to conquer. Virtually all Spaniards were fiercely pious, proud, and conservative. Napoleon's attack on the Catholic Church merely enraged ever more of them to the point where they joined the rebellion against their foreign oppressors.[130]

Word arrived that British General John Moore was advancing against General Nicholas Soult at Burgos. Napoleon quick-marched his troops from Madrid on December 21 in an attempt to cut off Moore and smash him against Soult. Moore learned of that threat and barely escaped westward across northern Spain. Napoleon urged his commanders to catch up to and destroy the British army. On January 11 Moore led his army into Coruna. There the British soldiers dug in and awaited the fleet which would take them to safety. The exhausted French army arrived before those entrenchments on January 16. Soult ordered an immediate assault, which was repulsed with heavy losses. Although Moore was killed in the battle, 26,000 British troops managed to board the transports and sail off to Lisbon.

It had been a narrow escape. Had Napoleon led the pursuit with his relentless vigor, his troops most likely would have run down the British and bagged the entire army. Indeed, that was his bitter reaction when he learned that Soult had bungled the job: "If I had had the time to pursue the English, not a single one would have escaped."[131] And that might have forced Britain finally to accept defeat and negotiate a lasting peace. The subsequent history of Napoleon, Europe, and the world would have been completely different.

But having raced from Germany to Spain to deal with a chronic worsening problem, he had then found it necessary to race back to Paris to overcome what appeared to be an even worse crisis. The latest spy reports revealed that not only was Austria definitely preparing for war, but a coterie was plotting to replace him. So on January 3, 1809, he had handed over the pursuit to Soult and headed toward his distant capital.

The conspiracy's instigator was none other than his own sister Caroline. She had bent heads with Talleyrand and Fouche over what to do should the emperor be killed in battle or assassinated. Napoleon had already mulled that possibility and had designated Joseph his successor. The conspirators would instead put Murat on the throne. To ensure that he got to Paris from Naples before Joseph arrived from Madrid, Talleyrand set up a series of post horses between the two capitals on which the cavalryman would gallop his way along.

But it was Napoleon who on January 23 arrived in Paris, not just alive but livid. Five days later he convened a council of state meeting at the Tuileries. During those intervening days he had tried but failed to amass hard evidence against the plotters. With only rumors to go on he could not press charges. Apparently he had more against Talleyrand than Fouche, because he singled out his former foreign minister for his assault. In a half-hour tirade, he blistered Talleyrand as a "thief . . . a coward, a faithless wench. . . . All your life you have failed to fulfill your duties, you have deceived and betrayed everyone. . . . I really don't know why I haven't had you hanged from the gates of the Carousel."[132]

Why not, indeed? Instead he merely stripped the title of Grand Chamberlain from the miscreant while allowing him to remain the Vice-Grand Elector. If he had hoped to make an example of Talleyrand, it backfired. Fouche was a direct witness to the tirade, and Caroline and Murat soon learned of it. But they had seen displays of the emperor's explosive temper before. For those who knew him it was not so much intimidating as embarrassing. And then, after the storm passed, there was calm, at least for a while. Given the lack of evidence, Napoleon may have had little choice but to let Talleyrand off so lightly. But to do so acted as an enticement rather a deterrent to further intrigues.

Talleyrand met with Metternich on January 30 with the words, "I am free now and our causes are joined." He then gave a prolonged seminar on how best to bring down Napoleon. His advice did not come cheap. Metternich wrote Vienna for 400,000 francs for Talleyrand to pocket. He added this succinct analysis: "The tension is getting extreme. Until now the emperor has not ventured to attack Fouche. His way of attacking Talleyrand proves how strong these men are positioned. The emperor is steeling himself; it would be a simple matter to render them powerless; presumably he dares not do so. The gauntlet is clearly thrown between them."[133]

The 1809 Campaign

It took nearly two weeks, from December 8 to 23, for Vienna's war hawks to talk Francis and a few reluctant advisors, most notably Archduke Charles, into seeking vengeance for all the past humiliations they had suffered at Napoleon's hands. Their choice seems foolhardy, even suicidal. To date Napoleon had been invincible, having inflicted devastating defeats on Austria in 1797, 1800, and 1805, on Prussia and Russia in 1806 and 1807, and on Egypt in 1798; and he was likely to do the same to Spain, sooner or later. He had repeatedly warned that if Austria started another war it would be dismembered and reduced to a rump state.

So, given all that, what explains the Austrian decision? It was partly cold calculation. The French army in Germany and Italy had been stripped to the bone to feed the war in Spain. Napoleon himself was in the Peninsula, and was likely to be there for some time; even he could not be in two places at once. Since the 1805 Treaty of Pressburg, Vienna had fleshed out its regiments, packed its warehouses with munitions and provisions, and replenished its treasury. But, most significantly, Austria's leaders decided to go to war because they had once again restored the hubris so vital to their self-image, even though it had repeatedly proved to be so self-defeating in the past. That hubris was thoroughly entangled with fatalism. Historian Paul Schroeder nicely captured Vienna's mindset: "Austria did not decide to go to war because it thought it would win; it thought it could win because it believed it had to go to war."[134]

And therein lies the psychological reason behind the decision. Although the Austrians had been the aggressors in every war they had fought against France since 1792, they refused to accept that reality. Instead they had convinced themselves that they were history's martyrs, continually victimized by a relentlessly imperialistic France. Honor demanded that they try once more to avenge all their past humiliations.

The Austrians pressed on with their decision, even when it became clear that they would have to war alone against the French empire. St. Petersburg and Berlin rebuffed Vienna's secret pleas for an alliance among them. While Alexander, Frederick William, and their respective state councils and courts passionately hated Napoleon, they feared him even more.

Britain at first refused to help the Austrians, for the opposite reason: it had already committed so many troops, treasure, and warships to the war on the Peninsula and elsewhere that it had nothing left to spare. So Foreign Secretary Canning explained that he had to reject Austria's first request in October 1808, because it was "utterly beyond the power of this country to furnish."[135] Word of the British army's retreat across Spain and evacuation from Coruna and the death of Moore caused Whitehall to rethink its strategy. Having tried and failed to defeat Napoleon directly on land, it made sense to resume the old policy of hiring others to do the job. So in February Canning sent a secret envoy to Vienna with a promise of 250,000 pounds sterling if Austria went to war. The Austrians complained that the amount was only a tenth of what they had previously requested. Eventually they talked the British into not only paying them another million once the war began and an additional four million, depending on how long the war lasted, but also into launching an invasion of Walcheren Island in the Netherlands to divert Napoleon's attention from the fighting in Germany and Italy.

Francis ordered his army's mobilization on February 8, 1809; it would take another two months before the army was ready to march. The Austrians helped instigate a revolt by Andreas Hofer against Munich's rule in the Tyrol that would spread Bavaria's army thin before the Austrian assault.

Napoleon was hardly surprised by Vienna's aggression. For months his spies had kept him informed of the Austrian debate and preparations for war. For well over a month he had been steadily mobilizing troops, supplies, and allies. He opened his diplomacy at Valladolid on January 15 when he sent letters to Eugene and all his German allies warning them of Austria's suspicious actions and asking them to ready their forces for a possible war. He sent an open appeal to the Rhine Confederation a month later, on February 15, warning them to ready themselves against the swelling Austrian threat. On February 23 he established an Army Corps of Observation on the Rhine and recalled Ambassador Antoine Andreossy from Vienna for consultations.[136]

The war began on April 10, when four Austrian armies attacked in different directions in a systematic attempt to regain what had been lost in previous wars and then prepare for Napoleon's inevitable counterattack. Archduke Charles led 200,000 troops into Bavaria, and within a week had routed all opposition and occupied most of the kingdom. General Jean Chasteler marched into the Tyrol with 20,000 troops, linked up with the Tyrolean rebel Hofer, and took over that territory. Archduke Ferdinand trounced Polish Prince Josef Anton Poniatowski's army at Raszyn, took Warsaw, and marched toward Thorn. Archduke John's 45,000 troops defeated an equal number of French and Italians commanded by Eugene at Sacile on April 16 in northeastern Italy. To tie down and ideally topple Jerome, Austrian-inspired revolts broke out in Westphalia.

Napoleon responded to the Austrian juggernaut with the full measure of his brilliance and energy. He sent orders to mobilize all the resources of France's beleaguered allies, the Rhine Confederation, Duchy of Warsaw, and Kingdom of Italy, for war against Austria. As for his "ally" Russia, Napoleon preferred that it stay out of the fight. His spies had kept him informed of the swelling rage in St. Petersburg against France. So he did not want to give Alexander an excuse to mobilize his army to launch against France rather than Austria. His ambassador at St. Petersburg, Armand de Caulaincourt, fulfilled his instructions nearly to the letter. Nonetheless the tsar felt compelled to make some sort of symbolic gesture toward his ally, so he sent 32,000 troops briefly over the Bug River into Austrian territory.[137]

As in 1805, the war's key theater would be the Danube valley. Napoleon arrived at Donauworth, where he quickly assessed the situation and sent couriers with orders galloping off to his corps commanders and the over

175,000 French and allied troops split among them. They defeated the Austrians at Thann, Abensberg, Landshut, Eckmuhl, Rastibonne, and Scharding from April 19 to 26. Napoleon led his troops triumphantly into Vienna on May 13. He immediately began mobilizing all the resources of the capital and the country under his control for his army and to maintain order.[138]

Also as in 1805, the Austrians refused to give up even though they had lost their capital and tens of thousands of troops. The word from Italy was just as demoralizing. Eugene had rallied his army, defeated John when he tried to cross the Adige, and then pursued him into northeastern Italy and Carinthia. In Dalmatia General Auguste Marmont routed the Austrians under General Andreas von Stoichewich and began marching north. Jerome crushed the revolts in Westphalia and awaited further orders.

Despite that string of defeats, the Austrian army still had plenty of fight left in it. Looking for a knockout blow, Napoleon led his army across the Danube on pontoon bridges near Vienna on May 21. His troops had spread out no more than a mile from shore at the villages of Aspern and Essling when the Austrians launched a massive counterattack: 94,000 troops and 280 guns against Napoleon's 62,000 troops and 60 guns. It was almost the emperor's Waterloo. His troops repelled repeated attacks, inflicting 23,000 casualties to their own losses of 16,000. For a while Napoleon was prevented from either receiving reinforcements or retreating when the Austrians launched rock-filled barges from upstream which smashed through his pontoon bridge, stranding him on the Danube's far shore. Herculean labors by his engineers managed to reconstruct the bridge within two days, which let his battered troops limp back to safety.[139]

For the next five weeks a stalemate prevailed on the Vienna front as each commander massed more troops and supplies and cast nervous glances elsewhere. The latest Austrian-inspired revolt broke out in Saxony. Napoleon sent Jerome to crush it in his first successful independent campaign. The emperor's worries that John might march north against his rear were relieved when he got word that Eugene had routed him at Raab on June 14 and captured that key fortress on June 23.

Napoleon attempted another assault across the Danube on the fourth of July. The Austrians had withdrawn their 145,000 troops and 256 guns to a string of hills and ridges a half dozen miles beyond the river. The emperor hurled his 180,000 troops and 488 guns against that well-chosen position. That epic two-day battle, then the largest in history, cost Napoleon 37,500 casualties and Charles 42,000. Although the French took the field, it was not quite the decisive battle that the emperor had desired. Napoleon pursued Charles, caught up at Znaim, and defeated him again. That was enough for Charles, even though Francis and most of his advisors urged him to keep fighting. Charles eagerly agreed to an armistice at Znaim on July 12.[140]

Francis reluctantly ratified the agreement on July 18. The Austrian monarch had good reason to fear the worst, given that it was the fourth war he had lost at Napoleon's hands. But the French emperor wrote him a conciliatory letter on July 22, expressing his hopes that this fourth peace treaty "would be the last, and reestablish in a durable manner tranquility on the continent which can shield itself from the provocations and intrigues of England. . . . I look at this time with strong pleasure because of the four wars that Your Majesty has made against France, the last three were . . . not useful or advantageous for England."[141]

A lot of sophisticated diplomacy was packed into those lines. Napoleon placed the moral guilt for the war and its resolution squarely on Francis' shoulders. Yet he offered his defeated opponent a face-saving dodge by scapegoating England as the ultimate villain. Finally he offered a vision that both men could work toward. It was a classic example of Napoleon's diplomatic style.

Nonetheless, after foreign ministers Champagny and Metternich began negotiations at Altenbourg and eventually moved to Vienna, it would take several months of hard bargaining before they struck a deal. While Champagny remained the French point man, Prince Johann von Lichtenstein and at times Prince Ferdinand von Budna von Littiz joined or replaced Metternich.

Napoleon immersed himself in the diplomacy's ends and means through detailed letters to Champagny. The first step was to demand that Francis halve the Austrian army, dissolve the militia, or landwehr, and expel all French exiles serving Austria. Once that was done they could begin discussing the amount of money and land Francis would have to relinquish as a penalty for his latest war of aggression. At crucial points Napoleon would directly intervene with letters to Francis or one of the key Austrian diplomats.[142]

While the Austrians had been defeated, if not crushed, the French were still struggling against Austria's allies, the British and Spanish. In the Peninsula, after garrisoning Coruna, Soult marched his army south to Oporto. Marshal Claude Victor headed west through central Spain and routed General Gregorio de la Cuesta at Medellin. The plan was for those two French armies, each numbering about 25,000 troops, to converge on the lower Tagus and then drive against Lisbon.

But that plan faced a formidable obstacle: Wellesley was back in Lisbon. With 20,000 British, 3,000 Hanoverians, and 16,000 Portuguese, his forces outnumbered either French army. He headed north to roust Soult out of Oporto and back up the Douro River into Spain. He then marched his footsore troops south to Abrantes on the Tagus, massed reinforcements and supplies, and led his army toward Spain on June 27. He joined hands with Cuesta on July 11, and attacked Victor at Talavera on July 28. King George awarded Wellesley for his victory by naming him the Viscount of Wellington; he would not become a duke until after the battle of Vitoria in 1813. Yet Talavera was hardly decisive. Victor regrouped and advanced again, but Wellesley defeated him at Cerro de Medellin on July 27. Then each army withdrew on its supply lines.

That year's largest British effort would be the Walcheren expedition, which included 40,000 troops commanded by General John Pitt, Earl Chatham. The plan was for Chatham to land his army there, then advance rapidly to drive the French from the Netherlands. His troops disembarked on July 29, opened a siege of Flushing on August 1, and received the surrender of its 6,000-man garrison on August 16. But after that successful beginning things began to go wrong. The fortresses of Batz and Cadzand defied his sieges. Louis meanwhile massed a Dutch and French army for a counterattack.

Fearing that his brother was not up to the job, Napoleon sent Bernadotte to act as his field commander. Ironically, Bernadotte was available because the emperor had dismissed him for his latest incompetence and arrogance during the Austrian campaign. Napoleon's attempt to give Bernadotte an opportunity to redeem himself would have bad diplomatic consequences. Louis retired to his palace for a prolonged sulk that would persist until he formally resigned his throne the next year. Bernadotte merely massed troops and waited for the "Walcheren fever" to take effect. During the entire campaign the British lost only 105 men in battle, but disease killed 4,000 and crippled 13,000 more. The British eventually evacuated their last troops from Walcheren on December 9.

That was not the only bad news for Whitehall. Austrian envoys had talked local British commanders into launching raids on Italy and Dalmatia to divert Eugene and Marmont. General l'Espine convinced Captain Hargood, the Adriatic squadron's commander, to sail north and harass French-controlled ports. Count de la Tour likewise got Ferdinand IV and General John Stuart to invade southern Italy. But neither effort realized Austrian hopes. Hargood sailed the northern Adriatic but dared not let his wooden warships get within cannon shot of the mighty fortresses guarding the ports. Stuart captured the islands of Ischia and Procida in Naples Bay, but at a cost of 1,500 men; those losses discouraged him from fulfilling a promise to land his expedition near Livorno or Genoa. The only success that year in the Mediterranean was when Admiral Collingwood's squadron captured Cephalonia, Ithaca, and Cerigo and began a siege of Corfu in the Ionian Islands. None of those campaigns relieved any of the mounting pressure on Austria to bow once more before the power of France.

Dark political events topped off that year's very mixed military results for Britain. The stress of directing an ever more unpopular global war that ate up vast amounts of men and money with no prospect of a decisive victory drove yet another British leader to an early grave. A stroke incapacitated Prime Minister Portland on August 11; he resigned on September 6 and died on October 30. Canning and Castlereagh then engaged in an unseemly grab for the empty seat. Fighting words led to a duel. Canning got away with a slight wound to his side, but the scandal forced both to resign. Instead Spencer Perceval headed the new government, while at the foreign ministry it would be first Lord Hawksbury (later Liverpool) and then Richard Wellesley who would spurn Napoleon's latest peace offerings.

Italian Affairs

As usual, Napoleon found time during his campaign to mull and act on a range of other pressing diplomatic and political issues of varying degrees of importance. That year he made what would be a lasting gift to Italy when he decreed that the Tuscan dialect, in which Dante had written his Divine Comedy, would be the realm's lingua franca. He chose Tuscan, however, for diplomatic rather than cultural reasons. Each region of the kingdom of Italy was clamoring for its dialect to be the national language. Since Tuscany was not part of the Italian kingdom, Napoleon used Tuscan to finesse charges of favoritism that would inevitably arise if he picked one of the Italian kingdom's dialects.

That was perhaps the emperor's only gentle diplomatic measure for Italy that year. His vision for the peninsula was not yet done. Over the previous dozen years he had toppled the rulers of the northern states and forged their lands into a kingdom whose crown he bore. He had chased Ferdinand IV from Naples to refuge in Sicily and put first his brother Joseph and then his brother-in-law Joachim Murat on that vacant throne. He had annexed Savoy, Piedmont, the Ligurian Republic, and several smaller principalities as departments of France. On May 24, 1808, he dissolved the Duchy of Parma and kingdom of Etruria and converted them into departments to be governed by Elisa, who would retain her title of duchesse.

When 1809 opened the only realm left with even nominal independence was the Papal States. The 1802 Concordat had papered over rather than ended the animosities between Paris and Rome. With time the relationship became locked into an ever more vicious cycle exacerbated by both unbridgeable differences on key issues and perceived slights. For instance, just a month after Austerlitz Napoleon replied to a letter from Pius VII containing a long list of complaints by scolding him for "lending an ear to the evil advice" of "the power of English gold which has organized a coalition against me." He then justified Ancona's reoccupation as a defensive measure against the English, Russians, and Neapolitans. Pius must think of Napoleon as his protector and benefactor. As usual, he had Cardinal Joseph Fesch, his uncle and ambassador in Rome, try to convert the pope to his views. Pius was hardly convinced.[143]

So Napoleon tried again. In his next letter he tried to make a theological case for cooperation against the English, who "from a religious point of view, are heretics and beyond the Church." Having tried to rally the pope to his crusade he then, in the next breath, dropped this bombshell: "All of Italy will be submitted under my law. . . . Your Holiness is the sovereign of Rome but I am its emperor. All my enemies must be yours. It is therefore not suitable that a single agent of Sardinia, England, Russia, and Sweden resides at Rome or in your states, or a single [enemy] ship appears in your ports." As usual, he sent a parallel letter to Cardinal Fesch with minute instructions on how to reinforce his diplomacy. Pius replied by asserting that not only would he not recognize a French takeover of the Papal States or Rome, but if Napoleon did so he risked being excommunicated.[144] Atop that the pope refused to annul Jerome's marriage, or recognize Joseph as the king of Naples or Napoleon's right to appoint French bishops.

That letter provoked rather than cautioned Napoleon. He had Talleyrand send a tough letter to Cardinal Giovanni Caprara, the papal foreign minister, condemning the "impertinence and bad faith of the Roman Court. . . . His Majesty will not recognize the Pope as a worldly prince, but only as a spiritual leader."[145]

For the next couple of years Napoleon's conflict with the Church was elbowed aside by a range of more pressing issues. But the tensions boiled over again in January 1808 over two issues: whether Rome would join the Continental System; and who should select France's prelates, with each claiming that power for himself. When Pius remained defiant, Napoleon sent orders to General Miollis to invade the Papal States and occupy Rome. Miollis immediately began to execute the orders after receiving them on January 21, 1808. By February 2, 1809, his troops had secured Rome and the Papal States.

Napoleon warned Pius that even worse would come if he did not yield: "If the Holy Father adheres to this position all is finished. . . . The result of war will be conquest, and the first result of the conquest will be a change in government. . . . What other guarantee would there be for the tranquility and security of Italy?"[146]

When that failed to move Pius, Napoleon signed a decree from the Schonbrunn Palace on May 17, 1809, by which the Papal States were annexed as departments of France. The pope henceforth would be solely a spiritual ruler; he would preside at the Vatican and reside at the Quirinale Palace, with an annual stipend of two million francs, courtesy of France. French troops carried out the takeover on June 10.[147]

That was the last straw for Pius VII. Ever since taking the papal throne he had endured one insult, manipulation, and loss after another at Napoleon's hands. On June 10 he issued a papal bull excommunicating all those who made or fulfilled the emperor's decree.

Now it was Napoleon's turn to be indignant. He fired off a letter to Murat, who as the neighboring King of Naples was designated the Papal States' "protector," to have him order the "arrest, even in the pope's palace, of all those who plot against public order and the safety of my soldiers." In a letter to General Miollis, the French commander in Rome, he called Pius a "madman who must be shut up," ordered the arrest of Cardinal Pacca, the power behind the papal throne, and even the pope himself if he "preaches revolt and wants to use the immunity of his palace to have circulars printed."[148]

That order certainly gave Miollis pause for thought as he contemplated the consequences of enduring the emperor's wrath for his lifetime if he did not obey the order, or God's wrath for eternity if he did. His second-in-command, General Etienne Radet, lost patience with his senior's Hamlet-like musings and took matters into his own hands. With a file of soldiers behind him, Radet strode into the Quirinale Palace to arrest not just Pacca but Pius himself on July 6. He had Pius sent under heavy guard to the Carthusian monastery of Certosa di Val d'Ema near Florence. That setting was familiar to the pope; the French had confined his predecessor, Pius VI, there during the winter of 1798-99. But this time it was just a brief rest stop; the pope was hurried onward.

Napoleon was stunned when he learned what had happened. To Fouche he wrote: "I am angry that the pope has been arrested, it is a piece of utter folly. Cardinal Pacca should have been arrested and the pope left peacefully at Rome. However, there is no way of remedying the matter; what is done is done. . . . I do not want the pope brought into France . . . the best place to put him would be Savona. . . . If he stops being foolish I should not be opposed to his being taken to Rome. . . . If he has already been brought into France, have him taken back toward Savona."[149]

The pope had indeed been brought into France, all the way to Grenoble, when the emperor's latest order caught up to his escort. Pacca was interned in the fortress of Fenestrelles in Savoy, while Pius was brought back to be lodged in the bishop's palace at Savona.

If Napoleon had hoped that the pope's arrest, peregrinations, and incarceration would force him to retract his bull of excommunication, he was wrong; those blows only hardened the pope's resolve. He would stay locked up at Savona until 1812, when the emperor ordered him taken to Fontainebleau for safer keeping and possibly negotiations.

In return for his excommunication, the emperor did get to annex the last semi-free states of the Italian peninsula to France. That meant imposing France's constitution and legal code, nationalizing most Church properties, disbanding the papal army, shutting down the papal press, and expelling all those clergymen who refused to swear allegiance to Napoleon. In all, fifteen bishops and about 900 priests swore the loyalty oath to the emperor, while nine bishops and 500 priests refused—and paid the consequences.[150]

Peace

The peace negotiations dragged on with no end in sight while both sides built up their forces in case they had to war again. When Francis appeared to have encouraged disruptions in French-held territory, Napoleon told Champagny to pass on the word that if that did not end he would simply annex those provinces to France, "render justice in my name, destroy feudal rights, and publish the Napoleonic Code." Then, once again, he tried a direct appeal to Francis himself: "Of all the calamities, war is the worst. Shame on those who provoke it! The blood and tears of the victims will fall upon them." After that guilt-inducing opening, he systematically dismantled each Austrian position and asserted his own. Finally, the emperor upped the pressure on Francis by having Champagny hint that Francis' burdens may have been too great, and perhaps he should be replaced with someone more flexible and farsighted, such as Archduke Charles or the Duke of Wurzburg.[151]

Sowing fear of a palace coup broke the diplomatic impasse. Francis dispatched Prince Johann von Liechtenstein to cut a deal with Napoleon. For months the emperor had been pondering whether to act on his promise to reduce Austria to a rump state which would never again threaten the peace of Europe. But in the end he decided to enlist Austria as an ally, and for that to be effective he had to keep it strong enough to give him diplomatic and military heft, but weak enough so that it did not again turn against him.

Those ideas formed the foundations for the Treaty of Schonbrunn signed on October 14, 1809. In return for letting Francis keep his throne, Napoleon carved from the Austrian empire Istria, Carniola, and the Littoral for France, Berchtesgaden, Salzburg, Bayreuth, Regensburg, and their surrounding lands for Bavaria, several border regions of Bohemia for Saxony, and much of Galicia for the Grand Duchy of Warsaw. That represented a loss of 3.5 million souls and enormous amounts of potential troops and taxes. Vienna would have to pay an indemnity of 400 million francs to France and its allies, and reduce its army to 150,000 men.

Austria was not the only country which was hurt by the peace. Napoleon penalized Prussia for its refusal to aid him against Austria by annexing Hamburg and the fortress of Glogau. Bavaria's advance eastward was offset by shedding a portion of Swabia to Wurttemberg and the Tyrol to the Kingdom of Italy.

Napoleon had scaled the summit of his power. His diplomacy in the coming years would determine whether he stayed there or tumbled himself and his empire into the abyss.

Chapter Four Endnotes: Napoleon Invincible

1. Napoleon to Joseph, January 27, 1806, Napoleon Bonaparte, Claude Tchou, ed., *Correspondance de Napoleon* (hereafter cited as *Correspondence*), 16 vols. (Paris: Bibliotheque des Introuvables, 2002), 9713.

2. Jean Hanoteau, ed., *With Napoleon in Russia: The Memoirs of General de Caulaincourt, Duke of Vicenza* (New York: William Morrow, 1935), 14.

3. For the best biography, see Carola Oman, *Napoleon's Viceroy: Eugene de Beauharnais* (London: Hodder and Stoughton, 1966).

4. Instructions for Prince Eugene, June 7, 1805, *Correspondence*, 8852.

5. Napoleon to Eugene, April 14, 1806, *Correspondence*, 10099.

6. Napoleon to Otto, July 12, 1804, *Correspondence*, 7856.

7. Napoleon to Bavarian Elector, December 21, 1805, *Correspondence*, 9599.

8. Napoleon to Eugene, December 31, 1805, January 33, 1806, *Correspondence*, 9636, 9638; Napoleon to Duroc, January 3, 1805, *ibid.*, 639.

9. Louis Constant, *Memoires Intimes de Napoleon Ier*, 2 vols. (Paris: Mercure de France, 1967), 1:359.

10. Message to the Senate, January 12, 1806, *Correspondence*, 9663.

11. Napoleon to Stephanie de Beauharnais, July 13, 1806, *Correspondence*, 10491; Decision to Adopt Stephanie, March 3, 1806, *ibid.*, 9914; see also, Napoleon to Baden Elector, January 4, 1804, *ibid.*, 9649; Napoleon to Baden Margrave, February 21, 1806, *ibid.*, 9862; Message to Senate, March 4, 1806, *ibid.*, 9923.

12. Napoleon to Talleyrand, December 14, 1805, *Correspondence*, 9573; Proclamation to the Army, December 27, 1805, *ibid.*, 9616; *Moniteur*, December 28, 1805.

13. Napoleon to Joseph Fesch, June 25, 1784, Thierry Lentz, ed., *Napoleon Bonaparte, Correspondance Generale (hereafter cited as General Correspondence)*, Tome Premier, *Les Apprentisages, 1784-1797* (Paris: Fayard, 2004), 1; Napoleon to Berthier, December 27, 1805, *Correspondence*, 9627; Napoleon to Joseph, December 31, 1805, January 12, 31, February 7, 9, March 2, 1806, *ibid.*, 9633, 9665, 9724, 9773, 9788, 99. For the best biography of Joseph in English, see: Owen Connelly, *The Gentle Bonaparte: A Biography of Joseph, Napoleon's Elder Brother* (New York: Macmillan, 1968).

14. Napoleon to Talleyrand, March 14, June 5, 1806, *Correspondence*, 9970, 10319; Bonaparte to Talleyrand, April 17, August 20, 1804, *ibid.*, 7718, 7946; Napoleon to Schimmelpenninck, May 12, 1805, *ibid.*, 8719.

15. Napoleon to Senate, June 5, 1806, *Correspondence*, 10317.

16. Constant, *Memoires*, 2:549.

17. Constant, *Memoires*, 137-44, 536-37.

18. Napoleon to Louis, July 21, 1806, *Correspondence*, 10534.

19. Napoleon to Louis, April 4, 1806, *Correspondence*, 12294.

20. Constant, *Memoires*, 1:139, 336-37, 429-35, 536-37.

21. Constant, *Memoires*, 434; John Bierman, *Napoleon III and His Carnival Empire* (New York: St. Martin's Press, 1988), 3-17.

22. Napoleon Message to Senate, March 18, 1805, *Correspondence*, 8447; Napoleon to Elisa, March 31, 1806, *ibid.*, 10036.

23. Napoleon to Elisa, May 24, June 13, September 4, 1806, *Correspondence*, 10265, 10359; Napoleon to Pius, May [n.d.], 1806, *ibid.*, 10266; Elisa to Pius, May 1806, *ibid.*,

10266; Napoleon to Archbishop of Lucca, May 1806, *ibid.*, 10267; Napoleon to Talleyrand, April 25, May 24, 1806, *ibid.*, 10133, 10264.

24. Constant, *Memoires*, 1:546.

25. Bonaparte to Pauline, April 6, 1804, *Correspondence*, 7674; Bonaparte to Fesch, April 10, 1804, *ibid.*, 7678.

26. Napoleon to Talleyrand, January 30, February 4, March 15, 1806, *Correspondence*, 9716, 9742, 9977; Napoleon to Berthier, February 14, 1806, *ibid.*, 9810; Napoleon to Maximilien Joseph, February 14, March 8, 1806, *ibid.*, 9811, 9942.

27. Napoleon to Frederick William III, April 4, 1806, *Correspondence*, 10051.

28. Note to Foreign Minister, July 2, 1806, *Correspondence*, 10448; Proposal for a Treaty with England, August 6, 1808, *ibid.*, 10604.

29. Napoleon to Murat, March 9, 15, 16, 23, April 4, 16, 1806, *Correspondence*, 9948, 9975, 9983, 10009, 10056, 10107; Decision, March 15, 1806, *ibid.*, 9976; Napoleon to Talleyrand, March 14, 15, April 7, May 31, 1806, *ibid.*, 9969, 9977, 10063, 10298.

30. Napoleon to Murat, August 2, 1806, *Correspondence*, 10587.

31. Napoleon to Talleyrand, March 14, 18, 1806, *Correspondence*, 9968, 9988, Napoleon to Eugene, March 17, 21, 26, April 21, 1806, *ibid.*, 9989, 10003, 10024, 10117; Napoleon to Berthier, March 24, 25, 1806, *ibid.*, 10016, 10017; Napoleon to Joseph, March 31, 1806, *ibid.*, 10044.

32. Napoleon to Otto, January 21, 1806, *Correspondence*, 9693; Napoleon to Talleyrand, April 10, May 31, June 23, 1806, *ibid.*, 10071, 10298, 10405.

33. Napoleon to Talleyrand, August 14, 1808, *Correspondence*, 10644; Napoleon to Dalberg, September 11, 1806, *ibid.*, 10762.

34. Napoleon to Talleyrand, August 22, 1806, *Correspondence*, 10683; Napoleon to Durand, September 12, 1806, *ibid.*, 10766.

35. Napoleon to Eugene, May 26, June 3, 1806, *Correspondence*, 10278, 10310; Napoleon to Berthier, June 7, 11, 1806, *ibid.*, 10331, 10348; Napoleon to Talleyrand, June 11, 1806, *ibid.*, 10346; Napoleon to Joseph, June 21, 1806, *ibid.*, 10395.

36. Napoleon to Talleyrand, June 11, 1806, *Correspondence*, 10346.

37. Thierry Lentz, *Nouvelle Histoire du Premier Empire* (Paris: Fayard, 2002), 239-47.

38. Napoleon to Turkish Ambassador, June 5, 1806, *Correspondence*, 10315; Napoleon to Talleyrand, May 21, June 11, 1806, *ibid.*, 10253, 10346; Napoleon to Selim, November 11, 1806, January 1, 1807, *ibid.*, 11232, 11533.

39. Emile Dard, *Napoleon and Talleyrand* (New York: D. Appleton Century and Company, 1937), 124-28.

40. Napoleon to Talleyrand, August 18, 1808, *Correspondence*, 10662; Talleyrand to Fox (copy to Napoleon), March 5, 1806, *ibid.*, 9926.

41. Napoleon to Frederick William, September 12, 1806, *Correspondence*, 10764; Napoleon to Laforest, September 12, 1806, *ibid.*, 10765.

42. Frederick William to Napoleon, September 25, 1806, Leon Lecestres, ed., *Lettres Personelles des Souverains a l'Emperor Napoleon 1st* (Paris: Plon, 1939), 318-25.

43. 1st Bulletin of the Grand Army, October 8, 1808, *Correspondence*, 10967; Napoleon to Bavarian King, September 21, 1806, *ibid.*, 10850; Napoleon to Wurttemberg King, September 21, 1806, *ibid.*, 10851; Napoleon to Baden Prince, September 28, *ibid.*, 10886.

44. Napoleon to Talleyrand, October 7, 1806, *Correspondence*, 10953.

45. To the People of Saxony, October 10, 1808, *Correspondence*, 10978; 2nd, 5th, 6th, 7th, 8th, 10th Bulletins of the Grand Army, *ibid.*, 10987, 11009, 11013, 11016, 11018, 11028; Napoleon to Frederick William, October 12, 1806, *ibid.*, 10990; Napoleon to Talleyrand, October 15, 1808, *ibid.*, 11007; Decret on Requisitions, October 15, 1806, *ibid.*, 11010.

46. Napoleon to Talleyrand, August 8, 22, 1806, *Correspondence*, 10624, 10683.

47. Napoleon to Frederick William, October 19, 1806, *Correspondence*, 11031.

48. 27th, 29th, 31st Bulletins of the Grand Army, November 4, 1806, *Correspondence*, 11167, 11223, 11246.

49. 18th Bulletin of the Grand Army, October 26, 1806, *Correspondence*, 1806.

50. 19th, 21st Bulletins of the Grand Army, October 27, 1806, *Correspondence*, 11097, 11102.

51. 33rd Bulletin of the Grand Army, *Correspondence*, 11277; Napoleon to Frederick William, December 6, 1806, *ibid.*, 11394.

52. Note for Attendant General, November 2, 1806, *Correspondence*, 11142; Napoleon to Talleyrand, December 10, 1806, *ibid.*, 11426.

53. Berlin Decree, November 21, 1806, *Correspondence*, 11283; Napoleon to Talleyrand, December 3, 1806, *ibid.*, 11283, 11379.

54. Lentz, *Premier Empire*, 1:256-76.

55. 36th, 45th, 47th Bulletin of the Grand Army, December 1, 1806, *Correspondence*, 11349, 11511, 11521,

56. Napoleon to Talleyrand, December 15, 1806, *Correspondence*, 11476; Napoleon to Champagny, July 30, 1807, *ibid.*, 13226; Napoleon to Charles IV, January 20, 1807, *ibid.*, 11672; Napoleon to Queen of Spain, January 20, 1807, *ibid.*, 11673; Napoleon to Godoy, January 21, 1807, *ibid.*, 11674.

57. Napoleon to Murat, December 2, 1806, *Correspondence*, 11350.

58. Napoleon to Saxon elector, December 2, 1806, January 24, 1807, *Correspondence*, 11359, 11686.

59. Order for the Polish Army, January 2, 1807, *Correspondence*, 11536; Decret for Poland, January 29, 1807, *ibid.*, 11732; Napoleon to Talleyrand, April 5, 1807, *ibid.*, 12301.

60. Constant, *Memoires*, 1:409-15, 602-03; Lentz, *Premier Empire*, 1:277-81.

61. 58th Bulletin of the Grand Army, February 7, 1807, *Correspondence*, 11796.

62. Instructions for Bertrand, February 13, 1807, *Correspondence*, 11810; Napoleon to Frederick William, February 26, 1807, *ibid.*, 11890.

63. Napoleon to Talleyrand, April 16, 1806, *Correspondence*, 12390.

64. Napoleon to Selim, April 3, 1807, *Correspondence*, 12277.

65. Napoleon to Shah, April 3, 7, 20, 1807, *Correspondence*, 12278, 12324, 12429; Napoleon to Talleyrand, April 3, 5, 12, 1807, *ibid.*, 12276, 12302, 12354; Instructions to General Gardane, May 10, 1807, *ibid.*, 12563.

66. Napoleon to Josephine, May 10, 1807, *Correspondence*, 12562.

67. Napoleon to Talleyrand, April 23, 1807, *Correspondence*, 12453; 78th Bulletin of the Grand Army, June 12, 1807, *ibid.*, 12747.

68. Napoleon to Frederick William, April 29, 1807, May 17, 1807, *Correspondence*, 12487, 12594; Frederick William to Napoleon, May 10, 1807, May 21, 1807, *Lettres Personelles des Souverains a l'Emperor Napoleon I*, 335, 339; Napoleon to Talleyrand, April 24, 1807, *Correspondence*, 12464.

69. 78th, 79th, and 80th Bulletins of the Grand Army, June 12, 17, 1807, *Correspondence*, 12747, 1276, 12775.

70. 82nd Bulletin of the Grand Army, *Correspondence*, 12801; Armistice, June 27, 1807, *ibid.*, 12834.

71. Henri Troyat, *Alexander of Russia: Napoleon's Conqueror* (New York: E.P. Dutton, 1982), 105; Robert Asprey, *The Reign of Napoleon* (New York: Basic Books, 2001), 75. For the most comprehensive analysis of their relationship, see Albert Vandal, *Napoleon et Alexander I: L'Alliance Russe sous le Premier Empire*, 2 vols. (Paris: Plon, 1896); for an excellent description of the spectacle, see 86th Bulletin of the Grand Army, June 25, 1807, *Correspondence*, 12827.

72. Troyat, *Alexander*, 103.

73. For the grand vision that the emperor shared with the tsar and got him to go along with, see: Napoleon to Alexander, July 4, 6 (2 letters), 9, 1807, *Correspondence*, 12849, 12862, 12865, 12884.

74. Napoleon to Josephine, July 7, 8, 1807, *Correspondence*, 12869, 12875.

75. Constant, *Memoires*, 1:426-27.

76. Troyat, *Alexander*, 105.

77. H. Butterfield, *The Peace Tactics of Napoleon* (New York: Octagon Books, 1972), 235.

78. Convention of Konigsberg, July 12, 1807, *Correspondence*, 12895; William Shanahan, *Prussian Military Reforms, 1786-1813* (New York: AMS Press, 1945), 98.

79. For excellent summaries of his diplomatic achievements and the state of the empire, see: Report of the Emperor before the Legislative Corps, August 16, 1807, *Correspondence*, 13034; Exposé of the Empire's Situation, August 24, 1807, *ibid.*, 13063.

80. Troyat, *Alexander*, 106.

81. Charles Maurice de Talleyrand Perigord, *Memoires du prince de Talleyrand* (Paris: Calmann-Levy, 1891), 2:316.

82. Alan Schom, *Napoleon Bonaparte* (New York: HarperCollins, 1997), 479.

83. Jean Hanoteau, ed., *Memoires du General de Caulaincourt, Duc de Vincence, Grand Ecuyer de l'Emperor*, 3 vols. (Paris: Plon, 1933), 2:257, 3:447.

84. Talleyrand, *Memoires*, 2:318.

85. Westphalian Constitution, November 15, 1807, *Correspondence*, 13362.

86. Napoleon to Talleyrand, July 30, 1804, *Correspondence*, 7884; Napoleon to Pius VII, May 24, 1805, *ibid.*, 8781; Napoleon to Jerome, May 30, 1805, *ibid.*, 8811.

87. Napoleon to Jerome, August 19, November 15 (2 letters), 1807, *Correspondence*, 13050, 13361, 13363;

88. They begin with Napoleon to Jerome, December 17, 1807, *Correspondence*, 13403.

89. Napoleon to Daru, August 12, 16, 1807, *Correspondence*, 13025, 13037.

90. Napoleon to Talleyrand, August 9, 1807, *Correspondence*, 13012.

91. Napoleon to Daru, September 14, 26, 1807, *Correspondence*, 13148, 13186.

92. Rory Muir, *Britain and the Defeat of Napoleon, 1807-1815* (New Haven, Conn.: Yale University Press, 1996), 6.

93. Digby Smith, *The Greenhill Napoleonic Wars Data Book* (London: Greenhill Books, 1998), 254.

94. Jean Marie Rene Savary, *Memoires du Duc de Rovigo*, 8 vols. (Paris: Imprimerie de Cosson, 1829), 3:150; Napoleon to Savary, July 13, 1807, *Correspondence*, 12902; Talleyrand to Savary, *Correspondence*, 12910.

95. Napoleon to Savary, September 28, November 1, 1807, *Correspondence*, 13190; Napoleon to Alexander, December 7, 1807, *ibid.*, 13383.

96. Napoleon to Savary, November 7, 1807, *Correspondence*, 13339.

97. Napoleon to Talleyrand, July 19, 1807, *Correspondence*, 12928.

98. Napoleon to John, the regent, September 8, 1807, *Correspondence*, 13132; Napoleon to Charles IV, October 12, 1807, *ibid.*, 13243; Napoleon to Champagny, October 12, 20, 1807, *ibid.*, 13235, 13274; Napoleon to Junot, October 17, 1807, *ibid.*, 13267.

99. Proposed Convention, October 23, 1807, *Correspondence*, 13287; Secret Convention, October 27, 1807, *ibid.*, 13300; Convention Relative to Portugal's Occupation, Treaty of Fontainebleau, October 27, 1807, *ibid.*, 13301; Napoleon to Charles IV, October 12, 1807, *ibid.*, 13243.

100. Napoleon to Junot, October 31, November 12, 1807, *Correspondence*, 13314, 13351; Napoleon to Charles IV, November 13, 1807, *ibid.*, 13355.

101. Napoleon to Junot, December 20, 1807, *Correspondence*, 13406.

102. Napoleon to Alexander, February 2, 1808, Alexander to Napoleon, March 13, 1808, in Michael Kerautret, ed., *Les Grand Traites de l'Empire, 1804-1810* (Paris: Nouveau Monde Editions/Fondation Napoleon, 2004), 358-61; Adam Zamoyski, *Moscow 1812: Napoleon's Fatal March* (New York: HarperCollins, 2004), 34-35; Sergei Spiridonovich Tatischeff, ed., *Alexander Ier et Napoleon d'apres leur correspondence inedite, 1801-1812* (Paris: Librarie Academique Didier, 1891), 372.

103. Napoleon to Charles IV, January 10, February 25, 1808, *Correspondence*, 13443, 13604.

104. Napoleon to Charles IV, January 10 (2 letters), 1808, *Correspondence*, 13443, 13444; Jacques Chastenet, *Manuel de Godoy et l'Espagne de Goya* (Paris: Hachette, 1961), 156-86.

105. Napoleon to Murat, February 20 (2 letters), March 6, 8, 9, 14, 29, 1808, *Correspondence*, 13588, 13589, 13626, 13628, 13632, 13652, 13696; Napoleon to Champagny, March 9, 1808, *ibid.*, 13620.

106. Napoleon to Murat, May 2, 1808, *Correspondence*, 13081; Napoleon to Joseph, May 11, 1808, Joseph Bonaparte, *Memoires et Correspondence Politique et Militaire du Roi Joseph*, 10 vols. (1853-54), 4:228.

107. Napoleon to Murat, March 29, 1808, *Correspondence*, 13696.

108. Napoleon to Murat, March 29, 1808, *Correspondence*, 13696; for a comprehensive foreign ministry analysis of Spain, see Report to the Emperor, April 24, 1808, *ibid.*, 13776.

109. Napoleon to Ferdinand, April 16, 1808, *Correspondence*, 13750; Napoleon to Murat, April 9, 10, *ibid.*, 13730, 13733.

110. Constant, *Memoires*, 475-88.

111. Napoleon to Talleyrand, May 1, 1808, *Correspondence*, 13797.

112. Napoleon to Murat, April 25, 1808, *Correspondence*, 13780.

113. Charles to Ferdinand, May 2, 1808, *Correspondence*, 13801; Ferdinand to Charles, May [n.d.], 1808, *ibid.*, 13817; Proclamation of Charles to the Spanish people, May 4, 1808, *ibid.*, 13809; Charles to Junta, May 4, 1808, *ibid.*; Charles to the Supreme Council, May 8, 1808, *ibid.*, 13856; Napoleon's Proposed Act of Mediation, May [n.d], 1808, *ibid.*, 13814; Napoleon to Talleyrand, May 6, 9, 1808, *ibid.*, 12815, 13834; Proclamation to the Spanish, May 25, 1808, *ibid.*, 13989.

114. Napoleon to Louis, March 27, 1808, *Correspondence* (unnumbered), 8:500-01; Napoleon to Joseph, May 10, 1808, *ibid.*, 13844.

115. Napoleon to Murat, May 8, 1808, *Correspondence*, 13830; Napoleon to Bessieres, May 8, 1808, *ibid.*, 13831; Deputy Address to the Junta, June 18, 1808, *ibid.*, 14066; Junta Proclamation, June 7, 1808, *ibid.*, 14071.

116. John Sherwig, *Guineas and Gunpowder: British Foreign Aid in the Wars with France, 1793-1815* (Cambridge, Mass.: Harvard University Press, 1969), 198-203.

117. Napoleon to Junot October 19, 1808, *Correspondence*, 14386.

118. Hubert Cole, _The Betrayers: Joachim and Caroline Murat_ (New York: Saturday Review Press, 1972).

119. Claude Francois de Meneval, _Memoires pour servir a l'Histoire de Napoleon Ier_ (Paris: E. Dentu, 1894), 3:219.

120. Laura Junot, _At the Court of Napoleon: Memoirs of the Duchesse d'Abrantes_ (New York: Doubleday, 1989), 291.

121. Constant, _Memoires_, 1:627.

122. Charles Maurice de Talleyrand, _Memoires Completes et Authentiques de Charles Maurice de Talleyrand_, 6 vols. (Paris: Chez Jean de Bonnot, 1967), 1:408; Emmanuel de Waresquiel, _Talleyrand: Le Prince Immobile_ (Paris: Fayard, 2003), 387-88.

123. Talleyrand, _Memoires_, 1:408.

124. Clement von Metternich, _Memoires, Documents, et Ecrits Divers Laisses par le Prince Metternich_ (Paris: Plon, 1881), 2:248; Waresquiel, _Talleyrand_, 388.

125. Troyat, _Alexander_, 121.

126. Napoleon, _Lettres d'Amour a Josephine_ (Paris: Fayard, 1981), 311; Constant, _Memoires_, 1:499-507, 631, 2:7-17.

127. Georg Lacour-Gayet, _Talleyrand_ (Paris: Payot, 1990), 632, 635; Dard, _Napoleon and Talleyrand_, 191.

128. Convention of Alliance, October 12, 1808, _Correspondence_, 14372.

129. Napoleon and Alexander to George III, _Correspondence_, 14373.

130. Proclamation to the Spanish, December 7, 1808, _Correspondence_, 14537; Response to the Madrid Corregidor, December 9, 1808, _ibid._, 14543; Order for the Spanish National Guard, December 15, 1808, _ibid._, 14569.

131. A.M. Roederer, ed., _Oeuvres du Comte P.L. Roederer_ (Paris: Firmin, Didot Freres, 1858), 3:537.

132. Waresquiel, _Talleyrand_, 400. See also, Lentz, _Premier Empire_, 1:428-34; Tulard, _Fouche_, 217-28;

133. Waresquiel, _Talleyrand_, 402-03.

134. Paul Schroeder, _The Transformation of European Politics, 1763-1848_ (New York: Oxford University Press, 1994), 355.

135. Sherwig, _Guineas and Gunpowder_, 208.

136. Napoleon to Eugene, January 15, 1909, _Correspondence_, 14715; Napoleon to Jerome, January 15, 1809, _ibid._, 14718; Napoleon to Louis X, Grand Duke of Hesse-Darmstadt, January 15, 1809, _ibid._, 14719; Napoleon to Maximilien Joseph, January 15, 1809, _ibid._, 14720; Napoleon to Frederick Augustus, January 15, 1809, _ibid._, 14721; Napoleon to Frederick, King of Wurttemberg, January 15, 1809, _ibid._, 14722; Napoleon to Charles Frederick, Grand Duke of Baden, January 15, 1809, _ibid._, 14723; Napoleon to Charles, Prince Primate of the Rhine Confederation, January 15, 1809, _ibid._, 14725; Napoleon to Rhine Confederation princes, February 15, 1809, _ibid._, 14782.

137. Napoleon to Campagny, March 21, 1809, *Correspondence*, 14933; Napoleon to Alexander, July 9, 1809, *ibid.*, 15508.

138. 1st, 7th Bulletins of the Army of Germany, April 24, May 13, 1809, *Correspondence*, 15112, 15202.

139. 10th, 13th Bulletins of the Army of Germany, October 23, 1809, *Correspondence*, 15246, 15272.

140. 25th Bulletin of the Army of Germany, July 8, 1809, *Correspondence*, 15505; Suspension of Arms, July 13, 1809, *ibid.*, 15517.

141. Napoleon to Francis, July 23, 1809, *Correspondence*, 15578.

142. Napoleon to Champagny, July 24, August 19, September 10, 21 (2 letters), 22, October 1, 1809, *Correspondence*, 15584, 15683, 15778, 15832, 15833, 15835, 15888.

143. Napoleon to Pius VII, January 7, 1806, *Correspondence*, 9655; Napoleon to Fesch, January 7, 1806, *ibid.*, 9656; Robin Anderson, *Pope Pius VII* (Rockford, IL: Tan Books, 2000).

144. Napoleon to Pius VII, February 13, 1806, *Correspondence*, 9805; Napoleon to Fesch, February 13, 1806, *ibid.*, 9806; Lentz, *Savary*, 282.

145. Napoleon to Talleyrand, May 16, 1806, *Correspondence*, 10237; Napoleon to Fesch, May 16, 1806, *ibid.*, 10239; Napoleon to Talleyrand, June 19, 1806, *ibid.*, 10378.

146. Napoleon to Champagny (letter and annex), April 1, 1808, *Correspondence*, 13709; see also Napoleon to Champagny, April 2, 1808, *ibid.*, 13714.

147. Decree, May 17, 1809, *Correspondence*, 15219.

148. Napoleon to Murat, June 19, 1809, *Correspondence*, 15383; Napoleon to Miollis, June 19, 1809, *ibid.*, 15385.

149. Napoleon to Fouche, July 18, 1809, *Correspondence*, 15555.

150. Owen Chadwick, *The Popes and the European Revolution* (Oxford: Clarendon Press, 1981), 513.

151. Napoleon to Champagny, August 19, September 10, 1809, *Correspondence*, 15683, 15778; Napoleon to Francis, September 15, 23, 1809, *ibid.*, 15823, 15837.

Imperial Zenith

1810-1812

*"Neutrality no longer exists. Britain doesn't recognize
it, neither can I. . . . Open war or else reliable peace.
Choose now."*

*"My power depends on my glory and my glories on the victories
I have won. My power will fail if I do not feed it on new
glories and new victories. Conquest has made me what I am
and only conquest can enable me to hold my position."*

"That is just the kind of womb I want to marry."

*"I have made a great blunder; but I shall
have the means to retrieve it."*

—Napoleon Bonaparte

The French Empire

By 1810 Napoleon had constructed an empire for which relatively little
diplomacy was necessary within or beyond. More than half of Europe's
population lived either in a greatly aggrandized France or one of its

protectorates. France itself expanded from 29 million people in 83 departments in 1790 to 44 million in 134 in 1812, at the empire's height; few people in those new departments actually spoke French. And then there were the new kingdoms of Italy, Naples, Spain, Holland, and Westphalia, and protectorates over the Rhine Confederation, Switzerland, and smaller realms. Much of that transfer of lands and peoples over the previous dozen years had been at the expense of Austria and Prussia, which were reduced to rump states and unwilling French allies. Although Russia had not suffered any territorial loss to Napoleon's ambitions, Alexander had committed his realm to his Continental System dedicated to economic warfare against Britain.

The Napoleonic Empire conferred various benefits and costs on its members. Most enjoyed more efficient rule and greater prosperity at the expense of a steady drain of troops and taxes. Napoleon abolished feudalism; imposed French-style constitutions and law codes; secularized society, allowed freedom of worship and nationalized most Church property; reduced or eliminated trade barriers and developed transportation and communication systems within and among regions; and promoted enterprise, education, and merit. All those acts were clearly progressive.

Economically, the empire had contradictory effects. Its larger markets and the insatiable demand of the states for more products and services related to war stimulated the creation and distribution of more wealth. Careers mostly were more open to talents. Productivity and wages tended to rise as the state conscripted ever more men from farms and work benches, because those workers left behind could demand more coin for their efforts. That in turn forced owners to find more ingenious ways to boost productivity and profits. The Continental System, however, devastated the maritime economy, turning ports into graveyards of rotting ships and empty workshops. At the same time it stirred entrepreneurs to make and sell substitutes for foreign products which had either disappeared or could be had only for sky-high prices from smugglers.[1] Virtually everyone condemned the ever-higher taxes. The imperial budget rose steadily from 588,066,203 francs in 1804 to 876,266,180 francs in 1812 (compared to Louis XVI's last budget of 298 million francs in 1789); the newly won areas of the empire paid for about a quarter of that.[2] Inflation was yet another force that eroded the wealth created from a relatively unified empire; wages and prices elbowed each other to get ahead in a constant race upwards.

As for political liberty, perhaps only the Dutch suffered a distinct loss; most other people hardly noticed the difference. Liberals may have at first embraced the revolutionary constitutional, institutional, and legal changes brought by Napoleon. Dissidents, however, swiftly discovered that they still suffered under a police state; the emperor's version was simply more efficient than the one it had supplanted.

Nationalism, like liberalism, was at once promoted and thwarted within the empire. Napoleon's consolidation and reorganization of Italy and Germany powerfully advanced the notion of what it meant to be Italian or German for ever more of those peoples. His invasions of Spain and Russia provoked a greater sense of being Spanish or Russian. French nationalism itself became the model for those who sought a nation for people sharing a common language and culture across a broad territory. Yet the promotion of nationalism, like liberalism, was a vocation for only a tiny if growing sliver of any population. And if those sentiments ever appeared to threaten French rule, the police ruthlessly suppressed them.

As Napoleon showed, making and breaking states was easy enough. Nations, however, demand generations and sometimes centuries to evolve. Across Europe four out of five people were illiterate peasants whose identity was rooted in their clan and village. It was the onerous presence of French troops and tax collectors which inadvertently sowed nationalism's seeds in that indifferent cultural soil. The oppressed soon recognized that they shared the same abject conditions with others of similar dialects and customs far beyond the horizon. The worse the exploitation, the more people began to mutter that they had to rise collectively in revolt against their oppressors. Obviously a revolt's chances of succeeding swells with the number of people and the width of the region which embraces it. Yet no matter what the revolt's results, afterwards most people quickly settled back into their traditional patterns of life and loyalty. Genuine nationalism is possible only with a modern state which mobilizes people behind a common identity and endeavors to unite them through a mass army, school system, literacy, propaganda, literature, arts, music, and heroes. That certainly was what Napoleon was trying to do in France.

If the empire's effects on its subordinate entities were at best mixed, France itself largely benefited. Napoleon definitely understood how to stimulate and guide France's economy. He was a pioneer of the muscular, problem-solving state with its streamlined administration, efficient revenue collection, and fiscal austerity. Over the years the emperor wrestled with slowing the national debt's rise, and eventually reduced it. Interest rates subsequently fell as the public sector competed less with the private sector for scarce capital. That in turn

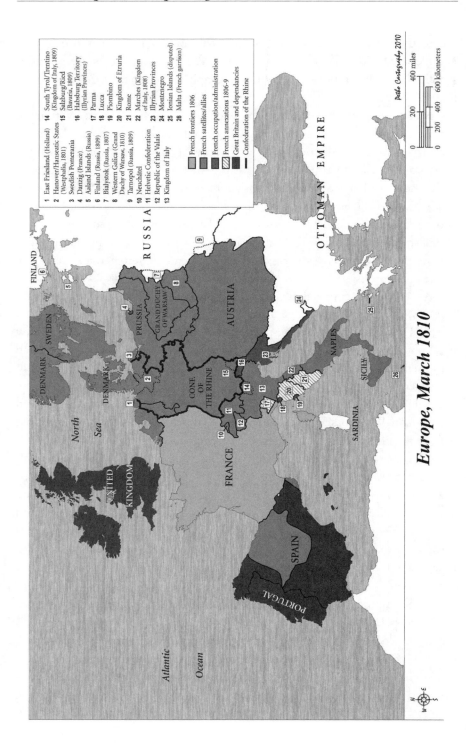

Europe, March 1810

1   East Friesland (Holland)
2   Hanover/Hanseatic States (Westphalia, 1801)
3   Swedish Pomerania
4   Danzig (France)
5   Aaland Islands (Russia)
6   Finland (Russia, 1809)
7   Bialystok (Russia, 1807)
8   Western Galica (Grand Duchy of Warsaw, 1810)
9   Tarnopol (Russia, 1809)
10 Neuchâtel
11 Helvetic Confederation
12 Republic of the Valais
13 Kingdom of Italy
14 South Tyrol/Trentino (Kingdom of Italy, 1809)
15 Salzburg/Ried (Bavaria, 1809)
16 Habsburg Territory (Illyrian Provinces)
17 Parma
18 Lucca
19 Piombino
20 Kingdom of Etruria
21 Rome
22 Marches (Kingdom of Italy, 1808)
23 Illyrian Provinces
24 Montenegro
25 Ionian Islands (disputed)
26 Malta (French garrison)

French frontiers 1806
French satellites/allies
French occupation/administration
French annexations 1806-9
Great Britain and dependancies
Confederation of the Rhine

Pablo Cartography, 2010

0   200   400 miles

0   200   400   600 kilometers

stimulated the economy as more entrepreneurs borrowed and invested more money into established or new businesses. Revenues rose with the economy, which reduced parasitical borrowing. Thus did the emperor promote a virtuous economic cycle of higher growth, wages, revenues, employment, and investments, and lower interest rates, budget deficits, and national debt. He further stimulated French economic development by judicious public investments in both infrastructure and industries. For instance, he had 64,000 kilometers of roads straightened, widened, graded, and tree-lined.[3] In 1810 he founded the Consul General of Administration of Commerce and Manufacturing to stimulate industry and innovation. Most of his policies could be a model for more recent political leaders on both sides of the Atlantic.

The only policies that distorted France's economic development were the Continental System and war. Unfortunately, the former tended to breed the latter. Napoleon's obsession with bringing Britain to its knees by denying it Europe's markets would ultimately lead to his own downfall. Napoleon's five-year "Spanish ulcer" began as an attempt to force Portugal into the Continental System. As will be seen, Tsar Alexander's decision to drop out of the embargo was the most important reason why Napoleon chose to war against him in 1812.

Ironically, Napoleon broke his own embargo just when it neared the brink of success. Britain suffered a series of ever-worsening harvests starting in 1808 that reached its nadir from 1810 to 1812; this brought its population to the edge of mass starvation. Had the emperor offered a comprehensive peace settlement by which he made some genuine concessions along with ending the embargo, Whitehall might well have thrown in the towel. Britain was trapped in a vicious cycle of worsening joblessness, food shortages, inflation, private and national debt, homelessness, malnutrition, bankruptcies, despair, industrial strikes, and riots; from this, peace appeared to be the only way out to ever more people. What kept Britain going was trade and its accompanying state revenues, which expanded steadily as merchants shifted from European to global markets. Nonetheless, Britain could not grow enough food to feed itself, and crop failures brought famines in a context of tight international markets in which communication and transportation were as slow as gusting winds or pounding hooves.

Napoleon saved Britain by offering to sell enough grain at inflated prices to alleviate the shortage. Then, when the inevitable protests rose from exporters of other goods, he began to relax some restrictions on them as well. He first loosened the Continental System on April 14, 1809, when he issued a list of products that could be exported if the merchant bought a special license, although direct trade with Britain was still forbidden. The decisive steps came the following year. On July 3, 1810, he lifted all export restrictions on French goods. On July 25 he placed all of the French Empire's commerce directly under his own control. On August 1 he allowed trade with Britain as long as the merchandise was carried in French ships, was sold for money rather than credit, and was authorized by a license issued in the emperor's own hand. The Trianon Decree of August 5 specified the exact cost of the fees for each good sold. Finally, the Fontainebleau Decree of October 19 tightened up the customs system to better ensure that licensed traders sailed and smugglers were nabbed. That "cash and carry" policy gave a boost to the empire's depressed ports while the state benefited both from the license fees and tariffs. While at first Napoleon favored French merchants, he gradually extended that trading privilege to other states in the Continental System—except, inexplicably, Russia.

The emperor further stimulated the maritime economy in April 1811 when he announced a naval buildup to 103 ships of the line and 76 frigates by 1814. His primary purpose was military rather than economic. He genuinely believed that if he could somehow just match the British fleet in the Channel he could eventually prevail. As he put it, "in four years I shall have a fleet. When my squadrons have three or four years at sea we shall measure swords with England. I know I may lose three or four engagements . . . [but] we shall succeed. Before ten years are passed, I shall have conquered England."[4] But like the Continental System, that naval buildup ultimately undermined French power, by funneling scarce resources into the delusion that he could somehow catch up with a nation whose wealth and power depended on its command of the seas.

Marie Louise

In late 1809, having won his war with Austria, another diplomatic problem loomed ever larger in Napoleon's mind: he needed a new wife. Or, to be more precise, a womb, within which he could plant an enduring dynasty of Bonapartes to rule the French empire.[5] Although for some time he had toyed with the idea of divorcing Josephine and marrying another, news from Warsaw settled the matter: his faithful mistress Marie Walewska was pregnant. Until then he was not completely certain that he could seed a child; a mistress and Hortense (if his valet Louis Constant was correct) had borne children, but there was a chance they were not his. Clearly, however, Josephine had conceived two children with her first husband but none with him.

Dissolving his marriage would be a sticky diplomatic matter.[6] First of all he had to convince Josephine to yield her crown for the good of France. Although divorce itself was a simple civil act, they then had to convince the Church that their marriage should be annulled.

Profoundly complicating all that was his deep love for Josephine. The nature of that love, however, as with most relationships, had changed with the years. His fiery passion for her during their initial sojourn as lovers had died with news of her infidelity. Eventually he forgave her, but his love for her thereafter was transformed into a deep affection.

Josephine undoubtedly sensed that something serious was troubling her husband after they were reunited at Fontainebleau on October 26. He was distant and irritable. How much of his behavior was a conscious attempt to harden her before giving her the crushing news and how much reflected his inability to quell a troubled conscience is impossible to say. He put off telling her for nearly a month. Hortense refused his plea that she act as his messenger. Asking Josephine for a divorce on November 30 was among his life's most wrenching emotional experiences.[7]

Two weeks later, on December 14, 1809, tears streamed down their faces when they appeared before the Bonaparte clan and State Council. Each read a statement explaining why a divorce was essential for the interests of France. Napoleon praised their thirteen years of marriage and the wonderful role Josephine had played as empress, but lamented her inability to provide an heir for the throne. The next day the documents were sent on to the Senate, which granted its approval. Napoleon was typically generous in his final settlement with Josephine: she would be compensated with Malmaison, the Elysee palace as a Parisian home, the extinguishment of all her existing debts, and an annual allowance of three million francs.

But the dissolution of their marriage was hardly done. It was essential that an annulment follow the divorce. According to Catholic doctrine, someone who remarries without an annulment is a bigamist. Few fecund princesses would be interested in marrying Napoleon with that stigma beclouding him. On December 22 Archchancellor Jean Jacques Regis Cambaceres filed on behalf of the couple for an annulment to the ecclesiastical court of Paris.

The Bonapartes did have a good case for annulment. Their civil marriage on March 6, 1796, had been certified with false documents that shrank the six-year age gap between Josephine and Napoleon to one. The official who performed the marriage was apparently unqualified to do so, and the person who witnessed it was underage. As for their church marriage on December 1, 1804, none of those who watched the ceremony signed their names as witnesses.

However, getting the pope to go along could not have been more diplomatically awkward. After all, it was under Napoleon's orders that Pius VII had been abducted from his palace in Rome and eventually incarcerated in the bishop's palace at Savona. When asked, his response was a curt no.

Once again French clerics were caught in a wrenching political tug-of-war between the emperor and the pope. On January 3, 1810, in Paris Napoleon was finally able to arm-twist a makeshift group, which included two cardinals, an archbishop, and four bishops, to issue an opinion favoring an annulment. That helped push the ecclesiastical court into granting an annulment on January 14.

It might be thought that finding a pretty, fertile royal wife would be an easy and enjoyable task. Surely virtually all of Europe's eligible princesses would line up for a chance to become the French empress? But that was not the case. The trouble was that not just any royal princess would do. Ideally the marriage would bind France with one of the other great powers. Over the months during which Napoleon shed his first wife, he supervised a diplomatic offensive to find her successor.

A Russian princess was clearly a prime choice. Indeed, Napoleon had first informally raised the issue with Alexander at Erfurt in October 1808 and had Caulaincourt make another query in November 1809. Each time the tsar must have inwardly shuddered with disgust at the image of one of his beloved sisters married to a man whom he increasingly despised as "the Minotaur."[8]

Napoleon had certainly given Alexander ample cause for complaint. At Tilsit and Erfurt the tsar had witnessed the emperor's displays of false charm dissolving at times into boorish outbursts of rage. Indeed, at times Napoleon had treated him more like a child than a sovereign. Even worse than those personal affronts was the cost of the alliance to Russia. The Continental System was a steadily tightening vice on the Russian economy. Ever more voices from his state council and the court, and from powerful merchants and manufacturers beyond, called for Russia to break with France and resume trade with Britain. But Alexander and most of his advisors agreed that the time was not yet ripe for that.

So instead Alexander's diplomatic response was essentially the same as the one that Talleyrand had fed him during the congress at Erfurt in October 1808, when Napoleon first casually broached the notion. The tsar explained: "If only I were concerned I would gladly give my consent, but mine is not the only one that must be obtained. My mother has retained an authority over her daughters which it is not for me to contest. I can try to give her some guidance."[9] He then "discovered" that his mother had already promised his sister to another. There was some truth in that; at least the idea of Catherine marrying Frederick George de Holstein, the heir to the duchy of Oldenburg, had been considered. Now it was consummated with a hasty wedding. As for the tsar's younger sister, Anne, she was then only thirteen, and Napoleon would have had to be patient for three or four years until she came of age. That was an easy promise for the tsar to make, since he knew that patience in anything, especially diplomacy, was not among the emperor's gifts. Caulaincourt's report reached the Tuileries on January 22, 1810.

A similar informal probe over whether one of Francis I's eligible daughters, most notably Marie Louise, the eldest, would be willing to marry Napoleon was raised with Austrian Ambassador Karl Philip, Prince Schwarzenberg, on December 20, 1809. He immediately passed on word to Chancellor Metternich, who raised the issue with Francis and his other advisors. The political wisdom of such a marriage would be a recurring and heated issue in the Hofburg Palace over the next couple of months. A consensus in favor of the marriage for reasons of state gradually emerged. It would take far longer, perhaps forever, for Francis to reconcile sacrificing his daughter.

It was not much easier for Napoleon to forge a consensus over the best candidate among his own family and advisors. The issue arose numerous times over the months, but it was not until January 28, 1810, that they reached a consensus.[10] Napoleon had narrowed his first-round picks to three kingdoms—Russia, Prussia, and Saxony. Perhaps from embarrassment, he had Foreign Minister Jean Baptiste de Nompere Champagny present those choices and guide the subsequent discussion. The ministers split over which liaison would render France the most political advantages. Cambaceres initiated the debate with an appeal that, for strategic reasons, it made sense for Napoleon to wait until Anne came of age. Lebrun countered with an argument for a Saxon. Murat and Fouche rallied to Cambaceres. Talleyrand typically thought outside Napoleon's box and called for an Austrian wife.

The emperor's first response to Talleyrand was to snort that a marriage alliance with Russia was strategically far more important than one with Austria;

and besides, Anne was much prettier than Marie Louise. He softened when Talleyrand explained just how fertile Habsburg girls were. Suddenly he exclaimed: "That is just the kind of womb I want to marry."[11]

Napoleon's choice of the envoy who would officially convey his proposal to marry Marie Louise appears rather insensitive. It was Eugene, Josephine's son, who presented the letter to Ambassador Schwarzenberg on February 7. While that formal request upset Francis and Marie Louise, Metternich could not have been more pleased. That marriage could be the first step in restoring a portion of the prestige and power Austria had lost over the past dozen years to Napoleon. However, it took no little effort on Metternich's part to talk the girl's father into yielding his "adorable doll," his favorite among his thirteen children, to a man whom he loathed as much as Alexander did. Once that mission was accomplished, Metternich then sent word to Paris that Francis was reluctant but not firmly opposed to the match. That letter marked the start of the diplomatic haggling.[12]

Napoleon replied with a hint that he might be willing to swap Illyria for Marie Louise and Galicia. That was a good deal for Austria, economically: the Illyrian coast was dotted with prosperous ports yielding high revenues. Why would the emperor be willing to part with that for the impoverished, remote region of Galicia? The only reason was strategic: invasions of either Russia or Austria could be launched from the latter land. That in turn would boost his power to pressure both realms diplomatically and war against them if need be. Metternich agreed to the trade. Those were the most important deals struck. It then remained to work out all the protocol for the array of ceremonies and celebrations that lay ahead to unite the two royal families. Somewhat ominously, the planners used the procession of Marie Antoinette from Vienna to Paris to guide the equivalent passage for her niece.[13]

With the terms settled, on February 23 Napoleon wrote to Francis a formal letter asking for his daughter's hand in marriage, and a separate letter to Marie Louise asking her to marry him. His letter to his future wife is touching; he recognized her doubtlessly mixed feelings and expressed his hope that one day she might genuinely love him. His chief of staff, Marshal Louis Alexandre Berthier, handed the respective proposals to the father and daughter at the Hofburg Palace on March 8. Although the decision had already been made, Marie Louise and Francis gave their formal consent.[14]

A proxy wedding was held on March 11. Originally Berthier was to stand in for Napoleon. But from sensitivity to his bride, respect for the valiant and skilled general he had bested the previous year, and as a conciliatory gesture to

Austria's court and people, the emperor allowed Archduke Charles to fill in for him. The bride's father expressed his feelings about losing Marie Louise to "the minotaur" through his choice of the opera performed that night as part of the marriage celebrations: "Iphigenia in Aulis" is the story of King Agamemnon's sacrifice of his daughter so that the gods would let him and his armada sail on to Troy, which the Greeks would finally conquer only after a grueling decade of war. Not much escaped Napoleon, but the irony of that choice evidently did; that same opera would be performed at St. Cloud following the civil marriage ceremony two and a half weeks later.[15]

The following day Marie Louise and Francis set off with a caravan of carriages toward Paris. Caroline Bonaparte and a French caravan met them at Branau on the frontier between Austria and Bavaria on March 16. The transition for Marie Louise was abrupt. Caroline rather brusquely took charge of her, helped her change into French-style clothing, and began instructing her on how to please her husband and his court. To ensure that spies did not infiltrate the Tuileries, Napoleon insisted that none of her ladies in waiting or even her governess would accompany her to Paris. Francis and his entourage mournfully bade his daughter farewell at the frontier and turned back toward Vienna. Metternich would lead an Austrian delegation on to Paris.

Napoleon fervently hoped that his bride would genuinely love him as a man. He was all too aware of the age gap between them—he was forty-one and she was eighteen. Despite the splendor of his court, he had retained his simple tastes in clothing; yet to please his young wife, he was willing to sacrifice that comfort. He brought in haberdashers who advised him on the latest clothing styles; he then ordered an entire new wardrobe. Although he disliked dancing, he got Hortense to give him lessons. Each day after their proxy marriage Napoleon wrote Marie Louise a love letter and sent a courier galloping off to hand-deliver it.[16]

Indeed, Napoleon was so excited at the thought of his pretty new bride that he impatiently refused to await her in Paris for the official ceremony. Instead he met her near the chateau of Compiegne and whisked her off to the imperial bedchamber. He could not have been happier. To Francis he later wrote a thank-you note in which he gushed that "she fulfills all my hopes. For two days we have not stopped exchanging proofs of the most tender feelings which unite us. We suit each other perfectly."[17] Although Francis was undoubtedly relieved that his daughter appeared to be happy, Napoleon offered details that would have made most fathers squirm.

Napoleon and his probably blushing bride wed in a civil wedding at St. Cloud on April 1 and a religious wedding presided over by Cardinal Fesch in the Louvre's Salon Carré the next day. Later that month they enjoyed a prolonged honeymoon tour of Brussels, Antwerp, and other recently acquired departments of France in the Low Countries. Napoleon remained thrilled with his new wife. Metternich reported that the emperor "is so much in love with her that he cannot hide the fact even when in public," and that Marie Louise said that she was "not in the least afraid of the Emperor but I begin to think that he is afraid of me."[18]

The most important event—indeed, the point of the marriage—was yet to come. On March 20, 1811, the emperor's hopes were fulfilled when a healthy son was born. It was not, however, an easy delivery for Marie Louise. At one point when her life appeared to be in danger, Napoleon gave permission for the doctor to sacrifice his child to save his wife. Fortunately that proved to be unnecessary, but it was a sign of how deeply he loved Marie Louise. The son was named Napoleon Francois Joseph Charles and received the title the King of Rome.[19]

Betrayals

Napoleon had ample reason to be pleased as 1810 unfolded. He was passionately in love with his pretty young bride and marveled at her swelling pregnancy. Peace and prosperity reigned over most of the empire. Reports indicated progress in the horrendous war in Spain. He could finally enjoy a prolonged stay in Paris where he could devote himself to governing the realm and savoring domestic bliss. Yet just below that relatively placid political surface lurked cancerous forces that were eating away at his rule.

It was customary for rulers to celebrate a joyous occasion with some act of benevolence, usually charity for the needy or amnesty for the condemned. The emperor marked his marriage by re-embracing Talleyrand into his inner circle. Once again he completely misjudged both his own powers and Talleyrand's character. He deluded himself that his humiliation of Talleyrand the previous year had finally chastised him into submission, but instead the tongue-lashing and demotion Talleyrand had received had fired in him an undying contempt and desire for vengeance. Within weeks he was selling out Napoleon by exchanging secret information for cash with Metternich. Talleyrand's treason did not end with Vienna. By early 1810 he was also peddling intelligence to the Russian and British governments, the Bourbon exiles, and even key leaders in the Rhine Confederation.

Oblivious to the relationship between Metternich and Talleyrand, Napoleon trusted and respected the Austrian ambassador. Metternich had returned to Vienna in the summer of 1809 but reappeared as Marie Louise's escort to her husband in April 1810. He remained in Paris another seven months, during which the two men met frequently.

Just behind Metternich in importance in Talleyrand's web of conspiracy was Russian diplomat Karl Nesselrode, who was ostensibly in Paris to negotiate a bilateral trade treaty. To Talleyrand he explained: "Officially speaking I am working under [ambassador] Prince Kurakin, but it is to you to whom I am really accredited. I am to correspond privately with the tsar who has sent you this letter by me."[20] Those words were certainly music to Talleyrand's ears. The greater his importance, the greater the price he could demand for his services. That September he stunned Alexander by requesting that 1,500,000 francs be deposited in the Bethmann Bank at Frankfort in October. In doing so, Talleyrand had uncharacteristically committed a grave error. With that damning letter the tsar thereafter had Talleyrand in his pocket. He would never have to play that trump card. Although he denied that extravagant demand, over the years he would subsidize Talleyrand's sybaritic lifestyle with lesser payments.[21]

Napoleon did suspect treason, but it was his brother King Louis of Holland whom he accused of betrayal. Louis was hardly guiltless. He turned a deaf ear to Napoleon's demands that he vigorously enforce the trade embargo and fill troop and tax quotas. But Louis argued that he had good reason to do so: those policies were strangling his kingdom's prosperity. The emperor responded to each refusal by annexing to France more of the king's territory. He first took the region between the Scheldt and Meuse rivers, and then the province of Flessingen.

That enraged Louis, but rather than square off with his brother he bullied the wife whom Napoleon had imposed upon him. Hortense fled with her first child Napoleon Charles for the safety of the emperor's Tuileries Palace. There she gave birth to Charles Louis Napoleon on April 24, 1808. Louis angrily summoned her and their two sons back to The Hague; Hortense refused. The emperor allowed Hortense and the child to stay in Paris for the present. They would later return to Holland.

Louis redoubled his passive aggressiveness. When the British invaded Walcheren Island in August 1809, he dragged his feet mobilizing his troops and only mustered a portion of what the emperor demanded. When Napoleon sent Bernadotte to take charge of Holland's defenses, Louis petulantly isolated himself in his palace.

The emperor decided to give his brother one last chance to conform. He summoned the king for consultations. Louis arrived in Paris on December 1 for what would be a series of bitter exchanges between the two over various issues. Napoleon finally issued, on December 21, 1809, a demand that Louis end all smuggling and privileges for the nobility, and expand the army to 25,000 troops and the fleet to fourteen ships of the line, seven frigates, and seven brigs. Louis remained the defiant martyr.

In January 1810 Napoleon began mobilizing an army to pressure Louis. On March 16, 1810, he forced Louis to sign a treaty that ceded Zeeland, Brabant, and Gelderland south of the Waal to France, and let French customs officials enforce the Continental System in what few provinces remained to him. Although Louis would attend Napoleon's April wedding in Paris and greet the imperial couple at Antwerp on May 5 during their extended honeymoon, the relationship was soured forever.[22]

During the months while Napoleon was repeatedly humiliating Louis for his defiance, he gave his brother yet another opportunity for redemption. The emperor composed a peace proposal that the king would sign and pass to the merchant Pierre Laboucherie, who had ties with the British financier Alexander Baring, who in turn would hand it to Foreign Secretary Richard Wellesley.[23]

But it seems that Fouche and Talleyrand were once again a step or two ahead of the emperor. In November 1809 they had initiated their own secret peace probe by sending a letter to Wellesley via a released British officer. They dangled the carrots of a free trade treaty and the creation of a South American empire governed by Ferdinand of Spain and freely trading with all. Wellesley replied through French financier Gabriel Ouvrard, a political enemy of Napoleon. Louis was well aware of these intrigues because he had allowed them to play out through Dutch ports.[24]

Napoleon was enraged when he learned of the Ouvrard channel on March 22, 1810. He tongue-lashed Louis for his complicity during their meeting at Antwerp on May 5. As with the previous plot of Fouche and Talleyrand, he tried to amass more evidence before he struck. This time Talleyrand apparently left no trail, but Fouche did. The emperor finally confronted his police minister at a Council of State meeting on June 2, 1810. He concluded his damning case with the words "You ought by rights to be executed." He then left it up to his ministers to decide Fouche's fate. That inspired a quip from Talleyrand: "No doubt Monsieur Fouche has made a grand mistake. As for me, I would replace him. But the only person to replace him is Fouche himself."[25]

Typically Talleyrand had laid bare a knotty problem with searing wit and truth. Fouche knew too much and commanded too vast a network of not just informers but quite possibly very well paid assassins who had already been contracted to avenge him should he ever be executed. So Napoleon chose a middle course. He paid off Fouche's early retirement with a huge pension and replaced him with the ever-faithful General Jean Savary. His letter to Fouche clearly explained why he was being fired: "The position of the police minister demands an entire and absolute confidence. . . . In important circumstances you have compromised the tranquility of myself and the state; that does not excuse in my eyes legitimacy of the motives. A negotiation was opened with England; meetings took place with Lord Wellesley. That minister knew that the envoy was speaking on your behalf; he had to believe that it was also on my behalf. And that totally upset all my foreign relations. . . . I cannot hope that you would change your manner of acting, since for several years . . . I have expressed my dissatisfaction."[26]

Fouche's golden parachute was severed before he could safely hit the ground. On June 18 Napoleon asked him to hand over all his papers; he was especially eager to get his hands on any incriminating documents concerning his extended family. Fouche replied that he had burned them. He actually had consigned some damning documents to the flames, but had switched the numbers and locations of other critical dossiers.

That news at once enraged and frightened the emperor. Napoleon exiled Fouche to his country home; but Fouche did not stop there. Fearing for his life, he fled to Italy, where he redoubled his intrigues with disgruntled Bonaparte family members including Lucien, Caroline, Murat, and, soon, Louis. When in September Napoleon recalled him to serve in the Senate, Fouche obeyed. He would keep a low profile and bide his time for the next chance to return to power. He would not have too long to wait.

As for the two peace feelers, the British spurned them with the same disdain that they had all the preceding ones.

While those intrigues were playing out, Napoleon was busy extinguishing his brother's last grip on Holland. The catalyst was a disturbing incident on May 23 when assailants dragged the emperor's ambassador to the king from his coach and severely beat him. Napoleon demanded that Louis bring the assailants to justice before June 1, or else he would send in Marshal Nicholas Oudinot at the head of 60,000 French troops to restore order. The deadline passed with no satisfaction, either because the king was unable or unwilling to provide it.[27]

Instead Louis mobilized his own army at the frontier and barred Oudinot and his troops. That infuriated the emperor, but the last thing he wanted was a war between men who were ostensibly brothers and states which were ostensibly allies. Oudinot demanded that his army be allowed to enter on June 23. Louis remained defiant, but ever more of his ministers begged him to yield. Louis finally abdicated on July 2 and, like Lucien, went into exile. Unlike his brother, Louis abandoned his family; accompanied by a few attendants, he made the round of spas in Germany, while Hortense and her two sons sought refuge with Josephine at Malmaison.

After spending a week fruitlessly searching for a willing and appropriate replacement, Napoleon announced on July 9 that the rest of Holland would be annexed to France. He would even attach the Dutch Royal Guard regiment to his own Imperial Guard. He put the best spin he could on his brother's abdication. To Constant, he remarked: "I had foreseen this stupidity of Louis but I didn't believe that he was so eager to do it. . . . Monsieur Constant, tell me, do you know the three capitals of the French Empire? . . . Paris, Rome, Amsterdam. That makes a nice effect, does it not?"[28]

As if that prolonged conflict with Louis was not embarrassing enough, Napoleon faced ever more grief from another royal sibling. The troubles started when Queen Caroline had conspired with Talleyrand and Fouche to put herself and her husband in power rather than the designated successor Joseph if Napoleon died. Then Caroline heatedly protested Napoleon's intention to divorce Josephine in preference for a fertile wife. Succession rather than sentiment provoked that outburst. She detested Josephine but preferred that barren woman as empress because it shortened the succession line to Joachim and Caroline. After Marie Louise gave birth to Napoleon II in March 1811, Caroline pettily refused to return to Paris to serve as one of the royal godmothers.

If Caroline's unseemly intrigues and spites were irritating, Murat's had a more substantive bite. Like virtually every ruler in the French empire, Murat benefited from widespread smuggling and corruption in his realm. That was not all. He refused to publish imperial decrees with which he disagreed, invade Sicily, or repay any of the five million francs his kingdom owed France.

Napoleon's first step in response was to declare persona non grata Murat's ambassador in Paris and recall his own from Naples. Murat not only remained defiant but, on June 24, 1811, fired a group of officials that Napoleon had imposed on him to enact imperial decrees and pass intelligence back to the Tuileries. That prompted Napoleon to dash off a stern warning to Murat: "You are surrounded by men who hate France and who want you to lose. Recall that I made you king for the interest of my system. Don't fool yourself; if you cease to be French, you will be nothing to me."[29] Pointing to the fate of Louis and Holland, he promised to do the same to Murat and Naples if his demands were not fulfilled. He transferred command of all French troops in the kingdom from Murat to General Paul Grenier and designated them an "army of observation." Finally he decreed that French law extended to all French citizens anywhere, even those who denounced their nationality.

To all those humiliations and pressures, Murat expressed a lament universal among Napoleon's puppet sovereigns: "He should be our mentor, not our master; it is not a king's duty to obey." He later asserted that Napoleon "shouts loud enough that he made us kings, but was it not us who made him emperor? My blood, my sword, and my life are the Emperor's. If he summons me to a field of battle . . . I am no longer a king but a marshal of the empire once more—but . . . at Naples I will be king, and I do not intend to sacrifice the existence, welfare, and interests of my subjects to his policies." To such sentiments, Napoleon had Berthier reply that Murat "has done nothing to be king: he owes that to his marriage with my sister."[30]

Probably as much to revive his own sagging glory as to relieve the pressure from Napoleon, Murat prepared for an invasion of Sicily. The chance came on September 17, 1811, after a tempest blew away the British fleet guarding the Straits of Messina. The result was an utter disaster. General Jacques Cavaignac set sail with his Neapolitan division from Reggio. General Grenier, who commanded Napoleon's troops in the kingdom, refused to join him without imperial orders. The British attacked the Neapolitans shortly after they landed on a beach south of Messina and captured over 800 of them, including Cavaignac.

That military disaster was humiliating enough. Nearly simultaneously Murat suffered a marital disaster as well when he received the devastating news that Jean Paul Daure, his minister of war, marine, and police, was cuckolding him. Before Murat's wrath Daure fled. Caroline denied any wrongdoing, but the king could not be placated. So the queen set sail on September 17 and, with favorable winds and roads, reached Paris two weeks later, on October 2.

Napoleon embraced her and her story that she had done nothing wrong. However, she was no sooner settled in Paris than she began to take on other lovers, including Metternich. Yet to all those rumors the emperor turned a deaf ear. He was always quick to forgive his wayward sister, no matter how often she disappointed or outright betrayed him. With her powerful mind, Machiavellian instincts, and insatiable passions, Caroline was the one among his seven siblings who most closely resembled him.[31]

Murat meanwhile wrote to Caroline a letter beseeching her to talk her brother into letting them retain their crowns. That was easy enough. The price that the emperor demanded was the couple's public reconciliation and Murat's promise that henceforth he would faithfully follow imperial orders. The royal couple eagerly pledged to do both; but promises were as easy to make as to break.

The Spanish Ulcer

All along, the worst problem festering within the French empire was not the defiance or even treason of some of its highest officials, but the chronic and worsening drain on the empire's wealth, power, and prestige by the quagmire in Spain. From 1808 to 1813 the French maintained from 250,000 to 300,000 troops there. Yet even with those extraordinary numbers they could barely cling to that land. Each year battles, skirmishes, diseases, and desertions devoured at least 50,000 soldiers, which Napoleon had somehow to replace by scraping up, training, equipping, and sending new men to that charnel house. Spain was an even more voracious consumer of cash. During their entire five years in power there the French were only able to extract about 32 million francs from that land stricken by poverty and war, while the emperor funneled into Spain more than twenty times that amount. In all, from 1808 to 1813 Spain's domestic debt would soar from 9.6 million francs to 87.2 million, and its debt to France from 28.5 million francs to 864.5 million francs.[32]

Joseph was sincerely doing his best to reign over Spain, but the challenge was beyond both his talents and powers. He got even nominal support from only a sliver of the population, that handful of liberals known as "afrancesados" who benefited from his implementation of the 1808 Constitution which Napoleon had unveiled at Bayonne. Assisting Joseph's rule was a Cortes with 80 members whom he appointed and 92 members chosen by an electoral college composed mostly of rich landowners and merchants. He also struggled to implement those constitutional tenets which abolished feudal and church privileges, and guaranteed such rights as jury trials and freedom from arrest without official charges. With the proceeds from confiscating and selling church property, he intended to fund industries, schools, orphanages, hospitals, science institutes, poor relief, and other public works. But those sales and ever more burdensome taxes never filled more than a fraction of all his fiscal needs. Instead they provoked ever more rage and resistance from ever more Spaniards. As if all that were not discouraging enough, the land which Joseph was directly responsible for governing kept shrinking.

This was because Napoleon granted full powers to the marshals or generals commanding field armies to mobilize the resources of the lands in which they camped or marched. On February 8, 1810, he designated Catalonia, Navarre, Aragon, and Biscay as military districts, each ruled by a governor-general. In May he did the same for Burgos and Valladolid. He began to convert all the land north of the Ebro River into departments of France. In all, Napoleon fragmented rather than unified both the military and administrative command over the Peninsula. In doing so he violated a fundamental military principle such that he continuously gave Wellington the opportunity to wield his superior strategic and tactical gifts, beating each French army in turn.

Compounding all that was the emperor's attempt to micromanage the war, administration, and diplomacy in Spain. By using Joseph and the generals solely as conduits for his own commands, he denied them their initiative as field commanders. So, in order not to incur the emperor's rancor, they lost opportunities as they awaited his latest order. Those instructions were nearly always obsolete. He made decisions on often sketchy or false information that was weeks old. Then his subsequent decisions took weeks to get to the recipient.

Despite all that, the initial news from the Peninsula in 1810 was heartening. The French captured Seville on January 31 and marched on to besiege Cadiz from February 3. Having routed all the Spanish armies and driven their remnants to the country's far corners, the French now appeared to control most of Joseph's kingdom. But those gains proved to be delusions. Ever more guerrillas destroyed ever larger detachments and supply convoys linking the field armies and garrisons with France.

More decisively, there was Wellington. Portugal's Council of Regency named Wellington generalissimo, which granted him dictatorial powers to muster men and provisions under his direct command. Wellington built a Portuguese army that was nearly as well-trained, -equipped, and valiant as the British army. Alas for the allied war effort, the Cortes at Cadiz denied him similar powers to perform similar wonders with Spanish troops. Although over five years the British would distribute millions of pounds sterling of coin, arms, munitions, and provisions through the Cortes or Spanish generals, nothing alleviated the dismal performance of Spain's armies in the field. Nonetheless, by mid-summer Wellington had readied his army in Portugal to meet the latest French invader.

Napoleon handed orders on April 16, 1810, to Marshal Andre Massena to journey to Salamanca, take command of the Army of Portugal, and march on Lisbon. Massena launched his campaign shortly after reaching Salamanca on May 15. The first step was to capture the fortresses of Cuidad Rodrigo and Almeida, which barred the path to Portugal. Each siege took nearly a month to complete, with Cuidad Rodrigo yielding on July 10 and Almeida on August 26. Massena then invaded Portugal.

Although Massena was among the emperor's finest marshals, he was no more capable of resolving the essential dilemma of fighting in the Peninsula than any of his colleagues. The further he marched from his base across that hostile land, the more troops he had to leave behind to defend his supply lines. He started out with 86,000 troops but had only about 40,000 by the time he collided with Wellington at Bussaco on September 25. After blunting Massena's assault, Wellington prudently withdrew, leaving nothing but scorched earth behind, all the way to the Torres Vedras line of fortifications that stretched from the Tagus River well east of Lisbon to the Atlantic Ocean fifty-three miles away.

Massena's troops reached that line on October 14 and could go no further. Stalled before those seemingly impregnable defenses, the French army withered away from disease, desertion, and starvation. Massena finally ordered a withdrawal to Santarem on November 14. In all, he had lost 25,000 troops, of which the British inflicted 10,000 casualties while attrition claimed the rest.

That wretched news was alleviated by word from another marshal. Nicolas Soult received orders from Napoleon to relieve Massena. On the last day of 1810 he marched his army from Seville, captured Olivenza with its 4,000 defenders on January 22, and then Badajoz with its 16,000 troops on March 12, 1811. But he had to beat a hasty retreat when he learned that three armies were converging on Seville, one under General Francisco Ballesteros from Andalusia, a mixed force under General Thomas Graham which had broken the siege of Cadiz, and finally that of General Manuel La Pena along the coast. Soult left General Adolphe Mortier in command of that stretch of frontier and hurried back to Seville. Ballesteros retreated at word of Soult's arrival. Graham stood firm at Barossa until Soult routed his army there on March 5. Pena then withdrew to safety.

Wellington's well-rested, -equipped, and -fed army marched after Massena's scarecrows in late February 1811. Massena withdrew from Santarem on March 3. Wellington caught up to Massena and defeated him at Sabugal on April 3. Massena did not stop retreating until his battered army reached Salamanca, where desperately needed reinforcements and supplies awaited him. Wellington halted his pursuit to besiege Almeida. In late April Massena led 48,000 troops westward to relieve Almeida. Leaving a small force at the siege, Wellington marched eastward and awaited Massena at Fuentes d'Onoro. Massena hurled his army at Wellington on May 3 and then again the following day. But with his army badly battered, Massena ordered a retreat back to Salamanca on May 8. The French garrison at Almeida punched free through the thinly defended siege lines during the night of May 10; a slow-burning fuse detonated the powder magazine behind them.

Wellington followed up those victories by dispatching General Beresford and his division against the French fortress at Badajoz. Learning of that advance, Soult quick-marched his army to its relief. Outnumbered, Beresford withdrew to the fortress of Elvas, where he awaited Spanish armies under generals Francisco Castanos and Joachim Blake. With his army now numbering 35,000 troops, of whom 10,000 were British, 10,000 Portuguese, and 15,000 Spanish, Beresford once again marched toward Badajoz.

Soult flung his 24,000 troops against Beresford, was repulsed, and then withdrew to Merida. There he was joined by Marshal Auguste Marmont and his corps. With 60,000 troops between them, they marched to Badajoz. Beresford again lifted his siege and withdrew to Elvas. Soult and Marmont relieved Badajoz on June 20.

The stalemate persisted elsewhere in Spain in 1811. General Rowland Hill routed General Girard at Arroyo dos Molinos before withdrawing to Portugal. That year's only unqualified French success was when Marshal Louis Suchet asserted control over most of Catalonia and Valencia, first by capturing Tarragona on June 28 and then by routing the Spanish at Saguntum on October 25.

All along the emperor's only diplomacy in the Peninsula was with his brother, the King of Spain. Against all contrary evidence, Napoleon insisted that only the harshest measures could cow the Spanish: "If you hang a few of them they will begin to tire of their game and become submissive and humble like they should be." Joseph tried to explain that such harsh measures actually provoked the guerrilla movement. The only policy which he believed could work was to inspire the Spanish to love rather than hate and fear him.[33] When Napoleon dismissed such notions, Joseph defied his order to stay in Spain and traveled all the way to France to plead his case. He caught up to Napoleon at the palace of Rambouillet on May 16, 1811. After six hours of often rancorous haggling, the emperor wearily agreed to let the king govern the Spanish and command the French armies as he saw fit. But Napoleon reneged on their deal shortly after Joseph returned to Madrid on July 16.

The War with the Church

Spain was not the only conflict in which a decisive victory eluded Napoleon. As with the Spanish, the emperor believed that only harshness worked with Pope Pius VII. Yet so far the pontiff had refused to recant his excommunication of the emperor and his minions in 1809 for their policies which sharply diminished the Catholic Church's power and wealth. Indeed, the pope appeared more rather than less defiant after suffering at French hands his kidnapping and incarceration in the bishop's palace at Savona in northwestern Italy.

For Napoleon the only thing left to do was to strip the pope of his last claim to worldly power. On February 17, 1810, the emperor decreed that the Papal States would be converted into French departments; Rome would be the French empire's second capital; the imperial prince would be the King of Rome and crowned there; the Catholic Church would receive a yearly stipend of two million francs; and its authority would be confined to solely spiritual matters. As he had put it in a letter to Pius a month earlier, "I recognize you as my spiritual chief, but I am your emperor." He justified that policy by arguing that Pius had "intrigued against my authority, excommunicated my ministers, my armies, and nearly everyone in the empire. . . . Is there a . . . means of punishing a pope who preaches revolt and civil war? . . . I know that one must render unto God the things that are God's, but the pope is not God."[34]

Yet some ranking Church officials still found ways to defy the emperor with passive resistance. He invited twenty-eight cardinals to witness his civil and religious weddings with Marie Louise; all twenty-eight attended the former, but thirteen skipped the latter. The "no shows" did so because they believed that

Napoleon had not received a legitimate annulment from his first marriage, and thus was committing the grave sin of polygamy by contracting a second.

The sight of those thirteen empty seats at his wedding enraged the emperor. He could have turned the cheek to that snub; instead he chose to retaliate in an extremely petty way. He invited all twenty-eight cardinals to a reception, then kept the thirteen so-called "black cardinals" waiting in a freezing room for two hours before ordering them dismissed from the palace. Fouche later sent word to the cardinals that the emperor would forgive them only if they sent him an official letter of apology for missing his wedding. They replied that they could hardly attend a wedding which the pope himself refused to bless. For that the emperor had the cardinals stripped of their positions and exiled to remote parts of France. Thereafter Pius added that treatment of the cardinals to the list of things that the emperor would have to reverse if he wanted his excommunication lifted.

Napoleon responded with yet another demand. He insisted that Pius officially agree that France's bishops henceforth could approve his list of nominations for new bishops if the pope did not do so within six months. That would have ended the papacy's last vestige of power over the church in France. On May 19 Pius wearily said he would go along, but refused to sign a proffered document which would have made that policy official.

The emperor issued an invitation to France's remaining cardinals and 95 bishops to meet with him on June 17, 1811. He appointed his uncle Cardinal Fesch to preside over the meeting. In one of his more outrageous acts of flimflam, Napoleon claimed to have a letter from the pope in which he agreed to the policy on the approval of new bishops. Although the letter was from Pius, it was merely a greeting to the bishops and cardinals. Napoleon then called on the assembled Church leaders to vote in favor of that fictitious papal blessing. They did so, with undoubtedly many going along from fear that if they did otherwise they would suffer the same fate as the "black cardinals."

Upon hearing of the deception, Pius declared that the council had acted illegally. Napoleon ordered the bishops and cardinals to disregard the pope's message. At this point most of the church leaders dug in their heels. Napoleon ordered a recess for the council on July 10 and had three of the most defiant bishops arrested and imprisoned in the chateau of Vincennes. Over the next four weeks he got 85 of the bishops to accept a compromise. When he reconvened the council on August 5, those bishops voted to approve the emperor's proposed procedure for new bishops—if the pope officially agreed.

Pius eventually sent back word that he would do so, but refused to recognize any bishops from the former papal states as part of France.

That put Napoleon in a diplomatic bind. If he went along with the pope's concession he would undermine the legitimacy of his annexation of the papal states. So he shelved his proposal and dismissed the council. For now he would let Pius languish in French custody in hopes that one day the pope would bow to all his demands.

At this point Cardinal Fesch finally remonstrated with Napoleon. For years he had been torn between his duty to the Church and his duty to his emperor and nephew. All along he had been vital in cloaking many of Napoleon's acts with a semblance of Church approval. But Napoleon's refusal to accept any temporal power for the pope and Church deeply troubled the cardinal. Their meetings increasingly broke down into shouting matches. Napoleon exiled his uncle to his diocese at Lyons on March 1, 1812.[35]

Napoleon was not done with Pius. Learning of rumors that the British might try to rescue the pontiff, he interrupted his feverish preparations for his Russian campaign with an order on May 21, 1812, that Pius be brought to France.[36] The pope arrived at the chateau of Fontainebleau on June 19, 1812. Although he was further than ever from Rome, his latest surroundings were certainly more pleasant that the austere palace at Savona. But Pius would be no more willing than he had been previously to surrender his last vestiges of papal authority and dignity.

Diplomatic Opportunities or Traps

If the pope remained resistant to the emperor's pressure, a seemingly even more implacable opponent gave signs that she was willing to deal. Few prominent people had better reasons to hate France than Queen Marie Caroline of the Kingdom of the Two Sicilies. First, the revolution had beheaded her sister, Marie Antoinette. A French-backed Neapolitan revolution had chased her, her husband Ferdinand IV, and their court from Naples to refuge in Sicily in 1799. Although that liberal revolution was short-lived and the Bourbons returned to power the following year, Napoleon forced them into exile in 1806 and plopped another couple on their thrones. Only British naval superiority deterred a French army from conquering Sicily where the royal family lived at the palace in Palermo. She was among that era's queens who figuratively wore the pants in the family. Like Louise of Prussia, Maria of Spain, and Caroline of Naples, Marie Caroline henpecked her mild-mannered husband into taking tougher policies than he would otherwise have pursued. And her hatred of Napoleon seemed endless.

So Napoleon was astonished when in 1810 he got a secret message that the queen wanted to talk. What could explain that turnabout? In a word: power. Napoleon seemed omnipotent. He had dashed his enemies' hopes when he defeated Austria the previous year. His Continental System, despite widespread smuggling, was certainly crimping Sicily's economy. The British, meanwhile, appeared ever more as much the royal family's jailors as protectors. Ambassador William, Earl Amherst, and Admiral Martin forced her to disperse her fleet to distant ports and connived with liberals to soften her spend, borrow, and tax policies that they claimed were squeezing merchants and peasants alike to the breaking point. Rather than help her and her husband retake southern Italy, the British merely held Sicily and poured all their efforts into driving the French from Spain.

Unfortunately, the details of Marie Caroline's proposed deal have been lost to history. Years later in exile at St. Helena, Napoleon mentioned something about her request for help in driving the British from Sicily. But he did not say just what she was willing to give for that aid or why she was willing at that point to trust the French—who had conquered half her realm—more than the British—who had saved the other half. The appeal appears bizarre, the product of a troubled, unstable mind. That is certainly how Napoleon treated it, dismissing the notion. The British would find out about the aborted plot and eventually use it against her and the conservative camp at court.

Around that same time another intriguing diplomatic opportunity arose from Europe's north side. Although Napoleon would take advantage of this one, ultimately it would backfire against him. In a coup on March 13, 1809, conspirators murdered Gustav IV, Sweden's deranged king, and replaced him with his senile but complacent uncle, who was crowned Charles XIII. The childless king was forced to adopt as his son and successor Christian Auguste d'Augustenborg, a Danish prince. The trouble was that the crown prince died on May 28, 1810, so that Sweden's Riksdag, or national assembly, faced the same problem of succession.

Napoleon naturally saw an opportunity in their plight. He had Foreign Minister Champagny pass the word that he would certainly look with favor upon a French candidate for the new crown prince; he envisioned Eugene for the post. He would also be happy to bless the marriage of a French princess into the Swedish royal family.

The Swedes felt pressured to at least discuss the notion. On January 6, 1810, a treaty was signed binding France to return Pomerania and Rugen Island to Stockholm, while Sweden would join the Continental System. (Although Napoleon would live up to his end of the bargain, Stockholm would not.) The Swedes then agreed to take a French candidate.

But they pointedly chose Napoleon's most inept and disloyal marshal over his faithful stepson.[37] The Riksdag formally elected Jean Baptiste Bernadotte as crown prince on August 21, 1810. That same day Charles XIII informed Napoleon of that choice and asked him to permit Bernadotte to accept that role. "I was little prepared for this news," Napoleon admitted, "since Your Majesty had let me know that he wanted to propose and get elected a brother of the last royal prince. However, I appreciate the sentiments which have carried the Swedish nation to give such a proof of their esteem to my people and my army."[38]

Although uneasy with the choice, Napoleon accepted it—for two sets of reasons, one personal, the other geopolitical.

Bernadotte's wife, Desiree, had been Napoleon's first love, and he still deeply cared for her despite all the intervening years, loves, and lusts. Not only that, but Desiree's sister had married Joseph. So there were sentimental and family considerations.

More importantly, it would seem to advance French interests to have any prominent Frenchman, even someone as unreliable as Bernadotte, in line for Sweden's throne. If Napoleon protested the choice of Bernadotte, the Swedes might well choose a candidate from another and, most likely rival, power. Before giving his blessing he got Bernadotte to promise that he would never war against France. With Bernadotte as crown prince it was more likely that Sweden would enforce the Continental System against Britain. Finally, the Russians would certainly worry about a potential alliance between Sweden and France and a two-front war for Russia should its relations with France ever break down. That possibility just might keep the Russians in line, although Napoleon of course sent his reassurance that they should fear nothing with Bernadotte in Stockholm. Yet whatever use Bernadotte might be to French interests posed a diplomatic dilemma for Napoleon. He had promised Charles XIII that he would conduct relations only through him or official diplomatic channels. That meant he would not write directly to Bernadotte, despite the numerous letters he received from him.[39]

As for Bernadotte, after conversion to Lutheranism and a prolonged tutoring in Swedish court etiquette and national interests, he received his title on March 16, 1811. Once in power, Bernadotte soon realized Napoleon's fears that he would be a loose cannon. At first he appeared to promote French interests by helping strengthen Sweden's commitment to the Continental System and allying with Saxony and Poland. But Bernadotte did so only because he and his advisors perceived those policies to be in Sweden's interests. The first contentious issue was Bernadotte's demand that Sweden be allowed to take Norway from Denmark in compensation for its loss of Finland to Russia. In return, Sweden would join France if it ever warred against Russia.[40]

But for Napoleon to go along would alienate his allies Denmark and Russia. He sent word that "my relations with Russia are good, and that I fear a war with that power." Likewise, he would not tolerate any Swedish aggression of Denmark over Norway. He abruptly dismissed the notion of any kind of alliance: "France has no need of Sweden."[41] Finally, he instructed his ambassador, Charles Alquier, henceforth to deal only with the king.

But Bernadotte continued to press his policy. When Napoleon angrily refused to betray the tsar with a secret alliance, Bernadotte pointedly spread the word to Swedish merchants that customs officials would turn a blind eye to violations of the Continental System. In response the emperor sent repeated protests to Stockholm. Finally, he summoned Sweden's ambassador and blustered that "neutrality no longer exists. Britain doesn't recognize it, neither can I. . . . Open war or else reliable peace. Choose now."[42]

When Stockholm remained defiant, Napoleon ordered his troops to take over Pomerania in January 1812. That let Bernadotte off the hook of his promise never to war against France. He sent envoys to St. Petersburg and London for an alliance. Eventually he would turn against France—at the point when he could inflict the worst possible strategic damage to Napoleon.

Meanwhile, the emperor sought assurances that another Baltic power, Prussia, was not conspiring to betray him. Frederick William III and his ministers had embarked on far-reaching military and economic reforms. Napoleon pointedly demanded an explanation for those reforms. The king replied in June 1810 with a promise that "I dare guarantee your majesty that [I] will work zealously . . . to advance and affirm the system . . . and the most intimate ties between France and Prussia."[43] Although Napoleon could do little but thank the king for his pledge, his spies continued to pass on information that the Prussians were secretly violating their obligations under the 1807 Tilsit treaty and subsequent agreements to limit their army's size and deployment.

Like the Swedes, the Prussians sent secret envoys to London, St. Petersburg, and Vienna to discuss forming a coalition against France.

Napoleon wrote to Frederick William conveying a demand that he halt those violations and join the Rhine Confederation or else face war. When the king denied any wrongdoing, the emperor had his letters published in Berlin and St. Petersburg. Frederick William then promised to comply with the emperor's demands, but only if Napoleon guaranteed Prussia's existing territory. The emperor refused, believing that he kept Prussia in line by threatening to dismember that realm and feed its parts to his eager allies if Frederick William grossly violated his promises. Although he could have written that into a treaty, the emperor preferred a non-legal means of coercing the Prussians.

To Russia, with War

Of all of Napoleon's blunders, none was more self-destructive than his decision to invade Russia. What was he thinking?

The issues that split Napoleon and Alexander were relatively minor and could have been finessed with face-saving measures by both sides. But a deadly mix of intractable false principles and false pride in both the emperor and tsar led those problems to fester rather than heal. The result was among history's most tragic examples of when leaders involved in a conflict did not want war but each deluded himself into believing that he had no choice other than to fight. The emperor and tsar straitjacketed themselves into a classic "security dilemma," in which the defensive measures each took to deter the other instead provoked the very war each hoped to avoid. In other words, the principle of "peace through strength" proved to be a chimera.

Ironically Napoleon himself eventually realized that. He sought to break that spiral with an appeal on April 6, 1811: "The effect of my military preparations will make Your Majesty increase his own; and when I learn of that here, that will force me to raise more troops: and all this over nothing!"[44] But Alexander did not respond, and fourteen months later Napoleon marched.

The ultimate problem was Napoleon's obsession with his Continental System. Alexander, like virtually all rulers—including, recently, the emperor himself—turned a blind eye to the massive smuggling. Yet Napoleon kept nagging Alexander to live up to the promises he had made in the 1807 Tilsit treaty and subsequent agreements.[45] The tsar understandably wearied of the pressure and hypocrisy.

The acrimonious impasse over the embargo conflict poisoned other issues. For instance, Napoleon may not have intended his decree on December 13, 1810, whereby he ordered the annexation of Hamburg, Lubeck, Bremen, and the Duchy of Oldenburg, as a direct affront to Alexander, but that was the effect. Those states were subsumed because all had violated the Continental System. The emperor reasoned that he could curtail the smuggling if French rather than local officials manned the customs service and coast guard. The tsar rightfully protested that the emperor's annexation of Oldenburg to his brother Jerome's kingdom of Westphalia violated the Tilsit treaty's article 27. Adding insult to injury was the bizarre twist that George, Duke Oldenburg, was Alexander's uncle, while the duke's son, having married the tsar's sister Catherine, was both his cousin and son-in-law. Napoleon countered that the duke had forfeited his own right to rule by violating the promise binding Oldenburg to the Continental System.

But even before the tsar learned that Napoleon had annexed Oldenburg he deliberately committed his own provocation toward the emperor. On December 31, 1810, Alexander decreed that he would raise tariffs on imports coming to Russia by wagon and lower them on those borne by ship. That was intended deliberately to hurt French exporters, since many of them conveyed most of their products to Russia by land and river rather than sea to avoid getting confiscated by British warships and privateers on the long, perilous voyage. Napoleon protested, to no avail.[46]

Those merchants who subsequently suffered sharp reductions in sales to Russia pressured the emperor to compensate them with sales elsewhere. That was among the reasons why Napoleon loosened his own Continental System to allow licensed sales to Britain itself. But that in turn understandably provoked Alexander and other rulers snared in the embargo to cry foul, and then loosen or end their own enforcement.

The emperor had another diplomatic bone to pick with the tsar. Ever since the French Revolution broke out émigrés had fled to Russia and offered their services. Naturally they were among those who advocated the hardest line against France. The most brilliant and bitter of those exiles was Charles Andre Pozzo di Borgo, a Corsican whose hatred of Napoleon went back to the days when they were political rivals over the fate of their native land. In 1807 the tsar had reluctantly bowed to the emperor's demand to expel the Corsican from Russia; in 1812, Alexander defiantly recalled Pozzo di Borgo to his service.

The fate of Poland was yet another contentious issue. Napoleon had created the Duchy of Warsaw after the 1807 Treaty of Tilsit, largely at Prussia's expense, and after the 1809 Treaty of Schonbrunn had split Austria's Galicia between Poland and Russia, with 1.5 million people going to the former and 400,000 to the later. Napoleon's gift to Russia was actually generous considering that Alexander's efforts during the 1809 war against Austria involved mostly minor movements and skirmishes. Yet Alexander complained that the creation and then augmentation of the Duchy of Warsaw and its alliance with France was a direct threat to Russia.

Alexander had his foreign minister, Nicolas Rumiantsev, draft a treaty whereby Napoleon promised that not only would he oppose Poland's transformation into a kingdom but would war against the Poles should they try to create one. Believing that the emperor would approve that diplomatic gesture, Ambassador Armand de Caulaincourt, who had served at St. Petersburg since November 1807, endorsed the treaty.[47]

But Napoleon rejected the treaty, arguing that he needed to keep his diplomatic options open. He tried to soften that blow by feeding Foreign Minister Champagny an argument to convey to St. Petersburg: "Russia wants to be reassured on my intentions toward Poland: Events prove my intentions. If I had wanted to reestablish Poland at Tilsit, instead of making peace I would have crossed the Niemen." He elaborated that argument in a direct message to Caulaincourt: "I do not want to reestablish Poland but I can not dishonor myself by declaring that the kingdom of Poland will never be reestablished."[48]

That necessarily unwritten and secret understanding should have been enough to allay the tsar's fears—had the relationship between them been healthy. But by now Alexander interpreted everything Napoleon did in the worst possible way. And Napoleon, of course, amply returned that distrust. When Champagny suggested that Napoleon make even more concessions to arrest and ideally reverse those suspicions, the emperor angrily fired him. In his place Napoleon put Hugues Maret, Duke Bassano, who would be more likely to simply implement rather than challenge his decisions.

The tsar replied with a list of complaints against French policies, and renewed his demand that Napoleon sign the treaty. Upon receiving the demarche on June 30, the emperor angrily summoned Ambassador Prince Alexander Kurakin and demanded answers: "What does Russia mean by such language? Does she want war? Why these persistent complaints? Why these insulting suspicions? Had I wished to restore Poland I would have done so and would not have withdrawn my troops from Germany. Is Russia trying to prepare me for her defection? I will be at war with her the day she makes peace with England." He then fired off a letter to Caulaincourt telling him to warn the tsar that war would result if he broke Tilsit and aligned with Britain.[49] Actually, the war would come even before Alexander openly allied with Britain.

Napoleon foresaw that the deteriorating relationship made war ever more likely, so he prepared emotionally and eventually diplomatically and militarily for the worst. Planning for a future war with Russia began officially with an order from the emperor to War Minister Henri Clarke on February 18, 1811.[50]

Yet Napoleon still hoped to avoid war altogether. He sought to forge an understanding with Alexander on all matters in a long letter sent in February 1811.[51] Most of his letter was taken up with his rationales for his own acts and criticisms of those of Alexander in regard to the Continental System, Poland, Oldenburg, Sweden, and Turkey. He tried to reassure the tsar that he would not recreate the kingdom of Poland and would compensate Duke Oldenburg.

But at times he explored the deeper reasons for their conflicts, which he found rooted in the psychology of the international system. Each leader, however seemingly all-powerful, was bound by expectations, fears, and other forces largely beyond his control. He and the tsar seemed to be nearing a point of no return when any suggestion of compromise, however sensible, would be seen as a sign of weakness which might encourage even stronger measures by the other leader and other potential enemies: "In a former time, before taking such measures against my commerce, I would have perhaps suggested ways by which we could have fulfilled our main goal and prevented the appearance that we had changed the system in the eyes of Europe. All Europe has seen that our alliance no longer exists. . . . If Your Majesty would permit me to say frankly: he has forgotten the good that he had drawn for the alliance which has fallen by the wayside since Tilsit." He ended with a plea that they could resolve their differences "in the intimacy of a relationship which for four years has been so happy."

Those dilemmas haunted Caulaincourt as well. He continued to do all he could to reverse the drift toward war. He sent back long reports analyzing the darkening outlook toward France among the tsar and ever more of his advisors, and made repeated requests for minor concessions to bolster the peace party against the war party. But the emperor rejected that advice. He believed that even the most symbolic of conciliatory gestures would simply invite Alexander to demand more. Only intimidation, not compromise, would keep the peace. Caulaincourt finally could take no more. The emperor's recalcitrant attitude, atop word that he had fired Champagny and banished his fiancée, Adrienne de Cansy, from Paris, prompted him to resign, ostensibly for health reasons.[52]

Napoleon replaced Caulaincourt with General Jacques de Lauriston, another yes-man like Maret. In May 1811 the new ambassador carried to the tsar a mostly conciliatory letter from the emperor. Napoleon insisted on his friendship for Alexander and his intention not to transform Poland into a kingdom. Yet he also admonished the tsar for violating the embargo and building up his army on the Polish frontier.[53]

The tsar replied with perfunctory professions of amity that he felt compelled to state but hardly felt. With those diplomatic niceties out of the way, he dispatched Alexander Chernyshev and Karl von Nesselrode to Paris with what amounted to an ultimatum. He demanded that Napoleon withdraw his troops from Danzig, the Duchy of Warsaw, and along the Oder River, and compensate Duke Oldenburg for the confiscation of his realm. Those requests were at once reasonable and provocative.

Napoleon was debating with himself over how to respond when Caulaincourt returned to Paris on June 5. The former ambassador could not have been more pessimistic. War could only be averted, he insisted, if Napoleon sacrificed Poland to Russia.[54]

That message infuriated the emperor and prompted him to fire off his sternest message yet. He assured the tsar that he recognized Russia's recent takeover of Finland, Wallachia, and Moldavia. That was hardly a concession, since those were all European realms that could not be more distant from France's spheres of influence. Indeed, for that very reason it was in French interests to encourage the tsar to get as deeply involved as possible—in fact, bogged down—in those remote lands. But, as a gesture to his Austrian ally Francis, he warned the tsar not to expand further into the Balkans.

When the tsar treated that warning with contemptuous silence, Napoleon ordered armies of observation established on the Elbe, Rhine, and Piave—all certainly far removed from the Niemen, yet there was no mistaking the diplomatic message. He highlighted his efforts to reinforce Marshal Louis-Nicolas Davout's Army of North Germany and get Rhine Confederation members to ready their forces. When Wurttemberg's King Frederick I protested, the emperor warned him to follow orders or face annexation; the monarch bowed to power. In July 1811 Napoleon ordered depots and magazines set up across the Duchy of Warsaw toward the Russian frontier. Word of both policies was deliberately leaked to intimidate Alexander into making concessions; instead those acts merely hardened the resolve of the tsar and his advisors.[55]

The pressure to launch a war he did not want was building on Napoleon. He vented some of his fury during a reception for the diplomatic corps on his birthday on August 15, 1811. When Russian ambassador Kurakin appeared, Napoleon blasted him in a prolonged harangue capped by the vow that "even if your armies camp on the heights of Montmartre I will never cede an ounce of Polish territory!"[56] Within less than three years Russian troops, along with other allied troops, would indeed battle for the Montmartre heights overlooking Paris.

As with a similar tirade against the British ambassador during a reception in 1803, Napoleon's latest outburst was not merely embarrassing but a major step toward war. As Alexander explained to Lauriston, "I would have wished that exchange to be kept secret but all the salons of St. Petersburg know about it and that new event only renders more implacable the determination of my nation, if not in provoking war but in defending its dignity and independence to the death."[57]

With his rage spent, Napoleon recognized his blunder and summoned Kurakin. He not only apologized but tried to assuage Russian honor by promising that not only would he sign a treaty guaranteeing that he would not convert the Duchy of Warsaw into a kingdom, but would get Vienna to do so as well.

Word of that concession arrived too late in St. Petersburg. By the late summer of 1811 Alexander and his advisors had essentially already decided to war against the French empire. The only deal that might prevent that war would be for Napoleon to let the Russian empire devour the Duchy of Warsaw; and that was something Napoleon would never allow. St. Petersburg, however, had to overcome two vital diplomatic challenges before it was ready to square off with the French empire. One was to find allies, and the other was to win its latest war with the Ottoman Empire. It would take until the spring of 1812 before Alexander achieved both.

Napoleon's ubiquitous spies sent word of St. Petersburg's attempts to entice Berlin and Vienna to join Russia against France. The emperor sent letters to each of his supposed allies asking whether the rumors were true. Both the Prussian and Austrian sovereigns vigorously denied any conspiracy. Frederick William III offered the typical diplomatic reply that "I dare flatter myself that Your Imperial Majesty could not have an instant of doubt of the purity of my intentions."[58]

Nonetheless, the secret Russian talks with the Prussians and Austrians over an alliance continued. On October 17, 1811, foreign ministers Nicolas Rumiantsev and Gerhard Scharnhorst actually signed a treaty committing Prussia to fall on Napoleon's rear should he invade Russia. But the king refused to ratify that deal unless Francis of Austria too agreed to stab Napoleon in the back. That was a step that Francis was not yet willing to make. After all, he would not only be violating a range of treaties binding Austria to France and warring against his own daughter's husband, but should he suffer his fifth defeat at Napoleon's hands he would undoubtedly lose his crown and see his realm entirely dismembered.

Alexander's appeal to London was initially no more successful. Stratford Canning, Britain's ambassador to St. Petersburg, was instructed to agree to help negotiate a peace settlement rooted in uti possedetis, or "to the victor goes the spoils." The amount and conditions for British financial and military aid, however, would take months to negotiate. If the reluctance of Frederick William and Francis to rush to Alexander's aid was understandable, the lack of enthusiasm with which the British cabinet greeted the tsar's appeal for aid, an alliance, and mediation of an end to the war between Russia and Turkey may appear puzzling. Had not Whitehall been the paymaster for a succession of wars against France over the previous two decades?

That, indeed, was the root of the problem. The British Empire in 1812 was teetering on the brink of economic, political, and psychological collapse. The national debt, interest rates, taxes, prices, joblessness, bankruptcies, and body counts soared while business investments, personal income, and morale plummeted. People hungry for jobs rampaged through factories destroying the machinery they believed stole their livelihoods. People hungry for food pillaged shops and warehouses to fill their pinched bellies. While there was no genuine threat of a French-style revolution, the war was certainly consuming Britain's leaders. Three prime ministers and a foreign minister had died within the last half dozen years. Strokes killed prime ministers William Pitt and William Henry Cavendish, the Duke of Portland, in January 1806 and September 1809, respectively, and foreign minister Henry Fox in September 1806, while an assassin shot to death prime minister Spencer Percival on May 11, 1812. Although the war had not caused King George III's latest bout of madness, which began in 1810 and would persist until his death a decade later, his affliction seemed eerily symbolic of the political insanity into which Europe had plunged since 1792 or, most would argue, 1789.

Yet Whitehall hung on defiantly and ever more desperately to war with France. While the British welcomed Napoleon's licensing of shipments of grain and other vital products in 1810 and 1811, they spurned his hints that he would be willing to discuss peace. The only recent negotiations had blossomed briefly in September and October 1810 before withering. The emperor had prompted those meetings after learning how harshly the British were treating French prisoners of war. But Whitehall killed his hopes for better conditions and an exchange, which might have served in turn as a foundation for a general peace. Napoleon later explained his failure to the Senate: "I had hoped to be able to establish a cartel for exchanging prisoners between France and England, and by extension profit from the sojourn of the two commissioners in Paris and London to reach a rapprochement between the two nations. My hopes have been deceived. I discovered in the British way of negotiations that trick of bad faith."[59]

If the Russians were running into diplomatic roadblocks in their search for allies, they were far more successful against the Turks. The only trouble was that Istanbul refused to accept defeat. The Russian victory at Roustachouk on July 4, 1811, was the war's turning point. The Russians marched on, conducted a bloody siege of Slodzie, and afterward captured 36,000 Turkish troops on December 7, 1811. In February 1812 the Russians launched an offensive that broke the back of Turkish resistance the following month. Under the treaty of Bucharest signed on May 28, the Sultan recognized Russia's takeover of Bessarabia and protectorates over Wallachia and Moldavia. Alexander could now begin marching most of his regiments from the Balkans to western Russia.

As St. Petersburg was resolving its Turkish war, it received an unexpected ally. On January 27, 1812, Napoleon had ordered French troops to reoccupy Pomerania as punishment for Sweden's break with the Continental System, its granting of permission to British warships to shelter in its ports, and its demand to take Norway from French ally Denmark. The French action in turn pushed Sweden into the arms of Russia. Under a treaty signed on April 5, Stockholm and St. Petersburg agreed to supply 30,000 and 20,000 troops, respectively, to an invasion of northern Germany should Napoleon march into Russia.[60]

Napoleon succeeded in arm-twisting Austria and Prussia to formally ally with France against Russia and supply armies for the invasion under the emperor's operational control. Under a treaty signed on February 24, 1812, Prussia would allow allied forces free passage through its territory and supply 20,000 troops to the invasion. Austria pledged 30,000 troops with a treaty signed on March 14. Between those deals Napoleon further shored up his vulnerable rear by getting Danish King Frederick VI on March 7 to mobilize 15,000 troops on the Holstein and Schleswig frontier to deter a possible landing there by British, Swedish, and/or Russian troops.

Napoleon's deals with Austria and especially Prussia were much less than they seemed, although they were the best he could get under the circumstances. Neither power wanted to war against Russia. The Prussians, as has been seen, would have preferred to attack France. Scharnhorst carried a letter from Frederick William to Alexander pledging that "if war breaks out we shall do each other only such harm as is strictly necessary. We shall always remember that we shall be united, that one day we are to become allies again and while yielding to irresistible necessity, we shall preserve the freedom and sincerity of our feelings."[61]

As if relations were not tense enough, a spy scandal exacerbated the animosities. In February 1812 Colonel Alexander Chernyshev, the tsar's special envoy to Napoleon, was nabbed bribing a foreign ministry clerk. Although Napoleon gave him a polite send-off and entrusted him with his latest appeal to Alexander, the damage had been done.[62]

Napoleon made once last attempt at peace with Britain. In April 1812 Foreign Minister Maret sent his counterpart Robert Stuart, Viscount Castlereagh, a set of peace proposals that included acceptance of Joseph as Spain's constitutional monarch, ruling with the Cortes; an independent Portugal; and the kingdom of Naples split between Murat ruling southern Italy and Ferdinand over Sicily. But Castlereagh dismissed Napoleon's latest initiative.[63]

As spring blossomed in St. Petersburg, the reality that he would soon be leading his empire to war loomed ever darker in Alexander's mind. The tsar was starting to second-guess the decision to take on a military genius with more than half a million troops at his command. Perhaps war could still be averted. Regardless, he wanted to ensure that Russia would be viewed as the victim rather than the aggressor. To Napoleon, Alexander wrote that he "would not draw the first sword. I have no intention of being held responsible in the eyes of Europe for the blood this war will cause to be shed. You have been threatening me for eighteen months now. French troops . . . line my frontiers. But I remain in my capital, arming and fortifying."[64]

Lest that message be interpreted as a sign of weakness, Alexander and his advisors chose to follow it up with an ultimatum. On April 18 ambassador Kurakin presented Napoleon with the demand that the tsar would only open talks with the emperor if he withdrew his troops from central Europe beyond the Rhine; joined a defensive alliance with Russia, Prussia, and Austria; compensated Duke Oldenburg; and converted the Continental System into a licensed trade system with Britain.[65]

Napoleon ignored those demands and simply stated that he would agree not to transform the Duchy of Warsaw into a kingdom. He then let Kurakin cool his heels before he saw him again on April 27. When Kurakin refused to retract any of the tsar's demands, Napoleon took his only concession off the table. Kurakin asked for and received his passport to return to St. Petersburg.

Napoleon had his aide Louis de Narbonne carry to Alexander a letter that he wrote on May 3 but backdated to April 25. He conveyed "my desire to avoid war and the persistence of my sentiments at Tilsit and Erfurt.. . . If fate must make war between us inevitable, it would not change any of the sentiments which Your Majesty inspired in me." Missing from the letter was any proposal to resolve the issues which divided them.[66]

War now was virtually inevitable. As Napoleon launched himself into the latest stage of mobilization, Caulaincourt undoubtedly recalled Alexander's parting warning to him:

> The Spanish have often been beaten, and they are neither defeated nor subdued. Yet they are not so far from Paris as we; they have neither our climate nor our resources. We shall take no risks. We have plenty of space and we shall preserve a well-organized army. . . . I shall not be the first to draw my sword, but I shall be the last to put it back in its sheath. . . . Our climate, our winter will fight for us. With you, wonders occur only when Your Majesty is present. But you cannot be everywhere at once; you cannot be absent from Paris year after year.[67]

In the months ahead those words would haunt the emperor.

An Unexpected Ally

Napoleon's strategy of trying to stretch Britain militarily, economically, and politically to the snapping point while periodically sending peace feelers across the Channel got a boost in early summer of 1812. Word would catch up to him in Russia that on June 18 the United States had declared war on Britain, a state of affairs that Napoleon had tried diplomatically to nurture.

Whether warring against Britain enhanced or harmed the national interests of the United States, the Americans certainly had ample cause for complaint. Since the outbreak of war in Europe two decades earlier American trade had been ravaged by blockades, embargoes, and outright confiscations of ships, cargoes, and even crew members. For half a dozen years leading up to June 1812, the Americans had tried to deter that aggression by wielding its economic power. In February 1806 President Thomas Jefferson got Congress to pass the Non-Importation Act, which cut off trade with any countries at war. With the Embargo Act of December 1807, the president and Congress stupidly cut off all foreign trade with all countries. That spared Americans those humiliating seizures at sea, but at the far worse cost of a harsh economic depression, especially in the nation's seaports. President James Madison and Congress restored a bit of sanity to their nation's foreign policy with the March 1809 Non-Intercourse Act, which restored trade with countries not at war.

But the depredations by both British and French ships continued, with the former taking, on average, twice as many American prizes. While France's confiscations sporadically supplied the country with scarce goods, Napoleon increasingly mulled whether it would make more sense to entice the United States into alliance rather than alienate it. In January 1810 he summoned John Armstrong, America's minister, and offered to stop seizing American ships.[68]

Although President James Madison did not respond directly to Napoleon's offer, he did get Congress to pass Macon's Bill Number Two that May. By its provisions the United States would restore trade with whichever country, Britain or France, was the first to promise to respect America's freedom of the seas.

Napoleon leapt at that opportunity. On August 2, 1810, he authorized Champagny to promise Armstrong that if the United States restored trade with France, France would stop confiscating American ships bound for British ports as of November 1. Yet Napoleon also issued the Trianon Decree, which repudiated any American claims against France for previous seizures. Nonetheless, he had his foreign minister convey the following reassuring sentiments to the Americans: "His Majesty likes the Americans; he regards their prosperity and their trade as favorable to his policies. American independence is one of the principal titles of glory of France; since the emperor has been pleased to aggrandize the United States, and, in any event, this will augment the property of his country and assure its happiness, the emperor always regards our relationship to his interests and his most cherished affections."[69]

President Madison responded on November 2, 1810, by announcing that the United States would restore diplomatic and trade relations with France. He also sent Britain an ultimatum to end its assaults against American shipping and sailors by February 2, 1811. That deadline passed with nothing but contemptuous silence from across the Atlantic, and the depredations continued. After enduring those losses for another sixteen months, Madison finally concluded that he had no honorable choice but to ask Congress for a declaration of war. The House of Representatives voted in favor on June 4 and the Senate on June 16. When Madison signed the bill on June 18, 1812, the United States was officially at war with Britain.

Napoleon realized how important that event was to his own efforts, although he could do little to aid the Americans.

The Fire in the Rear

As he had three years earlier when he warred against Austria, Napoleon needed to keep looking back over his shoulder as he headed east in 1812. In Spain Wellington and his commanders were preparing for their latest offensive, while Whitehall had nixed Napoleon's latest offer of peace based on uti possedetis. Castlereagh would open negotiations only with the understanding that Ferdinand VII was the sole legitimate king of a united Spain.

For Napoleon to accept that would have meant snatching away his own brother's crown and writing off as an utter, tragic waste the deaths of over 100,000 French and allied troops in the Peninsula over the previous four years. That he would not do. So the war dragged on there for another two years before Wellington finally reconquered all of Iberia and led his army into southwestern France.

Napoleon made that conquest easier by mining his army there for tens of thousands of troops for both his 1812 campaign in Russia and his 1813 campaign in Germany. Of course, had he accepted peace in Spain on Castlereagh's uncompromising terms, Napoleon could have transferred most of the over 200,000 veterans in Spain to Germany by 1813, and that most likely would have tipped the strategic balance to him.

Wellington's 1812 campaign in Spain was decisive. He opened it with an offensive in December 1811 to recapture the frontier fortresses of Cuidad Rodrigo and Badajoz; after bloody sieges he took the former on January 19, the latter on April 6. His losses were so heavy, however, that he needed two months to rebuild his army before he could march eastward.

Marshal Auguste Marmont hurled his army at Wellington's near Salamanca on July 22, but lost 14,000 troops while inflicting only 5,000 casualties. When Marmont retreated back across the Douro River, Joseph panicked and abandoned Madrid. The allies marched into the capital on August 12. That forced Soult to raise his siege of Cadiz and withdraw all the way to Valencia. Wellington marched on to Burgos, but lacked sufficient heavy siege guns to take the fortress and enough troops and supplies to ward off Joseph and Marmont, who were advancing on his rear with 50,000 troops. Wellington withdrew his army back to the frontier citadels that he had captured earlier that year. Joseph resettled more uneasily than ever in his Madrid palace.

Although Wellington and his army wintered far away in western Spain, the war in the Peninsula had decisively shifted in the allies' favor. Henceforth the initiative would be in Wellington's hands. And that was not all. In September, Spain's Cortez did what Portugal's government had done three years earlier: it offered Wellington actual command over all Spanish forces. Theoretically, Wellington would for the first time be able to coordinate the operations of the Spanish armies scattered across the peninsula. Although the effort proved about as easy as herding cats, his combined armies would overrun nearly all of Spain by the end of 1813.

The 1812 Campaign

Strategically, war with Russia made little sense for France. Trying to feed a fighting force capable of conquering Russia compounded the dilemma that Napoleon faced in Spain. The longer the supply lines, the more regiments had to be hived off to protect it, which correspondingly reduced those who could directly fight the Russians. And what would happen if the Russians did not stand and fight but simply traded land for time and awaited the arrival of their greatest ally, winter? Would the remnants of the French armies starve to death as snowstorms and partisans destroyed or delayed those vital supply caravans from reaching the front? If so, would Prussia and Austria take advantage of that disaster to break their alliance with France and attack Napoleon when he was at his weakest?

It was not as if Napoleon did not know what to expect beyond the Niemen. He need have only recalled the logistical nightmare of his winter campaign in Poland in 1807, and then compound that many times for the distances and poverty that awaited him in Russia. For months he had been stockpiling provisions, fodder, munitions, wagons, and draft animals in fortresses including Danzig, Stettin, and Custrin in Poland and in a network of depots leading back to France. But he was well aware that getting all that was needed to the front would be ever more challenging the further east he marched.

The only sensible strategy was to sit tight in eastern Poland with the bulk of his army and launch provocative but limited offensives across the frontier so as to goad the Russians into attacking. If Alexander was foolish enough to do so, then Napoleon could most likely inflict a devastating defeat on the Russians on ground of his own choosing with troops well-rested, -equipped, -trained, and eager. But Napoleon, of course, did not do that.

Yet it was hard not to be optimistic. Napoleon stage-managed his journey from Paris to the Russian front as a triumphal diplomatic procession. When the emperor and empress boarded their carriage at Saint Cloud and clattered eastward on May 9, 1812, they were accompanied by a score of other carriages filled with much of his court and escorted by a detachment of the Chasseurs a Cheval of the Imperial Guard cavalry. En route they were received by the local sovereigns and their courts. The climax of that procession came after they arrived in Dresden on May 16. Awaiting him were not just Frederick Augustus, the King of Saxony and Duke of Poland, but also Francis II of Austria, Frederick William III of Prussia, and most of the other allied sovereign leaders. What followed were almost two glittering weeks of summits, banquets, balls, hunts, and concerts. As Eugene later wistfully recalled: "Napoleon was indeed God at Dresden, the king among kings. It was, probably, the high point of his glory: he could have held on to it, but to surpass it seemed impossible."[70]

One sovereign notably absent from Dresden was the King of Naples. Napoleon had long suspected Murat and Caroline of playing both sides of the diplomatic fence. He had forbidden Murat from attending the glittering diplomatic summit at Dresden on the eve of his Russia campaign. His excuse was that somehow Murat's presence would remind Francis of the loss of Austrian possessions in Italy. That, of course, was an absolutely absurd notion, since it was Napoleon who was the king of an Italian state which had annexed former Austrian territory; Murat's kingdom had no such lands. The real reason, as Caulaincourt revealed, was that Napoleon "did not want Murat to establish relations with the Austrians. . . . If he had come to Dresden his vanity and

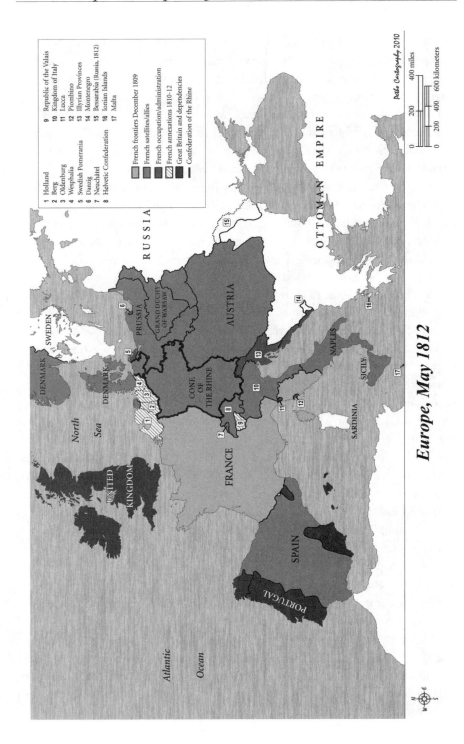

Europe, May 1812

Legend:

1 Holland
2 Berg
3 Oldenburg
4 Wesphalia
5 Swedish Pomerania
6 Danzig
7 Neuchâtel
8 Helvetic Confederation
9 Republic of the Valais
10 Kingdom of Italy
11 Lucca
12 Piombino
13 Illyrian Provinces
14 Montenegro
15 Bessarabia (Russia, 1812)
16 Ionian Islands
17 Malta

French frontiers December 1809
French satellites/allies
French occupation/administration
French annexations 1810–12
Great Britain and dependencies
Confederation of the Rhine

Pole Cartography 2010

0   200   400 miles
0   200   400   600 kilometers

self-interest would have led him into countless follies in trying to manage the Austrians." To Caulaincourt, Napoleon complained that Murat "was no longer a Frenchmen and had forgotten what he owed to his country and his benefactor. . . . He has a good heart. . . . When he sees me he is mine; but away from me, he sides, like all spineless men, with anyone who flatters . . . him." But it was not just Murat who worried Napoleon. Caroline "is ambitious and has stuffed his head with foolishness. He wants to have the whole of Italy; that is his dream." The Emperor also worried that Caroline had compromised herself with her well-known love affair with Metternich when he was ambassador in Paris.[71]

Napoleon still hoped to snatch peace from the jaws of war before it was too late. Amidst the two weeks of festivities at Dresden, he awaited word of Narbonne's last appeal to the tsar. Alexander received Narbonne at his Vilna headquarters on May 18. After again demanding that Napoleon disband his army and withdraw beyond the Rhine, the tsar issued this warning: "Tell the Emperor that I will not be the aggressor. He can cross the Niemen but never will I sign a peace dictated on Russian territory. [And] if, after a few defeats, I retreat, sweeping along the population, if I leave it to time, to the wilderness, to the climate to defend me, I may yet have the last word over the most formidable army of modern times."[72] And that, of course, was exactly what happened. Narbonne returned to Dresden with the tsar's ominous message on May 26.

As if Napoleon's diplomatic orgy in Dresden had not been heady enough, there was that vast group of armies awaiting him along the Russian frontier after he left Dresden on May 29. Never before had one man headed so many troops. When he crossed the Niemen River on June 24, he commanded 611,900 soldiers, including 513,500 infantry and foot artillery and 98,400 cavalry and horse artillery. There were 1,242 field artillery pieces, 130 siege guns, and 32,700 military vehicles drawn by 333,911 draft animals. Less than half of the army, 302,000 men, were from French territory, and only a third spoke French as their native tongue; the rest were recruited from across Europe. The French territorial forces numbered 265 infantry battalions and 219 cavalry squadrons compared to foreign, "empire" troops of 291 infantry battalions and 261 cavalry squadrons. Those foreigners included the corps of Viceroy Eugene with 80,000 mostly Italian troops, General Gouvion St. Cyr with 80,000 mostly Bavarian troops, General Josef Poniatowski with 60,000 Poles, King Jerome's 70,000 Westphalians, Saxons, Hessians, Dutch, Swiss, and Poles, General Johann Yorck with 20,000 Prussians, and General Karl von Schwarzenberg with 30,000 Austrians. There were even regiments of Lithuanians, Illyrians,

Spanish, and Portuguese. In all, 29 states had contributed varying numbers of troops, animals, and supplies. Massing, feeding, and equipping all those troops from so many nationalities was a logistical and diplomatic triumph.[73]

Napoleon split his command into five armies which totaled 450,000 troops to march eastward and 165,000 to guard depots and convey supplies to the ever-more-distant front. Napoleon himself would lead the center army of 250,000 troops, flanked on the south by Eugene's 80,000 and the north by Jerome's 70,000, and much further by MacDonald's 30,000 along the Baltic and Schwarzenberg's 30,000 below the Pripet Marshes.

The Russians then had 409,000 troops, of which 211,000 faced Napoleon just beyond the Niemen, 45,000 lay further east in various reserve forces, and 153,000 were deployed along the Turkish and Persian frontiers. On the western front the Russians were split into 127,000 led by Prince Peter Bagration and 48,000 led by Baron Mikhail Barclay de Tolly, while smaller forces were deployed elsewhere. Alexander himself had joined Barclay de Tolly's army at Vilna in April.

With the Russians initially outnumbered at least two to one along the frontier, how could they possibly check, let alone defeat, Napoleon's vast horde? Alexander and his generals did exactly what months earlier the tsar had told Caulaincourt he would do. The Russians withdrew steadily before the French, fighting an occasional rear-guard battle while gleaning the countryside of any food, fodder, or water that could succor the enemy. Ever more Cossacks and partisans began attacking isolated supply caravans, units, and couriers.

Thus, to win Napoleon somehow had to outmarch, encircle, and destroy Bagration and Barclay de Tolly not far from the frontier, and then invite Alexander for a peace conference at Smolensk, or winter there if the tsar spurned the offer. In any event, he was confident of victory. He boasted to Metternich that "it was only a matter of time."[74]

Upon reaching his army Napoleon spent the next several weeks wrapping up his campaign preparations. On June 24 he led his own army across the Niemen River while the other armies did so that day or soon thereafter. The invasion started out well enough. Both Russian armies just barely escaped the net on June 28. Jerome's tardiness was a major reason why. When Napoleon sharply criticized him, the king resigned in a huff and returned to Westphalia. Andoche Junot replaced him as that army's commander.

The emperor continued to mix diplomacy and war. He wrote Alexander his latest long letter on July 1 urging him to rekindle the spirit of Tilsit and forge a lasting peace. That message sandwiched a long list of grievances by which he justified his invasion. He got no reply.[75]

The emperor sped his soldiers onward, yet the Russians managed to slip out of the closing jaws of his weary columns at Mohilev on July 23, Polotsk on July 18, and Vitebsk on July 27. By early August exhaustion, disease, and battle had deprived the invaders of over 100,000 troops. Napoleon's own army now numbered 185,000 compared to the combined Russian army of 135,000 just beyond the horizon.

The Russian retreat stopped briefly at Smolensk. Napoleon drove them from the city in a pitched battle on August 17 and 18, but his troops were too spent to pursue. Rather than wait there, as he had initially planned, Napoleon pushed his army onward in quest of that elusive decisive battle. His commanders complained that the army was melting away and that the Russians would just keep withdrawing until they enjoyed superior numbers, then turn and destroy the French and their allies.

What drove Napoleon onward, against all reason? Caulaincourt reveals the emperor's mindset: "He believed in a battle because he wanted one, and he believed that he would win it because that was what he needed to do. He did not for a moment doubt that Alexander would be forced by his nobility to sue for peace, because that was the whole basis of his calculations." Napoleon offered his own explanation: that his military and diplomatic victories were inseparable. Russia and Spain were the "two ulcers which ate into the vitals of France and . . . she could not bear them both at once.. . . [There was] no time to be lost. We must extract peace; it is in Moscow. Besides, this army cannot now stop: with its composition and in its disorganization, motion alone keeps it together. One may advance at the head of it, but not stop to go back." Or, even more succinctly, he explained: "The very danger of the situation impels me towards Moscow. I have exhausted all the objections of the wise. The die is cast."[76]

Napoleon's irritation and impatience worsened the further he penetrated into Russia. He complained bitterly that Alexander neither let his army stand and fight nor sent him a delegation to discuss peace. Yet he missed some key diplomatic and strategic opportunities during his campaign's first phase.

He blew the only chance he would have to begin a process that might have led to serious talks. On June 26 Alexander sent Napoleon his police minister Alexander Balashov with a letter which condemned his invasion, warned him to turn back before it was too late, declared he would not negotiate until the invaders withdrew from Russian territory, and asked him to "spare mankind the calamities of another war."[77] That was actually a concession on the tsar's part;

previously he had demanded that Napoleon withdraw from Poland before he would talk, now he would be content with a withdrawal back into Poland.

Balashov was ushered into Napoleon's presence on July 1. After reading the message, had Napoleon countered by dispatching an envoy bearing word that he would halt his army in place if Alexander immediately accepted an armistice as the prelude to a summit between them to resolve their differences, the tsar might well have agreed. Instead Napoleon threw a temper tantrum. After he cooled off, he dictated a conciliatory reply: "War therefore is declared between us. . . . But my ear will always be open to peace negotiations. . . . If Your Majesty wants to end the war, you will find me ready . . . as at Tilsit and Erfurt, full of friendship . . . and desirous to prove it to you."[78]

Again after capturing Vilna, he could have halted his corps at good positions and sat tight, while transforming the Duchy of Warsaw into the Kingdom of Poland and uniting it into a confederation with the Grand Duchy of Lithuania. That would have outraged his allies, the Austrians and Prussians, but he could have mollified them by returning to them some of the Polish lands they had previously stolen. That would have at once secured his rear, and most likely provoked Alexander to order his armies to counterattack.

A delegation of Poles arrived at Vilna to plead with him to do just that. He kept them waiting for three days before receiving them on July 14, and then "was so evasive that it chilled and dissatisfied the most zealous." He told them that he thoroughly understood their sentiments and would have wanted the same had he been in their shoes, but alas their time had not yet come. He disappointed prominent and hopeful Lithuanians with the same message.[79]

Yet another vital diplomatic card that Napoleon never played was to free the serfs. He might never have had to cross the Niemen had he threatened Alexander with converting his campaign into a crusade. Faced with a "war of liberation," the tsar might well have folded. Although during the campaign Napoleon spoke of issuing an emancipation proclamation, he never did so.[80]

Actually, the effectiveness of doing so diminished with each day his army rampaged across Russia. His soldiers' actions destroyed the elation among those who initially greeted them as liberators. Defying strict orders and penalties, they pillaged, burned, raped, and murdered their way forward. Tens of thousands of other men deserted and marauded their way back to their distant homes. As in Spain, ever more partisan bands formed and struck back at the hated invaders, cutting the throats of stragglers and couriers. So much for the "hearts and mind" question.

The Grand Army was melting away from desertion, disease, starvation, and battle. Napoleon's advisors seized "every opportunity of enlightening His Majesty about the real state of affairs. . . . Never was the truth so dinned into the ear of a sovereign—though alas to no effect." Instead Napoleon angrily dismissed the warnings and insisted that any day he would decisively defeat the Russians and bring Alexander begging for terms. He said repeatedly that "Peace lies in Moscow."[81]

While the Russian armies had successfully evaded the attempts by the French to encircle and destroy them, they were experiencing their own unique problem. Alexander tended to meddle in military matters which were far beyond his competence. That was confusing and irritating enough to the field generals, but they also feared that their moody tsar would lose heart and open negotiations. Under the pressure of his generals and his sister Catherine, Alexander left the army on July 14 for the long road first to Moscow and eventually St. Petersburg.

Once Alexander was away from the war zone he could devote himself to diplomacy. He worked to unify Russia's efforts with those of the Swedes and British. In August he traveled across the Baltic to Abo (Turku), Finland, where he met with Bernadotte and British envoy William Cathcart. They struck deals whereby the British would supply St. Petersburg with muskets, munitions, and money, and launch offensives elsewhere around the fringe of Napoleon's empire to divert his attention and resources. Sweden and Russia entered a formal alliance with the Treaty of Abo on August 30.

After Smolensk, Alexander replaced Barclay de Tolly with Mikhail Kutuzov at the army's head. Although Kutuzov wanted to withdraw all the way to Moscow and even beyond, his commanders convinced him to halt their 120,000 troops at Borodino, seventy miles west of the Kremlin.

Napoleon had only 130,000 troops when he arrived near Borodino on September 7. He might have won a decisive battle—the one he had been searching for—had he tried to encircle the entrenched Russians or hurl his Imperial Guard against them late in the day when the enemy was wavering. But instead, after a massive bombardment he marched his army directly against the Russians in charge after charge. The result was a bloodbath in which each side lost over 30,000 men. Napoleon justified holding back his elite Old Guard with the fear that if they were repulsed all might well be lost this far into Russia's depths.

The emperor led his army into an undefended Moscow on September 14. Within a few days the Russian scorched-earth policy reached a crescendo when

Governor Feodor Rostopchin ordered arsonists to burn the city. Had Napoleon at that time withdrawn to Smolensk or marched southwest to the huge stores of munitions and provisions at Tula, he would have saved most of his 95,000 troops.

Instead Napoleon lingered in the ruined city for another five weeks in the vain hope that Alexander would sue for peace. As Caulaincourt pointed out, that was an utter delusion. It was obvious to everyone but the emperor that "it was scarcely probable that the Tsar would have set fire to his capital with the object of signing a peace among the ruins."[82]

Indeed, no Russian envoys appeared in Moscow. On September 20 Napoleon summoned Russian noble Ivan Yakovlev, and with mingled anger and despair explained: "I have no reason to be in Russia. I want nothing from her, as long as the treaty of Tilsit is respected. I want to leave, as my only conflict is with England. . . . If Tsar Alexander wants peace, he need only let me know." He then handed Yakovlev a letter for the tsar and released him and his family on the road to St. Petersburg. He was nearly as blunt with the tsar. After a pleasant opening, he stated: "The beautiful and superb city of Moscow no longer exists. Rostopchin had it burned. . . . How could he destroy one of the world's most beautiful cities for such a trivial goal? But that has been the conduct since Smolensk. . . . If I thought you were behind those orders I would never have written you this letter. . . . I have warred against you without animosity. . . . If Your Majesty would share with me his former sentiments, he will accept with good will this letter." That failed to move Alexander, who returned the letter unopened and ordered Kutuzov not to accept any more.[83]

Increasingly desperate, Napoleon sent Lauriston with his latest plea to Alexander on October 5; undoubtedly the emperor's parting words to Lauriston echoed repeatedly: "I want peace, I need peace, I must have peace! Just save my honor." Following orders, Kutuzov barred Lauriston from heading on to Alexander and rejected his requests for a cease-fire and prisoner exchange. He did finally relent and agree to forward Napoleon's letter. Once again, the tsar refused to reply.[84]

Throughout his five weeks in Moscow, Napoleon was mired in Hamlet-like indecision. He weighed and re-weighed all his options, and none were promising. Should he withdraw? If so, how far and by what route? Should he instead march on St. Petersburg with his diminished army to pressure the tsar into peace talks? Or would that just harden Alexander's resolve never to negotiate as long as a single foreign soldier stood on Russian soil? Regardless, did he even have enough troops to launch an offensive around Moscow, let alone toward St. Petersburg? Should he simply declare victory and lead his men back to winter cantonments in Poland? Should he establish a Kingdom of Poland that embraced much of western Russia? Should he hunker down in Moscow for the long cold winter?[85]

All along the hourglass of good marching and camping weather was running out. Indian summer was waning. Frost blanketed the earth each morning. The first snow flurries blew on October 12. Meanwhile, like vultures waiting for a wounded animal to die, the Russian corps were deployed in a crescent of camps within a score of miles from Moscow. One of those corps, commanded by General Levin Bennigsen, took a lunge at General Joachim Murat's 25,000 troops at Vinkovo south of Moscow on October 18 and routed them.

That blow roused Napoleon from his somnolence. He began to withdraw his army on October 20. His plan was to march south and then west through undevastated regions, but Kutuzov massed his army and blocked him at Maloyaroslarets. Although the French took the town, their losses were so great that Napoleon ordered his army to march west along the same route they had used to reach Moscow, now littered with rotting corpses, trampled fields, and burnt villages.

Kutuzov's troops were hard on the French army's heels, and swiftly other Russian forces converged to try to cut off the enemy's retreat. The weather steadily worsened; the first snowstorm engulfed them on November 6, and from that day the temperature was always well below freezing. Napoleon left a thickening trail behind him of men killed by freezing, starving, gunshots, or sword thrusts. The Russians nearly trapped Napoleon and the remnants of his army at the Berezina River, but the emperor inspired his 40,000 troops to hold off the enemy, build makeshift bridges, and stumble across to the western shore.

All along, as Caulaincourt noted, the "Emperor rose superior to the mischances which had befallen him. These reverses, instead of disheartening him, brought out more than ever his characteristic energy; he showed what sublime courage and a brave army are capable of. . . . The Emperor showed himself a match for each emergency. . . . If only he could have presumed no further upon Fortune, Glory, and Mankind. But hope, the merest inkling of success, elated him more than the severest setback could depress him." Essentially, "the Emperor deluded himself; and our ruin followed on his misfortune."[86]

As if his Russian campaign had not been disastrous enough, the emperor learned on November 7 that he had nearly been deposed in Paris. On October 23 General Claude de Malet tried to mount a coup d'etat by claiming that Napoleon had been killed and asserting powers to take over the government. War Minister Henri Clarke managed to rally enough troops to arrest Malet and 84 other suspects; eventually Malet and fourteen conspirators went to the scaffold.

That determined Napoleon to get back to Paris as soon as possible. He needed to reassert power and build another army for the next year's campaign. At Smorgorni on December 5 he passed command of his "army"—only 7,000 scarecrows remained of the 250,000 troops who had been under his immediate command on June 24—to Murat and raced off by sledge to his capital. Murat kept withdrawing further west until he reached Posen on January 16. The following morning he turned over command of the "army" to Eugene and cantered off toward Naples.

What had become of the 600,000 troops who had crossed the Niemen the previous June? The Russians registered over 136,000 prisoners, cremated or buried 308,000 corpses, and captured 900 cannons. But the unofficial losses may well have been over 570,000 troops, 200,000 horses, and 1,000 cannons.[87]

Sooner or later those horrendous losses would become well known. Napoleon sought to prepare the French public by issuing an official explanation a couple of days before his arrival in Paris. For those who could read between the lines, Bulletin 29 revealed that the army had suffered heavy losses and was forced to abandon Moscow and retreat all the way to Poland. The bulletin's last line was not meant to be ironic, but could not have been more so: "The health of His Majesty has never been better."[88]

Napoleon had suffered a vital loss that went beyond the destruction of the mightiest army the world had yet known. In the minds of ever more Europeans, the myth of Napoleon's invincibility had perished with his soldiers on the Russian steppes. As Empress Dowager Maria Fedorovna put it: "He is no longer an idol, but has descended to the rank of men, and as such he can be fought by men.[89]

The Emperor's carriage rattled into the Tuileries Palace courtyard on the evening of December 18. There was no time to rest. Somehow by spring he had to build an army of 250,000 men and plant it in the heart of Germany. Only that, along with diplomacy that involved significant concessions, could possibly save his empire and probably his throne. As Napoleon admitted to his ministers, "I have made a great blunder; but I shall have the means to retrieve it."[90] That, however, remained to be seen.

Chapter Five Endnotes: Imperial Zenith

1. E. F. Hecksher, *The Continental System: An Economic Interpretation* (Oxford: Oxford University Press, 1922); Francois Crouzet, "Wars, Blockade, and Economic Change in Europe, 1792-1815," *Journal of Economic History*, 24, 1964; Francois Crouzet, *L'Economie Britannique et le Blocus Continental* (Paris: Economica, 1987).

2. Alan Schom, *Napoleon Bonaparte* (New York: HarperCollins, 1997), 564.

3. Robert B. Holtman, *The Napoleonic Revolution* (New York: Louisiana State University Press, 1979), 111.

4. Albert Fournier, *Napoleon I: A Biography* (Paris: Holt & Company, 1911), 2:145.

5. For the best book on the subject, see Alan Palmer, *Napoleon and Marie Louise: The Emperor's Second Wife* (New York: St. Martin's Press, 2001).

6. For a very good overview of their marriage and divorce, see Evangeline Bruce, *Napoleon & Josephine: An Improbable Marriage* (New York: Scribner, 1995).

7. Jean Hanoteau, ed., *Memoires de la Reine Hortense*, 3 vols. (Paris: Plon, 1927), 1:226.

8. Napoleon to Champagny, February 6, 1810, Claude Tchou, ed., *Correspondence de Napoleon* (hereafter cited as *Correspondence*), 16 vols. (Paris: Bibliotheque des Introuvables, 2002), 16210; Fournier, *Napoleon*, 2:145.

9. Henry Troyat, *Alexander: Conqueror of Napoleon* (New York: E. P. Dutton, 1982), 123.

10. Jean Jacques Regis Cambaceres, *Memoires Inedit*, 2 vols. (Paris: Perin, 1999), 2:326-29; Charles Maurice de Talleyrand, *Memoires Complet et Authentiques de Charles Maurice de Talleyrand,* 6 vols. (Paris: Calmann Levy, 1891-92), 2:7-10.

11. Robert Asprey, *The Reign of Napoleon Bonaparte* (New York: Basic Books, 2001), 192.

12. Metternich to Schwarzenberg, January 27, 1810, Clement Wenceslas Lothaire, prince de Metternich, *Memoires, Documents, Ecrits Divers Laisses par le Prince de Metternich*, 8 vols. (Paris: Plon, 1880-84), 2:318; Adam Zamoyski, *Moscow 1812: Napoleon's Fatal March* (New York: HarperCollins, 2004), 4.

13. Napoleon to Champagny, February 7, 1810, *Correspondence*, 16218.

14. Napoleon to Francis, February 23, 1810, *Correspondence*, 16287; Napoleon to Marie Louise, February 23, 1810, *ibid.*, 16288; Napoleon Message to Senate, February 27, 1810, *ibid.*, 16297.

15. Carola Oman, *Napoleon's Viceroy: Eugene de Beauharnais* (London: Hodder and Stroughton, 1966), 299; Napoleon to Archduke Charles, March 28, 1810, *Correspondence*, 16364.

16. Louis Constant, *Memoires Intimes de Napoleon Ier*, 2 vols. (Paris: Mercure de France, 1967), 2:118-25.

17. Napoleon to Francis, March 29, 1810, *Correspondence*, 16361; Constant, *Memoires*, 2:125-32.

18. Palmer, *Napoleon and Marie Louise*, 105.

19. Constant, *Memoires*, 2:151-59, 160-68, 168-77, 195-204, 573-74.

20. Emile Dard, *Napoleon and Talleyrand* (New York: D. Appleton Century and Company, 1937), 217.

21. Emmanuel de Waresquiel, *Talleyrand, Le Prince Immobile* (Paris: Fayard, 1999), 414.

22. Napoleon to Champagny, January 6, 9, 12, 19, February 12, March 13, 1810, *Correspondence*, 16113, 16118, 16133, 16148, 16243, 16330; Napoleon to Clarke, January 18, 27, February 16, 1810, *ibid.*, 16145, 16173, 16216.

23. Napoleon to Louis, March 20, April 3, 20, May 12, 1810, *Correspondence*, 16352, 16366, 16395, 16467; Napoleon to Champagny, February 17, 1810, *ibid.*, 16266.

24. Jean Tulard, *Joseph Fouche* (Paris: Fayard, 1998), 243-55; Waresquiel, *Talleyrand*, 402-12; Thierry Lentz, S*avary, le Seide de Napoleon* (Paris: Fayard, 2001), 231-34, 243; Thierry Lentz, *Nouvelle Histoire du Premier Empire: L'Effondrement du Systeme Napoleonien, 1810-1814* (Paris: Fayard, 2004), 2:512-16; Napoleon to Champagny, June 2, 1810, *Correspondence*, 16528.

25. Waresquiel, *Talleyrand*, 411.

26. Napoleon to Fouche, June 3, 1810, *Correspondence*, 16529.

27. Napoleon to Clarke, June 23, 24, 1810, *Correspondence*, 16580, 16586; Napoleon to Champagny, June 24, 1810, *ibid.*, 16583.

28. Constant, *Memoires*, 2:141-42; Instructions for Prince Lebrun, July 9, 1810, *Correspondence*, 16620; Napoleon to the Government Commission, July 9, 1810, *ibid.*, 16621; Napoleon to Lebrun, July 10, 15, 22, 1810, *ibid.*, 16622, 16660, 16701; Napoleon to Champagny, July 21, 1810, *ibid.*, 16692.

29. Napoleon to Murat, August 30, 1811, quoted in Lentz, *Nouvelle Histoire*, 2:46-47.

30. Hubert Cole, *The Betrayers: Joachim and Caroline Murat* (New York: Saturday Evening Press, 1972), 150, 159, 166.

31. Schom, *Napoleon Bonaparte*, 571-75.

32. Napoleon to Joseph, January 10, 1809, Leon Lecestre, ed., *Lettres Inedites de Napoleon I* (Paris: Plon, 1897), 1:266; Joseph to Napoleon, February 19, 1809, Albert du Casse, ed., *Memoires et Correspondance Politique et Militaire du Roi Joseph*, 10 vols. (Paris: Perrotin Libraire, 1954-55), 5:60.

33. Notes on a letter to Pope, January [n.d.], 1810, *Correspondence*, 16194; Explanation to Senate for Annexation of Rome, February 17, 1810, *ibid.*, 16263; Senate-Consul Ratification of Annexation of Rome, *ibid.*, 16264; Napoleon to religious affairs committee, March 16, 1811, *ibid.*, 17478.

34. Constant, *Memoires*, 2:207, 577-78.

35. Napoleon to Savary, May 21, 1812, *Correspondence*, 18710.

36. Napoleon to Champagny, May 16, 19, 1810, *Correspondence*, 16476, 16488.

37. Napoleon to Charles XIII, September 6, 1810, *Correspondence*, 16875.

38. Napoleon to Bernadotte, September 10, 1810, Lecestre, *Lettres Inedites de Napoleon I*, 2:66; Napoleon to Champagny, September 7, December 22, 1810, *Correspondence*, 16876, 17229.

39. Napoleon to Maret, July 15, 1811, *Correspondence*, 17916.

40. Napoleon to Champagny, February 25, 1811, *Correspondence*, 17386, Napoleon to Alquier, December 22, 1810, *Correspondence*, 17229.

41. Paul Britten, *1812: Napoleon's Invasion of Russia* (London: Greenhill Books, 2000), 27.

42. Frederick William to Napoleon, June 17, 1810, *Lettres Personelles des Souverains a l'Emperor Napoleon I* (Paris: Plon, 1939), 378.

43. Napoleon to Alexander, April 6, 1811, *Correspondence*, 17579.

44. Napoleon to Alexander, October 23, 1810, *Correspondence*, 17071; Note to Prince Kurakin, December 2, 1810, *ibid.*, 17179.

45. Napoleon to Champagny, February 17, 1811, *Correspondence*, 17366.

46. Napoleon to Champagny, February 10, 1811, *Correspondence*, 17346.

47. Unratified Treaty, February 9, 1810, *Correspondence*, 16178.

48. Napoleon to Champagny, February 6, April 24, 1810, *Correspondence*, 16178, 16180; Napoleon to Caulaincourt, July 1, 1810, *ibid.*, 16181.

49. Napoleon to Caulaincourt, July 1, 1810, *Correspondence*, 16281.

50. Zamoyski, *Moscow 1812*, 61.

51. Napoleon to Alexander, February 28, 1811, *Correspondence*, 17395.

52. Caulaincourt had been in love with Adrienne de Canisy, one of Josephine's ladies in waiting. Alas, she was trapped in a marriage with her uncle whom she was forced to wed at age thirteen to keep the family estate unified. Napoleon refused to allow her a divorce for fear that would be the precedent for a wave of divorces among unhappy couples at his court. In late 1810 Napoleon exiled Adrienne from his court to her country estate.

53. Napoleon to Alexander, April 6, 1811, *Correspondence*, 17579.

54. Rather than listen carefully to his regime's expert on Russia, Napoleon vented his anger on him in petty, mean-spirited ways. According to Caulaincourt, "the Emperor, besides persecuting my friends, inflicted on me every sort of vexation which he could

inflict on a State official, even to the extent of withholding payments to which I was entitled." Jean Hanoteau, ed., *With Napoleon in Russia: The Memoirs of General de Caulaincourt, Duke of Vicenza* (New York: William Morrow, 1935), 15.

55. Napoleon to Maret, June 22, 1811, *Correspondence*, 17839.

56. Lentz, *Nouvelle Histoire du Premier Empire*, 2:233.

57. Lentz, *Nouvelle Histoire du Premier Empire*, 2:233.

58. Frederick William to Napoleon, September 12, 1811, *Lettres Personelles des Souverains a l'Emperor Napoleon*, 380.

59. Napoleon to Senate, December 10, 1810, *Correspondence*, 17200. For the treatment of prisoners, see Napoleon to Talleyrand, March 10, 1800, Decres, September 19, 1809, July 14, 1809, Clarke, August 15, 1811, *Correspondence*, 4655, 8032, 18033. For negotiations, see Napoleon to Daru, April 1, 1811, *Correspondence*, 17540.

60. Napoleon to Maret, December 27, 1811, *Correspondence*, 18378.

61. Troyat, *Alexander*, 140.

62. Napoleon to Alexander, February 24, 1812, *Correspondence*, 18523; Napoleon to Maret, March 2, 1812, *ibid.*, 18538; Napoleon to Kurakin, March 3, 1812, *ibid.*, 18541.

63. Maret to Castlereagh, April 17, 1812, *Correspondence*, 18652.

64. Armand Augustin Louis Caulaincourt, Duc de Vincence, *Memoires du General de Caulaincourt, duc de Vincence, Grand Ecuyer de l'Empereur* (hereafter cited as Caulaincourt, *Memoires*), 3 vols. (Paris: Plon, 1933), 1:330.

65. Lentz, *Premier Empire*, 2:248-49.

66. Napoleon to Alexander, April 25 (actual date May 3), 1812, *Correspondence*, 18669.

67. Caulaincourt, *Memoires*, 1:293.

68. Note Pour le General Armstrong, January 23, 1810, *Correspondence*, 16168; Projet de Note au Ministre Amerique, January 25, 1810, *ibid.*, 16169.

69. Proposal to Minister Armstrong, August 2, 1810, *Correspondence*, 16743.

70. Eugene de Beauharnais, *Memoires et Correspondance Politique et Militaire du Prince Eugene, annotes et mis en ordre par A. du Casse*, 10 vols. (Paris: Perrotin, 1858-60), 7:340.

71. Hanoteau, *With Napoleon in Russia*, 39.

72. Zamosky, *Moscow 1812*, 129, 130.

73. For the following statistics on French and Russian forces, see Richard K. Riehn, *1812: Napoleon's Russian Campaign* (New York: John Wiley, 1991), 441. For a discussion of the various estimates for the number of troops and casualties for both sides at the campaign's beginning, see Zamoyski, *Moscow 1812*, 116-19, 139-40.

74. Metternich, *Memoires*, 1:122.

75. Napoleon to Alexander, July 1, 1812, *Correspondence*, 18878.

76. Caulaincourt, *Memoires*, 1:407; Philippe Paul de Segur, *A History of Napoleon's Expedition to Russia*, 2 vols. (London: Michael Joseph, 1858), 1:252; Jean Francois Agathon Fain, *Manuscrit de Mil Huit Cent Douze*, 2 vols. (Paris: Delauney, 1827), 1:323.

77. Lentz, *Premier Empire*, 2:272-73.

78. Napoleon to Alexander, July 1, 1812, *Correspondence*, 18878.

79. Hanoteau, *With Napoleon in Russia*, 56; Constant, *Memoires*, 2:220-30; Zamoyski, *Moscow 1812*, 158-64.

80. Hanoteau, *With Napoleon in Russia*, 162-64.

81. Hanoteau, *With Napoleon in Russia*, 70.

82. Hanoteau, *With Napoleon in Russia*, 141.

83. Fain, *Manuscrit*, 2:104; Napoleon to Alexander, September 20, 1812, *Correspondence*, 19213.

84. Segur, *A History of Napoleon's Expedition*, 5:75.

85. Notes, October [n.a.], 1812, *Correspondence*, 19237.

86. Hanoteau, *With Napoleon in Russia*, 239, 209.

87. Muir, *Britain and the Defeat of Napoleon*, 229; Lentz, *First Empire*, 2:319-21; Zamoyski, *Moscow 1812*, 536-40.

88. 29th Bulletin of the Grand Army, December 3, 1812, *Correspondence*, 19365.

89. Zamoyski, *Moscow 1812*, 544.

90. Hanoteau, *With Napoleon in Russia*, 399.

Imperial Collapse

1813-1814

"If only Talleyrand were here—he would get me out of this."

"One can win back space but never time."

—Napoleon Bonaparte

The Power And Destruction Of Myth

No ruler before and few since Napoleon have matched his understanding of the relationship between physical and psychological power. The emperor was a master of manipulating images to create belief in his omnipotence, on and off the battlefield. Ideally, that propaganda established a self-fulfilling prophesy whereby others feared to challenge his rule, and thus unwittingly fed the myth.

That myth should have died a definitive death along with half a million men and women on the sun-baked or frozen Russian steppes. Yet the Napoleonic legend's grip on the imaginations of most elites and masses alike in France and beyond lingered. Why do people cling to a myth even after it has been exposed as false?

Many people, perhaps most, prefer blind belief to critical thought. It is so much easier and satisfying to merge one's own identity with someone or something believed to be far greater than oneself. To do so not only boosts one's self-esteem but abdicates one from the moral duty to understand and make hard choices in a complex, paradoxical, and often outright contradictory world. The devotion to some godlike leader and the state, religion, group, and/or movement that he personifies may persist even when resentment or outright hatred mingles with love for the object of one's devotion. The insatiable demands of that god for endless sacrifices and worship along with his thinly veiled egomania and megalomania may at times provoke fleeting doubts or questions among his devotees. Yet few ever abandon their faith; their own identities have become so strait-jacketed with that of their god that to even mull the notion of apostasy would leave the disciples teetering at the brink of psychological collapse.

But the carefully contrived aura of invincibility and the human need to believe in someone or something greater than oneself only partly explains why the subject states and peoples did not rise against the French empire after Russia. First of all, the relative economic, political, and emotional costs and benefits from being part of the French empire varied greatly from one state, region, class, and individual to another. Who would gain and who would lose, should the French empire collapse? Then, for those willing to throw off French rule, there was the practical question of whether this was the right time. The full extent of Napoleon's defeat, and thus his vulnerability, would not be known for months. Meanwhile, there were still enough French troops scattered in garrisons and fortresses across central Europe to intimidate local rulers. Each realm itself had suffered losses in the Russian campaign which would take months to replace. A revolt's chance of success obviously rose with the number and power of the states which joined it. Prussia and Austria would have to break first with France before the smaller states would be willing to risk the emperor's wrath. And finally, there was the question of honor. The rulers had signed treaties committing their realms to the alliance, and none wanted to be the first to sully his honor by breaking his word. For the present, it was easier to wait and see rather than act with unforeseen consequences.

It would soon be increasingly obvious to ever more statesmen that Napoleon no longer mastered events but was mastered by them. Indeed, he was a slave to his own delusions concerning his power. He refused to assess the worsening military odds against him and then make the appropriate diplomatic compromises that might have preserved much of his empire. That denial of reality would accelerate his empire's unraveling and eventual destruction. Napoleon was the ultimate dupe of his own carefully contrived mythology.

The Defection of Prussia and Austria

No state had better reasons and more power to try to overthrow French domination than Prussia. Napoleon, of course, understood that. He had his embassy in Berlin channel his psychological muscle at Frederick William III. He acted as though the losses in Russia were trifling, and that he would bring about a decisive victory in the spring. He demanded that the king supply another 30,000 troops for the 1813 campaign. Of course, Napoleon had no choice but to play such a role: to admit defeat might embolden the Prussians to break with him then and there.

And the king and his advisors played their role as well, that of displaying an adulation and confidence completely contrary to their true feelings. They too had little choice. The Prussian king and court were literally under the gun: Marshal Charles Augereau commanded 19,300 troops in and around Berlin. To resist at that point would have been to commit political suicide.

Prince Karl von Hardenburg, then the king's closest advisor, stifled his rage at Napoleon's arrogance and his own longing to immediately avenge 1806 and all the humiliations Prussia had suffered since. Instead, he urged his fellow advisors to muster similar restraint, arguing that national honor and political expediency combined to demand that, for the present, they had to act out the pantomime: "It is of the utmost importance to show for the present the greatest devotion to Napoleon's system and alliances, and to give to all our measures the appearance that they are being taken to support France."[1] Frederick William, always among the last to join the war party among his advisors, was happy to go along with Hardenburg. He went so far as to send to Napoleon a New Year's Eve message in which he reassured the emperor of "his constant attachment to the alliance and the [Continental] system." That convinced a grateful Napoleon of his "good faith."[2]

But not everyone was willing to submit. General Johann Yorck, who had withdrawn his 20,000-man corps from Russia intact into winter cantonments, was the first to break with the alliance. With the power of his troops behind him he could boldly sign, on December 30, 1812, a convention with the Russians by which he withdrew his corps from alliance with Napoleon into neutrality. The king publicly condemned but privately thrilled at York's unauthorized act. General Frederich von Bulow resisted Yorck's calls to join him openly, but did send secret word to the Russians of his own corps' neutrality in the coming spring campaign.

That inspired Frederick William to take a couple of decisive steps in January 1813 toward an open break with Napoleon. He sent Prince Hatzfeldt to Paris with demands that the emperor immediately pay a 90 million franc bill for supplies he had requisitioned for the Russian campaign, release back to Prussia all the lands that had been confiscated since 1807, and lift the legal manpower limit on the Prussian army. Meanwhile, the king sent Karl von Knesebeck to Vienna to entice Francis I into jointly breaking with France.

Austrian Foreign Minister Clement von Metternich deflated that Prussian hope. He explained that for practical, legal, and familial reasons the time was not yet ripe for Austria to revolt against the French empire. Yet he encouraged Frederick William to do so, and hinted that Austria would sit on the sidelines during the coming campaign.

Frederick William's demands posed a dilemma for Napoleon. A compromise might retain Prussia as an ally, but also might simply empower it to break sooner with France. Given that uncertainty, it was better to err on the side of caution. That meant yielding nothing while insisting that Berlin uphold the sanctity of the existing treaties. So he dismissed Knesebeck and his message, and sent orders to Eugene, who was then in Berlin, to requisition yet more supplies.

Rejecting Frederick William's demands proved to be a gross diplomatic blunder; yet Napoleon felt he had no choice. He would not violate his own honor by sacrificing the Duchy of Warsaw he had created to a Prussia he had conquered, even if that most likely would have kept Russia's armies at bay and allowed him to retain his empire over western and central Germany.

That rejection would give Frederick William the final excuse to break with France and ally with Alexander. But he still needed time. So at first he reacted as Napoleon had hoped, by promising support and requisitions. That was the last bone he tossed the emperor as he wiggled free of his grasp.

The king, family, and court fled from Berlin on January 21 and reached the fortress at Breslau four days later. From there Frederick William penned a proposal: that he would offer to mediate an end to the war, in return for which Prussia would expand to engulf all lands between the Elbe and Vistula rivers. Meanwhile he sent Knesebeck to Alexander with an appeal for an alliance, in return for the return of Prussia to its pre-1806 frontiers. On February 8 he bolstered his bargaining power by ordering universal conscription for all able-bodied men.

Under the Treaty of Kalisch, secretly signed on February 28, the tsar and king pledged to field 150,000 and 80,000 troops respectively, and to war until they had destroyed Napoleon and his empire; Russia would gain central Poland while Prussia took Saxony. The king took another two weeks to prepare Prussia's army before, on March 16, he revealed the alliance he had forged with Russia and formally declared war on France. The following day he issued an appeal "To My People," which called for a nationalistic levee-en-masse against France. On March 19 the king and tsar fleshed out their goals for a post-Napoleon Europe with the Treaty of Breslau, which would dissolve the Rhine Confederation and Westphalia kingdom and restore to Prussia its pre-1806 territories. The monarchs still had some crucial diplomatic details to work out. Frederick William was now determined to turn France back to its frontiers of May 1789, while Alexander was content to live with a France within its 1792 borders. On that, for the present, they agreed to disagree.

Strategic triumphs soon followed those diplomatic triumphs. On March 22 the two monarchs rode into Berlin, which Eugene and Augereau had prudently abandoned a couple of weeks earlier. The culmination of this first stage of diplomatic cooperation between Prussia and Russia came on March 25 with an ultimatum entitled a "Proclamation to the German People and Princes," which demanded that they either join Berlin and St. Petersburg or be destroyed. On April 24 they led their combined armies into Dresden, which they would make their headquarters for the spring campaign. They sent a renewed appeal to Austria to join them. They pressured Saxon King Frederick Augustus to turn his coat in their favor. They got King Maximilien Joseph and his foreign minister Count Maximilien de Monteglas to declare Bavaria's neutrality on April 25.

Most of Austria's inner circle, including the king and his chancellor, were still not yet willing to go that far. Under Metternich's guidance, Francis was skillfully playing his own diplomatic double game. In mid-December Napoleon wrote a letter to his father-in-law declaring his confidence in his loyalty and asking him to double Schwarzenberg's corps from 30,000 to 60,000 troops. Metternich dispatched to Paris Count Ferdinand von Bubna von Littitz to convey the king's desire for peace and his intention soon to declare neutrality. The emperor reacted badly to that message when Bubna delivered it on December 31. He angrily dismissed the envoy and fired off to Francis a letter filled with bluster about destroying Russia and warnings about what he would do to those who betrayed him.[3]

Metternich replied in a January 23 letter that Francis had decided to increase Schwarzenberg's corps to 150,000 troops. After giving Napoleon a day to mull the significance of that, he penned another letter announcing that

Vienna would sign an armistice with St. Petersburg and withdraw Schwarzenberg's corps to Austria. As soon as those troops touched their native soil, they would no longer be considered an auxiliary corps under Napoleon but simply an Austrian army under Francis. Napoleon would soon learn of the Convention of Zeyes signed between Austrian and Russian envoys on January 30.

Metternich followed that up by sending envoys to all four of the other great powers, France, Russia, Prussia, and Britain, offering to mediate the war's end, and to the minor powers of Poland, Saxony, Bavaria, the Rhine Confederation, and Naples, calling on them to join Austria in a neutrality pact. With those decisive steps, Metternich had positioned himself to arbitrate peace for Europe.

The trouble was that for now both sides scorned any notion of compromise. They valued Austria as a partner not for peace but for war. But Napoleon failed to make Francis an offer he could not refuse in return for an alliance. Alexander submitted his bid in a March 29 letter in which he promised to restore all those lands to Austria which it had lost since 1805.

Metternich expressed gratitude, yet still played hard to get. For him the tsar's offer was the first step in a carefully choreographed diplomatic dance that would restore to Vienna all that had been lost and much more. But that was inseparable from forging a lasting peace based on a balance of power and cooperation among the five key states. Francis boosted his foreign minister's power and international prestige by making him chancellor as well. No one had held that much power in Austria since Count Wenzel von Kaunitz, who had dominated Vienna's foreign policy during the latter half of the eighteenth century.

The Austrians would soon be enticed from another direction. Robert Stewart, Viscount Castlereagh, was appointed foreign secretary in 1812 and would dominate British diplomacy until his death in 1822. On April 25 his envoys William Cathcart and his half-brother Charles Stewart presented to their counterparts, Nesselrode and Hardenburg, a package deal. The key element was a two million pound sterling subsidy to be split between Russia and Prussia in a two-to-one ratio if they kept 160,000 and 80,000 troops respectively in the field against France; in addition, Whitehall would provide a 500,000 pound sterling subsidy to Russia's fleet, which had wintered in the British Isles. Finally, Britain would extend them a five million pound sterling paper security loan at five percent, whose payments would not begin until a half year after a final peace treaty or July 1, 1815, whichever came first. What the British asked in return was relatively modest: that Hanover be restored to independence and aggrandized by Minden, Hildescheim, and Ravensburg, three minor Prussian dependencies. Despite Britain's generosity, the Prussians agreed only to disgorge but not to aggrandize Hanover. The dispute would take months to resolve.

Castlereagh struck a swifter deal with Sweden, mostly because he promised much and demanded nothing of substance. On March 3 Prince Jean Baptiste Bernadotte signed a treaty with Castlereagh's envoy, Alexander Hope, whereby Sweden could take Norway from Denmark, Guadeloupe from France, and one million pounds sterling from Britain to join the alliance, and another million pounds sterling to keep 30,000 troops in the field against Napoleon.

Comeback

During his dash from the Russian steppes to the Tuileries, Napoleon typically had plotted in his mind a detailed plan for recruiting, training, supplying, and launching an army into the heart of Germany and defeating his enemies. As always, he would try to boost those efforts by manipulating the hearts and minds of his subjects, allies, and enemies alike. It was essential to spin the illusion that Russia had been a grave but reversible setback; that was the message he had his diplomats and publishers spread as widely as possible. He tried to appear a model of confidence and command as he addressed the Senate and State Council on December 20, and hosted the diplomatic community and his aristocracy at a grand, glittering reception on New Year's Day, 1813.[4]

Two days later Napoleon convened a council of his key foreign policy experts: Jean de Cambaceres, Charles de Talleyrand, Gerard Duroc, Hugues Maret, Armand de Caulaincourt, and Alexandre d'Hauterive. He wanted not their advice but their approval and implementation of decisions that he had already made. He made short work of the pleas by Talleyrand and Caulaincourt to cut a deal with Alexander even if it meant writing off chunks of the empire. While diplomacy would, as always, accompany war, generosity would be appropriate only after the war was won. France's enemies would see any concession before then as a sign of weakness, and thus be emboldened and more difficult ultimately to defeat; allies or neutral states would demand more to maintain their status; soon there would be nothing more to give. By the meeting's end, the emperor had forged a strained consensus. He and his government then threw themselves into creating an army and everything that it needed, virtually from scratch.[5]

Given the array of enemies allying against France, diplomacy would be even more crucial in this campaign than previously. And for that Napoleon recognized that he needed the very best diplomat possible as his foreign minister. But Talleyrand bluntly rejected the emperor's offer with the words: "I will not assume office because I believe that your views are contrary to what I believe to be for the glory and the happiness of my country."[6]

Napoleon had little more luck trying to harness his youngest brother into the war effort. The emperor had created the kingdom of Westphalia expressly for Jerome. In return, he expected Jerome to follow his directives. But, like his fellow fraternal monarchs, Jerome had become ever more independent after taking the throne. The crucial break had come during the Russian campaign the previous summer when Jerome had resigned his command and returned to Westphalia after Napoleon criticized his generalship and tried to subordinate him to Marshal Louis Davout.

Napoleon intended to use part of Westphalia as the staging ground for his 1813 campaign.[7] That gave Jerome enormous bargaining power, and he made the most of it. Typically his demand involved sexual rather than state politics. That notorious womanizer had fallen madly in love with the Bavarian countess Lowenstein-Wertheim and begged Napoleon to secure his divorce from Queen Catherine. Jerome's diplomacy did not end with the emperor. He also asked Bavarian King Maximilien Joseph to declare his lover a princess and Pius VII to grant him an annulment. While the king agreed, the pope and emperor rejected Jerome's requests; Napoleon chastised Jerome "for losing precious time with discussions" when he should be readying his realm for an invasion. He also gently encouraged Jerome's estranged wife Catherine to stay at the palace of Compiegne where she had sought refuge, ostensibly for her safety but as much so that she would not return to Cassel and distract Jerome from his duties.[8]

As the emperor prepared once again for war, he worried more than ever about the mortality of himself and his empire. The Russian debacle and General Malet's attempted coup were brutal wakeup calls. What would be his family's fate if he were killed or overthrown in a coup when he was far away on campaign? His Austrian wife was unpopular and mistrusted beyond her own coterie within the court. His son was only two years old. Should he die, they would undoubtedly be trampled figuratively, and perhaps even literally, beneath the stampede of ambitious factions eager to rule France.

An elaborate coronation for his wife and son might bolster their chances of survival. But would the pope go along this time? Napoleon wrote a request to Pius VII, who had been transferred from Savona to Fontainebleau in June 1812.

"Perhaps we can reach the goal we so desire of ending all the differences that divide the state and church," he suggested.[9] He entrusted Bishop Duvoisin with delivering the message and trying to open negotiations. The pope was willing, but the cardinals who represented him and Duvoisin soon deadlocked over who should govern the Catholic Church in France.

Napoleon wanted to talk directly with Pius, but feared losing face if it appeared that he was doing so out of desperation. Nor did he want to invite the pope to the Tuileries because of the political waves such a state visit would stir. So on January 18 he used the excuse of an imperial hunt at Grossbois near Fontainebleau to drop in and pay him an informal visit.

Napoleon spent a crucial week there trying to break the impasse. After being subjected to the "Napoleon treatment" of nearly incessant harangues and enticements, the exhausted pope signed a protocol on January 25, 1813, which essentially reiterated the principle that Rome reigned over the French Church but Paris ruled it. As for the appointment of bishops, the pope could either approve the choices submitted by Paris or accept their automatic approval after six months. Finally, he agreed to preside over the coronation. But he spurned three of the emperor's demands: that he rescind the excommunication of Napoleon and his officials, transfer the Holy See from Rome to Paris, and renounce temporal power over the Papal States.[10]

Ultimately, any deal with the pope would be more symbolic than substantive. If the pope would not bless the titles of his wife and child, Napoleon would find a more concrete way to secure them. He devised and on February 5 sent to the Senate for its approval a plan for a regency that would govern whenever he was away on campaign and would assume power should he die. The empress would be the official regent and president of the Senate. Assisting her would be all the imperial princes and grand dignitaries.

Then, two months later on March 24, Pius announced that the protocol had been induced under duress, and thus was null and void. The timing could not have been worse. The coronation took place anyway as scheduled, at the Elysee Palace on March 30. On that day the Empress Marie Louise was declared the queen regent over her son and future emperor; all French soldiers and officials everywhere would declare a loyalty oath to them. The pope's refusal to preside over the coronation certainly diminished its legitimacy in the eyes of many. But there was an even more glaring catch: the French Constitution forbade a woman from acting as regent; the whole coronation was thus illegal. That, however, did not stop Napoleon from going through with it.

The coronation was partly designed to assuage his father-in-law. All along Napoleon walked a diplomatic tightrope with Vienna. His letters to Francis were filled with respect, and he got Marie Louise to write to her father frequent emotional appeals for help.[11] Yet, given the history of Austrian aggression against France, Napoleon naturally mistrusted Vienna. His spies brought him word that the Austrians were once again playing a double game. To help deter a betrayal, Napoleon ordered Bavarian King Maximilien Joseph, Neapolitan King Joachim Murat, and Italian Viceroy Eugene to muster armies of observation. The danger was, of course, that such moves might provoke rather than deter Austrian aggression.

Against mounting evidence that it just was not so, Napoleon continued to believe that his relations with Francis remained iron-clad. On April 7 he wrote that the new Austrian ambassador, Karl von Schwarzenberg, "arrives today: the most intimate relations exist between the two courts." During their first meeting on April 9, Schwarzenberg presented a friendly but noncommittal letter from Francis. Napoleon in turn called on the Austrians to mass their army in Bohemia to threaten the swelling Russian and Prussian forces. Once again that latest request played nicely into Metternich's plans. Austria would happily go along, since that army could just as easily threaten Napoleon as it did his enemies.[12]

Metternich sent word urging Napoleon to compromise and spare Europe yet another round of disastrous war. In reply to Metternich and others, the emperor explained that he saw his choice as all or nothing: "I cannot take the initiative, that would be like capitulating . . . it is for the others to send me their proposals. If I concluded a dishonorable peace, it would be my overthrow."[13]

For Napoleon, that rationale was more than mere hyperbole. He had somehow survived the decade of revolutionary convulsions in which state terror or enraged mobs had murdered tens of thousands. Since taking power he had narrowly escaped several assassination attempts. He seems to have convinced himself that if he gave up some of his conquests he would somehow encourage his enemies to overthrow him; whereas, it was much more likely that a comprehensive peace which restored France to its "natural frontiers" would win him the gratitude of a people exhausted by two decades of wars that had been voracious of lives and wealth.

Hubris rather than fear better explains why Napoleon fought on. He believed that it was his destiny to rule as much of Europe as possible, either directly or through surrogates. Had he not been victorious in all his campaigns except in Russia? He was fearless on the battlefield and did not blink an eye as he sent countless others to their deaths. To fulfill his ambition and restore his crumbling empire meant risking everything in one last gamble that he could win another decisive campaign against his enemies.

The 1813 Campaign: The First Phase

Once again Napoleon had done the seemingly impossible.[14] Within four months he had mustered, supplied, and dispatched nearly 180,000 troops to camps around Mainz. About 137,000 of those troops were raw, young conscripts. He leavened that barely trained horde with 20,000 veterans from Spain and 20,000 gunners from the fortresses and warships guarding France's blockaded seaports. He then had the toughest and tallest soldiers among them pulled out of line and sent off to flesh out the surviving bare bones of his Imperial Guard battalions.

Although Napoleon's latest army had a backbone of veterans, most of his troops lacked training, muskets, uniforms, non-commissioned officers, cannons, and, most glaringly, horses. With so few cavalry, the emperor would be hard-pressed to find the enemy, and when he did would be unable to convert limited into decisive victories. In all, he had only about 20,000 mostly poorly trained and mounted cavalrymen who were less than 10 percent of his total forces, compared to the usual proportion of around 20 percent.

And then there was a problem of leadership. His marshals were exhausted and showed little élan for their emperor's latest round of war. Atop that Napoleon made poor use of them. Inexplicably, in 1813 (as well as 1814 and 1815) he would all but sideline his best general, Louis Davout, with the limited mission of retaking and holding Hamburg, rather than joining with his emperor on the crucial central front. Instead Napoleon would rely on Marshal Michel Ney, who was as unreliable in following orders or acting independently as he was truly courageous.

It was essential to rally all of France's satellites and allies behind the spring campaign. The most powerful states had already defected: Prussia had joined Russia, and Austria was on the diplomatic fence, but leaning toward the other side; Napoleon counted on Caroline and Jerome, along with his own kingdom of Italy, to devote all that they could. He fired off letters to the sovereigns reigning in Copenhagen, Dresden, Stuttgart, Munich, and Wurzburg, asking for troops and provisions. Yet all the leaders of those states, whether or not they were Napoleon's siblings, naturally balked at sacrificing any more of their men to a French war machine that appeared likely to be crushed in the coming campaign. To varying degrees they replenished their regiments, but most hesitated for the present to send them off to the not-so-Grand Army. Instead, one by one, most would open secret talks with Russian and Prussian envoys.[15]

For several tense days in mid-March it appeared as if at least some of the army might have to be diverted to defending southwestern France. Royalists took over Bordeaux on March 12 and declared that seaport open to a task force of British and exile troops. But time was not on the rebels' side. Such an allied expedition might take months before it dropped anchor before Bordeaux. Instead, within days the National Guard crushed that revolt and reestablished control. Yet that premature and misguided grab for power was a harbinger of far more serious revolts to come.

Meanwhile Eugene was withdrawing ever further westward as ever more enemy troops massed against him. He led his small army over the Oder River on February 18. He ordered Augereau to abandon Berlin on March 4 and join him beyond the Elbe River in Westphalia. General Gouvion Saint Cyr abandoned Hamburg on March 12; six days later a Russian army led by General Tettenborn marched into that vital seaport. That severed northern Germany's subjection to the French empire and the Continental System. General Jean Reynier withdrew his troops from Dresden on March 27; a month later, on April 24, the tsar and king led their combined forces into that city.

In all, Eugene had performed a minor miracle in the three months since Murat had tossed him the reins of what was left of the army that had invaded Russia. By mid-March he had scraped together over 80,000 troops from those shards and various garrisons and depots. Soon he would begin receiving the contingents Napoleon was gathering in France. Another 30,000 French or allied troops, however, were scattered in isolated fortresses across east Prussia and the Duchy of Warsaw.

Napoleon left Paris on April 15 for his headquarters at Mainz, spent ten days there trying to boost his army's supplies, munitions, and morale, then on April 25 led them eastward. The army under his direct command numbered 120,000, Eugene led 58,000 on his north flank toward Berlin, and Davout had 20,000 to recapture Hamburg. For now Napoleon's forces outnumbered the enemy within striking distance—the Russian army of 106,000 commanded by Prince Ludwig von Wittgenstein. But Wittgenstein, who had replaced Kutusov, who had died suddenly on April 28, would soon be reinforced by other Russian and Prussian forces.

Napoleon defeated the allies at Wissenfels on April 29 and Lutzen on May 2, retook Dresden on May 8, then marched further east and won victories at Bautzen on May 20, Wurschen on May 21, and Leipnitz on May 27. Davout secured his northern flank by retaking Hamburg on May 30 and chased Bernadotte with his 24,000 Swedish troops toward Lubeck.

But those victories won Napoleon little more than the blood-soaked fields on which the battles were fought; his casualties exceeded those of the enemy. Without enough cavalry, he was unable to make any victory decisive.[16]

The victories did swing a few minor powers back toward Napoleon's side. Saxon King Frederick Augustus sheepishly reembraced the emperor after the latter retook Dresden. Bavarian King Maximilien Joseph abruptly dropped talks with the Austrians over joining the coalition and reopened communication with the French. Danish king Frederick VI sent 12,000 troops to join Davout.[17]

But the further east Napoleon marched, the more nervous he got about the Austrian army swelling on his southern flank. On May 12 he sent Eugene back to Milan to prepare the Kingdom of Italy for the possibility of the latest war with Austria. On May 16 he received a jolt when Count Bubna appeared at his headquarters with a peace proposal from Francis. The terms his father-in-law offered enraged Napoleon. He would have to dissolve the Grand Duchy of Warsaw, release all the territories he had annexed to France since 1811, and return Illyria to Austria; he would make those concessions at a general peace congress at Dresden.

Nonetheless, the reply Napoleon dictated the next day was polite and positive: "I desire peace more than anyone. I consent to the opening of negotiations for a general peace and the meeting of a congress. . . . As soon as I learn that England, Russia, Prussia, and the allies have accepted this proposal, I will hasten to send a plenipotentiary to the congress, and shall urge my allies to do the same. I would even be willing to admit representatives of the Spanish insurgents to the congress so that they can present their interests."[18]

The dilemma, of course, was that the emperor's enemies had no reason to join a peace congress unless he crushed them in battle, and his army was incapable of doing that. Alexander and Frederick William remained fiercely determined to fight until Napoleon was destroyed, and then dictate the French empire's fate. Indeed, they had Napoleon's chief diplomat, Caulaincourt, turned back to the French lines after Napoleon dispatched him to the Russian camp on the eve of the battle of Bautzen.

But even if the allied leaders had then agreed to a congress, Napoleon had no intention of making any serious concessions. Metternich discovered that when he visited the emperor at Dresden on May 27. The chancellor proposed a peace based on Napoleon agreeing to dissolve the Duchy of Warsaw, restore all land taken from Austria since the Treaty of Luneville, and denounce all claims to land east of the Rhine and in Italy. Had Napoleon agreed to those terms, he could have saved his throne and a France enlarged by the Low Countries. But the notion enraged him into a tirade in which he swore to "sacrifice a million men yet if necessary. . . . You wish to tear Italy and Germany from me. You wish to dishonor me, monsieur. Honor before all!"[19] Tragically, nearly half a million more men would be slaughtered or maimed before the question of Napoleon's "honor" was finally settled once and for all.

Armistice

Napoleon's victories at Lutzen and Bautzen and his capture of Dresden were encouraging, if far from decisive. Without cavalry for a relentless pursuit, the emperor could only fume as the allied armies withdrew beyond easy striking distance or even observation. Under those circumstances, an armistice seemed like a sensible interlude in which to dredge up more horsemen, footmen, provisions, and munitions. Then, as soon as the truce expired, Napoleon planned to launch a campaign designed to land that elusive knockout blow. As for negotiations, he was open to the idea only if they were rooted in the mutual understanding that the French empire would remain intact.[20]

The allies were even more eager for a breather, for time was on their side: the longer they dragged out the clock, the more troops they could mass to hem in and eventually throttle Napoleon. For that, Austria was the key. It had shifted from French ally to neutral, and would undoubtedly turn against the French if the despot kept spurning Metternich's proposals. The French would then be threatened from three sides. The enticement of Bavaria into the alliance would be the strategic icing on the cake. The Bavarian army could march across Napoleon's rear, snapping his supply lines and completing the encirclement.

Napoleon sent Caulaincourt to negotiate the terms of an armistice. On June 4 a deal was finalized and signed at Pleiswitz for a six-week armistice that would expire on July 20. Napoleon regretted that deal not long after the ink had dried. Had he ruthlessly pursued Alexander he might have inflicted a decisive defeat, or so he believed. Instead he had certainly surrendered the initiative to his enemies. They would gleefully make the most of it.[21]

Besides the emperor, only the British resisted the notion. They feared that the time-out would weaken rather than strengthen the coalition and make the temptation of a separate peace more likely. So Whitehall cut off its subsidies to the allies for the armistice's duration.

But the British had misjudged the fierce desire of the Russians and Prussians, along with the Austrians—as soon as they dropped their diplomatic fig-leaf to join the crusade—to destroy the upstart once and for all. It did not take long for the Russians, Prussians, and Austrians to convince the British of their determination. Under the Treaty of Kalisch, signed on June 14, Britain formally allied with Russia and Prussia; under the Reichenbach treaties with Prussia that same day and Russia the next, the British promised 666,000 pounds sterling and one million pounds sterling respectively to those allies if they fought for the war's duration.

Meanwhile the Russians, Prussians, and Austrians worked out a peace plan which Metternich would submit to Napoleon. The Duchy of Warsaw would be eliminated and split among the three regimes. Prussia would replant its flag in Danzig and East Prussia, while Austria would retake Illyria and Dalmatia. The Rhine Confederation would be abolished and its members would once again be free states. Austria's border with Bavaria would be redrawn westward. Left unsaid was the status of the Low Countries and northern Italy. The implication was that they would remain under France's influence; but that was negotiable.

Metternich unveiled the plan to Napoleon at his headquarters at the Marcolini Palace in Dresden on June 26. The emperor angrily rejected the plan and unleashed a long tirade against Austrian policies: "If you wanted peace, why did you come so late. We have already lost a month, and your intervention is nearly becoming hostile. . . . In letting me exhaust myself . . . you count on speedier results. . . . I won two battles; my enemies are weakened to the point of getting over their illusions. Suddenly you slip into our midst and speak of an armistice and mediation, and everything was mixed up. Without your disastrous intervention, the allies and I would be at peace today. . . . You are no longer impartial. You are my enemy."[22]

After that initial storm passed, the two talked for eight and a half hours. Napoleon offered Austria Illyria if it would remain neutral, but that was not enough to satisfy Metternich; he also demanded the cession of half of Italy, the pope's return to Rome, independence for the Papal States, and French withdrawal from Poland, Spain, Switzerland, the Rhine Confederation, and Holland.

The emperor's rage burst again: "This pretension is an outrage! And it's my own father-in-law who greets me with such a scheme! . . . Ah, Metternich, how much England has given you to get you to play such a game against me."

The emperor refused to make any other concessions, partly because he clung to the delusion that all he needed was one grand victory to retrieve his empire, but mostly because he figured that he had nothing to lose.

"What then do they want of me? That I dishonor myself? Never! . . . I will not give up an inch of territory. Your sovereigns were born on the throne and they can be beaten twenty times and still regain their capitals. But as for me, I am an upstart soldier. My reign will not outlast the day when I have ceased to be strong and therefore to be feared." Despite his brilliant diplomatic gifts, Metternich failed to open Napoleon's mind to the reality that just the opposite was true. His parting words were designed to jolt the emperor: "You are lost, Sire. I had the presentiment of it when I came; now, in going, I have the certitude."[23]

That warning was powerfully bolstered the next morning when Count Philip Stadion, representing Austria, signed with Nesselrode and Hardenburg the Treaty of Reichenbach, whereby Austria would join 150,000 troops to the alliance if Napoleon did not join a peace congress that would convene at Prague on July 5 and unconditionally accept Metternich's peace plan by July 20.

That development briefly cleared some of the delusion from the emperor's mind. He sent word to Metternich that he wanted to see him again, and they met on June 30. The emperor asked for Austria to act formally as the diplomatic go-between. Metternich replied that Austria would do so if Napoleon formally absolved Vienna of any lingering military obligations to France. Napoleon did so, promised to send an envoy to the congress when it opened on July 5, and asked for the armistice to be extended until August 10. Metternich was sure he could talk the Russians and Prussians into approving the extension. Napoleon then followed that up with a letter to Francis in which he typically praised himself and blamed his enemies for the war: "I desire peace. If the Russians were as moderate as me, it would be promptly concluded. If, in contrast, they want to take from me concessions that sully my honor and the interests of my allies, they will completely fail."[24]

How different history would read had Napoleon promptly sent Caulaincourt to the conference when it opened and armed him with full diplomatic powers to cut the best deal possible. Instead he dragged his feet. He did not get around to dispatching Caulaincourt, assisted by Louis de Narbonne, to Prague until July 28, three weeks after the conference had opened, and refused to grant those envoys full plenipotentiary powers. As a result, he squandered crucial time before the conference and thereafter as messages were conveyed by couriers galloping between Dresden and Prague.

Napoleon's foot-dragging is even more inexplicable when one recalls that around that time he got news of the latest disaster from Spain. On January 4 the emperor had reluctantly ordered Joseph to abandon Madrid and concentrate his forces at Valladolid in northern Spain. Joseph turned his back on his capital for the last time on March 17. In May Wellington opened his latest campaign by leading 100,000 troops toward Burgos. For the first time his forces outnumbered the enemy's. Joseph and Marshal Jean Baptiste Jourdan had only 70,000 troops, and retreated from Burgos without a fight. Wellington caught up to Joseph at Vitoria on June 19. The king and marshal agreed to make a stand there. Wellington ordered a carefully planned attack on June 21 that nearly destroyed the French army. Joseph fled with the remnants of his troops to the French frontier. Other than Marshal Louis Suchet's firm command over much of Catalonia, the French merely clung to Pamplona and San Sebastien in the north.

Upon learning of that disaster, Napoleon sent orders to Marshal Nicholas Soult to take charge of the armies in northern Spain. But Soult would be no more successful than Jourdan in staving off Wellington. Soult gathered the remnants of the French army in northern Spain and marched it into a series of defeats at the hands of Wellington between July 11 and July 25, known collectively as the Battle of the Pyrenees. Once again, Wellington not only trounced a French commander but inflicted twice as many casualties as he suffered, 13,000 to 7,000. He then routed Soult at San Marcial on August 31. Soult withdrew to the Nivelle River and St. Jean de Luz on the French frontier.

Castlereagh meanwhile followed up Vitoria by formally articulating Britain's war aims and sent them to Cathcart at Prague. Essentially, the British agreed with their allies to turn back the clock to 1792 by returning to the kings of Portugal, Spain, the Two Sicilies, Piedmont-Sardinia, and Sweden all the lands they had held at that time, while Hanover and Holland would be restored to independence. The Rhine Confederation, Kingdom of Italy, and Duchy of Warsaw would be dissolved.[25]

At Prague the allies understandably believed that the emperor was not serious, that he was merely trying to divert their attention and weaken their resolve with completely unnecessary, time-wasting nonsense. It had the opposite effect: Alexander and Frederick William became more determined than ever to cut through any more diplomatic niceties. They had their respective diplomats, Johann von Anstett and Karl von Hardenberg, inform Caulaincourt that Napoleon had to either accept France's reduction to its 1792 borders or ready himself for a fight to the death. Napoleon ignored the ultimatum and instead sent word to Caulaincourt to criticize Austria for impartiality during the talks, as if that technicality would somehow get him off the hook.[26]

In response to the astonishment of his fellow diplomats at the emperor's obstinacies, Metternich revealed his insight into the man: "Napoleon is deluding himself completely about the real situation. All his calculations having long since been frustrated, he now clings to those ideas which flatter his preoccupations. He seems just as convinced now that Austria will never take up arms against him, as he was in Moscow that Alexander would negotiate."[27]

The Prussian, Russian, and Austrian monarchs put the finishing touches to their preparations for the resumption of the fighting. On August 6 they agreed that General Karl von Schwarzenberg would command the allied armies. On August 8, Francis sent an ultimatum to Napoleon to either accept the peace plan or expect war. Once again the emperor replied with a contemptuous silence—then had alarming second thoughts. The armistice expired at noon on August 10. The following day Napoleon sent a courier galloping with his own offer to Prague. Metternich penned the allied reply: "Yesterday we were mediators, but not today. French propositions must henceforth be addressed to the three Allied Courts."[28] Napoleon would receive the official Austrian war declaration from his father-in-law on his birthday, August 15.

The 1813 Campaign: The Second Phase

The allied plan to defeat Napoleon was simple: withdraw before him, entice him further east, attack his subordinates, and finally converge with overwhelming numbers. Four major allied armies marched against the 250,000 troops commanded by Napoleon and his marshals: Schwarzenberg's 240,000 Austrians from the south, Bennigsen's 60,000 Russians and Blucher's 95,000 Prussians from the east, and Bernadotte's 100,000 Swedes and Prussians from the north.

Napoleon spent eighteen-hour days devising an elaborate plan, which ideally would inflict a series of decisive blows on the allies.[29] Amidst those preparations, Murat showed up at his headquarters at Dresden on August 14 with a handful of Neapolitan troops. Napoleon only poorly disguised his anger as he greeted him. His spies had informed him that Murat was flirting with the allies, but could not uncover the sordid extent. Actually, Murat was willing to betray Napoleon and join the allies if they recognized not only his throne but his sovereignty over all of Italy below the Po River. Fearing to alienate his fickle brother-in-law should the reports be exaggerated, Napoleon did not then reveal what he knew and demand answers. Instead he tried to work his old magic on Murat by giving him command of the Imperial Guard, then, a few days later, asked him more appropriately to head his cavalry.

Napoleon opened the campaign by quick-marching his army against Schwarzenberg at Dresden and routing him on August 27, inflicting 36,000 casualties while sustaining only 10,000. But it was his last large-scale victory. First sickness cost him several crucial days in bed. Then all that Napoleon had won at Dresden was more than wiped out by allied defeats of Oudinot at Grossbeeren on August 23, MacDonald at Katzbach on August 26, Vandamme at Kulm on August 30, and Ney at Dennewitz on September 6. The three monarchs capped those victories on September 9 with the Treaty of Teplitz, whereby each pledged to keep at least 150,000 troops in the field for the duration. Then there was a lull for several weeks in September as each side tried to replenish depleted regiments and depots.[30]

The first follow-up offensive was Russian General Alexander Chernyshev's invasion of Westphalia. On September 27 he and his army appeared before Cassel, where he issued an allied ultimatum to Jerome to withdraw into neutrality or else suffer conquest. Jerome refused. Chernyshev attacked and captured Cassel on September 30. Jerome fled, but sent General Allix against Chernyshev. Allix drove off Chernyshev on October 7, and Jerome sat once again upon his throne by October 16.

All along the allies tried to entice those states that were neutral or still supporting Napoleon to switch sides. King Maximilien Joseph of Bavaria joined the allies by signing the Treaty of Reid on October 8. He readied his 36,000-man army, soon to be reinforced by 25,000 Austrians, to cut across Napoleon's rear. A week later Wurttemberg's King Frederick joined the alliance. In both cases national interests trumped sentiment in guiding the defections of those monarchs; as Napoleon had discovered with his own father-in-law, the fact that Maximilien Joseph and Frederick had each married off a beloved daughter to Eugene and Jerome as sons-in-law meant little.

The allies were now confident that they were ready to march against Napoleon himself. The commanders led their armies toward Leipzig, where the emperor had foolishly taken a stand. The three days of battle that raged there from October 16 to 19 pitting the 150,000 French and their allies against 250,000 coalition troops was the largest and bloodiest of the Napoleonic wars. In all, while Napoleon and his army barely escaped complete destruction, they lost over 75,000 men, of whom 40,000 were prisoners.[31]

Napoleon gained some grim satisfaction in routing General Karl Philip Wrede and his Bavarian army at Hanau on October 30 and escaping across the Rhine at Mainz on November 2. After reorganizing his troops and defense, he hurried on to Paris and reached the Tuileries on November 9.

But bad news continued to chase him as the allies crushed one of his scattered forces after another, with the worst loss being Saint Cyr's capitulation with 30,000 troops at Dresden on November 11. Under the terms Saint Cyr signed with the besieging general, he and his troops could head for home. But the sovereigns rejected the capitulation, and instead ordered that army interned for the war's duration. Before Napoleon heard about that deceit, he had his chief of staff Louis Alexander Berthier sign with Schwarzenberg a convention by which the French turned over the fortresses along the Oder and Vistula Rivers and marched back to France, while he retained the fortresses along the Elbe. The allies would be just as duplicitous in enticing those garrisons to surrender with false promises.[32]

The word from Spain was nearly as dismal. Wellington built up his army along the Nivelle River near the French frontier and sent forces to besiege San Sebastien and Pamplona, which surrendered on September 9 and October 31, respectively. Wellington had now liberated all of Spain except for Suchet and his 25,000 troops around Barcelona and a French garrison at Tarragona. He sent three Spanish armies against Suchet.

Wellington finally led his army across the Nivelle on November 10 and routed Soult. He marched on another score of miles to Bayonne. Rather than assault it, he isolated the 15,000-man garrison in a series of battles from December 9 to 13. Soult withdrew the battered remnant of his army deeper into southwestern France.

In the new year, Napoleon and Soult would try desperately to hold the allies at bay at opposite ends of France itself.

Defectors and Rejections

Napoleon's empire collapsed behind him as he rushed back to Paris to raise the latest army. The German sovereigns were desperate to switch sides before an allied force marched in and imposed a victor's justice. They raced off couriers with flattering letters requesting that the coalition embrace them.

The old rivalry between Prussia and Austria over Germany would reemerge from the ruins of France's short-lived hegemony over central Europe. Metternich swiftly and decisively took the lead in laying the groundwork for the reassertion of Austrian supremacy over Germany. His first coup came on November 2 when he signed the Treaty of Fulda by which Wurttemberg joined the coalition. On November 4 he orchestrated Francis I's triumphal parade into Frankfort, the Rhine Confederation's capital. From November 20 to 23 he negotiated and signed separate treaties with all the Rhine Confederation leaders.

In contrast, Hardenberg typically was not thinking, let alone acting, that far ahead. Since the British insisted that Hanover be restored to independence, he was obsessed with taking over Saxony to partially compensate Prussia for all it had suffered. For the present, Frederick William and his advisors were focused on winning the war; after all, Napoleon was at large, armed and dangerous.

Bernadotte had his own interests in mind as he marched an army across northern Germany. The Danes gave up after he invaded Holstein on January 7, 1814. Under the treaty of Kiel he traded Pomerania and Rugen Island to Denmark for Norway. Thus did he shed to Copenhagen those lands which had been a perennial source of tension with Berlin. Bernadotte hoped to curry more favor with the Prussians so that he might enlist them behind his ultimate ambition: being named the new king of France.

Napoleon would try to exploit those and other diplomatic tensions within the allied camp. Yet he would fail miserably because he clung to the delusion that he could retain some portion of the French empire. An unsigned peace offering issued by the allies at Frankfort on November 9 arrived in Paris by the hand of French diplomat Nicholas St. Aignan. Under it, Napoleon could keep his throne if he accepted a France with frontiers pared back to 1792.

Although that was unacceptable to Napoleon, not everyone agreed. When the emperor found Foreign Minister Maret's backbone to be sagging, he replaced him with Caulaincourt on November 20. The emperor's December 1 reply could not have been more unrealistic, given the circumstances. He refused to consider surrendering those regions of the Low Countries, Saarland, Switzerland, and Italy which he had incorporated as departments of France unless the other great powers were willing to reduce their realms to their own respective "natural frontiers."[33]

Metternich penned the allies' reply after Napoleon's message reached their headquarters at Frankfort on December 4, but he backdated it to December 1 so it would appear to be an independent statement which followed up the proposal of November 9. In the latest Frankfort Declaration the allies would not hold any talks with the French unless Napoleon accepted a return to France's 1792 frontiers as the foundation for peace. Metternich explained that "the allied powers desire that France will be great, strong, and happy. . . . The powers confirm that the French empire will have a territory that was never known under the kings." He then followed up that reassuring statement with the vow that "the allied powers will never rest their arms without achieving that grand and worthy result."[34]

Constant recalls Napoleon's reaction: "It did not take long to figure out that the proposals . . . were nothing but a lure, an old diplomatic ruse by which the foreigners would have won time while cradling the emperor in a false sense of security. . . . Far from entering negotiations with His Majesty, they tried to separate his cause from that of France."[35]

But what could be done? For Napoleon, the strategic situation was grim, and getting worse. The allied juggernaut steadily swelled with the defections. Denmark became the latest turncoat, enticed by a British offer of 400,000 pounds sterling for 10,000 Danish troops. The allies would open a third front against France in northwest Europe in December. In Holland riots broke out on November 15; two days later, French governor General Lebrun succumbed to a demand by Dutch leaders to withdraw with his troops. The new government invited back William V, the prince of Orange, who was in exile in London. William, accompanied by British envoy Richard, Earl Clancarty, arrived in Amsterdam on November 6. It took exactly a month for the first contingent of British troops to step ashore on December 6; General Graham landed with 1,500 troops on December 17. Meanwhile, rather pathetically, Louis, who had been in exile the last three years, issued a statement reclaiming his throne; no one else took it the least bit seriously. On January 7, 1814, Castlereagh reached the Hague for talks with William over how much of the United Provinces' former empire would be restored and under what terms, along with what military forces the Dutch might be able to provide the coalition. But the British lacked the manpower to spare for that front. The Prussians took advantage of that void when General Bulow marched his corps into the Low Countries in January and joined forces with Graham.

As Napoleon retreated back to Paris after Leipzig he had issued a stream of orders to mobilize all sectors of society and raise yet another army, this time to repel an invasion of France itself.[36] On December 2 he convoked the Legislative Corps to approve his measures and symbolize a France unified against its enemies.

Calling up the Legislative Corps seemed to make sense at the time. But Napoleon mistook intimidation for loyalty. Over the years he had bullied the Legislative Corps, as he had all other potential sources of opposition, into a strained public silence. But his ability to cow the legislators had diminished with news of each decisive defeat. A majority now were desperate to speak their minds. And they were not alone; ever more people wanted peace at virtually any price. Even prominent members of Napoleon's inner circle, most notably Jean Savary, were quietly discussing just how to talk the emperor into sacrificing the empire on the altar of peace.

So after the legislators assembled they did not meekly rubber-stamp the imperial decrees, as before. Instead the Legislative Corps, along with the Senate, asked the emperor to hand over all his diplomatic papers. Each house then nominated a five-man commission to examine them as a first step in the debate over just what was needed to negotiate a lasting peace.

The members of the Senate, Legislative Corps, and State Council were polite enough when the emperor addressed them collectively on December 19. But for most his words rang utterly hypocritical and hollow, and inspired not loyalty but bitter contempt and resentment:

> Striking victories have lustered French arms in this campaign. Unprecedented defections rendered those victories useless. Everything has turned against us. France itself will be in danger without the energy and union of the French. In these grand circumstances, my first thought has been to call you beside me. My heart needs the presence and affection of my subjects. . . . I have nothing against reestablishing peace. I know and share the sentiments of the French. But I say to the French, that peace can only be based on honor. It is regrettable that I am asking this generous people for new sacrifices, but they are commanded by the most noble and dear of interests.[37]

Napoleon then agreed to a grand swap with his legislators: he ordered his foreign ministry to share all the demanded diplomatic documents—if they passed his latest round of decrees. What the commissioners found and reported enraged nearly all the legislators. The documents revealed a series of missed opportunities for settlements and the subsequent, ever-harsher allied demands. The Senate was relatively diplomatic in expressing its concern and advice when its commission headed by Talleyrand met with Napoleon on December 29. The Legislative Corps chose a blunter approach by adopting, by a vote of 223 to 51, a resolution that condemned the "ambitious actions over twenty years so fatal to all the people of Europe." They demanded that the emperor immediately open negotiations and accept the allied terms.[38]

That was the last advice the emperor wanted to hear. So he dissolved the Legislative Corps on December 31, 1814. When the members defied him and met on New Year's Day, he appeared fierce-faced before them and declared: "You are trying to separate the sovereign and the nation. Only I am the representative of the people. . . . The throne itself, what is it? . . . The throne is a man and that man is me!"[39] That was offensive enough, but he heaped fuel on those flames by smearing all who opposed him as traitors who aided the nation's enemies, a not-uncommon ploy for leaders who have plunged their countries into unnecessary, unwinnable, and unpopular wars. He then had the police forcefully eject the legislators.

The worst emotional if not strategic blow came in late January when Napoleon learned that his own sister and brother-in-law had betrayed him. On January 8 Murat had signed a treaty with the Austrians by which he promised to lead 80,000 troops against Eugene and the kingdom of Italy in return for taking all of the Italian peninsula up to the Po River. The Austrians also promised to get the British to recognize him and get the pope to cede his lands to Murat's kingdom. In return, Murat agreed to give up his claim to Sicily to Ferdinand IV.

Napoleon believed he knew who was really to blame. "His wife made him defect," he explained. "Caroline my sister has betrayed me."[40] Although he knew well his sister's character, it actually was Murat who had first opened secret negotiations with the Austrians. This occurred as early as December 1812, after Murat took command of the remnants of the army which stumbled out of Russia. Murat and Caroline continued those discussions with Austria's ambassador to Naples, Count Mier, in April 1813. That spring he also opened a secret channel with William Bentinck, the British plenipotentiary to Ferdinand IV's exiled court at Palermo, Sicily; he offered the British to lead an army north against Eugene and the kingdom of Italy if they guaranteed that he could retain his throne at Naples. Bentinck was unwilling to be as generous as the Austrians; he said Murat must return his throne to Ferdinand, but might receive a realm elsewhere if he broke with Napoleon and joined the Coalition.

Murat carried on his intrigues even after joining Napoleon for the second phase of the 1813 campaign. On October 7 he secretly received his ambassador to Vienna, Mario Schinina, who brought the latest offer dangled by the Austrians for him to switch sides. After the debacle at Leipzig, Napoleon released Murat from service to ready his kingdom for the inevitable allied assault. Murat reached Naples on November 4; four days later he met with Austrian ambassador Mier. Never one for subtlety, Murat blurted out what he was willing to do: "I want to unite with the allies, defend their cause, and help them chase the French from Italy. I want to link myself with Austria and act entirely in its cause, provided that they support me."[41] He asked Mier personally to deliver his offer to Vienna. Meanwhile, he sent Schinina to ask Bentinck for a similar deal.

Murat's offer would provoke a mix of responses. Upon hearing Mier's account, Metternich replied that he would be delighted to take on Murat and would offer him recognition and all of Italy south of the Po river. Bentinck, however, sent word that he would not deal with Murat, since he had fought in the 1813 campaign. Nonplused, Murat chose to switch sides anyway.

Murat announced his defection in a January 15 letter to Napoleon: "I have just concluded a treaty with Austria. He who has fought so long beside you, your brother-in-law and your friend, has signed an act which seems to be hostile to you. . . . Your Majesty can appreciate . . . the necessity with which I gave in and the pain which I endure. It would be useless to recall the past. . . . If neutrality had been possible, I would have taken it . . . but . . . it was necessary to sign a treaty with your enemies. . . . This peace will especially have the good effect of consolidating my throne, of being recognized by all of Europe, and assuring my independence founded on the same interest as the other powers." He then landed an even more stinging blow: he demanded that Napoleon renounce his Italian crown and yield all Italian lands that he had annexed to France. Finally, he offered the stunning and sincere hope that his decision would only momentarily cool relations between them: "[M]ust those of friendship and family be broken too? I need to know you are still my friend, for I shall always be yours."[42]

Napoleon did not reply to Murat, but among those to whom he vented his fury was Joseph Fouche, to whom he swore his hope "to live long enough to avenge myself and France on such an outrageous and ungrateful horror."[43] Ironically, he made the remark about Murat's betrayal to the man who was the linchpin in an expanding plot to overthrow him. But Fouche's devious efforts would be surpassed by another conspiracy, spun by yet another man sidelined by Napoleon for his intrigues and then welcomed back to his government: Talleyrand.

What was Fouche doing back beside Napoleon? The emperor had plucked his former police minister from disgrace and exile with a letter dated May 10, 1813, ordering him to Dresden. Fouche arrived on June 10 and met with Napoleon, but did not learn exactly why he had been summoned until July 17, when Napoleon appointed him governor of Illyria and recalled General Andoche Junot from that post to his side. But on Fouche's way to his post, Napoleon bade him stop in Prague to confer with Metternich. Metternich used the opportunity of their meeting on July 19 not just to reiterate his terms but to try to induce Fouche to spy for him. Fouche refused, but skipped that whole subject of discussion in his letter to Napoleon. He headed on to Laybach (Ljubljana), Illyria's capital, where he arrived on July 29. It was an extraordinary turnabout for Fouche's fortunes. Now he had a half-way house back to Paris, either to assist a triumphant Napoleon or help overthrow him if he were decisively defeated. In October 1813 Fouche fled Illyria ahead of an Austrian army and made his way to Venice, Milan, and finally Bologna, where a letter from the Emperor caught up with him. Rather than condemn his flight, Napoleon named Fouche his plenipotentiary for Italy. He ordered him first to journey to Naples and talk Murat into fulfilling his request to march to the Po river at the head of 25,000 troops.

That played perfectly into the ambitions of both Fouche and Murat. After arriving on November 29, Fouche bent his head with Murat to develop the budding betrayal. To buy time, he wrote to Napoleon not to worry about a thing, Murat would soon join the campaign. What he did not say, of course, was that Murat would do so not against the Austrians but against Eugene and the kingdom of Italy. Fouche lingered in Naples until December 17, then headed back to Paris via diplomatic assignments Napoleon gave him in Rome, Florence, and Milan. All along the way he spun a web of fellow conspirators who would secretly work for Napoleon's downfall and their own seizure of power. In Lyons he met with Senator Jean Antoine Chaptal, who for years had quietly opposed Napoleon and would be a key player in the network.[44]

Napoleon still had a few diplomatic cards, literally in his hands, to play, although they were of little value. On November 12 he sent his former ambassador to Spain, Antoine Laforest, to open talks with Ferdinand VII, whom he had kept in splendid captivity at Talleyrand's chateau of Valencay since 1808. It took a month of haggling to cut a deal. On December 10 Ferdinand signed the Treaty of Valencay whereby he would be free to return to

Madrid and take the throne in return for peace with France, the withdrawal of Spanish troops from France, pardon for all who had collaborated with the French regime, and the removal of all foreign troops from Spain. Ferdinand hurried off his envoy, Duke San Carlos, to Madrid to present his treaty to the Cortes. Then he and his entourage had their belongings packed and set off on the long road to his capital.

Although Ferdinand was content with the deal, he did not get all he had wanted. As in 1807, he had asked the emperor to marry him to a French princess. That had made no sense for Napoleon then, since he was about to depose the Spanish crown prince, but certainly would advance French interests now, with Ferdinand replacing Joseph on the throne. But when Napoleon raised the notion of Joseph marrying off his daughter Zenaide to Ferdinand, the latter angrily dismissed it, let alone the idea of surrendering his own claim to the throne.

That was not Ferdinand's only disappointment. The Cortes rejected the treaty when San Carlo presented it on February 2, 1814. What's more, the Cortes would not grant Ferdinand the crown unless he accepted the liberal constitution of 1812. Ferdinand refused, and once again was in political limbo.[45]

Napoleon tried the same thing with Pius VII. He journeyed to Fontainebleau to meet with the pope on January 20, 1814, just before he left for his campaign. In return for his freedom to return to Rome, Pius made only one concession: he would allow nominations for French bishops to be automatically approved after six months, if the pope had not decided. Napoleon released Pius on January 22. That gesture did nothing to advance Napoleon's cause—at least on this earthly plane.

Given the military odds against him, Napoleon was well aware that his fate now most likely rested in the hands of the allied powers themselves. And that definitely worried him: "I think it doubtful that the allies are in good faith, and that England wants peace; as for me, I want it, but solid and honorable. . . . I accepted the Frankfort terms but it is probable that the allies have different ideas. . . . Their positions will be based on military events." He felt he could not compromise on the basis of anything less than a France with its "natural frontiers," which would run from the Rhine's west bank to its mouth and include parts of western Switzerland and northwest Italy. Otherwise he feared being overthrown because "there is not a French heart which would not feel disgust . . . and condemn the government which was cowardly enough to sign such a treaty."[46]

Diplomatically all he could do was to send Caulaincourt off to find the allied sovereigns and open talks with them. He did so on January 4, with a detailed list of what he wanted to keep, which included his version of natural borders for France plus Corsica and Elba, and independence for all of Italy north of the kingdom of Naples and west of the Adige river (the duchy of Lucca would remain in Elisa's hands). Austrian territory would begin east of the Adige, but if Metternich insisted on territory west of that river, then France would expand to engulf all of Piedmont, Genoa, and even down the coast to Spezia, with a rump Italian state between the two empires. If the allies demanded that Holland be severed from France, then Caulaincourt was to insist that it be an independent republic. If the allies wanted to split up Italy, then Joseph would get Tuscany.[47]

Caulaincourt reached the Army of Bohemia's advance guard at Luneville on January 6, but was prevented from proceeding. After writing to Metternich for permission, he received a reply saying that he would have to await the latest offer from the sovereigns. Caulaincourt would cool his heels at Luneville for weeks until the allied leaders had hammered out a consensus on their latest vision for peace.

Impatient with the delays, Napoleon wrote Metternich a letter on January 16 asking him to consider the consequences for Austria and Europe's balance of power if France were completely subjected; he implied that Austria might well ultimately lose if Prussia and Russia expanded over Germany and eastern Europe respectively. He then called for an armistice. But, as usual, Napoleon conceded nothing of substance, and Metternich never replied.[48]

At one point during these tense days Napoleon was heard to murmur: "If only Talleyrand were here—he would get me out of this."[49] In reality, only Napoleon could save himself. And that was by immediately and unconditionally accepting the allied terms. He would soon learn just what those terms were.

By mid-January, the four allied leaders—Alexander, Hardenberg, Metternich, and Castlereagh—who would determine the fate of Europe gathered at Langres, France, behind the lines of Schwarzenberg's army. There they reached the latest consensus on their negotiating position. Now they would accept peace only if France was reduced to its 1789 borders.

Yet they differed over other key issues. As for Napoleon, only Metternich would let him retain his crown; the other three wanted him to go, but differed over what to do with him and who would replace him. Obviously, Louis XVIII was the leading, although hardly the sole, contender; Castlereagh and Hardenberg backed his return to Paris. Alexander despised the Bourbons and preferred placing Bernadotte on the throne. But the tsar argued that any candidate had to be popular, or else France would likely suffer the same political convulsions that had ignited the revolutionary wars and eventually brought Napoleon to power. Regardless of whom they eventually chose to replace Napoleon, they first had to remove him from power; but that was just a matter of time and will.

Napoleon faced overwhelming military odds. Against the crumbling remnants of the French empire the allies had mustered nearly a million troops in field armies and rear echelon detachments. Napoleon would command the army blocking the route to Paris targeted by two massive armies marching through eastern France, Blucher's Army of Silesia and Schwarzenberg's Army of Bohemia, whose combined 200,000 troops outnumbered his own 70,000 by nearly two and a half to one. There were six other fronts. A Prussian army led by General Bulow and a British army under General Graham was assigned to conquer the Low Countries defended by General Maison. An Austrian army marched against the upper Rhone valley and Lyon defended by Marshal Augereau. In the southwest, Wellington led his army against Marshal Soult in the Gironde River valley. Of the French empire, only three regions remained defended. Marshal Davout was bottled up in Hamburg by superior allied forces. Marshal Suchet still held out in Barcelona against Spanish forces. Eugene would defend the kingdom of Italy from, eventually, four armies, an Austrian army led by General Heinrich Bellegarde east of the Mincio, an Austrian army led by Laval von Nugent, a Neapolitan army led by King Joachim Murat from south of the Po, and a British and Sicilian army led by William Bentinck from Livorno. Only miracles of Napoleonic diplomacy and arms could defeat that onslaught.[50]

Before departing for the front, Napoleon implemented the regency on January 23, 1814. Theoretically, the most prominent figure "assisting" Marie Louise would be Joseph who, after losing his throne in Spain, would in 1814 watch helplessly as his brother lost his. As a consolation prize to Joseph for renouncing his claim, Napoleon had granted him the title Lieutenant-General of the Empire, with the command of the national guard and the power at regency council meetings to sit beside the empress and guide her reign. But the real power behind that throne—and the fox in the henhouse—would be Talleyrand.[51]

The 1814 Campaign

Napoleon's 1814 campaign opened on January 25 when he left Paris for the front and ended on April 11 when he abdicated. Although he ultimately lost, that campaign is reckoned among his most brilliant. By exploiting interior lines and quick-marching his troops from front to front, he inflicted stinging, although far from decisive, defeats on the two converging, lumbering, larger allied armies led by Schwarzenberg and Blucher. But ultimately he would be overwhelmed by superior numbers along with intercepted orders, hesitant subordinates, and the intrigues of Talleyrand and his coterie in Paris.

Diplomacy played little role in the 1814 campaign. The reason was simple: the allies had decided that Napoleon must go, and to that end they would keep fighting until the deed was done. Caulaincourt was not even allowed to join the allied headquarters, then at Chatillon, until January 23. There he was kept waiting in diplomatic limbo as the leaders planned, negotiated, and intrigued. The formal setting for all that was the Congress of Chatillon, which opened on February 5 and included Count Philip Stadion representing Austria, Baron Wilhelm von Humboldt for Prussia, Count Andreas Razumovsky for Russia, and William Shaw Cathcart, Sir Charles Stewart, and George Hamilton Gordon, the Earl of Aberdeen, for Britain. Two days later the Congress summoned Caulaincourt and allowed him to speak. Knowing that if he presented Napoleon's dream list he would be dismissed, Caulaincourt simply and humbly asked for a France with 1792 borders ruled by Napoleon. They insisted that they would accept nothing more than a France within its 1789 borders, and for now would keep the fate of Napoleon dangling. They implied, however, that Napoleon might save his crown if he immediately bowed to their terms.

Caulaincourt promptly informed the emperor and asked for carte blanche. Perhaps to the emissary's surprise, Napoleon just as promptly granted it. A recent defeat on February 1 at La Rothiere, a few miles from his boyhood military school at Brienne, had plunged him into a deep depression. The allies meanwhile set up a new headquarters at Troyes. There, on February 10, Caulaincourt requested an armistice based on the immediate surrender of the Elbe fortresses and Italian possessions, and acceptance of Napoleon ruling a France with 1789 borders.[52]

The allied leaders, emboldened by battlefield victories and marches ever closer to Paris, rejected any notion of allowing Napoleon to rule, but split over whether to grant an armistice. They debated that issue from February 11 to 14, with Alexander opposed and Metternich, Hardenberg, and Castlereagh in favor. Alexander gave in when Metternich bluffed with a threat to withdraw from the coalition and sign a separate peace. Those debates came as each day couriers galloped up with news of the latest in a string of victories by Napoleon that sent the allied armies reeling in retreat. The monarchs sent Count Paar, an aide of Schwarzenberg, to Napoleon with a request for a brief truce.

Alas, those victories—in which Napoleon won five of six battles in mid-February—went to his head. So, at first he did not reply when Paar appeared with his message on February 17. Instead he fired off a triumphant letter to Caulaincourt telling him to hold out firmly for peace on the basis of the Frankfort Declaration and Napoleon as emperor. He explained his reasoning in a letter to Joseph: "That was the minimum I can accept with honor. . . . If I accepted the old frontier [of 1789], I would have been forced to resort to arms again in a couple of years to regain that land." As for the proposed armistice, Napoleon rejected the notion unless "they were entirely purged from my territory." He boasted that since the enemy was "completely discouraged . . . I hope to be able to make such a peace that every reasonable person would desire, and my desire is to accept nothing less than the Frankfort Declaration."[53]

Napoleon conveyed that same argument in a letter to Francis. Anything less than a France with 1792 borders would lead to "a peace that would not last long" because it would disrupt the "equilibrium of Europe." He tried to play on the divisions within the allied camp and Austrian fears of a more powerful Russia and Prussia. His latest burst of diplomacy did not end there. He had Marie Louise write to her father an emotional appeal asking him "not to force a dishonorable peace on the French people" and "to put yourself in my position, dear papa, and think of me and of my son." Under Metternich's direction, Francis issued a noncommittal reply to both his son-in-law and daughter.[54]

The allies promptly sent Prince Lichtenstein after Napoleon. He caught up to the emperor on February 23. Napoleon patiently listened to the terms—1789 frontiers for France—but held out for 1792. The next day he had Berthier write to Schwarzenberg with suggestions for lines for the armistice. Then, after reaching Troyes on February 24, he sent General Flahault with a formal request for an armistice based on the allies' withdrawal back to Alsace, Lorraine, and Franche Comte, the staging area for their offensive in January. But by now the allies had regained their confidence, regrouped their armies, and were marching once again westward. The chance for an armistice was dead and buried.[55]

That in turn prompted Napoleon to act. On March 2 he sent an aide with his latest instructions to Caulaincourt. This time his envoy was free to cut the best deal possible, as long as it included a France with natural borders and himself as emperor. But he also called for a general peace congress to be attended by all the major and minor European states to settle outstanding international problems after a generation of war. It would be more than a week before he received the latest rejection.[56]

All along, as Napoleon tirelessly marched, fought, planned, improvised, and haggled, he had to keep looking over his shoulder at affairs in Paris. He had left in charge a Regency Council which included only four people upon whom he could reasonably depend: his brother Joseph, Jean de Cambaceres, Henri Clarke, and Marie Louise. But the Council was packed with other people who were conspiring against him and for a Bourbon restoration. With Talleyrand at their head, the conspirators included Duke Francois de Montesquieu, Baron Joseph Louis, Francois Jaucourt, Archbishop Dominique de Pradt, and, especially, Duke Emmerich de Dalberg. Napoleon knew all too well that only his victories checked the ambitions of those men. His fear was that the Council would get cold feet if he were defeated and pull the political rug out from beneath him. French diplomat Nicholas St. Aignan confirmed those fears when he arrived at Troyes on February 24. The emperor "could not count on the spirit of the capital; that they were grumbling over the war's duration, and would like the emperor to seize the first chance to make peace."[57]

For months Talleyrand had been carefully laying the groundwork for Napoleon's overthrow and replacement with himself, either as the head of government or foreign minister. After Leipzig he had pushed his intrigues to a higher level when he sent birthday greetings to Louis XVIII, whose court was then in residence at Hartwell, England. In November 1813 Talleyrand had rejected the emperor's appeal that he return to serve as his foreign minister. Later he wrote of the irony that Napoleon wished "to be reconciled with me at the very moment he had become most suspicious about me."[58] But he did accept a position on the Regency Council, and used his power to pack it with his own men. So he and the royalists would be perfectly placed to welcome back the Bourbons when Napoleon was finally defeated. To the allied headquarters he sent a secret envoy, Baron Eugene de Vitrolles, with a blunt message dictated by him and signed by Dalberg: "You stumble along like children when you must walk forward on stilts. You can do what you want to do. . . . Have confidence."[59]

Napoleon's intransigence and Talleyrand's intrigues stiffened the will of the allied leaders to, literally, stick to their guns. Napoleon received word on March 8 that the allies were dead set to depose him and were writing that goal into a treaty. Indeed, under the Treaty of Chaumont, which the allies signed on March

9 but backdated to March 1, each vowed to keep 150,000 troops in the field until they had crushed Napoleon, and then retain 60,000 troops each to keep the peace; Britain promised to subsidize that crusade with five million pounds sterling.

After defeating Blucher in series of battles during the first week of March, the Emperor hoped to deliver the coup de grace at Laon on March 9. But Blucher's army swelled with reinforcements and subsequently drove Napoleon's puny force from the field. Yet despite that—or, more likely, because of it—Napoleon continued to act as though victory in his campaign was only a matter of time. On March 15 he sent word to Caulaincourt that he would accept nothing less than his personal rule over a France with 1792 borders, Eugene as the king of Italy in a realm whose eastern border was the Adige and included the Ionian Islands, and his sister Elisa in her continued reign over Lucca and Piombino, as well as the restoration to their respective thrones of his faithful allies the king of Saxony and the duke of Berg, whom the coalition had deposed. But he was still willing to compromise.

He issued that demand atop not only his own mixed record of minor victories and defeats but amid word mostly of routs and retreats on other fronts. Wellington's army was advancing deeper into southwestern France, having defeated Soult at Orthez on February 27, captured Bordeaux on March 12 after another uprising declared for Louis XVIII, and marched up the Gironde valley toward Toulouse, which he would seize on April 10. Bulow and Graham had scattered the Low Countries' defenders by April 1. In Italy Eugene initially displayed superior skill against his converging enemies. He crossed the Mincio and defeated Bellegarde, but then had to turn and race westward against Nugent, who had taken Parma and crossed the Po at Piacenza; Nugent retreated back across the Po. Bentinck captured Livorno on March 9, then sailed on to take Genoa on April 9. Elsewhere Augereau sat immobile around Lyon while Suchet and Davout clung to Barcelona and Hamburg, respectively, as enemy forces swelled around them.

As for the turncoat Murat, he sent word on January 21 to Eugene that he would not attack him without warning, and even after he officially issued a war declaration on February 15 he remained south of the Po. Yet his very presence forced Eugene to withdraw from the Adige to the Mincio. Napoleon nurtured a false hope that should Eugene be defeated, the subsequent conflict over who got what in Italy might well lead to war. Indeed, there were tensions among the allies. Bentinck had warned Murat to evacuate Tuscany and issued a call for Italian unification, presumably under British protection. To exacerbate that diplomatic tug-of-war, Napoleon had Joseph write to Murat and Caroline separate letters condemning them for their "iniquitous conduct," but offering to reaccept them into the French and family camps. Then he decreed on March 10 that the Papal States would revert to the Catholic Church. That could do nothing to help his own lost cause, but would sow dissent among the allies as Vienna, Rome, and Naples tussled over the territory.[60]

His setbacks pressured Napoleon to send secret instructions to Caulaincourt on March 19 to concede, if need be, Belgium and the Saarland, as long as France kept Antwerp, Mainz, and Alessandria. However, Cossacks captured that courier with Napoleon's diplomatic game plan. He also sent word to Eugene to strike a deal with Murat for all of Italy south of the Po in return for an alliance.

But it was far too late for all that. Caulaincourt had already written up Napoleon's latest instructions into a draft treaty of twenty-nine articles, which he presented to the allies on March 15. Three days later they not only rejected his proposal but terminated the negotiations. A stunned Caulaincourt had no choice but to hurry back to Napoleon.

Napoleon himself suffered a decisive defeat at the hands of Schwarzenberg in the two-day battle of Arcis-sur-Aube on March 20 and 21. Adding salt to those wounds, Caulaincourt finally caught up to Napoleon on the evening of March 24 and presented the bad news that talks had ended. An enraged emperor retorted that if the allies were determined to destroy him, he had nothing to lose but to fight to the bitter end. He clung to the delusions that had plagued him since his 1812 war against Russia: "If I win a battle, as I am sure I will, I will be the master of demanding the best conditions. . . . I have prepared everything and victory will not elude me." After venting a portion of his rage and delusions, a bit of the overwhelming reality re-intruded; he quietly admitted: "I lost everything at Arcis."[61]

Indeed he had, or nearly so. After routing Napoleon, Schwarzenberg marched westward and joined forces with Blucher before Paris on March 29. Learning of that advance, Napoleon dispatched Caulaincourt to Paris to urge the Regency Council to hold out until he could come to their rescue. Caulaincourt would get there just in time to witness the allies march triumphantly into the capital and a provisional government led by Talleyrand vote to depose Napoleon. Caulaincourt then galloped off to Fontainebleau with news of that latest catastrophe.[62]

What caused that finale? As the allied juggernaut neared Paris, Joseph convened the Regency Council on March 28 and presented February 8 and

March 16 letters from Napoleon instructing him to convey the queen, heir, and government to safety westward if the enemy threatened the capital. Joseph entrusted the defense of Paris to marshals Auguste Marmont and Adolphe Mortier, and, if need be, the terms of its surrender. He then fled with Marie Louise and her son, along with most of the rest of the government, for Blois in the Loire valley.[63]

Although Marmont and Mortier rallied their men and repelled the initial allied attack on March 30, the enemy's capture of Paris was only a matter of days. On March 31 Marmont negotiated with Count Alexis Orlov, the tsar's envoy, a ceasefire and the handover of Paris to the allies.

For half a dozen years Talleyrand had been waiting for just such an opportunity to take power; he made the most of it. That evening Talleyrand greeted the monarchs as they marched at the head of their armies into Paris, and even invited into his home Alexander and his entourage. The following day, on April 1, Talleyrand got the Senate to convene and name him the president of a provisional government; in so doing, they effectively deposed Napoleon. Then, on April 2, President Talleyrand and the Senate deprived Napoleon of his command over the army. The final act came the next day when the Senate declared that Napoleon was stripped of all powers because he "had violated his oath and criminally violated the rights of the people."

Napoleon was then at Fontainebleau with the remnants of his army. Upon learning of these events from Caulaincourt, he played his last diplomatic card. On April 4 he signed a statement that he was willing to abdicate in favor of his son: "The powers having declared that the Emperor Napoleon was the sole obstacle to the reestablishment of peace in Europe, the Emperor Napoleon, faithful to his oath, declares that he is ready to descend from the throne, leave France, and even give his life for the good of his country, inseparable from the rights of his son and that of the regency."[64] He then returned Caulaincourt along with marshals Ney and Macdonald to Paris with that pledge.

That provoked the latest debate among the allied leaders. Alexander was the most intrigued with the idea. He despised the Bourbons as effete, inept, and corrupt, and feared that if they retook power they would sooner or later provoke another revolution and round of wars with Europe.

Once again Talleyrand took the lead in guiding a decision. He convinced the allied leaders that the Bonapartes had to be purged from France and the Bourbons installed in their place. He then got the Senate on April 6 to vote for a slightly revised version of the 1791 Constitution, one which established a constitutional monarchy, and then issue a declaration that "The French people freely call to the throne of France Louis-Stanislaus Xavier of France, brother of the last King—and after him the other members of the House of Bourbon in the old order."

The key diplomatic question for the allies now was what to do with the man they had finally defeated. The options ranged from executing to freeing him. Caulaincourt pressed them to grant Napoleon rule over Corsica, Sardinia, or Corfu. Alexander devised the eventual compromise of letting him rule the much smaller island of Elba off Italy's west coast.

The three envoys returned with their bad news to Napoleon. Numb after years of disasters and stress, he took it quietly. He asked Caulaincourt to draft a treaty and take it back to the allies. Caulaincourt did so, and then spent several days haggling with Metternich, Hardenberg, Nesselrode, and Castlereagh over the details. Each signed the Treaty of Abdication at Talleyrand's home on April 11. The declaration itself was straightforward enough: "The allied powers having proclaimed that the Emperor Napoleon was the sole obstacle to the reestablishment of peace in Europe, the Emperor Napoleon, faithful to his oath, declares that he will renounce for himself and his descendants the thrones of France and Italy, and that there is not a single personal sacrifice, including even his life, that he is unwilling to make for the interests of France."[65]

It was the elaborate side agreement that took so long to negotiate. Essentially, the allies and provisional French government agreed to give Napoleon and his family a golden parachute for their forced retirement. In return for surrendering any claim to rule France, Napoleon could retain his imperial title and was given the island of Elba to rule along with an annual stipend of two million francs from France. His wife Marie Louise would annually receive one million and the Italian duchies of Parma, Piacenza, and Gustalla on the nearby mainland. The other Bonapartes also received yearly stipends, including 500,000 francs each for Joseph, Jerome, and Madame Mere, 400,000 for Hortense, 300,000 for Elisa and Pauline, and 200,000 for Louis; Eugene would receive "a suitable realm" outside France. The provisional French government promptly ratified the treaty.[66]

Although all the allied leaders, including Alexander, had varying degrees of doubts about the deal they had cut, they also had what appeared to be good political reasons for going through with it. The treaty swiftly got rid of Napoleon and allowed the leaders to concentrate on beginning the complex, controversial, and ultimately impossible mission of purging liberalism and nationalism from Europe so as to restore the continent to the political and ideological conditions that had prevailed before 1789.

For the present, Napoleon was philosophical about his downfall. To Caulaincourt he remarked: "I am not holding on to power. Born a soldier, I can without pitying myself once again become a civilian."[67] That vision of simple retirement would not last long.

He had some parting advice for his successors: "If the Bourbons are wise, they will change only the sheets on my bed: they will give employment to the men whom I have trained. Their followers are nothing but passions and grudges with clothes on. With men such as those, they can do nothing unless it is reactionary and they will ruin themselves."[68] That view was prescient.

Napoleon viewed his official abdication as a temporary expedient. He was well aware that it was the best deal possible under the circumstances. He understood the hatred and desire for vengeance among most of his enemies and how many advocated that he be executed or exiled to a distant prison far from Europe. For now he would lie low and wait while the national interests which the allies had set aside to defeat their common enemy reemerged and split them bitterly apart once again. Then perhaps he could make one last lunge for power over France.

That made political sense. But the enormity of his defeat plunged him into a deep depression. On the night of April 13 he penned a suicide note to his beloved Marie Louise: "I love you more than anyone else in the world. My misfortunes hurt me only because of the pain they cause you. Love your most tender husband always. Give a kiss to my son."[69] On a cord around his neck was a vial of poison he had carried since the Russian campaign. He put the vial to his lips and drained its contents. But the poison had lost its potency and merely made him severely sick; he would live another half dozen years.

During those years he would once again briefly bring mass death to Europe. And all along he would have to mull a lifetime of great achievements overshadowed by blunders, crimes, delusions, and crushing defeats.

Chapter Six Endnotes: Imperial Collapse

1. Paul R. Sweet, *Wilhelm von Humboldt: A Biography*, 2 vols. (Columbus: Ohio State University, 1980), 2:120.

2. Frederick William to Napoleon, December 31, 1812, Leon Lecestre, ed., *Lettres Personelles des Souverains a l'Emperor Napoleon I* (Paris: Plon, 1939), 387; Napoleon to King

of Saxony, January 22, 1813, Claude Tchou, ed., *Correspondance de Napoleon Ier* (hereafter cited as *Correspondence*), 16 vols. (Paris: Bibliotheque des Introuvables, 2002), 19481.

3. Napoleon to Francis, December 14, 1812, *Correspondence*, 19385.

4. Response to the Senate, December 20, 1812, *Correspondence*, 19389; Response to the State Council, December 20, 1812, *ibid.*, 19390; Presentation to the legislative Corps, February 14, 1813, *ibid.*, 19581.

5. For just a sampling, see: Notes to the Finance Council, December 22, 1812, *Correspondence*, 19391; Napoleon to Clark, January 4, 1813, *ibid.*, 19416; Napoleon to Berthier, January 9, 1812, *ibid.*, 19437; Napoleon to Eugene, January 24, 1812, *ibid.*, 19500; Napoleon to Mollien, February 27, 1813, *ibid.*, 19621.

6. Duff Cooper, *Talleyrand* (New York: Grove Press, 1932), 212.

7. Napoleon to Jerome, January 18, March 2, 1813, *Correspondence*, 19462, 19648.

8. Napoleon to Jerome, March 12, 1812, *Correspondence*, 19706; Napoleon to Catherine, Westphalian queen, March 17, 1813, *ibid.*, 19726.

9. Napoleon to Pius, December 31, 1812, *Correspondence*, 19402.

10. Concordat of 1813, *Correspondence*, 19511.

11. Napoleon to Francis, April 13, 1813, *Correspondence*, 19859; Napoleon to Marie Louise, April 7, 1813, Louis Madelin, ed., *Lettres Inedites de Napoleon I a Marie Louise* (Paris: Editions des Bibliotheque Nationales de France, 1935), 135; Francis to Napoleon, April 26, 1813, Jean Hanoteau, ed., *Lettres Personelles des Souverains a l'Emperor Napoleon* (Paris: Plon, 1939), 97-101.

12. Napoleon to Prince Lebrun, April 7, 1813, *Correspondence*, 19820; Napoleon to Francis, April 13, 1813, *ibid.*, 19859; Napoleon to Frederick, Wurttemberg king, April 24, 1813, *Correspondence*, 19902.

13. Meeting of the Emperor with Metternich, June 23, 1813, *Correspondence*, 20175.

14. Unless otherwise noted, military details for the 1813 campaign were gleaned from David Chandler, *The Campaigns of Napoleon: The Mind and Method of History's Greatest Soldier* (New York: Macmillan, 1966); J.P. Riley, *Napoleon and the World War of 1813: Lessons in Coalition War Fighting* (London: Frank Cass, 2000); Michael V. Leggiere, *Napoleon and Berlin: The Franco-Prussia War in North Germany, 1813* (Norman: University of Oklahoma Press, 2002).

15. Napoleon to Melzi, January 4, 1813, *Correspondence*, 19420; Napoleon to Caroline, January 4, 1813, *ibid.*, 19421; Napoleon to Frederick VI, Danish king, January 5, 1813, *ibid.*, 19424; Napoleon to Frederick Augustus, Saxon king, January 22, 1813, *ibid.*, 19481; Napoleon to Frederick, Wurttemberg king, March 2, 1813, *ibid.*, 19650; Napoleon to Maximilien Joseph, Bavarian king, March 2, 1813, *ibid.*, 19651; Napoleon to Ferdinand Joseph, Wurzburg grand duke, March 2, 1813, 19652.

16. Napoleon to Eugene, March 9, 15, 1813, *ibid.*, *Correspondence*, 19688, 9721.

17. Bulletin of the Grand Army, May 2, 24, 1813, *Correspondence*, 19951, 20042.

18. Napoleon to Francis, May 17, 1813, *Correspondence*, 20019.

19. Richard Mowat, *The Diplomacy of Napoleon* (London: Edward Arnold, 1924), 277-78.

20. Napoleon to Caulaincourt, May 26, June 1 (2 letters), 2, 3, 1813, *Correspondence*, 20052, 20066, 20067, 20069, 20072.

21. Napoleon to Caulaincourt, June 4, 1813, *Correspondence*, 20083.

22. Fain's Account of a Meeting with the Emperor, June 23, 1813, *Correspondence*, 20175.

23. Clement Wenceslas Lothaire, prince de Metternich, *Memoires, Documents, Ecrits Divers Laisses par le Prince de Metternich*, 8 vols. (Paris: Plon, 1880-84), 2:462-63.

24. Napoleon to Francis, June 30, 1813, *Correspondence*, 20198.

25. Castlereagh to Cathcart, July 5, 1813, Charles K. Webster, ed., *British Diplomacy, 1813-1815: Select Documents Dealing with the Reconstruction of Europe* (London: G. Bell, 1921), 6-10.

26. Napoleon to Narbonne, August 5, 1813, *Correspondence*, 20330. For a more systematic condemnation of Austria, see Observations, August 14, 1813, *ibid.*, 20376; Note by the Emperor, August 17, 1813, *ibid.*, 20395.

27. Henry Kissinger, *A World Restored: Metternich, Castlereagh, and the Problems of Peace, 1812-22* (London: Weidenfeld & Nicolson, 1957), 81.

28. Kissinger, *World Restored*, 82.

29. Napoleon to Clarke, August 18, 1813, *Correspondence*, 20410.

30. On the General Situation of My Affairs, August 30, 1813, *Correspondence*, 20492; Bulletin of the Grand Army, October 15, 1813, *ibid.*, 20813.

31. Bulletin of the Grand Army, October 24, 1813, *Correspondence*, 20830; Observations of the Emperor, November 3, 1813, *ibid.*, 20850.

32. Louis Constant, *Memoires Intimes de Napoleon I par Constant son Valet de Chambre* (Paris: Mercure de France, 1967), 2:411; Napoleon to Caulaincourt, December 18, 1813, *Correspondence*, 21018.

33. Napoleon to Metternich, December 1, 1813, *Correspondence*, 20956.

34. Frankfort Declaration, December 1, 1813, in Michel Kerautret, ed., *Les Grand Traites de l'Empire* (Paris: Nouvelle Monde Editions/Fondation Napoleon, 2004), 97-98.

35. Constant, *Memoires*, 2:363.

36. Napoleon to Clarke, November 10, 11, 16, 28, December 24, 25, 1813, *Correspondence*, 20874, 20880, 20898, 20948, 21033, 21035; Instructions for General d'Anthoudard, November 20, 1813, *ibid.*, 20928; Observations on the 1814 Budget, November 26, 1813, *ibid.*, 20947; Napoleon to Montalivet, December 17, 1813, *ibid.*, 21015; Decree for a Levee en Masse, January 4, 1814, *ibid.*, 21061.

37. Constant, *Memoires*, 2:392-93; Emperor to the Legislative Corps, December 19, 1813, *Correspondence*, 21021.

38. Emperor to Senate, December 30, 1813, *Correspondence*, 21053.

39. Constant, *Memoires*, 2:659, 396-408.

40. Owen Connelly, *Napoleon's Satellite Kingdoms* (New York: The Free Press, 1965), 304.

41. Jean Tulard, *Joseph Fouche* (Paris: Fayard, 1998), 287.

42. Murat to Napoleon, January 14, 1814, Archive Nationale, 31, Archive Politique, 20 (300).

43. Napoleon to Fouche, February 13, 1814, *Correspondence*, 21239.

44. Tulard, *Fouche*, 269-75, 283-93.

45. Napoleon to Maret, November 12, 1813, Leon Lecestres, ed., *Lettres Inedites de Napoleon Ier* (Paris: Plon, 1897), 2:295; Napoleon to Ferdinand, November 12, 1813, *Lettres Inedites de Napoleon*, 2:296; Roederer to Joseph, December 3 and 5, 1813, A.M. Roederer, ed., *Oeuvres du Comte P.L. Roederer*, 8 vols. (Paris: Firmin, Didot Freres, 1853-59), 3:584-85.

46. Napoleon to Caulaincourt, January 4, 1814, *Correspondence*, 21062.

47. Napoleon to Caulaincourt, January 4, 1814, *Correspondence*, 21063.

48. Napoleon to Metternich, January 16, 1814, *Correspondence*, 21101.

49. Cooper, *Talleyrand*, 217.

50. Note on France's Present Situation, January 12, 1814, *Correspondence*, 21089.

51. Napoleon to Joseph, January 24, 1814, *Correspondence*, 21134.

52. Napoleon to Caulaincourt, February 4, 5, 1814, *Correspondence*, 21178, 21179.

53. Napoleon to Caulaincourt, February 17, 19, 1814, *Correspondence*, 21285, 21315; Napoleon to Joseph, February 18, 1814, *Ibid.*, 21293.

54. Napoleon to Francis, February 21, 1814, *Correspondence*, 21344; Alan Palmer, *Napoleon and Marie Louise: The Emperor's Second Wife* (New York: St. Martin's Press, 2001), 164-65; Francis to Napoleon, February 27, 1814, *Lettres Personelles des Souverains a l'Emperor Napoleon*, 115-18.

55. Instruction to General Flahault, February 24, 1814, *Correspondence*, 21359; Berthier to Schwarzenberg, February 26, 1814, *ibid.*, 21344.

56. Napoleon to Caulaincourt, March 2, 1814, *Correspondence*, 21407.

57. Constant, *Memoires*, 2:438.

58. Emile Dard, *Napoleon and Talleyrand* (New York: D. Appleton and Company, 1937), 285-86.

59. Emmanuel de Waresquiel, *Talleyrand, Le Prince Immobile* (Paris: Fayard, 2003), 437.

60. Napoleon to Joseph, February 26, 1814, *Correspondence*, 21381; Hubert Cole, *The Betrayers: Joachim and Caroline Murat* (New York: Saturday Evening Press, 1972), 204.

61. Constant, *Memoires*, 2:448, 682.

62. Napoleon to Caulaincourt, March 31, 1814, *Correspondence*, 21546.

63. Napoleon to Joseph, February 8, March 16, 1814, *Correspondence*, 21210, 21497.

64. Declaration, April 4, 1814, *Correspondence*, 21555.

65. Act of Abdication, April 11, 1814, *Correspondence*, 21558.

66. Act of Abdication, April 11, 1814, *Correspondence*, 21558.

67. Constant, *Memoires*, 2:688.

68. Jean Hanoteau, ed., *No Peace With Napoleon!: Concluding the Memoirs of General de Caulaincourt, Duke of Vicenza* (New York: William Morrow, 1936), 192.

69. Napoleon to Marie Louise, April 19, 1814, *Correspondence*, 21560. For a discussion of the different versions of just when and how Napoleon tried to kill himself, see Constant, *Memoires*, 2:691-92.

Denouement

1814-1821

*"True conquests—the only ones which leave no regret—
are those made over ignorance."*

"Time overthrows all empires. . . . Glory or death is my destiny."

"In my retirement I will substitute the pen for the sword."

"It is but a step from the sublime to the ridiculous."

"Six feet of earth is good enough for a man."

—Napoleon Bonaparte

Push and Pull

Napoleon practiced very little diplomacy in the last half dozen years of his life. He had virtually no international contacts during his nine months' sojourn on Elba or his fleeting hundred days' comeback as head of France once again. Nor could he offer more than bitter complaints as he suffered various indignities at the hands of Governor Hudson Lowe, his sadistic jailor on St.

Helena. Nonetheless, if he offered no significant diplomatic initiatives of his own, he certainly provoked them in others.

It was the sheer weight of the Russian tsar's personality and the national power behind him that bent his allies to grudgingly accept his proposal to send Napoleon to rule Elba rather than imprison him on a far more remote island or place him against a wall with a blindfold over his eyes. The deal was no sooner signed than everyone, including the tsar, began to regret that decision. It was the impression that they were about to act on those second thoughts that would convince Napoleon that he had nothing to lose by sailing back to France.

So why then did the allies agree on Elba? It was a classic compromise that initially dissatisfied and eventually unnerved nearly everyone. The other leaders essentially held their noses when they signed off on Napoleon's comfortable retirement while Alexander did the same for Louis XVIII's ascendance to the French throne. Each tried to justify those choices by examining the larger diplomatic picture. France was deeply and bitterly divided. Although the emperor's popularity had plummeted after three years of devastating defeats, he still had a fervent core of supporters. Meanwhile, few people would enthusiastically welcome the Bourbons back to power. Thus it made much more political sense to make Napoleon a minor figurehead rather than a martyr. In all, it was believed that a conciliatory rather than a punitive peace would be more likely to endure.

Tragedy came when the allies refused to live up to their end of the deal. A gross failure of allied diplomacy made the Hundred Days all but inevitable. What they did was essentially to leave the cage unlocked while tormenting its occupant. Would Napoleon have flown the coop had his wife and son been allowed to join him in his retirement? Would he have stayed put had Louis XVIII not broken the Treaty of Fontainebleau that bound Paris to grant the ex-emperor an annual two million franc stipend? And what about all that quite serious talk among the great powers at Vienna—that filtered back to Elba—of revoking their deal, stripping Napoleon of his sinecure, and shipping him off to the ends of the earth?

Those were the most serious offenses. Then there were the lesser but still painful affronts. His fellow sovereigns refused to reply to his letters. Even worse were the agonizing rumors that Colonel Adam von Neipperg, whom Francis had assigned as Marie Louise's escort, had become her lover. Marie Louise's letters to Napoleon became less frequent and more emotionally distant until she stopped writing altogether.[1]

Finally, there were the increasingly bitter divisions among the great powers themselves. The heady triumph of marching into Paris and vanquishing Napoleon dissipated when the allied leaders reconvened at Vienna to settle a quarter century of revolutions and wars that had ravaged Europe. Without a common enemy they resorted to intriguing against one another. Austria and Prussia bickered over the fate of Germany in general and Saxony in particular; Russia, Prussia, and Austria over Poland; Austria, Britain, and France over who would rule Naples; Russia and Austria over the Balkans; Austria, Prussia, Russia, and Britain over whether to bow to Talleyrand's persistence that they welcome France into their great-power club.

Indeed, at one tense point the five nearly came to blows when the Prussians defied the others and insisted that they would annex Saxony. On January 3, 1815, Castlereagh, Metternich, and Talleyrand signed a secret treaty in which each pledged to field 150,000 troops against Prussia if it did not accept their compromise over Saxony. After several weeks of hard bargaining, the five great powers worked out a grand deal that embraced Saxony, Poland, Hanover, and Pomerania.

The clash of rival bloated egos exacerbated that clash of rival empires. The stage became quite cramped for the likes of Alexander, Metternich, and Talleyrand, to name the most spectacular vanities. Not only was each an unrepentant scene-stealer, but some, such as Metternich, even vied for his rivals' mistresses. Perhaps Friedrich von Gentz put it best with his reaction to the interactions between his boss Metternich and Talleyrand: "I sensed as never before the futility of human endeavor, the failings of men who hold the fate of the world in their hands . . . the fine-sounding nonsense of these gentlemen enveloped my mind in a fog of unreality."[2]

Given all that, it is hardly surprising that from Elba those divisions appeared to be devouring the coalition. What Napoleon could not see or refused to see was that the Congress of Vienna was actually astonishingly successful. The great powers cut relatively cordial and swift deals on most crucial issues, including the fate of France, the Netherlands, Spain, Italy, Sweden, and Piedmont-Sardinia. Likewise, the occasional temper tantrum over an unwanted compromise or tug-of-war over a coquette was soon diluted in the nearly non-stop swirl of exhilarating if exhausting social events, including balls, banquets, concerts, hunts, excursions, and seductions, from the time the first delegates began to gather in Vienna in September 1814 until the appropriately named Final Act in June 1815.

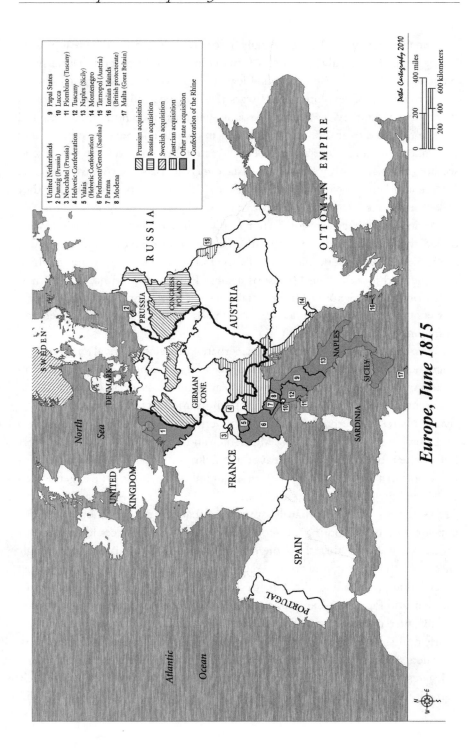

1 United Netherlands
2 Danzig (Prussia)
3 Neuchâtel (Prussia)
4 Helvetic Confederation
5 Valais
  (Helvetic Confederation)
6 Piedmont/Genoa (Sardinia)
7 Parma
8 Modena
9 Papal States
10 Lucca
11 Piombino (Tuscany)
12 Tuscany
13 Naples (Sicily)
14 Montenegro
15 Tarnopol (Austria)
16 Ionian Islands
   (British protectorate)
17 Malta (Great Britain)

Prussian acquisition
Russian acquisition
Swedish acquisition
Austrian acquisition
Other state acquisition
Confederation of the Rhine

Europe, June 1815

The great powers may have determined Europe's fate, but they rarely lost sight of the reality that they were acting out both the substance and style of their diplomacy before a live and quite critical audience. In all, five monarchs, 216 princes, and hundreds of lesser nobles and others attended part or all of the Congress of Vienna. Representatives of Europe's host of smaller states were there not just for a good time but to lend their voices to issues that directly affected them, as well as eventually to rubber-stamp the decisions made by the Big Five.

Rumors of discord came to Elba not just from Vienna. The word was that Louis XVIII and his court were rapidly alienating ever more people in Paris and beyond. Here again, Napoleon and his followers heard what they wanted to hear.

Bourbon rule was actually quite mild, despite the fire-breathing rhetorical cries for vengeance by a few hotheaded ultra-royalists such as the king's brother, Charles, Count Artois, or the king's closest advisor, Pierre, Count Blacas. The Charter that Louis had granted France and his policies were actually less repressive than those of his predecessor. After taking the throne, the king authorized no purges or confiscations against those who had benefited from the revolution. And above all, the nation was finally at peace. Yet most soldiers and republicans chafed under the new order, more from hurt pride than anything substantial. Word of their ever more bitter complaints reached Elba.

The ultimate reason for Napoleon's decision to return was rooted in his own psyche. Under any circumstances it would have been virtually impossible for anyone with his insatiable intelligence, energy, and ambitions to stay put on such a tiny island with so little to do and so little power to wield. After stepping ashore on Elba as its emperor on May 4, 1814, he engaged in a whirlwind of political, economic, and social reforms; but it did not take him long to exhaust the possibilities. As he later put it to Emmanuel de Las Cases on St. Helena, "when you are on a small island, once you have set in motion the machinery of civilization, there is nothing left to do but perish from boredom or to get away from it by some heroic venture."[3]

But it was not just boredom and claustrophobia that pushed him toward France. He sought somehow to make amends for his succession of stupid decisions, especially toward Spain and Russia, that had cost him his throne and shattered the lives or limbs of a million less fortunate others. He would return to Paris with promises of peace, prosperity, and liberty for all.

The decisive pull came on February 15 when a man posing as an Italian sailor was secretly ushered before Napoleon. He was actually Fleury de

Chaboulon, with a message from former foreign minister Hugues Maret. The time had come for the emperor to return to his rightful throne. If he did so, the French people would enthusiastically welcome him back. Over the next eleven days Napoleon and his followers busied themselves plotting their escape to France.

His timing made tactical rather than strategic sense. He waited until Colonel Neil Campbell, his genial but perceptive British minder, had departed for the mainland for a week or so to visit his mistress. For all the allied nightmares of Napoleon reappearing on the throne of France, Campbell was the only one of the four commissioners who had escorted him from Paris to Portoferraio to linger on Elba and ensure he did not escape. Campbell would be embarrassed but not surprised when he got word of what had happened; he had seen it coming for some time. As early as November 1814 he had warned Castlereagh: "If pecuniary difficulties press upon him so as to prevent his vanity from being satisfied by the ridiculous establishment of a Court . . . in Elba, I think he is capable of crossing over."[4]

But had the emperor waited a few weeks, the Congress of Vienna itself would have broken up after the representatives had signed or shaken hands over the last flurry of treaties and secret deals, with each leader returning to his own realm. That would have delayed any sort of coordinated response to Napoleon's return for perhaps a crucial month or so more. And that might have meant the difference between his gamble's ultimate failure and success.

The Hundred Days

Napoleon's last tragic mass waste of lives and wealth began as a mixed version of "Don Quixote" and "The Mouse That Roared." On the morning of February 26 the emperor and 1,026 other men, including 650 Old Guard grenadiers and 108 Polish lancers, packed themselves aboard three small ships and set sail for the Riviera. Even if everything else would go disastrously wrong, his proclamation to his followers was at least prescient: "I have taken into account the surprise that will seize on men, the state of public feeling, the resentment against the allies, the love of my soldiers, in time all the Napoleonic elements that still germinate in our beautiful France. I shall reach Paris without firing a shot."[5]

Four days later, on March 1, Napoleon led his men ashore at Frejus. His first step in trying to win back the French people, along with his former officials, officers, and soldiers, was to distribute a notice explaining why he had returned and what he hoped to do. His declaration "To the French People" condemned all the disruptions and betrayals since he had lost power, reminded them of the plebiscites by which they had elected him to rule over them and of the glory that he had brought them when he led France, and asked them to accept him again as their emperor. The language was typically Napoleonesque: "French people, in my exile I have heard your complaints and your desires. You will reclaim a government of your choice, which can only be legitimate. . . . You have asked me to sacrifice my retirement and return for the grand interest of the country. . . . France is but a single nation. . . . It is to you and the army alone that I make and will remake glory in all my power." He issued a similar declaration to the army: "Soldiers, we have been conquered. . . . In my exile I have heard your voices. I have arrived after having traversed all obstacles and perils. Your general, called to the throne by the choice of the people, gives himself to you. Come and join him. . . . Come and rally beneath the flags of your commander. His existence is inseparable from yours; his interest, his honor, his glory and yours are one."[6]

The second step in his return to power was literal. He made a key decision to head for Paris via the mountainous, sparsely populated and garrisoned eastern route rather than up the Rhone valley. Had he done otherwise he most likely would have faced swift extinction. But instead he sidestepped the thousands of troops already stationed there along with the tens of thousands more who would be sent down that valley after the word reached Paris that he had landed.

The turning point in Napoleon's bid for power could not have been more dramatic or poignant. On the morning of March 7 he and his men marched onto the windswept Laffey Pass a dozen miles south of Grenoble. Awaiting them with loaded muskets was the 5th Regiment.

Napoleon deployed his own troops, then strode confidently down the road between the two forces. Well within musket shot he stopped, looked up and down the ranks before him, opened his greatcoat, and shouted:

"I am your emperor. If there is a single soldier who wants to kill his emperor, here I am!"

"Vive l'empereur!" someone cried, echoed by countless others. The men broke ranks and surged joyfully around him.[7]

Word of the 5th Regiment's defection spread swiftly. Ever more regiments greeted Napoleon with ecstatic cheers and swelled his ranks, turning his trek to Paris into a triumphal procession. Those who had opposed his return to power either fled Paris or remained silent. Later, on St. Helena, when he was asked what was his happiest time, Napoleon replied, "The march from Cannes to Paris."[8]

How could the new Bourbon regime have been uprooted so easily? The news that Napoleon was back on French soil first reached Paris on March 5. Louis XVIII ordered his war minister, Marshal Nicolas Soult, to capture or kill the upstart and his followers. Soult sent couriers galloping to muster the kingdom's army and gave the field command to Marshal Michel Ney. Both Soult and Ney had initially intended to do their duty; indeed, Ney swore he would bring the rebel back in an iron cage. Yet over the following days the power of Napoleon's charisma, reports of ever more defecting regiments, contempt for the effete, haughty Bourbons, and the fear of being on history's wrong side ate away at them both. Eventually they quietly let it be known that they too would welcome back their former commander. Ney embraced Napoleon at Auxerre on March 17; Soult would greet him in Paris.

So, with that ever more powerful political storm surging toward them, Louis and his court packed into a cavalcade of carriages and fled on March 20. They did not stop running until they reached Ghent, well behind the lines of allied troops and, if need be, with easy access to fast vessels that could sail them to safety in England.

The shocking news that Napoleon was missing from Elba first reached Vienna on March 6. Where could he have gone, and what did he plan to do? That question was partly answered on March 11 when the ever more worried delegates learned that he had landed in France. The great powers' first collective act was to declare Napoleon an international outlaw on March 13. As word of ever more defections reached Vienna, they renewed, on March 25, the Treaty of Chaumont that committed each to fielding 150,000 troops to crush Napoleon. Their hopes that the French army would hunt him down died on March 28 when word arrived that Louis had escaped to his latest exile and Napoleon was back in power. The allies then threw themselves into planning the diplomatic and military strategy for crushing Napoleon once again and for all time.

Napoleon, meanwhile, was trying to consolidate his rule and avert a war. He swiftly acted on his promises that he would restore the revolution's ideals and French glory. To that end he busied himself reorganizing France politically and mobilizing it against the all-but-inevitable allied onslaught. He had done a lot of soul searching during his long months in exile, and was sincere in his intention to devote his rule to liberty, peace, and prosperity. He even abolished slavery on March 29, because it was morally and philosophically the right thing to do, not because it would win him any extra support.[9]

As for a government, he formed a State Council with Armand Caulaincourt heading the ministry of foreign affairs, Lazare Carnot interior, Jean Cambaceres justice, Martin Gaudin finance, Hugues Maret state, Louis Davout war, Denis Decres navy, and Joseph Fouche police, along with his brothers Joseph and Jerome as advisors. He charged liberal Benjamin Constant with drafting a constitution that provided for civil liberties and a two-house parliament. A plebiscite would later ratify the constitution with an official vote of 1,532,357 for and only 4,802 against.[10]

That lackluster turnout reflected the general attitude toward Napoleon's return to power. While few people had supported the Bourbons, not many more were eager to embrace the man who had brought such devastation to France. Most adopted a nervous wait-and-see attitude. They hoped for the best but feared the worst. Those fears would soon be tragically realized, first with civil and then international war. The announcement of conscription once again provoked the Vendee to revolt. The 20,000 troops that Napoleon diverted to crush that rebellion might have overwhelmed Wellington at Waterloo. In contrast, the junta that took over Corsica and demanded autonomy was dispersed peacefully and rule by Paris was reestablished.[11]

While the emperor's sincere attempts to provide France with a government that was at once strong and just were commendable, he made several extremely poor choices to man it. The most notorious was recalling Joseph Fouche as police minister; Fouche immediately began using his powers to undermine and destroy Napoleon. Just as wrong-headed were his tappings of Louis Davout as war minister, Louis Suchet to command the Army of the Alps, and Michel Ney and Emmanuel de Grouchy to command the wings of the army he would lead against the British and Prussians in Belgium. What was wrong with those choices? Davout and Suchet were outstanding generals whose talents were wasted in Paris and Lyon respectively, far from the decisive battlefields. As for Ney and Grouchy, while their courage was uncontestable, their respective careers should have armed Napoleon with ample evidence that they lacked the strategic and tactical gifts for such crucial commands. Had Davout and Suchet rather than Ney and Grouchy commanded his two wings, Napoleon most likely would have crushed Wellington and Blucher.

Napoleon hoped ideally to avert a war altogether, or at least to delay it as long as possible. He wrote to his estranged father-in-law on April 1, justifying his actions, calling for peace, and asking that his wife and son be allowed to return to him. He had Caulaincourt dispatch secret envoys to Sweden, Naples, Holland, Saxony, and all the German states to solicit their recognition of, and even better their active support for, his latest regime. On April 4 he wrote to each of the four great-power leaders pledging that "the first need of my heart is to devote myself completely to maintaining an honorable tranquility," for the good of the French people who had recalled him to power and for all the peoples of Europe. In his letter to the tsar he included a copy of the secret treaty signed by France, Britain, and Austria on January 3 against Prussia and Russia. Those would be his last significant international diplomatic initiatives.[12]

No sovereign replied; how could they communicate with a man they had declared an international outlaw? Alexander assured the British, Austrians, and exiled French leaders that he would forgive their secret alliance against Russia and Prussia. Napoleon had Caulaincourt publish in the *Moniteur* the lack of response, but if he hoped that gesture would embarrass those states, it backfired.[13]

What else could Napoleon do diplomatically, at least for now? He asked Caulaincourt to have his foreign ministry officials compile an analysis of his foreign policy from the time he took power until he lost it, and then the major decisions and controversies of the Congress of Vienna. His primary reason for doing so was to publish the work and remind the people of all the past glories he had brought them. But also, like a lawyer having his assistants prepare a legal brief, he apparently wanted to provide a document that systematically revealed how just and progressive his policies had been and how unjust and regressive were those of his enemies against him, at least in his own mind.[14]

As for allies, who would dare stand with him against the collective weight of Europe led by the great powers? Realistically, there was only one possibility, and it was a long shot. During his exile on Elba he had sent first his sister Pauline and then his mistress Marie Walewska to Naples to offer forgiveness and seek some as yet unspecified future help from Joachim and Caroline Murat, who had betrayed him the previous year. Napoleon dispatched Colonna d'Istria to Murat with a letter thanking him for his kindness to Marie Walewska and "her" son, expressing love to his sister and their children, and most importantly urging a reconciliation and cooperation between them. Murat and Caroline reacted predictably to those entreaties, with the volatile king displaying very mixed emotions and the cynical queen openly dismissive.[15]

After settling at the Tuileries Napoleon wrote to Murat that "I am at peace with everything. I will support you with all my power. I am counting on you." The emperor called on the king to send a ship to Marseilles so that they could establish regular communications. But there was not the slightest hint of any call to arms. Alas, by the time the letter reached Naples, Murat was long gone.[16]

Where had that volatile, impetuous, and rather dim-witted man gone? Murat was eager to compensate for his betrayal of Napoleon the previous year. He also felt he had nothing to lose. His spies at Vienna had passed word that the great powers were conspiring to topple him and return Ferdinand IV to power in Naples. So, rather than sit tight, he jumped the gun. On March 15, after learning that Napoleon had made it to Grenoble—which was still a long way from Paris—Murat marched north at the head of his army. Four days later he stopped briefly in Rome to announce his takeover of the Papal States. Then, at Rimini on March 30, he declared himself the king of Italy "from the Alps to the straits of Scilla," and called on all patriotic Italians to rally to his rule. The first battles occurred on April 2 and 4 when his troops routed small Austrian forces outside Bologna and Modena, respectively. Those would be his last victories.

The Austrians launched a counter-offensive. They defeated Murat at Occhiobello on April 10 and destroyed his army in two days of fighting at Tolentino on May 2 and 3. Murat abandoned his troops and reached his capital on May 18. Four days later the Austrian army marched into Naples. Murat escaped by disguising himself as a sailor and sneaking aboard a vessel bound for France through the British blockade. The British would soon restore Ferdinand IV and his court to power in Naples.

An enraged Napoleon publicly repudiated Murat's actions even before his defeat was known, and he had Murat arrested when he landed at Cannes. He ordered his officials to "make it clear to him that he ruined France in 1814; in 1815, he has compromised her and ruined himself."[17] He was then released with the warning to stay away from Paris. After Waterloo Murat fled first to Corsica, where he plotted with a few devoted followers. In October they landed near Pizzo down toward the toe of Italy in an utterly harebrained scheme to retake his kingdom. He was swiftly captured by local militia, tried in a court martial, found guilty of treason, and executed on October 8, 1815.

Had Murat been clever rather than foolish, he might have played off Napoleon and the allies against each other, to his own benefit. By pretending to lean toward Paris he could have engaged the British and Austrians in negotiations that could well have resulted in a treaty reaffirming his rule.

Instead, his premature attack led not just to his rapid and humiliating demise, but let the allies concentrate their attention and forces on defeating Napoleon.

The allies had over half a million troops immediately available to march against France. Their plan was for Arthur Wellesley, the Duke of Wellington, and Gebhard Blucher to hold Belgium with their respective armies of 92,300 and 130,200 troops while Karl von Schwarzenberg and Mikhail Barclay de Tolly headed toward eastern France with their respective armies of 225,000 and 168,000 troops.

Time and numbers were clearly on the allied side. That made it imperative for Napoleon somehow to invade Belgium and rout Wellington and Blucher before turning on Schwarzenberg and Barclay de Tolly. The first phase of that war would be challenging enough. The combined armies of Wellington and Blucher numbered 222,500 to Napoleon's 124,000 troops, a nearly two-to-one superiority.

Nonetheless, Napoleon had at least three possible advantages. Wellington commanded a mongrel army, with fewer than half his troops first-rate British and German troops, the rest untested Belgians and Dutch. The two armies were scattered in an arc that covered several different approaches to Brussels. Finally, there was a gap between Wellington's left flank and Blucher's right.

Given the enemy's deployment, superior numbers, and time advantage, Napoleon's resultant plan was the only one that made sense. He would mass his troops and hurl them directly at that gap between the two armies in hopes of decisively defeating each in turn. The plan might have succeeded had he and his subordinates not made a series of very bad decisions.

Napoleon's 1815 campaign would last only four days, from June 15 when his army invaded Belgium through June 18 when he was routed at Waterloo.[18] All along Ney would be the worst culprit. During the first two days he dragged his feet getting to the front and sending his wing forward, and then on June 16 he paused before the crossroads of Quatre Bras during the crucial hours when his forces outnumbered the enemy's. By the time Ney ordered an attack, Wellington had raced up enough troops so that he actually outnumbered him.

That same day a dozen miles eastward, Napoleon launched a massive attack against Blucher around the town of Ligny. A French corps commanded by General Jean d'Erlon was positioned between Quatre Bras and Ligny, and could have crushed either Wellington's left or Blucher's right. Instead that corps spent the day marching and counter-marching between the two battles as d'Erlon obeyed conflicting orders from Ney and Napoleon. So that night Wellington and Blucher withdrew with their armies beaten but intact.

While Napoleon joined Ney in pursuit of Wellington, he sent Grouchy at the head of 30,000 troops to hound Blucher's retreat and prevent him from linking forces with Wellington. Grouchy blundered by mistaking one of the Prussian corps for Blucher's entire army and trailing it northeast. Blucher instead withdrew most of his army directly north to stay parallel with and eventually join Wellington.

Rainstorms on the 17th slowed the pursuit. That evening when Napoleon finally caught up to Wellington's army it was drawn up on a low ridge a mile south of the village of Waterloo. The following morning, that of the 18th, he had to delay his attack until early afternoon until the ground dried out enough for his artillery to be brought up. The two armies were almost exactly matched in numbers, with Napoleon and Wellington commanding about 74,000 troops each, although the former had 254 cannons to the latter's 157.

The biggest difference between Napoleon and Wellington at Waterloo was how each commander handled the battle. Wellington carefully deployed his troops to best cover the terrain he had chosen and then just as carefully made vital tactical decisions. Napoleon, in contrast, essentially handed over the battle to Ney, issuing only half a dozen written or verbal orders to his field commander during the entire day.

Wellington brilliantly countered every move that Napoleon and Ney made. When Napoleon ordered a bombardment shortly after noon, Wellington simply withdrew his army to relative shelter on the reverse slope of the ridge; most of the cannon balls either plopped harmlessly into the mud or sailed overhead. The "Iron Duke" then ordered his troops back atop the ridge to rout a massive French attack, first by infantry and then by cavalry, on his center. Anchoring the British right flank was the walled chateau of Hougoumont; the troops valiantly defended that position against repeated attacks by Jerome's division. Meanwhile, Blucher was marching to the rescue. By late afternoon his troops had routed the French at Plancenoit and were surging against Napoleon's right flank. In a desperate last roll of the dice, Napoleon threw his best troops, the Old Guard, against the British center. The British routed that attack and then counterattacked just as the Prussians were rolling up the French right. As the remnants of his army fled, Napoleon abandoned them and hurried to Paris.

When Napoleon reached the capital it was no longer his. Upon learning of Waterloo, Fouche engineered a bloodless coup d'etat modeled upon that of Talleyrand the previous year. Fouche forged a consensus, first in the State Council and then the two chambers of parliament, that Napoleon must abdicate. On June 22 Napoleon did so in favor of his son, with the words: "I hereby offer to sacrifice myself to the hatred of the enemies of France. My political life is over, and I proclaim my son under the title of Napoleon II, Emperor of the French."[19]

The Senate then appointed Fouche, Caulaincourt, and Carnot to lead a government and open negotiations with the allies who were steadily approaching Paris. Although Grouchy had managed to rally 50,000 troops and was skillfully leading a fighting withdrawal, it would only be a matter of time before Wellington and Blucher, with overwhelming numbers of troops and cannons, reached Paris. A delegation reached the allied camp near Laon with two requests: an armistice and free passage for Napoleon to seek exile in America. Wellington and Blucher bluntly rejected both requests and ordered their armies forward.

With the political rug pulled from beneath him, Napoleon lingered with his mother and Hortense at Malmaison until June 29. Josephine had died there the previous year during his exile on Elba. What bittersweet memories must have kaleidoscoped through his mind during that brief sojourn.

With a handful of followers he set off for Rochefort in hopes of there slipping aboard a ship bound for the New World, but he found the bay blockaded by British warships when he arrived on July 3. For a week from July 8 he holed up at the fortress on the Ile d'Aix and mulled his choices. He finally accepted the inevitable on July 15 when he sent word to Captain Frederick Maitland of the HMS *Bellerophon* that he was willing to surrender in return for safe passage to America. Maitland welcomed him aboard and sailed off for England. They dropped anchor briefly at Torbay and then for six weeks at Plymouth as the British government and allied envoys tried to figure out what to do with him.

Napoleon asked for asylum in England. To George, the prince regent, he wrote: "Exposed to the factions which distract my country and to the enmity of the greatest powers of Europe, I have closed my political career, and I come, like Themistocles, to throw myself upon the hospitality of the British people. I put myself under the protection of their laws which I claim from your Royal Highness, as the most powerful, the most constant, and the most generous of my enemies."[20] Once again he did not receive a direct reply.

He learned his fate on August 4, shortly after Maitland received orders from Admiral George Keith, the Channel Fleet commander. Napoleon typically did not go quietly: "I solemnly protest here, before God and humanity, against the violation of my most sacred rights which have been taken by force from my person and my liberty. I came freely aboard the *Bellerophon*. I am a prisoner. I am the hostage of England. . . . I appeal to history."[21]

His protest was officially ignored. Maitland ordered the anchor hoisted and sails unfurled on August 7. He set course for St. Helena, far in the south Atlantic and nearly equidistant from South Africa, South America, and Antarctica.

Napoleon Bonaparte would first set foot on that starkly beautiful island on October 16, 1815. There he would spend the rest of his days, reviled or adored but hardly forgotten. He was accompanied by a dwindling band of followers and, from April 1816, increasingly hounded by Hudson Lowe, the sadistic governor. His death on May 5, 1821, was the anticlimax to an era that had begun with the Bastille and ended at Waterloo. He will eternally remain among history's greatest yet most controversial generals and diplomats. Indeed, in both the related fields of war and diplomacy, Napoleon Bonaparte's failures were as resounding as his triumphs.

Chapter Seven Endnotes: Denouement

1. Alan Palmer, *Napoleon and Marie Louise: The Emperor's Second Wife* (New York: St. Martin's Press, 2001), 177-88.

2. Alan Palmer, *Metternich: Councilor of Europe* (New York: Phoenix Giant, 1997), 14.

3. Steven Englund, *Napoleon: A Political Life* (New York: Scribner, 2004), 421. For a brief selection of some of his reform orders, see: Orders to General Drouot, May 7, 1814, Claude Tchou, ed. *Correspondance de Napoleon Ier* (hereafter cited as *Correspondence*), 16 vols. (Paris: Bibliotheque des Introuvables, 2002), 21685; Notes, [n.d.], *ibid.*, 21567; Orders, May 10, 1814, *ibid.*, 21568; Napoleon to Bertrand, June 24, 1814, *ibid.*, 21582.

4. Neil Campbell, *Napoleon at Fontainebleau and Elba, Being a Journal of Occurrences in 1814-1815* (London: John Murray, 1869), 233, 317; Fernand Beaucour, *Une Visite a Napoleon a l'ile d'Elbe d'un membre du Parlement Anglais* (Paris: C.E.N., 1990), 304.

5. John Holland Rose, *The Life of Napoleon*, 2 vols. (London: George Bell & Sons, 1903), 2:445.

6. Napoleon to the French People, May 1, 1815, *Correspondence*, 21681; Napoleon to the Army, March 1, 1815, *ibid.*, 21682.

7. Report on Napoleon's March, *Le Moniteur*, March 23, 1815.

8. Englund, *Napoleon*, 429.

9. Decree, March 13, 1815, *Correspondence*, 21686; State Council Response, March 26, 1815, *ibid.*, 21716; Notes to Finance Council, April 29, 1815, *ibid.*, 21853; Decree Abolishing Slavery, March 29, 1815, *ibid.*, 21743.

10. Constitutional Act, April 23, 1815, *Correspondence*, 21839; Emperor's Speech to the Electoral College, June 1, 1815, *ibid.*, 21997; Speech to the National Assembly, June 7, 1815, *ibid.*, 22023; Alan Schom, *Napoleon Bonaparte* (New York: HarperCollins, 1997), 733.

11. Napoleon to Carnot, April 10, 1815, *Correspondence*, 21793; Napoleon to Davout, May 3, 1815, *ibid.*, 21874; Napoleon to General Corbieau, May 21, 1815, *ibid.*, 21944.

12. Napoleon to Francis, April 1, 1815, *Correspondence*, 21753; Napoleon to Caulaincourt, April 3, 1815, *ibid.*, 21759; Circular Letter to Sovereigns, April 4, 1815, *ibid.*, 21769.

13. Napoleon to Caulaincourt, April 7, 1815, *Correspondence*, 21777.

14. Napoleon to Caulaincourt, March 28, 1815, *Correspondence*, 21739.

15. Napoleon to Murat, February 17, 1815, Archive Nationale, 20/334 (I).

16. Napoleon to Murat, March [n.d.], 1815, *Correspondence*, 21745.

17. Note for the Foreign Minister, April 15, 19, 1815, *Correspondence*, 21809, 21826; Hubert Cole, *The Betrayers: Joachim and Caroline Murat* (New York: Saturday Evening Press, 1972), 243.

18. Order of the Day, June 13, 1815, *Correspondence*, 22049; Order of Movement, June 14, 1815, *ibid.*, 22053; Napoleon to Ney, June 16, 1815, *ibid.*, 22058; Napoleon to Grouchy, June 16, 1815, *ibid.*, 22059; Army Bulletin, June 20, 1815, *ibid.*, 22061.

19. Declaration to the French People, June 22, 1815, *Correspondence*, 22063; Message to the Chamber of Representatives, June 21, 1815, *ibid.*, 22062; Napoleon to the Army, June 25, 1815, *ibid.*, 22065.

20. Rory Muir, *Britain and the Defeat of Napoleon, 1807-1815* (New Haven, Conn.: Yale University Press, 1996), 367-68.

21. Napoleon Protest, August 4, 1815, *Correspondence*, 22067.

Acknowledgements

I must first express my deepest gratitude to Dr. Thierry Lentz, who directs the Napoleon Foundation in Paris, for all his brilliant scholarship, guidance, and kindness. Dr. Lentz is one of the world's leading scholars of Napoleon, and it was an honor and pleasure for me to spend some time with him. I would also like to thank Dr. Peter Hicks, the author of many fine publications as well as the Napoleon Foundation's outstanding newsletter, for all the insights he shared with me during my stay. I am grateful to the rest of the Napoleon Foundation's staff for all their cheerful and patient assistance. The Napoleon Foundation is truly a paradise for researchers. I thank David Markham, the President of the International Napoleonic Society and President Emeritus of the Napoleon Historical Society, for taking time from his busy schedule to read my manuscript and give his very enthusiastic endorsement for its publication. I deeply appreciate the efforts of Rob Ayer and Lee Merideth for their respective editing and typesetting of my book. Finally, I applaud Jason Petho for his latest series of wonderful maps.

Dr. William R. Nester
St. John's University
November, 2011

Bibliography

Primary Sources

Addington, Henry. *The Life and Correspondence of the Right Honorable Henry Addington, 1st Viscount Sidmouth*. 3 vols. Ed. George Pellew. London: J. Murray, 1847.

Alexandre Ier et le Prince Czartoryski. *Correspondance Particuliere et Conversations, 1801-1823*. Ed. Prince Ladislas Czartoryski. Paris: Michel Levy Freres, 1865.

Barras, Paul Jean Francois Nicolas de. *Memoires de Barras, Membre du Directoire*. 4 vols. Paris: Hachette, 1895-96.

Beaucour, Fernand. *Une Visite a Napoleon a l'ile d'Elbe d'un Membre du Parlement Anglais*. Paris: C.E.N., 1990.

Beauharnais, Eugene de. *Memoires et Correspondances Politique et Militaire du Prince Eugene*. 10 vols. Ed. Albert du Casse. Paris: Perrotin, 1858-60.

Beauharnais, Hortense de. *Memoires de la Reine Hortense*. 3 vols. Paris: Plon, 1927.

Bertrand, Henri Gatien. *Cahiers de Sainte Helene*. 3 vols. Paris: Sulliver, 1958.

Blaze, Elzear. *Life in Napoleon's Army: The Memoirs of Captain Elzear Blaze*. London: Greenhill Press, 1995.

Bonaparte, Jerome. *Memoires et Correspondance du roi Jerome et de la reine Catherine*. 7 vols. Ed. Albert du Casse. Paris: Dentu, 1861-66.

Bonaparte, Joseph. *Memoires et Correspondance Politique et Militaire du roi Joseph*. 10 vols. Ed. Albert du Casse. Paris: Perrotin, 1853-54.

Bonaparte, Lucien. *Memoires Secretes sur la vie privee, politique, et literaire de Lucien Bonaparte, prince de Canino*. Paris: Delaunay, 1818.

Bonaparte, Napoleon. *Correspondance de Napoleon*. 32 vols. Paris: Imprimerie Imperiale, 1858-1870.

------. *Correspondance de Napoleon*. 16 vols. Ed. Claude Tchou. Paris: Bibliotheque des Introuvables, 2002.

------. *Correspondance Inedite de Napoleon I*. 5 vols. Paris: Henri Charles-Lavauzelle, 1912-25.

------. *Ecrits Personnelles de Napoleon*. 3 vols. Ed. Jean Tulard. Paris: Introuvable de l'Histoire, 2001.

------. *The Letters and Dispatches of the First Napoleon*. 3 vols. London: Chapman and Hall, 1884.

------. *Lettres Inedites de Napoleon I*. Ed. Leon Lecestre. Paris: Plon, 1897.

------. *Lettres Inedites de Napoleon I a Marie-Louise*. Ed. Louis Madelin. Paris: Bibliotheque Nationales de France, 1935.

------. *Lettres Personnelles des Souverains a l'Emperor Napoleon I*. Paris: Plon, 1939.

------. *Memoirs of Napoleon I*. New York: Duffield, 1929.

------. *Memoires*. 5 vols. Paris: Club du Livre, 1969.

------. *Memorial de Sainte-Helene*. 2 vols. Ed. Emmanuel de Las Cases. Paris: Editions Garnier Freres, 1961.

------. *Napoleon Bonaparte: Correspondance Generale*. 6 vol. Ed. Thierry Lentz. Paris: Fayard, 2004-2009.

------. *Napoleon Lettres d'Amour a Josephine*. Ed. Jean Tulard. Paris: Fayard, 1981.

------. *Oeuvres Litteraires et Ecrits Militaires*. 3 vols. Paris: Bibliotheque des Introuvables, 2001.

------. *Oeuvres Litteraires et Ecrits Militaires*. 3 vols. Ed. Jean Tulard. Paris: Introuvables de l'Histoire, 2001.

Boulay de la Merthe, A. "Correspondance de Talleyrand avec le Premier Consul Pendant la Campagne de Marengo." Extrait de la *Revue d'Histoire Diplomatique*. April 1892.

------. *Documents Sur la Negotiation du Concordat entre la France et la Saint-Siege, 1800-1801*. 6 vols. Paris: E. Leroux, 1890.

Bourrienne, Louis Antoine Fauvelet. *Memoires de M. de Bourrienne sur Napoleon, le Directoire, le Consulat, l'Empire, et la Restauration*. 5 vols. Paris: Garnier, 1899-1900.

Broglie, duc de, ed. *Souvenirs du Prince de Talleyrand*. 5 vols. Paris: Calmann-Levy, 1891-92.

Browning, O., ed. *Despatches from Paris, 1784-1790*. 2 vols. London: Offices of the Society, 1909-10.

------. *England and Napoleon in 1803; Being the Dispatches of Lord Whitworth and Others*. London: Longmans, Green, and Co., 1887.

Cambaceres, Jean Jacques Regis. *Cambaceres: Memoires Inedits*. 2 vols. Paris: Perrin, 1999.

Campbell, Neil. *Napoleon at Fontainebleau and Elba, Being a Journal of Occurrences in 1814-1815*. London: John Murray, 1869.

Canning, George. *Some Official Correspondence of George Canning.* 2 vols. London: Longmans, Green, and Co., 1887.

Carnot, Lazare N.M. *Memoires Historiques et Militaires.* Paris: Baudoin Freres, 1824.

Castlereagh, Robert Stewart, Viscount. *Correspondence, Despatches, and other Papers of Viscount Castlereagh.* 12 vols. Ed. Charles William Vane. London: John Murray, 1850-53.

Catinat, Michael et Bernard Chevalier, eds. *Correspondance de l'Imperatrice Josephine.* Paris: Payot, 1996.

Caulaincourt, Duke of Vicenza, Armand de. *Memoirs.* 3 vols. London: Cassell, 1950.

Caulaincourt, Armand Louis Augustin. *Memoirs of General de Caulaincourt, Duke of Vicenza.* 3 vols. Paris: Plon, 1933.

Caulaincourt, Armand de. *With Napoleon in Russia: The Memoirs of General de Caulaincourt, Duke of Vicenza.* Ed. Jean Hanoteau. New York: William Morrow, 1935.

———. *No Peace with Napoleon: Concluding the Memoirs of General Armand de Caulaincourt, Duke of Vicenza.* Ed. Jean Hanoteau. New York: William Morrow, 1936.

Champagny, Jean Baptiste Nompere de. *Souvenirs de M. de Champagny, duc de Cadore.* Geneva: Slakine-Megariotis Reprints, 1975.

Chaptal, Jean Antoine. *Mes Souvenirs sur Napoleon.* Paris: E. Plon, Norrit, et Cie, 1893.

Chateaubriand, Francois Rene de. *Memoires d'Outre-Tombe.* 3 vols. Paris: Livre de Poche, 1973.

Cobbett, William, ed. *The Parliamentary History of England, from the Earliest Period to the Year 1803.* London: R. Bashaw, 1806.

Constant, Benjamin. *Memoires sur les Cent-Jours.* Paris: J.J. Pauvert, 1961.

Constant, Louis Constant Wairy. *Memoires Intimes de Napoleon I par Constant, son Valet de Chambre.* 2 vols. Paris: Mercure de France, 2000.

Correspondance Authentique de la Cour de Rome avec la France. 1814.

Czartoryski, Prince Adam. *Memoirs of Prince Adam Czartoryski and his Correspondence with Alexander I.* 2 vols. Ed. C. de Mazade. London: Remington, 1888.

Davout, Louis Nicolas. *Correspondance de Marechal Davout, Prince d'Eckmuhl, ses Commandements, son Ministere, 1801-1815.* Paris: Plon, 1885.

Desmarest, Pierre Marie. *Temoignages Historiques, ou, Quinzes Ans de Haute Police sous le Consulat et l'Empire.* Paris: Levasseur, 1833.

Diesbach, Ghislain de. *Memoires d'Une Femme de Qualite sur le Consulat et l'Empire.* Paris: Mercure de France, 1987.

Du Casse, Albert. *Histoire des Negotiations Diplomatiques Relative aux Traites de Mortefontaine, de Luneville, et d'Amiens.* Paris: E. Dentu, 1855.

Ducrese, Georgette, ed. *Memoires Sur l'Imperatrice Josephine.* Paris: Mercure de France, 2004.

Fain, Agathon Jean Francois. *The Manuscript of 1814.* London: H. Colburn, 1823.

———. *Manuscrit de 1812*. 2 vols. Paris: Delauney, 1827.

———. *Manuscrit de 1813*. Paris: Delauney, 1829.

———. *Manuscrit de 1814*. Paris: Delauney, 1830.

———. *Memoires du Baron Fain*. Paris: Arlea, 2002.

Fouche, Joseph. *Joseph Fouche, Ministre de la Police, Memoires*. Ed. Edwy Plenel. Paris: Arlea, 1993.

Fox, Charles James. *The Memorials and Correspondence of Charles James Fox*. 4 vols. Ed. John Russell. New York: AMS Press, 1970.

George III. *The Later Correspondence of George III*. 5 vols. Ed. A. Aspinall. Cambridge: Cambridge University Press, 1962-70.

George IV. *The Correspondence of George, Prince of Wales, 1770-1812*. Ed. A. Aspinall. London: Cassel, 1965.

Gourgand, Gaspard. *Journal de Sainte Helene*. 2 vols. Paris: Flammarion, 1947.

Guizot, Francois. *Memoires pour servir a l'histoire de mons temps*, vol. 1. Paris: Michel Levy, 1858.

Hauterive, Ernest et J. Grassion, eds. *La Police Secrete du Premier Empire: Bullitines Quotidiens Addresses par Fouche a l'Emperor, 1809-1810*. 5 vols. Paris: Perrin et Cie, 1964.

Jaucourt, A. F., Comte de. *Correspondance du Comte de Jaucourt, ministre interimaire des affaires etrangeres, avec le prince de Talleyrand pendant le Congres de Vienne*. Paris: Plon, Nourrit, et Cie, 1905.

Junot, Laura. *At the Court Napoleon: Memoirs of the Duchesse d'Abrantes*. New York: Doubleday, 1989.

Kerautret, Michel. *Les Grands Traites du Consulat, 1799-1804*. Paris: Nouveau Monde Editions/Fondation Napoleon, 2002.

———. *Les Grands Traites du Empire, 1804-1810*. Paris: Nouveau Monde Editions/Fondation Napoleon, 2004.

———. *Les Grands Traites du Empire, 1810-1815*. Paris: Nouveau Monde Editions/Fondation Napoleon, 2004.

La Fayette, Gilbert de. *Memoires, Correspondances et Manuscripts du general de La Fayette*. 6 vols. Paris: Fournier Aine, 1837-38.

La Forest, Antoine Rene. *Correspondance du Comte de la Forest, Ambassadeur de France en Espagne, 1808-1813*. Paris: Alphonse Picard et Fils, 1913.

La Garde-Chambonas, Comte Auguste de. *Souvenirs du Congres de Vienne, 1814-1815*. Paris: Emil-Paul, 1904.

La Tour du Pin, Madame. *Memoirs: Laughing and Dancing Our Way to the Precipice*. London: Harvill Press, 1999.

Las Cases, Emmanuel Auguste Dieudonne. *Memorial de Sainte Helene*. Paris: Editions de Seuil, 1968.

Londonderry, Robert Stewart, second Marquess of. *Correspondence, Despatches, and Other Papers of Viscount Castlereagh, Second Marquess of Londonderry.* 12 vols. London: H. Colburn, 1851-55.

Louis-Philippe d'Orleans. *Mon Journal.* 2 vols. Paris: Michel Levy, 1849.

Luvaas, Jay, ed. *Napoleon on the Art of War.* New York: Touchstone, 1999.

Malmesbury, James Harris, Earl. *The Diaries and Correspondence of James Harris, Earl of Malmesbury.* London: Richard Bentley, 1845.

Marie Caroline. *Correspondance Inedite de Marie Caroline, Reine de Naples et de Sicile avec le Marquis de Gallo.* 2 vols. Paris: Emile Paul, 1911.

Meneval, Claude Francois de. *Memoires pour Servir a l'Histoire de Napoleon I.* 2 vols. Paris: E. Dentu, 1894.

Metternich, Prince Clement Wenceslas Lothaire von. *Memoires, Documents, Ecrits Divers Laisses par le Prince de Metternich, 1773-1815.* 8 vols. Paris: Plon, 1880-1884.

Miot de Melito, Andre Francois. *Memoires du Comte Miot de Melito, Ancien Ministre, Ambassadeur, Conseiller d'Etat et Membre de l'Institut, 1788-1815.* New York: Charles Scribner's Sons, 1881.

Murat, Joachim. *Correspondance de Joachim Murat.* Paris: E. Plon, Nourrit, et Cie, 1897.

Nelson, Horatio. *The Dispatches and Letters of Vice Admiral Lord Viscount Nelson.* Ed. Sir Nicolas Harris Nicolas. London: Henry Coburn, 1945.

Nesselrode, Karl Robert. *Lettres et Papiers du Chancelier Comte de Nesselrode, 1760-1850.* 11 vols. Paris: Lahure, 1904-12.

Ouvrand, Gabriel Julian. *Memoires de J.-G. Ouvrand sur sa Vie et ses Diverses Operations Financieres.* Paris: Moutardier, 1826-27.

Pitt, William. *The Speeches of the Right Honorable William Pitt in the House of Commons.* 2 vols. New York: Kraus Reprint Company, 1972.

Poniatowski, Joseph. *Correspondance du Prince Joseph Poniatowski avec la France.* Poznan, Poland: Societe Scientifique, 1921.

Pozzo di Borgo, Charles Andre. *Correspondances diplomatique du comte Pozzo di Borgo, ambassadeur de Russie en France, et du comte de Nesselrode, 1814-1818.* Paris: Calmann-Levy, 1890.

Roederer, Pierre Louis. *Memoires Pour Servir a l'Histoire de Napoleon I depuis 1802 jusqua 1815.* 8 vols. Paris: Firman, 1853-59.

Savary, Anne Jean Marie Rene. *Memoires du Duc de Rovigo pour Servir a l'Histoire de l'Empereur Napoleon.* 8 vols. Paris: Boussage, 1829.

Scott, James Brown, ed. *The Armed Neutralities of 1780 and 1800: A Collection of Official Documents.* New York: Oxford University Press, 1918.

Segur, Philippe Paul de. *Histoire et Memoires.* 8 vols. Paris: Firmin Didot, 1873.

———. *A History of Napoleon's Expedition to Russia.* 2 vols. London: Michael Joseph, 1858.

Sidmouth, Henry Addington, first Viscount. *The Life and Correspondence of the Right Honorable Henry Addington, First Viscount Sidmouth.* Ed. George Pellew. London: J. Murray, 1847.

Smith, William Sydney. *The Letters of Sydney Smith.* 2 vols. Oxford: Clarendon Press, 1953.

Talleyrand-Perigord, Charles Maurice de. *Correspondance inedite du Prince de Talleyrand et du Roi Louis XVIII pendant le Congres de Vienne.* Paris: Plon, 1881.

———. *La Mission de Talleyrand a Londres en 1792: Correpondance Inedite de Talleyrand avec le Departement des Affaires Etrangeres.* Ed. George Pallain. Paris: Plon, 1889.

———. *Le Miroir de Talleyrand: Lettres Inedites a la Duchess de Courlande Pendant le Congres de Vienne.* Paris: Libraire Academique Perrin, 1976.

———. *Lettres Inedites de Talleyrand a Napoleon. 1800-1809.* Paris: J. de Bonnot, 1967.

———. *Lettres Inedites de Talleyrand a Napoleon, 1800-1809.* Ed. Pierre Bertrand. Paris: Perrin, 1889.

———. *Lettres de Napoleon a Talleyrand.* Ed. Pierre Bertrand. Paris: Perrin, 1989.

———. *Memoires Complet et Authentiques de Charles Maurice de Talleyrand.* 6 vols. Paris: Calmann-Levy, 1891-92.

———. *Memoires Complet et Authentiques de Charles Maurice de Talleyrand-Perigord, 1754-1815.* 6 vols. Paris: Plon, 1982.

Tatichtchev, Sergie Spiridonovich, ed. *Alexander I et Napoleon. d'apres leur Correspondance inedited, 1801-1812.* Paris: Libraire Academique Didier, 1891.

Theibault, Paul Charles Henri. *The Memoirs of Baron Theibault.* 2 vols. London: Smith, Elder, 1896.

Webster, Charles K., ed. *British Diplomacy, 1812-1815: Select Documents Dealing with the Reconstruction of Europe.* London: G. Bell, 1921.

Weil, M. H., ed. *Les Dessous du Congres de Vienne d'apres des documents Originaux des Archives du Ministere Imperial et Royale de l'Interior a Vienne.* 2 vols. Paris: Payot, 1917.

Wellesley, F.A., ed. *The Diary and Correspondence of Henry Wellesley, First Lord.* London: Hutchinson & Co., 1936.

Wellesley, Richard. *The Despatches and Correspondence of the Marquess Wellesley, K.G., During His Lordship's Mission to Spain as Ambassador Extraordinary to the Supreme Junta in 1809.* London: John Murray, 1838.

———. *The Memoirs and Correspondence of...Richard Marquess Wellesley.* 3 vols. London: Richard Bentley, 1843.

Wellington, Arthur Wellesley, Duke. *The Dispatches of Field Marshal the Duke of Wellington during his various Campaigns in India, Denmark, Portugal, Spain, the Low Countries, and France from 1799 to 1818.* 8 vols. Ed. John Gurwood. London: Parker Furnivall and Parker, 1857-72.

Wickham, William. *The Correspondence of the Right Honorable William Wickham from the Year 1794.* 2 vols. London: R. Bentley, 1870.

Wilson, Robert. *Narrative of Events During the Invasion of Russia.* London: Kimber, 1960.

Secondary Sources

Acerra, Martine, et Jean Meyer. *Marines et Revolution.* Rennes: Ouest France, 1988.

Acton, Harold. *The Bourbons of Naples, 1734-1825.* London: Methuen and Company, 1957.

Adams, Ephraim D. *The Influence of Grenville on Pitt's Foreign Policy, 1787-1798.* Washington, D.C.: Carnegie Institute, 1904.

Adams, Michael. *Napoleon and Russia.* London: Hambledon Company, 2006.

Adkins, Roy and Leslet. *The War for all the Oceans: From Nelson at the Nile to Napoleon at Waterloo.* New York: Penguin, 2006.

Aftalion, Florin. *The French Revolution: An Economic Interpretation.* Cambridge: Cambridge University Press, 1990.

Albion, Robert G. *Forests and Sea Power.* Cambridge, Mass.: Harvard University Press, 1926.

Alexander, John T. *Catherine the Great: Life and Legend.* New York: Oxford University Press, 1989.

Alexander, R. S. *Bonapartism and Revolutionary Tradition in France: The Federe of 1815.* New York: Cambridge University Press, 1991.

Amini, Iradj. *Napoleon et la Perse.* Paris: Nouveau Monde Editions, 1995.

Anderson, Matthew S. *The Eastern Question, 1774-1923: A Study in International Relations.* London: Macmillan, 1966.

Anna, Timothy. *Spain and the Loss of America.* Lincoln: University of Nebraska Press, 1983.

Anstey, Roger. *The Atlantic Slave Trade and British Abolition, 1760-1810.* Atlantic Highlands, NJ: Humanities Press, 1978.

——. "A Reinterpretation of the Abolition of the British Slave Trade, 1806-1807." *English Historical Review.* 87:304-32.

Arboit, Gerald. "L'Impossible Reve Oriental de Napoleon." *Revue du Souvenir Napoleonien*, n. 402, Juillet-Aout, 1995. 27-37.

Arjuson, Antoine de. *Castlereagh.* Paris: Tallandier, 1995.

Arnold, Eric. *Fouche, Napoleon, and the General Police.* Washington, DC: University Press of America, 1979.

Arnold, James R. *Napoleon Conquers Austria: The 1809 Campaign for Vienna.* Westport, Conn.: Greenwood Publishing, 1995.

Arringon, L.-J. *Une Amie de Talleyrand: La Duchess de Courland, 1761-1821.* Paris: Flammarion, 1946.

Asprey, Robert. *The Reign of Napoleon Bonaparte.* New York: Basic Books, 2001.

———. *The Rise of Napoleon Bonaparte.* New York: Basic Books, 2001.

Ashenazy, Szyman M. *Napoleon et la Pologne, 1806-1807.* Bruxelles: Editions de Flambeau, 1925.

Atkin, Muriel. "The Pragmatic Diplomacy of Paul I: Russia's Relations with Asia, 1796-1801." *Slavic Review*, 38/1, March 1979. 60-74.

———. *Russia and Iran, 1780-1828.* Minneapolis: University of Minnesota Press, 1980.

Atteridge, A. Hilliard. *Marshal Murat.* London: Nelson, 1912.

Auriol, G. L. *La France, L'Angleterre, et Naples de 1803 a 1806.* 2 vols. Paris: Plon, Nourrit, et Cie, 1904.

Austin, Paul Britten. *1812: Napoleon's Invasion of Russia.* London: Greenhill Books, 2000.

Aymes, Jean-Rene. *La Guerre d'Independence Espagnolle, 1808-1814.* Paris: Bordas, 2003.

Bac, Ferdinand. *Le Secret de Talleyrand.* Paris: Hachette, 1933.

Bagally, John W. *Ali Pasha and Great Britain.* Oxford: Basil Black, 1938.

Baker, Keith M. *The Political Culture of the French Revolution.* New York: Elsever Science & Technology Books, 1988.

———, ed. *The French Revolution and the Creation of Modern Political Culture.* 4 vols. New York: Pergamon Press, 1987-94.

———, et al. *Inventing the French Revolution.* New York: Cambridge University Press, 1990.

Bakshi, S. R. *British Diplomacy and Administration in India, 1807-13.* New Delhi: Imprint, 1971.

Barahona, Renato. "The Napoleonic Occupation and Its Political Consequences in the Basque Provinces, 1808-1813." *The Consortium on Revolutionary Europe*, 1985.

Barbier, J., and H. Klein. "Revolutionary Wars and Public Finances: The Madrid Treasury, 1784-1807." *Journal of Economic History*, 41/2, 1981.

Bardet, Jean-Paul, ed. *Histoires des Populations de l'Europe: La Revolution Demographique, 1750-1914.* Paris: Fayard, 1998.

Barnes, Donald G. *George III and William Pitt, 1783-1806.* Stanford, Calif.: Stanford University Press, 1939.

Barrow, John. *The Life and Correspondence of Sir William Sydney Smith.* 2 vols. London: Richard Bentley, 1848.

Bartlett, C. J. *Castlereagh.* New York: Charles Scribner's Sons, 1966.

Bartlett, R. P., et al. *Russia and the World of the Eighteenth Century.* Columbus: Ohio University Press, 1986.

Barlette, Ruhl J. *The Record of American Diplomacy.* New York: Knopf, 1964.

Barton, Sir Dunbar Plunkett. *Bernadotte: Prince and King, 1810-1844.* London: John Murray, 1925.

Barton, H. A. "Late Gustavian Autocracy in Sweden: Gustavus IV, Adolf and His Opponents, 1792-1809." *Scandinavian Studies*, vol. 46, 1974. 265-84.

Baumgart, Winfried. *The Peace of Paris: Studies in War, Diplomacy, and Peacemaking.* Santa Barbara, Calif.: Clio Books, 1981.

Beales, Derek E. D., and T. C. W. Blanning. "Prince Kaunitz and the Primacy of Domestic Policy." *International History Review*, vol. 2, 1980. 618-24.

Beales, D. *Joseph II.* New York: Cambridge University Press, 1987.

Bearce, George D. *British Attitudes toward India.* New York: Oxford University Press, 1961.

Beaucour, Fernand. "Le Grand Projet Napoleonien d'Expedition en Angleterre: Myth ou Realite." *Proceedings, Consortium on Revolutionary Europe,* 1982. 225-45.

Behrens, Catherine. *Society, Government, and the Enlightenment: The Experience of Eighteenth Century France and Prussia.* London: Thames and Hudson, 1985.

Bell, David A. *The First Total War: Napoleon's Europe and the Birth of Warfare as We Know It.* New York: Houghton Mifflin, 2007.

Bely, Lucian, ed. *Dictionaire de l'Ancien Regime.* Paris: Puf, 2003.

Bennett, Geoffrey. *Nelson the Commander.* New York: Scribner's Sons, 1972.

Benoist-Mechin. *Bonaparte en Egypte et en Syrie, 1798-1800.* Paris: Perrin, 1978.

Berdalh, Robert M. *The Politics of the Prussian Nobility, 1770-1848.* Princeton, NJ: Princeton University Press, 1989.

Bergeron, Louis. *L'Episode Napoleonien: Aspects Interieurs, 1799-1815,* 2 vols. Paris: Seuil, 1972.

Bernard, J.F. *Talleyrand, A Biography.* New York: G.P. Putnam's Sons, 1973.

Bernard, Paul. *Joseph II and Bavaria: Two Eighteenth Century Attempts at German Unification.* The Hague: M. Nijhoff, 1965.

Bertaud, Jean-Paul. *1799: Bonaparte Prend le Pouvoir.* Paris: Jean Picollec, 1997.

——. *The Army of the French Revolution: From Citizen-Soldiers to Instruments of Power.* Princeton, NJ: Princeton University Press, 1988.

——. *La Revolution Armee: Les Soldat-Citoyens et la Revolution Francaise.* Paris: R. Laffont, 1979.

——. *Le Duc d'Enghien.* Paris: Fayard, 2001.

Bertier de Sauvigny, Guillaume de. "The Bourbon Restoration: One Century of French Historiography." *French Historical Studies.* 12:41-67.

——. *La Restauration.* Paris: Fayard, 1999.

——. *Metternich.* Paris: Fayard, 1986.

——. *Metternich et la France apres la Congress de Vienne.* 3 vols. Paris: Hachette, 1968-71.

——. *Metternich et son temps.* Paris: Fayard, 1959.

Best, Geoffrey. *War and Society in Revolutionary Europe, 1770-1870*. Leicester: Leicester University Press, 1982.

Bierman, John. *Napoleon III and His Carnival Empire*. New York: St. Martin's Press, 1988.

Billinger, Robert D. *Metternich and the German Question*. Newark: University of Delaware, 1991.

Bindel, V. *Le Vatican a Paris, 1809-1814*. Paris: Editions Alsatia, 1942.

Birke, Adolf, and Eckhart Hellmuth, eds. *The Transformation of Political Culture: England and Germany in the Eighteenth Century*. Oxford: Oxford University Press, 1990.

Biro, Sydney S. *The German Policy of Revolutionary France*. 2 vols. Cambridge, Mass.: Harvard University Press, 1957.

Black, Jeremy. *British Foreign Policy in an Age of Revolutions, 1783-1793*. Cambridge: Cambridge University Press, 1994.

———. *European Warfare, 1660-1815*. New Haven, Conn.: Yale University Press, 1994.

———. *Natural and Necessary Enemies: Anglo-French Relations in the Eighteenth Century*. Athens: University of Georgia Press, 1986.

———. *War and the World: Military Power and the Fate of Continents, 1450-2000*. New Haven, Conn.: Yale University Press, 1998.

Black, Jeremy, and Philip Woodfine, eds. *The British Navy and the Use of Naval Power in the Eighteenth Century*. Leicester: Humanities Press International, 1988.

Blanc, Oliver. *Les Espions de la Revolution et de l'Empire*. Paris: Perrin, 1995.

Blanning, T. C. W. "The Abortive Crusade." *History Today*, 39, May, 1989.

———. "The French Revolution and Europe." In C. Lucas, ed., *Rewriting the French Revolution*. New York: Oxford University Press, 1991. 183-206.

———. *The French Revolution: Aristocrats Versus Bourgeois?* London: Palgrave Macmillan, 1996.

———. *The French Revolution in Germany: Occupation and Resistance in the Rhineland, 1792-1802*. New York: Oxford University Press, 1983.

———. *The French Revolutionary Wars, 1787-1802*. New York: St. Martin's Press, 1996.

———. "German Jacobins and the French Revolution." *The Historical Journal*, 1980. 23: 985-1002.

———. *Joseph II*. London: Longman, 1994.

———. "Liberation or Occupation? Theory and Practice in the French Revolutionaries' Treatment of Civilians Outside France." *In Civilians in the Path of War*, ed. Mark Grimsley. Lincoln: University of Nebraska Press, 2002.

———. *The Origins of the French Revolutionary Wars*. London: Longman, 1986.

———. *The Rise and Fall of the French Revolution*. Chicago: University of Chicago Press, 1996.

Bluche, Francois. *Danton*. Paris: Fayard, 1984.

Blumenthal, Henry. *France and the United States: Their Diplomatic Relations, 1789-1914*. Chapel Hill: University of North Carolina Press, 1970.

Bois, Jean-Pierre. *Nouvelle Histoires des Relations Internationales: De la Paix des Rois a l'Ordres des Empereurs, 1714-1815*. Paris: Seuil, 2003.

Bond, Gordon C. *The Grand Expedition: The British Invasion of Holland in 1809*. Athens: University of Georgia Press, 1979.

———. "Louis Bonaparte and the Collapse of the Kingdom of Holland." *Proceedings, Consortium on Revolutionary Europe*, 1974. 141-53.

Bonnel, Ulane. *La France, les Etat-Unis, et la Guerre de Course, 1797-1815*. Paris: Nouvelles Editions Latines, 1961.

Boppe, Auguste. *L'Albanie et Napoleon, 1797-1814*. Paris: Hachette, 1914.

Bosher, J.F. *The French Revolution*. London: Weidenfeld & Nicolson, 1989.

Botzenhart, Manfred. "Metternich and Napoleon." *Francia, 1973*. 1:584-94.

Boudon, Jacques-Oliver. *Le Consulat et l'Empire*. Paris: Mont Chrétien, 1997.

———. *Histoire du Consulat et de l'Empire*. Paris: Perrin, 2000.

———. *Napoleon et les Cultes: Les Religions en Europe a l'Aube du XIX Siecle*. Paris: Fayard, 2002.

Boulay de la Merthe, Comte. *Le Directoire et L'Expedition d'Egypte*. Paris: Hachette, 1885.

Bouloiseau, Marc. *The Jacobin Republic, 1792-1794*. New York: Cambridge University Press, 1984.

Bowden, Scott. *Napoleon's Grande Armee of 1813*. Chicago: The Emperor's Press, 1990.

Bowman, Albert Hall. *The Struggle for Neutrality: Franco-American Diplomacy during the Federalist Era*. Knoxville: University of Tennessee Press, 1974.

Branda, Pierre, and Thierry Lentz. *Napoleon, l'Esclavage, et les Colonies*. Paris: Fayard, 2006.

Brauer, K., and William E. Wright, eds. *Austria in the Age of the French Revolution, 1789-1815*. Minneapolis: University of Minnesota Press, 1990.

Brett-James, A. *Europe Against Napoleon*. Cambridge: Cambridge University Press, 1987.

———. *Wellington at War, 1794-1815*. London: Macmillan, 1961.

Breunig, Charles. *The Age of Revolution and Reaction, 1789-1850*. New York: W. W. Norton, 1977.

Brewer, John. *The Sinews of Power: War, Money, and the English State, 1688-1783*. Cambridge, Mass.: Harvard University Press, 1989.

Britten, Paul. *1812: Napoleon's Invasion of Russia*. London: Greenhill Books, 2000.

Broers, Michael. *Europe Under Napoleon, 1799-1815*. New York: St. Martin's Press, 1996.

———. *The Napoleonic Empire in Italy, 1796-1814: Cultural Imperialism in a European Context?* New York: Palgrave Macmillan, 2005.

Bromley, J. S. "The Second Hundred Years War, 1689-1815." In Douglas Johnson, Francois Crouzet, and Francois Bedaria, eds., *Britain and France, Ten Centuries.* Folkstone: Dawson, 1980. 164-72.

Brooke, John. *King George III.* London: Constable, 1972.

Brown, Howard. *War, Revolution, and the Bureaucratic State: Politics and Army Administration in France, 1791-1799.* New York: Oxford University Press, 1995.

Brown, William Garrott. *The Life of Oliver Ellsworth.* New York: Macmillan, 1905.

Bruce, Evangeline. *Napoleon & Josephine: An Improbable Marriage.* New York: Scribner, 1995.

Bryant, Arthur. *The Years of Endurance, 1793-1802.* London: Book Club Associates, 1975.

———. *The Years of Victory, 1802-1812.* London: Book Club Associates, 1975.

Buckland, C. S. B. "An English Estimate of Metternich in 1813." *English Historical Review,* vol. 39, 1924. 256-58.

———. *Metternich and the British Government from 1809 to 1813.* London: Macmillan, 1932.

Buckland, Charles S. B. *Friedrich von Gentz: Relations with the British Government, 1809-13.* London: Macmillan, 1933.

Burne, Alfred H. *The Noble Duke of York: The Military Life of Frederick Duke of York and Albany.* London: Staples Press, 1949.

Burton, June K. *Napoleon and Clio: Historical Writing, Teaching, and Thinking During the First Empire.* Durham, N.C.: Carolina Academic Press, 1979.

Burton, R.G. *Napoleon's Campaigns in Italy, 1796-1797, and 1800.* London: George Allen, 1912.

Butterfield, Herbert. *The Peace Tactics of Napoleon, 1806-1808.* New York: Octagon Books, 1972.

Caldwell, R. J. *The Era of Napoleon: A Bibliography of the History of Western Civilization, 1799-1815.* 2 vols. New York: Scholastic, Inc., 1991.

Carr, Raymond. "Gustavus IV and the British Government, 1804-9." *English Historical Review,* vol. 60, 1945. 36-66.

Carrington, Dorothy. *Napoleon et ses Parents: Au Seuil de l'Histoire.* Paris: Editions Alain Piazzola & La Marge, 2000.

Casaglia, Gheraldo. *Le Partage du Monde: Napoleon et Alexandre a Tilsit.* Paris: S. P. M., 1998.

Cate, Curtis. *The War of the Two Emperors: The Duel Between Napoleon and Alexander: Russia 1812.* New York: Random House, 1985.

Cecil, Algernon. *Metternich, 1773-1859: A Study of his Period and Personality.* London: Eyre & Spottiswoode, 1933.

Cerami, Charles A. *Jefferson's Great Gamble: The Remarkable Story of Jefferson, Napoleon, and the Men Behind the Louisiana Purchase.* Naperville, Ill.: Sourcebooks, 2003.

Chadwick, Owen. *The Popes and European Revolution*. Oxford: Clarendon Press, 1981.

Chair, Somerset de, ed. *Napoleon on Napoleon: An Autobiography of the Emperor*. London: Caswell, 1992.

Chamberlain, Muriel E. *Lord Aberdeen: A Political Biography*. London: Longman, 1983.

Chandler, David. *The Campaigns of Napoleon*. New York: Macmillan, 1966.

———. *Dictionary of the Napoleonic Wars*. London: Arms and Armour, 1979.

———, ed. *Napoleon: The Final Verdict*. London: Arms and Armour Press, 1996.

Chardigny, Louis. *L'Homme Napoleon*. Paris: Perrin, 1999.

Charles-Roux, F. *Bonaparte: Governor of Egypt*. London: Methuen, 1937.

Chastenet, Jacques. *Manuel de Godoy et l'Espagne de Goya*. Paris: Hachette, 1961.

Chaumie, J. *Les Relations Diplomatique entre la France et l'Espagne: De Varennes a la Mort de Louis XVI*. Bordeaux: Feret, 1957.

Chevalier, Bernard, et Christophe Pincemaille. *L'Imperatrice Josephine*. Paris: Payot, 1996.

Chiappe, Jean-Francois. *George Cadoudal ou la Liberte*. Paris: Perrin, 1990.

Child, John. *Armies and Warfare in Europe, 1648-1789*. New York: Holmes and Meier, 1982.

Christiansen, Eric. *The Origins of Military Power in Spain, 1800-1854*. London: Oxford University Press, 1967.

Christie, Ian R. *Stress and Stability in Late Eighteenth Century Britain: Reflections on the British Avoidance of Revolution*. New York: Oxford University Press, 1984.

———. *Wars and Revolutions: Britain, 1760-1815*. Cambridge, Mass.: Harvard University Press, 1982.

Chuquet, Arthur. *La Jeunesse de Napoleon*. 3 vols. Paris: Armand Collin, 1898-99.

Clausewitz, Karl von. *The Campaign of 1812*. London: John Murray, 1843.

———. *On War*. Ed. and trans. Michael Howard and Peter Paret. Princeton, NJ: Princeton University Press, 1976.

Clement, G. *Napoleon en Allemagne: La Campagne de 1813*. Paris: Le Livre Chez-Vous, n.d.

Cobb, Richard. *The People's Armies*. New Haven, Conn.: Yale University Press, 1987.

———. *Reactions to the French Revolution*. New York: Oxford University Press, 1972.

Cole, Hubert. *The Betrayers: Joachim and Caroline Murat*. London: Saturday Review Press, 1972.

———. *Fouche: The Unprincipled Patriot*. London: Eyre and Spottiswoode, 1971.

Coles, Harry L. *The War of 1812*. Chicago: University of Chicago Press, 1965.

Colley, Linda. *Britons: Forging the Nation, 1707-1837*. New Haven, Conn.: Yale University Press, 1992.

Collins, Anna. *Slavery and the French Revolutionists, 1788-1805*. Lewiston, N.Y.: Edwin Mellen Press, 1988.

Collins, Irene. *Napoleon and His Parliaments 1800-1815*. New York: St. Martin's Press, 1979.

Collins, James B. *The Ancien Regime and the French Revolution*. Belmont, Calif.: Wadsworth Learning, 2002.

Connelly, Owen. *Blundering to Glory: Napoleon's Military Campaigns*. Wilmington, Del.: Scholarly Resources, 1987.

———. *The French Revolution and Napoleonic Era*. New York: Harcourt Brace, 2000.

———. *The Gentle Bonaparte*. New York: Macmillan, 1968.

———. *Napoleon Satellite Kingdoms*. New York: Macmillan, 1966.

———, ed. *Historical Dictionary of Napoleonic France*. Westport, Conn.: Greenwood Publishers, 1985.

Contaimine, Henry. *Diplomatie et Diplomates sous la Restauration, 1814-1830*. Paris: Hachette, 1970.

Cookson, J. E. *British Armed Nation, 1793-1815*. New York: Oxford University Press, 1997.

———. *The Friends of Peace: Anti-War Liberalism in England, 1793-1815*. New York: Cambridge University Press, 1982.

———. *Lord Liverpool's Administration: The Crucial Years, 1815-1822*. Edinburgh: Scottish Academic Press, 1975.

———. "Political Arithmetic and War in Britain, 1793-1815." *War and Society*, vol. 1, no. 2, 1983. 37-60.

Cooper, Duff. *Talleyrand*. New York: Grove Press, 1934.

Coquelle, R. *Napoleon and England, 1803-1810*. London: G. Bell, 1904.

Cormack, William S. *Revolution and Political Conflict in the French Navy, 1789-1794*. Cambridge: Cambridge University Press, 1995.

Corvoisier, Andre. *Armies and Societies in Europe 1494-1789*. Bloomington: University of Indiana Press, 1976.

Costeloe, Michael P. *Response to Revolution: Imperial Spain and the Spanish America Revolutions, 1810-1840*. New York: Cambridge University Press, 1986.

Craig, Gordon. *The Politics of the Prussian Army, 1640-1945*. Oxford: Oxford University Press, 1964.

———. "The Problems of Coalition Warfare: The Military Alliance Against Napoleon, 1808-1814." *U.S. Air Force Academy*, 1965.

———. *War, Politics, and Diplomacy*. London: Weidenfeld and Nicolson, 1966.

Crawley, C. W. "England and the Sicilian Constitution of 1812." *English Historical Review*, vol. 55, April 1940. 251-74.

———. "English and French Influences in the Cortes of Cadiz." *Cambridge Historical Journal*, vol. 4, 1939. 176-206.

Crimmins, P. "The Royal Navy and the Levant Trade, 1795-1805." In J. Black and P. S. Woodfine, eds., *The British Navy and the Use of Naval Power in the Eighteenth Century*. Leicester: Humanities Press Inc., 1988. 221-36.

Cronin, Vincent. *Napoleon*. London: HarperCollins, 1994.

Crook, M. H. "Federalism and the French Revolution: The Revolt of Toulon in 1793." *History*. 65: 583-97.

Crosby, A. W. *America, Russia, Hemp, and Napoleon: American Trade with Russia and the Baltic, 1783-1812*. Columbus: Ohio State University Press, 1965.

Cross, A. G., ed. "Russian Perceptions of England and Russia, and Russian National Awareness at the End of the Eighteenth and the Beginning of the Nineteenth Centuries." *Slavonic and East European Review*. 61: 89-106.

Crossley, Ceri, and Ian Small, eds. *The Revolution and British Culture*. New York: Oxford University Press, 1989.

Crouzet, Francois. *Britain Ascendant: Comparative Studies in Franco-British Economic History*. Cambridge: Cambridge University Press, 1990.

———. *De la Superiorite de l'Angleterre sur la France: L'Economique et l'Imaginaire*, XVII-XX Siecles. Paris: Perrin, 1999.

———. "The Impact of the French Wars on the British Economy." In H. T. Dickinson, ed., *Britain and the French Revolution, 1789-1815*. New York: St. Martin's Press, 1989. 189-210.

———. *L'Economie Britannique et le Blocus Continental*. Paris: Economica, 1987.

———. *L'Economique Britannique et le Blocus Continental, 1803-1813*. 2 vols. Paris: Economica, 1997.

———. "Wars, Blockades and Economic Change in Europe, 1792-1815. *Journal of Economic History*, vol. 24 (1964). 567-88.

Crowhurst, Patrick. *The French War on Trade: Privateering, 1793-1815*. London: Scholar Press, 1989.

Cubberly, Ray E. *The Role of Fouche During the Hundred Days*. Madison: University of Wisconsin Press, 1969.

Cunningham, Audrey. *British Credit in the Last Napoleonic War*. Cambridge: Cambridge University Press, 1934.

Dainville, Francois de, et Jean Tulard. *Atlas Administratif de l'Empire Francaise d'apres l'Atlas Redige par Ordre du Duc de Feltre en 1812*. Genève: Droz, 1973.

Dallas, Gregor. *The Final Act: The Roads to Waterloo*. New York: Henry Holt and Company, 1996.

Daly, Robert W. "Operations of the Russian Navy during the Reign of Napoleon I." *Mariner's Mirror*, vol. 34, July 1948. 169-83.

Dann, Otto, and John Dinwiddy, eds. *Nationalism in the Age of the French Revolution*. London: Hambledon, 1988.

Dard, Emile. *Napoleon and Talleyrand*. New York: D. Appleton-Century & Company, 1937.

Davies, D. W. *Sir John Moore's Peninsula Campaign, 1808-1809*. The Hague: Martinus Nijhoff, 1974.

Davies, Godfrey. "The Whigs and the Peninsula War, 1808-1814." *Transactions of the Royal Historical Society*, 2nd Series, vol. 4, 1919. 114-31.

Davies, Norman. *God's Playground: A History of Poland*, vol. 2. New York: Oxford University Press, 1981.

Davis, H. W. C. "The Great Game in Asia, 1800-44." *Proceedings of the British Academy*. 12: 227-56.

Davis, Walter W. *Joseph II: An Imperial Reformer for the Austrian Netherlands*. The Hague: Nijhof, 1974.

Dean, Rodney J. *L'Eglise Constitutionelle, Napoleon, et le Concordat de 1801*. Paris: University of Paris, Sorbonne, 2004.

Deane, Seamus. *The French Revolution and Enlightenment in England, 1789-1832*. Cambridge, Mass.: Harvard University Press, 1988.

Dechamps, J. *Entre la Guerre et la Paix: Les Isles Britanniques et la Revolution Francaise, 1798-1803*. Brussels: La Renaissance du Livre, 1949.

DeConde, Alexander. *The Quasi-War: The Politics and Diplomacy of the Undeclared Naval War with France, 1797-1801*. New York: Scribner, 1966.

Deprez, Eugene. "Les Origines Republicaines de Bonaparte." *Revue Historique*, 97, 1908.

Derogy, Jacques, et Hesi Carmel. *Bonaparte en Terre Sainte*. Paris: Fayard, 1992.

Derry, John W. *Castlereagh*. London: Allen Lane, 1976.

———. *Charles James Fox*. London: Batesford, 1972.

———. *Politics in the Age of Fox, Pitt, and Liverpool: Continuity and Transformation*. New York: Palgrave Macmillan, 1990.

———. *William Pitt*. London: Arco Publishing, 1962.

Desbiere, Edouard. *Trafalgar, la Campagne Maritime de 1805*. Paris: Chapelot, 1907.

Deutsch, Harold C. "Napoleonic Policy and the Project of a Descent upon England." *The Journal of Modern History*, vol. 2, no. 4, December 1930. 541-64.

———. *The Genesis of Napoleonic Imperialism*. Philadelphia: Lippincott, 1975.

Dhombres, Jean. *Lazare Carnot*. Paris: Fayard, 1997.

Dickinson, H. T. *British Radicalism and the French Revolution, 1789-1815*. New York: Oxford University Press, 1985.

———, ed. *Britain and the French Revolution, 1789-1815*. New York: Palgrave Macmillan, 1989.

Diesbach, G. de. *Histoire de l'Emigration, 1789-1814*. Paris: Perrin, 1998.

Donaghay, Maire. "The Marechal de Castries and the Anglo-French Commercial Negotiations of 1786-1787." *The Historical Journal*, vol. 22, no. 2, June 1972. 295-312.

Doyle, William. *The Oxford History of the French Revolution*. New York: Oxford University Press, 1989.

Driault, Eduoard. *La Politique Orientale de Napoleon, 1806-08*. Paris: Felix Alcan, 1904.

———. *Napoleon en Italie, 1800-1812*. Paris: Felix Alcan, 1905.

———. *Napoleon et l'Europe: Austerlitz, la Fin du Saint-Empire, 1804-1806*. Paris: Felix Alcan, 1912.

———. *Napoleon et l'Europe: La Chute de l'Empire, La Legende de Napoleon, 1812-1815*. Paris: Felix Alcan, 1927.

———. *Napoleon et l'Europe: Le Grand Empire, 1809-1812*. Paris: Felix Alcan, 1924.

———. *Napoleon et l'Europe: la Politique Exterieure de Premier Consul, 1800-1803*. Paris: Felix Alcan, 1910.

———. *Napoleon et l'Europe: Tilsit, France, et Russie sous le Premier Empire, la Question de Pologne, 1806-1809*. Paris: Felix Alcan, 1917.

Droz, Jacques. *Europe Between Revolutions, 1815-1848*. Ithaca, NY: Cornell University Press, 1980.

Ducere, E. *Napoleon a Bayonne*. Biarritz: Editions Harriet, 1994.

Duffy, Christopher. *The Army of Maria Theresa: The Armed Forces of Imperial Austria, 1740-1780*. London: Hippocene Books, 1977.

———. *The Military Experience in the Age of Reason*. London: Diane Publishing Company, 2003.

———. *Russia's Military Way to the West: Origins and Nature of Russian Military Power, 1700-1800*. London: Routledge, Kegan, & Paul, 1982.

Duffy, Michael. "British Diplomacy and the French Wars, 1789-1815." In H. T. Dickinson, ed., *Britain and the French Revolution, 1789-1815*. New York: Palgrave Macmillan, 1989. 127-45.

———. *Soldiers, Sugar, and Seapower: The British Expeditions to the West Indies and the War Against Revolutionary France*. New York: Oxford University Press, 1987.

———, ed. *The Military Revolution and the State*. Exeter: Exeter University Press, 1980.

Dufraisse, Roger. "Bonaparte, a-t-il Sacrifice le Rhin a l'Italie en 1796-1797?" *Revue du Souvenir Napoleonien*, n. 416, Janvier-Fevrier 1998. 5-20.

———. "La Contrebande dans les Departements Reunis de la Rive Gauche du Rhin a l'Epogue Napoleonaire." *Francia*, 1973. 1: 508-36.

———. "La Crise Economique de 1810-1812 en Pays Annexe: l'Exemple de la Rive Gauche de Rhin." *Francia*, 1978. 6: 407-40.

———. "Les Populations de la Rive Gauche du Rhin et le Service Militaire a la Fin de l'Ancien Regime et a l'Epogue Revolutionaire." *Revue Historique*, 1963. 231: 103-40.

———, et Michel Kerautret. *La France Napoleonienne: Aspects Exterieurs, 1799-1815*. Paris: Seuil, 1999.

Dugan, James. *The Great Mutiny*. New York: New American Library, 1966.

Dunan, Marcel. *L'Allemagne de la Revolution et de l'Empire*. Paris: Plon, 1954.

———. *Napoleon et Allemagne: le Systeme Continental et les Debuts du Royaume de Baviere*. Paris: Plon, 1942.

———, ed. *Napoleon et l'Europe*. Paris: Plon, 1961, 1943.

Dunant, Emile. *Les Relations Diplomatiques de la France et de la Republique Helvetique, 1798-1803*. Basle: Verlag der Basler Buch, 1901.

Dupont, Marcel. *Caroline Bonaparte, la Soeur Preferee de Napoleon*. Paris: Hachette, 1937.

Dupre, Huntley. *Lazare Carnot*. New York: Porcupine Press, 1975.

Durand, C. "Le Pouvoir Napoleonien et ses Legitimites." *Annales de la Faculte de Droit et de Science Politique d'Aix-Marseille*, 1972. 7-33.

Durant, Will and Ariel. *The Age of Napoleon: A History of European Civilization from 1789 to 1815*. New York: Simon and Schuster, 1975.

Dwyer, Philip G. "Duroc Diplomate: Un Militaire au Service de la Diplomatie Napoleonienne." *Le Souvenir Napoleonien*, vol. 58, 1995. 21-40.

———. "The Politics of Prussian Neutrality, 1795-1806." *German History*, 12 (1994). 351-74.

———. "Prussia and the Armed Neutrality: the Invasion of Hanover in 1801." *International History Review*, 15 (1993). 661-87.

———, ed. *Napoleon and Europe*. London: Longman, 2001.

Dziewanowski, M. K. *Alexander I: Russia's Mysterious Tsar*. New York: Hippocene Books, 1990.

Egan, C. L. *Neither Peace Nor War: Franco-American Relations, 1803-1812*. Baton Rouge: Louisiana State University Press, 1983.

Ehrman, J. *The British Government and Commercial Negotiations with Europe, 1783-1793*. Cambridge: Cambridge University Press, 1962.

Ehrman, John. *The Younger Pitt: The Consuming Struggle*. Palo Alto, Calif.: Stanford University Press, 1996.

———. *The Younger Pitt: The Reluctant Transition*. London: Constable Robinson, 1985.

———. *The Younger Pitt: The Years of Acclaim*. London: Constable & Company, 1984.

Elliot, D.C. "The Grenville Mission to Berlin, 1799." *Huntington Library Quarterly*, 18 (1954-55). 129-46.

Elliott, Marianne. "Ireland and the French Revolution." In H. T. Dickinson, ed., *Britain and the French Revolution, 1789-1815*. New York: St. Martin's Press, 1989. 83-101.

———. *Partners in Revolution: The United Irishmen and France*. New Haven, Conn.: Yale University Press, 1982.

Ellis, Geoffrey. *The Napoleonic Empire*. Atlantic Highlands, N.J.: Humanities Press International, 1991.

Emsley, Clive. *British Society and the French Wars, 1793-1815*. London: Palgrave Macmillan, 1979.

——. *The Longman Companion to Napoleonic Europe.* London: Longman, 1993.

Englund, Steven. *Napoleon: A Political Life.* New York: Scribner, 2004.

Epstein, R. M. *Napoleon's Last Victory and the Emergence of Modern War.* Lawrence: University of Kansas Press, 1994.

Esdaile, Charles J. *The Duke of Wellington and the Command of the Spanish Army, 1812-13.* Basingstoke: Macmillan, 1990.

——. *Fighting Napoleon: Guerrillas, Bandits, and Adventurers in Spain, 1808-1814.* New Haven, Conn.: Yale University Press, 2004.

——. "The Napoleonic Period; Some Thoughts on Recent Historiography." *European History Quarterly*, vol. 23, 1993. 415-32.

——. *Napoleon's Wars: An International History, 1803-1815.* New York: Viking, 2007.

——. *The Peninsula War: A New History.* London: Penguin Press, 2002.

——. *The Spanish Army in the Peninsula War.* Manchester: Manchester University Press, 1988.

——. "War and Politics in Spain, 1808-1814." *The Historical Journal*, vol. 31, no. 2, 1988. 295-317.

——. *The Wars of Napoleon.* New York: Longman, 1995.

——. "Wellington and the Military Eclipse of Spain, 1808-1814." *International History Review*, vol. 11, February 1989. 55-67.

Espitalier, A. *Napoleon and King Murat, 1808-1813.* New York: John Lane Company, 1912.

Esposito, Vincent J., and John R. Etling. *A Military History and Atlas of the Napoleonic Wars.* London: Greenhill Books, 1999.

Evans, Howard. "The Nootka Sound Controversy in Anglo-French Diplomacy, 1790." *Journal of Modern History*, vol. 46, no. 4, December 1974. 609-40.

Falk, Minna R. "Stadion, adversaire de Napoleon (1806-1809)." *Annales Historiques de la Revolution Francaise*, 169 (1962). 288-305.

Favier, F. "La Suede et le Blocus Continental." *Revue du Souvenir Napoleonien*, n. 389, Juin-Juillet, 1993. 25-29.

Feldbaek, Ole. "The Anglo-Russian Rapprochement of 1801: A Prelude to the Peace of Amiens." *Scandinavian Journal of History.* 3: 208-27.

——. *Denmark and the Armed Neutrality, 1800-1801.* Copenhagen: Akademisk Forlag, 1980.

——. "The Foreign Policy of Tsar Paul I, 1800-1801: An Interpretation." *Jahrbucher fur die Geschite Osteuropas.* 30: 16-35.

Ferrero, Guglielmo. *The Gamble: Napoleon in Italy, 1796-1797.* London: G. Bell and Sons, 1961.

——. *The Reconstruction of Europe.* New York: W. W. Norton and Company, 1961.

——. *The Two French Revolutions, 1789-1796.* New York: Basic Books, 1968.

Fierro, A., A. Paulleuel-Guillard, et Jean Tulard, eds. *Histoire et Dictionaire du Consulat et de l'Empire*. Paris: R. Laffont, 1995.

Finley, Milton. *The Most Monstrous of Wars*. Columbia: University of South Carolina Press, 1994.

Fisher, H.A.L. *Napoleonic Statesmanship: Germany*. Oxford: Clarendon Press, 1903.

Flayhart, William Henry. *Counterpoint to Trafalgar: The Anglo-Russian Invasion of Naples, 1805-1806*. Columbia: University of South Carolina Press, 1992.

Flick, Carolyn. *The Making of Haiti: The Saint Domingue Revolution from Below*. Knoxville: University of Tennessee Press, 1990.

Flockerzie, L. J. "Saxony, Austria and the German Question after the Congress of Vienna, 1815-1816." *International History Review*. 12: 661-87.

Fohlen, C. *Jefferson a Paris*. Paris: Perrin, 1995.

Ford, Franklin. "The Revolutionary and Napoleonic Era: How Much of a Watershed?" *American Historical Review*, vol. 49, no. 1, 1963.

Ford, Guy Stanton. *Hanover and Prussia, 1795-1803: A Study in Neutrality*. New York: AMS Press, 1967.

———. *Stein and the Era of Reform in Prussia, 1807-15*. New York: Peter Smith Publication Inc., 1965.

Forrest, Alan. *Conscripts and Deserters: The Army and French Society During the Revolution and Empire*. New York: Oxford University Press, 1989.

———. *Soldiers of the French Revolution*. Durham, NC: Duke University Press, 1990.

Forrester, C. S. *The Age of Fighting Sail: The Naval War of 1812*. London: Chapman Billes Inc., 1956.

Fortescue, John W. *British Statesmen of the Great War, 1793-1814*. Oxford: Oxford University Press, 1911.

Fournier, Albert. *Napoleon I: A Biography*. Paris: Holt & Company, 1911.

Fournoux, Amable de. *Napoleon et Venise, 1796-1814*. Paris: Fallois, 2002.

Franceschi, Michel, and Ben Weider. *The Wars Against Napoleon: Debunking the Myth of the Napoleonic Wars*. New York: Savas Beatie, 2008.

Fraser, Antonia. *Marie Antoinette: The Journey*. New York: Anchor Books, 2002.

Fregosi. *Dreams of Empire: Napoleon and the First World War, 1792-1815*. London: Hutchinson, 1989.

Frey, Linda and Marsha. "'The Reign of the Charlatans Is Over': The French Revolutionary Attack on Diplomatic Practice." *Journal of Modern History*, vol. 65, no. 4, December 1993. 706-44.

Fryer, W. R. *Republic or Restoration in France? 1794-1797*. Manchester, Eng.: Manchester University Press, 1965.

Fuente, Francisco de la. "Portuguese Resistance to Napoleon: Don Miquel Format and the Mobilization of Portugal." *The Consortium on Revolutionary Europe*, 1983.

Fugier, Andre. *Histoire de Relations Internationales: La Revolution Francaise et l'Empire Napoleonien.* Paris: Hachette, 1994.

———. *Napoleon et l'Espagne, 1799-1808.* 2 vols. Paris: Felix Alcan, 1930.

———. *Napoleon et l'Italie.* Paris: Hachette, 1947.

Fulford, Roger T. B. *Samuel Whitbread, 1764-1815: A Study in Opposition.* London: Macmillan, 1967.

Gagliardo, John C. *Reich and Nation: The Holy Roman Empire as Idea and Reality, 1763-1806.* Bloomington: University of Indiana Press, 1980.

Gallaher, John G. "Marshall Davout and the Second Bourbon Restoration." *French Historical Studies,* vol. 6, 1970. 350-64.

Galpin, W. F. *The Grain Supply of England During the Napoleonic Period.* Philadelphia: University of Pennsylvania Press, 1925.

Garnier, Michael. *Bonaparte et la Louisiane.* Paris: S. P. M., 1992.

Gash, Norman. "After Waterloo: British Society and the Legacy of the Napoleonic Wars." *Transactions of the Royal Historical Society.* 28: 145-38.

———. *Lord Liverpool: The Life and Political Career of Robert Jenkinson, Second Earl of Liverpool, 1770-1828.* Cambridge, Mass.: Harvard University Press, 1984.

———, ed. *Wellington: Studies in the Military and Political Career of the First Duke of Wellington.* Manchester: Manchester University Press, 1990.

Gat, Azar. *The Origins of Military Thought.* New York: Oxford University Press, 1989.

Gates, David. *The Napoleonic Wars, 1803-1815.* New York: St. Martin's Press, 1997.

———. *The Spanish Ulcer: A History of the Peninsula War.* New York: Da Capo, 1986.

Gayer, Arthur, W. Rostow, and A. Schwartz. *The Growth and Fluctuations of the British Economy, 1790-1850.* Oxford: Oxford University Press, 1973.

Geggus, David. "The Anglo-French Conflict in the Caribbean in 1790s." In Colin Jones, ed., *Britain and Revolutionary France: Conflict, Subversion, and Propaganda.* Exeter: University of Exeter Press, 1983. 27-39.

———. *Slavery, War, and Revolution: The British Occupation of Saint Dominique, 1793-98.* New York: Oxford University Press, 1982.

Geyl, Pieter. *Napoleon: For and Against.* New Haven, Conn.: Yale University Press, 1949.

Gill, Conrad. "The Relations Between England and France in 1802." *The English Historical Review,* vol. 24, no. 93, January 1909. 61-78.

Girod de l'Ain, Gerard. *Bernadotte: Chef de Guerre et Chef d'Etat.* Paris: Perrin, 1968.

———. *Joseph Bonaparte: Le Roi Malgre Lui.* Paris: Perrin, 1970.

Glover, Michael. "Arms and the British Diplomat in the French Revolutionary Era." *Journal of Modern History,* vol. 29, 1959. 199-212.

———. *Britain at Bay, Defense Against Bonaparte, 1803-1814.* London: George Allen and Unwin, 1973.

———. *Britannia Sickens: Sir Arthur Wellesley and the Convention of Cintra.* London: Leo Cooper, 1970.

———. "The French Fleet, 1807-1814: Britain's Problem and Madison's Opportunity." *Journal of Modern History*, vol. 39. 233-52.

———. *Legacy of Glory: The Bonaparte Kingdom of Spain, 1808-1813.* New York: Scribners, 1971.

———. *Napoleonic Wars.* New York: Hippocene Books, 1979.

———. *Peninsula Preparations: The Reform of the British Army, 1795-1809.* Cambridge: Cambridge University Press, 1963.

———. *A Very Slippery Fellow: The Life of Sir Robert Wilson, 1803-1814.* London: George Allen and Unwin, 1978.

Godechot, Jacques. *Les Commissaires aux Armees sous le Directoires.* 2 vols. Paris: Fustier, 1937.

———. *Le Comte d'Antraigues: Un Espions dans l'Europe des Émigrés.* Paris: Fayard, 1986.

———. *The Counter-Revolution: Doctrine and Action, 1789-1804.* Princeton, NJ: Princeton University Press, 1981.

———. *La Grande Nation: l'Expansion Revolutionaire de la France dans le Monde de 1789 a 1799.* 2 vols. Paris: Auber, 2004.

———. *Les Institutions de la France sous la Revolution et l'Empire.* Paris: Puf, 1981.

Godlewski, Guy. "Napoleon et Les-Etats-Amis." *La Nouvelle Revue Des Deux Mondes, Juillet-Septembre*, 1977.

Goebel, Dorothy B. "British Trade to the Spanish Colonies, 1796-1823." *American Historical Review*, vol. 43, 1937-38. 288-320.

Goetz-Bernstein, H. A. *La Politique Exterieure de Brissot et des Girondins.* Paris: Libraire Hachette, 1912.

Goldenberg, Joseph A. "The Royal Navy's Blockade in New England Waters, 1812-1815." *International History Review*, vol. 6, August 1984. 424-39.

Goncourt, E. et J. *Histoire de la Societe Francaise pendant le Directoire.* Paris: Gallimard, 1992.

Gotteri, Nicole. *La Campagne de Suisse en 1799: "Le Choc des Geants."* Paris: RMN, 2003.

———. *Napoleon et le Portugal.* Paris: Bernard Giovanangeli, 2004.

Grab, Alexander. "The Kingdom of Italy and Napoleon's Continental Blockade." *Proceedings, Consortium on Revolutionary Europe*, 1989. 18: 587-604.

Grainger, John D. *The Amiens Truce.* Rochester, NY: Boydell Press, 2004.

Grandmaison, Geoffrey de. *L'Espagne et Napoleon.* 3 vols. Paris: Plon, 1908.

Graubard, S. R. "Castlereagh and the Peace of Europe." *Journal of British Studies*, vol. 3, 1963. 79-87.

Gray, Denis. *Spencer Perceval: The Evangelical Prime Minister, 1762-1812.* Manchester: Manchester University Press, 1963.

Gray, D. S. "The French Invasion of Hanover in 1803 and the Origins of the King's German Legion." *Proceedings, Consortium on Revolutionary Europe,* 1980. 198-211.

Gray, Marion W. "Prussia in Transition: Society and Politics under the Stein Reform Ministry of 1808." *American Philosophical Society,* 76, 1986.

Graziani, Antoine Maria. *Pascal Paoli Pere de la Patrie Corse.* Paris: Talladier, 2002.

Greenbaum, Louis S. *Talleyrand, Statesman Priest.* Washington, DC: Catholic University Press, 1970.

Gregory, Desmond. *Sicily: The Insecure Base: A History of the British Occupation of Sicily, 1806-1815.* Teaneck, NJ: Fairleigh Dickinson University, 1988.

Grimsted, P. K. *The Foreign Ministers of Alexander I: Political Attitudes and the Conduct of Russian Diplomacy, 1810-1825.* Berkeley: University of California Press, 1969.

Grunwald, Constantin de. *Baron Stein: Enemy of Napoleon.* London: J. Cape, 1940.

Guillard, A. Palleul. *L'Episode Napoleonienne: Aspects Exterieurs.* Paris: Seuil, 1972.

Guillon, E. L. M. *Napoleon et les Suisses, 1803-1815.* Paris: Plon, 1910.

Guy, Alan J., ed. *The Road to Waterloo: The British Army and the Struggle Against Revolutionary and Napoleonic France, 1793-1815.* London: National Army Museum, 1990.

Haas, A. G. *Metternich, Reorganization and Nationality, 1813-1818: A Story of Foresight and Frustration in Rebuilding the Austrian Empire.* New York: Coronet Books, 1963.

Hagen, William W. "The Partitions of Poland and the Crisis of the Old Regime in Prussia, 1772-1806." *Central European History.* 9: 115-28.

Hales, Edward E. Y. *Napoleon and the Pope: The Story of Napoleon and Pius VII.* London: Eyre & Spottiswoode, 1961.

———. *Revolution and Papacy, 1767-1848.* Garden City, NY: Hanover House of Doubleday & Company, 1960.

Hall, C. D. *British Strategy in the Napoleonic War, 1803-15.* Manchester: Manchester University Press, 1992.

Hamilton-Williams, David. *The Fall of Napoleon: The Final Betrayal.* London: Arms and Armour Press, 1994.

———. *Waterloo, New Perspectives: The Great Battle Reappraised.* London: Arms and Amour Press, 1993.

Hampson, Norman. *Prelude to Terror: The Constituent Assembly and the Failure of Consensus, 1789-1791.* New York: Oxford University Press, 1988.

Harbron, J. *"Spain's Forgotten Naval Renaissance." History Today,* 40/8, 1990.

———. *Trafalgar and the Spanish Navy.* Annapolis, MD: Naval Institute Press. 1925.

Harford, Lee S. "Bavaria and the Tyrol Under Napoleon." *The Consortium on Revolutionary Europe,* 1989.

Haswell, Jock. *The First Respectable Spy: The Life and Times of Colquhound Grant.* London: Hamilton, 1969.

Hayman, Peter. *Soult: Napoleon's Maligned Marshal.* London: Arms and Armour, 1990.

Haythornthwaite, Philip J. *The Napoleonic Source Book*. London: Arms and Armour Books, 1990.

Heckscher, Eli F. *The Continental System*. Oxford: Clarendon Press, 1922.

Heles, Peter A. "Clausewitz and the Campaign of 1812 in Russia." *The Consortium on Revolutionary Europe*, 1989.

Helmuth, Eckhart, ed. *The Transformation of Political Culture: England and Germany in the Late Eighteenth Century*. Oxford: Oxford University Press, 1990.

Hemphill, W. Edwin. "The Jeffersonian Background of the Louisiana Purchase." *The Mississippi Valley Historical Review*, vol. 22, no. 2, September 1935. 177-90.

Henry, Nicholas, Fifth Earl Stanhope. *Notes of Conversations with the Duke of Wellington, 1831-1851*. London: Murray, 1888.

Henshall, Nicolas. *The Myth of Absolutism: Change and Continuity in Early Modern European Monarchy*. London: Longman Publishing, 1992.

Herr, Richard. *The Eighteenth Century Revolution in Spain*. Princeton, NJ: Princeton University Press, 1958.

Hibbert, Christopher. *George IV*. London: Penguin, 1976.

———. *Wellington: A Personal History*. Reading, Mass.: Perseus Books, 1997.

Hickey, Donald R. "The Monroe-Pinckney Treaty of 1806: A Reappraisal." *William and Mary Quarterly*, 1987. 35: 65-88.

———. *The War of 1812: A Forgotten Conflict*. Urbana: University of Illinois Press, 1990.

Hill, Peter P. *Napoleon's Troublesome Americans: Franco-American Relations, 1804-1815*. Washington, DC: Potomac Books, 2005.

———. *William Vans Murray*. New York: Macmillan, 1975.

Hinde, Wendy. *Canning*. Oxford: Blackwell, 1989.

———. *Castlereagh*. London: Collins, 1981.

Hitsman, J. Mackay. *The Incredible War of 1812*. Toronto: University of Toronto Press, 1965.

Hocquellet, R. *Resistance et Revolution durant l'Occupation Napoleonienne en Espagne, 1808-1812*. Paris: Boutique de Histoire, 2001.

Holbraad, Carsten. *The Concert of Europe: A Study in German and British International Theory, 1815-1914*. New York: Barnes and Noble, 1971.

Hollingsworth, Barry. "The Napoleonic Invasion of Russia and Recent Soviet Historical Writing." *Journal of Modern History*, vol. 38, no. 1, January 1966. 38-52.

Holtman, Robert B. *Napoleonic Propaganda*. Baton Rouge: Louisiana State University Press, 1950.

———. *The Napoleonic Revolution*. New York: Lippincott, 1967.

Hone, J. Ann. *For the Cause of Truth: Radicalism in London, 1896-1821*. Oxford: Clarendon, 1982.

Hope-Jones, Arthur. *Income Tax in the Napoleonic Wars.* Cambridge: Cambridge University Press, 1939.

Horne, Alistair. *How Far From Austerlitz? Napoleon, 1805-1815.* London: Macmillan, 1996.

Horsman, Reginald. *The Causes of the War of 1812.* London: Eyre and Spottiswoode, 1969.

Horwald, Donald D. "British Seapower and Its Influence Upon the Peninsula War, 1808-1814." *The Naval War College Review,* vol. 31, no. 2, Fall 1978. 54-71.

Hourtoulle, F.-G. *1814: La Campagne.* Paris: Histoire et Collections, 2005.

Houssaye, Henry. *1814.* Paris: Perrin, 1918.

———. *1815: La Premiere Restauration, Le Retour de l'ile d'Elbe, les Cents Jours.* Paris: Plon, 1920.

———. *1815: La Second Abdication, La Terreur Blanche.* Paris: Plon, 1918.

———. *Napoleon and the Campaign of 1814.* London: Hugh Rees, 1914.

Howard, Donald D. "Wellington and the Defense of Portugal (1808-1813)." *The Consortium on Revolutionary Europe,* 1989.

Howe, P. "Belgian Influence on French Policy, 1789-1793." *Proceedings, Consortium on Revolutionary Europe,* 1986. 16: 213-22.

Hueckel, Glenn R. *The Napoleonic Wars and their Impact on Factor Returns and Output Growth in England, 1793-1895.* New York: Hueckel, 1985.

Humphreys, Robert A., and J. Lynch, eds. *The Origins of the Latin American Revolutions, 1808-1826.* New York: Random House, 2000.

Hunt, Lynn A. *Politics, Culture, and Class in the French Revolution.* Berkeley: University of California, 1984.

———, D. Lansky, and P. Hanson. "The Failure of the Liberal Republic in France, 1795-1799: The Road to Brumaire." *Journal of Modern History.* 51: 734-59.

Hurt, M. *The Chouanerie and Counter Revolution: Puisaye, the Princes, and the British Government.* 2 vols. Cambridge: Cambridge University Press, 1965.

Huttenback, R. A. "The French Threat to India and British Relations with Sind, 1799-1809." *English History Review,* 1961. 76: 590-99.

Iiams, Thomas M. *Peacemaking from Vergennes to Napoleon: French Foreign Relations in the Revolutionary Era 1774-1814.* Huntington, NY: Praeger Publishing, 1979.

Imlah, Albert H. "Real Values in British Foreign Trade, 1798-1853." *Journal of Economic History,* vol. 7, 1948. 133-52.

Iung, Theodore. *Bonaparte et son Temps, 1769-1799.* 3 vols. Paris: Charpentier, 1880-81.

Jackson, W. G. F. *Attack in the West: Napoleon's First Campaign Re-read Today.* London: Eyre & Spottiswoode, 1953.

James, James Alton. "French Opinion as a Factor in Preventing War Between France and the United States, 1795-1800." *The American Historical Review*, vol. 30, no. 1, October 1924. 44-55.

——. "Louisiana as a Factor in American Diplomacy, 1795-1800." *The Mississippi Valley Historical Review*, vol. 1, no. 1, June 1914. 44-56.

James, Lawrence. *The Iron Duke: A Military Biography of Wellington*. London: Weidenfeld and Nicolson, 1992.

Jardin, Andre, and Andre-Jean Tudesq. *Restoration and Reaction, 1815-1848*. New York: Cambridge University Press, 1984.

Jarrett, Derek. *The Begetters of Revolution: England's Involvement with France, 1759-1789*. Totowa, NJ: Rowman & Littlefield, 1973.

Jenks, Leland H. *The Migration of British Capital to 1875*. New York: Barnes and Noble, 1971.

Jennings, Lawrence C. *French Reaction to British Slave Emancipation*. Baton Rouge: Louisiana State University Press, 1988.

Johnson, Paul. *The Birth of the Modern: World Society, 1815-1830*. London: Weidenfeld and Nicolson, 1991.

Johnston, Otto W. "British Espionage and Prussian Politics in the Age of Napoleon." *Intelligence and National Security: An Interdisciplinary Journal*, 2 (1987). 230-44.

——. *The Myth of a Nation: Literature and Politics in Prussia Under Napoleon*. Columbia: University of South Carolina Press, 1989.

Johnston, Robert M. "Lord William Bentinck and Murat." *English Historical Review*, vol. 19, 1904. 263-80.

Jomini, Antoine Henri. *The Political and Military History of the Campaign of Waterloo*. New York: Redfield, 1860.

Jones, Colin. *The Longman Companion to the French Revolution*. London: Longman, 1990.

——. "The Military Revolution and Professionalization of the French Army Under the Ancien Regime." In Michael Duffy, ed., *The Military Revolution and the State*. Exeter: Exeter University Press, 1980.

——, ed. *Britain and Revolutionary France: Conflict, Subversion, and Propaganda*. Exeter: Exeter University Press, 1983.

Josselson, Michael and Diana. *The Commander: A Life of Barclay de Tolly*. Oxford: Oxford University Press, 1980.

Jupp, Peter. *Lord Grenville, 1759-1834*. Oxford: Clarendon Press, 1985.

Kagan, Frederick W. *The End of the Old Order: Napoleon and Europe, 1801-1805*. New York: Da Capo, 2006.

Kaplan, Lawrence S. *Entangling Alliances with None: American Foreign Policy in the Age of Jefferson*. Kent, Ohio: Kent State University Press, 1987.

——. "France and the War of 1812." *Journal of American History*, vol. 57, no. 1. 36-47.

Kaplan, Steven. *Farewell Revolution: The Historians' Feud, France 1789/1989.* Ithaca, NY: Cornell University Press, 1995.

Karal, E. Z. "The Ottoman Empire and the Serbian Uprising 1807-1812." In W. S. Vucinich, ed., *The First Serbian Uprising.* Boulder, Colo.: Westview Press, 1982. 207-26.

Kaufmann, William W. *British Policy and the Independence of Latin America, 1804-1828.* New Haven, Conn.: Yale University Press, 1951.

Keep, John H. L. "Paul I and the Militarization of Government." In H. Ragsdale, ed., *Paul I: A Reassessment of His Life and Reign.* Pittsburg: University of Pittsburgh Press, 1979.

———. "The Russian Army's Response to the French Revolution." *Jahrbrucher fur die Geschichte Osteuropas.* 28: 500-23.

———. *Soldiers of the Tsar: Army and Society in Russia.* New York: Oxford University Press, 1985.

Kennedy, Paul. *The Rise and Fall of British Naval Mastery.* London: Humanities Book, 1976.

Kennedy, Roger G. *Mr. Jefferson's Lost Cause: Land, Farmers, Slavery, and the Louisiana Purchase.* New York: Oxford University Press, 2003.

Kerautret, M. "Napoleon, Frederic, et la Naissance du Wurttemberg Moderne." *Voies Nouvelles pour l'Histoire du Premier Empire: Territoires, Pouvoirs, Identites,* 2003. 75-98.

Kissinger, Henry. *A World Restored: Metternich, Castlereagh, and the Problems of Peace, 1812-1822.* London: Weidenfeld & Nicolson, 1957.

Klang, Daniel. "Bavaria and the War of Liberation, 1813-14." *French Historical Studies,* Vol. 4, 1965.

Kohn, H. *Prelude to Nation-States: The French and German Experience, 1789-1815.* Princeton, NJ: Van Nostrand, 1967.

Kosary, Domokos. *Napoleon et la Hongrie.* Budapest: Akademiai Kiado, 1979.

Kraehe, Enno E. "From Reinbund to Deutscher Bund: The Road to European Equilibrium." *Proceedings, Consortium on Revolutionary Europe,* 1977. 4: 163-75.

———. *Metternich's German Policy: The Congress of Vienna, 1814-1815.* Princeton, NJ: Princeton University Press, 1983.

———. *Metternich's German Policy: The Contest with Napoleon, 1799-1814.* Princeton, NJ: Princeton University Press, 1963.

———. "Raison d'Etat et Ideologie dans la Politique Allemande de Metternich, 1809-1820." *Revue d'Histoire Moderne et Contemporaine, 1966.* 13: 181-94.

———. "Wellington and the Reconstruction of the Allied Armies during the Hundred Days." *International History Review,* vol. 11, February 1989. 84-97.

Kukiel, Marian. *Czartoryski and European Unity, 1770-1861.* Princeton, NJ: Princeton University Press, 1955.

Kurtz, Stephen G. "The French Mission of 1799-1800: Concluding Chapter in the Statecraft of John Adams." *Political Science Quarterly*, vol. 80, no. 4, December 1965. 543-57.

Labarre de Raillecourt, Dominique. *Louis Bonaparte*. Paris: Peyronnet, 1963.

Lackland, H. M. "The Failure of the Constitutional Experiment in Sicily, 1813-14." *English Historical Review*, vol. 41, 1926. 210-36.

———. "Lord William Bentinck in Sicily, 1811-12." *English Historical Review*, vol. 42, 1927. 371-96.

Lacour-Gayet, Georges. *Talleyrand, 1754-1838*. 4 vols. Paris: Payot, 1933-34.

Lacour-Gayet, Michel. *Joachim et Caroline Murat*. Paris: Perrin, 1996.

———. *Marie-Caroline, Reine de Naples, Un Adversaire de Napoleon*. Paris: Tallandier, 1990.

Lafage, Franck. *L'Espagne de la Contre-Revolution: Development et Declin, XVIII-XX Siecle*s. Paris: L'Harmatlan, 1993.

Laissus, Yves. *L'Egypte: Une Adventure Savante, Avec Bonaparte, Kleber, Menou, 1798-1801*. Paris: Fayard, 1998.

La Jonquiere, C. de. *L'Expedition d'Egypte, 1798-1801*. 4 vols. Paris: Claude Lavauzelle, 1899.

Langlois, Claude. "Le plebiscite de l'an VIII ou le coup d'Etat du 18 pluvoise an VIII." *Annales historique de la Revolution Francaise*, 1972. 45-63, 231-46, 390-415.

Langsam, Walter C. *The Napoleonic Wars and German Nationalism in Austria*. Columbia: University of South Carolina Press, 1930.

Las Cases, Marie-Joseph Emmanuel Dieudonne, comte de. *Memorial de Sainte Helene*. 2 vols. Paris: Flammarion, 1951.

Latrille, Andre. *L'Eglise Catholique et la Revolution Francaises*. 2 vols. Paris: Editions du Cerf, 1970.

———. *Napoleon et la Saint-Siege, 1801-1808: L'Ambassade du Cardinal Fesch a Roma*. Paris: F. Alcan, 1935.

Laurens, Henry. *L'Expedition d'Egypte, 1798-1801*. Paris: Seuil, 1989.

Lavery, Brian. *The Ship of the Line: Design, Construction, and Fitting*. London: Brassey's, Inc., 1984.

Lebrun, F., and Roger Dupuy, eds. *Les Resistance a la Revolution*. Paris: Puf, 1987.

Lefebvre, Georges. *The French Revolution from 1793 to 1799*. London: Routledge, 1998.

———. *The French Revolution from Its Origins to 1799*. New York: Columbia University Press, 1965.

———. *Napoleon*. 2 vols. London: Routledge & Kegan Paul, 1969.

Leggiere, Michael V. *The Fall of Napoleon: The Allied Invasion of France, 1813-1814*. New York: Cambridge University Press, 2007.

———. *Napoleon and Berlin: The Franco-Prussia War in North Germany 1813*. Norman: University of Oklahoma Press, 2002.

Lemarchand, G. "La Grande-Bretagne Face a la France a la Fin du XVIII Siecle: Les Movements Paysan." *Annales Historique de la Revolution Francaise*, 1999. 97-126.

Lentz, Thierry. *Le 18-Brumaire: Les Coups d'Etats de Napoleon Bonaparte*. Paris: Jean Picollec, n.d.

———. *Dictionaire des Ministres de Napoleon*. Paris: JAS, 1999.

———. *Le Grand Consulat, 1799-1804*. Paris: Fayard, 1999.

———. *Napoleon et l'Europe*. Paris: Fayard, 2004.

———. *Nouvelle Histoire du Premier Empire: L'Effondrement du Systeme Napoleonien, 1810-1814*. Paris: Fayard, 2004.

———. *Nouvelle Histoire du Premier Empire: Napoleon et la Conquete de l'Europe, 1804-1810*. Paris: Fayard, 2002.

———. "Les Relations Americano-Francaises, de la Revolution a la Chute de l'Empire." *Revue du Souvenir Napoleonien,* Janvier-Fevrier, 1996.

———. *Savary: Le Siede de Napoleon*. Paris: Fayard, 2001.

Levillain, P., ed. *Dictionaire Historique de la Papaute*. Paris: French and European Publishers, 1994.

Levy, Arthur. *Napoleon et la Paix*. Paris: Plon, 1902.

Levy, Francis. *Alexandre Ier et sa Sainte-Alliance, 1811-1825*. Paris: Fischbacher, 1975.

Lewis, Michael. *A Social History of the Navy, 1793-1815*. London: Stackpole Books, 2004.

Lloyd, Christopher C. "Armed Forces and the Art of War: Navies." In *The New Cambridge History*, ed. C. W. Crawley, vol. 9, *War and Peace in an Age of Upheaval*. Cambridge: Cambridge University Press, 1965.

———. *Nelson and Sea Power*. London: English Universities Free Press, 1977.

———. "The Nile Campaign: Nelson and Napoleon in Egypt." New York: Barnes and Noble, 1973.

Lloyd, Peter A. *The French Are Coming: The Invasion Scare, 1803-05*. London: Hyperion Books, 1991.

Lobanov-Rostovsky, A.A. *Russia and Europe, 1789-1825*. Durham, NC: Duke University Press, 1947.

Lockhart, J. G. *The Peacemakers, 1814-1815*. London: Duckworth, 1932.

Longford, Elizabeth. *Wellington: Pillar of State*. New York: Harper & Row, 1972.

———. *Wellington: The Years of the Sword*. New York: Harper & Row, 1969.

Longworth, Philip. *The Art of Victory: The Life and Achievements of Generalissimo Suvorov*. New York: Holt, Rinehart, & Winston, 1966.

Lord, Robert Howard. *The Second Partition of Poland: A Study in Diplomatic History*. Cambridge: Harvard University Press, 1915.

Lovett, Gabriel H. *Napoleon and the Birth of Modern Spain*. 2 vols. New York: New York University Press, 1965.

Lovie, J., et A. Palluel-Guillard. *L'Episode Napoleonien: Aspects Exterieurs*. Paris: Parut, 1972.

Lucas, Colin, ed. *Rewriting the French Revolution*. New York: Oxford University Press, 1991.

Lukacs, John A. "Russian Armies in Western Europe, 1799, 1814, 1917." *American Slavic and East European Review*, vol. 13, 1954. 319-37.

Lynch, John. *Bourbon Spain, 1700-1808*. New York: Oxford University Press, 1989.

——. "British Policy and Spanish America, 1783-1808." *Journal of Latin American Studies*, vol. 1, no. 1, 1969.

——. *The Spanish American Revolutions, 1808-1826*. New York: W.W. Norton, 1973.

Lynn, John A. *The Bayonets of the Republic: Motivation and Tactics in the Army of Revolutionary France, 1791-1794*. Urbana: University of Illinois Press, 1984.

Lyon, E. Wilson. "The Franco-American Convention of 1800." *The Journal of Modern History*, vol. 12, no. 3, September 1940. 305-33.

——. *Louisiana in French Diplomacy, 1759-1804*. Norman: University of Oklahoma Press, 1934.

——. *The Man Who Sold Louisiana: the Career of Francois Barbe-Marbois*. Norman: University of Oklahoma Press, 1942.

——. "Milfort's Plan for a Franco-Creek Alliance and the Retrocession of Louisiana." *The Journal of Southern History*, vol. 4, no. 1, February 1938. 72-87.

Lyons, Martin. *Napoleon Bonaparte and the Legacy of the French Revolution*. New York: Palgrave, 1994.

Macartney, Carlyle A. *The Habsburg Empire, 1790-1912*. New York: Macmillan, 1969.

McGrew, Roderick E. *Paul I of Russia, 1754-1801*. New York: Oxford University Press, 1992.

McKay, Derek, and H. M. Scott. *The Rise of the Great Powers, 1648-1815*. London: Longman, 1983.

Mackenzie, Norman. *Escape From Elba: The Fall and Flight of Napoleon, 1814-1815*. New York: Oxford University Press, 1982.

Mackesy, Piers. "Collingwood and Ganteaume: The French Offensive in the Mediterranean, January to April 1808." *Mariner's Mirror*, 41, 1955.

——. "Problems of an Amphibious Power: Britain Against France, 1793-1815." *Naval War College Review*, 1978. 30:16-25.

——. *Statesmen at War: The Strategy of Overthrow, 1798-1799*. London: Longman, 1974.

——. *The War in the Mediterranean, 1803-1810*. Cambridge, Mass.: Harvard University Press, 1957.

——. *War Without Victory: The Downfall of Pitt, 1799-1802*. Oxford: Clarendon Press, 1984.

McLynn, Frank. *Napoleon*. London: Jonathan Cape, 1997.

McManners, John. *The French Revolution and the Church.* London: S.P.C.K., 1969.

Macmillan, D. S. "Russo-British Trade Relations under Alexander I." *Canadian-American Slavonic Studies,* 1973. 7: 68-77.

McNally, R. T. "The Origins of Russophilia in France: 1812-1830." *American Slavic and East European Review,* 1958. 17: 173-89.

McQuiston, J. R. "Rose and Canning in Opposition, 1806-1807." *Historical Journal, 1971.* 14: 503-27.

Madaraiga, Isabel de. *Russia in the Age of Catherine the Great.* London: Phoenix Press, 2002.

Madelin, Louis. *L'Apogee de L'Empire, 1809-1810.* 3 vols. Paris: Hachette, 1944.

———. *Histoire du Consulat et de l'Empire.* 16 vols. London: Heinemann, 1937-54.

Mahan, Alfred Thayer. *The Influence of Sea Power Upon the French Revolution and Empire, 1793-1812.* 2 vols. Westport, Conn.: Greenwood Publishing, 1968.

———. *The Influence of Sea Power Upon History, 1660-1783.* London: Dover Publishers, 1987.

———. *Nelson at Naples.* London: Reprint Services Corporation, 1997.

Manchester, Alan K. *British Preeminence in Brazil: Its Rise and Decline.* Chapel Hill: University of North Carolina Press, 1933.

Mansel, Philip. *The Eagle in Splendor: Napoleon and His Court.* London: George Philip, 1987.

———. "How Forgotten Were the Bourbons in France between 1812 and 1814?" *European Studies Review,* 1983. 13: 13-38.

———. *Louis XVIII.* London: Blond and Briggs, 1981.

———. "Wellington and the French Restoration." *International History Review,* vol. 11, February 1989. 76-83.

Marcum, J. W. "Catherine II and the French Revolution: A Reappraisal." *Canadian Slavonic Papers,* 1974. 16: 187-202.

Marcus, Geoffrey J. *The Age of Nelson and the Royal Navy.* New York: Viking Press, 1971.

Margerison, K. "P.-J. Roederer: Political Thought and Practice during the French Revolution." *Transactions of the American Philosophical Society,* 1983. 1: 1-164.

Markham, Felix. *Napoleon.* London: Weidenfeld, 1963.

Marlowe, John. *Perfidious Albion: The Origins of Anglo-French Rivalry in the Levant.* London: Elek, 1971.

Marriott, J. A. R. *The Eastern Question: An Historical Study in European Diplomacy.* Oxford: Oxford University Press, 1947.

Marshall-Cornwall, James. *Marshal Massena.* Oxford: Oxford University Press, 1965.

Martin, Jean-Clement. *La Contre Revolution: Revolution et Nation en France, 1789-1799.* Paris: Seuil, 1992.

———. *La Vendee et la France.* Paris: Seuil, 1986.

Martineau, Gilbert. *Lucien Bonaparte, Prince de Canino.* Paris: Editions France-Empire, 1989.

Mason, H. T., and William Doyle, eds. *The Impact of the French Revolution on European Consciousness.* Gloucester: Sutton Publishing, 1989.

Masson, Frederic. *Le Department des Affaires Etrangeres Pendant la Revolution, 1787-1804.* Paris: Societé d'Editions Litteraires et Artistique, 1903.

———. *Napoleon et Sa Famille.* 13 vols. Paris: Albin Michel, n.d.

Masson, P. "Napoleon et l'Angleterre: Napoleon contre la Marine Anglaise, 1797-1805." *Revue de Souvenir Napoleonien,* 400, Mars-Avril 1995. 27-45.

Matheson, Cyril. *Life of Henry Dundas, First Viscount Melville, 1743-1811.* London: Constable and Company, 1933.

Mathias, Peter. "Concepts of French in England and France in the Eighteenth Century." *Studies in Eighteenth Century Culture,* 1985. 15: 32-37.

———. "The Impact of the Revolutionary and Napoleonic Wars, 1793-1815, on the Long-Run Growth of the British Economy." *Review, Fernand Braudel Centre,* Paris, 1989. 12: 335-83.

———, and P. K. O'Brien. "Taxation in Britain and France, 1715-1810." *Journal of European Economic History,* vol. 5.

May, Arthur J. *The Age of Metternich, 1814-1848.* New York: Peter Smith Publishers, 1963.

Medelin, Louis. *Fouche, 1759-1820.* 2 vols. Paris: Plon et Nourrit, 1945.

Meinecke, Friedrich. *The Age of German Liberation, 1795-1815.* Berkeley: University of California Press, 1977.

Melchior-Bonnet, Bernadine. *Jerome Bonaparte.* Paris: Perrin, 1979.

———. *Napoleon et la Pape.* Paris: Laroussse, 1958.

Melvin, Frank E. *Napoleon's Navigation System: A Study of Trade Control During the Continental Blockade.* New York: D. Appleton and Co., 1919.

Meyer, Jack Allen. *Wellington's Generalship: A Study of His Peninsula Campaign.* Columbia: University of South Carolina Press, 1984.

Meyer, Jean. "La Marine Francaise au XVIIIe Siecle." *En De 1715 a 1871,* ed. Jean Delmas, vol. 2, *Histoire Militaire de la France,* ed. Andre Corvoisier. Paris: French and European Publishers, 1992.

Michalski, J., and M. Senkowska. "L'Historiographe Polonaise de la Revolution Francaise et de l'Epoque Napoleonienne." *Annales Historique de la Revolution Francaise,* 1981. 55: 608-15.

Michelet, Jules. *Histoires de la Revolution Francaise.* 2 vols. Paris: Robert Laffont, 1979.

Michon, George. *Robespierre et la Guerre Revolutionaires.* Paris: M. Riviere, 1937.

———. *Le Role de la Prusse en 1791-1792: La Declaration de Pillnitz et la Guerre.* Paris: T.E.P.A.C., 1941.

Middleton, Charles R. *The Administration of British Foreign Policy, 1782-1846*. Durham, NC: Duke University Press, 1977.

Mitchell, Brian R., and Phyllis Dean. *Abstract of British Historical Statistics*. Cambridge: Cambridge University Press, 1962.

Mitchell, Harvey. "Resistance to the Revolution in Western France." *Past and Present*, 1974. 63: 94-131.

——. *The Underground War Against France: The Missions of William Wickham, 1794-1800*. Oxford: Oxford University Press, 1965.

——. "The Vendee and Counterrevolution: A Review Essay." *French Historical Studies*, 1968. 5: 405-29.

Mitchell, Leslie G. *Charles James Fox*. New York: Oxford University Press, 1992.

——. *Charles James Fox and the Disintegration of the Whig Party, 1782-1794*. New York: Oxford University Press, 1971.

Molieres, Michel. *La Campagne de 1809: Les Operations du 24 Avril au 12 Juillet*. Paris: Le Livre Chez Vous, 2004.

Moloney, B. "Anglo-Florentine Diplomatic Relations and the French Revolution." *English Miscellany*, 1968. 11: 273-93.

Montague, Andrew J., ed. *The American Secretaries of State and Their Diplomacy*. New York: Knopf, 1927.

Montgomery, Frances. "General Moreau and the Conspiracy Against Napoleon in 1804: The Verdict of the Court and History." *The Consortium on Revolutionary Europe*, 1989.

Mooney, G. "British Diplomatic Relations with the Holy See 1793-1830." *Recusant History*, 1978. 14: 193-210.

Moran, D. J. "Goethe and Napoleon: The French Pursuit of the Allgemeine Zeitung." *Central European History*, vol. 14, 1978. 91-109.

Mori, Jennifer. *William Pitt and the French Revolution, 1785-1795*. New York: St. Martin's Press, 1997.

Morley, Charles. "Alexander and Czartoryski: The Polish Question from 1801 to 1813." *Slavonic and East European Review*, vol. 25, April 1947. 405-26.

Morris, Roger. *The Royal Dockyards During the Revolutionary and Napoleonic Wars*. Leicester: Leicester University Press, 1983.

Mosse, George L. *The Nationalization of the Masses: Political Symbolism and Mass Movements in Germany from the Napoleonic Wars through the Third Reich*. New York: Howard Fertig, 2001.

Mourousy, Paul. *Alexandre Ier, tsar de Russie: Un Sphinx en Europe*. Paris: Editions du Rocher, 2004.

——. *Le Tsar Paul I*. Paris: Editions du Rocher, 1997.

Mowat, Richard B. *The Concert of Europe*. London: Macmillan, 1930.

————. *The Diplomacy of Napoleon.* London: Edward Arnold, 1924.

Muir, Rory. *Britain and the Defeat of Napoleon, 1807-15.* New Haven, Conn.: Yale University Press, 1996.

Murphy, Orville T. *Charles Gravier, Comte de Vergennes: French Diplomacy in the Age of Revolution, 1719-1787.* Albany, NY: State University of New York Press, 1982.

————. "Louis XVI and the Pattern and Costs of a Policy Dilemma: Russia and the Eastern Question, 1787-1788." *Proceedings, Consortium on Revolutionary Europe*, 1986. 16: 264-74.

Naff, Thomas. *Ottoman Diplomacy and Great European Powers, 1797-1802.* London: University of London, 1960.

————. "Reform and the Conduct of Ottoman Diplomacy in the Reign of Selim III, 1789-1807." *Journal of the American Oriental Society*, vol. 83, no. 3. 295-315.

Nafziger, George F. *Napoleon's Invasion of Russia.* Novato, Calif.: Presidio Press, 1988.

Napier, Maj.-Gen. Sir W. F. P. *History of the War in the Peninsula and in the South of France, from the Year 1807 to the Year 1814.* 6 vols. London: Thomas and William Boone, 1853.

Narbonne, B. *La Diplomatie du Directoire et Bonaparte, d'Apre les Papiers Inedits de Reubell.* Paris: Presses Universitaire de France, 1951.

————. *Joseph Bonaparte: Le Roi Philosophe.* Paris: Hachette, 1949.

Nash, Howard P. *The Forgotten Wars: The Role of the U.S. Navy in the Quasi War with France and the Barbary Wars, 1798-1905.* New York: A.S. Barnes, 1968.

Nelson, A.P., and E. A. Benians, eds. *The Growth of the New Empire, 1793-1870.* Cambridge: Cambridge University Press, 1940.

Nichols, I. C. "Tsar Alexander I: Pacifist, Aggressor, or Vacillator?" *East European Quarterly*, vol. 16, 1982. 33-44.

Nicolle, Andre. "The Problem of Reparations after the Hundred Days." *Journal of Modern History*, 25 (1953). 343-54.

Nicolson, Harold. *The Congress of Vienna: A Study in Allied Unity, 1812-1822.* London: Constable, 1946.

Niven, Alexander C. *Napoleon and Alexander I: A Study in Franco-Russian Relations.* Washington: University Press of America, 1978.

Noble, Iris. *Rivals in Parliament: William Pitt and Charles Fox.* New York: J. Messner, 1970.

Norman, Barbara. *Napoleon and Talleyrand: The Last Two Weeks.* New York: Stein and Day, 1976.

O'Brien, P. "Public Finance in the Wars with France, 1793-1815." In H. T. Dickinson, ed., *Britain and the French Revolution, 1789-1815.* Basingstoke: Macmillan, 1989.

O'Dwyer, Margaret M. *The Papacy in the Age of Napoleon and the Restoration: Pius VII, 1800-1823.* Lanham, MD: University Press of America, 1985.

O'Gorman, Frank. *The Whig Party and the French Revolution.* New York: St. Martin's Press, 1967.

Oliver, Albert. *Le Dix-huit Brumaire.* Paris: Gallimard, 1959.

Olivier, Daria. *Alexandre Ier: Prince des Illusions.* Paris: Fayard, 1973.

Oman, Carola. *Napoleon's Viceroy: Eugene de Beauharnais.* London: Hodder & Stoughton, 1966.

Oman, Sir Charles. *A History of the Peninsula War.* 7 vols. Oxford: Clarendon Press, 1902-30.

———. *Studies in the Napoleonic Wars.* London: Methuen, 1929.

———. *Wellington's Army, 1809-1814.* London: Greenhill, 1986.

Orieux, J. *Talleyrand; ou, le Sphinx Incompris.* Paris: Flammarion, 1970.

Osiander, Andreas. *The States Systems of Europe, 1640-1990: Peacemaking and the Conditions of International Stability.* Oxford: Oxford University Press, 1994.

Padfield, Peter. *Guns at Sea.* New York: St. Martin's Press, 1973.

Pakenham, Thomas. *The Year of Liberty: The Great Irish Rebellion of 1798.* New York: Random House, 1993.

Palluel-Guillard, A. *L'Aigle et la Croix: Geneve et la Savoie, 1798-1815.* Geneve: Cabedita, 1999.

Palmer, Alan. *Alexander I: Tsar of War and Peace.* New York: Weidenfeld and Nicolson, 1974.

———. *Bernadotte: Napoleon's Marshal, Sweden's King.* London: John Murray, 1990.

———. *The Chancelleries of Europe.* London: Allen & Unwin, 1983.

———. *An Encyclopedia of Napoleon's Europe.* London: Weidenfeld and Nicolson, 1984.

———, et al. *Napoleon's Russian Campaign.* London: Carrol & Graf Publishers, 1967.

———. *The Lands Between: A History of Central Europe from the Congress of Vienna.* London: Macmillan, 1970.

———. *Metternich: Councilor of Europe.* New York: Phoenix Books, 1997.

———. *Napoleon and Marie Louise: The Emperor's Second Wife.* New York: St. Martin's Press, 2001.

Palmer, Robert R. *Twelve Who Ruled: The Year of Terror in the French Revolution.* Princeton, NJ: Princeton University Press, 1969.

Paoli, Francois. *La Jeunesse de Napoleon.* Paris: Tallandier, 2005.

Paret, Peter. *Clausewitz and the State.* New York: Oxford University Press, 1976.

———. *Yorck and the Era of Prussian Reform, 1807-1815.* Princeton, NJ: Princeton University Press, 1966.

———. "Napoleon's Philosophy of Governing Conquered Territories, 1805-1807." *South Atlantic Quarterly*, 1952. 51: 70-84.

———. "Why Did Napoleon Invade Russia?: A Study in Motivation and the Interrelations of Personality and Social Structure." *Journal of Military History*, 1990. 54: 131-46.

Parkinson, C. Northcote. *Britannia Rules: The Classic Age of Naval History, 1793-1815*. London: Weidenfeld and Nicolson, 1977.

———. *War in the Eastern Seas, 1793-1815*. London: G. Allen & Unwin, 1954.

———, ed. *The Trade Winds: A Study of British Overseas Trade During the French Wars, 1793-1815*. London: G. Allen & Unwin, 1948.

Parisian, Steven. *George IV: Inspiration of the Regency*. New York: St. Martin's Press, 2001.

Perkins, Bradford. *Castlereagh and Adams: England and the United States, 1812-1823*. Berkeley: University of California Press, 1964.

———. *The First Rapprochement: England and the United States, 1795-1805*. Berkeley: University of California Press, 1967.

———. *Prologue to War: England and the United States, 1805-1812*. Berkeley: University of California Press, 1968.

———, ed. *The Causes of the War of 1812: National Honor or National Interest?* Huntington, NY: R.E. Krieger, 1962.

Perrot, Jean-Claude, and Stuart Woolf. *State and Statistics in France, 1789-1815*. London: Harwood Academic, 1984.

Petre, F. L. *Napoleon and the Archduke Charles*. London: Arms and Armour, 1976.

———. *Napoleon at Bay, 1814*. London: Arms and Armour, 1977.

Philip, Mark, ed. *The French Revolution and British Popular Culture*. Cambridge: Cambridge University Press, 1991.

Phillips, Walter Alison. *The Confederation of Europe: A Study of the European Alliance, 1813-1823*. New York: Fertig, 1966.

Phipps, Ramsay Weston. *The Armies of the First French Republic and the Rise of the Marshals of Napoleon: The Armees de la Moselle, du Rhin, de Sambre-Meuse, de Rhine et Moselle*. Oxford: Oxford University Press, 1929.

Piechowiak, A. B. "The Anglo-Russian Expedition to Holland in 1799." *Slavonic and East European Review*, 1962-63. 41: 182-95.

Pienkos, A. T. *The Imperfect Autocrat: Grand Duke Constantine Pavlovich and the Polish Congress Kingdom*. Boulder, Colo.: Westview Press, 1987.

Pietromarchi, Antonello. *Lucien Bonaparte, Prince Romain*. Paris: Perrin, 1985.

Pillepich, A. Milan. *Capitale Napoleonienne, 1800-1814*. Paris: Lettrage Distribution, 2001.

———. *Napoleon et les Italiens: Republique Italienne et Royaume d'Italie, 1802-1814*. Paris: Nouveau Monde Editions/Fondation Napoleon, 2003.

Pinaud, P.-J. *Cambaceres: Le Premier Surveillant de la Franc-Maconnerie Imperiale*. Paris: Editions Maconnerie de France, 1996.

Pinguad, Alain. "Le Congres de Vienne et la Politique de Talleyrand." *Revue Historique*, 1899. 70: 1-52.

———. "La Politique Italienne de Napoleon Premier." *Revue Historique*, vol. 54, 1927. 20-33.

Pivka, Otto von. *Navies of the Napoleonic Era*. London: Hippocene Books, 1980.

Pluchon, Pierre. *Toussaint-L'Ouverture, de l'Esclavage au Pouvoir*. Paris: L'Ecole, 1989.

Polasky, Janet L. *Revolution in Brussels, 1787-1793*. Hanover, NH: University Press of New England, 1987.

Polowetzky, Michael. *A Bond Never Broken: The Relations Between Napoleon and the Authors of France*. Rutherford, N.J.: Fairleigh Dickinson University Press, 1993.

Poniatowski, Michel. *Talleyrand, et le Consulat*. Paris: Perrin, 1986.

Pope, Dudley. *The Great Gamble: Nelson at Copenhagen*. London: Weidenfeld & Nicolson, 1972.

Price, Munro. *Preserving the French Monarchy: The Comte de Vergennes, 1774-1797*. Cambridge: Cambridge University Press, 1995.

Puryear, Vernon J. *France and the Levant: From the Bourbon Restoration to the Peace of Kutiah*. Berkeley: University of California Press, 1941.

———. *Napoleon and the Dardanelles*. Berkeley: University of California Press, 1951.

Quynn, D. M. "The Art Confiscations of the Napoleonic Wars." *American Historical Review*, 1971. 50: 437-60.

Radvany, E. *Metternich's Projects for Reform in Austria*. The Hague: Nijhoff, 1971.

Ragsdale, Hugh. "Continental System in 1801: Paul I and Bonaparte." *Journal of Modern History*, vol. 42, 1970. 70-89.

———. *Detente in the Napoleonic Era*. Lawrence: University of Kansas Press, 1980.

———. "Russia, Prussia, and Europe in the Policy of Paul I." *Jahrbucher fur die Geschichte Osteurpas*, 1983. 31: 81-118.

———. "Russian Influence at Luneville." *French Historical Studies*, vol. 5, no. 3, Spring 1968. 274-84.

———. *Tsar Paul and the Question of Madness: An Essay in History and Psychology*. Westport, Conn.: Greenwood Press, 1988.

———. "Was Paul Bonaparte's Fool? The Evidence of Neglected Archives." In Hugh Ragsdale, ed., *Paul I: A Reassessment of His Life and Reign*. Pittsburgh: Pittsburgh University Press, 1979. 76-90.

———, ed. *Paul I: A Reassessment of His Life and Reign*. Pittsburgh: University of Pittsburgh Press, 1979.

Rambaud, Jacques. *Naples Sous Joseph Bonaparte, 1806-1808*. Paris: Nijhoff, 1911.

Ratchinski, Andre. *Napoleon et Alexandre I: La Guerre des Idees*. Paris: Giovanangelli, 2002.

Rath, R. J. "The Habsburgs and Public Opinion in Lombardy-Venetia, 1814-1815." In E. M. Earles, ed., *Nationalism and Internationalism.* New York: Octagon Books, 1974. 303-05.

Rath, Rueben J. *The Fall of the Napoleonic Kingdom of Italy, 1814.* London: Hippocene Books, 1971.

Regnault, J. "L'Emperor et l'Opinion Publique, 1813-1814." *Revue Historique de l'Armee,* vol. 13, 1957. 29-50.

Reihn, G. J. *Great Britain and the Establishment of the Kingdom of the Netherlands, 1813-15: A Study in British Foreign Policy.* London: Allen & Unwin, 1930.

Reihn, Richard K. *1812: Napoleon's Russian Campaign.* New York: John Wiley, 1991.

Reilly, Robin. *William Pitt the Younger.* New York: G. P. Putnam's Sons, 1979.

Reinhard, Marcel. *Le Grand Carot.* 2 vols. Paris: Hachette, 1950-52.

———. "La Guerre et la Paix a la fin de 1793: un Interview Inedits de Danton." *Annales Historiques de la Revolution Francaises,* 1953. 2: 97-103.

Reinnerman, A. J. *Austria and the Papacy in the Age of Metternich, 1809-1830.* 2 vols. Washington, D. C.: Catholic University Press, 1989.

———. "Metternich, Alexander I, and the Russian Challenge in Italy, 1815-20." *Journal of Modern History,* 1974. 46: 262-76.

———. "The Papacy, Austria, and the Anti-French Struggle in Italy, 1792-97." In K. Brauer and W. E. Wright, ed., *Austria in the Age of the French Revolution, 1789-1815.* Minneapolis: University of Minnesota Press, 1990. 47-68.

Renier, Gustave J. *Great Britain and the Establishment of the Kingdom of the Netherlands, 1813-1815.* London: G. Allen & Unwin, 1930.

Rials, S. *Revolution et Contre-Revolution au XIX Siecle.* Paris: Albatross, 1987.

Riehn, Richard K. *1812: Napoleon's Russian Campaign.* New York: John Wiley, 1991.

Riley, J. *The Seven Years' War and the Old Regime in France: The Economic and Financial Toll.* Princeton, NJ: Princeton University Press, 1986.

Riley, J.P. *Napoleon and the World War of 1813: Lessons in Coalition Warfighting.* London: Frank Cass, 2002.

Riley, Jonathon. *Napoleon as a General: Command from the Battlefield to Grand Strategy.* London: Hambledon, 2007.

Roach, E. E. "Anglo-Russian Relations from Austerlitz to Tilsit." *International History Review,* 1983. 5: 181-200.

Robert, Jacques-Henri. *Dictionaire des Diplomates de Napoleon.* Paris: Henry Veyrier editions, 1990.

Roberts, Michael. *The Whig Party, 1807-1812.* London: Frank Cass, 1965.

Robertson, William S. *France and Latin-American Independence.* London: Hippocene Books, 1967.

Robson, William H. "New Light on Lord Castlereagh's Diplomacy." *Journal of Modern History*, vol. 3, 1931. 198-218.

Rodger, A. B. *The War of the Second Coalition, 1798 to 1801: A Strategic Commentary.* Oxford: Oxford University Press, 1964.

Roger, Philippe. *L'Ennemi Americain: Genealogie de l'Anti-Americanism Francais.* Paris: Seuil, 2002.

Roider, Karl A. *Austria's Eastern Question, 1700-1790.* Princeton, NJ: Princeton University Press, 1982.

———. *Baron Thugut and Austria's Response to the French Revolution.* Princeton, NJ: Princeton University Press, 1987.

Rose, John Holland. "Canning and the Spanish Patriots in 1808." *American Historical Review*, 1906. 12: 39-52.

———. "The Conflict with Revolutionary France." In *The Cambridge History of the British Empire*, ed. J. Holland Rose, A. P. Nelson, and E. A. Benians, vol. 2, *The Growth of the New Empire, 1783-1870.* Cambridge: Cambridge University Press, 1940.

———. "France and the First Coalition Before the Campaign of 1796." *English Historical Review*, 1903. 18: 287-302.

———. *The Life of Napoleon.* 2 vols. London: George Bell & Sons, 1903.

———. *Pitt and Napoleon: Essays and Letters.* London: G. Bell, 1912.

———. *The Revolutionary and Napoleonic Era, 1789-1815.* Cambridge: Cambridge University Press, 1935.

———. *William Pitt and the Great War.* London: G. Bell, 1911.

———. *William Pitt and the Great War.* Westport, Conn.: Greenwood Publishers, 1971.

———. *William Pitt and the National Revival.* London: G. Bell, 1911.

Rosecrance, Richard, and Chih Cheng Lo. "Balancing, Stability, and War: The Mysterious Case of the Napoleonic International System." *International Studies Quarterly*, vol. 40, no. 4, 1996. 479-500.

Ross, Michael. *The Reluctant King: Joseph Bonaparte, King of the Two Sicilies and Spain.* New York: Mason/Charter, 1977.

Ross, Steven T. *European Diplomatic History, 1661-1799.* Garden City, NY: Doubleday, 1969.

———. *European Diplomatic History, 1789-1815.* Malabar, Florida: Krieger, 1981.

———. "The Military Strategy of the Directory: The Campaigns of 1799." *French Historical Studies*, vol. 5, 1967. 170-87.

———. *Quest for Victory: French Military Strategy, 1792-99.* New York: Oak Tree Publishers, 1973.

Rosselli, John. *Lord William Bentinck and the British Occupation of Sicily, 1811-1814.* Cambridge: Cambridge University Press, 1956.

Rossignol, M.-J. *La Ferment Nationaliste: Aux Origines de la Politique Exterieurs des Etats-Unis, 1789-1812*. Paris: Belin, 1994.

Rothenburg, Gunther. "Archduke Charles and the Question of Popular Participation in War." *Proceedings, Consortium on Revolutionary Europe*, 1982. 214-24, 263-68.

———. *The Art of Warfare in the Age of Napoleon*. Bloomington: University. of Indiana Press, 1978.

———. *Napoleon's Great Adversaries: The Archduke Charles and the Austrian Army, 1792-1814*. Bloomington: University of Indiana Press, 1982.

———. "The Origins, Causes, and Extension of the Wars of the French Revolution and Napoleon." *Journal of Interdisciplinary History*, vol. 19, no. 4, Spring 1988. 771-93.

Rude, George. *Revolutionary Europe, 1783-1815*. London: Blackwell Publishers, 1985.

Ruppenthal, R. "Denmark and the Continental System." *Journal of Modern History*, vol. 12, 1961. 123-40.

Ryan, A. "An Ambassador Afloat: Vice-Admiral Sir James Samaurez and the Swedish Court, 1808-1812." In J. Black and P. S. Woodfine, eds., *The British Navy and the Use of Naval Power in the Eighteenth Century*. Leicester: Leicester University Press, 1988. 237-58.

———. "The Causes of the British Attack Upon Copenhagen in 1807." *English Historical Review*, vol. 68, 1953. 37-55.

———. "The Defense of British Trade with the Baltic, 1808-1813." *English Historical Review*, vol. 74, 1959. 443-66.

Ryan, Frederick W. *The House of the Temple: A Study of Malta and Its Knights in the French Revolution*. London: Burns, Oates, & Washburn, 1930.

Rydjord, John. "British Mediation between Spain and Her Colonies, 1811-1813." *Hispanic American Historical Review*, 21 (1941). 29-50.

Sack, James J. *The Grenvillites, 1801-1829: Party Politics and Factionalism in the Age of Pitt and Liverpool*. Urbana: University of Illinois Press, 1979.

Saint-Hilaire, M. *Napoleon au Conseil d'Etat*. Paris: Victor Magen, 1843.

Saul, Norman E. "The Objectives of Paul's Italian Policy." In H. Ragsdale, ed., *Paul I: A Reassessment of His Life and Reign*. Pittsburgh: University of Pittsburgh Press, 1979. 31-44.

———. *Russia and the Mediterranean, 1797-1807*. Chicago: University of Chicago Press, 1979.

Sauvigny, Guillaume de. *Metternich and his Times*. London: Humanities Press, 1962.

Savant, Jean. *Les Espions de Napoleon*. Paris: Hachette, 1957.

Schama, Simon. *Citizens: A Chronicle of the French Revolution*. New York: Vintage, 1990.

———. *Patriots and Liberators: Revolution in the Netherlands, 1780-1813*. New York: Vintage, 1992.

Schenk, Hans G. *The Aftermath of the Napoleonic Wars*. New York: Howard Fertig, 1968.

Scher-Zembitska, L. *L'Aigle et le Phenix: Un Siecle de Relations Franco-Polonaises*. Paris: CNRS Editions, 2001.

Schneer, Richard M. "Arthur Wellesley and the Cintra Convention: A New Look at an Old Puzzle." *Journal of British Studies*, vol. 19, no. 2, Spring 1980. 522-40.

Schneid, Frederick C. *Napoleon's Conquest of Europe: The Third Coalition*. Westport, Conn.: Praeger, 2005.

Schom, Alan. *Napoleon Bonaparte*. New York: HarperCollins, 1997.

———. *One Hundred Days: Napoleon's Road to Waterloo*. New York: Oxford University Press, 1992.

Schroeder, Paul. "The Collapse of the Second Coalition." *Journal of Modern History*, vol. 59, 1987. 244-90.

———. "Did the Vienna System Rest Upon a Balance of Power?" *American Historical Review*, vol. 97, 1992. 683-706.

———. "Napoleon's Foreign Policy: A Criminal Enterprise." *Journal of Military History*, vol. 54, no. 2, 1990. 147-63.

———. "The Nineteenth Century International System: Changes in the Structure." *World Politics*, vol. 39, 1986. 1-26.

———. "The Nineteenth Century System: Balance of Power or Political Equilibrium?" *Review of International Studies*, vol. 15, 1989. 135-53.

———. *The Transformation of European Politics, 1763-1848*. New York: Oxford University Press, 1994.

———. "An Unnatural `Natural Alliance': Castlereagh, Metternich, and Aberdeen in 1813." *International Historical Review*, vol. 10, 1988. 522-40.

Schulze, H. *The Course of German Nationalism: From Fichte to Bismarck, 1763-1867*. New York: Cambridge University Press, 1991.

Scofield, Philip. "British Politicians and French Arms: The Ideological War of 1793-1795." *History*, vol. 77, 1992. 1183-1201.

Scott, Franklin D. *Bernadotte and the Fall of Napoleon*. Cambridge, Mass.: Harvard University Press, 1935.

———. "Bernadotte and the Throne of France, 1814." *Journal of Modern History*, vol., 5, 1933. 465-78.

Scott, Samuel F. *The Response of the Royal Army to the French Revolution: The Role and Development of the Line Army, 1787-1813*. New York: Oxford University Press, 1978.

———, and Barry Rothaus, eds. *Historical Dictionary of the French Revolution, 1789-1799*. 2 vols. Westport, Conn.: Greenwood Publishers, 1985.

Secher, Reynald. "Genocide and the Bicentenary: The French Revolution and the Revenge of the Vendee." *The Historical Journal*, 1987. 30: 60-77.

———. *Le Genocide Franco-Francais: La Vendee-Venge*. Paris: Presse Universitaires de France, 1986.

Sedouy, Jacques-Alain de. *Le Congres de Vienne: L'Europe Contre la France, 1812-1815.* Paris: Perrin, 2002.

Sen, S. P. *The French in India, 1763-1816.* Calcutta: Firma K.L. Mukhopadhyay, 1958.

Senkowski, Gluck M. "Pouvoir et Societe en Illyrie Napoleonienne." *Revue de l'Institut Napoleon,* 1980, no. 136. 57-78.

Severn, J. K. *A Wellesley Affair: Richard Marquis Wellesley and the Conduct of Anglo-Spanish Diplomacy, 1809-1812.* Gainesville: University of Florida Press, 1981.

Shanahan, William O. *Prussian Military Reforms, 1786-1813.* New York: AMS Press, 1945.

Shapiro, Barry M. *Revolutionary Justice in Paris, 1789-1790.* Cambridge: Cambridge University Press, 1993.

Shaw, S. J. *Between Old and New: The Ottoman Empire Under Sultan Selim III, 1798-1807.* Cambridge, Mass.: Harvard University Press, 1971.

———. "The Ottoman Empire and the Serbian Uprising, 1804-1807." In W. S. Vulcinich, ed., *The First Serbian Uprising, 1806-1809.* Boulder, Colo.: Westview Press, 1982. 71-94.

Sheehan, James J. *German History, 1770-1866.* New York: Oxford University Press, 1989.

Sherwig, John M. *Guineas and Gunpowder: British Foreign Aid in the Wars with France, 1793-1815.* Cambridge, Mass.: Harvard University Press, 1969.

———. "Lord Grenville's Plan for a Concert of Europe, 1797-1799." *Journal of Modern History,* vol. 34, 1962. 284-93.

Sher-Zembitska, Lydia. *L'Aigle et le Phenix: Un Siecle de Relations Franco-Polonaise, 1732-1832.* Paris: CNRS Editions, 2001.

Shneidman, J. L. "The Proposed Invasion of India by Russia and France in 1801." *Journal of Indian History,* 1957. 35: 167-75.

Shupp, Paul F. *The European Powers and the Near Eastern Question, 1806-1807.* New York: Columbia University Press, 1931.

Sibalis, Michael. "The Napoleonic Police State." In Philip G. Dwyer, ed., *Napoleon and Europe.* London: Longman, 2001.

Sieyes, Emmanuel. *What Is The Third Estate?* London: Pall Mall, 1963.

Silberling, Norman J. "Financial and Monetary Policy of Great Britain during the Napoleonic Wars." *Quarterly Journal of Economics,* 38 (1923-24). 214-33.

Simms, Brendan. *The Impact of Napoleon: Prussian High Politics, Foreign Policy, and the Crisis of the Executive, 1797-1806.* Cambridge: Cambridge University Press, 1997.

———. "'An Odd Question Enough': Charles James Fox, the Crown, and British Policy during the Hanoverian Crisis of 1806." *Historical Journal,* vol. 38, no. 3, 1995. 567-96.

———. "The Road to Jena: Prussian High Politics, 1804-1806." *German History,* 12 (1994). 374-94.

———. *The Struggle for Mastery in Germany, 1779-1850.* Cambridge: Cambridge University Press, 1998.

Sked, Alan, ed. *Europe's Balance of Power, 1815-1848.* London: Macmillan, 1979.

Slosson, Preston W. *Pitt and Fox.* New York: G. Wahr, 1978.

Smith, Digby. *The Greenhill Napoleonic Wars Data Book: Actions and Losses in Personnel, Colors, Standards, and Artillery, 1792-1815.* London: Greenhill, 1998.

———. *Navies of the Napoleonic Era.* London: Schiffer Publishing, 2004.

Sorel, Albert. *L'Europe et la Revolution Francaises.* 8 vols. Paris: Plon, 1893-1912.

———. *Europe and the French Revolution: The Political Transformation of the Old Regime.* London: Collins, 1969.

Sparrow, Elizabeth. *Secret Service: British Agents in France, 1792-1815.* Woodbridge, England: Boydell Press, 1999.

———. "The Secret Service Under Pitt's Administration, 1792-1806." *History,* April 1998. 290-94.

Squire, P. S. "Metternich and Benckendorff, 1807-1842." *Slavonic and East European Review,* 1967. 45: 135-62.

Stagg, J. C. A. *Mr. Madison's War: Politics, Diplomacy, and Warfare in the Early American Republic.* Princeton, NJ: Princeton University Press, 1983.

Stanhope, Philip. *Life of the Right Honorable William Pitt.* 4 vols. New York: AMS Press, 1971.

Stearns, Josephine. *The Role of Metternich in Undermining Napoleon.* Urbana: Illinois Studies in the Social Sciences, vol. 39, no. 4, 1948.

Stenberg, Richard. "The Boundaries of the Louisiana Purchase." *Hispanic American Historical Review,* vol. 14, no. 1. 32-64.

Stinchcombe, William. "The Diplomacy of XYZ Affair." *The William and Mary Quarterly,* vol. 34, no. 4, October 1977. 590-617.

Stone, Bailey. *The Genesis of the French Revolution: A Global Historical Interpretation.* Cambridge: Cambridge University Press, 1994.

Stone, Laurence. *An Imperial State at War: Britain from 1689 to 1815.* London: Routledge, 1994.

Sutherland, D. M. G. *France 1789-1815: Revolution and Counterrevolution.* New York: Oxford University Press 1986.

Sweet, Paul R. *Friedrich von Gentz: Defender of the Old Order.* Westport, Conn.: Greenwood Press, 1970.

———. *Wilhelm von Humboldt: A Biography.* 2 vols. Columbus: Ohio State University, 1980.

Taillemite, Etienne. *La Fayette.* Paris: Fayard, 1989.

Tangeras, L. "Castlereagh, Bernadotte, and Norway." *Scandinavian Journal of History,* 1983. 8: 193-223.

Thiers, Adolphe. *Histoire du Consulat et de l'Empire.* 20 vols. Paris: Paulin, 1845-62.

Thiesse, Anne-Marie. *La Creation des Identities Nationales, Europe XVIII-XX Siecle.* Paris: Seuil, 1999.

Thiry, Jean. *Le Concordat et le Consulat a Vie.* Paris: Berger-Levrault, 1956.

Thomas, Daniel H., ed. *The New Guide to the Diplomatic Archives of Western Europe.* Philadelphia: University of Pennsylvania Press, 1975.

Thompson, James M. *Napoleon Bonaparte.* New York: Oxford University Press, 1988.

Thompson, Norman, ed. *Wellington: Studies in the Military and Political Career of the First Duke of Wellington.* Manchester: Manchester University Press, 1990.

Thomson, Gladys Scott. *Catherine the Great and the Expansion of Russia.* New York: Colliers, 1962.

Thrasher, Peter A. *Pasquale Paoli: An Enlightened Hero, 1725-1807.* London: Constable, 1970.

Tracy, Nicolas. *Nelson's Battles: The Art of Victory in the Age of Sail.* Annapolis, MD: Naval Institute Press, 1996.

Tranie, Jean. *Napoleon et l'Angleterre, 1793-1815.* Paris: Pygmalion, 1994.

Tranie, Jean, et J.C. Carmigniani. *Bonaparte: La Campagne d'Egypte.* Paris: Pygmalion, 1988.

———. *Les Guerres de l'Ouest, 1793-1815.* Paris: Lavauzelle, 1983.

———. *Napoleon: 1ere Campagne d'Italie.* Paris: Pygmalion, 1990.

———. *Napoleon et l'Autriche: la Campagne de 1809.* Paris: Copernic, 1979.

———. *Napoleon: Bonaparte, 2eme Campagne d'Italie.* Paris: Pygmalion, 1991.

———. *Napoleon: La Campagne d'Espagne, 1807-1814.* Paris: Pygmalion, 1998.

Trevelyan, George. *George the Third and Charles Fox.* 2 vols. London: Longman Green, 1914.

Troyat, Henri. *Alexander of Russia: Napoleon's Conqueror.* New York: E.P. Dutton, 1982.

Trulsson, Sven G. *British and Swedish Policies and Strategies in the Baltic after the Peace of Tilsit in 1807.* Stockholm: C. W. K. Gleerup, Biblioteca Historica Lundensis, 40, 1976.

Tulard, Jean. *Le 18 Brumaire.* Paris: Perrin, 1999.

———. *Bibliographie Critique des Memoires sur le Consulat et l'Empire.* Paris: Droz, 1971.

———. *La France de la Revolution et de l'Empire.* Paris: Puf, 2004.

———. *Le Grand Empire.* Paris: A. Michel, 1982.

———. *Joseph Fouche.* Paris: Fayard, 1998.

———. *Murat ou l'Eveil des Nations.* Paris: Hachette, 1983.

———. *Napoleon ou le Mythe du Saveur.* Paris: Fayard, 1987.

———. *Nouvelle histoire de Paris: Le Consulat et l'Empire, 1800-1815.* Paris: Hachette, 1983.

———. "Simeon et l'Organization du Royaume de Westphalie, 1807-1813." *Francia,* 1973. 1: 557-68.

———, ed. *La Contre-Revolution: Origins, Historie, Posterite.* Paris: Perrin, 1990.

———, ed. *L'Europe de Napoleon.* Paris: Horvath, 1989.

———, et L. Garros. *Itineraire de Napoleon au Jour le Jour, 1769-1821.* Paris: Tallandier, 2002.

Turner, E. H. "The Russian Squadron with Admiral Duncan's North Sea Fleet, 1795-1800." *Mariner's Mirror,* 1963. 49: 212-22.

Turner, Frederick Jackson. "The Policy of France toward the Mississippi Valley in the Period of Washington and Adams." *The American Historical Review,* vol. 10, no. 2, January 1905. 249-79.

Turner, W. B. *The War of 1812: The War That Both Sides Won.* Toronto: Dundern Press, 2000.

Urban, Mark. *The Man Who Broke Napoleon's Codes.* New York: Faber and Faber, 2001.

Vandal, Albert. *Napoleon et Alexander I: L'Alliance Russe sous le Premier Empire.* 3 vols. Paris: Plon, 1891-96.

Vann, J. A. "Hapsburg Policy and the Austrian War of 1809." *Central European History,* vol. 7, 1974. 291-310.

Vidal, Florence. *Elisa Bonaparte: Soeur de Napoleon 1er.* Paris: Pygmalion, 2005.

Vidalenc, Jean. *Les Émigrés Francais, 1789-1825.* Caen: Universite de Caen, 1963.

Viennot, Odette. *Napoleon et l'Industrie Francaise: La Crise de 1810-1811.* Paris: Plon, 1947.

Villiers, Philippe de. *Napoleon Bonaparte et la Vendee.* Paris: Somogy Editions d'Art, 2004.

Vucinich, W. S., ed. *The First Serbian Uprising.* Boulder, Colo.: Westview Press, 1982.

Waliszewski, Kazimierz. *Paul the First of Russia, the Son of Catherine the Great.* London: Archon Books, 1969.

Walker, Mack, ed. *Metternich's Europe, 1814-48.* New York: Walker, 1968.

Walsh, J. M. *Edmund Burke and International Relations.* Basingstoke: Macmillan, 1995.

Ward, A. W., and G. P. Gooch. *The Cambridge History of British Foreign Policy.* 3 vols. Cambridge: Cambridge University Press, 1922.

Waresquiel, Emmanuel de. *Talleyrand, le Prince Immobile.* Paris: Fayard, 2003.

Warner, Oliver. *The British Navy: A Concise History.* London: Thames and Hudson, 1975.

Watson, G. E. "The United States and the Peninsula War." *The Historical Journal,* vol. 19, December 1976. 859-76.

Watson, J. Steven. *The Reign of George III 1760-1815.* Oxford: Oxford University Press, 1960.

Webb, Paul. "Construction, Repair, and Maintenance in the Battle Fleet of the Royal Navy, 1793-1815." In *The British Navy and the Use of Naval Power in the Eighteenth Century,* eds. Jeremy Black and Philip Woodfine. Leicester: Leicester University Press, 1988.

Webster, Charles K. *British Policy and the Independence of Latin America, 1812-1830.* 2 vols. New York: Frank Cass and Company, 2001.

———. *The Congress of Vienna, 1814-1815.* London: Thames and Hudson, 1965.

———. "The Duel between Castlereagh and Canning in 1809." *Cambridge Historical Journal,* vol. 3, 1929. 83, 95, 314.

———. *The Foreign Policy of Castlereagh, 1812-1815: Britain and the Reconstruction of Europe.* London: G. Bell, 1931.

———. *The Foreign Policy of Castlereagh, 1815-1822: Britain and the European Alliance.* London: G. Bell, 1925.

Wegert, Karl H. *German Radicals Confront the Common People: Revolutionary Politics and Popular Politics, 1789-1848.* Mainz: Verlag Philipp von Zaben, 1992.

Weil, M. H. *Le Prince Eugene et Murat, 1813-1814.* 5 vols. Paris: Ancienne Libraire Thorin et Fils, 1902.

Wells, Roger. *Wretched Faces: Famine in Wartime Britain, 1793-1801.* London: Palgrave Macmillan, 1988.

Whaley, Leigh Ann. *The Impact of Napoleon, 1800-1815: An Annotated Bibliography.* Lanham, Md.: Scarecrow Press, 1997.

Whitaker, Arthur Preston. "France and the American Deposit at New Orleans." *The Hispanic American Historical Review,* vol. 11, no. 4, November 1931. 485-502.

———. *The Mississippi Question, 1795-1803: A Study in Trade Politics, and Diplomacy.* New York: Appleton-Century, 1934.

Whitcomb, Edward A. *Napoleon's Diplomatic Service.* Durham, N.C.: Duke University Press, 1979.

White, D. Fedotoff. "The Russian Navy in Trieste during the Wars of the Revolution and the Empire." *American Slavic and East European Review,* vol. 6, December 1947. 25-41.

Williams, David Hamilton. *Waterloo: New Perspectives: The Great Battle Reappraised.* New York: Wiley, 1994.

Woloch, Isser. *The French Veteran from the Revolution to the Restoration.* Chapel Hill: University of North Carolina Press, 1979.

———. *Napoleon and His Collaborators: The Making of a Dictatorship.* New York: W. W. Norton and Company, 2001.

———. "Napoleonic Conscription: State Power and Civil Society." *Past and Present,* 1986. 111: 101-29.

———. *The New Regime: Transformations of the French Civil Code, 1789-1820s.* New York: W.W. Norton, 1994.

Woolf, Stuart. *Napoleon's Integration of Europe.* London: Routledge, 1991.

Wright, D.G. *Napoleon and Europe.* London: Routledge, 1991.

Zamoyski, Adam. *Moscow 1812: Napoleon's Fatal March.* New York: HarperCollins, 2004.

———. *Rites of Peace: The Fall of Napoleon & the Congress of Vienna.* New York: HarperCollins, 2007.

Zawadzki, W.H. *A Man of Honor: Adam Czartoryski as a Statesman of Russia and Poland, 1795-1831.* Oxford: Clarendon Press, 1993.

Zeigler, Philip. *Addington: A Life of Henry Addington, First Viscount Sidmouth.* London: Collins, 1962.

Zieseniss, Charles O. *Le Congres de Vienne et l'Europe des Princes.* Paris: P. Belfond, 1984.

Zimmerman, J. F. *The Impressment of American Seamen.* New York: Associated Faculty Press, 1966.

Index

4